2009

Britain

& Ireland

The most in-depth campsite guides

D1741816

INSPECTED
CAMPSITES
& SELECTED

Compiled by: Alan Rogers Guides Ltd

Designed by: Paul Effenberg, Vine Design Ltd

Additional photography: T Lambelin, www.lambelin.com
Maps created by Customised Mapping (01769 540044)
contain background data provided by GisDATA Ltd
Maps are © Alan Rogers Guides and GisDATA Ltd 2008

Published by: Alan Rogers Guides Ltd,
Spelmonden Old Oast, Goudhurst, Kent TN17 1HE
www.alanrogers.com Tel: 01580 214000

British Library Cataloguing-in-Publication Data:
A catalogue record for this book is available
from the British Library.

ISBN 978-1-906215-12-5

Printed in Great Britain by J H Haynes & Co Ltd

Contents

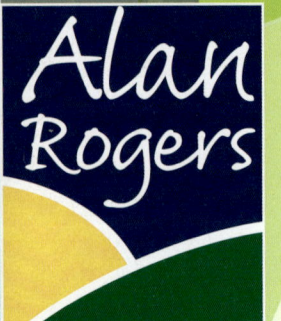

The Alan Rogers approach

Alan Rogers Guides were first published over 40 years ago. Since Alan Rogers published the first campsite guide that bore his name, the range has expanded and now covers 27 countries in five separate guides. No fewer than 20 of the campsites selected by Alan for the first guide are still featured in our 2009 editions.

There are well over 5,000 camping and caravanning parks in Britain and Ireland of varying quality: this guide contains impartially written reports on almost 600 (30 more then last year), including some of the very finest, each being individually inspected and selected. All the usual maps and indexes are also included, designed to help you find the choice of campsite that's right for you. We hope you enjoy some happy and safe travels – and some pleasurable 'armchair touring' in the meantime!

A question of quality

The criteria we use when inspecting and selecting parks are numerous, but the most important by far is the question of good quality. People want different things from their choice of campsite so we try to include a range of campsite 'styles' to cater for a wide variety of preferences: from those seeking a small peaceful campsite in the heart of the countryside, to visitors looking for an 'all singing, all dancing' park in a popular seaside resort. Those with more specific interests, such as sporting facilities, cultural events or historical attractions, are also catered for.

The size of the park, whether it's part of a chain or privately owned, makes no difference in terms of it being required to meet our exacting standards in respect of its quality and it being 'fit for purpose'. In other words, irrespective of the size of the park, or the number of facilities it offers, we consider and evaluate the welcome, the pitches, the sanitary facilities, the cleanliness, the general maintenance and even the location.

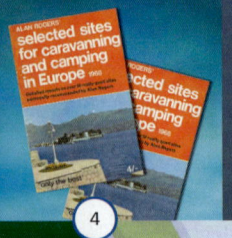

" ...the campsites included in this book have been chosen entirely on merit, and no payment of any sort is made by them for their inclusion."

Alan Rogers, 1968

Expert opinions

We rely on our dedicated team of Site Assessors, all of whom are experienced campers, caravanners or motorcaravanners, to visit and recommend parks. Each year they travel some 100,000 miles around Europe inspecting new campsites for the guide and re-inspecting the existing ones. Our thanks are due to them for their enthusiastic efforts, their diligence and integrity.

We also appreciate the feedback we receive from many of our readers and we always make a point of following up complaints, suggestions or recommendations for possible new parks. Of course we get a few grumbles too – but it really is a few, and those we do receive usually relate to overcrowding or to poor maintenance during the peak school holiday period. Please bear in mind that, although we are interested to hear about any complaints, we have no contractual relationship with the campsites featured in our guides and are therefore not in a position to intervene in any dispute between a reader and a campsite.

Independent and honest

Whilst the content and scope of the Alan Rogers guides have expanded considerably since the early editions, our selection of campsites still employs exactly the same philosophy and criteria as defined by Alan Rogers in 1968.

'telling it how it is'

Firstly, and most importantly, our selection is based entirely on our own rigorous and independent inspection and selection process. Campsites cannot buy their way into our guides – indeed the extensive Report which is written by us, not by the site owner, is provided free of charge so we are free to say what we think and to provide an honest, 'warts and all' description. This is written in plain English and without the use of confusing icons or symbols.

HIGHLY RESPECTED BY SITE OWNERS AND READERS ALIKE, THERE IS NO BETTER GUIDE WHEN IT COMES TO FORMING AN INDEPENDENT VIEW OF A CAMPSITE'S QUALITY. WHEN YOU NEED TO BE CONFIDENT IN YOUR CHOICE OF CAMPSITE, YOU NEED THE ALAN ROGERS GUIDE.

- PARKS ONLY INCLUDED ON MERIT
- PARKS CANNOT PAY TO BE INCLUDED
- INDEPENDENTLY INSPECTED, RIGOROUSLY ASSESSED
- IMPARTIAL REVIEWS
- OVER 40 YEARS OF EXPERTISE

INSPECTED
CAMPSITES
& SELECTED

Written in plain English, our guides are exceptionally easy to use, but a few words of explanation regarding the layout and content may be helpful. For England we have used official tourist board regions and the counties within them. For Wales, Scotland and Ireland (north and south) we use the counties.

Tourist Board area

The Reports – *Example of an entry*

Park Number | Park name
Postal address (including county)
Telephone number. Email address   alanrogers.com web address

A description of the park in which we try to give an idea of its general features – its size, its situation, its strengths and its weaknesses. This section should provide a picture of the park itself with reference to the facilities that are provided and if they impact on its appearance or character. We include details on pitch numbers, electricity (with amperage), hardstandings etc. in this section as pitch design, planning and terracing affects the park's overall appearance. Similarly we include reference to pitches used for caravan holiday homes, chalets, and the like. Importantly at the end of this column we indicate if there are any restrictions, e.g. no tents, no children, naturist sites.

Facilities
Lists more specific information on the park's facilities and amenities and, where available, the dates when these facilities are open (if not for the whole season). Off site: here we give distances to various local amenities, for example, local shops, the nearest beach, plus our featured activities (bicycle hire, fishing, horse riding, boat launching). Where we have space we list suggestions for activities and local tourist attractions.

Open: Park opening dates.

Directions
Separated from the main text in order that they may be read and assimilated more easily by a navigator en-route. Bear in mind that road improvement schemes can result in road numbers being altered.
O.S.GR: Ordnance Survey grid references are included for those using OS maps.
GPS: references are provided as we obtain them for satellite navigation systems (in degrees and minutes).

Charges 2009 (or a general guide)

Indexes
Our three indexes allow you to find parks by their number and name, by region and park name, or by the town or village where the park is situated. See also the handy Quick Reference sections at the back.

Campsite maps
The maps at the back of the guide relate to the geographical areas and will help you identify the approximate position of each campsite. The colour of the campsite number (in red) indicates if it is open all year. You will certainly need more detailed maps, for example the Ordnance Survey road atlas.

Facilities

Toilet blocks

We assume that toilet blocks will be equipped with WCs, washbasins with hot and cold water and hot showers with dividers or curtains, and will have all necessary shelves, hooks, plugs and mirrors. We also assume that there will be an identified chemical toilet disposal point, and that the campsite will provide water and waste water drainage points and bin areas. If not the case, we comment. We do mention certain features that some readers find important: washbasins in cubicles, facilities for babies, facilities for those with disabilities and motorcaravan service points. Readers with disabilities are advised to contact the site of their choice to ensure that facilities are appropriate to their needs.

Shop

Basic or fully supplied, and opening dates.

Bars, restaurants, takeaway facilities and entertainment

We try hard to supply opening and closing dates (if other than the campsite opening dates) and to identify if there are discos or other entertainment.

Children's play areas

Fenced and with safety surface (e.g. sand, bark or pea-gravel).

Swimming pools

If particularly special, we cover in detail in our main campsite description but reference is always included under our Facilities listings. We will also indicate the existence of water slides, sunbathing areas and other features. Opening dates, charges and levels of supervision are provided where we have been notified.

Leisure facilities

For example, playing fields, bicycle hire, organised activities and entertainment.

Dogs

If dogs are not accepted or restrictions apply, we state it here. Check the quick reference list at the back of the guide.

Off site

This briefly covers leisure facilities, tourist attractions, restaurants etc. nearby.

Charges

These are the latest provided to us by the parks. In those cases where 2009 prices are not given, we try to give a general guide.

Opening dates

These are advised to us during the early autumn of the previous year – parks can, and sometimes do, alter these dates before the start of the following season, often for good reasons. If you intend to visit shortly after a published opening date, or shortly before the closing date, it is wise to check that it will actually be open at the time required. Similarly some parks operate a restricted service during the low season, only opening some of their facilities (e.g. swimming pools) during the main season; where we know about this, and have the relevant dates, we indicate it – again if you are at all doubtful it is wise to check.

Sometimes, campsite amenities may be dependant on there being enough customers on site to justify their opening and, for this reason, actual opening dates may vary from those indicated.

Special pitches

We note an ever increasing number of 'special' pitches under a variety of fancy names (for example, Executive, Panorama, Super). These provide a range of extra facilities such as waste water disposal, TV and phone connections, hardstanding, patios, etc. and they are often booked up well in advance. Readers interested in such pitches should contact the park concerned to check exactly what is provided. People with disabilities are also advised to telephone before turning up to ensure that facilities are appropriate to their particular needs.

Whether you're an 'old hand' in terms of camping and caravanning or are contemplating your first trip, a regular reader of our Guides or a new 'convert', we wish you well in your travels and hope we have been able to help in some way.

We are, of course, also out and about ourselves, visiting parks, talking to owners and readers, and generally checking on standards and new developments.

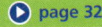 Holiday homes ▶ page 322

Our NEW Holiday Home section

Over recent years, more and more parks in Britain and Ireland have added high quality holiday home accommodation in the form of caravan holiday homes, chalets and lodges. In response to feedback from many of our readers, and to reflect this evolution in campsites, we have decided to introduce a separate section on caravan holiday homes and chalets (see page 322). If a park has decided to contribute to this section, it is indicated above our site report in the main body of the guide with a page reference where the full details are given. We feature parks offering some of the best accommodation available and have included full details of one or two accommodation types at these parks. Please note however that many other campsites listed in this guide may also have a selection of accommodation for rent.

We wish all our readers thoroughly enjoyable Camping and Caravanning in 2009 – favoured by good weather of course!

THE ALAN ROGERS TEAM

Regions

SCOTLAND

Northumbria

NORTHERN IRELAND

Cumbria

Yorkshire

North West England

Heart of England

REPUBLIC OF IRELAND

WALES

East of England

Southern England

London

South West England

South East England

Channel Islands

The Alan Rogers Awards

The Alan Rogers Campsite Awards were launched in 2004 and have proved a great success.

Our awards have a broad scope and before committing to our winners, we carefully consider more than 2,000 campsites featured in our guides, taking into account comments from our site assessors, our head office team and, of course, our readers.

Our award winners come from the four corners of Europe, from southern Portugal to Slovenia, and this year we are making awards to campsites in 13 different countries.

Needless to say, it's an extremely difficult task to choose our eventual winners, but we believe that we have identified a number of campsites with truly outstanding characteristics.

In each case, we have selected an outright winner, along with two highly commended runners-up.

Listed below are full details of each of our award categories and our winners for 2008.

Our warmest congratulations to all our award winners and our commiserations to all those not having won an award on this occasion.

THE ALAN ROGERS TEAM

Alan Rogers Progress Award 2008

This award reflects the hard work and commitment undertaken by particular site owners to improve and upgrade their site.

WINNER

PO8202	Turiscampo, Portugal

RUNNERS-UP

DE3202	Grav-Insel, Germany
IT60450	Marina di Venezia, Italy

Alan Rogers Welcome Award 2008

This award takes account of sites offering a particularly friendly welcome and maintaining a friendly ambience throughout reader's holidays.

WINNER

FR05000	Princes d'Orange, France

RUNNERS-UP

FR71110	Du Lac, France
DK2022	Vikær Diernæs, Denmark

Alan Rogers Active Holiday Award 2008

This award reflects sites in outstanding locations which are ideally suited for active holidays, notably walking or cycling, but which could extend to include such activities as winter sports or water sports

WINNER

FR07120 L'Ardéchois, France

RUNNERS-UP

SV4210	Sobec, Slovenia
AU0265	Park Grubhof, Austria

Alan Rogers Motorhome Award 2008

Motorhome sales are increasing and this award acknowledges sites which, in our opinion, have made outstanding efforts to welcome motorhome clients.

WINNER

UK0220 Trevornick, England

RUNNERS-UP

BE0655	De Lilse Bergen, Belgium
CZ4840	Oase Praha, Czech Republic

Alan Rogers 4 Seasons Award 2008

This award is made to outstanding sites with extended opening dates and which welcome clients to a uniformly high standard throughout the year.

WINNER

AU0440 Schluga, Austria

RUNNERS-UP

NL6520	BreeBronne, Netherlands
ES92950	Don Cactus, Spain

Alan Rogers Seaside Award 2008

This award is made for sites which we feel are outstandingly suitable for a really excellent seaside holiday.

WINNER

NL5735 Tempelhof, Netherlands

RUNNERS-UP

UK1070	Woolacombe Bay, England
CR6732	Polari, Croatia

Alan Rogers Country Award 2008

This award contrasts with our former award and acknowledges sites which are attractively located in delightful, rural locations.

WINNER

FR23030 Creuse Nature, France

RUNNERS-UP

ES90260	El Burro Blanco, Spain
IT62090	Vidor, Italy

Alan Rogers Rented Accommodation Award 2008

Given the increasing importance of rented accommodation on many campsites, we feel that it is important to acknowledge sites which have made a particular effort in creating a high quality 'rented accommodation' park.

WINNER

IT60370 Jesolo International, Italy

RUNNERS-UP

FR33300	La Jenny, France
NL5560	De Wijde Blick, Netherlands

Alan Rogers Unique Site Award 2008

This award acknowledges sites with unique, outstanding features – something which simply cannot be found elsewhere and which is an important attraction of the site.

WINNER

FR34070 Sérignan, France

RUNNERS-UP

IT60030	Pra' delle Torri, Italy
DE3182	Teutoburger Wald, Germany

Alan Rogers Family Site Award 2008

Many sites claim to be child friendly but this award acknowledges the sites we feel to be the very best in this respect.

WINNER

FR32010 Camp de Florence, France

RUNNERS-UP

ES80350	L'Amfora, Spain
IT62630	Bella Italia, Italy

Alan Rogers Readers' Award 2008

We believe our Readers' Award to be the most important. We simply invite our readers (by means of an on-line poll at www.alanrogers.com) to nominate the site they enjoyed most.

The outright winner for 2008 is:

WINNER

IT60200 Union Lido, Italy

Alan Rogers Special Award 2008

A special award is made to acknowledge sites which we feel have overcome a very significant setback, and have, not only returned to their former condition, but has added extra amenities and can therefore be fairly considered to be even better than before. In 2008 we acknowledged two campsites, which have undergone major problems and have made highly impressive recoveries.

UK2885	Warner Farm, England
FR32080	Le Talouch, France

MAPS 1 & 2

The West Country is a diverse region of beautiful sandy bea[ches], steep craggy cliffs, desolate moors and rolling green hills. Home of clotted cream teas, it also boasts a range of historical and modern attractions, including t[he] celebrated Eden Project.

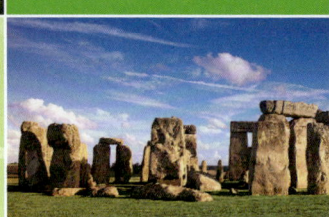

THE SOUTH WEST COMPRISES: CORNWALL, DEVON, SOMERSET, BATH, BRISTOL, SOUTH GLOUCESTERSHIRE, WILTSHIRE AND WEST DORSET.

With its dramatic cliffs, pounded by the Atlantic ocean, and beautiful coastline boasting warm waters, soft sandy beaches and small seaside towns, Cornwall is one of England's most popular holiday destinations. The coast is also a surfers' paradise, while inland the wild and rugged Bodmin Moors dominate the landscape. In Devon, the Dartmoor National Park has sweeping moorland and granite tors where wild ponies roam freely. Much of the countryside is gentle rolling green fields, dotted with pretty thatched cottages. The coastline around Torbay is known as the English Riviera which, due to its temperate climate, allows palm trees to grow. Stretching across East Devon and West Dorset is the fossil-ridden Jurassic Coast, a World Heritage Site. West Dorset is also home to Lyme Regis and Weymouth, which comes alive in summer when regular entertainment, including a carnival and fireworks, is held along the seafront. Famous for its cider and cheese, Somerset is good walking country, with the Exmoor National Park, which also straddles Devon. Wiltshire's natural attractions include the Marlborough Downs, Savernake Forest and the River Avon. It also boasts one of the most famous prehistoric sites in the world, the ancient stone circles of Stonehenge.

Places of interest

Bath: World Heritage Site full of Roman [a]. Georgian architecture, elegant streets su[ch as] the Circle and Royal Crescent, Roman ba[ths]

Bristol: steeped in maritime history with [the] world's first great Ocean Liner; Brunel's Clifton Suspension bridge; range of museums and art galleries.

Cornwall: seaside town of St Ives; Land's End; Eden Project; Penzance and St Michael's Mount.

Devon: popular seaside resorts of Torqu[ay] Paignton and Brixham; cities of Exeter a[nd] Plymouth.

Somerset: Weston-Super-Mare; Wells Cathedral; Cheddar Gorge and Wookey Hole caves.

West Dorset: Dorchester, home of Thom[as] Hardy; Isle of Portland; Abbotsbury villa[ge] with swannery.

Wiltshire: Salisbury; Glastonbury; Longle[at] manor house and safari park.

Did you know?

Chesil Beach is an 18 mile stretch of fortress-like walls of pebbles, formed 12,000 years ago.

There are numerous white horses carve[d] into the landscape across the South We[st]

The Jurassic Coast is a Natural World Heritage Site stretching for 95 miles.

The Black Death entered England throu[gh] the port in Weymouth in 1348.

Britain's oldest complete skeleton, Cheddar Man, was buried in Gough's C[ave] 9,000 years ago.

At 404 feet Salisbury Cathedral has the tallest medieval spire in the world.

Map 1 (North Cornwall / South West)

0380
BUDE
Devon

BOSCASTLE *

0360
* CAMELFORD
LAUNCESTON *

A30

A39

PADSTOW *
0430 0505
0500
0302
0230 0300
WADEBRIDGE
0805

SOUTH WEST

0306
* BODMIN
* LISKEARD
A38
0440

0205 0200
NEWQUAY 0170 0210
0220 0530
0310
0270
0280
0400
0285 0195
0190
0320
LOOE

0160 0165
0120 0140
Cornwall
0290
0145
0415
0255
0250
0400

0125
0510
0012
0010 * TRURO
0155
0150
MEVAGISSEY

0030
0040 ST IVES
0050
0035
A30
* REDRUTH
0016
0180

0018
0065 0060
0480
0025
PENZANCE
* HELSTON
0090

0450 0450
* FALMOUTH

0490 0070

RED TEXT DENOTES ALL YEAR SITE

0   5   10   Miles 15   20   25
0   8   2 16 Kms 4   32   40

Map 2 (Devon / Somerset / Dorset)

1145
ILFRACOMBE 1257
0720 1120
0730 0725
1070 1075
0735
1150
0690
0710
1140
0680
LYNMOUTH
1370
* MINEHEAD
1380
1480
A38
1560

0700

1360
1590
1350
Somerset

* BARNSTAPLE
0745
1355
SOUTH MOLTON
A361
1520
TAUNTON *
1340
A358

A39
1065
GREAT TORRINGTON *
* CHULMLEIGH
1060
TIVERTON *
0750
M5

SOUTH WEST
A377
1000
A30

0380
* BUDE
HONITON *
A35
Dorset West
1730
1760

* OKEHAMPTON
0760
EXETER *
1110 1020
1720
LYME REGIS
1810

LAUNCESTON *
A30
1250
Devon
1100
SIDMOUTH

A386
0940
0970
1010 1095

0300
0790
0800
0802
0960 0980
0950
0880 0915
0910
1080
NEWTON ABBOT

Cornwall
TAVISTOCK
0805
ASHBURTON
0900
TORQUAY

* LISKEARD
A38
0440
0865
0860 1130
0850 0870

0400 0320
LOOE
PLYMOUTH *
0810
TOTNES *
0820
0840
0845
0835
* DARTMOUTH

0300

KINGSBRIDGE *
0830
0825
0826
* SALCOMBE

RED TEXT DENOTES ALL YEAR SITE

0   5   10   Miles 15   20   25
0   8   16 Kms 24   32   40

WALES
South Wales

M4
CARDIFF
● 5925
● 5927

Gloucestershire
HEART
BRISTOL
● 1440
A4
● 1460 ✳ BATH
A36

WESTON-SUPER-MARE ✳
● 1530
● 1580
● 1570
● 1575
● 1510
A38

LYNMOUTH
● 0680
● 1370
✳ MINEHEAD
● 1380
● 1545
● 1430
● 1550
● 1490
A39
● 1690
A361

WELLS ✳
● 1560
GLASTONBURY ✳
● 1390
● 1540
● 1480
● 1360
● 1590
● 1355
● 1350

Somerset

● 0745
✳ SOUTH MOLTON
A361
● 1520
TAUNTON ✳
● 1340
M5
● 1500
A303

Devon
● 0750
TIVERTON ✳
● 1420
A358
✳ YEOVIL

SOUTHERN

● 1060
● 1000
A30
A37

HONITON ✳
Dorset
West
● 1770
Dorset
East

● 0760 EXETER ✳
● 1730
● 1760
● 1810
LYME REGIS ✳
● 1750
A35
DORCHESTER ✳
● 1100
● 1110
● 1020
✳ SIDMOUTH
● 1720
● 1740
● 1780

A377

RED TEXT DENOTES ALL YEAR SITE

Miles
0   5   10   15   20   25
0   8   16   24   32   40
Kms

● 0940
● 0970
A38
● 1010 ● 1095
● 1830 ● 1820
● 1800
✳ WEYMOUTH

● 4170
● 2570
RED TEXT DENOTES ALL YEAR SITE

Miles
0   5   10   15   20   25
0   8   16   24   32   40
Kms

● 4100

Oxfordshire
A34

A433   A429
HEART
Gloucestershire
SWINDON ✳

Berkshire
M4

● 1680
● BRISTOL
● 1440
✳ CHIPPENHAM
A4
● 1660
**SOUTH
WEST**

● 1460 ✳ BATH
● 1700
A346

● 1510
Wiltshire

Somerset
● 1630

A39
✳ WELLS
A361 ● 1690
✳ WARMINSTER
A303
SOUTHERN

● 1490
● 1540
A36

Hampshire

A350
SALISBURY
● 1650
WINCHESTER ✳
● 1500
A303
Dorset
East
A354
● 1670
● 2380

SOUTHERN
● 1640
● 2290
✳ YEOVIL
● 1655
● 2360
✳ SOUTHAMPTON

UK0010 Chacewater Park

Cox Hill, Chacewater, Truro TR4 8LY (Cornwall)

Tel: 01209 820762. Email: enquiries@chacewaterpark.co.uk   www.alanrogers.com/UK0010

For those who want to be away from the hectic coastal resorts and to take advantage of the peace and quiet of an 'adults only' park, this will be an excellent value-for-money choice. Chacewater has a pleasant rural situation and the site is run with care by Richard Peterken and his daughters Debbie and Mandy. It provides 100 level touring pitches, all with electricity (10A) and 80 with hardstanding, in two large field areas (slight slope) edged with trees or in small bays formed by hedges. There are 29 serviced pitches (with electricity, water, and drainage) and an area reserved for dog owners.

Facilities

The main toilet block provides well equipped showers and two en-suite units. Laundry room. Second fully equipped block near reception providing roomy showers open direct to outside. Gas supplies. Icepack service. Library in reception. Only adults are accepted (over 30 yrs). One dog (certain breeds) only by arrangement. Off site: Golf, riding and bicycle hire, all within 3 miles. Bus stop 100 yds.

Open: 1 May - 30 September.

Directions

On the A30 take A3047 signed Scorrier and continue under bridge to roundabout where left towards St Day. In 500 yards turn right at crossroads onto the B3298 signed St Day. After 1 mile turn left at crossroads and continue for a mile, then left at blue camping sign (by Truro Tractors). Site is next right. O.S.GR: SW742439. GPS: N50:15.048 W05:10.353

Charges guide

Per unit incl. 2 adults	£ 13.00 - £ 16.00
dog (one only)	£ 1.00
Discounts for senior citizens.	

UK0016 Lanyon Holiday Park

Loscombe Lane, Four Lanes, Redruth TR16 6LP (Cornwall)

Tel: 01209 313474. Email: jamierielly@btconnect.com   www.alanrogers.com/UK0016

Lanyon's location is a pleasant surprise after the somewhat grey landscape found in parts of the tip of Cornwall. Tucked away down a lane, the holiday caravans are attractively situated with hedged touring fields beyond. A neat tarmac road curves around to reception, the pub and an indoor pool. There are 25 large hedged touring pitches around the edge of two level fields and room for around 40 tents in high season in a separate field. A large play area for children is overlooked by the roof top terrace of the bar. This is a pleasant, nice relaxed destination for a family holiday with something for everyone and splendid views across the surrounding countryside to the sea.

Facilities

Three fully equipped toilet blocks, the one attached to reception with heating. The other two are of 'portacabin' type but well maintained. Showers may be in short supply at peak times. Laundry room. Bar serving meals (Spring BH, w/ends until mid-July). Heated indoor pool (10 x 4 m). Games room. Play area and trampoline. Off site: Riding 1 mile. Fishing and golf 2 miles. Bicycle hire 2.5 miles. Beach 5 miles. Watersports at St Stithian's reservoir 1 mile.

Open: Easter - 31 October.

Directions

From southwest side of Redruth take B3297 Helston road. After 1 mile enter Four Lanes village. Pass two shops then take second right into Loscombe Lane. Follow to park on right. O.S.GR: SW683387. GPS: N50:12.175 W05:14.732

Charges guide

Per person	£ 5.00 - £ 8.00
child (under 16 yrs)	£ 2.00 - £ 4.00
pitch incl. electricity	free - £ 3.00

UK0018 Bone Valley Caravan & Camping Park

Heamoor, Penzance TR20 8UJ (Cornwall)

Tel: 01736 360313. Email: enquiries@bonevalleycandcpark.co.uk   www.alanrogers.com/UK0018

A small garden-like park tucked away at the back of Penzance, Bone Valley has 5 caravan holiday homes to let and 17 touring pitches. There is also room for a few tents tucked behind hedges and all is accessed by a circular road. The park is surrounded by tall trees with fresh water in a small stream coming straight off the moors (good for keeping bottles cold). The philosophy of its owner can be summed up by his words, 'use your common sense and there is no need for rules and regulations'. A bus leaves from the village every half hour to Penzance but it only takes about 25 minutes to walk.

Facilities

The small toilet block is traditional in style, bright and cheerful. Washing machine, dryer with large sink. Reception carries some emergency supplies. Simple meals served in a pleasant room with TV/radio and small library. Kettle, tea ,coffee and sugar provided with a welcome drink on arrival. Off site: Village has shops, pub etc. Beach, boat launching, bicycle hire and fishing 1.5 miles.

Open: All year.

Directions

Take the A30 from Penzance and at second roundabout take fourth exit signed Madron. Take fourth turn right into Joseph's Lane signed Gulval, then next left signed Bone Valley. Park is 600 yards. O.S.GR: SW461318. GPS: N50:08.048 W05:33.156

Charges guide

Per person (over 15 yrs)	£ 3.00
pitch incl. electricity	£ 7.00 - £ 9.00

15

UK0012 Killiwerris Camping & Caravan Park

Penstraze, Chacewater, Truro TR4 8PF (Cornwall)

Tel: **01872 561356**. Email: **killiwerris @aol.com**

www.alanrogers.com/UK0012

Tucked down a Cornish lane, Killiwerris is a rare find. It has been developed from a large garden and the field surrounding the house into a small and delightful touring park which provides 20 good sized pitches for caravans and motorcaravans. Of these, 17 are semi-separated either by low fencing or hedging, all with hardstanding in the front field with flowering shrubs sheltered by Monteray pines and other indigenous trees. The birds love it, as do adult humans – the park is 'adult only' so it is very peaceful. Three further pitches are found in the back field. Electricity (10/16A) is available for all the pitches with water points between two.

Facilities

A small heated toilet block provides for all needs with one shower each for men and women and ladies having one toilet/washbasin cubicle. Grab rails for disabled visitors. Separate laundry room. Off site: Bus stop 8 minutes level walk. Chacewater village (shop, pub, etc.) 1 mile. Beach 4.5 miles. Fishing 2 miles. Golf 2 miles. Riding 1.5 miles. Bicycle hire 2-3 miles.

Open: Easter - end October.

Directions

Using the A30 in the direction of Penzance, exit at Chiverton Cross roundabout (this large roundabout is 28 miles west of Bodmin) signed for Truro and St Agnes. Take third exit for Blackwater and in 500 yards turn left into Kea Down Road. Park is 1 mile on right. O.S.GR: SW753455. GPS: N50:15.930 W05:09.300

Charges guide

Per unit incl. 2 persons, electricity and awning	£ 12.00 - £ 16.00
extra person	£ 3.50
dog (max. 2)	£ 0.50
No credit cards.	

UK0025 Roselands Caravan & Camping Park

Dowran, Saint Just, Penzance TR19 7RS (Cornwall)

Tel: **01736 788571**. Email: **info@roselands.co.uk**

www.alanrogers.com/UK0025

Roselands is a small, family owned park situated on the Cornish moors overlooking the village of St Just and with marvellous views of the sea and countryside around Lands End. In all there are 14 holiday homes to let, 17 level grassy touring pitches (all with 16A electricity) and some provision for tents. The owner's home provides a bar and conservatory, along with reception and a small shop, sit in the centre of the park. The conservatory acts as a community family room with games, internet facility and tourist information with a play area outside and a games room nearby. This area is very popular with walkers and birdwatchers. Bicycles are available to hire. The park itself originated in 1972 in old clay pits – the area where most of the holiday homes are located was one of the pits and is consequently very sheltered. Subsequent owners have added to the house and the new owners, Craig and Kerry with their young family do everything themselves. This includes running the little bar which also serves food and making suggestions for walks (with or without your dog) and what to see and do. Craig is very knowledgeable and will also organise fishing trips.

Facilities

Small traditional toilet block, fully equipped and can be heated. Laundry facilities. Small shop mainly for basics and gas. Bar with bar food served in conservatory (all year). TV and internet access. Play area. Games room. Bicycle hire. Off site: Fishing and Golf 1 mile. Riding 2 miles. Beach and surfing 2 miles at Sennen Cove. Boat launching 5 miles. Nearby Lands End and Cape Cornwall. Minack Outdoor Theatre.

Open: 1 January - 31 October.

Directions

Take the A3071 from Penzance for St Just. Follow for 5.5 miles and 0.5 miles before St Just turn left at sign for site. O.S.GR: SW386302. GPS: N50:06.794 W05:39.480

Charges guide

Per unit incl. 2 persons	£ 8.00 - £ 10.00
incl. electricity	£ 10.00 - £ 12.50
extra person	£ 2.00
child (under 5 yrs)	£ 1.00

You might also like to consider...

 www.alanrogers.com for latest campsite news

UK0040 Trevalgan Touring Park

Saint Ives TR26 3BJ (Cornwall)

Tel: **01736 792048**. Email: **recept@trevalgantouringpark.co.uk**   www.alanrogers.com/UK0040

Trevalgan is owned by the same family that owns Ayr Holiday Park. It is a quiet, traditional style of park, located on the cliffs 1.5 miles west of bustling St Ives. It is a truly rural location where you can enjoy spectacular views and an abundance of flora and fauna. There are 120 clearly marked pitches (88 with 16A electricity and some with water as well) in two level fields edged by Cornish stone walls – it could be a little exposed on a windy day. The park is very popular with walkers with direct access to the coastal path. A member of the Countryside Discovery group.

Facilities

A fully equipped toilet block includes a baby room and facilities for disabled visitors. Motorcaravan service point. Campers' kitchen. Small shop (in reception). Mobile shop calls daily. Gas supplies. Games field, adventure play area and crazy golf. Giant draughts and chess. Purpose built games room with TV and coffee machine. Off site: Fishing 3 miles. Bicycle hire 8 miles. Riding and golf within 2 miles. Regular bus service to St Ives and back (June - mid Sept). As well as the coastal path, a path leads to St Ives across the fields (30-40 minutes).

Open: 1 May - 30 September.

Directions

Approach site down a narrow Cornish lane from the B3306 St Ives - Lands End road, following sign. O.S.GR: SW490400. GPS: N50:12.461 W05:31.129

Charges guide

Per person	£ 3.25 - £ 4.50
child (5-16 yrs)	£ 1.50 - £ 2.50
pitch	£ 6.00 - £ 11.00
dog	£ 1.50 - £ 2.00

For a more rural experience

'A touring park just 2 miles from St.Ives town centre. Beautiful scenery, new facilities, serviced pitches, summer bus service to town. Ideal for families, walkers, cyclists - explore St.Ives and West Cornwall.'

www.trevalgantouringpark.co.uk   Telephone: 01736 792048

UK0050 Polmanter Tourist Park

Halsetown, Saint Ives TR26 3LX (Cornwall)

Tel: **01736 795640**. Email: **reception@polmanter.com**   www.alanrogers.com/UK0050

A popular and attractively developed park, Polmanter is located high up at the back of St Ives, with wonderful sea and country views. The Osborne family has worked hard to develop Polmanter as a complete family base. Converted farm buildings provide a cosy bar lounge with conservatory overlooking the heated swimming pool. The 250 touring pitches (no caravan holiday homes) are well spaced in several fields divided by established shrubs and hedges giving large, level, individual pitches with connecting tarmac roads. There are 87 serviced pitches with electricity, water, waste water and TV point, 10 with hardstanding. The remaining pitches all have 16A electricity. It is a busy park with a happy atmosphere within 1.5 miles of St Ives. A footpath leads from the park (20 minutes downhill) or there is a bus service from the park in high season (hourly, 10.00 - midnight). A member of the Best of British group.

Facilities

Three fully equipped toilet blocks can be heated and include en-suite family rooms. Facilities for disabled visitors. Baby room. Fully equipped laundry. Motorcaravan service point. Well stocked shop. Bar with food and family area (Whitsun - mid Sept). Takeaway. Heated swimming pool (Whitsun - mid Sept). Some entertainment (peak season). Tennis. Putting. Play area. Sports field. Games room. Off site: Golf 1 mile. Fishing, riding, bicycle hire and boat launching within 2 miles. Indoor pool and leisure centre at St Ives. Note: dogs are banned from the St Ives beaches in high season.

Open: 1 April - 31 October.

Directions

Take A3074 to St Ives from the A30 and then first left at a mini-roundabout taking 'Holiday Route' (B3311) to St Ives (Halsetown). At T-junction turn right for Halsetown, right again at the Halsetown Inn then first left. O.S.GR: SW509392. GPS: N50:11.771 W05:29.461

Charges guide

Per unit incl. 2 persons and awning	£ 13.00 - £ 23.00
incl. mains services	£ 16.00 - £ 26.00
extra person	£ 3.00 - £ 7.00
child (3-15 yrs)	£ 2.50 - £ 5.50
dog (max. 2)	free - £ 2.50

Camping Cheques accepted.

17

UK0030 Ayr Holiday Park

Higher Ayr, Saint Ives TR26 1EJ (Cornwall)

Tel: **01736 795855**. Email: **recept@ayrholidaypark.co.uk**   www.alanrogers.com/UK0030

Ayr Holiday Park has an unparalleled position overlooking St Ives Bay and Porthmeor beach and is a popular well cared for site. On first arrival it may seem to be all caravan holiday homes, but behind them is a series of naturally sloping fields with marvellous views providing a total of 90 pitches, of which 40 are for touring caravans and motorcaravans. These pitches are on grass, all with 16A electricity and several fully serviced. An extra field for tents is open in July and August. A 'state of the art' toilet block provides excellent facilities in a colourful and modern design. St Ives centre with restaurants, bars and supermarkets is within easy walking distance, as is the new Tate Gallery. There is direct access to the coastal footpath.

Facilities

The excellent toilet block includes two family shower rooms and facilities for baby changing and disabled people. Wetsuit showers. Fully equipped laundry room. Motorcaravan point. Games room with TV, hot drinks and snack machines. Adventure play area. Contact park if you wish to take a dog. Off site: Spa shop nearby. Tate Gallery and beaches within walking distance. Leisure centre with indoor pool nearby. Golf 1 mile. Riding 2 miles. Sea and coarse fishing 2-3 miles.

Open: All year.

Directions

Leave the A30 and in 300 yds turn left at mini-roundabout following signs for St Ives for heavy vehicles and day visitors (not town centre). After 2 miles this joins the B3311, then the B3306 1 mile from St Ives (an octagonal building on left). Still heading for St Ives turn left at a mini-roundabout following camping signs through residential areas. Park entrance is 600 yds at Ayr Terrace. O.S.GR: SW515388. GPS: N50:12.757 W05:29.357

Charges guide

Per person	£ 3.50 - £ 5.50
child (5-16 yrs)	£ 1.75 - £ 3.00
pitch	£ 7.00 - £ 18.00
services, plus	£ 3.75

UK0035 Little Trevarrack Holiday Park

Laity Lane, Carbis Bay, Saint Ives TR26 3HW (Cornwall)

Tel: **01736 797580**. Email: **info@littletrevarrack.co.uk**   www.alanrogers.com/UK0035

Little Trevarrack is a traditional Cornish park covering 20 acres, with wonderful views from the top of the site across St Ives bay towards Hayle and the surrounding countryside. It is owned by Neil, son of the owners of Polmanter Park, and Annette Osborne and has a smart, large reception and entrance. There are 234 pitches, in five open fields (the top ones with gentle slopes), 153 with 10A electricity and 15 with water and drain as well. Bushes and hedging have grown to provide individual pitches and give a continental appearance to the park. A smart heated outdoor pool also provides a paddling pool and sunbathing area. Landscaped and fenced, a new play area is alongside. Carbis Bay with its safe sandy beach is ideal for families with young children and is less than a mile away. In high season a bus runs hourly into St Ives. This is a developing park which will provide a quiet, peaceful base from which to explore St Ives and the southern tip of Cornwall.

Facilities

The large, central toilet block is modern and well equipped. Baby room and facilities for disabled visitors in the reception building. Laundry. Heated swimming and paddling pools. Games room. Internet access and WiFi. Play area and play field. Wild flower field with paths for dog walking. No kites allowed. Early and late arrivals area. Off site: Golf and riding 2 miles. Bicycle hire 4 miles. Beach and fishing 1 mile. Dogs are banned from the St Ives beaches in high season.

Open: 1 April - 30 September.

Directions

Follow signs for St Ives and take A3074 to Carbis Bay. Site is signed on left opposite junction to Carbis Bay beach. Follow road for 150 yds, cross small crossroads and site is the second turn on the right. O.S.GR: SW52737 GPS: N50:11.234 W05:28.250

Charges guide

Per unit incl. 2 persons and electricity	£ 15.00 - £ 25.50
incl. water and waste water	£ 17.50 - £ 29.50
extra person	£ 2.50 - £ 6.50
child (3-15 yrs)	£ 2.00 - £ 4.50
dog (max. 2)	£ 1.00 - £ 3.00

UK0060 **River Valley Country Park**

Relubbus, Penzance TR20 9ER (Cornwall)

Tel: **01736 763398**. Email: **rivervalley@surfbay.dircon.co.uk**   www.alanrogers.com/UK0060

River Valley is a quiet park set in the 18 acres of a partly wooded, peaceful river valley. It offers a mix of 75 timber lodges, caravan holiday homes and 50 touring pitches. The large, well spaced touring pitches are in small meadows or natural clearings. Most are clearly defined with shrubs, hedges or trees and 15A electrical connections are available. The caravan holiday homes and lodges, some privately owned, are in more or less separate areas, beside the river at the far end of the park or on the hillside at the back. A fence separates the park from the river and there is a pleasant walk for 2.5 miles alongside it, popular for walking dogs. Much of the valley is a protected nature reserve and the park encourages wildlife by not using weed killers and by leaving parts uncut – badgers, foxes, herons, kingfishers and glow-worms are regular visitors. St Michael's Mount is only 3 miles and can be reached by footpath. This is a very special park, very well run by Brian and Eileen Milsom. A member of the Surf Bay Leisure Group.

Facilities

Three well maintained toilet blocks include family shower rooms. Some private cabins for ladies and make-up room with hair dryers. Separate laundry facilities and baby bath. Motorcaravan service point. Shop/reception.
Off site: Bicycle hire 5 miles. Riding, fishing and golf 3 miles. Beach 3 miles.

Open: 31 March - 27 October.

Directions

From A30 at St Michaels Mount roundabout, take A394 towards Helston. At next roundabout take B3280 to Relubbus. In about 3 miles in village turn left just over a small bridge. O.S.GR: SW566320. GPS: N50:08.574 W05:24.761

Charges guide

Per unit incl. 2 persons and electricity	£ 8.50 - £ 17.50
extra person	£ 1.50 - £ 3.25
dog	£ 1.00
awning or pup tent	£ 2.00
Min. charge 2 adults per vehicle.	

UK0070 Silver Sands Holiday Park

Gwendreath, Ruan Minor, Helston TR12 7LZ (Cornwall)

Tel: **01326 290631**. Email: **enquiries@silversandsholidaypark.co.uk**

www.alanrogers.com/UK0070

Silver Sands is a small, peaceful 'away-from-it-all' park in a remote part of the Lizard peninsula, the most southerly part of mainland Britain and an 'area of outstanding natural beauty'. It is tucked away behind two other holiday home parks (possible noise in season). The park itself has 16 caravan holiday homes, along with 36 touring pitches of which 20 have 5A electrical hook-ups. The pitches are large, attractively situated and divided into individual bays by flowering shrubs and bushes. The adjoining tent field has similar pitches (4 with electricity) where the shrubs are growing (some pitches are slightly sloping). The park is only reached after passing Culdrose Naval Base and the Goonhilly Earth Station down a single track road. A half mile footpath leads down through a small valley to the twin beaches of Kennack Sands (one is dog-free) divided by a small headland. This is generally an unspoilt walking area with the coastal path passing through and under the care of English Nature. A member of the Countryside Discovery group.

Facilities

The fully equipped toilet block includes an en-suite room for disabled visitors, doubling as a family room. Some play equipment. An undeveloped 3 acre field can be used for walking, kite flying, etc. Off site: Restaurant nearby, pub within walking distance. Fishing 1 mile. Bicycle hire 5 miles. Boat launching 2 or 7 miles. Riding 5 miles. Golf 6 miles.

Open: Easter - mid September.

Directions

From Helston take A3038 Lizard road. After Culdrose turn left on B3293 passing Goonhilly after 4 miles. At next crossroads turn right (Kennack Sands), continue for 1.5 miles then left to Gwendreath on single track road – site is 1 mile. O.S.GR: SW732170. GPS: N50:00.540 W05:10.140

Charges guide

Per unit incl. 2 persons	£ 10.00 - £ 15.00
incl. electricity	£ 12.00 - £ 17.00
extra person	£ 2.50 - £ 3.90
child (under 16 yrs)	£ 1.50 - £ 2.20
dog	£ 1.50 - £ 2.20

Reductions for some bookings.

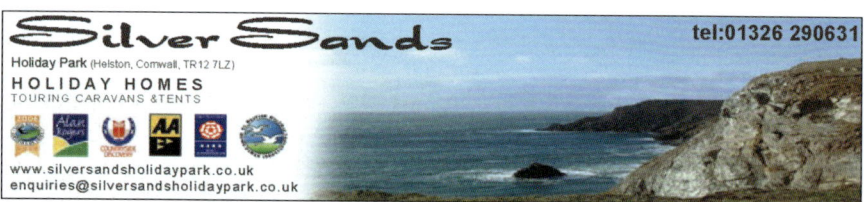

Silver Sands

Holiday Park (Helston, Cornwall, TR12 7LZ)

HOLIDAY HOMES
TOURING CARAVANS &TENTS

tel:01326 290631

www.silversandsholidaypark.co.uk
enquiries@silversandsholidaypark.co.uk

UK0065 Wayfarers Camping & Caravan Park

Relubbus Lane, Saint Hilary, Penzance TR20 9EF (Cornwall)

Tel: **01736 763326**. Email: **elaine@wayfarerspark.co.uk**

www.alanrogers.com/UK0065

Wayfarers is a neat and tidy garden-like park reserved for adults only in rural Cornwall. Sheltered by perimeter trees and consisting of two finely mown fields interspersed by shrubs and palm-like trees, 42 places are available for caravans (up to 23 ft. single axle), motorcaravans (up to 22 ft) and tents, plus 4 holiday caravans to rent. There are 36 pitches with 16A electricity with hardstanding available on 24. Should you enjoy walking you can follow the River Hayle down to St Erth. There are many more suggestions with maps and a good display of leaflets in the information room, including a star chart. The owners Elaine and Steve live on site and make you very welcome maintaining the park to a high standard. Do look at the dolls house in the shop. Built by Elaine's father the detail and furniture is amazing. The Lizard and Lands End with the Minnack Theatre wait to be explored and St Michael's Mount is only 2 miles away.

Facilities

The modern toilet block is fully equipped. Ladies have a wash cubicle and there are two smart en-suite shower rooms (key system). Fully equipped laundry. Dishwashing sinks in the house. Shop stocks basics. No twin axle caravans. Dogs are not accepted. Off site: Two pubs with food in Goldsithney 1 mile. Fishing 1 mile. Golf 1.5 miles. Riding 1 mile. Bicycle hire 2 miles. Boat launching 5 miles. Beach 2 miles. Sailing 5 miles.

Open: April - September.

Directions

Following the A30 (Penzance) take the A394 Helston road after the St Ives turning. Follow for 1 mile then turn left on the B3280 and pass through Goldsithney village and site is 1 mile further on left. O.S.GR: SW559314. GPS: N50:07.990 W05:25.010

Charges guide

Per unit incl. 2 persons and electricity	£ 11.00 - £ 19.00
extra person	£ 5.00

UK0090 Trethem Mill Touring Park

Saint Just-in-Roseland, Saint Mawes, Truro TR2 5JF (Cornwall)

Tel: **01872 580504**. Email: **reception@trethem.com**

The Akeroyd family are proud of their park and work hard to keep it really well maintained. They aim to attract couples and families who seek peace and tranquillity, and can manage without a bar and on-site entertainment. Trethem is a 'strictly touring' park with 84 pitches all with electricity, 15 with water and waste water. Over 60 are on hardstanding with TV connections. The pitches are large, most on slightly sloping ground, some terraced, with the lower field more level and sheltered. All are individual or in bays, divided by hedging (some still growing) giving your own area. Generally there is a good spacious feel. There is a circular tarmac access road and careful landscaping (the park is a mass of colour in season). The area around reception is particularly pretty where a small watermill has been built amongst the flowers – the sound of gently flowing water is very relaxing. Saint Mawes is a very popular, pretty village on the Roseland peninsula, which is itself an 'area of outstanding natural beauty'. Only three miles away, Trethem Mill is well placed for either sailing, walking the coastal path around the peninsula, visiting the gardens of Trelissick or Heligan, or simply lazing on the nearby beaches.

Facilities

The well equipped central toilet block is kept spotlessly clean and is heated in cooler weather. En-suite facilities for disabled visitors which can double as a family room. Baby room (under 4s). Reception/shop, only small but well stocked and licensed. Freezer for ice packs (free). Motorcaravan services. Well equipped, fenced adventure playground (closed at 21.00). Large field for ball games. Extra field for dog walking. WiFi throughout park. Off site: Fishing 1.5 miles. Boat launching 2 miles. Bicycle hire 2 miles. Golf 6 miles. Riding 8 miles.

Open: 1 April - 15 October.

Directions

From Tregony follow A3078 to St Mawes. About 2 miles after passing through Trewithian, watch for caravan and camping sign. O.S.GR: SW863264. GPS: N50:11.402 W05:00.058

Charges guide

Per unit incl. 2 persons and electricity	£ 15.00 - £ 21.00
incl. services	£ 19.00 - £ 25.00
extra person	£ 5.00
child (3-14 yrs)	£ 4.00
dog	£ 1.00

UK0125 Beacon Cottage Farm Holidays

Beacon Drive, Saint Agnes TR5 0NU (Cornwall)

Tel: **01872 552347**. Email: **beaconcottagefarm@lineone.net**   **www.alanrogers.com/UK0125**

Amazing views greet you as you arrive at Beacon Farm. The stark remains of Wheal Coates tin mine stand out against the cliffs and views over the sea stretch for 25 miles – as far as St Ives. A mixed beef and arable farm, Beacon has its own home bred herd of beef cows and calves. The buildings and the impressive stone walls are extremely well maintained. One large, sloping field and a smaller one enjoy sea views but can be less sheltered than the pitches in smaller paddocks which are sheltered by walls and trees. In all there are 70 pitches of varying size, 42 with 10A electricity. This is a truly popular area with walkers and birdwatchers. A 10 minute walk takes you to Chapel Porth beach an unspoilt sandy cove offering excellent swimming and surfing, with caves and rock pools to explore. St Agnes with good shops and restaurants is 1.5 miles away by car or you can walk through fields past the foot of St Agnes' Beacon. Beacon Farm has been in the same hands for many generations and has been welcoming visitors to stay since 1927. Two stone holiday cottages are available to rent.

Facilities

Good stone built toilet blocks are fully equipped and include a family room. Baby bath and changing mat. Laundry room. Fresh supplies are kept in reception (papers, milk, bread and eggs). Fish and chip van calls once a week. Play area with adventure type equipment. Off site: Fishing and beach 0.5 miles. Riding 1.5 miles. Bicycle hire 2 miles. Golf 3 miles.

Open: Easter/1 April - 30 September.

Directions

From the A30 travelling west take B3277 (signed St Agnes) at Chiverton roundabout. At roundabout approaching St Agnes, turn left for Chapel Porth and follow brown Beacon Cottage Farm signs. O.S.GR: SW705503. GPS: N50:18.340 W05:13.494

Charges guide

Per unit incl. 2 persons	£ 15.00 - £ 21.00
incl. electricity	£ 19.50 - £ 24.50
extra person	£ 5.50
child (2-12 yrs)	£ 3.00
dog	£ 2.00

UK0120 Silverbow Park

Goonhavern, Truro TR4 9NX (Cornwall)

Tel: **01872 572347**   **www.alanrogers.com/UK0120**

Silverbow has been developed by the Taylor family over many years and they are justifiably proud of their efforts. They believe Silverbow is a way of life and staying is an experience – they have certainly created a relaxed and tranquil atmosphere seeking to encourage couples and young families (teenagers are not accepted). Hard work, planting and landscaping has provided a beautiful environment set in 21 acres. There are 90 tourist pitches which are all of good size and include 69 'super' pitches in a newly developed area, with electricity, water and drainage, which are even larger. Many are on a slight slope with some attractive views. There are also 15 park-owned, high quality leisure homes. Much free space is not used for camping, including an excellent sports area with two grass and two all-weather tennis courts, as well as wild meadow and wooded areas ideal for walks. A natural area with ponds has been created to encourage wildlife. The park is 2.5 miles from the sandy beach at Perranporth (30 minutes walk away from traffic) and 6 miles from Newquay.

Facilities

Two good toilet blocks include private cabins, four family shower/toilet rooms, two accessible for wheelchairs, and a bath on payment. Laundry room. Motorcaravan services. Free freezer service. Shop for basics (mid May - mid Sept). Covered, heated swimming pool and small paddling pool (mid May - mid Sept) gated and sheltered by high surrounding garden walls. Games room. Adventure playground. Play field. Tennis. Off site: Gliding, riding and fishing nearby. Concessionary green fees are available at Perranporth golf club. Pub within walking distance.

Open: Early May - end September.

Directions

Entrance is directly off the main A3075 road 0.5 miles south of Goonhavern. O.S.GR: SW781531. GPS: N50:20.194 W05:07.238

Charges guide

Per unit incl. 2 persons	£ 10.00 - £ 20.00
extra person under 50 yrs	£ 3.00 - £ 6.00
extra child (2-12 yrs)	
or adult over 50 yrs	£ 2.50 - £ 4.50
full service pitch incl. electricity	£ 6.00
dog	free - £ 1.50

Children over 12 yrs with or without parents not accepted. Discounts available.

UK0140 Penrose Farm Touring Park

Goonhavern, Truro TR4 9QF (Cornwall)

Tel: **01872 573185**. Email: **penroseholidays@hotmail.co.uk**   www.alanrogers.com/UK0140

Penrose Farm, owned and run by the Welch family, has a quiet and comfortable atmosphere on the edge of the village of Goonhavern. The park is level and sheltered, with the pitches spread over five fields with flower beds and bushes set amongst them. These colourful flowers and those at the entrance give the park a neat and well cared for feel. There are over 100 pitches with 10A electricity, many with hardstanding, water and drainage, plus a few seasonal places and some privately owned caravan holiday homes. A play area will amuse children and the family are now offering a simple café menu, including breakfast. It is only a short walk to the village and its popular pub, and buses to Newquay stop in the village. The superb beach at Perranporth is only 2.5 miles. To retain the quiet family image, there are no plans for bars or entertainment. Only couples and families are welcome.

Facilities

The fully equipped and refurbished toilet block is well maintained and includes four en-suite family rooms. Facilities for disabled visitors. Well equipped laundry. Small shop. Gas supplies. Takeaway incl. breakfast. Playground. Caravan storage. Off site: Fishing or riding 0.5 miles, golf 1 mile.

Open: 1 April - 31 October.

Directions

Take A30 from Exeter past Bodmin and Indian Queens. Just after wind farm take the B3285 to Perranporth. Park is on the left as you enter Goonhavern village. O.S.GR: SW790535. GPS: N50:20.408 W05:06.394

Charges guide

Per unit incl. 2 persons and electricity	£ 12.00 - £ 21.00
incl. services	£ 14.00 - £ 25.00
extra person (5 yrs and over)	£ 3.00 - £ 3.50
dog	free - £ 2.00

Families and couples only.
Less 50p for over 60s if booked.

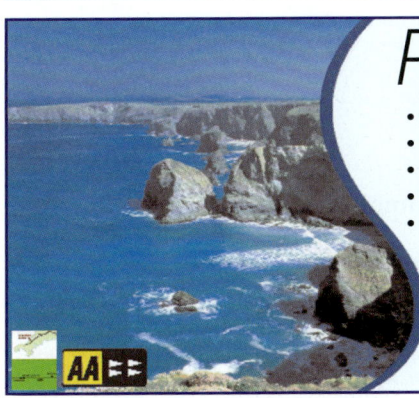

UK0145 Trewhiddle Holiday Estate

Pentewan Road, Saint Austell PL26 7AD (Cornwall)

Tel: **01726 879420**. Email: **holidays@trewhiddle.com**   www.alanrogers.com/UK0145

Trewhiddle Village is a traditional style holiday park, complete with a large number of caravan holiday homes and three camping fields, is now under the same ownership as Sea View International (UK0150). Plans are in hand to upgrade the park. The approach to the park is off the road leading from St Austell to Pentewan with an uphill driveway to what was formally the manor house, now an independently owned pub and restaurant in the centre of this 16 acre park. The touring fields cover six acres and provide about 112 pitches for all types of unit, with or without electricity. The fields are sloping and edged with tall, mature trees and stone walls.

Facilities

The toilet blocks were in need of some care and attention when we visited, but this work is planned. Laundry room. Shop with ice service. Trewhiddle pub provides a bar, restaurant and takeaway. Swimming pool. Play area. Games room and amusement arcade. Bicycle hire. Off site: Beach and sailing 1.5 miles. Golf 4 miles. Boat launching and fishing 5 miles. Riding 6 miles. Eden Project 5 miles. Lost Gardens of Heligan 2-3 miles. Cycle trail.

Open: All year excl. February.

Directions

From the St Austell ring road take the B3273 to Mevagissy. Park is just under 1 mile on the right. O.S.GR: SX006511. GPS: N50:19.473 W04:47.790

Charges guide

Per unit incl. 2 persons and electricity	£ 8.00 - £ 24.00
extra person (over 5 yrs)	£ 3.00 - £ 5.00
dog	£ 3.00

UK0155 Tregarton Park

Gorran, Mevagissey, Saint Austell PL26 6NF (Cornwall)

Tel: **01726 843666**. Email: **reception@tregarton.co.uk**   www.alanrogers.com/UK0155

Run by the welcoming Hicks family, Tregarton Park itself dates back to the 16th century. It is little wonder that the listed buildings have created some problems in providing modern facilities, although the Hicks have done well with their conversions to create a pleasing environment. The 12 acre caravan park is made up of four meadows, with wonderful rural views. The 125 pitches, all with electric hook ups (10A), are of generous size with most separated by either hedges or fencing. All have been terraced, as the park itself is quite hilly. Reception provides a well stocked shop, tourist information and a takeaway service offering freshly cooked food including a daily delivery of Cornish pasties. The large heated outdoor pool is surrounded by decked terraces, with tables and chairs where one can relax and watch the children – in fact, it is the focal point of the park. An adventure playground is in one of the meadows where there is also an impressive all-weather tennis court (free). Close to the small harbour town of Gorran and about 2.5 miles from Mevagissey, with several beaches close by, this is an ideal site for those who do not want lots of entertainment, but would enjoy the option of various activities available nearby.

Facilities

The tiled toilet block is fully equipped. Facilities for disabled visitors. Laundry room. Well stocked shop with groceries and camping supplies. Takeaway. Gas supplies. Heated swimming pool. Tourist information. Dog exercise meadow. Playground. Facilities are open Whitsun - mid Sept. Off site: Eden project 9 miles. Heligan Gardens 2 miles. Mevagissey 2 miles. Beaches 2 miles. Fishing trips available from Mevagissey and Gorran Haven.

Open: 7 April - 31 October.

Directions

Leave St Austell travelling south on the B3273 and pass through London Apprentice and Pentewen. Follow Tregarton Park's brown tourist signs by turning right at the crossroads at the top of the hill towards the Lost Gardens of Heligan and Gorran Haven. Do not go into Mevagissey.
O.S.GR: SW989435. GPS: N50:15.528 W04:49.765

Charges guide

Per unit incl. 2 persons, electricity and awning	£ 7.95 - £ 21.95
extra person (over 4 yrs)	£ 2.95 - £ 5.95
dog (max. 2)	free - £ 3.00

UK0180 Carnon Downs Caravan & Camping Park

Carnon Downs, Truro TR3 6JJ (Cornwall)

Tel: **01872 862283**. Email: **info@carnon-downs-caravanpark.co.uk**   www.alanrogers.com/UK0180

Carnon Downs is an excellent all year park run personally and enthusiastically by Simon Vallance, a very forward thinking owner. It has been thoughtfully laid out so that all pitches back onto attractive hedging or areas of flowering shrubs and arranged to provide some pleasant bays or other, more open grass areas. Gravel roads connect the 150 pitches, most with electricity (10/16A) and over 70 with hardstanding. Of these 55 are fully serviced, with the newer ones being exceptionally large and surrounded by young shrubs. On arrival you will receive a warm welcome, a neat layout plan of the park and a touring information pack. This includes comprehensive details on walks and cycle paths leading from the park. Some of the park's amenities are to be found in the round-house next to the TV and information room. The round-house used to house the donkeys that turned the mill which once operated on the site! Although one side of the park is next to the A39 road, it is well screened with a band of mature woodland so noise should be minimal. This quiet, quality family park is well situated to explore the tip of Cornwall. A member of the Best of British group.

Facilities

Two excellent modern, light and airy, heated blocks include en-suite units. Another well maintained block, also heated, includes some washbasins in cubicles and showers (unisex). Three good family bath/shower rooms, one suitable for use by disabled people or families. Mother and toddler room, two baby sinks and full sized bath. Two laundries with freezers. Motorcaravan service point (ask at reception). Gas, newspapers and caravan accessories. General room with TV. Good dog walks. Caravan storage. Off site: Pub/restaurant 100 yds across the road. Fishing 5 miles. Riding or bicycle hire 2 miles. Golf 1 mile. Walks direct from site.

Open: All year.

Directions

From Truro take A39 Falmouth road. After 3 miles, park entrance is directly off the Carnon Downs roundabout. O.S.GR: SW805406.
GPS: N50:13.517 W05:04.807

Charges guide

Per unit incl. 2 persons and electricity	£ 17.00 - £ 22.00
extra person	£ 3.00
child (5-14 yrs)	£ 2.50
all service hardstanding	£ 2.00

UK0150 Sea View International

Boswinger, Gorran Haven, Saint Austell PL26 6LL (Cornwall)
Tel: 01726 843425. Email: holidays@seaviewinternational.com
www.alanrogers.com/UK0150

Sea View is an impressive, well cared for park, its quality reflected in the awards it has won. The enthusiastic owners Mr and Mrs Royden and their team are continually improving the park with the aim of providing quality camping. A whole new area has been developed at the top of the park with uninterrupted views, 31 large, hedged, fully serviced grass pitches and a new toilet block providing excellent, en-suite family shower rooms. The remaining, established pitches (163, also with views) all have 16A electricity and 43 are fully serviced, including 12 hardstandings which are suitable for large motorhomes. There are 38 caravan holiday homes for hire in a separate area. Although somewhat exposed, the park is colourful with flower beds and flowering shrubs and has well manicured grass of exceptional quality. The area around the swimming pool is particularly attractive with sunbathing areas with free sunbeds on tiled terraces surrounded by flowers creating private little areas, all with magnificent views of the sea and the distant headland. A family barbecue area has been established in the large recreation field between the two areas. There is plenty to do and see in this area, from the gardens of Heligan and Trelissick, to Lanhydroc House and the seal sanctuary, not forgetting the safe beaches, one of which is only a half mile walk from the park.

Facilities

Excellent toilet facilities are well maintained and heated providing for all needs, including en-suite facilities, bathrooms (on payment), baby baths and facilities for disabled visitors. Campers' kitchen. Well equipped laundry. Motorcaravan service point. Shop and off-licence with gas (June - end Sept). Takeaway (Whit - mid Sept). Swimming pool (heated end May - mid Sept). Large playing field. Fenced play area for under 7s. Adventure playground. Games room. Bicycle hire. Certain breeds of dog are not accepted. Off site: Fishing 0.5 miles. Boat launching 2 miles. Riding 1 mile. Golf 9 miles. Community bus picks up at the park.

Open: 1 April - 31 October.

Directions

From St Austell take B3273 towards Mevagissey; 1 mile before Mevagissey village turn right at Gorran and camp sign and continue towards Gorran for 5 miles. Fork right at sign and follow signs to park. O.S.GR: SW991412. GPS: N50:14.214 W04:49.202

Charges guide

Per unit incl. 2 persons and electricity	£ 12.00 - £ 31.00
incl. water and drainage	£ 15.00 - £ 33.00
extra person (over 4 yrs)	£ 3.00 - £ 5.00
pup tent	£ 2.50
dog (limited breeds and numbers)	£ 3.00

Special off-peak offers.

25

UK0165 Monkey Tree Holiday Park

Rejerrah, Newquay TR8 5QR (Cornwall)

Tel: **01872 572032**. Email: **enquiries@monkeytreeholidaypark.co.uk**   www.alanrogers.com/UK0165

Monkey Tree covers 56 acres and boasts an impressive entrance and smart reception. There are 500 pitches with 450 for touring units and 50 caravan holiday homes to rent in their own area. The pitches in the original part of the park benefit from mature hedging which offers a degree of privacy which the newer ones lack, but all have been planted with individual hedges. The pitches are of a good size and most have electricity (13/16A). Serviced pitches with hardstanding are being developed including some extra large pitches which include the use of private facilities in the toilet block. During the holiday season there is much going on at Monkey Tree. All the family should find something to keep them happy. For the little ones there is a morning Kid's Club, for older children there are adventure playgrounds, well fenced for safety, trampolines, bouncy castles and an amusement arcade and pool tables. For everyone there is an outdoor heated pool, paddling pool and a sauna. The club and restaurant are popular with entertainment for children in the early part of the evening and bingo, karaoke, disco and cabaret acts to follow. Themed weekends are organised early and late in the season; Halloween is especially popular. There are wonderful beaches, watersports to enjoy and places such as the Eden Project and Flambards a must to visit.

Facilities

The original block (refurbished) supplements two new modern timber blocks with heating, providing for all needs including facilities for babies and disabled visitors. Private en-suite facilities for use with the super pitches. Laundry. Motorcaravan services. Gas supplies. Shop (mornings only in low season). Club with entertainment, bar and restaurant (main season and B.Hs). Takeaway (high season). Outdoor pool and paddling pool (Whitsun - end Sept). Trampolines (supervised, with charge). Bouncy castles. Three adventure play areas. Amusement arcade. Fishing lakes. Caravan storage. Off site: Golf, riding, boat launching and sailing 5 miles.

Open: All year.

Directions

Follow the A30 ignoring all signs for Newquay. At Carland Cross with windmills on the right, carry straight over following signs for Perranporth. After 1 mile turn right at Boxheater Junction on the B3285 signed Perranporth and Goonhavern. Follow for 0.5 miles then turn right into Scotland Road for 1 mile to park on the left. O.S.GR: SW801546. GPS: N50:21.133 W05:05.500

Charges guide

Per person	£ 3.75 - £ 6.20
child (3-14 yrs)	free - £ 3.75
pitch incl. electricity	£ 3.50
incl. services	£ 7.50 - £ 10.50

UK0190 Polruan Holidays Camping & Caravanning

Polruan-by-Fowey PL23 1QH (Cornwall)

Tel: **01726 870263**. Email: **polholiday@aol.com**   www.alanrogers.com/UK0190

Polruan is a rural site in an elevated position on the opposite side of the river to Fowey, 200 metres from the Coastal path. With 47 touring pitches and 10 holiday caravans to let, this is a very pleasant little site. The holiday homes are arranged in a neat circle, with a central area for some touring units, including 7 pitches with gravel hardstanding and electricity, one fully serviced. The remaining touring pitches are in an adjacent field with 8 electricity hook-ups, which is part level for motorcaravans and part on a gentle slope for tents. There are marvellous sea views, but it could be a little exposed when the wind blows off the sea. A raised picnic area gives more views across the estuary to Fowey.

Facilities

The fully equipped sanitary block has modern, controllable showers, large enough for an adult and child. Laundry room and dishwashing sinks. Motorcaravan service facilities. Reception (with a small terrace) doubles as a shop for everyday needs. Gas. Drinks machine and freezer for ice packs. Tourist information and bus timetables (for Looe, etc). Sloping field area with swings for children. Off site: Coastal path 200 m. Fishing 0.5 miles. Riding or bicycle hire 3 miles. Golf 10 miles.

Open: Easter - 1 November.

Directions

From main A390 at East Taphouse take the B3359 towards Looe. After 5 miles fork right signed Bodinnick and ferry. Watch for signs for Polruan and site to left. Follow these carefully along narrow Cornish lanes to site on right just before village. O.S.GR: SX133509. GPS: N50:19.655 W04:37.509

Charges guide

Per unit incl. 1 or 2 persons and electricity	£ 10.25 - £ 16.00
extra person	£ 3.00
child (2-16 yrs)	£ 1.75
No credit cards.	

UK0205 Treloy Touring Park

Newquay TR8 4JN (Cornwall)

Tel: 01637 872063. Email: treloy-tp@btconnect.com   www.alanrogers.com/UK0205

Just three miles from the wonderful beaches around Newquay, yet peacefully located away from the crowds, Treloy is a pretty park. Family owned and run, there are 197 pitches, many level, some slightly sloping, all with 16A electricity (new system) and 20 fully serviced. All are used for touring units and perhaps this contributes towards the relaxed family atmosphere. There are concrete hardstandings for caravans which are attractively interspersed with shrubs and form a pleasant landscape feature. Elsewhere hydrangea edge the roads around the more open pitches and more trees are being planted. St Mawgan, the RAF air sea rescue base and Newquay's airport are nearby but there is little disturbance. There is an hourly bus service to Newquay from the park entrance which means the coast and beaches can be enjoyed without taking the car. On return to Treloy there is the Park Chef and the Surfrider's Bar for meals and drinks. If you do not fancy the beach there is a pool on the park. This is a real family park providing for all ages.

Facilities

Two new toilet blocks, one with showers, the other with toilets and washbasins only. Baby room with two large sinks. En-suite facilities for disabled visitors (key). Laundry. Gas. Shop with all necessities. Bar (20/5-15/9). Pleasant café with a good reputation and including breakfast (20/5-1/9). Swimming pool (walled and gated). Play areas and field with goal posts. Nature trail. Family entertainment such as magic shows, bingo, folk and rock music. Off site: Fishing 1 mile. Golf 0.5 miles. Riding and boat launching 3 miles. Other beaches such as Watergate Bay, Mawgan Porth and Porth beach are a short car journey.

Open: 20 May - 15 September.

Directions

From A39 St Columb Major take the B3059 for Newquay. Park is signed after about 4 miles. O.S.GR: SW858625. GPS: N50:25.972 W05:00.750

Charges guide

Per person	£ 6.00 - £ 7.35
child (3-14 yrs)	£ 3.25 - £ 4.45
pitch incl. electricity	£ 3.75
incl. services	£ 5.75
dog	£ 1.00 - £ 2.50

See advertisement on page 30

www.alanrogers.com for latest campsite news

UK0170 Trevella Caravan Park

Crantock, Newquay TR8 5EW (Cornwall)

Tel: **01637 830308**. Email: **holidays@trevella.co.uk**

www.alanrogers.com/UK0170

One of the best known and respected of Cornish parks with its colourful flowerbeds (a regular winner of a 'Newquay in Bloom' award), Trevella is also one of the first to fill up and has a longer season than most. Well organised, the pitches are in a number of adjoining meadows, most of which are on a slight slope. Of the 250 pitches for touring units (any type), some 200 can be reserved and these are marked, individual ones. Over 200 pitches have electricity (10A), with 59 serviced pitches (with hardstanding, electricity and TV hook-ups, water, waste water), some extra large with sewage drain as well. Trevella is essentially a quiet family touring park. The accent is on orderliness and cleanliness with on-site evening activities limited, although Andy's Kitchen offers good home-cooked food. Access is free to two fishing lakes, (permits from reception); with some fishing instruction and wildlife talks for youngsters in season. There is a pleasant walk around the lakes, which are a haven for wildlife and a protected nature reserve. It is also possible to walk to Crantock beach but check the tides first. A member of the Best of British group.

Facilities

Kept very clean, three blocks provide good coverage with individual washbasins in private cabins for ladies, hairdressing room and baby room. Laundry. Freezer pack service. Well stocked supermarket (Easter - Oct). Café (including breakfast) and takeaway. Heated outdoor pool. Games room. TV room. Crazy golf. Pets corner. Large adventure playground. Play and sports area. Fishing. Off site: Shuttle bus service to Newquay in high season. Beach 0.5 miles on foot. Newquay 2 miles. Pubs and restaurants at Crantock, 1 mile. Riding 1 mile. Golf 3 miles.

Open: Easter - 31 October.

Directions

To avoid Newquay leave the A30 or A392 at Indian Queens, straight over crossroads with A39 and A3058, left at A3075 and first right at site sign. O.S.GR: SW802598. GPS: N50:23.838 W05:05.768

Charges guide

Per person	£ 4.20 - £ 7.30
child (3-16 yrs)	£ 2.30 - £ 5.20
pitch incl. electricity	£ 4.00
incl. services	£ 8.00 - £ 11.00

Families and couples only.

See advertisement on page 27

UK0220 Trevornick Holiday Park

Holywell Bay, Newquay TR8 5PW (Cornwall)

Tel: **01637 830531**. Email: **bookings@trevornick.co.uk**

www.alanrogers.com/UK0220

Trevornick, once a working farm, is a modern, busy and well run family touring park providing a very wide range of amenities close to one of Cornwall's finest beaches. A modern reception with welcoming staff sets the tone for your holiday. The park is well managed with facilities and standards constantly monitored. It has grown to provide caravanners and campers (no holiday caravans but 68 very well equipped 'Eurotents') with 440 large grass pitches (350 with 10A electricity and 55 fully serviced with electricity, water, drain and TV connection with DVD channel) on five level fields and two terraced areas. There are few trees, but some good views. Providing 'all singing, all dancing' facilities for fun packed family holidays, the farm buildings now provide the setting for the Farm Club. Recently refurbished, it provides much entertainment from bingo and quizzes to shows, discos and cabaret. The Stables Grill also opens for breakfast and the Hungry Horse provides takeaway food. The rest of the development provides a pool complex, an 18 hole golf course, with a small, quiet club house offering bar meals and lovely views out to sea and three fishing lakes. Next door is the Holywell Bay 'fun' park (reduced rates) and the sandy beach is five minutes by car or a short downhill walk. An innovative idea is the 'Hire shop' where it is possible rent anything you might have forgotten from sheets, a fridge, travel cot, etc. to a camera or a wet suit to catch the Cornish surf!

Facilities

Five modern toilet blocks provide showers (20p), two family bathrooms, baby bath, laundry facilities and provision for disabled visitors. Well stocked supermarket with bread made on site (both from late May). Hire shop. Bars (with TV), restaurant, cafe and takeaway. Entertainment (every night in season). Pool complex with heated outdoor pool, paddling pool, sunbathing decks, solarium, sauna and massage chair. Health and beauty salon. Super Fort Knox style adventure playground, crazy golf, Kiddies Club and indoor play area (supervised for 2-8 yr olds at a small charge). Amusement arcade and bowling alley. Teenage meeting room. 18-hole pitch and putt with golf pro shop. Bicycle hire. Coarse fishing with three lakes. Dogs accepted in one field only. Only limited facilities open at Easter and from 8 Sept. Off site: Riding within 1 mile. Bicycle hire and boat launching 4 miles.

Open: Easter - mid September.

Directions

From A3075 approach to Newquay - Perranporth road, turn towards Cubert and Holywell Bay. Continue through Cubert to park on the right. O.S.GR: SW776586. GPS: N50:23.099 W05:07.736

Charges guide

Per person	£ 4.95 - £ 9.30
child (4-14 yrs)	£ 1.30 - £ 6.55
electricity	£ 4.75
'super premium' or 'jumbo' pitch incl. electricity	£ 8.95
dog	£ 3.45 - £ 3.75

Families and couples only. Many special discounts.

UK0160 Newperran Holiday Park

Rejerrah, Newquay TR8 5QJ (Cornwall)

Tel: **01872 572407**. Email: **holidays@newperran.co.uk**   **www.alanrogers.com/UK0160**

Newperran is a large, level park in rural Cornish countryside. Being on high ground, it is quite open but this also gives excellent views of the coast and surrounding countryside. The owners, Keith and Christine Brewer, have rebuilt the reception, shop and pub to a very high standard. The traditional layout of the park provides a number of flat, well drained meadows divided into over 370 individual pitches with 10/16A electricity. Some fields have larger and reservable spaces with more free space in the centre. There are now 61 fully serviced pitches, some with hardstanding and a TV point. Newperran is only 2.5 miles from Perranporth beach, but there is a free heated swimming pool with sunbathing area and paddling pool on the park. A state of the art entrance barrier is now in place operating on recognition of your number plate. The pub, or Cottage Inn as it is called, is a very comfortable area with a log burner for low season warmth and family entertainment such as quiz nights in high season. A separate café operates on a franchise basis. This is a well run park with plenty of space and activities for families with a few caravan holiday homes to rent. There are plans to provide a specialist naturist area but advanced booking will be required.

Facilities

Toilet facilities comprise four clean blocks, two heated, all refurbished to a very high standard. Facilities include washbasins in cabins, family rooms, baby room, hairdressing room and a unit for disabled visitors. Laundry room. Well stocked self-service licensed shop. Licensed bar (mid May - Oct). Café (all season). New outdoor heated swimming pool with paddling pool (Whitsun - Sept). Adventure playground and separate toddlers' play area. Games room with TV. TV room. Off site: Riding or golf 2 miles. Fishing 1 mile. Goonhavern village within walking distance with pubs and post office. Beach 2.5 miles.

Open: Easter - October.

Directions

Turn off A3075 to west at camping sign 7 miles south of Newquay and just north of Goonhavern village. O.S.GR: SW794546.
GPS: N50:21.026 W05:06.109

Charges guide

Per person	£ 4.45 - £ 7.75
child (3-15 yrs)	£ 2.35 - £ 6.10
pitch incl. electricity	£ 4.25 - £ 12.00
car	£ 1.30

UK0210 Hendra Holiday Park

Newquay TR8 4NY (Cornwall)

Tel: **01637 875778**. Email: **jn@hendra.co.uk**   **www.alanrogers.com/UK0210**

Hendra is a long-established holiday park for all the family with a wide range of facilities and a comprehensive entertainment programme. There are comedians, show bands, cabaret, dancing, bingo, discos, plus a super pool complex. The 548 touring pitches are on well mown, slightly sloping grass fields with country views and mature trees, some more sheltered than others. There are 280 caravan holiday homes in separate fields (some are to rent). With tarmac roads and lighting, 311 pitches have electricity (16A) and 28 pitches are fully serviced including water, electricity, light, sewer drainage, satellite TV connections and some innovative awning pads (dogs are not accepted on these pitches). The entrance and reception are very attractive with a mass of well tended flower beds which, along with the other facilities, form an attractive, village-like centre to the park. The 'star of the show' at Hendra is the Oasis complex consisting of an indoor fun pool with flumes, river rapids and beach. It is open to the public – really a mini water-park. The outdoor heated pool with grass sunbathing area is free to campers and activities are well catered for with a range of amenities. The park is only 1.5 miles from Newquay and its fabulous surfing beaches and a bus to the town passes the gate. Hendra welcomes families and couples.

Facilities

Three modern fully equipped toilet blocks including facilities for babies and disabled visitors. Large launderette. Motorcaravan services. Gas supplies. Well stocked shop. Various bars and restaurants, open all season (limited hours in early season). Pizzeria (main season only). Takeaway. Outdoor swimming pool. Indoor pool complex (cost £2.50 per family group, max. 4 persons, under 5s free; timed sessions are if very busy). Various play areas including one for soft play. Tennis. Minigolf. Bowling. Off site: Fishing or riding 1 mile. Bicycle hire or golf 2 miles. Beach 1.5 miles.

Open: 23 March - 31 October.

Directions

Park is on left side of A392 Indian Queens - Newquay road at Newquay side of Quintrell Downs. O.S.GR: SW833601. GPS: N50:24.146 W05:02.949

Charges guide

Per person	£ 4.55 - £ 8.25
child (3-14 yrs)	£ 1.35 - £ 5.45
pitch incl. electricity	£ 4.99 - £ 5.99
vehicle	£ 1.30 - £ 1.85
incl. services	£ 12.00 - £ 14.00
Minimum charges at peak times.	

See advertisement on page 29

31

UK0230 Glenmorris Park

Longstone Road, Saint Mabyn PL30 3BY (Cornwall)

Tel: **01208 841677**. Email: **info@glenmorris.co.uk**

www.alanrogers.com/UK0230

The beaches of north Cornwall and the wilds of Bodmin Moor are all an easy drive from Glenmorris Park. The park is being gradually improved and carefully maintained by the Hayman family and it provides a spacious and relaxed atmosphere. There are 80 level pitches, 60 with 16A electricity, on well drained and well mown grass with 20 hardstandings. There are some caravan holiday homes to let. A nice, sheltered outdoor pool is an added attraction. However, there is no bar although the local village inn has a good reputation for food. The Camel Trail is only two miles, providing a means to cycle or walk all the way to Bodmin, Wadebridge or Padstow. Bodmin and Wadebridge are only five or six miles for supermarket shopping. It is also possible to telephone 'Cor Link' and they will arrange to transport you to the nearest bus route.

Facilities

The fully equipped modern toilet block includes an en-suite unit per sex. Laundry. Heated outdoor swimming pool and paddling pool (late May - early Sept), surrounded by a sheltered, paved and grass sunbathing areas. Good, fenced adventure play area with bark safety base. Play area for small children. Games room. Caravan storage. Off site: Fishing, riding or golf 3 miles. Bicycle hire 5 miles.

Open: 1 April - mid October.

Directions

From Bodmin or Wadebridge on A389, take B3266 north signed Camelford. At village of Longstone turn left signed St Mabyn and brown camping sign. Site is 400 yds. on right. Ignore all other signs to St Mabyn. O.S.GR: SX053732. GPS: N50:31.668 W04:44.711

Charges guide

Per person	£ 4.00 - £ 5.50
child (3-15 yrs)	£ 1.25 - £ 1.50
electricity (16A)	£ 3.30
dog	£ 1.00
Weekly rate available.	

UK0195 Penmarlam Caravan & Camping Park

Bodinnick-by-Fowey, Fowey PL23 1LZ (Cornwall)

Tel: **01726 870088**. Email: **info@penmarlampark.co.uk**   **www.alanrogers.com/UK0195**

Penmarlam is situated high above the estuary opposite Fowey, close to the village of Bodinnick which is famous for being the home of Daphne du Maurier. The original field is level and sheltered with a circular concrete access road and 30 pitches which are semi-divided by bushes. The newer field with 35 pitches has a slight slope, is divided with wild banks and enjoys good countryside views. All pitches have 16A electricity and 6 also have water and drainage. The modern reception, shop and the toilet facilities are well situated between the two fields. Reception is fitted with a loop system for deaf visitors and the owner can 'sign' as well as speaking French, Spanish and some German! Internet access is provided here, with wireless access possible from the pitches. Some of our readers will be attracted by easy access to a slipway and boat moorings near the park entrance, This also makes for a pleasant walk with picnic tables overlooking the river at the bottom.

Facilities

The modern, colourful and heated toilet block is fully equipped including a baby and toddler room in the ladies' and a separate en-suite unit for disabled visitors which can double as a family room. Laundry facilities. Well stocked licensed shop with fresh fruit and vegetables. Coffee machine (available for reduced hours in low season). Video, DVD and book library. Off site: Fishing and boat launching 500 m. Beach 1 mile. Riding 3 miles. Golf 6 miles. Car or passenger ferry for Fowey. Annual Daphne du Maurier Festival of Arts and Literature is held in Fowey (May). Fowey Regatta (mid August).

Open: 1 April - 31 October.

Directions

From the main A390 road at East Taphouse take B3359 towards Looe. After 5 miles fork right, signed Bodinnick and ferry. Site is signed on the right 1 mile past village of Lanteglos Highway, just before Bodinnick village. O.S.GR: SK130527. GPS: N50:20.660 W04:37.373

Charges guide

Per person	£ 3.00 - £ 5.50
child (3-15 yrs)	£ 1.50 - £ 2.75
pitch incl. electricity	£ 6.00 - £ 8.00
with water and drainage	£ 8.00 - £ 10.00

UK0200 Newquay Holiday Park

Newquay TR8 4HS (Cornwall)

Tel: **01637 871111**. Email: **enquiries@parkdean.com**   **www.alanrogers.com/UK0200**

Part of the Parkdean Group, Newquay Holiday Park lies peacefully on a terraced hillside only just outside the town, 2 miles from the beaches and town centre. Its main feature is an attractively laid out group of three heated swimming pools with a giant water slide (lifeguards in attendance) and 'green' sunbathing areas overlooked by a terrace for cool drinks. With a large proportion of caravan holiday homes (for let), there are still two fields used for touring units. These provide 187 marked pitches in hedged fields, some sloping, marked out by lines on ground but with nothing between them. Electricity (16A) is available. Family entertainment is provided each night with live music, discos etc. in the site's Fiesta Club which also has a bar, TV lounge and games room with pool and snooker tables. A bus service runs to Newquay from the main road at the site entrance.

Facilities

Two good sized, modern toilet blocks include a unit for disabled visitors and baby bath. An extra block is opened for the main season when facilities may be under pressure. Launderette. Well stocked self-service shop (gas from reception). Bar/lounge with Sky TV. New café/restaurant with all day food also 'pub grub' in evenings. Outdoor pool complex with slide (and lifeguards). Pitch and putt and crazy golf. Playground for little ones and adventure play area for older children. Children's club. Recreation field. Amusement arcade. Dogs or other pets are only permitted on certain pitches.

Open: Easter - October.

Directions

Park is east of Newquay on A3059 road 1 mile east of junction with A3058. O.S.GR: SW853626. GPS: N50:25.350 W05:01.470

Charges guide

Per unit incl. 4 persons	£ 7.00 - £ 27.00
incl. services	£ 10.00 - £ 30.00
extra person (over 3 yrs; up to 4 people)	£ 2.00 - £ 4.00
dog	£ 2.50

UK0250 Pentewan Sands Holiday Park

Pentewan, Saint Austell PL26 6BT (Cornwall)

Tel: **01726 843485**. Email: **info@pentewan.co.uk**   **www.alanrogers.com/UK0250**

Pentewan Sands is a popular, well managed family park with an ideal position right beside a wide sandy private beach. A busy, 32 acre holiday park with lots going on, there are 501 touring pitches, 401 with electricity, and 120 caravan holiday homes for hire. The good-sized pitches are on level grass with nothing between them. They are marked and numbered by frontage stones, mostly in rows adjoining access roads. A good heated pool with a paddling pool is beside the Beach Club. This contains a restaurant, two bars upstairs and a further one downstairs opening on to the pool area, open all day and serving good value food in season. A full entertainment programme, beach activities, scuba diving, windsurfing courses and a club for children are organised, and a small watersports centre is on the beach. Jet-skis are not permitted and 4WD vehicles are not allowed on the beach. The Pentewan Valley Trail, a six mile route for cycling or walking follows the old carriageway to Mevagissey with its throngs of tourists (two miles by the main road). The park and the beach have been owned by the Tremayne family for over 60 years.

Facilities

Four main toilet blocks receive heavy use in peak season but are maintained by individual cleaners. Two bathrooms, a baby room and facilities for disabled people. Well equipped laundry room. Motorcaravan service point. Large, self-service shop with off-licence, bistro and fast food (Whitsun - mid Sept). Bars, bar meals (Easter - mid Sept, limited hours early and late season). Entertainment programme. Swimming pools (supervised and open Whitsun - mid Sept). Playground. Games room. Tennis. Bicycle hire. Slipway and boat launching (Whitsun - mid Sept). Freezer service, battery charging service. Gas. Caravan and boat storage. Dogs are not accepted. Off site: Riding and golf 2 miles. Bicycle hire 0.5 miles.

Open: 18 March - 30 October.

Directions

From St Austell ring road take B3273 for Mevagissey. Park is 3.5 miles, where the road meets the sea. O.S.GR: SX018468. GPS: N50:17.297 W04:47.145

Charges guide

Per unit incl. 2 persons	
and electricity	£ 12.45 - £ 27.05
extra person	£ 1.80 - £ 4.60
child (3-15 yrs)	£ 1.10 - £ 3.45
extra small tent, boat or car	£ 1.70 - £ 2.40
Sea front pitch plus 10-20%.	

UK0255 Sun Valley Holiday Park

Pentewan Road, Saint Austell Bay, Mevagissey PL26 6DJ (Cornwall)

Tel: **01726 843266**. Email: **reception@sunvalleyholidays.co.uk**   **www.alanrogers.com/UK0255**

This very neat, tidy holiday park has been developed in the grounds of a country house which is now split into holiday apartments. Set in a sheltered situation on the road from St Austell to Pentewan, Sun Valley has the appearance of a park, helped by the wonderful mature cedars which are over 250 years old. Over 75 caravan holiday homes have been carefully landscaped into the 20 acres, together with 25 level touring pitches. Hardstandings and 10A electricity hook ups are available. Excellent facilities include a bar and restaurant where regular entertainment is arranged. There is an indoor heated swimming pool and tennis courts. Children are not forgotten either with a Kid's Club and other activities. There is a paddling pool, soft ball play area for little ones, a games room, an adventure play area plus equipment for under fives, not to mention Rabbit Land (with regular petting times) and Lilly and Milly, the resident goats. Bikes are available to hire on the park. There is much to do here, never mind the wonderful sandy beach down the road, and plenty of places to visit in the area including the Eden Project, Charlestown, Mevagissey, Fowey and the Lost Gardens of Heligan. A member of the Best of British group.

Facilities

Heated en-suite family rooms offer 'home from home' comfort with a baby changing station and ramped access for disabled people. New heated shower facilities. Fully equipped laundry in the pool block. Washing lines. Shop (limited hours in low seasons). Bar/restaurant with regular entertainment. Activities and club for children. Indoor pool (all season). Paddling pool. Play areas. Rabbit Land and goats. Tennis. Apartments and caravans to rent. Off site: Beach 1 mile. Golf 1.5 miles. Riding 5 miles. Bus stop at park entrance (hourly service).

Open: All year.

Directions

From the St Austell ring road take B3273 for Mevagissey. After village of London Apprentice watch for site entrance on right (about 1 mile). O.S.GR: SX006484. GPS: N50:18.030 W04:48.070

Charges guide

Per unit incl. 2 persons	
and electricity	£ 16.50 - £ 32.50
extra person	£ 3.00
child (2-12 yrs)	£ 1.50
dog	free - £ 1.00

UK0270 Mena Caravan & Camping Park

Lanivet, Bodmin PL30 5HW (Cornwall)

Tel: **01208 831845**. Email: **mena@campsitesincornwall.co.uk**   www.alanrogers.com/UK0270

A peaceful, simple park, Mena is tucked away in the Cornish countryside, yet close to the main routes, and a warm welcome await visitors. A few years ago it was a field for cows and with hard work and care it has been developed into a comfortable, yet natural site. Set in 15 acres of secluded countryside, it is spacious and never crowded offering only 25 level grass pitches on well drained, slightly sloping grass. There are 12 electricity connections (10A). The land includes a small fishing lake and a wooded area. Now open all year, developments include a new reception and shop. Mena means 'hilltop' in the Cornish language and the site is actually situated at the geographical centre of Cornwall, overlooked by Helman's Tor, one of the highest points on Bodmin Moor. It is also close to the Saints' Way, the pilgrim route from Ireland where they crossed by land from Padstow to Fowey on their way to France. With its position, visitors can choose between beaches on the north or south coast. Lanivet village has a shop and a pub serving meals.

Facilities

Four toilet and washbasin cabins are in an older wooden building. Two new showers and two toilets are behind the veranda building. On the opposite side of the site is a new en-suite facility for disabled visitors, part of a building housing a large games room with three quarter size snooker table, TV and darts. Shop (with gas). Swings, etc. for children in the central grass area. Fishing lake (licence required). Two mobile homes for hire. Off site: Lanivet village with shop and pub 2 miles. Riding 1 mile. Golf 2 miles. Bicycle hire 3 or 5 miles. Nearest beach 8 miles. Eden Project 4 miles.

Open: All year.

Directions

From the A30 Bodmin bypass, exit at the A30/A391 Innis Downs roundabout. Take the A389 north signed Lanivet and Bodmin. After 0.5 miles take first right (filter lane) and pass under the A30. Turn first left (Lostwithiel, Fowey) and in 0.25 miles turn right at top of hill (Celtic Cross on the left). Continue for 0.5 miles and take first right into lane and site in 100 yds. O.S.GR: SX041625. GPS: N50:25.816 W04:45.430

Charges guide

Per unit incl. 2 persons	£ 9.00 - £ 19.00
incl. electricity	£ 14.00 - £ 23.50
extra person	£ 4.00 - £ 5.00
child (3-16 yrs)	£ 1.50 - £ 2.50
dog	£ 1.00 - £ 2.00

No credit or debit cards.

UK0280 Powderham Castle Holiday Park

Lanlivery, Lostwithiel PL30 5BU (Cornwall)

Tel: **01208 872277**. Email: **powderhamcastletp@tiscali.co.uk**   www.alanrogers.com/UK0280

A pleasant, peaceful touring park, Powderham Castle has plenty of sheltered green space and a natural, uncommercialised atmosphere. This has been enhanced by careful planting of trees and shrubs to form a series of linked paddocks with an unfenced stream running through. The park has 35 private caravan holiday homes in a separate field and 56 numbered touring pitches spread round the perimeter of the paddocks, each with 10-15 pitches. There are 40 with electricity (5/10A) and 12 have hardstanding (groundsheets must be lifted on alternate days). A large, well equipped activity play area with adventure type equipment on grass is in one of the hedged paddocks. The park is now owned by Darron and Jenny Hopkins and their young family and they welcome families and couples to enjoy their park with its colourful trees and grassy paddocks. Indoor tennis courts (Bodmin) and a swimming pool are near. The village pub is within walking distance and there are several good local restaurants. The Eden Project is very close. The nearest beach at Par is some 4 miles.

Facilities

The single well equipped toilet block is quite a walk from some pitches. En-suite family washroom and unit for disabled visitors. Fully equipped laundry room. Motorcaravan service point. Gas supplies. Play area. TV room. Games room. Putting green. Torch useful. Off site: Fresh water fishing 1.5 miles or sea fishing 3 miles. Beach 4 miles. Bicycle hire 4 miles. Riding 2 miles. Golf 1.5 miles.

Open: Easter/1 April - 31 October.

Directions

Park approach road leads off A390 road 1.5 miles southwest of Lostwithiel. Follow white or brown camping signs. No other approach is advised. O.S.GR: SX083592. GPS: N50:24.115 W04:41.883

Charges guide

Per unit incl. 2 persons and electricity	£ 11.00 - £ 15.00
extra person	£ 1.50 - £ 2.00
child (4-15 yrs)	£ 1.00 - £ 1.50
dog	£ 1.00 - £ 2.00

No single sex groups (excl. bona fide organisations).

UK0285 Penhale Caravan & Camping Park

Fowey PL23 1JU (Cornwall)

Tel: **01726 833425**. Email: **info@penhale-fowey.co.uk**   www.alanrogers.com/UK0285

Penhale is a traditional campsite on four and half acres of rolling farmland with magnificent views across the countryside to St Austell Bay. The Berryman family run an arable and beef farm alongside the campsite. The atmosphere here is relaxed and there is plenty of room in the touring fields. The fields do slope but a number of pitches have been levelled. In total, there are 56 pitches for all types of units, 26 with 16A electricity hook-ups. Ten holiday caravans occupy a separate field. It is possible to walk to Polkerris beach a mile away and Fowey is just a mile and a half. The attractive, busy town of Fowey with its narrow streets is on the river of the same name and is a sailor's paradise (Regatta week is late August). Daphne du Maurier's association with the town is celebrated at the Literary Centre and with an annual Arts Festival in May. This is the landscape of wooded valleys, hidden coves and sandy beaches that inspired her books. There are many lovely walks and the site has produced directions. There are no public footpaths direct from the site but permission has been given to access the footpaths across private property.

Facilities

One fully equipped toilet block at the bottom of the touring fields. Laundry room. Reception at the farmhouse stocks basic necessities. Off site: Sandy beach, pub and watersports centre at Polkerris beach 1 mile (windsurfing, sailing, paddle surf, kayak). Fishing and boat launching 1.5 miles. Three golf courses within 7 mile. Shops and restaurants Fowey 1.5 miles. Garage with shop 600 yds.

Open: Easter/1 April - 8 October.

Directions

From the A390 take B3269 for Fowey and 1 mile before town turn right at roundabout by petrol station on the A3082 St Austell road. Site is about 600 yds on the left. O.S.GR: SK105526. GPS: N50:20.585 W04:40.109

Charges guide

Per person	£ 4.00 - £ 5.00
child (4-15 yrs)	£ 2.00
pitch	£ 1.00 - £ 5.00
incl. electricity	£ 3.00 - £ 7.00
dog	£ 1.00 - £ 2.00

UK0300 The Colliford Tavern Campsite

Colliford Lake, Saint Neot, Liskeard PL14 6PZ (Cornwall)

Tel: **01208 821335**. Email: **info@colliford.com**   www.alanrogers.com/UK0300

Colliford Tavern must be unique, quietly situated high on Bodmin Moor near Colliford Lake but hidden and protected by tall pines with a camping area and a tavern. The camping area is quiet and simple and has been kept very natural with short grass (helped by the rabbits) and sheltered from the moor by tall pines. The main field provides 40 fairly level pitches with 19 electric hook-ups (16A) and 6 hardstandings. Reception is in the tavern building. The tavern is run as a free house with a bar, dining room, a family room with outside terrace, garden, water wheel and a good, fenced play area with a Wendy House. It is open to campers and caravanners and the general public. The site gate is closed at night but there is a 24 hour bell. Ideally situated for Colliford Lake and the Moor, be it for walking, fly fishing (permits available) or birdwatching, the park is also suitable for excursions to both the north and south coasts.

Facilities

The pine-fitted, heated toilet block is fully equipped and includes a baby room and unit for disabled people (no shower). Service wash and tumble dry (Monday to Friday). Restaurant and bar. Play area. Some occasional family entertainment. Tickets for the Eden Project (20-30 minutes by car). Barbecues permitted with prior permission.

Open: All year.

Directions

Approaching on the A30 travelling south, pass the Jamaica Inn and site is signed a further 1-1.5 miles on the left. Follow for 0.5 miles and site is signed beside Colliford Lake Park. O.S.GR: SX168730. GPS: N50:32.216 W04:34.936

Charges guide

Per unit incl. 2 persons	£ 13.00
extra person (over 12 yrs)	£ 4.00
electricity (16A)	£ 3.00
child (5-12 yrs)	£ 2.00
dog	£ 0.50

UK0290 Carlyon Bay Caravan & Camping Park

Bethesda, Carlyon Bay, Saint Austell PL25 3RE (Cornwall)

Tel: **01726 812735**. Email: **holidays@carlyonbay.net**   www.alanrogers.com/UK0290

Tranquil open meadows edged by mature woodland, well cared for by the Taylor family, provide a beautiful holiday setting with the nearest beach five minutes walk from the top gate. The original farm buildings have been converted and added to, providing an attractive centre to the park, also home for the owners, with a certain individuality of design which is very pleasing, particularly in the impressively tiled toilet blocks which are of excellent quality. The 180 pitches in five areas are spacious and allow for a family meadow and a dog free meadow (high season only). All are on flat, terraced or gently sloping grass with flowers and flowering shrubs in some areas. The 115 pitches with electricity (10/16A) are marked and include 8 with full services, 6 with hardstanding. The attractive kidney shaped, heated swimming pool and a paddling pool, are walled and paved for sunbathing. This is part of the central, covered area where entertainment is provided in high season for families and children. A pleasant family pub and Ben's Playworld for children are within walking distance.

Facilities

Three individually designed, modern toilet blocks (one heated) provide a full range of comfortable facilities for all your needs. Fully equipped laundry room. Modern reception with little shop. Takeaway (May - mid Sept). Swimming and paddling pools (Whitsun - Sept). TV lounge. Crazy golf. Two play areas, one adventure type. Eden Project tickets. Off site: Golf. Riding 3 miles. Bicycle hire 4 miles. Sailing 2 miles. Boat launching 5 miles. Coastal footpath. Buses to St Austell and Fowey from park entrance. Eden Project 2 miles.

Open: Easter/1 April - end September.

Directions

From Plymouth direction on A390, pass Lostwithiel and 1 mile after village of St Blazey, turn left at roundabout beside Britannia Inn. After 400 yds turn right on a concrete road and right again at site sign. O.S.GR: SX053526. GPS: N50:20.451 W04:44.233

Charges guide

Per unit incl. 2 persons and electricity	£ 12.00 - £ 25.00
serviced pitch	£ 14.00 - £ 27.00
extra person	£ 5.00
child (3-17 yrs)	£ 3.00 - £ 4.00
dog (max 2)	£ 2.50
Camping Cheques accepted.	

UK0310 Trekenning Tourist Park

Saint Columb Major, Newquay TR8 4JF (Cornwall)

Tel: **01637 880462**. Email: **holidays@trekenning.co.uk**   www.alanrogers.com/UK0310

Trekenning is a very useful park with easy access just off the A39 roundabout at St Columb Major. It comprises a large sloping field with neatly cut grass and all the facilities tucked into the top corner. There are 75 pitches, 68 with 10A electricity and semi-terraced. The A39 runs parallel to one side of the site, so there may be road noise. The star of the show is undoubtedly the kidney shaped pool and paddling pool which are in a garden-like setting with gazebos and sun loungers surrounded by lawn and overlooked by a patio bar at the top – lovely for summer evenings.

Facilities

Two toilet blocks, one with showers and washbasins, the other with two en-suite bathrooms (50p) and six large family showers, well refurbished. Laundry room. Shop for basics (July/Aug). Bar with food on demand. Takeaway (B.Hs and July/Aug). Play area. Outdoor pool with poolside bar (Whitsun - end Aug). Games room. Off site: Fishing 1 mile. Riding and golf 2 miles. Bicycle hire 6 miles.

Open: All year.

Directions

Take A3059 turning to Newquay from St Columb Major then turn immediately left; park is signed. O.S.GR: SW907625. GPS: N50:25.309 W04:56.559

Charges guide

Per unit incl. 2 persons	£ 11.00 - £ 15.00
incl. electricity	£ 14.00 - £ 18.00
extra person	£ 4.50 - £ 6.50
child (3-15 yrs)	£ 2.00 - £ 4.50

37

UK0302 South Penquite Farm

South Penquite, Blisland, Bodmin PL30 4LH (Cornwall)

Tel: **01208 850491**. Email: **thefarm@bodminmoor.co.uk**

www.alanrogers.com/UK0302

South Penquite offers real camping with no frills, set on a 80 hectare hill farm high on Bodmin Moor between the villages of Blisland and St Breward. The farm achieved organic status in 2001 and runs a flock of 300 ewes and a herd of 40 cattle. The camping is small scale and intended to have a low impact on the surrounding environment. Tents or simple motorcaravans can pitch around the edge of three walled fields, roughly cut in the midst of the moor. You can find shelter or a view. Four Yurts (round Mongolian tents) are for rent, complete with wood burning stoves – quite original. You will also find horses, ponies, chickens, geese, ducks and, when we visited, a pair of turkeys which had escaped the Christmas cull and showed their approval or not by the skin around their necks changing colour! A farm walk of some two miles takes you over most of the farm and some of the moor taking in a Bronze Age hut settlement, the river and a standing stone. It is also possible to fish for brown trout on the farm's stretch of the De Lank river, a tributary of the Camel. Take a look at the farm's website which offers a fascinating insight into life and work at South Penquite.

Facilities

Simple but adequate, there are separate toilets and washbasins for men and women, plus four new large showers. Two outside Belfast sinks. Washing machine and dryer. LPG gas. Facilities for field studies and opportunities for educational groups and schools to learn about the local environment. Fishing (requires an EA rod licence and tokens available from the Westcountry Rivers Trust). Dogs are not accepted. Off site: Walking, riding and cycling. Sustrans Route 3 passes close by. North and south coasts within easy reach.

Open: 14 May - mid October.

Directions

On the A30 over Bodmin Moor pass Jamaica Inn and sign for Colliford Lake and watch for St Breward sign (to right) immediately at end of dual-carriageway. Follow this narrow road over open moor for 2 miles ignoring any turns to left or right. Also ignore right turn to St Breward just before the South Penquite sign. Follow track over stone bridge beside ford through farm gate and then bear to left to camping fields. Walk back to book in at Farm House.
O.S.GR: SX104752. GPS: N50:32.670 W04:40.310

Charges guide

Per person	£ 5.00
child (5-16 yrs)	£ 3.00
Less 10% for stays of 5 nights or more.	
No credit cards.	

UK0306 Ruthern Valley Holidays

Ruthernbridge, Bodmin PL30 5LU (Cornwall)

Tel: **01208 831395**. Email: **camping@ruthernvalley.com**

www.alanrogers.com/UK0306

This is a little gem of a site set in 7.5 acres of woodland, tucked away in a peaceful little valley not far from Bodmin. The park was landscaped over 30 years ago with an amazing range of trees and shrubs. It is now owned by Andrew and Nicola Johnson who will bring their talents and expertise to this tranquil small park. There are 16 touring pitches informally spaced but numbered in the main, tree-lined field, six with electricity, and a further 13 in smaller fields and alcove areas amongst the woods with a small stream meandering through and alive with bluebells when we visited. The landscaping lends itself to the informal layout of the level touring pitches and the self catering accommodation. Twelve wooden chalets and six caravan holiday homes blend into the natural wooded environment. A very good adventure play area is set away from the pitches, and a small, basic toilet block and a little shop complete the provision. This is a site for relaxing with time to enjoy simpler pastimes of walking or birdwatching. Over 40 different species of bird have been recorded.

Facilities

The small toilet block provides everything necessary including a shower each per sex plus washing machines, dryer. Newly built shower and solar hot water heating system. Shop with basic provisions shares with reception (reduced hours in low season). Barbecue hire. Play area with excellent equipment including five-a-side goal posts. Dogs are not accepted in touring areas during July/Aug. Bicycle hire (delivered to site). Off site: Nearest pub 3-4 miles. Riding 4 miles.

Open: April - October.

Directions

Approaching Bodmin from A30 or A38 turn right at first mini roundabout and proceed anti-clockwise on the inner ring road. Go straight over double mini-roundabout, leaving Bodmin on A389/A391 towards St Austell. Ignore first Nanstallon - Ruthernbridge sign, after 1.5 miles, at top of hill, turn right. At Nanstallon village sign (0.75 miles), turn left then filter left. Continue for 1 mile dropping down into Ruthernbridge. Turn left immediately before bridge. Site is on left in 300 yards. O.S.GR: SX012668. GPS: N50:27.873 W04:48.114

Charges guide

Per unit incl. 2 persons	£ 11.00 - £ 13.00
incl. electricity	£ 13.00 - £ 15.50
extra person over 4 yrs	£ 2.50

UK0320 Polborder House Caravan & Camping Park

Bucklawren Road, Saint Martins by Looe PL13 1NZ (Cornwall)

Tel: **01503 240265**. Email: **reception@peaceful-polborder.co.uk**   **www.alanrogers.com/UK0320**

Polborder House is a lovely site which may appeal to those who prefer a quiet, well kept little family site to the larger ones with many on-site activities. With good countryside views, up to 36 touring units can be accommodated on well tended grass. Pitches are marked with some hedging between pairs to give privacy. Most have electricity (16A), there are several hardstandings and 17 pitches are serviced. The owners, Amanda and Dale Byers, live on the park and are most helpful. The nearest beach is a 20-25 minutes walk. This is a good area for walking with links to the coastal path.

Facilities

The fully equipped sanitary block (key entry) includes a baby room, laundry, and covered sinks outside for dishwashing. En-suite toilet unit for disabled visitors with ramped access. Shop for gas and basics. Toddler's play area. Hut with tourist information. Off site: Fishing, golf and boat launching within 2 miles. Riding 6 miles. Restaurant 500 m. Diving school at Seaton 2 miles, scuba centre and fishing trips at Looe 2.5 miles.

Open: All year.

Directions

Park is less than 0.5 miles south of the B3253. Turn off 2 miles east of Looe and follow signs to park and Monkey Sanctuary at junctions; care is needed with narrow road. O.S.GR: SX283555.
GPS: N50:22.633 W04:25.110

Charges guide

Per unit incl. 2 persons	£ 10.00 - £ 17.00
extra person	£ 4.00 - £ 5.50
child (5-16 yrs)	£ 2.00 - £ 3.00

UK0360 Lakefield Caravan Park

Lower Pendavey Farm, Camelford PL32 9TX (Cornwall)

Tel: **01840 213279**. Email: **lakefield@pendavey.fsnet.co.uk**   **www.alanrogers.com/UK0360**

Lakefield is a small, simple touring park on what was a working farm. Now the main focus is on the BHS approved equestrian centre. With only 40 pitches, it is no surprise that the owners, Maureen and Dennis Perring, know all the campers. The well-spaced pitches backing onto hedges and with 24 electric hook-ups (16A) are in view of the small, fenced lake watched over by one of Cornwall's first wind farms. The white-washed café/reception, converted from one of the old barns is open all day offering traditional Cornish fare. Children will love the animals and 'Wabbit World'.

Facilities

Simple but adequate toilet block. Washing machine and dryer in the ladies' and a dishwashing sink and a laundry sink outside but under cover. Toilet for disabled visitors at Riding Centre. Shop and tea room. Picnic tables. Gas supplies. Torches may be useful. Off site: Fishing (sea 4 miles, coarse 5 miles). Golf 2 miles.

Open: 1 April - 30 September.

Directions

Follow B3266 north from Camelford. Park access is directly from this road on the left just before the turning for Tintagel, clearly signed.
O.S.GR: SX097852. GPS: N50:38.103 W04:41.259

Charges guide

Per unit incl. 2 persons	£ 6.00 - £ 10.00
extra person (5 yrs and over)	£ 1.00
electricity	£ 2.50

UK0400 Trelay Farmpark

Pelynt, Looe PL13 2JX (Cornwall)

Tel: **01503 220900**. Email: **stay@trelay.co.uk**   **www.alanrogers.com/UK0400**

Situated a little back from the coast, just over three miles from Looe and Polperro in a rural situation, this is a real gem of a park. Neat, tidy and quiet, despite the name, there is no farm. As you drive in, there are caravan holiday homes (15 privately owned, some let by the park), attractively arranged. The touring area is behind and slightly above, on level to gently sloping, neatly cut grass. A hardcore road connects the good sized, numbered pitches that border the site and back onto hedges, the majority with rural views. There are 43 pitches with electricity and a further 12 pitches for tents, etc.

Facilities

Excellent, spacious chalet-type toilet block, purpose built, heated, well equipped and maintained, with large cubicles. Some semi-private washbasins. En-suite unit with ramp for disabled visitors (key from reception); it includes a baby bath. Two dishwashing sinks and a laundry sink. Washing machine and dryer. Gas supplies. Free use of fridge/freezer and ice pack service. Tourist information including map sales and loan. Off site: Village with pub, shops and bus service 0.5 miles. Looe and Polperro within 3 miles. Bus service from the village.

Open: 30 March - end October.

Directions

From A390 Lostwithiel road take B3359 south at Middle or East Taphouse towards Looe and Polperro. Site is signed 0.5 miles past Pelynt on the left. From Looe take A387 towards Polperro and after 2 miles turn right onto B3359 towards Pelynt. Site is signed 1 mile on right. O.S.GR: SX210545.
GPS: N50:21.735 W04:31.133

Charges guide

Per unit incl. 2 persons	£ 7.50 - £ 12.00
extra person	£ 3.50
electricity	£ 2.00
No credit cards.	

UK0415 Trencreek Farm Country Holiday Park

Hewas Water, Saint Austell PL26 7JG (Cornwall)

Tel: 01726 882540. Email: reception@trencreek.co.uk

www.alanrogers.com/UK0415

Trencreek Farm is a friendly, well equipped park set in 56 acres of rolling Cornish countryside of woodland and lakes and is a wonderful place for a family holiday. Although no longer a working farm, there are some animals to see, including pot bellied pigs and pigmy goats, carefully kept in pens. The grassy pitches are of a good size, most with electrical connections and arranged around the edges of sloping fields. The camping fields surround the former, central farm buildings which have been converted to house all the amenities, including a heated swimming pool. Also very popular are four small course fishing lakes, each of which is stocked with a different range of fish. The park managers, Bev and Gary Cox, have worked hard to bring the park up to standard and encourage a happy and friendly atmosphere. In peak season they organise a club for children (15.00-17.00, Monday to Friday), along with quiz nights in the bar. The animals are an obvious attraction for children and the fishing lakes for fathers, but there is always the pool for the rest of the family. Mobile homes and chalets are available for hire. A member of the Surf Bay Leisure group.

Facilities

Two traditional style toilet blocks are supplemented by a chalet block containing five en-suite units per sex (charged). Launderette. Shop. Bar, restaurant. Takeaway food. Heated swimming pool. Tennis court. Sports field. Fishing (small charge). Adventure play area. TV and games room. Children's farm. Off site: Nearest beach 4 miles. Golf (18-hole) 3 miles. Riding and bicycle hire 4 miles. The Lost Gardens of Heligan 3 miles. Eden Project 3 miles.

Open: 7 April - 29 October.

Directions

Site is four miles west of St Austell. Take the A390 and then fork left to join the B3287 and the site is 1 mile further on the left. O.S.GR: SW965484. GPS: N50:18.045 W04:51.425

Charges guide

Per pitch incl. 2 persons	£ 8.50 - £ 16.00
incl. electricity	£ 10.45 - £ 18.00
extra person (over 3 yrs)	£ 1.50
dog	£ 1.00

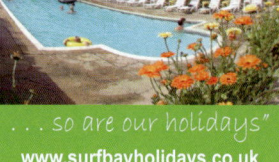
UK0410 Heligan Woods Holiday Park

Saint Ewe, Saint Austell PL26 6EL (Cornwall)

Tel: 01726 843485. Email: info@heliganwoods.co.uk

www.alanrogers.com/UK0410

A peaceful park in a mature garden setting, Heligan Woods complements its sister site, Pentewan Sands with its busy beach life and many activities. One can enjoy the mature trees and flowering shrubs here which have been further landscaped to provide an attractive situation for a number of holiday homes (some for rent, 5 privately owned). These face out over a part of the 'Lost Valley' of Heligan fame and are interspersed with touring pitches, with some below on sloping grass and others in a more level situation amongst trees and shrubs. In all, there are 100 good sized touring pitches, 80 with 16A electricity. The many facilities of Pentewan Sands are open to Heligan Woods visitors. There is access to the Pentewan Trail to ride or cycle into Mevagissey or Pentewan.

Facilities

Fully equipped and well kept, the modern, heated toilet block includes a unisex room with bath and small size bath. Fully equipped laundry room. Small shop (peak season only). Adventure playground. Off site: Riding 4 miles, golf 5 miles. Lost Gardens of Heligan next door.

Open: 1 February - 30 November.

Directions

From St Austell ring road take B3273 for Mevagissey. After 3.5 miles, pass Pentewan Sands, continue up the hill and turn right following site signs. O.S.GR: SW999464. GPS: N50:17.330 W04:48.725

Charges guide

Per unit incl. 2 persons	£ 9.95 - £ 22.95
extra person	£ 1.75 - £ 3.85
child (3-15 yrs)	£ 1.00 - £ 2.80

UK0380 Wooda Farm Holiday Park

Holiday homes ▶ page 324

Poughill, Bude EX23 9HJ (Cornwall)

Tel: 01288 352069. Email: enquiries@wooda.co.uk

www.alanrogers.com/UK0380

Wooda Farm is spacious and well organised, with some nice touches. A quality, family run park, it is part of a working farm, under two miles from the sandy, surfing beaches of Bude. In peaceful farmland with plenty of open spaces (and some up and down walking), there are marvellous views of sea and countryside. The 220 large pitches are spread over four meadows on level or gently sloping grass, 142 with 10A electricity, 73 hardstanding hedged 'premier' pitches (electricity, water, waste water) and 5 premier pitches with Sky TV, linked by tarmac roads. A late arrivals area has electricity. Beside the shop and reception at the entrance are 55 caravan holiday homes to let. A few friendly farm animals welcome assistance at feeding time! Tractor and trailer rides, archery and clay pigeon shooting with tuition are provided in season, plus woodland (to find the pixies) and orchard walks and excellent coarse fishing. There is much to do in the area – sandy beaches with coastal walks and Tintagel with King Arthur's Castle and Clovelly nearby. A member of the Best of British group.

Facilities

Three well maintained toilet blocks, one heated, include a unit suitable for disabled people, two baby rooms and five family bathrooms (small charge). Two laundry rooms. Motorcaravan services. Shop with licence (reduced hours out of season). Attractive courtyard bar with bar meals and restaurant. Play area. 9-hole 'fun' golf course (clubs provided). Games room with TV. Badminton. Tennis. Gym. Coarse fishing in 1.5 acre lake (permits £1.50/half day, £2.50/day). Certain breeds of dogs not accepted. WiFi. Internet access. Caravan storage. Off site: Village inn is 5 minutes walk. Leisure Centre and Splash Pool in Bude.

Open: 1 April - 31 October.

Directions

Park is north of Bude at Poughill; turn off the A39 on north side of Stratton on minor road for Coombe Valley, following camp signs at junctions.
O.S.GR: SS225080. GPS: N50:50.599 W04:31.114

Charges guide

Per unit incl. 2 persons	£ 12.00 - £ 19.00
incl. electricity	£ 14.00 - £ 21.00
incl. water and drainage	£ 16.00 - £ 26.00
extra person	£ 3.50 - £ 5.00
child (3-15 yrs)	£ 2.00 - £ 3.50

Camping Cheques accepted.

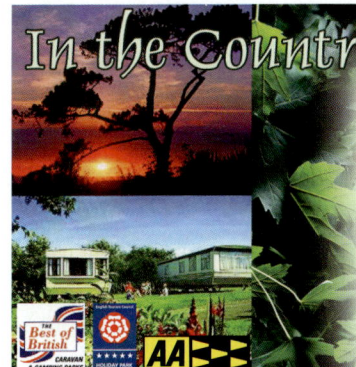

In the Countryside - Beside the Sea

The Colwill family welcome you to Wooda Farm Park set in 27 acres of parkland with spectacular views of sea and countryside - an excellent base for touring the delights of Cornwall and Devon.

- Fishing • Fun Golf • Family Bathrooms
- Heated Facilities • All-weather Pitches

www.wooda.co.uk
Tel: 01288 352069

Wooda Farm Park, Bude, Cornwall EX23 9HJ

UK0430 Padstow Touring Park

Padstow PL28 8LE (Cornwall)

Tel: 01841 532061. Email: mail@padstowtouringpark.co.uk

www.alanrogers.com/UK0430

Padstow Touring Park has wonderful views over the surrounding countryside. Originally open fields, bushes and shrubs have grown to break up the gently sloping fields. There are 150 pitches, over half with 10A electricity and some with hardstanding. 'Kernow' pitches have access to private, en-suite facilities. The site can accommodate up to 32-34 ft. motorhomes. Padstow itself is a mile away, either by public footpath through the fields (20-30 minutes) or by bicycles on the road. A bus service passes and reception holds timetables. Rick Stein's restaurant may tempt you – if you can get a reservation!

Facilities

Three toilet blocks, including one new with under-floor heating, en-suite shower rooms, facilities for disabled visitors and a family room. Exclusive washrooms for use with the 'Kernow' pitches. Full laundry facilities. Reception/shop for gas, camping equipment and provisions. Bread to order. Play area. WiFi access. Off site: Nearest beach is at Padstow, others are within 2 miles. Riding or fishing 2 miles. Golf 5 miles.

Open: All year.

Directions

Park is on the main A389 road into Padstow, on the right about 1 mile before the town. If towing or in a motorhome avoid the A389 between Wadebridge and St Issey; instead take the B3274.
O.S.GR: SW912739. GPS: N50:31.623 W04:56.951

Charges guide

Per unit incl. 2 persons	£ 10.00 - £ 26.50
extra person	£ 3.50 - £ 4.50
child (3-15 yrs)	£ 2.00 - £ 3.00

41

UK0440 Dolbeare Caravan & Camping Park

Saint Ive Road, Landrake, Saltash PL12 5AF (Cornwall)

Tel: 01752 851332. Email: reception@dolbeare.co.uk www.alanrogers.com/UK0440

Ian and Chris are now the proud owners of this small, but well kept park. Dolbeare is in a rural setting (but very easily accessible from the main A38) and consists of a large rectangular field of neat grass edged with trees and sloping slightly at the top, connected by a gravel road, and a camping paddock. All 66 pitches are on hardstanding and have 16A electricity connections. An extra field provides the camping paddock and can also be used for rallies. Part of it is set aside for a games field with a dog walk being developed at the top of the park. A new low level adventure play area has been added, along with giant chess and Connect 4 games. At reception, leaflets are provided on 'Where to Eat', 'Where to Walk' and 'Suggestions for what to do' with a good supply of tourist information and maps. This is a very usefully situated park said to be 20 minutes from everywhere – Plymouth, beaches, National Trust properties, Dartmoor and Bodmin Moor, etc.

Facilities

The fully equipped heated toilet block to one side of the field. Indoor dishwashing sinks. Laundry next to reception. Fridge and freezer in camping field. Motorcaravan services. Reception doubles as a small shop for basics including gas (limited hours out of main season). Site barrier (card system with £5 deposit). Off site: Fishing and riding 3 miles. Golf 5.5 miles. Nearest beach 8 miles.

Open: All year.

Directions

After crossing the Tamar Bridge into Cornwall, continue on A38 for a further 4 miles. In Landrake village turn right following signs and site is 0.75 miles on the right. O.S.GR: SX366616. GPS: N50:25.838 W04:18.331

Charges guide

Per unit incl. 2 persons and electricity	£ 13.20 - £ 18.60
extra person	£ 3.50
child (5-16 yrs)	£ 2.25

UK0450 Pennance Mill Farm Chalet & Camping Park

Maenporth, Falmouth TR11 5HJ (Cornwall)

Tel: 01326 317431 www.alanrogers.com/UK0450

Pennance Mill Farm has been in the hands of the Jewell family for three generations and is listed as a typical Cornish farmstead in an Area of Outstanding Natural Beauty (AONB) and you can enjoy the woodland walk with 200 year old beech trees. In the high season skittles, country games and barbecue evenings are organised, all in keeping with the relaxed and friendly atmosphere generated by the owners. The camping area is situated in four sheltered south-facing and fairly level fields with views over the countryside and providing for 75 pitches, all of which have 16A electricity and 8 hardstanding. Caravans are accepted however this is not a site for those who like neat manicured lawns and flower beds. An old mill wheel reminds one of the site's origins and you book in at the farmhouse. A private foot and cycle path takes you to the sandy beach at Maenporth safe for bathing, windsurfing and diving. An hourly bus service now runs to the beach and the town centre.

Facilities

The two toilet blocks are fully equipped. The first near the entrance is the original one but it is well kept with good hot water, washing machine, dryer, laundry and dishwashing sinks. The block in the top meadow is more modern, heated and includes dishwashing sinks. Small farm shop including some basic provisions (open 9.00-10.30 and 17.30-18.30). Gas supplies. Small play meadow with new play equipment. Off site: New Maritime Museum. Tennis courts, golf course and pitch and putt within walking distance. Coastal footpath to the Helford River.

Open: Easter - November.

Directions

From Truro, follow signs for Falmouth on A39. At first roundabout pass Asda then turn right at next roundabout signed Maenporth and industrial estates (on Bickland Water Road). Follow brown international camping sigps for 1.5 miles and continue down the hill to site on your left as the road bends to the right. O.S.GR: SW789307. GPS: N50:08.099 W05:05.560

Charges guide

Per person	£ 5.00 - £ 6.00
child (over 3 yrs)	£ 1.75 - £ 2.50
pitch incl. electricity	£ 6.50 - £ 7.50

 www.alanrogers.com for latest campsite news

UK0480 Boscrege Caravan Park

Ashton, Helston TR13 9TG (Cornwall)

Tel: 01736 762231. Email: enquiries@caravanparkcornwall.com   www.alanrogers.com/UK0480

A pretty little site covering 12 acres and hidden deep in the countryside in an area of outstanding natural beauty (AONB), Boscrege will suit those who want a quiet peaceful base for their Cornish holiday. The main large touring field nestles at the foot of Tregonning Hill with its striking hill top cross, and has neatly cut grass with a gentle slope from the top. The pitches are generously spaced around the edge, backing on to hedging and leaving plenty of room in the centre for ball games. Three small, attractive paddock areas, two with caravan holiday homes (26 in total), the other for touring units, complete the total provision of 51 pitches, 28 with 10A electricity. A nature trail has been developed which will help you identify the birds which can be seen around the park. This park is a welcome retreat for couples and families with young children.

Facilities

The traditional style toilet block is showing its age somewhat but is fully equipped including a smaller basin for children (M/F). Dishwashing sinks, laundry sink, washing machine and dryer and microwave. Reception keeps emergency supplies. Two play areas for smaller children and central ball area. Amusement machines, pool table and TV room. New nature trail. Off site: Godolphin House and garden. Whole of the tip of Cornwall easily accessible – the Lizard, Lands End. Nearest beach (Praa Sands) 2 miles. Fishing 1 mile. Golf and riding 2 miles. Bicycle hire and boat launching 5 miles.

Open: Easter/1 April - 31 October.

Directions

From Helston take A394 for Penzance. At top of Sithney Common Hill turn right just before Jet garage onto B3302 (Hayle) road. Pass Sithney Stores on left and take next left for Carleen and Godolphin Cross. Continue to Godolphin Cross village and turn left at side of Godolphin Arms signed Ashton. Proceed up hill bearing left at top until site signs where road turns sharply left and go straight over into lane leading to Boscrege. O.S.GR: 593305. GPS: N50:07.501 W05:22.051

Charges guide

Per unit incl. 4 persons	£ 8.00 - £ 15.95
electricity	£ 2.95
No charge for dogs (max. 3).	

UK0500 Trewince Farm Holiday Park

Saint Issey, Wadebridge PL27 7RL (Cornwall)

Tel: 01208 812830   www.alanrogers.com/UK0500

A well established and popular park, Trewince Farm is four miles from Padstow has been developed around a dairy farm with magnificent countryside views. Careful landscaping with flowering shrubs and bushes makes this an attractive setting. There are 35 caravan holiday homes discreetly terraced, some privately owned, some to let. Two touring areas on higher ground provide both hardstanding and level grass pitches with a sheltered tent area. Over half of the 120 touring pitches have electricity (10A) and 34 have water and drainage. The park's main feature is an excellent sheltered, walled and heated swimming pool with paddling pool, and paved sunbathing area. Farm rides and Cornish pasty suppers in the barn are organised in the high season.

Facilities

Two fully equipped, well maintained toilet blocks include washbasins in cabins, hair care rooms, dishwashing under cover and laundry rooms. Children's room with bath (20p) and facilities for disabled visitors. Well stocked shop (all season) by reception. Fish and chip van calls twice weekly, a butcher once a week. Swimming pool. Play area. Games room. Crazy golf. New fishing lake. Off site: Riding 3 miles. Golf and bicycle hire 3.5 miles. Beach 4.5 miles. Pubs and restaurants in village of St Issey. Camel Trail for walking or cycling (goes to Padstow).

Open: 23 March - 31 October.

Directions

From Wadebridge follow A39 towards St Columb and pick up the A389 for Padstow. Site signed on left in 2 miles. Follow for short distance to park entrance on right. O.S.GR: SW937715. GPS: N50:34.316 W04:54.793

Charges guide

Per unit incl. 2 persons	£ 9.00 - £ 14.00
incl. electricity	£ 10.00 - £ 15.50
hardstanding, drainage and electricity	£ 11.00 - £ 16.00
extra person	£ 3.50
child (3-15 yrs)	£ 1.85 - £ 2.90

UK0505 The Laurels Holiday Park

Padstow Road, Whitecross, Wadebridge PL27 7JQ (Cornwall)

Tel: **01209 313474**. Email: **jamierielly@btconnect.com**   www.alanrogers.com/UK0505

This is a small park in a garden-like setting of which the managers Edna and Ray are very proud. It is very well maintained and provides 32 level pitches with 16A electricity. Some have hardstanding and some are extra large. Neat hedging marks the pitches and the central area with shrubs and plants is kept clear for enjoyment. A good play area for children is well fenced from the A39 which could be the cause of some road noise. The Camel Trail for walking or cycling is close and follows the estuary from Wadebridge to Padstow. A bus stops outside the site.

Facilities

Well kept fully equipped toilet block. Laundry. Facilities for drying wetsuits. Freezer and communal fridge. Play area with trampoline. Off site: Shops 1 mile. Beach 4 miles. Riding, bicycle hire, boat launching 3 miles. Fishing 5 miles. Camel Trail (walking/cycling).

Open: Easter - 31 October.

Directions

Travelling west, bypass Wadebridge on the A39. Pass the Royal Cornwall showground on the left then turn right (A38) signed Padstow. Park entrance is immediately on the right. O.S.GR: SW958716. GPS: N50:30.496 W04:52.915

Charges guide

Per person	£ 5.00 - £ 8.00
child (under 16 yrs)	£ 2.00 - £ 4.00
pitch incl. electricity	£ 3.00 - £ 4.00

UK0490 Mullion Holiday Park

Helston TR12 7LJ (Cornwall)

~~0844 826 5595~~ 01326 240 000

Tel: **0870 4447774**. Email: **touring@weststarholidays.co.uk**   www.alanrogers.com/UK0490

For those who enjoy plenty of entertainment, both social and active in a holiday environment, Mullion would be a good choice. This holiday park is situated on the Lizard peninsula with its sandy beaches and coves. It has all the trimmings – indoor and outdoor pools, super play areas, clubs, bars and a wide range of nightly entertainment. Recent developments include a new look 'Stargate Club' and a 'village square' with a bandstand. These amenities form the core of the park and are well organised and managed. The touring area past the holiday homes has a more relaxed atmosphere and is set on natural heathland with clumps of bramble and gorse which provide breaks and recesses making for a more informal layout. Linked by a circular gravel road, all 160 pitches are numbered, 10 with hardstanding and 105 with electricity connections (16A). Land drainage could be a problem if there is heavy continuous rain. A resident warden is based at the entrance to the touring section. Eurotents are avaiable for hire. There is much to see in the area including Goonhilly Satellite Station and Flambards Village, the theme park, Lizard Point and Lands End.

Facilities

A central modern toilet block is fully equipped and includes a baby unit and bath. It is supplemented with additional 'portacabin' style facilities for high season. Dishwashing sinks under cover, two laundry sinks and two washing machines. Large launderette in main complex. Freezer pack service. Large supermarket with off licence. Pub with family room, restaurant and takeaway (half board or breakfast options). Stargate Club with live shows and cabarets, big screen satellite TV. Excellent outdoor play areas (fenced). Toddlers' soft play area. Amusement arcade, bowling alley. Heated outdoor pool and paddling pool (26/5-8/9). Heated indoor fun pool with slide, both supervised. Sauna and solarium. Crazy golf, pitch and putt. Barbecue.

Open: 20 May - 9 September.

Directions

From Helston take A3083 for The Lizard and continue for 7 miles. Site on left immediately after the right turning for Mullion. O.S.GR: SW698185. GPS: N50:01.267 W05:12.883

Charges guide

Per pitch	£ 12.75 - £ 27.50
incl. electricity	£ 15.75 - £ 30.50
super hook-up incl. electricity, TV point, fresh water	£ 17.25 - £ 32.00
awning	free - £ 5.00
dog (max 2)	£ 5.00

Half-board or breakfast options available. Free club membership included.

UK0510 Summer Valley Touring Park

Shortlanesend, Truro TR4 9DW (Cornwall)

Tel: **01872 277878**. Email: **res@summervalley.co.uk**   www.alanrogers.com/UK0510

Summer Valley is a quiet and mature, but very pleasant, small rural park suitable for visiting both the north and south coast of Cornwall. South facing, the park consists of a large well kept grass area with reception and facilities to one side. A tarmac road circles this and mature trees edge the whole site providing shelter but still allowing rural views. Caravans go on the central area which slopes gently and is divided down the centre with more mature trees and shrubs. The pitches around the perimeter area are semi-divided by shrubs and used more for tents. There is provision for 60 units of all types, but only 50 are used, 45 with electricity connections (10/16A).

Facilities

A good quality, solid toilet block is well maintained with ladies to the left and men to the right, plus unisex showers. Washbasins in cabins and one shower/toilet en-suite per sex. Laundry facilities. Campers' rest room with library. Reception/licensed shop (basics) with freezer pack service (reduced hours out of main season). Gas supplies. Small play area hidden in a corner but part of the central area is left for ball games. Off site: Village of Shortlanesend within walking distance with post office and pub. Fishing 2.5 miles. Golf 3 miles. Riding 5 miles. Bicycle hire 2.5 miles. Perranporth beach 6 miles (dogs are allowed away from the village end).

Open: 31 March - 31 October.

Directions

From Truro take B3284 north, signed Perranporth. Follow for 2.5 miles and site is signed on left just through the village of Shortlanesend.
O.S.GR: SW 800479. GPS: N50:17.459 W05:05.294

Charges 2009

Per unit incl. 2 persons	£ 11.50 - £ 15.00
extra person	£ 1.50
child (3-16 yrs)	£ 1.00
electricity	£ 2.00

UK0530 Trethiggey Touring Park

Quintrell Downs, Newquay TR8 4LG (Cornwall)

Tel: **01637 877672**. Email: **enquiries@trethiggey.co.uk**   www.alanrogers.com/UK0530

Trethiggey is a garden-like park with a ten month season, set some three miles back from the busy Newquay beaches and night life, with an enjoyable, informal style. With natural areas including a small wildlife pond and fishing lakes to enjoy, conservation is high on the agenda. There are 157 pitches, 110 with 16A electricity, some with hardstanding and a few also serviced with water and sewage connection. Some level pitches are formally arranged, with others more informal on gently sloping grass amidst 12 caravan holiday homes. A tent field is opened for the main season. A bistro and barbecue bar are very popular. Facilities maintain the informal touch with reception alongside the Trethiggey Trading Post which provides basic supplies, an off-licence and a small library. The bistro-style café and terrace operates in school holidays for breakfasts and simple evening meals, with children catered for. At weekends in peak season the barbecue bar is an added attraction.

Facilities

Two fully equipped, heated shower blocks, one in traditional style. En-suite facilities for families and disabled visitors. Baby bathroom. Motorcaravan service point. Laundry facilities and wet suit wash. Games room at each toilet block with TV and amusement machines. Shop. Café and takeaway. Adventure play area and recreation field. Coarse fishing. WiFi access. Off site: Riding 2 miles. Golf and bicycle hire 3 miles. All the delights of Newquay within 3 miles with nightly minibus service (book in shop). Pub within walking distance.

Open: 2 March - 2 January.

Directions

Site is a few hundred yards south of roundabout where A393 crosses the A3058 at Quintrell Downs (beside the A3058). O.S. GR:SW846596. GPS: N50:23.810 W05:01.698

Charges guide

Per person	£ 4.25 - £ 6.85
child (4-15 yrs)	£ 1.85 - £ 4.25
pitch incl. electricity	£ 3.20 - £ 6.00
dog	£ 1.80 - £ 2.50

See advertisement on page 30

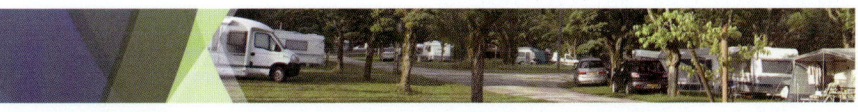

UK1070 **Woolacombe Bay Holiday Village**

Runner up Alan Rogers Awards 2008

Sandy Lane, Woolacombe EX34 7AH (Devon)

Tel: **01271 870343**. Email: **goodtimes@woolacombe.com**   www.alanrogers.com/UK1070

Woolacombe Bay Holiday Village, and its sister site Golden Coast Holiday Village nearby, are well known holiday parks providing a range of holiday accommodation from caravan holiday homes to luxury lodges, apartments and villas, with many on site amenities including pools, restaurants and bars, and providing a wide range of entertainment. A camping section at the Woolacombe Bay park caters for tents and trailer tents only, so touring visitors can enjoy all the activities and entertainment of both parks. Partly terraced out of the hillside and partly on the hill top with some existing pine trees but with many more trees planted for landscaping, the site has magnificent views out across the bay. Marked and numbered pitches have been provided on grass for 150 tents, 97 with electricity (10/16A). All should be level, having been terraced where necessary and they are connected by gravel roads. Some up and down walking is needed for the toilet block. A bus service (small charge) runs between the two parks, the third and fourth parks in the group (Twitchen Park and Easewell Farm) and the beach during the main season, although there is a footpath to the beach from the site. The three larger parks have varied entertainment programmes and children's clubs and Woolacombe Bay also boasts a health spa and beauty suite.

Facilities

A smart central toilet block has excellent facilities, including en-suite shower and washrooms and separate toilets, baby facilities, and also a sauna and steam room. Laundry rooms. Two units for disabled visitors. Supermarket. Bars, restaurant and entertainment. Indoor (heated) and outdoor pools with flumes and slides. Sauna and gym. Beauty and holistic treatments. Wide range of sporting activities. Tennis. ATM. Dogs are welcome at Woolacombe Bay but not at Golden Coast. Off site: Fishing and riding 1 mile. Beach 1 mile.

Open: 11 May - 21 September (camping).

Directions

Take A361 Barnstaple - Ilfracombe road through Braunton. Turn left at Mullacott Cross roundabout towards Woolacombe then right towards Mortehoe. Now follow the camping signs by turning left and park is on the left. O.S.GR: SS469443. GPS: N51:10.627 W04:11.479

Charges guide

Per caravan or motorcaravan	
incl. all persons	£ 15.00 - £ 50.00
serviced pitch	£ 18.00 - £ 52.00
tent - per person	£ 5.00 - £ 16.00
tent - child (5-15 yrs)	£ 2.50 - £ 8.00

UK1075 **Golden Coast Holiday Village**

Station Road, Woolacombe EX34 7HW (Devon)

Tel: **01271 870343**. Email: **goodtimes@woolacombe.com**   www.alanrogers.com/UK1075

The Golden Coast Holiday Village is part of the Woolacombe Bay Holiday Parks group that includes Woolacombe Bay, Twitchen Park and the recently acquired Easewell Farm Holiday Park. It predominantly comprises brick-built holiday accommodation, however, there are two small camping areas providing 91 pitches, 18 of which are fully serviced. The toilet block is adequate rather than good, and was quite clean at the time of our visit. Campers can enjoy an extensive program of entertainment for children and adults, and qualified nursery nurses run an OFSTED approved crèche. A shuttle bus runs between the four parks and to the beach several times a day (it costs £1 per person per holiday). A visit to the Old Mill Inn should not be missed; it serves bar meals, and has an excellent beer garden with adventure play area for the children. The range of amenities and facilities at this large park will suit families looking for a lively holiday filled with activities and entertainment.

Facilities

A fairly new building provides good facilities. Washing machine and dryer in the ladies' section. Large, well stocked supermarket, boutique and beauty salon. Indoor and outdoor swimming pools, outdoor flume, sauna and solarium. Bar, club, Old Mill Inn, restaurant and takeaway. Floodlit tennis court. Adventure playgrounds. Snooker. Games room. Soft play area and crèche. Ceramics studio. Learn to swim classes. 9-hole golf course. Indoor and outdoor bowls, ten-pin bowling complex. Fishing lake. Woodland walks. Shuttle bus. Dogs are not accepted. Off site: Woolacombe beach is about 2 miles. For walkers there is the coastal path. Amenities at sister parks available to all visitors.

Open: 12 February - 2 January.

Directions

From Barnstaple, take A361 (signed Braunton and Ilfracombe). Turn left on B3343 (signed Woolacombe) and follow the road towards the town. The park is on the left near the top of the hill. O.S.GR: SS480435. GPS: N51:10.350 W04:10.366

Charges guide

Per caravan or motorcaravan	
incl. services	£ 15.00 - £ 50.00
	£ 18.00 - £ 52.00
tent - per person	£ 5.00 - £ 16.00
tent - per child (5-15 yrs)	£ 2.50 - £ 8.00

BEST BEACH IN BRITAIN and awarded Family Resort of the Year

fun
filled holidays

See our advert under Woolacombe, Devon for further details

REGISTER ONLINE FOR LATEST OFFERS!!

woolacombe.com/ar
01271 870 343

WOOLACOMBE BAY

UK0720 Easewell Farm Holiday Park

Mortehoe, Woolacombe EX34 7EH (Devon)

Tel: **01271 870343**. Email: **goodtimes@woolacombe.com**　　　www.alanrogers.com/UK0720

Near the sandy beaches of Woolacombe, Easewell Farm is now part of the Woolacombe Bay Holiday Park group who own the Woolacombe Bay, Golden Coast and Twitchen parks. A shuttle bus runs between the four parks and to the beach (tickets £1 per person per holiday). This is a traditional style touring park which during the day is a hive of activity, but the nights are quiet and peaceful. The largest of the camping fields is sloping with superb views across the headland to the sea. Two smaller fields are terraced and one area has hardstandings. Together they provide 302 pitches, 124 with electricity connections (15A) and 20 also with TV and water connections. Also available are a lovely four bedroom farmhouse (sleeping ten), a pretty two bedroom cottage (five beds) and a caravan holiday home. The shop is well stocked (gas available), there is a takeaway and restaurant and an attractive bar with patio overlooking a small duck pond. The park has its own very well maintained 9-hole golf course which is popular and has reduced fees for campers. One of the huge redundant farm buildings has been put to excellent use: divided into three areas, it provides table tennis and pool, a skittle alley and two lanes of flat green bowling with changing rooms. Walks to the local village and along the coastal path are easy from the site and a bus to Ilfracombe and Barnstaple stops 100 yards from the entrance.

Facilities

The central toilet block has been regularly upgraded and can be heated. Two washbasins in the ladies have hoses for hair washing, controllable showers (no dividers). Small area with baby bath facilities. Laundry. These facilities are arranged around the farmhouse area and include a very well equipped unit for disabled people with everything in one large room including a hairdryer. Motorcaravan service point. Shop. Bar. Golf. Small heated indoor swimming pool is well used, as are games and TV rooms. Fenced play area with bark base. Indoor skittle alley. In high season only one dog per pitch is allowed. Off site: Fishing or riding 1 mile. Bicycle hire 3 miles. Tarka Trail for walking and riding. Boat trips to Lundy Island.

Open: Easter - end October.

Directions

From Barnstaple, take A361 Ilfracombe road through Braunton. Turn left at Mullacott Cross roundabout on B3343 to Woolacombe, turning right after 2-3 miles to Mortehoe. Park is on the right before the village. O.S.GR: SS465455. GPS: N51:11.118 W04:11.936

Charges guide

Per caravan or motorcaravan	£ 15.00 - £ 50.00
incl. services	£ 18.00 - £ 52.00
tent - per person	£ 5.00 - £ 16.00
tent - child (5-15 yrs)	£ 2.50 - £ 8.00

UK0730 Twitchen Park

Mortehoe, Woolacombe EX34 7ES (Devon)

Tel: **01271 870848**. Email: **goodtimes@woolacombe.com**　　　www.alanrogers.com/UK0730

Set in the grounds of an attractive Edwardian country house, Twitchen Park is owned by nearby Woolacombe Bay Holiday Parks. Its main concern lies in holiday caravans and apartments, although it also provides marked pitches, all for touring units, at the top of the park, with some views over the rolling hills to the sea. With a more recently developed touring field, they include 228 pitches with 16A electricity, many with tarmac hardstanding (not always level), mostly arranged around oval access roads in hedged areas. Further non-electric pitches are behind in two open, unmarked fields which are sloping (blocks are thoughtfully provided, stored in neat wooden boxes next to water points). A smart, modern entertainment complex incorporates a licensed club and family lounge with snacks, a restaurant, teenage disco room, cartoon lounge, outdoor pool and smart indoor pool complex. Twitchen is very popular for families with children. If they become bored, there are always the excellent beaches nearby with a footpath down to the sea. All the facilities of Golden Coast and Woolacombe Bay Holiday Villages and Easewell Farm are free to visitors at Twitchen, with a bus (small charge) running regularly between the four parks and to the beach.

Facilities

There are two toilet blocks. Dishwashing and laundry facilities at each block plus a good modern launderette at the central complex. Motorcaravan service point. Shop and takeaway. Club, bars, restaurant and entertainment for adults and children, day and evening. OFSTED approved crèche for children (charge). Outdoor pool (heated mid May - mid Sept). Attractive indoor pool with sauna, paddling pool, fountain and a viewing area. Putting green. Games rooms. Good adventure play area. ATM. American motorhomes are accepted (up to 30 ft). Off site: Beach 1 mile. Golf 1 mile. Fishing, riding and bicycle hire 2 miles.

Open: Easter- end October.

Directions

From Barnstaple take A361 towards Ilfracombe and through Braunton. Turn left at Mullacott Cross roundabout towards Woolacombe and then right towards Mortehoe. Park is on the left before village. O.S.GR: SS465451. GPS: N51:11.081 W04:11.862

Charges guide

Per caravan or motorcaravan	£ 15.00 - £ 50.00
incl. services	£ 18.00 - £ 52.00
tent - per person	£ 5.00 - £ 16.00
tent - child (5-15 yrs)	£ 2.50 - £ 8.00
Special offers available.	

UK0680 Channel View Caravan & Camping Park

Manor Farm, Barbrook, Lynton EX35 6LD (Devon)

Tel: **01598 753349**. Email: **relax@channel-view.co.uk**   **www.alanrogers.com/UK0680**

Channel View is a quiet, family run park situated in a sunny, south-facing position overlooking Lynton and Lynmouth. The gently sloping ground provides fairly level pitches which are mostly on hardstandings. The park is divided into two areas, an open area that is sheltered by bushes and trees and one that is more exposed but has views. There are 15 serviced pitches with electricity, water and a drain, and 60 with electricity (16A). The grass is well cared for and there is site lighting, although a torch would be useful. There is a café on the site that also offers takeaways. A small shop is located with reception and is well stocked. There is a freezer for ice packs, a public telephone and a children's play area. The Country Inn pub is nearby with bar food available.

Facilities

The modern and very clean toilet and shower block is partly tiled. Showers are free (here are three steps down to the ladies showers from the toilets). Baby changing/family washroom. Facilities for disabled visitors (Radar key). Laundry with washing machines, dryers and iron. Café. Small shop. Play area. Off site: Lynton and Lynmouth, Exmoor and the Doone Valley are nearby. Many walks can be started from the site. Riding 1 mile. Fishing 1 mile. Golf 15 miles. Beach 2 miles.

Open: 15 March - 15 November.

Directions

Take the A399 from Ilfracombe. Turn left on the A39 and continue past the turn for Lynton to site on the left after 2 miles. It is not advisable to approach from Lynton and Lynmouth. O.S.GR: 724482. GPS: N51:13.080 W03:49.758

Charges guide

Per unit incl. 2 persons	£ 10.00 - £ 15.00
incl. electricity	£ 12.00 - £ 14.00
extra person	£ 3.00 - £ 4.00
child (6-16 yrs)	£ 1.00 - £ 3.00

UK0700 Greenacres Touring Caravan Park

Bratton Fleming, Barnstaple EX31 4SG (Devon)

Tel: **01598 763334**   **www.alanrogers.com/UK0700**

A neat, compact, rural park on the edge of Exmoor, Greenacres is managed and run alongside, but separately from, the farm owned by the family. Drive through the farm access to the park (clearly signed) – you will need to go back and call at the house to book in. No tents are taken. The site has 30 very large, well drained pitches (all with 16A electricity hook-ups) with connecting gravel paths to the road – in theory you can get to your unit without stepping on the grass. The top area is level, the lower part next to the beech woods is semi-terraced to provide six hardstandings and some hedged places. There are marvellous views outside the beech hedge that shelters the site. To the west of Exmoor, the park is very suitable for the coast at Ilfracombe and Combe Martin, or for exploring the moor. The family has opened up a woodland walk through newly planted trees and across the fields to a secluded valley picnic area beside a stream to take advantage of the marvellous views and surroundings. The West Country cycle way passes within a mile of the park and the area is the setting for the classic novel, 'Lorna Doone'.

Facilities

The neat, clean toilet block with showers (1M, 1F) on payment (20p). Units for disabled visitors (and general use in peak times). Laundry room, with sink, spin dryer, iron and board, and dishwashing room. Washing lines provided. Gas supplies. Tourist information kiosk. Area for children with football and volleyball nets and swings, separated by a Devon bank from the 2 acre dog exercise field. Off site: Fishing 3 miles. Riding 6 miles. Golf 12 miles. Pubs, restaurants and takeaways within 3 miles.

Open: Easter/1 April - 19 October.

Directions

From North Devon link road (M5, exit 27) turn north at South Molton onto A399. Continue for 9 miles, past turning for Exmoor Steam Centre and on to Stowford Cross. Turn left towards Exmoor Zoological Park and Greenacres Farm is on the left. O.S.GR: SS660404. GPS: N51:08.858 W03:55.051

Charges guide

Per unit incl. 2 persons	£ 6.50 - £ 10.25
incl. electricity	£ 8.25 - £ 12.00
extra person	£ 1.50 - £ 2.25
child (under 7 yrs)	free
dog	free

No credit cards.

www.**alanrogers**.com for latest campsite news

UK0710 Hidden Valley Touring & Camping Park

West Down, Ilfracombe EX34 8NU (Devon)

Tel: **01271 813837**. Email: **relax@hiddenvalleypark.com**   **www.alanrogers.com/UK0710**

The owners, Martin and Dawn Fletcher, run this aptly named family park to high standards. In a sheltered valley setting between Barnstaple and Ilfracombe beside a small stream and lake (with ducks), it is most attractive and is also convenient for several resorts, beaches and the surrounding countryside. The original part of the park offers some 67 level pitches (standard, large, 'super' and 'premium' pitch options) on three sheltered terraces. On hardstanding, all have electricity (16A) and TV connections (leads for hire), with a water point between each pitch. Kingfisher Meadow, a little way from the main facilities and reached by a tarmac road, provides a further 58 pitches. These are entirely on grass (so suitable for campers with tents) and all have electricity, water, drain and TV hook-up. Two good adventure play areas have wooden equipment and safe bark surfaces (one near a fast flowing stream which is fenced). There is a well stocked, licensed shop, a coffee shop serving breakfast and lunch and therapy suite with a fully qualified therapist. Essentially this is a park for those seeking good quality facilities in very attractive, natural surroundings, without too many man-made distractions – apart from some traffic noise during day time. It provides a relaxed setting with woodland walks direct from the site.

Facilities

Two modern toilet blocks (one for each area, one heated) are tiled and have non-slip floors. Some washbasins in cubicles, some en-suite with toilets in the Kingfisher Meadow block. Bathroom (tokens). Baby room. Complete facilities for people with disabilities. Laundry facilities. Supplementary clean 'portacabin' style facilities in the original area. Motorcaravan service facilities. Gas supplies. Shop. Coffee shop (breakfast and lunch). Therapy suite. Play areas. Up to two dogs are accepted (otherwise by prior arrangement). Caravan storage. Off site: Fishing or golf 2 miles. Bicycle hire 4 miles. Riding 5 miles. Beach 5 miles.

Open: All year.

Directions

Park is on the A361 Barnstaple - Ilfracombe road, 3.5 miles after Braunton. O.S.GR: SS499408. GPS: N51:08.792 W04:08.733

Charges guide

Per unit incl. 2 persons	£ 15.00 - £ 38.00
extra person	£ 3.00 - £ 5.00
child (3-15 yrs)	£ 2.00 - £ 4.00
dog	£ 0.50 - £ 2.00
Discounts for over 50s.	
Camping Cheques accepted.	

UK0735 Woolacombe Sands Holiday Park

Beach Road, Woolacombe EX34 7AF (Devon)

Tel: **01271 870569**. Email: **lifesabeach@woolacombe-sands.co.uk**   **www.alanrogers.com/UK0735**

With sea views and within walking distance of Woolacombe's lovely sandy beach, this family park has been terraced out of the valley side as you drop down into the village. Apart from its smart entrance, it has been left natural. The pond and stream at the bottom are almost hidden with gated access to the National Trust fields across the valley. The 200 terraced level grass pitches all with 10A electricity are accessed by gravel roads with some good up and down walking needed to the toilet blocks (probably not the best environment for disabled people). Some 50 mobile homes and 14 bungalows are in the more central area, and tents tend to be placed on the bottom terraces. The park boasts both indoor and outdoor pools (accessed by code) with a full time attendant. Evenings see Woolly Bear emerge from his 'shack' to entertain children, with adult family entertainment later. A good plus factor is the fact that all facilities open when the site opens. A useful path leads from the site to the beach via the car park and the walk is said to take 15 minutes.

Facilities

Four basic toilet blocks with good hot water are spread amongst the terraces. The newer shower block has separate toilets opposite. Shop. Self-service food bar providing good value meals and breakfast (main season and B.Hs). Two bars and full entertainment programme. Heated indoor and outdoor pools both with paddling pool areas. Fenced play area on bark with plenty of equipment. Ball area with nets. Crazy golf. 'Kingpin' bowling. Off site: Beach 15 minutes walk or 0.5 miles. Riding next door. Golf, bicycle hire and freshwater fishing 0.5 miles.

Open: 1 April - 1 November.

Directions

Follow A361 from Barnstaple through Braunton towards Ilfracombe. At Mullacott Cross roundabout turn left for Woolacombe (B3343). Site clearly signed on left as you go down the hill into the village. O.S.GR: SS468436. GPS: N51:10.287 W04:11.510

Charges guide

Per person	£ 5.00 - £ 15.00
child (5-16 yrs)	£ 2.50 - £ 7.50
dog	£ 5.00
Electricity included.	

UK0690 **Stowford Farm Meadows**

Berry Down, Combe Martin, Ilfracombe EX34 0PW (Devon)

Tel: **01271 882476**. Email: **enquiries@stowford.co.uk**   www.alanrogers.com/UK0690

Stowford Farm is a friendly, family park set in 500 acres of the rolling North Devon countryside, available for recreation and walking, yet within easy reach of five local beaches. The touring park and its facilities have been developed in the fields and farm buildings surrounding the attractive old farmhouse and provide a village like centre with a comfortable spacious feel. There are 710 pitches on five slightly sloping meadows separated by Devon hedges of beech and ash. The numbered and marked pitches, some with hardstanding, are accessed by hard roads, most have electricity (10/16A) and there are well placed water points. The Old Stable Bar offers entertainment in high season including barn dances, discos, karaoke and other musical evenings. There is also much for children to do, from the indoor heated pool and under cover mini-zoo (Petorama) where they can handle many sorts of animals (on payment), to the wide range of organised activities on offer. In low season some facilities may only open for limited hours. Stowford also provides plenty to keep the whole family occupied without leaving the park, including woodland walks and horse riding from the park's own stables. However, it is also a good base for exploring the North Devon coast and Exmoor. A new development of 40 very smart holiday lodges with wonderful views has been added to the park.

Facilities

Five identical toilet blocks, each looked after by resident wardens, are fully equipped and provide good, functional facilities, each block with laundry facilities and dishwashing. The newest block (in field 5) has under-floor heating and includes facilities for disabled visitors. Extra good facilities for disabled visitors and private family washrooms are beside reception. Well stocked shop (with holiday goods and gas). Good value takeaway with restaurant area. Bars and entertainment in season. Indoor pool (22 x 10 m; heated Easter - Oct) at a small charge (£1.25). Riding. 18-hole pitch and putt. Crazy golf. Bicycle hire. 'Kiddies kar' track (all charged). Games room. Large play area. Games and activities organised in high season. ATM. Woodland walks. Dogs welcome in three sections (max. 2 per pitch). Summer parking and winter caravan storage. Caravan centre with sales, workshop, accessories and repair centre. Off site: Fishing, boat launching 4 miles.

Open: All year.

Directions

From Barnstaple take A39 towards Lynton. After 1 mile turn left on B3230. Turn right at garage on A3123 and park is 1.5 miles on the right. O.S.GR: SS565438. GPS: N51:10.499 W04:03.285

Charges guide

Per unit and car incl. 2 persons	
and electricity	£ 8.80 - £ 27.00
extra person	free - £ 4.50
child (5-12 yrs)	free - £ 2.50
dog	£ 1.50 - £ 2.50

Low and mid season discounts for over 50s.

UK0725 **Warcombe Farm Camping Park**

Station Road, Mortehoe EX34 7EJ (Devon)

Tel: **01271 870690**. Email: **info@warcombefarm.co.uk**   www.alanrogers.com/UK0725

This park is set in a quiet position on a hill above Woolacombe. It is a large, fairly open site on gently sloping land. There are 250 level or fairly level pitches, some secluded, others extra large with hardstanding and with electricity, and others fully serviced. Shrubs and trees help to divide some of the pitches. Two hardstanding pitches are designed to provide facilities and access for disabled campers. In total, 160 pitches have electricity hook ups (16A). The site has panoramic views across to the sea and at its centre has a fully fenced lovely well kept lake that is a haven for wildlife. Fishing is permitted in the lake with free lessons sometimes available for those who want to learn. An adjoining, newly planted wood of 14 acres is available for walks and dog walking. There is an adventure playground for children under 14 and space for ball games. The reception area also acts as a small shop with basics including bread and milk, also providing internet access. A takeaway beside reception is opened at weekends in the low season, full time in high season.

Facilities

Two modern toilet blocks are spotlessly clean, with free preset showers. En-suite facilities in one block. Family bathrooms and facilities for disabled visitors (coded locks). Laundry with washing machines, dryers and iron. Motorcaravan services. Shop. Takeaway (w/ends only in low season). Play area. Fishing. Torches useful. Off site: Woolacombe beach is 1.5 miles. Public footpaths and cycle trails (the Tarka Trail is on the doorstep). Riding and golf 1 miles. Bicycle hire 4 miles.

Open: 15 March - 31 October.

Directions

Approaching from Barnstaple on A361 follow signs for Ilfracombe. At Mullacott Cross (10 miles from Barnstaple) turn left and follow B3343 for Woolacombe. After 1.8 miles turn right for Mortehoe. Park is the first on the right in 500 yards. O.S.GR: SS477457. GPS: N51:11.426 W04:10.838

Charges guide

Per unit incl. 2 adults	
and electricity	£ 12.00 - £ 27.00
serviced pitch	£ 15.00 - £ 29.00
extra person	£ 4.00
child	free - £ 2.00

Stowford Farm Meadows

Stowford Country Holidays
A complete service for the touring caravanner

Open All Year Round

Park Facilities

Hard Standing Available

- Indoor Heated Swimming Pool
- Shop for food & supplies
- Take-Away Cafe & 'The Pantry'
- Old Stable & Old Barn Bars
- Family Orientated Entertainment
- Horse Riding Centre & Cycle Hire
- Kiddies' Cars
- 'PETORAMA' Undercover Mini-Zoo
- 18 Hole Fun Golf
- 9 Hole Crazy Golf
- Sports Field & Play Areas
- Extensive Woodland Walks
- **Storage Available**
- **Seasonal Pitches Available**

Stowford Farm Meadows is an award winning touring caravan and camping site close to Combe Martin in the beautiful surroundings of the North Devon countryside.

The site also comprises an award winning caravan sales centre from where we supply Bailey, Elddis & Coachman.

Also, be sure to visit our brand new, air conditioned caravan accessory shop with awning display.

To book call us on

☎ **01271 882476**

Combe Martin Devon EX34 0PW
www.stowford.co.uk

UK0745 Riverside Caravan Park

Marsh Lane, North Molton Road, South Molton EX36 3HQ (Devon)

Tel: **01769 579269**. Email: **relax@exmoorriverside.co.uk**   www.alanrogers.com/UK0745

A very impressive purpose-built campsite beside the River Mole, all the 44 pitches at this park have hardstanding, 16A electricity connection, water, drain and TV aerial socket. Neat grass, tarmac roads and growing trees and hedges contribute to the attractive, overall impression. The heated toilet block gleams but the highlight must be the chemical disposal point which has its own special house and is tiled with a washbasin (would they were all like that!) The owners, Joy and Nicky Penfold, are not resting on their laurels and are currently developing fishing lakes down by the river and a play area on the opposite bank. The ancient market town of South Molton is a mile away and a bus stops outside the entrance. Exmoor is on hand to explore, as are the North Devon resorts of Woolacombe, Ilfracombe, Combe Martin and Lynton, not to mention the surfing paradise of Croyde Bay.

Facilities

Modern, fully equipped and heated toilet block accessed by code. Facilities for disabled visitors. Laundry room. Shop (limited hours in low season). Play area planned. Fishing. Caravan storage. Off site: Riding 2 miles. Golf 5 miles. Boat launching and beach 12 miles.

Open: All year.

Directions

From M5 exit 27 take the North Devon Link road A361. Near South Molton watch for site sign (direction North Molton). O.S.GR: SS723270. GPS: N51:01.852 W03:49.123

Charges guide

Per unit incl. 2 adults	
and 2 children	£ 10.00 - £ 16.00
incl. electricity	£ 12.00 - £ 27.00
extra person	£ 3.00

UK0750 Minnows Touring Caravan Park

Sampford Peverell, Tiverton EX16 7EN (Devon)

Tel: **01884 821770**   www.alanrogers.com/UK0750

Minnows is an attractive, neat small park with views across the Devon countryside, separated from the Grand Western canal by hedging. Easily accessible from the M5, it is suitable as an ideal touring centre for Devon and Somerset, for cycling or walking, or simply for breaking a long journey. A small, neat park, open for eight months of the year, it provides 45 level pitches all with 16A electricity and hardstandings for all weather. A further 3.5 acres have been added to the park providing space for more and larger pitches, a tent area, a playground and a large field for ball games, etc. The village of Sampford Peverell, with pub and farm shop, is only a half mile walk via the towpath, with Tiverton 7.5 miles. In fact, there are 12 miles of level walking on the towpath or one can take a trip on a horse-drawn barge. The site is also on the Sustran cycle route (route 3). Tiverton Parkway station (BR) is less than one mile and buses run from the village to Tiverton. Coarse fishing permits for the canal are available from reception. A Caravan Club affiliated site, non-members are also very welcome. There could be some road noise from the adjacent A361.

Facilities

The heated toilet block has been refurbished with tiled floors, new pressurised showers and 2 cubicles for ladies. It is clean and comfortable with all modern facilities and constant hot water. Facilities for disabled visitors and babies. Laundry with washing machine, dryer and ironing. Motorcaravan service point. Gas supplies. Newspaper delivery arranged. Play area. Bicycle hire (delivery to site). American RVs accepted (up to 36 ft), advance booking necessary. All year caravan storage. Site gates closed 21.00 and locked 23.00-7.30 hrs. Off site: Boat slipway, golf driving range and 9-hole course 400 yds, full course 4 miles. Riding 6 miles.

Open: 10 March - 3 November.

Directions

From M5 junction 27 take A361 signed Tiverton. After 600 yds take first exit signed Sampford Peverell. After 100 yds. turn right at roundabout and cross bridge over A361 to second roundabout. Go straight ahead and park is immediately ahead. From North Devon on A361 go to M5 exit 27 and return back up the A361 as above. O.S.GR: ST042148. GPS: N50:55.501 W03:21.871

Charges guide

Per person	£ 3.95 - £ 5.50
child (5-16 yrs)	£ 1.30 - £ 2.15
pitch	£ 4.30 - £ 7.10
dog	free - £ 1.00
Credit cards accepted for £10 or more.	

UK0790 Harford Bridge Holiday Park

Holiday homes ▶ page 324

Peter Tavy, Tavistock PL19 9LS (Devon)

Tel: 01822 810349. Email: enquiry@harfordbridge.co.uk

www.alanrogers.com/UK0790

Harford Bridge has an interesting history – originally the Wheal Union tin mine until 1850, then used as a farm campsite from 1930 and taken over by the Royal Engineers in 1939. It is now a quiet, rural, mature park inside the Dartmoor National Park. It is bounded by the River Tavy on one side and the lane from the main road to the village of Peter Tavy on the other, with Harford Bridge, a classic granite moorland bridge, at the corner. With 16.5 acres, the park provides 120 touring pitches well spaced on a level grassy meadow with some shade from mature trees and others recently planted; 47 pitches have electrical hook-ups and 10 have 'multi-services', 5 with hardstanding. Out of season or by booking in advance you may get one of the delightful spots bordering the river (these are without electricity). Some holiday caravans and chalets are neatly landscaped in their own area. At the entrance to the park a central grassy area is left free for games, which is also used by the town band, village fete, etc. While the river (unfenced) will inevitably mesmerise youngsters, a super central adventure play area on a hilly tree knoll will claim them. In early summer there are chicks to watch, horses to make a fuss of and the park ducks are a feature. To celebrate the park's anniversary, a wonderful wild flower habitat has been created. There are seven willow structures resembling wig-wam shaped tents on the main entrance shrub bed. With its own and the local history, plus its situation, this is a super place to stay.

Facilities

The single toilet block is older in style but fully equipped and well kept, with free hot water and showers all year. Facilities for disabled visitors and babies. Good launderette and drying room. Freezer. Motorcaravan service point. Games room and separate TV room. Play area. Tennis (free). Two barbecue areas. Fly fishing (by licence). WiFi planned. Off site: Bicycle hire, riding and golf, all within 2.5 miles. West Devon cycle way adjacent to park.

Open: All year.

Directions

Two miles north of Tavistock, off A386 Tavistock - Okehampton road, take the road to Peter Tavy. O.S.GR: SX504768. GPS: N50:34.278 W04:06.840

Charges guide

Per unit incl. 2 persons	£ 10.50 - £ 14.75
incl. electricity	£ 13.50 - £ 17.75
with full services	£ 15.00 - £ 19.25

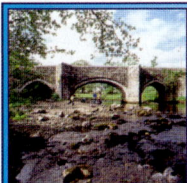

UK0760 Barley Meadow Camping & Caravan Park

Crockernwell, Exeter EX6 6NR (Devon)

Tel: 01647 281629. Email: welcome@barleymeadow.com

www.alanrogers.com/UK0760

This peaceful little park is located on the northern edge of Dartmoor with easy access from the A30. It is sheltered from the weather by good hedging and, although not always visible from the pitches, there are open views across the moorland to the south. The 60 pitches are mostly on level grass, well spaced, most with hardstandings (some taken by seasonal units), and 36 electric hook-ups (10/16A). Shrubs have now been planted to divide the pitches. The site would be a suitable base for visiting Exeter, Okehampton and Plymouth, hiking over the moors, or just enjoying the local area. The Two Moors Way for walkers is only 400 yards from the site.

Facilities

The single heated toilet block is well maintained and provides all facilities including a well equipped room for disabled campers and babies. Laundry. Small shop for basic groceries, small camping items and gas. Games room with pool table and TV. Playground. Small library and information chalet. Only small American RVs (up to 30 ft.) accepted. Off site: Fishing 1 mile (river) or 2 miles (lake). Golf 2.5 miles. Riding 2 miles. Nearby is Castle Drogo, the youngest castle in the U.K. At Fingle Bridge there are walks and an Inn. Further afield is Canonteign Falls, home of England's highest waterfall. Okehampton 15 minutes.

Open: 15 March - 2 November.

Directions

From M5 exit 31, take A30 towards Okehampton. After 10 miles turn left towards Cheriton Bishop. After 0.5 miles pass through village, and continue for 1 mile towards Crockernwell, and site entrance is on your left. From the west on A30, at the 'Merry Roundabout' at Whiddon Down, take first left towards Cheriton Bishop. Continue for 2 miles and site entrance is on right. O.S.GR: SH742924. GPS: N50:43.052 W03:46.995

Charges guide

Per unit incl. 2 persons and electricity	£ 13.00 - £ 17.00
extra person	£ 3.00
child (3-15 yrs)	£ 1.50

UK0802 Langstone Manor Holiday Park

Moortown, Tavistock PL19 9JZ (Devon)

Tel: **01822 613371**. Email: **web@langstone-manor.co.uk**   **www.alanrogers.com/UK0802**

Situated on the southwest edge of Dartmoor, this holiday park has been developed in the grounds of the old Langstone Manor house. The touring pitches are tucked into various garden areas with mature trees and flowering shrubs, or in the walled garden area with views over the moor. In all there are 42 level grass pitches which vary in size (20 with 16A electricity). A new camping area has been terraced and has open views over farmland and the moor. You pass through a number of holiday caravans on the way to reception and the touring pitches where you will also find some holiday cottages and flats for rent. The 'pièce de resistance' is the unexpected traditional bar and restaurant in the Manor House, complete with a terrace that catches the evening sun (try the 'jail ale' made in Princetown). Open in high season and on demand in low season it has an open fire (if needed). Approaching over a short section of the moor, you realise how well Langstone Manor is situated to explore Dartmoor by foot, by car or on bike (the park has direct access). The market town of Tavistock is 3 miles away and there is a wealth of National Trust Houses and Gardens to visit.

Facilities

The toilet block is set to one side of the walled garden area, fully equipped and well maintained. Showers on payment (20p tokens from reception or bar). Fully equipped laundry room. Changing mat for babies in the ladies. Basic supplies kept in reception (order bread the day before). Bar/restaurant. Play area. Off site: Leisure centre and pool 2 miles. Golf 1 mile. Fishing 2 miles. Bicycle hire 3 miles. Boat Launching 10 miles. Sailing 15 miles.

Open: 15 March - 29 October.

Directions

From Tavistock take the B3357 Princetown road. After about 2 miles turn right at crossroads (site signed). Pass over cattle grid onto the moor and follow site signs. O.S.GR: SX524738
GPS: N50:32.694 W04:05.050

Charges guide

Per unit incl. 2 persons	£ 12.00 - £ 14.00
electricity	£ 2.00
child	£ 2.00 - £ 3.00
awning	£ 1.00 - £ 2.00

UK0800 Higher Longford Caravan Park

Moorshop, Tavistock PL19 9LQ (Devon)

Tel: **01822 613360**. Email: **stay@higherlongford.co.uk**   **www.alanrogers.com/UK0800**

This attractive well organised, family run park is situated within the Dartmoor National Park boundaries with views up to the higher slopes of the moor. A neat, sheltered field provides 40 level pitches arranged on each side of a circular access road, with three smaller touring areas for a further 12 units, a small terraced camping field with good views and a seasonal camping field for a further 40. Facilities include 65 electrical hook-ups (16A), several multi-serviced pitches and an area of hardstanding for motorcaravans in poor weather. Some attractive converted cottages form a courtyard area with the farmhouse and reception. Within the 14th century farmhouse is a small licensed shop with gas and some farm produce, and a takeaway including breakfast items and fresh bread. It adjoins a pleasant, cosy campers' lounge with pool table and TV which is open all day. Higher Longford is an ideal centre for touring Dartmoor, either by car, on foot, or astride a local pony (riding stables nearby). Plymouth and the cross-channel ferries are a 30 minute drive, Tavistock is 3 miles, with a good market and Goose Fair in October.

Facilities

A heated toilet block provides excellent full en-suite facilities (amongst the best we have seen) plus extra toilets and washbasins. Family bathroom and baby changing. Full laundry facilities. Motorcaravan services. Ice block service. Shop and takeaway (hours limited in winter). Campers' lounge with pool and TV. Large recreation field with adventure play area in centre. Nature area. Adventure trail for children and walks. Caravan storage. Off site: Bus service outside park. Game or coarse fishing 3 miles, Tavistock golf course 1 mile. Bicycle hire 2.5 miles. Riding 5 miles. Beach 15 miles.

Open: All year.

Directions

Park is clearly signed from the B3357 Princetown road, 2 miles from Tavistock. O.S.GR: SX520747.
GPS: N50:33.210 W04:05.623

Charges guide

Per person	£ 3.50 - £ 6.00
child (5-16 yrs)	£ 1.10 - £ 3.00
pitch incl. electricity	£ 4.50 - £ 10.00
tent pitch	£ 5.50 - £ 7.00

UK0805 Woodovis Park

Woodovis House, Gulworthy, Tavistock PL19 8NY (Devon)

Tel: 01822 832968. Email: info@woodovis.com

www.alanrogers.com/UK0805

Woodovis Park is set in the grounds of Woodovis House, owned in the 19th century by a mine captain in the days when the valley had a thriving copper mining industry. It nestles in a sheltered wooded position covering 14 acres, by the edge of the Tamar Valley on the borders of Devon and Cornwall. John and Dorothy Lewis have been running Woodovis Park since 1999, helped by their very welcoming staff. There are 50 good sized pitches, all with 10A electricity and 19 with hardstanding. Split over two fields, most are on level, neatly mown grass, some are gently sloping. Landscaped in between are 35 caravan holiday homes, 17 privately owned and 18 for hire. The whole area is sheltered by thick hedges and woodland but in places you can see across the valley to Cornwall. An indoor heated swimming pool complete with spa pool and sauna are a welcome attraction, as are the freshly baked morning croissants or bread ordered the night before at reception. The approach to the site is down a tree lined lane with passing places. This is a peaceful spot with some nice touches, run to a very high standard. Try exploring Dartmoor and become addicted to 'Letterboxing'. A member of the Best of British group.

Facilities

A purpose built, modern toilet block is fully equipped. Bathroom (coin operated) could be used by disabled people or for babies. Family cubicles. Toilet for disabled visitors at the pool. Fully equipped laundry. Motorcaravan service point. Shop for basics with off licence doubles with reception. Indoor heated swimming pool (no swimming alone). Good games room including large size 'Connect 4'! Fenced play area. Minigolf. Archery and 'water-walking' organised weekly. Frames for disposable barbecues. Off site: Pub within walking distance. Tamar valley. Fishing 1.5 miles. Golf, riding and bicycle hire 3 miles. Boat launching 6 miles. Tavistock 4 miles.

Open: 15 March - 30 October.

Directions

From Tavistock follow the A390 for Liskeard. After 3 miles turn right at Gulworthy roundabout signed Chipshop, Lamerton and Caravan Park. After 1 mile entrance is signed on left. O.S.GR: SX431743. GPS: N50:32.932 W04:12.951

Charges guide

Per person (over 5 yrs)	£ 5.00
pitch incl. electricity	£ 7.00 - £ 15.50
awning	£ 2.00

UK0810 Riverside Caravan Park

Leigham Manor Drive, Marsh Mills, Plymouth PL6 8LL (Devon)

Tel: 01752 344122. Email: info@riversidecaravanpark.com

www.alanrogers.com/UK0810

As you leave the A38 for Plymouth and negotiate the Marsh Mills roundabout you can have no idea that there is a lush green touring park tucked away from the modern, out-of-town shopping units in a quiet green valley. There are 232 pitches for caravans or motorcaravans, 150 of which have electricity (10A) and 60 are on hardstanding – especially useful as the site is open all year round. There is further provision for 60 tents. Hidden behind a high, evergreen hedge are an attractive swimming pool and children's pool. A play area is nearby and a pleasant restaurant with bar and games room provide welcome facilities and entertainment in high season. Twenty seven years ago it was a cornfield but, with careful development by its owner, it now provides a welcome oasis from which to explore Dartmoor, to enjoy the amazing views from Plymouth Hoe or even to overnight quietly before catching the ferry to France. The wooded valley sides give way to level grass where the trees and shrubs planted all those years ago have matured to give a park-like feel. The River Plym runs down one side of the site but it is carefully fenced.

Facilities

Three modern, fully equipped toilet blocks include cubicles with toilets and washbasins. Laundry room. Motorcaravan service point. Gas supplies. Basics are kept in reception (more in high season). Bar, restaurant and takeaway (B.Hs and high season) with family entertainment included. Heated swimming pool and children's pool. Games room with TV. Play area. Off site: Fishing possible in River Plym. Sea fishing 3.5 miles. Golf and riding 5 miles. Bicycle hire and boat launching 3.5 miles. Beach 10 miles. Dry ski slope and supermarket within walking distance. Bus stop 10 minutes.

Open: All year.

Directions

From the A38 Marsh Mills roundabout for Plymouth take the third exit. After a few yards turn left following caravan signs, then right alongside the River Plym to the park. O.S.GR: SX518576. GPS: N50:23.890 W04:05.240

Charges guide

Per person	£ 3.25 - £ 5.50
child (3-10 yrs)	£ 1.75 - £ 2.50
pitch incl. electricity	£ 5.50 - £ 7.50
tent pitch	£ 3.50 - £ 6.50
dog, pup tent, extra car or boat	£ 1.00 - £ 2.00

UK0820 Moor View Touring Park

California Cross, Modbury PL21 0SG (Devon)

Tel: **01548 821485**. Email: **info@moorviewtouringpark.co.uk**   www.alanrogers.com/UK0820

Moor View has a gently sloping position with terraced, individual, fairly level grass pitches with marvellous views across to the Dartmoor Tors. It provides 68 pitches of varying size, connected by hardcore roads. All are on hardstanding with 10A electricity, water and drainage. Bushes and shrubs planted between the pitches are growing well giving the park a more mature feel. This is a park in a lovely corner of Devon, run personally by the enthusiastic owners, Edward and Liz Corwood. A member of the Countryside Discovery group and an 'adults only' park.

Facilities

Traditional style, heated toilet facilities have access from a courtyard area and are kept clean, providing all necessary facilities including a laundry room and sink, and covered dishwashing sinks. Shop. Takeaway in season (to order, 18.30-20.30). TV room. WiFi. Off site: Golf 5 miles, riding and fishing 6 miles. Country pub within walking distance. Modbury is 3 miles. Burgh Island and Bigbury Bay are nearby, Dartmoor is within striking distance.

Open: All year.

Directions

Leave the A38 at Wrangaton Cross, signed Ermington, Modbury and Yealmpton. Turn left and follow straight on at crossroads (Kitterford Cross) signed Modbury, Loddiswell, Kingsbridge for 3 miles to California Cross. Leave garage on left and follow towards Modbury (B3207). Park is 0.5 miles on left. O.S.GR: SX705533. GPS: N50:21.821 W03:49.047

Charges 2009

Per unit incl. 2 persons and electricity	£ 7.95 - £ 20.95

UK0826 Higher Rew Caravan & Camping Park

Malborough, Kingsbridge TQ7 3BW (Devon)

Tel: **01548 842681**. Email: **enquiries@higherrew.co.uk**   www.alanrogers.com/UK0826

The Squire family have developed this rural park on their farm which is located about a mile up a single track lane from South Sands, near Salcombe. South Sands is ideal for boating, sailing and windsurfing as well as providing safe bathing. A ferry runs to Salcombe town. The rural views from the park are amazing but you have to climb a little higher to see the sea. The coastal path can be reached by footpaths from the park. A large, sloping, open field has been terraced to provide 90 grass pitches, 60 of which have 16A electricity.

Facilities

Toilet facilities have been completely refurbished to a high standard. Unisex showers are in a separate, light and airy part. Showers are metered (20p for 4 minutes). Freezer for ice packs. Reception with shop for basics. Play area. Tennis court. Skittle alley. Caravan storage. Off site: Beach, fishing and sailing 1 mile. Boat launching 3 miles. Riding 5 miles. Golf 4-5 miles.

Open: Easter - October half term.

Directions

Park is clearly signed from Malborough. Follow signs to Soar for 1 mile. Turn left at Rew Cross, then first right for Higher Rew. Take care with single track roads, although there are plenty of passing places. O.S.GR: SX73381. GPS: N50:13.810 W03:48.339

Charges guide

Per unit incl. 2 persons	£ 5.00 - £ 14.00
electricity	£ 2.00
No credit cards.	

UK0830 Slapton Sands Camping & Caravanning Club Site

Middle Grounds, Slapton, Kingsbridge TQ7 2QW (Devon)

Tel: **01548 580538**   www.alanrogers.com/UK0830

Slapton is a charming village with tiny lanes and cottages and two historic pubs, one dominated by the ruined tower of an old monastery. This site is situated on the road which leads from Slapton Sands, on a well kept meadow overlooking the bay – the sea views are panoramic from some areas of the site, with shelter provided by some large bushes and the surrounding hedge. There are 115 grass pitches, some with a slight slope, and electricity (16A) is available for 46 (including 10 with hardstanding). Motorcaravans, trailer tents and tents are accepted without problems but the planners will only permit 8 caravan pitches which are kept for club members.

Facilities

The modern toilet block is central, can be heated and is kept very clean, with washbasins in private cabins. Useful parent and child room and separate unit for disabled visitors (with key). Washing machine and dryer (and outside lines). Motorcaravan service point. Small library, gas and freezer. Small play area. Off site: Riding 0.5 miles. The Field Studies Centre arranges guided walks and can issue fishing permits.

Open: March - October.

Directions

From the A38 take A384 to Totnes. Just before town, turn right on A381 to Kingsbridge, then the A379 through Stokenham to Slapton Sands. Half way along the beach road turn left. Site is 200 yds. Avoid the narrow Five Mile Lane from the A381. O.S.GR: SX825450. GPS: N50:17.439 W03:39.035

Charges guide

Per person	£ 4.90 - £ 8.25
pitch (non-member)	£ 5.65

UK0825 Karrageen Caravan & Camping Park

Bolberry, Malborough, Kingsbridge TQ7 3EN (Devon)

Tel: 01548 561230. Email: phil@karrageen.co.uk

www.alanrogers.com/UK0825

Karrageen is to be found in a wonderful area of Devon, near Kingsbridge and Salcombe, with a mixture of rolling countryside, hidden coves, cliff tops and sandy beaches. You can walk, sail, surf or just relax and enjoy the wonderful scenery. This is a small family park run personally by the Higgin family situated in the hamlet of Bolberry, one mile up the lane from Hope Cove. The main camping field slopes gently with either sea or rural views. It has been terraced with hedging to provide 70 grassy pitches with 54 electricity connections (10A). There are some 20 places specifically designed for touring caravans. Six caravan holiday homes to let complete the provision in a separate field which houses the modern toilet block. The family home across the road provides reception, a licensed shop and a takeaway facility which includes vegetarian, Indian or Oriental options.

Facilities

The attractively decorated toilet block includes two curtained washbasins for privacy. En-suite provision for disabled visitors doubles as a family shower room. Parent and baby room. Laundry room. Separate dishwashing (metered as it is spring water, 20p). Freezer for ice packs. Shop including some basic camping equipment. Fresh baguettes and croissants daily. Calor and camping gas. Takeaway (evenings only, last orders 19.00). No play area as such but two open areas for ball games. Off site: Fishing, boat launching and beach 1 mile. Golf 3 miles. Riding 6 miles. Salcombe, sailing Mecca and fishing port with sandy beaches 3.5 miles. Kingsbridge, ancient market town 6 miles.

Open: Easter - 29 September.

Directions

Travelling south from Exeter on the A38, take the A3121 (signed Ermington and Modbury). Follow signs to Kingsbridge and Salcombe. At Malborough, turn sharp right through the village, following signs for Bolberry for 0.6 mile. Turn right to Bolberry, then after 0.9 miles the park is on the right. On the left is a concrete drive to Karrageen House and reception. Take care with single track lanes, although there are plenty of passing places. O.S.GR: SX692391. GPS: N50:14.357 W03:50.402

Charges guide

Per unit incl. 2 adults, 2 children	£ 11.00 - £ 19.00
extra person	£ 3.00 - £ 5.00
child (under 17 yrs)	£ 1.00
electricity	£ 2.00 - £ 3.00

No credit cards.

UK0835 Little Cotton Caravan Park

Dartmouth TQ6 0LB (Devon)

Tel: 01803 832558. Email: enquiries@littlecotton.co.uk

www.alanrogers.com/UK0835

This lovely, family run park on the outskirts of Dartmouth is ideally situated for exploring this attractive area of South Devon. Well tended and immaculate, the 7.5 acre park is open and grassy. On level and gently sloping ground, it is situated on a hilltop and has views across the other fields. There are 95 pitches, all with electricity (16A) and mostly level with some hardstanding available. The park is divided into four areas with one dedicated to rallies. A dog walking area is to one side. Located next to the Dartmouth 'park and ride', it is easy get into Dartmouth (tickets can be bought from reception) and a path leads from the site to the bus stops. Dartmouth has very limited parking so this is really the best way to visit. A site shop in reception is well stocked with foods, camping (including gas) and other items all at very reasonable prices.

Facilities

The modern, heated toilet block is centrally situated. It is very clean, light, airy and warm. Some washbasins are in cubicles. Free showers are preset. Excellent facilities for disabled visitors. Laundry facilities. Unisex baby room. Well stocked shop in reception. Bread and sandwiches to order. Freezer. Barbecues are allowed off the ground. Off site: Dartmouth Castle and the steam railway can be easily accessed by ferry. Beach, fishing and boat launching 2 miles. Golf 3 miles.

Open: 15 March - 31 October.

Directions

Park is on the outskirts of Dartmouth on the A3122 next to the Dartmouth 'park and ride'. From Totnes take A381 (Kingsbridge) and turn left at Halwell on A3122. Site is on right just before entering Dartmouth. O.S.GR: SX857508. GPS: N50:20.706 W03:36.456

Charges guide

Per unit incl. 2 persons	£ 11.25 - £ 15.75
incl. electricity	£ 13.50 - £ 18.00
extra person	£ 3.00
child (3-14 yrs)	£ 2.00

UK0845 Hillhead Caravan Club Holiday Park

Hillhead, Brixham TQ5 0HH (Devon)

Tel: 01803 853204. Email: enquiries@caravanclub.co.uk   www.alanrogers.com/UK0845

Hillhead is a fully refurbished Caravan Club park set in 22 acres of beautiful Devon countryside. Originally developed in the 1960s within what is now a coastal protection area two miles from Brixham, the park has benefited from a £3 million redevelopment. Unusually for a Caravan Club site, it offers a full entertainment programme in peak season. Hillhead comprises 239 pitches, all with electrical hook-ups and many with fine views. Amenities are to a uniformly high standard, notably the main complex based around an attractive courtyard, and housing a shop, bar, games room and restaurant. The children's play area is outstanding with a range of imaginative items including a large wooden fort. Hillhead is rightly proud of its strong commitment to sound environmental practice, with a plan to promote species diversity and the encouragement of good practice by site workers and visitors alike.

Facilities

The two sanitary blocks are new and maintained to a high standard. Each block includes 3 special private family bathrooms (key from reception) and facilities for disabled visitors. Laundry facilities. Motorcaravan service point. Shop. Bar and restaurant. Swimming pool (heated May - Sept) with children's pool adjacent. Large play area. Skateboard ramp. Games room. TV. Entertainment in season. Games field. Dog walking area. WiFi.
Off site: Nearest beach and coastal path 2 miles. Bus stop at site entrance. River Dart boat trips. Paignton, Torquay and Brixham. Golf (18-hole) and riding 2 miles. Bicycle hire 2.5 miles.

Open: 14 March - 5 January.

Directions

Site is well signed from the A379 Paignton - Dartmouth road and is on the B3205 (Slappers Hill Road). Entrance is on the left after 400 yards. O.S.GR: SX904534. GPS: N50:22.177 W03:32.689

Charges guide

Per person	£ 4.70 - £ 7.50
child (5-16 yrs)	£ 1.80 - £ 4.50
pitch	
incl. electricity (non-member)	£ 10.90 - £ 17.00

UK0850 Galmpton Park

Greenway Road, Galmpton, Brixham TQ5 0EP (Devon)

Tel: 01803 842066. Email: galmptontouringpark@hotmail.com   www.alanrogers.com/UK0850

Within a few miles of the lively amenities of Torbay, Galmpton Park lies peacefully just outside the village of Galmpton, overlooking the beautiful Dart estuary just upstream of Dartmouth and Kingswear. A family park, some 120 pitches (60 marked for caravans) are arranged on a wide sweep of grassy, terraced meadow, each pitch with its own wonderful view of the river. Situated on the hillside, some parts have quite a slope, but there are flatter areas (the owners will advise and assist). There are 90 electrical connections (10A) and 23 pitches have water and drainage. There is a separate tent field. Galmpton is a quiet and simple park (with the gates closed 11.15 pm - 7.30 am) in a most picturesque setting, within easy reach of all the attractions of South Devon. A member of the Countryside Discovery group.

Facilities

A central, substantial looking toilet block provides clean facilities including three washbasins in cabins, a very attractive under 5's bathroom (key), baby unit and hair care areas. Dishwashing room also with washing machine, dryer, iron and ironing board. Reception/shop sells a wide range of basics including gas. Bread to order. Good adventure play equipment. Dogs (max. 2 per unit) are accepted at the owner's discretion and not mid July and August. Motorhomes over 21 ft. are not accepted. Off site: Local pub is 5 minutes walk.

Open: Easter - 30 September.

Directions

Take A380 Paignton ring road towards Brixham until junction with the Paignton - Brixham coast road. Turn right towards Brixham, then second right into Manor Vale Road. Continue through the village, past the school and site is 500 yds. on the right. O.S.GR: SX885558. GPS: N50:23.499 W03:34.084

Charges guide

Per unit incl. 2 persons and electricity	£ 11.00 - £ 16.40
de-luxe pitch plus	£ 13.10 - £ 19.40
extra person	£ 2.50
child (5-16 yrs)	£ 1.50
Various discounts available.	

UK0840 ## Woodlands Leisure Park

Blackawton, Totnes TQ9 7DQ (Devon)

Tel: **01803 712598**. Email: **fun@woodlandspark.com**

www.alanrogers.com/UK0840

Woodlands is a pleasant surprise – from the road you have no idea of just what is hidden away deep in the Devon countryside. To achieve this, there has been sympathetic development of farm and woodland to provide a leisure centre, open to the public and with a range of activities and entertainment appealing to all ages. The site overlooks the woodland and the leisure park, taking 350 units on three sloping, grassy fields, the original terraced one maturing well. One of the others has been fully terraced to provide groups of four to eight flat, very spacious pitches (90% with 10A electricity and a shared water tap, drain and rubbish bin). The newest field has 120 pitches (with electricity) designed with a more open feel to provide space for larger groups or rallies. Children (and many energetic parents too!) will thoroughly enjoy a huge variety of imaginative adventure play equipment, amazing water coasters, toboggan runs, the new 'Sea Dragon Swing Ship', a white knuckle monster, the 'Avalanche' and much more, hidden amongst the trees. Those more peacefully inclined can follow woodland walks around the attractive ponds. The 'Empire of the Sea Dragon', an indoor play centre, provides marvellous wet weather facilities comprising five floors of play areas and amazing slides. With a two night stay, campers on the touring park are admitted free of charge to the leisure park. A popular touring park, early reservation is advisable.

Facilities

Three modern, heated toilet blocks, include private bathrooms (coin-operated, 20p) and 16 family shower cubicles. Two laundry rooms. Freezer for ice packs. Baby facilities. The leisure park café provides good value meals and a takeaway service for campers. Café opening hours and camping shop (with gas and basic food supplies) vary according to season and demand. TV and games room. Dogs are accepted on the campsite but not in the leisure park (kennels available). Caravan storage. Off site: The charming town of Dartmouth and the South Hams beaches are near. Fishing 4 miles. Golf 0.5 miles. Riding 5 miles. Beach 4 miles.

Open: Easter - 1 November.

Directions

From A38 at Buckfastleigh, take A384 to Totnes. Before the town centre turn right on A381 Kingsbridge road. After Halwell turn left at Totnes Cross garage, on A3122 to Dartmouth. Park is on right after 2.5 miles. O.S.GR: SX813521. GPS: N50:21.474 W03:40.500

Charges guide

Per unit incl. 2 persons	
and electricity	£ 14.50 - £ 21.00
extra person over 2 yrs	£ 6.75
awning or extra small pup tent	£ 2.50
large tent or trailer tent (120 sq ft plus)	£ 2.50
dog (contact site first)	£ 2.50

UK0860 Whitehill Country Park

Stoke Road, Paignton TQ4 7PF (Devon)

Tel: **01803 782338**. Email: **info@whitehill-park.co.uk**

www.alanrogers.com/UK0860

Whitehill Country Park is beautifully situated in rolling Devon countryside, just 2.5 miles from the nearest beaches. Extending over 40 acres, a definite sense of space characterises this park and 10 acres of ancient woodland are available for walks and attract a great deal of wildlife. Whitehill is a friendly park with 320 large grassy pitches which are located in separate fields around the site with evocative names, such as Nine Acres, Sweethill and Coombe Meadow. Most pitches have electrical connections (16A). Around 60 pitches are used for caravan holiday homes. The park boasts an attractive swimming pool (max. depth 1.3 m) with a children's paddling pool alongside, as well as a good range of other leisure facilities, notably The Hayloft bar (with satellite TV), a café and an extensive decking area for outside eating.

Facilities

Two brand new sanitary blocks include private, individual washing facilities for ladies. Ample laundry facilities. Gas supplies. Shop. Bar. Café (24/5-1/9). Swimming and paddling pools (heated 17/5-1/9). Three play areas. Electronic games. Craft centre for children. Dogs and other pets are not accepted. Off site: Paignton 2.5 miles. Beach 3 miles. Fishing and golf 2 miles. Riding 4 miles. Torquay, Dartmoor, Quay West Aqua Park. Bus stop at site entrance.

Open: Easter - 30 September.

Directions

Turn left at The Parkers Arms off the A385 Paignton to Totnes road, signed Stoke Gabriel. Site is 1 mile along this road. O.S.GR: SX857587. GPS: N50:25.072 W03:36.540

Charges 2009

Per unit incl. 2 persons and electricity	£ 14.50 - £ 26.50
Camping Cheques accepted.	

UK0865 Byslades International Touring Park

Totnes Road, Paignton TQ4 7PY (Devon)

Tel: **01803 555072**. Email: **info@byslades.co.uk**

www.alanrogers.com/UK0865

Byslades is a large, well maintained touring park covering 23 acres on the side of a valley. The site is cut into terraces on the steepest slopes, so that most of the pitches are level. Many of the pitches (grass and hardstanding) have a lovely view across the valley to the fields on the other side. There are 190 pitches, 150 with electricity (10/16A). There is a security barrier at the entrance to the park and CCTV has been installed. A large heated outdoor swimming pool, with a special area for toddlers. A café is nearby which also sells bread, milk and a few essentials.

Facilities

Two modern toilet blocks are kept very clean, with some washbasins in private cubicles and free showers (with dividing curtain). Facilities for disabled visitors (access by key). Baby changing facilities in the Ladies. Laundry with washing machines, dryers and irons. Freezer for ice packs. Motorcaravan waste disposal point. Café with takeaway and basic supplies. Club house with bar. Swimming pool. Play area. Off site: Bus stop near park entrance (Totnes and Paignton). Fishing ajacent. Beach 3 miles.

Open: May - September.

Directions

Leave the A38 near Buckfastleigh (A384) or near South Brent (A385) signed for Totnes. Leave Totnes on the A385 signed for Paignton and the site is about 3 miles from Totnes on the left. O.S.GR: SX845597. GPS: N50:25.798 W03:37.021

Charges guide

Per unit incl. 2 persons	£ 6.00 - £ 12.50
extra person	£ 3.00 - £ 5.00
child (3-12 yrs)	£ 2.00 - £ 3.50
electricity	£ 2.00

UK0870 Beverley Park Holiday Centre

Goodrington Road, Paignton TQ4 7JE (Devon)

Tel: **01803 661978**. Email: **info@beverley-holidays.co.uk**   www.alanrogers.com/UK0870

Beverley Park, a good quality holiday centre, celebrated its 50th anniversary in 2008. This popular, busy park is attractively landscaped and has marvellous views over Torbay. The park and its amenities are all run in an efficient and orderly manner. The park has 195 caravan holiday homes and 23 lodges, mainly around the central complex. There are 187 touring pitches in the lower areas of the park, all reasonably sheltered, some with views across the bay and some on slightly sloping ground. All pitches can take awnings and have 16A electricity (15 m. cable), 38 have hardstanding and 42 are fully serviced. Tents are accepted and a limited number of tent pitches have electrical connections. The park has a long season and reservations are essential for caravans. Entertainment is organised at Easter and from early May in the Starlight Cabaret bar. There are indoor and outdoor pools, heated and supervised. The Oasis fitness centre provides a steam room, jacuzzi, sunbed and an excellent fitness room. The park is in the heart of residential Torbay, with views across the bay to Brixham and Torquay, and sandy beaches less than a mile away. There is a regular bus service to Paignton, Torbay and Brixham and minibus service to the beach and town. This popular park has lots to offer and is well maintained and run. A member of the Best of British group.

Facilities

Good toilet blocks are well maintained and heated with roomy showers, some with washbasins en-suite. Baths on payment. Unit for disabled visitors. Facilities for babies. Laundry. Gas supplies. Large general shop (17/3-31/10). Motorcaravan service point. Restaurant, bars and takeaway (all Easter, then 30/5-26/10). Swimming pools. Fitness centre. Tennis. Crazy golf. Playground. Nature trail. Amusements. Soft play area. Dogs are not accepted. Off site: Minibus service to Paignton (timetable at reception). Fishing, bicycle hire, riding and golf 2 miles.

Open: All year.

Directions

Park is south of Paignton in Goodrington Road between A379 coast road and B3203 ring road and is well signed on both. O.S.GR: SX882584. GPS: N50:24.812 W03:34.120

Charges 2009

Per unit incl. 2 persons and electricity	£ 15.00 - £ 32.00
tent pitch incl. 2 persons	£ 12.50 - £ 28.00
extra person	£ 4.70
child	£ 3.50

Max. 6 persons per reservation.

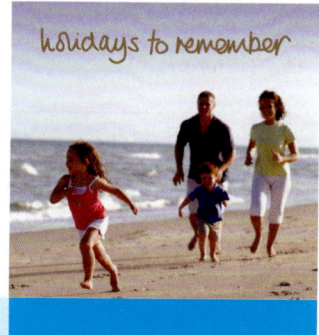

UK1130 Hoburne Torbay

Goodrington, Paignton TQ4 7JP (Devon)

Tel: **01803 558010**. Email: **enquiries@hoburne.co.uk**   www.alanrogers.com/UK1130

Situated to the south of central Paignton, this Hoburne park's major interest is a complex of 560 holiday homes (120 to let). However, there are 60 touring pitches (no tents) on flat grass by the entrance. The pitches are of a reasonable size and all have 10A electricity. For those who like entertainment, the central club complex is the park's best feature, with a good-sized heated outdoor pool (80 x 40 ft) and a super indoor pool with views across the bay, a flume, sauna and steam room.

Facilities

Two modern toilet blocks. Large launderette. Well stocked shop. Motorcaravan service point. Restaurant/bar. Takeaway. Club room. Heated outdoor pool. Indoor pool with flume, sauna and steam room. Bowling. Crazy golf. Amusement arcade. Adventure playground. TV room. Indoor soft adventure play area. Children's entertainment. American motorhomes 25 ft. max. Pets are not accepted.

Open: 14 February - 15 January excl. 2 weeks at Xmas.

Directions

Park is signed from the outer Paignton ring road. Look for left turn into Goodrington Road, then left into Grange Road. O.S.GR: SX890585. GPS: N50:25.191 W03:34.070

Charges guide

Per unit incl. up to 6 persons	£ 11.50 - £ 27.50

63

UK0910 Ross Park

Park Hill Farm, Ipplepen, Newton Abbot TQ12 5TT (Devon)

Tel: **01803 812983**. Email: **enquiries@rossparkcaravanpark.co.uk**   www.alanrogers.com/UK0910

Ross Park has to be seen to appreciate the amazing floral displays with their dramatic colours, that are a feature of the park. These are complemented by the use of a wide variety of shrubs which form hedging for most of the 110 pitches to provide your own special plot, very much as on the continent. Many pitches have wonderful views over the surrounding countryside and for those who prefer the more open style, one small area has been left unhedged. The owners, Mark and Helen Lowe, continue to strive to provide quality facilities and maintain standards, and this is reflected in the awards they have won. The New Barn provides a comfortable lounge, a mezzanine bar with bar snacks and a restaurant with extra seating in the conservatory which is home to some exotic and colourful plants. The touring area is divided into bays or groups by hedging and shrubs and provides 110 pitches all with electricity (16A). Some 82 of these have a hardened surface, some made larger with a further gravel area. An orchard area alive with daffodils in the spring and a conservation area with information on wild flowers and butterflies, and with extended views, completes these environmentally considered amenities. Barn dances are organised on Sundays in high season. This is a well cared for park worthy of consideration. A member of the Best of British group.

Facilities

Seven well equipped, heated en-suite units, one with baby facilities, two suitable for disabled people. Further separate shower, washbasin and toilet facilities. Extra heated block with toilets, washbasins in cabins and hair-care centre. Fully equipped laundry room. Utility room with dishwashing, freezer and battery charging. Dog shower. Motorcaravan services. Recycling bins. Reception with licensed shop. Gas supplies. Bar, bar snacks and restaurant with a la carte menu (all April - end Oct, plus Christmas and New Year). New conservation and tourist information room. Games room. 7 acre park area for recreation. Croquet green. Badminton. Large well equipped playground. Caravan storage. Off site: Dainton Park 18-hole golf course is adjacent. Fishing 3 miles. Riding 1 mile. Beach 6 miles.

Open: All year excl. January and February.

Directions

From A381 Newton Abbot - Totnes road, park is signed towards Woodland at Park Hill crossroads and Jet filling station. O.S.GR: SX845671. GPS: N50:29.516 W03:38.054

Charges guide

Per unit incl. 2 persons	£ 10.50 - £ 20.00
incl. electricity	£ 11.50 - £ 21.00
extra person	£ 3.25 - £ 5.30
child (4-16 yrs)	£ 1.50 - £ 2.50

Christmas packages available.
No credit cards.

UK0900 Widdicombe Farm Tourist Park

The Ring Road, Compton, Paignton TQ3 1ST (Devon)

Tel: **01803 558325**. Email: **info@widdicombefarm.co.uk**   www.alanrogers.com/UK0900

Widdicombe Farm is only three miles from Torquay and with easy access from the A380, is well situated for the Torbay area. There are 194 numbered pitches, 160 with electricity (10A) of which most have hardstanding and 20 are fully serviced. Surrounded by farmland, the pitches are on terraces with open views across the countryside. Many trees and shrubs have been planted and there are tarmac access roads. There may be some background traffic noise but it is not too intrusive. Touring areas are separated into sections for families, couples, tent campers, etc.

Facilities

Three older style toilet blocks are kept very clean. The original heated block near reception is fully equipped and includes facilities for disabled people, dishwashing area and laundry room. Shop and 'Poppy' restaurant (evening meals, breakfasts, cream teas and takeaway) and family bar (all Easter, then spring B.H - mid Oct). Games room. Play area and recreation field for ball games. Certain breeds of dog are not accepted. Caravan storage. Off site: Fishing, bicycle hire, riding and golf within 2 miles.

Open: 24 March - 15 October.

Directions

From Newton Abbot take A380 south for about 5 miles; site is well signed off this road. O.S.GR: SX874641 GPS: N50:28.025 W03:35.208

Charges guide

Per unit incl. 2 persons	£ 7.50 - £ 15.50
incl. electricity	£ 9.50 - £ 20.00
extra person	£ 3.50 - £ 3.00
child (3-16 yrs)	£ 2.50

Bargain breaks available.

www.**alanrogers**.com for latest campsite news

UK0880 Dornafield

Two Mile Oak, Newton Abbot TQ12 6DD (Devon)

Tel: 01803 812732. Email: enquiries@dornafield.com
www.alanrogers.com/UK0880

The entrance to Dornafield leads into the charming old courtyard of a 14th Century farmhouse giving a mellow feeling that is complemented by the warm welcome from the Dewhirst family. Having booked in, continue down the lane (with a tree covered bank alive with wild flowers) to the Buttermeadow, a tranquil valley providing 75 individual pitches on flat grass, separated by grassy ridges and in some places, wild rose hedges. You pass the walled Orchard, secluded and cosy for tents. Or take the road up the hill to Blackrock Copse with large luxury pitches with all facilities including a chemical disposal point and cleverly concealed TV connections. Electricity points are 10A. Whilst having been carefully designed, the environment remains natural. Both Buttermeadow and Blackrock have super, well maintained woodland adventure play areas. The reception, shop, tourist information/ecology room have been sympathetically converted from farm outbuildings, with the games room from the old milking parlour, complete with stalls. Dornafield is a member of the Caravan Club's 'managed under contract' scheme, with both members and non-members made welcome. The rural situation is delightful and, being away from the coast and without any evening activities, it is a haven for those seeking a quiet, restful holiday. This is a park that is well worth consideration. A member of the Best of British Group.

Facilities

Both modern toilet blocks are excellent and heated, with some washbasins in cubicles and comfortable roomy showers, but the new block up the hill could be said to be 'state of the art' with under-floor heating and a heat recovery system. Both blocks have facilities for disabled visitors and babies. Laundry rooms. Shop. Gas supplies. All-weather tennis court. Games room. Play areas. All year caravan storage. Off site: Local inn 0.5 miles. Fishing 2.5 miles. Golf 1 mile.

Open: 15 March - 3 January.

Directions

Park is northwest of A381 Newton Abbot - Totnes road. Leave A381 at Two Mile Oak Inn, opposite garage, and turn left at crossroads after about half a mile. Entrance is on the right. O.S.GR: SX848683. GPS: N50:30.019 W03:38.230

Charges guide

Per person	£ 3.50 - £ 9.00
child (5-16 yrs)	£ 1.50 - £ 3.50
pitch	£ 5.00 - £ 11.00
dog	£ 1.00 - £ 2.00

UK0915 Woodville Caravan Park

Totnes Road, Ipplepen, Newton Abbot TQ12 5TN (Devon)

Tel: 01803 812240. Email: info@woodvillepark.co.uk
www.alanrogers.com/UK0915

A lovely little site for 'adults only', Woodville is in a sheltered situation, attractively laid out with a wide variety of shrubs and trees. There are 26 pitches all with hardstanding and 16A electricity. They are accessed by a circular road which provides a central lawned area. A caravan storage area is to one side. This is a quiet site with few services, although the park is adjacent to a garden centre which also sells food and drinks. Dainton Park golf course is directly opposite and Ipplepen village is within walking distance and has three pubs. The owners live on site and take a pride in their park.

Facilities

A fully equipped toilet block also provides a separate unit for visitors with disabilities. Washing machine and freezer. Vans selling fish and chips and eggs call weekly. Wooden chalet with tourist information doubles as reception open for an hour or two each morning. Off site: Shop and golf course adjacent. Three pubs within walking distance. Bus service on main road. Fishing 5 miles. Beach and boat launching 7 miles.

Open: 1 March - 1 January.

Directions

From Newton Abbot follow A381 Totnes road for about 3 miles. Site is on the right just after Fermoys Garden Centre. The site gate is kept closed. O.S.GR: SY296913. GPS: N50:29.703 W03:37.779

Charges guide

Per unit incl. 2 persons	£ 13.50 - £ 14.50
extra person	£ 3.00 - £ 3.50
pet	£ 0.50

UK0960 ## Parkers Farm Holiday Park

Higher Mead Farm, Ashburton, Newton Abbot TQ13 7LJ (Devon)

Tel: **01364 654869**. Email: **parkersfarm@btconnect.com**

www.alanrogers.com/UK0960

Well situated with fine views towards Dartmoor, Parker's Farm is a modern touring site on a working farm. Close inspection reveals a unique chance to experience Devon country life at first hand, with pigs, sheep, goats, calves and rabbits to feed and touch. The 100 touring pitches are set directly above the farm buildings on broad terraces giving groups of flat pitches, all with good views across the valley (over the A38 which may give some road noise). Electricity (12A) is provided throughout and hardstandings are available. Trees and hedges have matured nicely on the terraces, with many more planted. Caravan holiday homes are available to hire. In addition the Parker family has added a family bar which provides entertainment during the main season (live singers, family bingo, children's entertainers) and a restaurant using locally sourced ingredients. Farm walks are tremendously popular and take place three evenings a week in high season, on request at other times. Parker's Farm provides a warm welcome – in the words of one camper, 'You come here and feel you belong'.

Facilities

Two modern and clean shower and toilet blocks provide good facilities with two family shower rooms. Baby bathroom. En-suite room for disabled visitors. Laundry. Shop (Easter - mid Oct). Restaurant, comfortable bar with family room (Easter, then Whitsun - mid Sept) and entertainment. Games room. Indoor play and TV area. Large outdoor play area. Trampolines. Caravan storage. Caravan holiday homes to hire. Rallies welcome. American motorhomes accepted by prior arrangement. Off site: Bicycle hire 5 miles. Golf 4 miles. Riding 5 miles.

Open: Easter - 31 October.

Directions

From Exeter on A38, 26 miles from Plymouth, turn left at Alston Cross signed Woodland Denbury. Site is 400 yards. O.S.GR: SX757702. GPS: N50:31.667 W03:43.451

Charges guide

Per unit incl. 2 persons	£ 7.00 - £ 16.00
incl. electricity	£ 9.00 - £ 23.00
extra person	£ 3.00
child (3-15 yrs)	£ 2.00
dog	£ 1.50

UK0980 ## Lemonford Caravan Park

Bickington, Newton Abbot TQ12 6JR (Devon)

Tel: **01626 821242**. Email: **info@lemonford.co.uk**

www.alanrogers.com/UK0980

Lemonford is a well run, neat and tidy site for all ages and families on the southern edge of the National Park, some three miles from both Ashburton and Newton Abbot. It has the look and atmosphere of the 'cultivated' caravan park, close to the main road, yet set in a sheltered, peaceful dip bordered by the pretty River Lemon. There are 85 pitches (about 40 used as seasonal pitches) on level grass and grouped in four areas. Most pitches have 10A electricity, over 55 have hardstanding. A good pub is within walking distance, along the banks of the river. Well mown grass and smart, trimmed hedges create the tranquil, attractive atmosphere the owners work hard to maintain.

Facilities

Two modern toilet blocks, one new, can be heated and provide some large private cabins, a ladies' bathroom (£1 payment) and a family bathroom. The new block has facilities for disabled visitors. Laundry facilities. Shop. Gas supplies. Freezer service. Play area. No commercial vehicles are accepted. Off site: Fishing 4 miles, riding and bicycle hire 3 miles, golf 2 miles. Leisure pool in Newton Abbot.

Open: End March - 31 October.

Directions

Travelling from Exeter, turn off A38 Plymouth road at A382 (Drumbridges) exit signed Newton Abbot, Bovey Tracey, Mortonhampstead. At roundabout take third exit to Bickington. Continue for 3 miles and park is on left at the bottom of the hill. From Plymouth, take A383 (Goodstone) exit, cross the A38 and take first left to Bickington to site on right. O.S.GR: SX793723. GPS: N50:32.346 W03:42.240

Charges guide

Per unit incl. 2 persons	£ 10.00 - £ 15.00
electricity	£ 2.50

Special low season offers.

UK0940 Holmans Wood Holiday Park

Harcombe Cross, Chudleigh TQ13 0DZ (Devon)
Tel: **01626 853785**. Email: **enquiries@holmanswood.co.uk**

www.alanrogers.com/UK0940

Close to the main A38 Exeter - Plymouth road, with easy access, this attractive, neat park makes a sheltered base for touring south Devon and Dartmoor. The hedged park is arranged on well kept grass surrounding a shallow depression, the floor of which makes a safe, grassy play area for children. Many attractive trees are growing and the park is decorated with flowers. In two main areas and accessed by tarmac roads, there are 116 level pitches (including a number of seasonal pitches) and 25 smart mobile homes in a private area. There are 100 pitches with 10A electrical hook-ups and 70 with hardstanding, electricity, water and drainage. A picturesque 8 acre meadow is provided for tents. Play equipment is provided for children, with badminton and tennis nets and an extra meadow for recreation. There may be some traffic noise on pitches to the west of the park. This is a pleasant, well run park which would suit couples or families who prefer a peaceful stay.

Facilities

The single, good quality toilet block includes facilities for babies and disabled visitors. Laundry room. Play area. Caravan storage. Dogs are not accepted. Off site: Pub/restaurant nearby in Chudleigh village. The beach or Dartmoor are 7 miles and Haldon Forest for walks is 2 miles. Sunday market at Exeter Racecourse (2 miles). Fishing 1 mile, golf or riding 4 miles.

Open: Mid March - end October.

Directions

From Exeter on A38 Plymouth road, 0.5 miles after the racecourse and just after a garage, take Chudleigh exit (signed). Park is immediately on the left. From Plymouth turn off A38 for Chudleigh/Teign Valley, then right for Chudleigh. Continue through the town and park is 1 mile. O.S.GR: SX882811. GPS: N50:37.191 W03:34.970

Charges guide

Per unit incl. 2 persons and electricity	£ 12.00 - £ 17.00
'de-luxe' pitch	£ 13.00 - £ 18.00
extra person	£ 2.20 - £ 3.00
child (4-14 yrs)	£ 1.90 - £ 2.00

UK0950 River Dart Country Park

Holne Park, Ashburton TQ13 7NP (Devon)
Tel: **01364 652511**. Email: **enquiries@riverdart.co.uk**

www.alanrogers.com/UK0950

The park is marketed as 'River Dart Adventures', where campsite and adventure experiences are enjoyed by old and young from all over Europe. It does become busy at weekends and school holidays with supervised activities for 7 year olds and upwards, such as climbing and canoeing. The camping and caravanning area is in the more open parkland overlooking the woods and is mainly on a slight slope with some shade from mature trees. There are 185 individual pitches of very reasonable size, marked by lines on the grass, some slightly sloping, with 105 electrical connections (10/16A) and 12 hardstandings. Once part of a Victorian estate with mature woodland on the edge of Dartmoor in the beautiful Dart valley, the park and its activities are now open to the general public on payment. It features a variety of unusual adventure play equipment arranged amongst and below the trees, 'Lilliput Land' for toddlers, Jungle Fun, streams and a lake, all free for campers.

Facilities

Two wooden toilet blocks, one quite smart, the older a little tired, can both be heated. Washbasins in cubicles, baby facilities, laundry, freezer, en-suite unit for disabled visitors (access by key), family bathroom and drying room. Motorcaravan service point. Shop. Restaurant, bar. Takeaway (20/7-31/8). Large TV and games room. Indoor climbing room (some of these open all year for the activities on offer). Small, heated swimming pool. Tennis. Max. two dogs per pitch. Off site: Bicycle hire or riding 4 miles. Golf 6 miles.

Open: 1 April - 30 September.

Directions

Signed from the A38 at Peartree junction, park is about 1 mile west of Ashburton, on the road to Two Bridges. Disregard advisory signs stating 'no caravans' as access to the park is prior to narrow bridge. O.S.GR: SX734701. GPS: N50:31.019 W03:47.321

Charges guide

Per unit incl. 2 persons	£ 11.50 - £ 20.50
incl. electricity	£ 14.50 - £ 23.50
extra person (over 3 yrs)	£ 5.50 - £ 7.00
dog (max. 2)	£ 2.00 - £ 3.00
Camping Cheques accepted.	

UK1080 Coast View Holiday Park

Torquay Road, Shaldon, Teignmouth TQ14 0BG (Devon)

Tel: **01626 872392**. Email: **info@coastview.co.uk**   www.alanrogers.com/UK1080

On the coast road between Teignmouth and Torquay with magnificent views over Lyme Bay, this family run park has a section of caravan holiday homes and chalets with the touring area higher on the hillside. There are 18 pitches with hardstanding and 16A electricity, and a number with water in a further area. A level area is kept for motorcaravans. Over 100 pitches for tents are on part sloping, part terraced grass on the hillside with adequate protection from the prevailing southwest winds and marvellous views. To the right of the park entrance is an attractive indoor swimming pool. and an entertainment area comprising a clubroom with a bar. Bar meals, snacks and takeaway food are served here. Entertainment is organised each evening and activities in the mornings for children. All these facilities are open all season. Various themed weekends are organised, for example Jazz and Rock and Roll. The park is conveniently located for the beach (1.5 miles) and the coastal footpath is adjacent. Torbay is 5 miles. A bus service stops at the gates. Good for holidaymakers of all ages, this park offers superb views with a range of facilities.

Facilities

The modern toilet block is spacious with free hot showers and open washbasins. Baby room. Laundry facilities. Licensed shop for basic provisions. Indoor pool and children's pool. Clubroom with bar, restaurant, takeaway, games room and TV room. Full entertainment programme and themed weekends. Adventure playground and indoor soft play area. Crazy golf. Off site: Beach 1.5 miles. Fishing and golf 1 mile. Riding 3 miles.

Open: 15 March - 18 October.

Directions

From A380 Exeter - Newton Abbot road, take the A381 to Teignmouth. On entering town turn right over Shaldon Bridge on B3199 for Torquay. Park is on right in about 1.5 miles. O.S.GR: SX932714. GPS: N50:32.073 W03:30.190

Charges guide

Per unit incl. up to 5 persons	£ 13.00 - £ 23.00
servced pitch	£ 17.00 - £ 37.00

UK1095 Leadstone Camping

Warren Road, Dawlish Warren, Dawlish EX7 0NG (Devon)

Tel: **01626 864411**. Email: **info@leadstonecamping.co.uk**   www.alanrogers.com/UK1095

Leadstone provides traditional camping at its best in a series of hedged grass fields, sloping in parts, in a natural, secluded bowl. In an area of designated outstanding natural beauty, the beach and sand dunes of Dawlish Warren are only a half mile walk. The area can get somewhat frenzied in peak holiday times but Leadstone provides a haven of peace and tranquillity. Owned by the same family since 1974, the Leadstone welcome is personal and the site totally relaxed. In all, there are 137 pitches, 102 with 16A electricity. A regular bus service passes the gate every 15 minutes. The toilet facilities are centrally situated but of the 'portacabin' variety. This is due to the site's situation on the seaward side of the Warren road where it is subject to Coastal Preservation regulations (it must be possible to move buildings within 24 hours). However, the provision is good under the circumstances, if somewhat short on toilets. Extra toilet pods are brought in for peak times. The site is only open for a short season but popular and well run. Dawlish Warren is renowned for its good weather and average temperatures of over 70 degrees are not uncommon.

Facilities

Fully equipped, centrally located 'portacabin' style provision is well kept. Unisex showers (20p for 5-6 minutes). Washing machines. Basic supplies and gas from reception. Play area with real tractor. Off site: Beach with shops, cafés, etc at Dawlish Warren 0.5 miles. Golf 0.5 miles. Bicycle hire 2 miles. Riding 5 miles. Boat launching 7 miles.

Open: 13 June - 7 September.

Directions

From Exeter follow the A379 Teignmouth road (M5 exit 30). After Starcross watch for left turn to Dawlish Warren and site is on right after 0.5 miles. O.S.GR: SX973780. GPS: N50:35.638 W03:27.097

Charges guide

Per person	£ 6.25 - £ 7.75
child (3-14 yrs)	£ 2.40 - £ 2.75
pitch	£ 4.00 - £ 4.50
electricity	£ 3.00

UK0970 Cofton Country Holidays

Holiday homes ▶ page 325

Starcross, Dawlish EX6 8RP (Devon)

Tel: **01626 890111**. Email: **info@coftonholidays.co.uk**

www.alanrogers.com/UK0970

A popular, family run park for families only, Cofton is 1.5 miles from a sandy beach at Dawlish Warren. It has space for 450 touring units on a variety of fields and meadows with beautiful country views. Although not individually marked, there is never a feeling of overcrowding. The smaller, more mature fields, including a pleasant old orchard for tents only, are well terraced. While there are terraces on most of the slopes of the larger, more open fields, there are still some quite steep gradients to climb. There are some 300 electrical connections (10A) and a few hardstandings. One area has 66 park-owned, holiday homes for let. A well designed, central complex overlooking the pool and decorated with flowers and hanging baskets, houses reception, a shop and off-licence and a bar lounge, the 'Cofton Swan', where bar meals are usually available (all Easter - 30 Sept). A family room and bar are on the first floor of this building and there is an outdoor terrace and some light entertainment in season. The adjacent supervised kidney-shaped heated pool with paddling pool, has lots of grassy space for sunbathing. Coarse fishing is available in three lakes on the park. The adjoining unspoilt woodland of 50 acres provides wonderful views across the Exe estuary and a woodland trail of 2 miles to Dawlish Warren.

Facilities

Toilet facilities comprise four blocks, well placed for all areas, and another new one of very high standard has just been completed. Facilities for disabled visitors and babies. Hair dryers. In addition three 'portacabin' style units with basic toilet facilities are provided for the peak season. Two launderettes. Gas available. Ice pack hire service. Bar lounge. TV. Shop. Fish and chip shop also serving breakfast. Swimming pool (overall length 100 ft. open Spr. B.H - mid Sept). Games room (busy in high season). Adventure playground in the woods overlooking the pools and two other well equipped play areas. Pony rides in high season. Coarse fishing (from £20 per rod for 7 days, discount for senior citizens outside July). Winter caravan storage. Off site: Beach 1.5 miles. Woodland walks/pub 0.5 miles. Golf 3 miles.

Open: 1 April - 31 October.

Directions

Access to the park is off the A379 road 3 miles north of Dawlish, just after Cockwood harbour village. O.S.GR: SX965797. GPS: N50:36.756 W03:27.628

Charges guide

Per unit incl. 2 persons and electricity	£ 13.00 - £ 26.00
hardstanding pitch	£ 15.00 - £ 26.00
extra person (over 2 yrs)	£ 2.00 - £ 4.00

Small low season discount for Senior Citizens. Camping Cheques accepted.

See advertisement on the back cover.

A glorious corner of Devon
Please see our advert on the back cover
0800 085 8649 www.coftonholidays.co.uk

UK1010 Lady's Mile Holiday Park

Exeter Road, Dawlish EX7 0LX (Devon)

Tel: **01626 863411**. Email: **info@ladysmile.co.uk**   www.alanrogers.com/UK1010

Lady's Mile is a popular, large family touring park that caters well for children. It has extensive grassy fields (with some trees for shade), in addition to the main, landscaped camping area which is arranged in broad terraces. There are 486 pitches, mostly marked by lines but with nothing between them, and most with electricity (10A). It is a 20 minute walk to a good sandy beach at Dawlish Warren and 10 minutes to Dawlish beach, but the park also has a good sized, free outdoor swimming pool with 200 ft. plus slide, paddling pool and a paved surround plus a super heated indoor pool (20 x 10 m) with 100 ft. flume and separate paddling pool (both with lifeguards). A large and attractive bar complex has a family area overlooking the indoor pool and an entertainment programme. Below is a spacious games room including pool tables and video games, and a new separate disco and bar. A sloping recreation field is ideal for kite flying and the large fenced adventure playground has a safe, sand surface. A 9-hole golf course is on site (free but with small charge for hire of clubs) and a multisports pitch. The park is popular over a long season, with reservation necessary for high season.

Facilities

Four toilet blocks of various ages and styles, but of a good standard, are well spaced around the main areas of the park with an additional shower block. Facilities for disabled people. Four family bathrooms (50p). Dishwashing sinks under cover. Two launderettes. Shop. Fish and chip takeaway. Bars and entertainment programme. Restaurant and carvery (half-board option available). All these Easter - mid Sept. Indoor (Easter - Oct) and outdoor (May - Sept) pools. Adventure play area. Games room. Golf (9-hole). Ball area with nets. Tarmac area at reception for late arrivals. Winter caravan storage. Off site: Riding and bicycle hire 1 mile. Fishing 3 miles.

Open: 13 March - 31 October.

Directions

Park is 1 mile north of Dawlish with access off the A379 (Exeter - Teignmouth) road.
O.S.GR: SX969778. GPS: N50:35.715 W03:27.568

Charges guide

Per unit incl. 2 persons	£ 11.50 - £ 27.00
incl. electricity	£ 12.50 - £ 29.50
extra person over 2 yrs	£ 1.50 - £ 3.50
dog	£ 1.50 - £ 3.50

Low season special offers
and low season discount for OAPs.

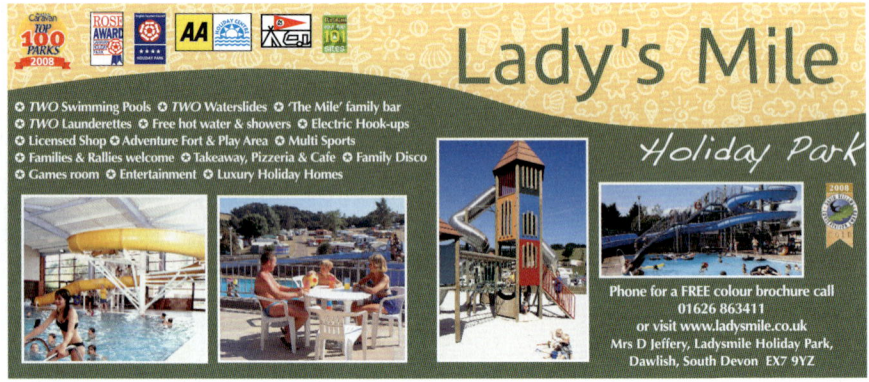

Lady's Mile Holiday Park

○ *TWO* Swimming Pools ○ *TWO* Waterslides ○ 'The Mile' family bar
○ *TWO* Launderettes ○ Free hot water & showers ○ Electric Hook-ups
○ Licensed Shop ○ Adventure Fort & Play Area ○ Multi Sports
○ Families & Rallies welcome ○ Takeaway, Pizzeria & Cafe ○ Family Disco
○ Games room ○ Entertainment ○ Luxury Holiday Homes

Phone for a FREE colour brochure call
01626 863411
or visit www.ladysmile.co.uk
Mrs D Jeffery, Ladysmile Holiday Park,
Dawlish, South Devon EX7 9YZ

fUn filled holidays
WOOLACOMBE BAY
REGISTER ONLINE FOR LATEST OFFERS woolacombe.com/ar

UK1100 Webbers Caravan & Camping Park

Castle Lane, Woodbury, Exeter EX5 1EA (Devon)

Tel: **01395 232276**. Email: **reception@webberspark.co.uk**   www.alanrogers.com/UK1100

Set in a lovely location in East Devon, with rural views, this family run park has developed over 20 years to one that can boast spacious, modern facilities, yet still retain its relaxed, rural atmosphere. The 115 marked, grass pitches are large, with the majority level and a few gently sloping. Some of the higher pitches have marvellous views across the Exe river valley. There are 100 electricity connections (10/16A). The park is surrounded by fields and visitors can watch the wildlife and grazing sheep from a fenced walk around the park perimeter. Within the park is a 'pets paddock' with a friendly donkey, Shetland pony and goats. A short drive takes you to the two miles of glorious sand at Exmouth or the delightful pebble beach at Budleigh Salterton. Woodbury Common for excellent heathland walks is just over a mile away whilst, for a little city life, Exeter is also nearby. A member of the Countryside Discovery and Best of British groups.

Facilities

There are three modern toilet blocks, one is a light and airy building with 4 family shower rooms, a bathroom (£1) and a unit for disabled visitors (WC, shower and washbasin). Laundry facilities. Unusual in terms of number, are seven chemical disposal points, located at each water point (and adequately separated). Small shop at reception for essentials. Ice pack service. Gas supplies. Motorcaravan service point. Play area and games field. All year caravan storage. Off site: Woodbury village within walking distance with excellent pub/restaurant, post office, etc. Exeter 6 miles. Fishing or golf (Woodbury Park Golf Club) 1 mile. Riding 4 miles. Bicycle hire or boat launching 5 miles.

Open: April - October.

Directions

From M5 exit 30 take the A3052 (Sidmouth) for 5 miles and turn right at Halfway Inn. From the A30, Daisymount exit, take B3180 for 3 miles to Halfway Inn and go straight across at crossroads. All routes then follow B3180 (Budleigh Salterton and Exmouth). After 2 miles turn right into lane (signed Woodbury, golf and caravan parks). Follow for 1 mile to park on left just before Woodbury village. O.S.GR: SY017874. GPS: N50:40.685 W03:23.521

Charges guide

Per pitch incl. 2 persons, electricity	£ 12.00 - £ 18.00
extra person (over 3 yrs)	£ 3.00

Min. booking of 4 nights in high season.

UK1020 Oakdown Touring & Holiday Caravan Park

Weston, Sidmouth EX10 0PT (Devon)

Tel: **01297 680387**. Email: **enquiries@oakdown.co.uk**   www.alanrogers.com/UK1020

Oakdown is a very attractive, well planned park and the Franks family and their team continue to work hard to provide a warm welcome. The attention to detail is evident at this award-winning park as soon as you arrive. The park has easy access, beautiful floral displays and a spacious feeling. The 100 level touring pitches are arranged in landscaped bays, screened by a growing range of trees and shrubs and linked by a circular road. All have 16A electricity, all have hardstanding and many have water and drainage. Two bays have 16 caravan holiday homes for rent and Oak Grove, a neat area contains 46 privately owned holiday homes. The field trail, a haven for wild flowers and birds leads to the nearby Donkey Sanctuary. Recent additions include a lake, dew pond and further wild flower areas and there is a 9-hole, par 3 Approach golf course. Continual improvements make this park an excellent choice for visitors with disabilities. A Best of British Group member.

Facilities

The central toilet block provides well maintained, fully equipped, heated sanitary facilities. One private cabin for ladies. Two unisex family bathrooms (bath, shower, toilet, washbasin and coin-operated entry), double as units for disabled people. Laundry facilities plus free freezer and microwave. Motorcaravan service point. Internet room. Fax service. TV room. Two adventure play areas and castle. No cycling, skate-boarding or kite flying is permitted. Caravan storage. Off site: Riding 6 miles. Golf adjacent. Swimming 1 mile. Beach 2 miles.

Open: 14 March - 2 November.

Directions

Turn south off the A3052 (Exeter - Lyme Regis) road between Sidford and Colyford, 2.5 miles east of the A375 junction and park is on left. O.S.GR: SY167902. GPS: N50:42.336 W03:10.838

Charges guide

Per pitch incl. 2 persons	£ 10.80 - £ 16.60
incl. electricity	£ 14.30 - £ 20.25
incl. mains services	£ 20.00 - £ 26.00
extra person (5 yrs and over)	£ 2.95
awning	£ 2.95

Less 70p for senior citizens in low season.

UK1110 Salcombe Regis Camping & Caravan Park

Salcombe Regis, Sidmouth EX10 0JH (Devon)

Tel: **01395 514303**. Email: **contact@salcombe-regis.co.uk**

www.alanrogers.com/UK1110

On the edge of Salcombe Regis village, 1.5 miles from Sidmouth and less than a mile from the sea. Salcombe Regis Park covers 16 acres of land. It is surrounded by farmland with views of the combe and the sea beyond. The focal point of the main camping area is a large 'village green' where the play area and pitch and putt are located. The reception and pitches are arranged around the green, all connected by a tarmac road. The 110 pitches are level and have their own water supply, with 98 electricity hook-ups (16A). A 25 minute walk across fields takes you to a small secluded beach, although the walk there is fairly steep – we are told there are 129 steps that take you down to the beach! There are many footpaths and coastal walks nearby, protected by the National Trust and with views of Sidmouth and Weston Mouth. Sidmouth town, originally a small fishing town but now a seaside resort, is host to the annual International Folk Festival, where for one week in summer the town is filled with folk artists from all over the world.

Facilities

The traditional style toilet block (to one side of the site and a longer walk for some) is kept spotlessly clean by the resident wardens and includes a bathroom for families and disabled visitors. Shop at reception selling basic supplies and local produce. Dishwashing area under cover. Laundry room with washing machines, dryers and ironing board. Motorcaravan service point. Play area. Pitch and putt. Caravan storage. Torches useful. Off site: Fishing, bicycle hire and golf 1.5 miles. Riding 3 miles. Sidmouth and beach 1.5 miles.

Open: Easter - 28 October.

Directions

Park is well signed on the A3052 Exeter - Lyme Regis road. From the east, take first left after Donkey Sanctuary. From the west proceed up the hill out of Sidford. Do not take first road signed Salcombe Regis, but take the next right at top of hill. Follow road round to site on left after golf range. O.S.GR: SY149892. GPS: N50:41.743 W03:12.322

Charges guide

Per unit incl. 2 persons	£ 10.50 - £ 15.50
incl. electricity	£ 14.00 - £ 19.00
extra person	£ 3.65
child (5-15 yrs)	£ 2.25

UK1250 Woodland Spring Touring Park

Venton, Drewsteignton EX6 6PG (Devon)

Tel: **01647 231695**. Email: **enquiries@woodlandsprings.co.uk**

www.alanrogers.com/UK1250

Hidden away in a corner of the Dartmoor National Park, Woodlands Springs is a haven of peace and tranquillity. Set in a dip, it is sheltered by woodland with some views across the rural countryside. It provides 85 fairly level, grass pitches (39 with hardstanding) and 53 with electricity (10A), with a circular gravel access road and a central toilet block. Bare essentials are kept in reception and a large field provides good dog walking. The resident owners provide a warm welcome on this quiet park that only accepts adults. With 600 miles of public right-of-way on Dartmoor, there is plenty to keep walkers busy. Over 50 species of birds have been seen on the park over the last few years so it would also be a good base for bird watching.

Facilities

A new toilet block should be ready for the 2009 season including full facilities for disabled people. Chemical disposal. Fishing, riding and bicycle hire can be arranged. Dog kennels for rent. Off site: Fishing 3 miles. Riding 5 miles. Golf 9 miles. Castle Drogo and Stone Wall Gardens nearby.

Open: All year.

Directions

From M5 exit 31 follow the A30 towards Okehampton. After 15 miles at Whiddon Down junction turn on A382 Moretonhampstead road. Stay on A382 for 0.5 miles then left at roundabout. After 1 mile turn left at brown caravan sign, then left and park is 150 yds down drive. O.S.GR: SX694911. GPS: N50:42.385 W03:51.040

Charges 2009

Per unit incl. 2 persons	£ 11.00 - £ 16.00
incl. electricity	£ 14.00 - £ 19.00
extra person	£ 2.00

UK1000 Forest Glade Holiday Park

Cullompton EX15 2DT (Devon)

Tel: **01404 841381**. Email: **enquiries@forest-glade.co.uk**   **www.alanrogers.com/UK1000**

Forest Glade, owned and run by the Wellard family, is set in the Blackdown Hills (designated an area of outstanding natural beauty), deep in mid-Devon away from the more hectic life on the coast. A sheltered site set amongst woodland with extensive walking without using your car, there are 80 level touring pitches, 68 of which have 10/16A electricity connections, 4 have full services and 42 have hardstanding. Touring caravans must book in advance and the easiest route for them will be explained then (phone bookings accepted). Although set in the country, the beaches of East Devon are a fairly easy drive away. There is a small heated, covered pool with a paddling pool and patio area outside, and a large games room (up a flight of steps, so not suitable for visitors with disabilities). The surrounding forest makes this a dog lover's paradise (dogs are accepted).

Facilities

One main toilet block, heated in cold weather, with some washbasins in cubicles. Separate suite for visitors with disabilities. Laundry facilities. Baby room. Extra facilities with toilets, washbasins and showers are at the swimming pool. Drain for motorcaravan tanks. Shop is quite well stocked including gas, bread and pastries with a takeaway (open evenings except Sunday). Microwave. Adventure playground. Games room. Swimming pool. Sauna. All weather tennis. Ball games. WiFi internet access. Caravan storage. New wildlife information room. Off site: Fishing or riding 1.5 miles. Golf 6 miles. Beach 17 miles.

Open: Mid March - end October.

Directions

Park (at the top of a steep hill) is 5.5 miles from the M5 exit 28. Take A373 for 3 miles, turning left at camp sign, just past thatched pub on right, towards Sheldon. Park is on left after 2.5 miles. This access is not suitable for touring caravans owing to a steep hill – phone the park for alternative route details. O.S.GR: ST101073. GPS: N50:51.470 W03:16.651

Charges 2009

Per unit incl. 2 persons and electricity	£ 12.75 - £ 17.50
extra person	£ 2.80
child (4-9 yrs)	£ 1.40

UK1065 Smytham Manor Leisure

Smytham Manor, Little Torrington EX38 8PU (Devon)

Tel: **01805 622110**. Email: **info@smytham.co.uk**   **www.alanrogers.com/UK1065**

A family owned, rural retreat of 25 acres, Smytham Manor is hidden away in its own valley, some 10 miles south of Bideford and 18 miles north of Okehampton. Part landscaped with neat grass and magnificent trees, the house is to one side of the valley with some privately owned mobile homes and more to the other side with pretty gardens. Tents have space in the walled garden where the swimming pool is situated and caravans go on terraced grass opposite. There is room for 45 units, of which 31 can have 16A electricity connections. Some pitches have gravel hardstanding. Lower down, the valley becomes more natural and wooded, with lakes and a path leading down to the Tarka Trail.

Facilities

Very smart, heated toilet block with every modern facility, including provision for disabled visitors which double as a baby room. Recycling pavilion. Bar with terrace (open evenings, weekends only low season). Milk, bread and daily essentials at reception. Swimming pool (solar heated May - Sept). Games room. Adventure playground. Walks. Off site: Fishing, golf and bicycle hire 2 miles. Riding 4 miles. Beach 8 miles. Boat launching/sailing 9 miles. Restaurants and pubs 2 miles or along the Tarka Trail.

Open: March - October.

Directions

From Bideford follow the A386 Okehampton road through Great Torrington. Turn right to park after 2 miles. From A30 pick up the A386 south of Okehampton and go north for 18 miles towards Great Torrington. O.S.GR: SS484163. GPS: N50:55.508 W04:09.460

Charges guide

Per unit incl. 2 persons	£ 8.00 - £ 18.00
extra person	£ 1.00 - £ 2.00
electricity	£ 2.00

73

UK1060 Yeatheridge Farm Caravan Park

East Worlington, Crediton EX17 4TN (Devon)

Tel: **01884 860330**. Email: **yeatheridge@talk21.com**   www.alanrogers.com/UK1060

Yeatheridge is a friendly, family park with riding, fishing lakes, and indoor pools. Based on a 200 acre farm, 9 acres have been developed over many years into an attractive touring park. Around the site there are views of the local hills and Dartmoor away to the south, and Exmoor lies to the north. You can explore three woodland walks ranging from 1 to 2.5 miles and the banks of the River Dalch. There are two deep coarse fishing lakes (bring your own rod), the top one offering family fishing and the lower one for serious fishing (age 14 or over and free of charge). Horse riding is available on site (best to bring your own hat) with hour-long and park rides available. The ponies and goats are also popular with adults and children alike. The touring area is very neat and tidy with a spacious feel to it as units are sited around the perimeter or back onto hedges, leaving open central areas. The 85 numbered, grass pitches are flat, gently sloping or on terraces and are sufficiently large, 80 with electricity connections (10A). Seasonal tourers take up 25 pitches and in addition there are 4 caravan holiday homes. The owners, Geoff and Liz, are constantly upgrading the park (recently opening a new reception and amenity building) and they try very hard to make everyone feel at home.

Facilities

Two toilet blocks provide family rooms, washbasins in cubicles, showers and facilities for babies. En-suite room for disabled visitors. Dishwashing (hot water 10p) and laundry. Motorcaravan service point. Shop. Bar, restaurant and snack bar (hours vary acc. to season). Unsupervised indoor swimming pools, toddlers' pool and water slide open daily, 10.00-20.00 hrs. Fenced play area with fort for under 10s (parental supervision). Football field. TV room. Pool table, table tennis and skittles. Fishing. Riding.

Open: 22 March - 29 September.

Directions

Park is off the B3042 Witheridge - Chawleigh (not in East Worlington). From M5 take exit 27 onto the A361 to Tiverton. Turn left onto A396 for 0.5 miles then right on B3137 almost to Witheridge, then left on B3042 for 3 miles to site, well signed down concrete roadway on left. O.S.GR: SS770114. GPS: N50:53.322 W03:45.006

Charges guide

Per unit incl. 2 persons	£ 7.50 - £ 13.50
extra person over 4 yrs	£ 2.20
electricity	£ 1.30
awning or pup tent	£ 1.00 - £ 2.00
dog (first two)	£ 0.50 - £ 1.00

Yeatheridge Farm Caravan & Camping Park
01884 860330
www.yeatheridge.co.uk
If you are a country lover, there is everything to interest you here.
2 ½ miles of wood & riverside walks. If you wish to explore beautiful Devon,
then there could not be a better location.
NEW ON-SITE RESTAURANT

UK1257 Watermouth Cove Holiday Park

Ilfracombe EX34 9SJ (Devon)

Tel: **01271 862504**. Email: **info@watermouthcoveholidays.co.uk**   www.alanrogers.com/UK1257

This park is set in a lovely position, being at the side of a stream as it flows into the harbour and sea at Watermouth Cove. It has its own private beach from where there are lovely views across the sea to Hangman's Hill. Part of the park is arranged on the fairly level valley floor, whilst the tent area is on the side of the private headland with beautiful views of the coast from the higher ground. Electricity hook-ups (10A) are available. Children will enjoy fishing from the rocks, there is an adventure play area and during high season activities are organised for them.

Facilities

New heated facilities are provided in good quality 'portacabin' style units arranged in a U-shape with decking and seating joining them together. Showers are preset, have non-slip bases and a glass partition. The camping field has its own toilets. Laundry with washing machines, dryers and a free iron and board. Drinks machines, one providing hot drinks. Shop. Bar, restaurant and takeaway (weekends only in low season). Play area and activities for children (high season). Entertainment. Off site: Ilfracombe is nearby, Lynton and Lynmouth, Exmoor and Combe Martin within easy reach. Coastal roads and paths are numerous.

Open: 16 March - 28 October.

Directions

From M5 exit 27 follow signs for Barnstaple A361. At South Molton roundabout turn right signed A399 and continue for 16 miles following signs to Combe Martin. Go through Combe Martin on A399. After 2 miles Watermouth Cove is clearly signed on the right. O.S.GR: SS557482. GPS: N51:12.749 W04:04.278

Charges guide

Per unit incl. 2 persons	£ 7.50 - £ 23.00
incl. services	£ 10.50 - £ 26.00
extra person	£ 2.00
child (under 8 yrs)	free - £ 1.00

UK1120 Napps Touring Holiday Park

Old Coast Road, Berrynarbor, Ilfracombe EX34 9SW (Devon)

Tel: **01271 882557**. Email: **info@napps.fsnet.co.uk**   **www.alanrogers.com/UK1120**

Set in an idyllic location in North Devon, this popular, family-run site offers peace and quiet on site, with plenty to see and do off site. A path just outside the gates leads down to a private beach with safe bathing; although it is only 200 yards to the gate, there are 200 steps down to the beach so it is not suitable for wheelchair users. Combe Martin and Ilfracombe beaches are also close by. The 200 touring pitches, most with views of Watermouth Bay, are terraced and spacious, many are serviced with electricity, water tap and waste point, and over 150 more have a 10A hook-up.

Facilities

Two modern toilet blocks include open plan washbasins, showers and family wash cubicles. Laundry. Licensed shop. Gas supplies. Bar with terrace and entertainment in high season. Takeaway. Heated outdoor pool with paddling pool. Tennis. Ceramics studio for children. Games room. Adventure play area. Caravan storage. Off site: Beach and fishing 200 yds. Golf and boat launching 1.5 miles. Bicycle hire and riding 5 miles.

Open: 1 March - 15 November.

Directions

Leave M5 at exit 27, take A361 to South Molton and then A399 to Combe Martin. Site is 1.5 miles west of Combe Martin on the A399 (signed).
O.S.GR: SS559475. GPS: N51:12.511 W04:03.845

Charges guide

Per unit incl. 2 persons	£ 10.00 - £ 20.00
incl. electricity	£ 9.00 - £ 24.00
extra person (over 5 yrs)	free - £ 3.00
awning	£ 1.00 - £ 3.00

UK1140 Lobb Fields Caravan & Camping Park

Saunton Road, Braunton EX33 1EB (Devon)

Tel: **01271 812090**. Email: **info@lobbfields.com**   **www.alanrogers.com/UK1140**

Lobb Fields has two camping areas providing 180 pitches on sloping grass, with a few hardstandings. Twelve pitches are reserved for seasonal caravans, and 61 have 16A electricity hook-ups. A third field is open for campers for 28 days only in high season. The pitches are marked and grass roads lead to the amenities. As the two toilet blocks are at the very bottom or very top of the fields, some up and down walking is inevitable. Although close to many activities, it is peaceful here for a quiet holiday.

Facilities

Two elderly toilet blocks (one in each field) have all the usual facilities. Two family/baby rooms. Laundry. Cleaning and maintenance can be variable. The lower block can be heated and has good facilities for disabled visitors. Hair dryers and irons available from reception (£5 deposit). Play area. Surf shop. Off site: Nearest shops less than a mile. Fishing, golf, riding and bicycle hire 1 mile. Boat launching 1.5 miles.

Open: 29 March - 29 October.

Directions

Take A361 Barnstaple to Braunton road, then the B3231 (signed Croyde) to Braunton. Park is 1 mile from Braunton on the right - take care through Braunton as roads are quite narrow and busy.
O.S.GR: SS474370. GPS: N51:06.699 W04:10.874

Charges guide

Per unit incl. 2 persons	£ 6.00 - £ 18.00
prime pitch	£ 9.00 - £ 23.00
extra person	£ 3.00 - £ 5.00

UK1145 Hele Valley Holiday Park

Hele Bay, Ilfracombe EX34 9RD (Devon)

Tel: **01271 862460**. Email: **holidays@helevalley.co.uk**   **www.alanrogers.com/UK1145**

Hele Valley is a well-established park which has been in the same family for over 30 years. Located a mile from Ilfracombe in a wooded valley, it is only a few minutes walk from Hele Bay beach. Apart from the 80 attractively laid out caravan holiday homes (20 available for rent), the park caters for tents and motorcaravans only due to difficult access. Some 50 pitches are set in two lush green fields. Eight dedicated grass pitches for motorcaravans have electricity and 50 for tents have hook-ups.

Facilities

The bright, airy and modern toilet block (access by key with deposit required) provides a mixture of open and enclosed washbasins; plus long mirrors and free hairdryers. Separately, a deluxe baby changing room, complete with pretty frieze and chiming mobiles and a well-fitted unit for disabled visitors. Laundry areas. Modern reception with tourist information. Two good adventure play areas and a play field. Parents must keep children away from the steep-sided stream running the length of the park. Off site: Shop, pubs and cafés 5 minutes walk. Fishing, sea fishing, sailing, many shops in Ilfracombe 1 mile. Beach and golf 400 yards. Riding 4 miles. Bus service in main road.

Open: 24 May - 7 September.

Directions

From Ilfracombe, take A399 east towards Combe Martin. With Ilfracombe swimming pool on the left, proceed down hill 400 m. and, at Hele Valley sign, take a very sharp right turn (easier to approach from Combe Martin). Down steep road and continue to T-junction (right-angled and narrow). Turn right to the park. From Combe Martin follow A399 west for 8 miles, past Ilfracombe golf course on left. Continue down hill and turn left at brown sign. Then as above.
O.S. GR: SS533474. GPS: N51:12.667 W04:06.000

Charges guide

Per pitch incl. 2 persons	£ 12.00 - £ 24.00
incl. electricity	£ 16.00 - £ 28.00
extra person	£ 4.00 - £ 6.00

75

UK1150 Ruda Holiday Park

Parkdean Holidays, Croyde Bay, Croyde EX33 1NY (Devon)

Tel: **01271 890477**. Email: **enquires@ruda.co.uk**   www.alanrogers.com/UK1150

Ruda Holiday Park is a recent addition to Parkdean Holidays, now comprising 12 parks in Scotland, Wales and southwest England. Ruda is right beside a Blue Flag beach and provides 313 camping and touring pitches in two distinct areas. A large camping area divided into four sections is reserved for tent campers and motorcaravans (there are some electricity hook-ups around the perimeter and it is served by two toilet blocks that are aging but clean). Touring caravan and motorcaravan pitches, all with 13A connections, are in a separate field across the road and have direct access to the beach. A central complex (well away from the camping fields) houses food outlets, and the entertainment clubs and bars. The Cascade Tropical Pool is a fun pool with flume and water featuress. There's plenty of walking on the sand dunes and around the park, and Croyde Bay is renowned for surfing.

Facilities

Two blocks in the camping fields provide toilets, showers with preset controls, and communal washbasins; these are aging but were clean at the time of visit. A separate bathroom with toilet can be accessed by wheelchairs (key from reception), however there are no aids for visitors with disabilities. A third, modern building provides all facilities in the touring field. Laundry facilities. Bar, restaurant, snack bar and takeaway. Amusement arcade. Cascade Tropical pool. Adventure playground. Tennis. Sports field. Fishing lake. Supermarket, boutique and hire centre. Surfing equipment for hire. Direct access to beach. Caravan holiday homes and lodges for hire. Dogs are not accepted. Off site: Surfing. Lundy Island excursion.

Open: March - November.

Directions

From Barnstaple, take A361 signed Braunton and Ilfracombe. At Braunton, take sharp left (narrow road) towards Croyde (signed) and follow the road all the way to the beach. Entrance to Ruda is on the right. O.S.GR: SS561331.
GPS: N51:08.111 W04:14.112

Charges guide

Per pitch incl. 4 persons	£ 9.00 - £ 30.00
pitch with services	£ 12.00 - £ 38.00

Prices are for pitch and up to four persons; maximum of eight persons per pitch.

IN THE HEART OF EXMOOR COUNTRY

Burrowhayes Farm
Caravan & Camping Site & Riding Stables

Popular Site in delightful National Trust setting on Exmoor.
A walkers paradise. Pony trekking from site. Sites for touring caravans, tents & motorhomes. Caravans for hire. Heated toilet & shower block with disabled facilities

Tel: 01643 862 463 www.burrowhayes.co.uk

UK1370 Burrowhayes Farm Caravan & Camping Site

West Luccombe, Porlock, Minehead TA24 8HT (Somerset)

Tel: **01643 862463**. Email: **info@burrowhayes.co.uk**   www.alanrogers.com/UK1370

This delightful park with riding stables on site, is on the edge of Exmoor. The stone packhorse bridge over Horner Water beside the farm entrance sets the tone of the park, which the Dascombe family have created over the last thirty years having previously farmed the land. The farm buildings have been converted into riding stables with escorted rides available (from April). Touring and tent pitches are on partly sloping field with marvellous views or a flatter location in the clearing by the river, while 20 caravan holiday homes are in a separate area. Electrical hook-ups are available (10A), although some long leads may be needed. With walking, bird watching, plenty of wild life to observe, pretty Exmoor villages and Lorna Doone country nearby there is much to do. Children can ride, play in the stream or explore the woods at the top of the site. Limited trout fishing is available in Horner Water (NT permit) alongside the park.

Facilities

The heated toilet block provides controllable hot showers, one washbasin cubicle for each sex, hairdressing and shaving areas. In the reception and stable block area are a laundry room, unit for disabled visitors and babies, and an indoor dishwashing room. A second older block is opened in high season with extra WCs and washbasins. Motorcaravan service point. Well stocked shop doubles with reception (from 1/4). Dogs must be kept on leads at all times and exercised off site. Off site: Beach 2 miles. Fishing 2 miles. Bicycle hire 5 miles. Golf 6 miles. Minehead 5 miles. Local pub 20 minutes walk.

Open: 15 March - 31 October.

Directions

From A39, 5 miles west of Minehead, take first left past Allerford to Horner and West Luccombe. Site is on right after 400 yards. O.S.GR: SS899461.
GPS: N51:12.212 W03:34.668

Charges guide

Per unit incl. 1 or 2 persons	£ 8.50 - £ 12.00
incl. electricity	£ 10.50 - £ 14.00
extra person	£ 3.50 - £ 4.50
child (3-15 yrs)	£ 2.00 - £ 2.50
dog	free

UK1340 Cornish Farm Touring Park

Shoreditch, Taunton TA3 7BS (Somerset)

Tel: **01823 327746**. Email: **info@cornishfarm.com**   www.alanrogers.com/UK1340

This neat little park, which opened for its first full season in 2006, is on level ground and conveniently located close to the M5 motorway. There are 49 pitches, all with 10A electricity, of which 25 are on gravel hardstanding. Most pitches are accessed from a gravel road with plenty of fresh water taps, site lighting and some picnic tables. A separate area for tents is close to the toilet block. With its colourful flowerbeds and old apple trees this makes a pleasant stop-over. Light power cables cross the site and there is some background motorway noise. Maximum length for motorhomes is 30ft, unless by arrangement with the wardens. To the left are the barns that house the Van Bitz workshops producing security systems for motorcaravans. The centrally situated, modern toilet block is of a high standard including under-floor heating, designed by the owners who are campers and caravanners themselves. There are no other facilities on the park but a cycle path and a footpath will take you into Taunton, the county town of Somerset. This park is a good base for visiting Cheddar Gorge, Wookey Hole, and Clarke's shopping village at Street.

Facilities

One central block with under-floor heating and modern fittings. Large dual purpose room providing facilities for disabled visitors and small children. Dusk to dawn low energy lighting. Laundry room. Dishwashing sinks outside under cover at one end of the building. Motorcaravan service point. Off site: Level cycle/footpath into Taunton (2 miles) which has a castle, museum, and markets. Tesco Express 1 mile. Golf 2 miles. Bicycle hire 2 miles.

Open: All year.

Directions

From M5 exit 25 follow signs for Taunton. At first set of traffic lights turn left signed Corfe (B3170). Take third left (Ilminster Road). Bear right at roundabout onto Blackbrook Way. Bear left at next roundabout and follow to T-junction (B3170). Turn right then next left (Killams Drive). Take second left (Killams Ave) and cross motorway bridge. Site is immediately after the bridge (second entrance). O.S.GR: ST 234 219. GPS: N50:59.520 W03:05.554

Charges guide

Per unit incl. 2 persons and electricity	£ 13.00 - £ 15.00

Luxury Camping in the Heart of Somerset

Cornish Farm Touring Park, Shoreditch, Taunton TA3 7BS Tel: 01823327746 **www.cornishfarm.com**

"The best we've ever seen" - a frequent comment from happy customers about our facilities. Level gravelled hard standings. Only two miles away from town centre. Follow Racecourse signs from M5 or town centre until you pick up Cornish Farm brown signs. Rallies welcome. Large well equipped fully tiled and heated family/disabled shower room. Book exchange. Laundry room. Washing-up area. Low energy dusk to dawn lights for your security and safety.

UK1380 Hoburne Blue Anchor

Blue Anchor Bay, Minehead TA24 6JT (Somerset)

Tel: **01643 821360**. Email: **enquiries@hoburne.com**   www.alanrogers.com/UK1380

Although mainly a holiday park, with almost 300 caravan holiday homes, Blue Anchor nevertheless offers good facilities for 103 touring units. Trailer tents are accepted but not other tents (other than pup tents with a touring booking). Virtually in a separate touring area, the level pitches all have 16A electricity and hardstanding for cars and motorcaravans (with caravans going on the adjacent grass). A feature of the park is a good sized indoor swimming pool with an area for small children, complete with fountain. Restaurants and takeaways are within easy walking distance.

Facilities

Toilet facilities provide large, free hot showers. Fully equipped launderette. Indoor heated swimming pool. Excellent adventure-style play area. Crazy golf. Small supermarket with coffee shop. American motorhomes accepted (max. 36 ft). Dogs are not accepted. Off site: Beach 100 yds. Riding and bicycle hire 5 miles. Golf 6 miles.

Open: 1 March - 31 October.

Directions

From M5 junction 25, take A358 signed Minehead. After 12 miles turn left onto A39 at Williton. After 4 miles turn right onto B3191 at Carhampton signed Blue Anchor. Park is 1.5 miles on right. O.S.GR: ST024535. GPS: N51:10.932 W03:23.837

Charges guide

Per unit incl. up to 6 persons, electricity and awning	£ 9.50 - £ 19.50

77

UK1355 Lowtrow Cross Caravan Site

Upton, Wiveliscombe, Taunton TA4 2DB (Somerset)

Tel: **01398 371199**. Email: **info@lowtrowcross.co.uk**   www.alanrogers.com/UK1355

Situated just inside Exmoor National Park, Lowtrow Cross is a small park for adults only and ideal for dogs owners. It is quietly located on a hillside giving lovely views north towards the Brendon Hills. There are 23 generously sized pitches, of which two are occupied by caravan holiday homes and two are seasonal. An adjacent meadow can be used for tents. There are four hardstandings otherwise the pitches are on sloping grass. There are 17 electricity hook-ups (16A) each with a TV socket (aerial cables on loan). Although there is no bar or restaurant on site there is a pub at the gate with local cask beers and excellent food. Lowtrow Cross is well situated for walking and cycling in the beautiful Exmoor countryside with its wide variety of wildlife. Close by Haddon Moor, with its own herd of ponies and buzzards overhead, overlooks Wimbleball Lake where one can enjoy boating, fishing and nature trails. Not far away are Dunster Castle, Porlock and the West Somerset Steam railway. The area is well known for its cider and there is a museum of cider-making at Taunton.

Facilities

Traditional heated, well equipped, toilet block but no facilities for disabled visitors. Excellent laundry room. Freezer and microwave. Small shop in reception; basic foodstuffs, milk, bread, free range eggs, frozen ready meals, toiletries. Off site: Lowtrow Cross Inn at gate. Garage 750 m. Fishing and boating 3 miles. Golf and riding 10 miles.

Open: 16 March - 31 October.

Directions

From M5 junction 25 follow signs for Minehead (A358) through Taunton, then 5 miles from Taunton turn west (left) on B3224 signed Raleigh Cross. Shortly after passing Raleigh Cross Inn turn south on B3190 signed Bampton. Site is on right in 4 miles just before Upton village. O.S.GR: ST007292. GPS: N51:03.201 W03:25.195

Charges guide

Per unit incl. 2 adults	£ 10.00 - £ 13.00
extra adult	£ 4.00
electricity (16A)	£ 2.50
awning	£ 0.50 - £ 1.00

Lowtrow Cross

Upton, Nr. Wiveliscombe, Taunton
Somerset, TA4 2DB

A small, quiet, adults only site
set in a secluded area on the
edge of Exmoor National Park

Email: info@lowtrowcross.co.uk
www.lowtrowcross.co.uk

* Spotless facilities
* Electric/TV hook ups
* Hardstandings
* Laundry
* Microwave/Freezer
* Small shop
* Wi Fi
* Tourist info
* Dogs Welcome free

Tel: (01398) 371199

UK1360 Halse Farm Touring Caravan & Camping Park

Winsford, Minehead TA24 7JL (Somerset)

Tel: **01643 851259**. Email: **ar@halsefarm.co.uk**   www.alanrogers.com/UK1360

A truly rural park with beautiful, moorland views, you may be lucky enough to glimpse red deer across the valley or be able to see ponies and foals grazing outside the main gate which is adjacent to the moor. Two open, neatly cut fields (level at the top) back onto traditional hedging and slope gently to the middle and bottom where wild flowers predominate. One field provides electricity points (10A) and is used for motorcaravans and caravans, the other is for tents. There is no reception – you leave your unit by the toilet block and walk down to the farm kitchen to book in. The pretty village of Winsford is one mile (footpath from farm) with a post office, shop, pub and restaurant. A member of the Countryside Discovery group.

Facilities

The central toilet block is of good quality and heated. Well equipped and maintained, it includes a toilet, washbasin and shower for visitors with disabilities, washing machine, dryer and iron, and tourist information. Gas is available at the farm. Play equipment. Off site: Fishing 4 miles, bicycle hire 5 miles, riding 2 miles. Tarr Steps and Barle Valley 3 miles. Winsford village 1 mile.

Open: 18 March - 1 November.

Directions

Turn off A396 Tiverton - Minehead road for Winsford (site signed). In Winsford village turn left in front of the Royal Oak (not over ford) and keep on uphill for 1 mile (go slowly round the sharp bend at the bottom). Cross cattle grid onto moor and turn immediately left to farm. Caravans should avoid Dulverton – keep to the A396 from Bridgetown. O.S.GR: SS898342. GPS: N51:05.863 W03:34.799

Charges guide

Per unit incl. 2 persons and electricity	£ 12.00 - £ 14.00
extra person	£ 5.00 - £ 6.00
child (5-16 yrs)	£ 1.00 - £ 2.00
Less 10% for 7 days paid in advance.	

UK1350 Quantock Orchard Caravan Park

Crowcombe, Taunton TA4 4AW (Somerset)

Tel: 01984 618618. Email: qocp@flaxpool.freeserve.co.uk   www.alanrogers.com/UK1350

Quantock Orchard, nestles at the foot of the Quantocks in quiet countryside, close to many of the attractions of the area. Attractively developed, mature apple trees, recently planted trees, shrubs and pretty flower beds with a nice use of heathers, make a pleasant environment and the clock tower on the wooden sanitary block adds interest. With access from fairly narrow gravel roads, there are 55 touring pitches, part separated by growing shrubs and hedging, of which 20 are for tents. Of various sizes, all touring pitches have 10A electricity hook-ups, 20 have hardstanding, 4 have TV hook-up and 5 are fully serviced (two extra large, with patio and barbecue). Levelling blocks may be required on some pitches. Only 'air-flo' style groundsheets are permitted on grass pitches. A leisure suite provides a sauna, steam room, jacuzzi, minigym and conservatory rest area (this facility is open to the public; visitor membership optional with a range of tariffs; children under 16 not admitted). It is complemented by the outdoor heated swimming pool, open to all, which is walled with paved sunbathing surrounds.

Facilities

The central, heated sanitary block is very well maintained. Two showers each for ladies and men. Some washbasins in curtained cubicles for ladies, excellent family bathroom and separate baby rooms. Microwave. Laundry facilities. Drain for motorcaravan waste water tanks. Well stocked licensed shop includes camping accessories. Mountain bike hire (some with buggies for children). Fish and chip van visits (twice weekly in summer). Swimming pool (40 x 20 ft. and open May - Sept). Leisure suite. Games room, Sky TV. Fenced safe-based play area. Caravan storage Oct. - March. Off site: The West Somerset Steam Railway in Crowcombe 1 mile. The Carew Arms serve meals.

Open: All year.

Directions

Park is west off A358 road (Taunton - Minehead), about 1 mile south of Crowcombe village.
O.S.GR: ST140363. GPS: N51:06.504 W03:13.587

Charges guide

Per unit incl. 2 persons and electricity	£ 12.95 - £ 17.95
tent pitch, car and 2 persons	£ 11.95 - £ 16.95
extra person	£ 3.49
child (3-15 yrs)	£ 1.49 - £ 2.49
backpacker or cyclist	£ 3.95 - £ 7.00

You might also like to consider...

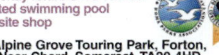
79

UK1390 The Old Oaks Touring Park

Wick Farm, Wick, Glastonbury BA6 8JS (Somerset)

Tel: **01458 831437**. Email: **info@theoldoaks.co.uk**   www.alanrogers.com/UK1390

The Old Oaks, an 'adults only' park, is tucked below and hidden from the 'Tor', in a lovely secluded setting with views across to the Mendips. In total there are 100 large pitches in a series of paddocks, the majority with 10A electricity, hardstanding and several with fully serviced (including sewage). Mainly backing on to hedges, they are attractively arranged and interspersed with shrubs and flowers in a circular development or terraced with increasing views. A quiet orchard area or a separated hedged paddock for camping and a larger field with chemical disposal facilities complete the provision. Mature trees and hedging combine with the mellow farm buildings to give a sense of timelessness, tranquillity and peace. Whether you fish or not, the pond which is well stocked with carp, roach and tench is worth a visit not only for its view of the Tor, but also to see the ducks and the chickens on your way. There is parking for disabled visitors within 25 yards of the pond. In an area steeped in history and legend, this is a very well equipped and maintained park which should meet the needs of the discerning camper or caravanner. A member of the Best of British group.

Facilities

The heated toilet block, converted from the old stables, is of excellent quality and well equipped. Neatly paved outside, it has digital security locks (a public footpath from the Tor passes through the farm). Some washbasins are in cubicles. Two en-suite rooms and a bathroom (£1). Disabled visitors have two rooms. Fully equipped laundry room. Motorcaravan service facilities. Freezer for ice packs (free). Useful dog wash. Licensed shop for basics (limited hours). Library room. Bicycle hire (with helmets). Fishing. Only adults are accepted (18 yrs and over). Internet access at reception. Off site: Riding 5 miles. Golf 6 miles. Market day is Tuesday.

Open: 1 March - 17 November, 22 December - 3 January.

Directions

Park is north off A361 Shepton Mallet - Glastonbury road, 2 miles from Glastonbury. Take narrow unclassified road signed Wick for 1 mile and park is on the left. O.S.GR: ST521394. GPS: N51:09.158 W02:40.818

Charges guide

Per unit incl. 2 persons and electricity (10A)	£ 14.50 - £ 19.00
with full services	£ 17.50 - £ 23.00
extra person	£ 4.50
dog	£ 1.00

UK1420 Southfork Caravan Park

Parrett Works, Martock TA12 6AE (Somerset)

Tel: **01935 825661**. Email: **southforkcaravans@btconnect.com**   www.alanrogers.com/UK1420

Don't be put off by the address which is historic – this was once a 17th century flax mill. Michael and Nancy Broadley now own and run this excellent, modern, well drained site just outside the lovely village of Martock. With 27 touring pitches on grass with a gravel access road (21 with 10A electrical hook-ups and 2 with water and waste water), it is an orderly, quiet park on two acres of flat, tree lined meadow near the River Parrett. All the expected facilities are close to the entrance and as the owners live on the premises, the park is open all year. Most things are available, including an NCC approved caravan repairs/servicing centre. Despite the rural setting, the A303 trunk road is just five minutes away. This area of South Somerset contains much of interest, including gardens, historic houses and sites, the Fleet Air Arm Museum, Haynes Motor Museum and Cricket St Thomas Wildlife Park. Information about access to many cycle routes and numerous walks, including the Parrett Trail, is available from reception.

Facilities

The heated well maintained toilet block is fully equipped and includes some washbasins in cabins. Laundry room with washing machine and dryer. Shop and limited off-licence with gas and comprehensive camping accessories. Play area. Off site: Fishing (with licences) on the River Parrett a few yards from the park. Golf 5 miles. Bicycle hire 8 miles. Riding 10 miles. Pubs with good food in South Petherton and Martock, less than 2 miles in each direction.

Open: All year.

Directions

From A303 between Ilchester and Ilminster turn north at the roundabout signed for South Petherton. At T-junction in middle of village, turn right towards Martock. Park is at Parrett Works midway between the two villages (about 1.5 miles from South Petherton). O.S.GR: ST446187. GPS: N50:57.922 W02:47.389

Charges guide

Per unit incl. 2 persons	£ 9.00 - £ 13.00
incl. electricity (10A)	£ 11.50 - £ 15.50
extra person	£ 1.75
child (under 5 yrs)	free
dog	£ 1.00

UK1440 Baltic Wharf Caravan Club Site

Cumberland Road, Bristol BS1 6XG (Somerset)

Tel: **01179 268030**. Email: **balticwharf@caravanclub.co.uk**   www.alanrogers.com/UK1440

This excellent Caravan Club site in Bristol's redeveloped dockland, is well laid out and maintained to a high standard. It is screened from the road by a high wall with a boatyard on one side and residential apartments on the other, with access via a lockable gate to the Baltic Wharf dockside. The view across the dock towards Clifton village and Bristol is unique and you can even glimpse the suspension bridge. The 55 pitches are accessed by a circular tarmac road, all on stone chippings and ideal for all year round use (steel pegs are sold at reception). Awnings are prohibited on 16 pitches to meet fire regulations. All have electricity (16A) and TV aerial points (reception is poor). It is a 30 minute walk to the city centre, a daily ferry runs throughout the year or there's a regular bus service. An extra ferry runs from the SS Great Britain to Templemeads. This is a popular site in a popular location so advance booking is essential. Arrive between 12 noon and 20.00. There is no space for trailers, boats, etc. and tents and units over 28 ft. long are not accepted.

Facilities

The toilet block provides good clean facilities including controllable showers and washbasins in cubicles (heated in winter). Good facilities for disabled visitors, plus toilets and showers for the walking disabled in the main block. Dishwashing under cover. Fully equipped laundry room. Motorcaravan service point. Tourist information room. Dogs are welcome but there is no dog walk. Wardens live on the site. Off site: Fishing and boating (permits from Harbour Master's office) 400 yards.

Open: All year.

Directions

From M5, J18, take A4 (signed Bristol West). Follow signs for Historic Harbour and SS Great Britain under Clifton Suspension Bridge and through Hotwells (about 5.5 miles). Cross over Dock bridge and site is about 500 yds. on left. From opposite direction (from East) follow signs for Historic Harbour and SS Great Britain. Site on right just to the west of SS Great Britain. Look carefully for the Caravan Club sign – site is behind a high wall. There are no brown signs. O.S.GR: ST574721. GPS: N51:26.792 W02:36.855

Charges guide

Per person	£ 4.70 - £ 6.20
child (5-16 yrs)	£ 1.50 - £ 3.00
pitch incl. electricity (non-member)	£ 10.90 - £ 15.30

UK1520 Waterrow Touring Park

Wiveliscombe, Taunton TA4 2AZ (Somerset)

Tel: **01984 623464**. Email: **waterrowpark@yahoo.co.uk**   www.alanrogers.com/UK1520

Beside the River Tone in a pretty part of South Somerset, Tony and Anne Taylor have enthusiastically developed Waterrow into a charming, landscaped touring park for adults only. Nestling in a little sheltered valley, it is very peaceful and possible for an overnight stop (just over 30 minutes from the M5) or ideal as a base for exploring nearby Exmoor and the Brendon Hills. There are 48 touring pitches, all of which are on level hardstandings, including 5 with full services. All have electricity (16A), spring and mains water are available and TV aerial points have been installed (your own lead is required, sometimes quite long). A small area has been set aside for tent campers. Converted barns have been put to good use, providing local tourist information, a small library and a visual record of the park's development. Further down the park, below the touring area, wide steps lead to a private nature reserve where you can find the Otter Holt, go fly fishing for wild brown trout (tuition available), take a riverside walk or just relax and watch the birds. This 'adult only' site is open all year. A member of the Best of British group.

Facilities

A modern, clean toilet unit, well fitted out and with heating, provides WCs and washbasins, some in curtained cubicles. New heated shower block. Facilities for disabled people (key). Laundry facilities. Motorcaravan service point. Limited provisions are available in reception. Order jacket potatoes before lunchtime for the evening for just £1.20. Water colour, drawing and fly fishing holidays arranged at certain times. WiFi. Caravan storage with 'store and stay' system. Site is not suitable for large American motorhomes. Luxury holiday home for hire. Off site: Fishing 5 miles. Golf 7 miles. Bicycle hire 10 miles. Riding 12 miles. The Rock Inn is a short walk and provides good meals and real ales. Wiveliscombe 3 miles.

Open: All year.

Directions

From M5 exit 25 take A358 (signed Minehead) round Taunton for 4 miles, then at Staplegrove onto the B3227 for 11.5 miles to Wiveliscombe where straight over at lights to Waterrow (still on the B3227). Park is on left shortly after the Rock Inn. Do not use satellite navigation for this site as it takes you on roads unsuitable for caravans. O.S.GR: ST052250. GPS: N51:00.990 W03:21.163

Charges guide

Per unit incl. electricity and 2 persons (adults only)	£ 13.00 - £ 21.00
extra person	£ 5.00

UK1460 Newton Mill Camping Park

Newton Road, Bath BA2 9JF (Somerset)

Tel: **01225 333909**. Email: **newtonmill@hotmail.com**   **www.alanrogers.com/UK1460**

In a peaceful valley two miles from the centre of the historic city of Bath and with direct access to the local cycle track network, Newton Mill is an excellent base from which to explore the city and the area. The site accepts 105 tents and also has 90 caravan pitches (with 30 long stay) which are located at the other end of the valley. All of these have hardstandings, with 16A electricity and satellite TV hook-ups. This end of the park is closest to the main Bristol - London railway line, not visually obtrusive but occasional rail noise may be noticeable. The site has been created around an old mill, the bar and restaurant now occupying part of the original building, and there is a modern timber chalet style reception building with a small, well stocked shop. The restaurant (open evenings all year) serves good value, speciality meals. Breakfasts are available (weekends Easter - October, daily in summer). The tent meadow is in an elevated position, or alternatively you may prefer the paddock, a small field alongside the stream which is a car free zone with a separate parking area.

Facilities

Two new heated toilet blocks provide excellent modern facilities with some washbasins in cubicles, free hot showers, bathrooms (on payment), baby rooms and a good suite for disabled campers. Launderette. Basic motorcaravan service point. Shop, bar, restaurant with garden seating area. Play area. Boules court. Fishing. Off site: Bus service into Bath runs every 10 minutes from Twerton village which is a 10 minute walk. Nearby Bristol and Bath Railway Path (a traffic free cycle way) links to the West Bath Riverside Path, and the Kennet and Avon towpath. Thursday market in Twerton.

Open: All year.

Directions

Site is 2 miles west of Bath city centre, about 1 mile southeast of the roundabout where the A4 meets the A39. From the north take M4 exit 19, turn on to M32 and almost immediately take A4174 (Avon ring road) for 7.5 miles to the A4. Turn left towards Bath and after 5 miles at second roundabout, take second exit signed Newton St Loe and pass The Globe public house. Site entrance is on the left after about 1 mile. O.S.GR: ST713647. GPS: N51:22.688 W02:24.649

Charges guide

Per person	£ 5.00
child (3-16 yrs)	£ 2.50
pitch incl. car	£ 3.00 - £ 8.00
awning	£ 2.00
dog	£ 0.75

We invite you to visit our family owned Park which lies in an idyllic setting in a hidden valley close to the centre of Britain's most elegant city

www.campinginbath.co.uk   tel 01225 333909   newtonmill@hotmail.com

FREQUENT BUSES & TRAFFIC-FREE CYCLE PATH TO BATH AND BRISTOL CITY CENTRES

UK1430 Cheddar, Mendip Heights Camping & Caravanning Club Site

Priddy, Wells BA5 3BP (Somerset)

Tel: **01749 870241**. Email: **cheddar@campingandcaravanningclub.co.uk**   **www.alanrogers.com/UK1430**

Historic Priddy is the highest village in the Mendips and is famed for its annual Sheep Fair in August. Nearby are extensive Roman lead-workings, Bronze Age burial mounds, the Priddy Circle and access to Swildons Hole, one of the popular cave systems in the Mendips. Formerly Mendip Heights Caravan Park, this well kept site is half a mile from the village with tranquil views across the Mendip fields. It has a simple charm with field margins left natural to encourage wildlife. Three fields provide space for 90 units on mostly slightly sloping short grass with 56 electricity hook-ups (16A), 36 with hardstanding, 8 serviced pitches with electric and water and 5 seasonal pitches.

Facilities

The refurbished toilet block with all facilities is bright, cheerful and heated. Two family rooms (one with high and low toilet and shower). Facilities for disabled visitors. Dishwashing and laundry facilities. The reception/licensed shop doubles as the village shop and is therefore open all season selling groceries, Calor gas, etc. Tourist information. Motorcaravan service point. Wendy house, swings and table tennis for children. Torches useful. Off site: Two traditional village pubs with very different characters stand by the village green within walking distance (0.5 miles). Bicycle hire and golf 5 miles. Fishing 6 miles, riding 2 miles.

Open: 2 March - 14 November.

Directions

From M5 exit 21 take A371 to Banwell. Turn left on A368, right on B3134 and right on B3135. After 2 miles turn left at camp sign. From M4 westbound exit 18, A46 to Bath, then A4 towards Bristol. Take A39 for Wells and right at Green Ore traffic lights on B3135; after 5 miles left at camp sign. From Shepton Mallet, follow A37 north to junction of B3135 and turn left. Continue on B3135 to lights at Green Ore. Straight on and after 5 miles left at camp sign. O.S.GR: ST522518. GPS: N51:15.816 W02:41.123

Charges guide

Per person	£ 6.05 - £ 8.40
child	£ 2.25 - £ 4.80
pitch with services incl. electricity	£ 3.25

UK1480 Home Farm Holiday Park & Country Club

Edithmead, Burnham-on-Sea TA9 4HD (Somerset)

Tel: **01278 788888**. Email: **SITE@hfhp.co.uk**   **www.alanrogers.com/UK1480**

Home Farm is neatly and attractively laid out covering 44 acres, and is convenient for those using the M5. The 780 level pitches (including 180 privately owned holiday homes and a number of seasonal units) laid out on level mown grass are all clearly marked, accessed by tarmac roads and divided into various sections, such as an area for those with pets. Including 183 pitches with hardstanding, there are 20 serviced pitches for RVs and motorcaravans. Tents are not accepted. Electrical connections (10A) are available everywhere. A large, modern pool with paved surrounds and a paddling section is neatly walled and a new indoor pool and leisure centre will open for the 2009 season. There is early evening entertainment for children, plus amusement machines and pool tables. The club house (with free membership) provides meals, entertainment, wide screen TV, an attractive conservatory and outside barbecue area. In all, it is an excellent provision. Burnham-on-Sea is only a mile away – there is a footpath from the site crossing the railway line. With Berrow Sands and Brean Down there is over seven miles of beach to choose from! There is some road and rail noise but this quietens at night.

Facilities

Two main, refurbished toilet blocks are heated and well situated for touring areas. Hot showers in one block are larger, but minus dividers. Bathrooms (key with £5 deposit). Baby room. Well equipped laundry. Facilities for disabled visitors. Dog shower. Shop with groceries, camping accessories and camping gaz. Bar. Restaurants, takeaway. Swimming pool (May - Sept). Indoor pool. Play area. ATM. Internet access and WiFi zone. Security patrols at night. Barrier card (£2). Off site: Boat launching 1 mile. Golf 2 miles. Riding 3 miles. Beach 3 miles.

Open: 10 February - 6 January.

Directions

Home Farm is 400 yards from M5 exit 22 and the A38. It is signed from the B3140 into Burnham-on-Sea. O.S.GR: ST328493.
GPS: N51:14.325 W02:57.850

Charges guide

Per pitch incl. 2 persons, electricity and awning	£ 8.00 - £ 25.00
extra person	£ 3.00 - £ 5.25
child (4-17 yrs)	£ 1.50 - £ 4.50
dog	£ 1.00 - £ 2.00

Special breaks available.

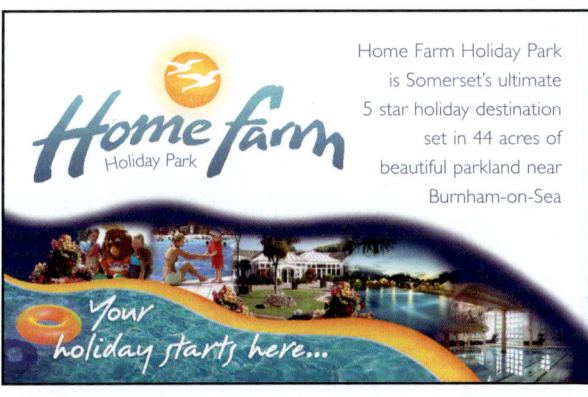

Home Farm Holiday Park is Somerset's ultimate 5 star holiday destination set in 44 acres of beautiful parkland near Burnham-on-Sea

Home Farm has everything you need for a fabulous family holiday, including:

- Swimming pool
- Children's adventure playground
- Lounge bar /Large entertainment venue
- Fishing lake /Dog walk

Brand new indoor Leisure Centre opening in January 2009!

BOOKING HOTLINE 01278 788888
www.homefarmholidaypark.co.uk

UK1510 Bath Chew Valley Caravan Park

Ham Lane, Bishop Sutton BS39 5TZ (Somerset)

Tel: **01275 332127**. Email: **enquiries@bathchewvalley.co.uk**   **www.alanrogers.com/UK1510**

A small and secluded garden site for adults only, Chew Valley has been developed with much tender love and care by the Betton family and is now affiliated to the Caravan Club. Caravans are sited on neat lawns amongst colourful beds of flowers and the cars are tucked away on the nearby car park, providing a tranquil and restful atmosphere. The warden will assist you in placing your caravan. Groundsheets are not permitted on the grass in order to protect it. There are neat hardstandings (which motorcaravans must use) and 17 spacious, fully serviced pitches.

Facilities

The heated toilet block provides all the fittings that make life comfortable. Eight separate en-suite units each with WC, basin and shower. Facilities for disabled visitors. Utility room with laundry facilities. Motorcaravan service point. Internet access and WiFi. Off site: Village 100 yds with pubs, post office, general store and newsagent. Supermarkets 15 minutes drive. Fishing 1 mile. Golf 5 miles. Riding 8 miles. Beach 15 miles.

Open: All year.

Directions

From Bath on A368 turn right opposite Red Lion pub in Bishop Sutton. Road appears a little narrow but continue past small track to the left (50 yds) for a further 50 yds. Park entrance is on the left. O.S.GR: ST584599. GPS: N51:20.195 W02:35.831

Charges guide

Per person	£ 4.50
standard pitch incl. electricity, awning and pets	£ 11.00

UK1530 Slimeridge Farm Touring Park

Links Road, Uphill, Weston-super-Mare BS23 4XY (Somerset)

Tel: **01934 641641**

www.alanrogers.com/UK1530

This small touring site is next to the beach in Uphill village at the southern end of Weston Bay. There are 56 pitches (many taken on seasonal lets), on level grass with electricity (16A) available, separated from the beach by stone walling. The view across the bay is quite something, with Brean Down and Steep Holm Island standing out. With its close proximity to the beach, the site could be affected by the tide in extreme adverse winter weather conditions. A tarmac road connects the marked and numbered pitches (eight with hardstandings for motorcaravans). Arrive between 11.00 and 17.00 hrs.

Facilities

A modern toilet block with electronic code entry system is well equipped and includes en-suite shower facilities that are also provided for handicapped visitors. Laundry room. Chemical disposal unit also used for waste water. Off site: Post office, general stores and pubs within close walking distance. Golf (note: golfers have right of way to cross the park as the golf course is split by the site).

Open: 1 March - 30 October.

Directions

Site is south of Weston-super-Mare. From the A370 follow sign for Uphill village and sands. O.S.GR: ST312588. GPS: N51:19.433 W02:59.342

Charges guide

Per unit incl. 2 persons, electricity and awning	£ 10.00 - £ 20.00
extra person	£ 1.50 - £ 3.00

No credit cards.

UK1490 Greenacres Camping

Barrow Lane, North Wootton, Shepton Mallet BA4 4HL (Somerset)

Tel: **01749 890497**

www.alanrogers.com/UK1490

Greenacres is a rural site in Somerset countryside for tents, trailer tents and small motorcaravans only. Hidden away below the Mendips and almost at the start of the 'Levels', it is a simple green site – a true haven of peace and quiet. The grass is neatly trimmed over the 4.5 acres and hedged with mature trees, though there is a view of Glastonbury Tor in one direction and of Barrow Hill in the other. All of the 30 pitches are around the perimeter of the park, leaving a central area safe for children to play. Wild life abounds.

Facilities

The central toilet block is simple but perfectly acceptable and kept clean. Hot showers are accessed directly from the outside. Spin dryer. Play equipment, badminton net and play house. The park office is across the lane (gate is usually keep shut), at the owner's bungalow. Here too are fridges and freezers for campers' use, a library, tourist information and bicycle hire. Batteries may be charged or borrowed. Dogs are not accepted. Off site: North Wootton within 1 mile with large pub/restaurant and a vineyard. Fishing and riding nearby.

Open: March - October.

Directions

From A39 Glastonbury - Wells road turn east at Brownes Garden Centre and follow camping signs. From A361 Glastonbury - Shepton Mallet road follow camp signs from Pilton or Steanbow. Roads are narrow with few passing places. O.S.GR: ST553416. GPS: N51:10.342 W02:38.513

Charges guide

Per person	£ 6.50
child (4-16 yrs)	£ 2.00

No credit cards.

UK1540 Batcombe Vale Campsite

Batcombe Vale, Shepton Mallet BA4 6BW (Somerset)

Tel: **01749 831207**. Email: gary.butler1@virgin.net

www.alanrogers.com/UK1540

Set in a secluded valley with fields gently rising around it, contented cows grazing with watchful buzzards cruising above and views across the distant hills, this is a very special place. Descending slowly down the narrow drive you see the pitches, attractively set and terraced where necessary, in an oval with the lakes below. The grass is left natural around the 32 pitches (20 with 10A electricity) and paths mown where needed. Batcombe Vale House is an attractive, mellow building covered with wisteria, to one side of the valley overlooking the lakes and the 'wilder' landscape.

Facilities

The small rustic toilet block covered in honeysuckle meets all needs, including a freezer and dishwashing sinks. Groundsheet awnings must be lifted daily. Fishing. Caravan storage. One dog per pitch is welcome (no dangerous breeds). Bed and breakfast available in Batcombe Vale House. No commercial vehicles or motorcycle 'packs', family groups only. Off site: Golf, riding and bicycle hire 5 miles. Bruton (for shops, etc.) is 2 miles. Launderettes at Shepton or Frome.

Open: Easter - end September.

Directions

Bruton is south of Shepton Mallet and Frome and north of Wincanton where the A359 intersects the B3081. Access to the site must be via Evercreech or Bruton (B3081), then follow the brown and white camping signs. The access drive is steep. O.S.GR: ST684376. GPS: N51:08.188 W02:27.190

Charges guide

Per unit incl. 2 persons and electricity	£ 18.00
extra person	£ 4.50

No credit cards.

UK1500 Long Hazel Park

High Street, Sparkford, Yeovil BA22 7JH (Somerset)

Tel: 01963 440002. Email: longhazelpark@hotmail.com

www.alanrogers.com/UK1500

Pamela and Alan Walton are really enthusiastic about their neat, small, adult only park in the Somerset village of Sparkford where they will make you most welcome. This level, landscaped park is surrounded by beech hedging, silver birches and many other ornamental trees and has a relaxed, comfortable feel. It provides 50 touring pitches for all types of units with electrical hook-ups (16A), 40 pitches with hardstanding, some extra long with grass lawns, and the entrance has been widened for easier access. Part of the park is being developed with holiday lodges for private ownership.

Facilities

The well equipped toilet block is neat, tidy and heated in winter. Good en-suite facilities for visitors with disabilities. Washing machine and dryer. Motorcaravan waste water discharge. Gas supplies. Pitches suitable for American style motorhomes. Cycle routes and walks. Caravan storage. Off site: Bus service. Spar shop, post office and MacDonalds 400 yards. Village inn 100 yds. Riding or fishing 8 miles. Golf 5 miles. Haynes Motor Museum and Yeovilton Fleet Air Arm Museum.

Open: All year.

Directions

At roundabout on A303 take road into village of Sparkford and park is signed on the left 100 yds before the Inn. O.S.GR: ST604263. GPS: N51:02.064 W02:34.118

Charges guide

Per unit incl. 2 persons and electricity	£ 16.00 - £ 18.00
extra person	£ 2.00

No credit cards.

UK1545 Cheddar Bridge Touring Park

Draycott Road, Cheddar BS27 3RJ (Somerset)

Tel: 01934 743048. Email: enquires@cheddarbridge.co.uk

www.alanrogers.com/UK1545

Within easy walking distance of Cheddar village, this is an adult only (over 18 yrs) park. A compact site, there are 50 pitches, mostly on level grass, with 45 electricity hook-ups (16A) and 10 gravel hardstandings. A separate area for a few tents is on the river bank. Reception keeps basic supplies and gas cylinders. Note: the site access is over a fairly narrow bridge with low stone walls, passable for double axle caravans, but more difficult for American RVs and very large motorcaravans. Cheddar village has a small supermarket with ATM, garage, pubs, restaurants and a leisure centre.

Facilities

Attractive heated sanitary block (close to site entrance, some distance from most of the pitches) with washbasins in cubicles, large showers, and family bathroom with shower over the bath. Utility room with laundry facilities. Hot water is restricted to 07.00-12.00 and 16.00-21.00. Fishing. Off site: Cheddar Gorge and village. Swimming pool 0.5 miles. Golf 3 miles. Riding 3 miles.

Open: 1 March - end October.

Directions

Site entrance is about 100 yards south of village on A371, on right, next to Cheddar Football Club. O.S.GR: ST461530. GPS: N51:16.389 W02:46.475

Charges guide

Per unit incl. 2 persons and electricity	£ 7.00 - £ 17.00
extra person	£ 2.00
dog	£ 1.00

UK1550 Bucklegrove Caravan & Camping Park

Wells Road, Rodney Stoke, Cheddar BS27 3UZ (Somerset)

Tel: 01749 870261. Email: info@bucklegrove.co.uk

www.alanrogers.com/UK1550

Bucklegrove is set right in the heart of Somerset on the southern slopes of the Mendip Hills and close to the tourist attractions of Cheddar Gorge, Wookey Hole, and Wells. The 125 touring pitches, 80 of which have 10A electricity connections, are split between two fields joined by a woodland walk. The top slightly undulating field is more suitable for tents and caravans, while the lower field with some short hardstandings is a little more level and would be suitable for caravans and smaller motorhomes. A new play area with safety surface includes a multiplay unit, slide and spring riders.

Facilities

Two bright and cheerful toilet blocks include some washbasins in cubicles and some spacious showers. The larger, heated block also provides bathrooms (50p) with baby changing facilities, and a room for visitors with disabilities. Laundry rooms. Well stocked shop. Indoor swimming pool and paddling pool with terrace bar. Games room. Play area (under 14s). Dogs accepted in low season only. Off site: Riding 2 miles. Golf 3 miles. Fishing 5 miles. Beach at Weston-Super-Mare 12 miles. Cheddar 7 miles. Bus to Wells stops at the entrance.

Open: 1 March - 14 December.

Directions

Take A371 Wells to Cheddar road. Park is on right about 1 mile past Westbury village. Take care as the road between Wells and Cheddar is rather narrow through some of the villages. O.S.GR: ST490496. GPS: N51:14.599 W02:43.938

Charges guide

Per unit incl. 2 persons	£ 8.00 - £ 21.00
incl. electricity	£ 12.00 - £ 25.00
extra person	£ 4.00
child (4-17 yrs)	£ 1.00 - £ 3.00
dog (off peak only)	£ 2.00

UK1560 The Fairways International Touring Park

Bath Road, Bawdrip, Bridgwater TA7 8PP (Somerset)

Tel: 01278 685569. Email: holidays@fairwaysinternational.co.uk   www.alanrogers.com/UK1560

A level 5.5 acre park set in rural Somerset, Fairways is owned and run by the Walker family. There are plans for major upgrading and expansion over the next few years. So far, improvements include new electricity points, 90 hardstanding pitches (4 for American style motorhomes), and an improved site entrance and roads. More pitches and a kitchen for backpackers are planned. There are 200 pitches on well drained grass and of these about 50 are seasonal. There are 150 with electricity (10A). Families with children are directed to pitches close to the play area in the centre of the park.

Facilities

A central toilet block houses both washbasins in cubicles and open plan, showers (push-button control). Baby bath/shower room. Unit for disabled visitors. A wheelchair is provided for visitors to use if required. Good laundry facilities. Shop with gas. Freezer and microwaves (free of charge). Central play area. Games room TV and electronic games. Caravan storage. Electronic barrier. Off site: Beaches at Burnham-on-Sea 8 miles. Walking in the Quantock Hills within 10 miles. Glastonbury, Cheddar Gorge and Wookey Hole. Cycle routes and footpaths are within a mile of the park.

Open: All year.

Directions

From M5 exit 23, take A39 in the direction of Glastonbury. Turn left just before Texaco garage on B3141 towards Woolavington and site is about 50 yards on the right. O.S.GR: ST348402. GPS: N51:09.416 W02:56.091

Charges guide

Per unit incl. 2 persons	£ 10.00 - £ 14.00
incl. electricity	£ 13.50 - £ 17.00
extra person	£ 2.50
child (3-15 yrs)	£ 1.50

Euros accepted.

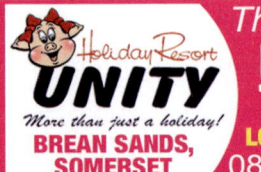
UK1575 Holiday Resort Unity

Coast Road, Brean Sands TA8 2RB (Somerset)

Tel: 01278 751235. Email: rjh@hru.co.uk   www.alanrogers.com/UK1575

Holiday Resort Unity offers everything for everyone, from young children to the 'young at heart'. Apart from the extensive on-site amusements and entertainment programme, campers can also use the swimming pools, funfair and other leisure pursuits at the adjoining Brean Leisure Centre (owned by the same family), some free of charge and others by paying a small fee. Three large touring fields provide pitches that are flat and open, mostly grass but some on concrete hardstandings (motorcaravans up to 30 ft. can be accommodated). Most pitches have 16A electricity hook-ups. A separate warden looks after each camping field. Ready equipped tents and a substantial number of caravan holiday homes are available for rent. Access to the five mile stretch of sandy beach is via a footpath opposite the site entrance. Fishing (with a licence) is permitted from Unity Lake in the Yellow Field. RJ's is a club with bars, food and nightly entertainment for the whole family. 'Sarah's Pantry' offers takeaway or sit-down meals (including the Sunday roast), while fish and chips are available at Porkers Bar.

Facilities

Three good toilet blocks provide ample facilities and include en-suite units. Some toilets and washbasins have been adapted for people with disabilities (key from reception). Well equipped laundries. Motorcaravan service point, recycling station, jet spray to wash vehicles. Well stocked shop. Gas exchange. RJ's Club, Sarah's Pantry and Porkers fish and chip bar. Large adventure play area. Cyber Zone (high season; £1 for 10 minutes). Buster's Work Out Gym, Sally's sun beds. Monday market, Sunday car boot sales. All facilities open during high season, most open during mid season and at weekends in low season. Torches advisable at night. Off site: Walking access from park to Brean Leisure Centre (pool, funfair etc); riding, cycling, cinema, walks, golf. Bus and land-train services vary according to season. Beach 100 m.

Open: 10 February - 20 November.

Directions

From M5 exit 22, follow signs for Burnham-on-Sea (B3140), Berrow and Brean. Holiday Resort Unity is on right along the main street of Brean – it is well signed. Take care as road through Berrow and Brean is rather narrow. O.S.GR: ST290539. GPS: N51:16.829 W03:00.733

Charges guide

Per standard pitch	£ 6.00 - £ 28.00
serviced pitch	£ 8.00 - £ 30.00
incl. hardstanding	£ 10.00 - £ 32.00

Price includes unit, 4 persons, awning, entertainment/swimming and 'Piglet Club'. Deduct 25% if only two people occupy the pitch.

UK1590 Exe Valley Caravan Site

Bridgetown, Dulverton TA22 9JR (Somerset)

Tel: 01643 851432. Email: paul@paulmatt.fsnet.co.uk   www.alanrogers.com/UK1590

Occupying a prime position in a wooded valley alongside the River Exe, within the National Park. Exe Valley Caravan Site is ideally situated for visiting the Doone Valley, Tarr Steps, Dulverton and many other beautiful venues in the area. This four acre 'adult only' campsite is owned and managed by Paul and Christine Matthews. Set beside the River Exe or the millstream, there are 50 large pitches (mostly grass but with some hardstandings at the top end), of which 41 have 10A electricity and TV hook-ups. Reception forms part of the owner's home which is an old mill, complete with water wheel and grindstones that are in working order. Open for visits every Sunday at 10.00, CCTV has been installed so campers may watch the bat colony in the loft from a screen in the mill. Reception also houses a small shop stocking basic provisions. Fly fishing along the River Exe is possible from the site or at Wimbleball Reservoir just over four miles away. This part of Somerset is a haven for walking, cycling, pony trekking, or as a place to just sit and relax.

Facilities

The refurbished toilet block houses the usual facilities and an en-suite room for disabled visitors (quite short steep ramp to enter). Excellent laundry with domestic washing and drying machines, plus a microwave (free). Motorcaravan service point. Small shop with basic provisions. Bicycle hire. Gas supplies. Free fly fishing. WiFi. This is an adult-only park. Off site: Riding 4 miles. Golf 12 miles. Pub at Bridgetown. Winsford village has a general stores, pub and tea rooms.

Open: 14 March - 13 October.

Directions

Bridgetown is roughly midway between Dunster and Tiverton on the A396. As you enter Bridgetown from Tiverton, look for site sign and turn left on minor road. Site is 100 yards on the right. O.S.GR: SS923332. GPS: N51:05.292 W03:32.325

Charges guide

Per unit incl. 2 persons	£ 8.00 - £ 14.00
extra person	£ 3.00
electricity (10A) and TV hook-up	£ 2.50
awning	£ 1.00
dog	£ 1.00

No credit cards.

UK1570 Northam Farm Touring Caravan Park

Brean Sands, Burnham-on-Sea TA8 2SE (Somerset)

Tel: 01278 751244. Email: enquiries@northamfarm.co.uk   www.alanrogers.com/UK1570

Brean has been a popular holiday destination for decades and many large campsites have evolved. Northam Farm is one of them; it is a large family park with good facilities and an ongoing programme of improvements. Of the 750 pitches, 350 are for seasonal units and these are separated from the four touring fields. Pitches are large so you won't feel cramped and 154 have block paved hardstanding. There are two play areas for youngsters, a sports field, bicycle track, and cricket pitch for teenagers, and fishing on the lake for adults. The owners and staff are always available to help visitors enjoy their stay.

Facilities

Three good toilet blocks, well maintained and within reasonable distance of all pitches, provide ample toilets, washbasins (newest block has curtained cubicles) and spacious showers (50p pull cord operation). Bathrooms (£1 charge). Baby room. Rooms for visitors with disabilities (opened by key). Laundry. Motorcaravan service point. Dog shower. Licensed shop well stocked with food, holiday gear and accessories. Snack bar/takeaway. Free entry to live entertainment at The Seagull. Games room. Two play areas. Sports field. Fishing lake. Caravan workshop for repairs and servicing. Caravan storage. Dogs are not accepted in one field. Off site: Burnham-on-Sea and Weston-Super-Mare nearby. Golf and riding 0.5 miles.

Open: March - October.

Directions

From M5 exit 22 follow signs to Burnham-on-Sea, Berrow and then Brean. Continue through Brean and Northam Farm is on the right, half a mile past Brean Leisure Park. O.S.GR: ST297556. GPS: N51:17.694 W03:00.610

Charges guide

Per unit incl. 2 persons	£ 6.75 - £ 15.50
incl. electricity	£ 8.75 - £ 18.00
extra person	£ 2.00 - £ 2.50
child	£ 0.75 - £ 1.00
dog, awning, fishing	free

UK1580 Warren Farm Holiday Centre

Warren Road, Brean Sands, Burnham-on-Sea TA8 2RP (Somerset)

Tel: **01278 751227**. Email: **enquiries@warren-farm.co.uk**   www.alanrogers.com/UK1580

Warren Farm is a popular venue for family campers who want the beach, fun and entertainment. With over 1,000 pitches, the park is divided into several fields, with touring and seasonal pitches kept well apart; Sunnyside, part of Warren Farm, is about 200 yards further down the road and has its own warden. Access roads are wide and all the 565 touring pitches are grassy and level, with 16A electric hook-ups. There are no hardstandings so motorhomes may have difficulties in extremely wet weather. Ranch-style wooden fences break up the camping fields and couples usually park around the perimeter overlooking fields and views of the Mendip Hills.

Facilities

Several toilet blocks of varying styles provide WCs, showers (on payment) and mostly communal washbasins. Showers are of adequate size (one block with no dividers); the new building in field 4 has larger ones and facilities for babies. Facilities for disabled visitors in some blocks. Four laundries. Motorcaravan service points. Two shops, snack bar and Chinese takeaway. Fish bar. Beachcomber Inn. Play equipment. Play barn. Sports field. Fishing lake. WiFi. Off site: Burnham-on-Sea, Weston-super-Mare, Cheddar, Wells and Glastonbury. Golf and riding 1.5 miles.

Open: 28 March - 31 October.

Directions

Leave M5 at junction 22 and follow the B3140 to Burnham-on-Sea, then to Berrow and Brean. Continue through Brean and Warren Farm is on the right about 1.5 miles past Brean Leisure Park. O.S.GR: ST297564. GPS: N51:18.149 W03:00.590

Charges guide

Per unit incl. 2 persons	£ 7.00 - £ 15.00
extra person	£ 2.00
electricity (16A)	£ 2.50

UK1660 Piccadilly Caravan Park

Folly Lane West, Lacock, Chippenham SN15 2LP (Wiltshire)

Tel: **01249 730260**. Email: **piccadillylacock@aol.com**   www.alanrogers.com/UK1660

Piccadilly Caravan Park is set in open countryside close to several attractions, notably Longleat, Bath, Salisbury Plain, Stourhead, and Lacock itself. You will receive a warm welcome from the owner at this small, quiet family owned park that is beautifully kept. Well kept shrubs, plants and trees have been landscaped to give the impression of three separate areas and create a very pleasant ambience. There are 40 well spaced, clearly marked pitches, 12 of which have hardstanding, and two good areas for tents. Electrical connections (10A) are available on 34 pitches.

Facilities

The one toilet block is well maintained and equipped, should be adequate in size for peak periods and can be heated in cool weather. Laundry room with baby changing facilities. Ice pack service. Small, bark-based playground and a large, grass ball play area. Limited gas supplies. Papers can be ordered. Off site: Bus service from Lacock village to Chippenham. Fishing 1 mile. Bicycle hire 6 miles. Riding 4 miles. Golf 3 miles.

Open: Easter/1 April - October.

Directions

Park is signed west off A350 Chippenham - Melksham road (turning to Gastard with caravan symbol) by Lacock village. 300 yds. to park. O.S.GR: ST911683. GPS: N51:24.828 W02:07.781

Charges 2009

Per unit incl. 2 persons	£ 14.00
extra person over 5 yrs	£ 2.00
electricity	£ 2.00
No credit cards.	

UK1680 Plough Lane Caravan Site

Plough Lane, Kington Langley, Chippenham SN15 5PS (Wiltshire)

Tel: **01249 750146**. Email: **enquiries@ploughlane.co.uk**   www.alanrogers.com/UK1680

Catering for adults only, this is a good example of a well designed, quality, modern touring site. The 50 pitches (all for touring units) are attractively laid out over four acres, access roads are gravel and the borders are stocked with well established shrubs and trees. The pitches are half grass, half hardstanding and all have electricity (16A), with 25 having full services. The site entrance has a barrier system for security. This site is an ideal base for visiting north Wiltshire and south Gloucestershire.

Facilities

The sanitary building is heated, spacious, light and airy, and has all the usual facilities including some washbasins in cubicles. Separate en-suite room for disabled visitors with ramp access. Fully equipped laundry. Max. 2 dogs per unit. This park is for adults only (over 18 yrs). Barrier card deposit £10. Off site: Supermarket, two pubs and two garages (both with gas). Golf less than 1 mile.

Open: Easter - October.

Directions

From M4 exit 17 turn south on A350 for 2 miles, then left at traffic lights (site signed). From Chippenham head north on A350 (towards M4), approaching traffic lights (signed for site). O.S.GR: ST914764. GPS: N51:29.182 W02:07.542

Charges guide

Per unit incl. 2 persons	£ 16.00 - £ 19.00
extra person (max. 2 extra)	£ 5.00
No credit cards.	

UK1640 Greenhill Farm Camping & Caravan Park

New Road, Landford, Salisbury SP5 2AZ (Wiltshire)

Tel: 01794 324117. Email: greenhillcamping@btconnect.com www.alanrogers.com/UK1640

Located on the northern edge of the New Forest National Park, this is an attractive, uncommercialised, hide-away for adults only (over 18 yrs), set around two small lakes, one of which is reserved for coarse fishing. The 100 level pitches, 35 hardstanding (the rest on grass), come complete with 16A electric hook-ups, and are attractively spread around the 14 acre site. An area for tents is in a separate hill-top meadow with views over the nearby forest and its own fishing lake. There is also a separate area set aside for pets. Local attractions include Paultons Park, Breamore House, Downton Moot and the New Forest. Several local pubs serving meals are close by and a bus stop outside the site entrance provides services to Salisbury or Southampton.

Facilities

Portacabin-type units of varying ages located around the site perimeter provide basic facilities and can be heated when necessary. No dedicated facilities for disabled persons. Laundry with washing machine and dryer. Gas supplies. Milk, eggs, gifts, maps etc. stocked. Coarse fishing lakes (£3.60 per rod per day). Torches useful. One vehicle only per camping unit (others to remain in car park). CCTV on access road and car park areas. American motorhomes not accepted. Off site: Landford village has a bakery, post office, off-licence and general stores (15 minute walk). Golf 3 miles. Riding 4 miles. Bicycle hire 8 miles.

Open: 25 January - 22 December.

Directions

From M27 exit 2 take A36 north towards Salisbury for about 6 miles. Pass through West Wellow and after passing a B.P. garage on left, take next left into New Road, and continue for under 1 mile to site entrance on left. O.S.GR: SU264184.
GPS: N50:57.867 W01:37.545

Charges 2009

Per unit incl. 2 persons, awning	
and electricity	£ 15.00
tent incl. 2 persons	£ 10.00
extra person	£ 4.00

Greenhill Farm Camping & Touring Park

Adult only hideaway site on the edge of the New Forest with level hard standings and hookups. Access to the Commons and New Forest and within easy reach of the cities Salisbury, Southampton and Winchester. Onsite toilets, showers, laundry, purchasable gas and fishing. Offsite facilities close by, including food shop, bar, restaurant, swimming pool, beaches and golf course. Separate area for visitors without dogs.

Landford, Nr Salisbury, Wiltshire • Contact Mrs Jenny Osman on 01794 324117

UK1655 Church Farm Caravan & Camping Park

Sixpenny Handley, Salisbury SP5 5ND (Wiltshire)

Tel: 01725 552563. Email: churchfarmcandcpark@yahoo.co.uk www.alanrogers.com/UK1655

Church Farm offers 35 spacious pitches (including two hardstandings), all with 16A electricity hook-ups, arranged around the perimeter of two fields, plus a tent field. Although the site is fairly open the farm buildings and thick hedges do give some shelter from the prevailing wind. Breakfasts are available in the main season from a snack bar with a new café opening soon. Sixpenny Handley is a Saxon hilltop village and St Mary's church dates back some 900 years. From the site you can hear the bells and the chimes of its clock. The Roebuck Inn in the High Street offers a varied menu. This is a quiet corner right on the Wiltshire - Dorset border but within day trip distance of many of the area's finest attractions. There are some fine country walks available on nearby Cranborne Chase.

Facilities

A small modern building provides clean facilities and a dedicated room for disabled campers. Laundry with washing machine and dryer in a separate building. Freezer for ice packs. Gas supplies. Rather basic motorcaravan service point (may be difficult to access for some units). Breakfast snack bar, café planned. Off site: The village has a bus stop, a number of small shops, a small supermarket and Post Office. Tennis courts (hire equipment from site). Golf 4 miles. Riding 5 miles. Fishing 10 miles.

Open: All year.

Directions

To avoid the village centre, 1 mile south of Handley Hill roundabout on A354 turn towards Sixpenny Handley, then right by the School and site 300 yards by the Church. O.S.GR: ST996173.
GPS: N50:57.319 W02:00.413

Charges guide

Per person	£ 6.00 - £ 7.00
child (3-14 yrs)	£ 1.50
serviced pitch	£ 2.50
awning	£ 1.00

UK1690 Longleat Caravan Club Site

Warminster BA12 7NL (Wiltshire)

Tel: **01985 844663**

www.alanrogers.com/UK1690

What a magnificent situation in which to find a caravan park, amidst all the wonders of the Longleat Estate including the Elizabethan House, gardens designed by Capability Brown and the Safari Park. Visitors can roam the woodlands (leaflets are available on a range of walks) and enjoy the views, watch the wildlife and marvel at the azaleas, bluebells, etc. according to the season or listen to the occupants of the Safari Park. The site itself, well managed by Caravan Club wardens, is situated in 10 acres of lightly wooded, level grassland within walking distance of the house and gardens. There are 165 generous pitches (101 with hardstanding and 64 on grass), all with 16A electricity connections. Water points and re-cycling bins are neatly walled with low night lighting. Two new buildings provide immaculate facilities, whilst the former toilet block now houses further services, a family room and tourist information. Tents are not accepted (except trailer tents).

Facilities

Two heated toilet blocks provide washbasins in cubicles, controllable showers and a vanity section with mirrors and hairdryers. Baby/toddler room, suite for disabled visitors, laundry and dishwashing room and a family room with a DVD player. Two motorcaravan service points. Play area. Office is manned 09.00-18.00 and stocks basic food items, papers can be ordered and gas is available. Paperback exchange library. Fish and chip van calls some evenings. Late arrivals area. Off site: Longleat House and its attractions. Frome 7 miles.

Open: 17 March - 30 October.

Directions

The main entrance to Longleat which caravans must use is signed from the A362 Frome - Warminster road near where it joins the A36 Warminster bypass. Turn into the estate and follow the Longleat House route through the toll booths for 2 miles then follow caravan club signs for 1 mile. There are shorter ways to leave the site. O.S.GR: ST806434.
GPS: N51:11.442 W02:16.711

Charges guide

Per person	£ 4.70 - £ 6.20
child (5-16 yrs)	£ 1.50 - £ 3.00
pitch incl. electricity	
(non-member)	£ 10.90 - £ 15.30

UK1700 Devizes Camping & Caravanning Club Site

Spout Lane, Seend, Melksham SN12 6RN (Wiltshire)

Tel: **01380 828839**

www.alanrogers.com/UK1700

First opened in 1998, this site occupies a level field with gravel roads and centrally located facilities. It is also adjacent to the Kennet and Avon Canal (opened in 1810 and recently extensively restored) and the towpath now provides a traffic-free route passing the Caen Hill flight of 29 locks into Devizes (4 miles). In the other direction the towpath runs towards Melksham (also 4 miles). There are 50 hardstanding and 40 grass pitches, 80 with electricity (16A). The Millennium Wood on the site contains more than 1,000 trees. The site is central for visiting many places of interest including the stone circles at Stonehenge and Avebury. A more unusual outing is to Sandridge Farm, renowned for its speciality bacons, hams and sausages. The farm shop is open daily, May to Sept. and visitors can see the pigs and piglets (admission free – wellies advisable). The Vale of Pewsey cycle route can be accessed from the canal towpath to the east of Devizes, and runs for 41 miles between Great Bedwyn and Corsham.

Facilities

The modern, heated toilet block provides spacious hot showers, washbasins in cubicles, laundry, dishwashing room and a baby room. Facilities for disabled visitors are in a suite (with alarm system) by reception. Motorcaravan services (in the late arrivals area). Small playground. Reception opens 09.00-10.00 and 16.00-17.30, and stocks basic foods and drinks, snacks and gas supplies, fishing licences and local tourist information. Off site: Farmers' Market second Friday each month.

Open: All year.

Directions

From Devizes take A361 westbound, and 0.5 miles before Seend village, take A365 towards Melksham. Cross the canal bridge, take next left by 'Three Magpies' and the site entrance is on the right. From M4 exit 17, use A350 to Melksham and A365 to the site. O.S.GR: ST950620.
GPS: N51:21.390 W02:04.335

Charges guide

Per person	£ 6.30 - £ 7.25
child	£ 2.15 - £ 2.25
pitch (non-member)	£ 5.65

UK1630 Brokerswood Country Park

Brokerswood, Westbury BA13 4EH (Wiltshire)

Tel: **01373 822238**. Email: **info@brokerswood.co.uk**   **www.alanrogers.com/UK1630**

This countryside campsite is located in an 80 acre country park, with ancient broadleaf woodland, plenty of marked walks, a woodland railway which also runs 'Santa Specials' (bookings taken from 1 August). The campsite has 65 pitches arranged around an open meadow area, served by a circular gravel roadway, with low level site lighting. There are 25 hardstanding pitches, and 44 electricity hook-ups (10A). Although fairly recently laid out, the site is maturing well. American RVs and other large units should use the coach entrance and they (and all other arrivals after 18.00) are asked to phone ahead so that arrangements can be made for the barrier. The gift shop has a special Christmas theme from the end of October. The park also has adventure playgrounds and play trails amongst its many activities for the family. Most are free for campers, except for the train. Fishing in the lake is available, ask at reception. Cycling in the park is forbidden. In the interest of environmental conservation it has its own biological waste management system.

Facilities

Two well insulated and heated, timber clad buildings are at one end of the site. Some washbasins in cubicles, large, controllable hot showers. Family rooms (on payment). Fully equipped suite for disabled people with ramped approach and alarm. Laundry and ironing facilities. Motorcaravan services. Gas. Milk, bread, newspapers to order from reception/shop. Café (all day). Takeaway (Aug). Fishing. Entry barrier (key code). No cycling on site. Off site: Golf 6 miles. Pub with excellent meals 400 yds.

Open: All year.

Directions

From Trowbridge take A361 south for 2 miles, turning left (east) at Southwick, and follow signs to Country Park. O.S.GR: ST840524.
GPS: N51:16.217 W02:13.885

Charges guide

Per pitch	£ 10.00 - £ 25.00
incl. electricity	£ 12.00 - £ 27.00
extra person	£ 3.50 - £ 3.00
dog	£ 1.00

BROKERSWOOD
COUNTRY PARK

Superb facilities in a beautiful woodland setting near Westbury, off the A36 between Bath & Salisbury.

- Caravan and Camping Park open all year round
- Level pitches with 10 amp electric hook-ups
- Centrally heated toilet and shower block
- Private family bathroom facilities
- Free unlimited access to the Country Park
- 2 adventure playgrounds and nature trail
- Barbecue and picnic areas
- Narrow gauge railway (seasonal)
- Onsite café and shop
- Booking essential, dogs welcome

Brokerswood, Westbury, Wiltshire. BA13 4EH

Book online at www.brokerswood.co.uk - Email info@brokerswood.co.uk - Tel 01373 822238

UK1650 Coombe Touring Park

Coombe Nurseries, Race Plain, Netherhampton, Salisbury SP2 8PN (Wiltshire)

Tel: **01722 328451**   **www.alanrogers.com/UK1650**

A true touring park with outstanding views over the Chalke Valley, Coombe is adjacent to Salisbury racecourse. There are 100 spacious pitches all on level, well mown grass, 50 with electric hook-ups (10A). The tent pitches are generally around the outer perimeter. Many pitches are individual and sheltered by hedging. Reception also has a small shop, there are supermarkets in Salisbury (4.5 miles), and pubs in Netherhampton and Coombe Bissett (2 miles) both serving meals.

Facilities

A well built, modern, centrally heated sanitary unit, provides an ample supply of WCs, spacious press button showers, washbasins in cubicles for the ladies, and a family room (with bath) has facilities for disabled persons, babies and toddlers. Dishwashing room. Laundry facilities. Small shop (May-Sept). Open grass play area. Gas available. Off site: Nearby attractions include Wilton House, Wilton Carpet Factory and the Wilton Shopping Village, Salisbury Cathedral, Stonehenge. Golf 400 yards. Riding and tennis in Wilton 2.5 miles. Indoor pool, leisure centre and cinema in Salisbury 4.5 miles.

Open: 1 January - 20 December.

Directions

From the A36, 2 miles west of Salisbury (just east of Wilton roundabout), turn south on A3094 towards Netherhampton and Harnham. After 0.5 miles on sharp left bend, turn right to Stratford Tony and Racecourse. Continue to top of hill by racecourse entrance, and turn left on narrow lane behind racecourse for 700 yards to site entrance.
O.S.GR: SU098282. GPS: N51:03.257 W01:51.655

Charges guide

Per unit incl. 2 persons	£ 11.00 - £ 13.00
extra person	£ 3.00

No credit cards.

91

UK1670 Alderbury Caravan & Camping Park

Southampton Road, Whaddon, Salisbury SP5 3HB (Wiltshire)

Tel: **01722 710125**. Email: **alderbury@aol.com**   **www.alanrogers.com/UK1670**

At the southern end of Alderbury/Whaddon village, this small, simple touring park is conveniently located for visiting Salisbury and the New Forest. Situated on level ground, there is a gravel access road to the 39 numbered pitches; 26 with electricity (10A) and 12 on hardstanding. The park has some mature trees for shade, as well as younger trees, shrubs and flowers. The village shop and post office, a pub serving meals and a bus stop are within easy level walking distance of the entrance. There are hourly bus services to Salisbury, Southampton and Romsey. The country lanes around the area are good for cycling and walking. Salisbury Museum, the Cathedral and its Close are all well worth a visit. There is some road noise, most noticeable at the far end of the park.

Facilities

The central toilet block is practical, but has hard use all year round and would benefit from some refurbishment. Showers in cubicles with curtain, separate unit for disabled visitors, dishwashing sink, freezer, washing machine and microwave also in a separate room. Gas supplies. American motorhomes accepted by prior arrangement. New children's pool. Music room (1/7-30/8). In high season children's entertainment and sporting activities. Off site: Fishing 1 mile. Bicycle hire 3 miles. Riding 2 miles. Golf 5 miles.

Open: All year.

Directions

From Salisbury take A36 towards Southampton and, after 3 miles (at far end of the dual-carriageway), turn left (Alderbury and Whaddon), then right, over bridge, and left for park entrance. From Southampton on A36 towards Salisbury, continue past A27 (Romsey) junction and over Pepperbox Hill. At end of a downhill straight, left on slip road marked Alderbury, park is signed. O.S.GR: SU198263. GPS: N51:02.072 W01:43.169

Charges guide

Per unit incl. 2 persons	£ 11.00 - £ 12.00
electricity (16A)	£ 14.00 - £ 15.00
extra person	£ 2.25 - £ 2.50
child (under 14 yrs)	£ 1.25 - £ 1.50
No credit cards.	

UK1730 Monkton Wyld Farm Caravan Park

Monkton Wyld Farm, Charmouth DT6 6DB (Dorset)

Tel: **01297 631131**. Email: **holidays@monktonwyld.co.uk**   **www.alanrogers.com/UK1730**

Monkton Wyld Farm is a combination of two sites, one the original site developed by Simon and Joanna Kewley, the other a Camping & Caravanning Club site developed by the Kewleys for the club. The family runs the two sites together, with the reception and the shop on the club side. Both sites have matured into attractive, comfortable, garden-like parks, with trees and flowering shrubs such as hydrangea and lavender creating a colourful, scented backdrop. Mature trees around the perimeter of the park provide shade. Plenty of space between the 180 pitches gives a feeling of spaciousness, all pitches have 16A electricity and 93 have hardstanding. A woodland walk has been created in 80 acres of the beautiful countryside surrounding the park. On site facilities are limited but there are two play areas, one at the top of the original park with good space for ball games, a climbing frame, trampoline, etc. If you fancy a holiday with a difference, try staying in a 'yurt' – the site offers one of these fully equipped, Mongolian style tents for rent. There is also a ground floor flat for rent. A select development of caravan holiday homes for private ownership is being developed to one side of the club site.

Facilities

Two well built, heated toilet blocks are fully equipped. Family room with baby changing facilities (can also be accessed by wheelchairs). Laundry area. Gas supplies. Shop (Easter - end Sept). Takeaway (May - Aug). Play areas. Caravan storage. Gate locked at 23.00. Off site: Fishing and riding 2 miles. Bicycle hire, golf and boat launching 3 miles. Shops and local pubs within 1 mile. Charmouth and Lyme Regis 3 miles (buses leave from just along the road to both towns). The X53 Jurassic Coast bus stops at the end of the lane.

Open: 14 March - 10 November.

Directions

Park is signed on A35 between Charmouth and Axminster, about 2.5 miles west of Charmouth. Turn right at Greenway Head (B3165 signed Marshwood) and park is on the left. Approach reception through the Club site entrance. Don't go to Monkton Wyld hamlet - the road is very steep. O.S.GR: SY329966. GPS: N50:45.920 W02:57.150

Charges guide

Per unit incl. 2 persons	£ 13.20 - £ 23.20
incl. electricity	£ 16.10 - £ 26.10
extra person	£ 6.60 - £ 8.60
child (6-17 yrs)	£ 2.25 - £ 2.35

UK1760 Wood Farm Caravan Park

Axminster Road, Charmouth DT6 6BT (Dorset)

Tel: **01297 560697**. Email: **holidays@woodfarm.co.uk**   **www.alanrogers.com/UK1760**

Wood Farm is an excellent, family run park, maintained to high standards and with an indoor swimming pool. On sloping, well landscaped ground, the park has splendid rural views across the Marshwood Vale. There are 196 pitches for touring units, all with 10A electricity of which 25 are for tents on a grassy, terraced field. The standard pitches are neat, level all-weather pitches with hardstanding, electricity (10A) and TV connections, and provision for awnings. Some are divided by neat, box-like leylandii hedging, some are terraced. There are 57 'premium' pitches with water, waste water and TV connections. Around 80 caravan holiday homes are in separate areas. Excellent provision is made for disabled visitors, although there is considerable up and down walking due to the terrain. Situated on the western side of Charmouth beside the A35 (some road noise may be expected), the park is only a mile or two from Lyme Regis and its beaches. This area is now part of England's first natural World Heritage site, the Jurassic Coast. Wood Farm is part of the Caravan Club's 'affiliated' scheme (non-members are very welcome). A member of the Best of British group.

Facilities

Four modern, well equipped toilet blocks can be heated and include some washbasins in cubicles, en-suite family rooms charged). Excellent facilities for disabled people. Baby unit. Laundry rooms. Motorcaravan service point. Shop by reception. Fish and chip van several times weekly. Good heated indoor pool (charged). Recreation hall. Internet access. Bridge club. Outdoor draughts. Tennis. Play field. Two coarse fishing ponds (carp, rudd, roach, tench, perch) adjacent (licence from park). Off site: Golf 1 mile. Riding 4 miles. Beaches and shops 1 and 2 miles. X53 Jurassic Coast bus to explore the coast.

Open: 13 March - 2 November.

Directions

Park is 0.5 miles west of Charmouth village with access near the roundabout at the A35 and the A3052 (Lyme Regis) junction. O.S.GR: SY356940. GPS: N50:44.530 W02:54.953

Charges guide

Per person	£ 4.50 - £ 6.50
child (5-16 yrs)	£ 2.00 - £ 3.00
pitch incl. 10A electricity	£ 5.00 - £ 10.50
'premium' pitch	£ 10.50 - £ 15.50
pup tent, dog, extra car	£ 2.00

Special senior citizens low season discounts.

UK1720 Shrubbery Caravan & Camping Park

Rousdon, Lyme Regis DT7 3XW (Dorset)

Tel: **01297 442227**. Email: **info@shrubberypark.co.uk**   **www.alanrogers.com/UK1720**

Three miles west of historic Lyme Regis in a good situation to explore the Jurassic Coast, this well cared for park has distant views of the surrounding countryside. There are 120 generous pitches with more than enough room to pitch for most units. On slightly sloping, neatly cut grass which undulates in places, they are accessed by tarmac roads and all have 10A electricity. The pitches back on to well cut shrubs or the perimeter trees. A modern reception area is welcoming and stocks basic supplies and local provisions. This is a comfortable park where couples and families with young children are welcomed. The X53 Jurassic Coastal bus which runs from Poole to Exeter passes the door. A general store and petrol station are adjacent to the site entrance. In the local area you can search for fossils, visit the donkey sanctuary or ride the miniature train at Pecorama in Beer. The Cob at Lyme Regis evokes memories of 'The French Lieutenant's Woman', whilst the unique Undercliff National Nature Reserve is popular with naturalists and walkers.

Facilities

Excellent heated toilet blocks, the newest (part of the reception building) with en-suite units, bathroom and laundry facilities. Two further blocks nearer the top of the park. Facilities for disabled visitors. Simple shop. General store at adjacent fuel station. Play area. Crazy golf. Off site: Beach 3 miles. Fishing 1 mile. Golf 3 miles. The X53 Jurrassic Coastal bus service passes the door.

Open: Mid March - end October.

Directions

From the A35 near Axminster follow the A358 south towards Seaton. At T-junction turn left on A3052 signed Rousdon. Site is on left entering the village. O.S.GR: SY298913. GPS: N50:43.040 W02:59.713

Charges guide

Per unit incl. 2 persons	£ 8.75 - £ 14.25
extra person	£ 2.00 - £ 3.00
electricity	£ 2.75

UK1740 **Golden Cap Holiday Park**

West Dorset Leisure Holidays, Seatown, Chideok, Bridport DT6 6JX (Dorset)

Tel: **01308 422139**. Email: **holidays@wdlh.co.uk**   **www.alanrogers.com/UK1740**

Golden Cap, named after the adjacent high cliff (the highest in southern England) which overlooks Lyme Bay, is only 150 yards from a shingle beach at Seatown and is surrounded by National Trust countryside and the Heritage Coastline. The park is arranged over several fields on the valley floor, sloping gently down towards the sea. It is in two main areas, having once been two parks, each separated into fields with marvellous views around and providing 108 touring pitches. All have electricity and 30 also have hardstanding with drainage and gravel awning area. An extra sloping tent area is used for peak season (torch useful), although it is a five minute walk from here to the toilet blocks and shop. There are 219 caravan holiday homes in their own areas. A coarse fishing lake has been opened and the indoor pool at Highlands End (under the same ownership, 3 miles away) is open for campers at Golden Cap on payment. Beaches are nearby, sea fishing, boat launching, riding or fossil hunting are possible in the area, plus good walks including access to the coastal path.

Facilities

The modern toilet block is of good quality with spacious shower cubicles (some with toilet and washbasin). Facilities for disabled visitors. Baby room. Two other smaller blocks around the park. Laundry room. Motorcaravan service point. Useful and well stocked shop (all season). Gas supplies. Small play area. Fishing lake (day tickets from shop). American motorhomes are not accepted. Off site: Pub with food service close. Beach 150 yds. Golf 2 miles. Bicycle hire, boat launching 3 miles.

Open: 20 March - 8 November.

Directions

Turn off A35 road at Chideock (a bigger village) 3 miles west of Bridport, at sign to Seatown opposite church. Park is less than 1 mile down narrow lane. O.S.GR: SY423919. GPS: N50:42.920 W02:49.300

Charges guide

Per unit incl. 2 persons	
and electricity	£ 13.25 - £ 22.00
extra person	£ 3.50 - £ 4.00
child (4-17 yrs)	£ 2.00 - £ 2.50
all service pitch	£ 15.25 - £ 24.00
pitch with sea view	£ 19.25 - £ 28.00

Highlands End and Golden Cap Holiday Parks

Tel: 01308 422139 Email: holidays@wdlh.co.uk
Eype, Bridport, Dorset DT6 6AR

www.wdlh.co.uk

A World Heritage Coastline on your doorstep

WEST DORSET LEISURE HOLIDAYS

UK1750 **Highlands End Holiday Park**

West Dorset Leisure Holidays, Eype, Bridport DT6 6AR (Dorset)

Tel: **01308 422139**. Email: **holidays@wdlh.co.uk**   **www.alanrogers.com/UK1750**

On slightly sloping ground with superb open views, both coastal and inland, Highlands End is quietly situated on the Dorset Heritage Coastline. With access to the coastal path, a path in front of the park runs along the cliff top and then leads down to a shingle beach a little further along. It is a good quality park with 180 caravan holiday homes, mostly privately owned, and 195 touring pitches in two areas nearest to the sea – one has to travel through the holiday homes to reach them. All have electricity and 45 also offer water, drainage, hardstanding and a gravel awning area. A further area is used for tents in high season. A modern, attractive building houses a lounge bar, good value restaurant with takeaway facility, family room and games room with some musical evenings in high season. The park's amenities also include an excellent, air-conditioned indoor heated pool, a tennis court and pitch and putt (all charged). The owners have a long term interest in the fire brigade and an historic fire engine (1936 Leyland Pump Escape) along with memorabilia make an interesting display in the bar. A well run park and a member of the Best of British group.

Facilities

Two toilet blocks near the touring sections are well maintained and can be heated. Some washbasins in cubicles with toilets, large, roomy showers. En-suite facilities for disabled visitors. Baby care room. Laundry room. Motorcaravan service point. Well stocked shop including gas supplies. Bar, restaurant and takeaway (evenings and Sunday lunch). Indoor pool (20 x 9 m), gym, sauna/steam room. Games room. 9-hole pitch and putt. Two adventure play areas. Large sloping field for ball games. Off site: Beach 0.5 miles. Bicycle hire and golf 2 miles. Fishing 3 miles.

Open: 20 March - 8 November.

Directions

Follow Bridport bypass on A35 around the town and park is signed to south (Eype turning), down narrow lane. There is a new exit road. O.S.GR: SY452914. GPS: N50:43.520 W02:46.620

Charges guide

Per unit incl. 2 persons	
and electricity	£ 13.25 - £ 22.00
all services and hardstanding	£ 15.25 - £ 24.00
extra person	£ 3.50 - £ 4.00
child (4-17 yrs)	£ 2.00 - £ 2.50
dog	£ 2.00 - £ 2.50

UK1810 Newlands Caravan Park

Charmouth DT6 6RB (Dorset)

Tel: **01297 560259**. Email: **enq@newlandsholidays.co.uk**

Holiday homes ▶ page 326

www.alanrogers.com/UK1810

Newlands is well situated on the Jurassic Coast, the first natural world heritage site in England. A family owned park, it is run with care and enthusiasm, occupying a prominent position beside the road into Charmouth village with rural views southwards to the hills across the valley. The terrain is terraced in two fields to provide over 200 well spaced places for touring units, some for seasonal units and over 80 for caravan holiday homes (some for hire). The mainly sloping tent field also has super views towards the sea and Lyme Regis. Electricity (10A) is provided on 160 pitches and 30 have hardstanding, water and drainage. Other accommodation includes smart pine lodges, apartments and motel rooms. All the facilities are located in a modern building to one side of the wide tarmac entrance. The club bar opens each evening and lunch times to suit. Family entertainment includes a children's club during school holidays with 'Dino Dan' dinosaur. An indoor pool adjoins the bar area and an adjacent outdoor pool is walled, paved and sheltered. A large play area in the field below the tent field is open dawn to dusk. This is a comfortable site for families with the beach and village within easy walking distance, with some evening and family activity.

Facilities

Two modern, heated toilet blocks (both refurbished) provide roomy showers and adjoining covered dishwashing areas and laundry rooms. Baby room. Well stocked shop (March - Nov). Licensed club bar (limited hours Nov - March). Restaurant (open 18.00-21.00. March - Nov plus Xmas/New Year) including takeaway. Outdoor heated pool (supervised in high season; the entrance is key coded). Indoor pool and jacuzzi (small charge, open all year, limited hours Nov - March). 9-pin bowling alley for hire at £5 per half hour. Play area. Off site: Beach 0.5 miles. Fishing 1 mile. Riding 3 miles. Golf 2 miles. Charmouth is known for its fossil finds and its connection with Jane Austen

Open: 1 February - 1 December (also 27 Dec. - 3 Jan).

Directions

Approaching from Bridport leave the A35 at first sign for Charmouth at start of the bypass and site almost directly on your left. O.S.GR: SY373935. GPS: N50:44.310 W02:53.390

Charges guide

Per unit incl. up to 6 persons and awning	£ 10.00 - £ 25.00
incl. electricity	£ 15.00 - £ 27.00
serviced pitch	£ 14.00 - £ 30.00
dog (max. 2)	£ 1.00 - £ 3.00
extra pup tent	£ 5.00

Only one van or tent per pitch.
Camping Cheques accepted.

UK1770 Bingham Grange Touring & Camping Park

Melplash, Bridport DT6 3TT (Dorset)

Tel: **01308 488234**. Email: **enquiries@binghamgrange.co.uk**   **www.alanrogers.com/UK1770**

Bingham Grange is an attractive, purpose built park, for adults only (formerly Bingham's Farm). In a pleasant, rural situation 2 miles from the market town of Bridport, there are views seaward towards West Bay and inland across Beaminster Downs and Pilsdon Hill. The park provides an area of individual pitches with 10A electricity and over 50 hardstandings, nicely landscaped with shrubs and trees growing between the pitches, plus an open sloping field overlooking the valley with serviced pitches and space for tents. A path is provided to the river which links with the main footpaths for Bridport (20 minutes). Local hostelries are also within reach. A limited bus service runs on the main road. The Brit Valley is an unspoilt area of West Dorset with an ancient heritage and coastal West Bay is only a couple of miles. The facilities at this park are good, having been converted from original farm buildings. The present owners are working hard to maintain and improve them.

Facilities

Well equipped toilet block, with under floor heating and a separate, fully equipped room for the less able with ramped access and 5 luxury shower rooms (also with washbasin and 4 with WC). Laundry room with microwave and freezer. Reception keeps simple supplies. Restaurant serving home cooked food seems to be very popular. Gas available. Only adults (over 18 yrs) are accepted. Off site: Sea fishing and golf 3 miles.

Open: Easter - October, Xmas and New Year.

Directions

At the roundabouts on the A35 road, on the east side of Bridport, follow signs for Beaminster on the A3066. After about 2 miles watch for site entrance on the left. O.S.GR: SY482963. GPS: N50:45.905 W02:44.455

Charges guide

Per unit incl. 2 persons and electricity (10A)	£ 12.50 - £ 26.00
tent pitch incl. 2 persons	£ 12.00 - £ 19.50
extra person	£ 5.00
awning	£ 2.00
dog	£ 2.00

UK1820 Bagwell Farm Touring Park

Chickerell, Weymouth DT3 4EA (Dorset)

Tel: **01305 782575**. Email: **ar@bagwellfarm.co.uk**   **www.alanrogers.com/UK1820**

A pleasant, large, family park, Bagwell Farm is situated between Weymouth and Abbotsbury, close to Chesil Beach. In a valley, yet with an open aspect, there are 280 numbered touring pitches, some taken up by seasonal units. There are 260 electricity connections (10A) and 9 serviced pitches. Some of the terraced pitches have beautiful views of Chesil Bank and the sea. In addition there is a traditional camping field with a campers' shelter and a barbecue, plus a rally field with electricity hook-ups. An attractive bar has been converted from farm buildings where meals are served.

Facilities

Traditional style toilet blocks are supplemented by a new heated block. Unisex bathrooms on payment. Laundry. Motorcaravan service point. Shop with off-licence. Bar and grill with takeaway (open mid/high seasons, check when booking). Games room. Play area. Pets corner. Caravan storage. Off site: Riding 1 mile. Golf, fishing and bicycle hire 5 miles. Weymouth beach 5 miles with bus service. Abbotsbury with Swannery and Tropical Gardens 4 miles. Two pubs are within walking distance.

Open: All year.

Directions

Follow the B3157 from Weymouth towards Bridport. Park is 2 miles after passing Chickerell village. The entrance is on the brow of a hill – care is needed. O.S GR: SY627816. GPS: N50:37.853 W02:31.199

Charges guide

Per unit incl. 2 persons and electricity	£ 12.50 - £ 22.00
incl. services	£ 14.50 - £ 25.00
extra person	£ 4.00 - £ 5.00
child (5-16 yrs)	£ 1.00 - £ 1.50

UK1780 Freshwater Beach Holiday Park

Holiday homes ▶ page 325

Burton Bradstock, Bridport DT6 4PT (Dorset)

Tel: **01308 897317**. Email: **enquiries@freshwaterbeach.co.uk**

www.alanrogers.com/UK1780

Family run parks for families with direct access to their own private beach are rare in Britain and this one has the added advantage of being in beautiful coastal countryside in West Dorset. The site is next to the sea and a beach of fine pebbles, sheltered from the wind by pebble banks. The River Bride edges the park and joins the sea here. Approached by a fairly steep access road, the park itself is on level, open ground. The 500 plus touring pitches, 400 with 10A electricity, are on an open, undulating grass field connected by tarmac or hardcore roads. Caravan pitches (10 x 11 m.) are marked and evenly spaced in lines. Some tent pitches are in the main field, with others well spaced on a newly terraced extra field. In separate areas there are 270 caravan holiday homes, with 40 for hire. This lively holiday park has an extensive range of facilities which include an outdoor pool, a good value licensed restaurant and newly refurbished bars with an evening entertainment programme in season. Daytime entertainment caters for all ages – don't miss the donkey derby! Footpaths lead to the thatched village of Burton Bradstock or West Bay. The overall impression is of a large, busy holiday park with a friendly reception and happy atmosphere.

Facilities

Two fully equipped toilet blocks serve the caravan fields and a third newer block is in the tent field. It is a good provision for a busy beach park. Facilities for disabled people (Radar key), and a baby care room (key system). Laundry and dishwashing sinks cope well at peak times. Launderette. Bars with wide variety of entertainment and evening shows. Licensed restaurant (weekends only in late season; closed Mondays all season). Good value supermarket and takeaway. Heated and supervised outdoor swimming and paddling pools (15/5-30/10) with lessons available. New indoor games room with pool table, music, TV, amusements and soft drinks bar. Activities for children. Two play areas. High season pony trekking (stables on site). Off site: Golf course 0.5 miles. Fishing possible from Chesil Bank. Abbotsbury Sub-Tropical Gardens and Swannery 8 miles.

Open: 17 March - 12 November.

Directions

Park is immediately west of the village of Burton Bradstock, on the Weymouth - Bridport coast road (B3157). O.S.GR: SY980898.
GPS: N50:42.300 W02:44.320

Charges guide

Per unit incl. up to 6 persons, car and awning	£ 15.00 - £ 33.00
extra person, car or boat	£ 2.00
electricity	£ 2.00
small tent incl. 2 persons	
walking or cycling	£ 4.00 - £ 16.00
dog	£ 2.50

Single sex groups are not accepted.

UK1800 East Fleet Farm Touring Park

Fleet Lane, Chickerell, Weymouth DT3 4DW (Dorset)

Tel: **01305 785768**. Email: **enquiries@eastfleet.co.uk**   **www.alanrogers.com/UK1800**

East Fleet Farm has a marvellous situation on part level, part gently sloping meadows leading to the shores of the Fleet, with views across to the famous Chesil Bank with the sea beyond. This park has been developed by the Whitfield family within the confines of their 300 acre organic arable farm in keeping with its surroundings, yet with modern amenities. It is maturing well as bushes and trees grow. The 400 pitches back onto hedges and are a comfortable size so there is no feeling of crowding. Of these, 280 are level and marked with 10/16A electricity hook-ups, 100 also having hardstanding. The terraced bar with views over the Fleet was converted from the barn and features original beams and brickwork. Part of the World Heritage Jurassic Coast, the Fleet is a lagoon renowned for its wildlife and popular with bird watchers. The busy resort of Weymouth with its safe bathing beaches and many watersports facilities is only three miles away (bicycle hire and boat launching possible). In peak season a regular bus service runs to Weymouth and the nearby Abbotsbury Swannery and Gardens.

Facilities

Two fully equipped toilet blocks include family rooms. The newest one is very smart in a Norwegian log cabin. En-suite unit for disabled visitors. Laundry room. Motorcaravan service point. Reception plus shop with basic groceries, bread, papers and gas. Bar serving food with terrace (Easter - Sept). Games room. Fenced play area (remember, elsewhere this is a working farm). Games field. Nature watch boards. Off site: Riding and golf 2 miles. Access to the Fleet and coastal path.

Open: 15 March - 31 October.

Directions

Park is signed at traffic lights on B3157 Weymouth - Bridport road, about 3 miles west of Weymouth beside Territorial Army base. Fleet Lane has been widened with plenty of passing places and speed bumps (20 mph). O.S.GR: SY639798. GPS: N50:37.156 W02:30.024

Charges guide

Per unit incl. 2 persons	£ 8.00 - £ 18.00
incl. electricity	£ 12.00 - £ 22.50
extra person	£ 1.00 - £ 4.50
child (5-12 yrs)	£ 0.25 - £ 0.50

UK1830 Sea Barn & West Fleet Holiday Farms

Fleet, Weymouth DT3 4ED (Dorset)

Tel: **01305 782218**. Email: **enquiries@seabarnfarm.couk**   **www.alanrogers.com/UK1830**

Sea Barn and West Fleet are located just half a mile apart in delightful countryside overlooking the Fleet Lagoon, Chesil Bank and Lyme Bay – all part of the Jurassic coast. Only tents, trailer tents and motorcaravans with tents and awnings are accepted. The parks share some facilities. An outdoor pool and clubhouse are at West Fleet, along with the new smart toilet block. Both have their own reception with well stocked shops. Sea Barn is quieter and popular over a longer period with spectacular views, whereas West Fleet attracts families. Both are popular with birdwatchers, walkers and fishermen. West Fleet has 250 pitches, 60 with electricity, Sea Barn the same number of pitches but only 45 electric hook ups. These are situated in grassy meadows some sloping, some protected by trees and hedging, many with wonderful views.

Facilities

Traditional simple toilet blocks, brightly painted and clean. New block at West Fleet with en-suite room for disabled visitors and two bathrooms (free). Laundry facilities at both sites. Heated pool at West Fleet (May - Sept). Bigger shop offering wider range at West Fleet which also has the Club House (evenings), in reality an open ended barn and outdoor area which works well (home produced steaks the speciality). Breakfast served. Family entertainment. Adventure play area at Fleet and smaller area at Sea Barn. Games field. Torches useful. Off site: Access to South West Coastal path. Fishing at Chesil Bank. Riding 1 mile. Golf, bicycle hire, boat launching and beach all at Weymouth 5 miles. Abbotsbury with Swannery and sub-tropical gardens 7 miles.

Open: March - October.

Directions

From Wemouth take the B3157 coast road for Bridport. Pass Chickerell and turn left at mini-roundabout to Fleet. Pass church on right and continue to top of hill. Sea Barn is to the left, West Fleet to the right. O.S.GR: SY626805. GPS: N50:37.523 W02:32.319

Charges guide

Per unit incl. 2 persons and electricity	£ 12.00 - £ 18.00
extra person	£ 3.00 - £ 4.50
child (2-15 yrs)	£ 1.00 - £ 2.50
dog (max 2)	£ 1.00 - £ 2.00

MAP 2

Southern England

Rich in maritime heritage and historical attractions, the Southern region comprises tranquil English countryside boasting picture-postcard villages, ancient cities and towns, formidable castles and grand stately homes, coupled with a beautiful coastline and lively seaside resorts.

THIS REGION INCLUDES: EAST DORSET, HAMPSHIRE, ISLE OF WIGHT, OXFORDSHIRE, BERKSHIRE AND BUCKINGHAMSHIRE

The south coast is a popular holiday destination for those looking for a beach holiday. Seaside resorts include Swanage, and Bournemouth, with its seven miles of golden sand. Also along this coastal stretch is Durdle Door, a natural arch that has been cut by the sea, and Europe's largest natural harbour at Poole Bay. Nearby, the Isle of Purbeck is not actually an island, but a promontory of low hills and heathland that juts out below Poole Harbour. Across the water is the Isle of Wight, easily reached via a short ferry trip across the Solent. Rural Southern England comprises green rolling hills and scenic wooded valleys, with numerous walking and bridle paths passing through picturesque villages with quintessential English pubs. The New Forest, well known for its wild roaming ponies, is a distinctive, peaceful retreat. The River Thames weaves its way through the Thames basin and Chilterns area, passing charming riverside villages, castles, stately homes and beautiful countryside, including that around Oxford. This city of dreaming spires has lovely scenic walks, old university buildings to explore, plus a huge selection of restaurants, pubs and shops. Along the river you can go punting, hire a rowing boat, or take one of the many river-boat trips available.

Places of interest

East Dorset: Monkey World in Wareham; village of Cerne Abbas, with Cerne Giant.

Hampshire: historic Winchester; Portsmouth, home of the Mary Rose; Southampton maritime museum.

Isle of Wight: Cowes; Sandown with Dinosaur Isle; Shipwreck Centre in Ryde; Smuggling Museum in Ventnor; Carisbrooke Castle in Newport.

Oxfordshire: Blenheim Palace; Didcot Railway Centre; historic market town of Chipping Norton.

Berkshire: Windsor, with Legoland, Windsor Castle; Reading.

Buckinghamshire: Bletchley Park near Milton Keynes; county town of Aylesbury; Beaconsfield, once home to Enid Blyton, and now housing the world's first model village.

Did you know?

The Cerne Giant is thought to have represented a pagan god dating back to pre 13th century.

Gosport is home to one of the worlds largest sundials covering 40 metres.

T.E Lawrence 'Lawrence of Arabia' was a fellow of All Souls College in Oxford and lived in Dorset.

Remains of over 20 species of dinosaur have been recovered on the Isle of Wight.

The annual Olney Pancake Race in Bucks has been running since around 1445.

Author Charles Dickens was born in Portsmouth, the house where he was born is now a museum.

Windsurfing was invented on Hayling Island by Peter Chilvers in 1958.

Southern England

Worcestershire
Warwickshire
Northamptonshire
4185 4180 2600
4190 4150 2610
4140 4130
Buckinghamshire
* CHELTENHAM
2580 2590
GLOUCESTER *
HEART 2620
AYLESBURY *
A40 A41
4170 2570 * OXFORD
Gloucestershire Oxfordshire
4100 M40
2750
A433 2700
SWINDON * SOUTHERN
A34
1680 M4 READING *
* CHIPPENHAM Berkshire
1660
BATH * 2690
1460 1700 SOUTH WEST
A346 BASINGSTOKE * M3 Surrey
Somerset 1630 Wiltshire GUILDFORD *
A303
1690 Hampshire A3
1540 A31
SALISBURY WINCHESTER * SOUTH EAST
A303 1650 1670
A350 A354 2380 West Sussex
1640
1655 2290 * SOUTHAMPTON 2320 * CHICHESTER
2360 2350 2300 2895
Dorset East 2150 LYNDHURST 2315 2885
BLANDFORD FORUM * 2340 2310 PORTSMOUTH *
2070 2060 2285 * RINGWOOD
2080 2530 RYDE
2050 2120 2250 2520 2495 2515
2030 2180 2130 2280 NEWPORT 2500 2450 2470 SANDOWN
DORCHESTER * 2100 * POOLE BOURNEMOUTH 2480 2475
2090 Isle of Wight
* WEYMOUTH 2020

Miles
0 5 10 15 20 25
0 8 16 24 32 40
Kms

RED TEXT DENOTES ALL YEAR SITE

UK2030 Wareham Forest Tourist Park

North Trigon, Wareham BH20 7NZ (Dorset)

Tel: **01929 551393**. Email: **holiday@warehamforest.co.uk**   www.alanrogers.com/UK2030

This peacefully located and spacious park, on the edge of Wareham Forest, has 200 pitches and is continually being upgraded by its enthusiastic owners, Tony and Sarah Birch. The focal point of the park is the modern reception and shop, located by the pools. Four main areas provide a wide choice of touring pitches from grass to hardstanding and luxury, all with 16A electricity. Tenters have their own choice of open field or pinewood. The site has provided direct access for walkers into the forest or the seven miles of the Sika cycle trail may be used. The lovely market town of Wareham is accessible by bike without having to use the roads. This park has an almost continental feel, with plenty of space. Even when it is busy, it is calm and peaceful in its forest setting. In low season you may be lucky enough to spot the herd of Sika deer which live in the forest. The park is well situated to explore the Dorset coast and Thomas Hardy country. A member of the Best of British Group.

Facilities

Two well maintained toilet blocks are of a good standard with some washbasins in cubicles for ladies. The block used in the winter months is centrally heated. Facilities for disabled people. Well equipped laundry rooms. Motorcaravan service point. Small licensed shop with gas. Swimming pool (60 x 20 ft), heated 20/5 - early Sept. Large adventure play area. Barrier closed 23.00-07.00. Resident wardens on site. Caravan storage. Off site: Cycle trail and walking in the forest. Bicycle hire and golf 3 miles. Fishing 5 miles. Riding 8 miles.

Open: All year.

Directions

From A31 Bere Regis, follow A35 towards Poole for 0.5 miles and site is well signed to the right for a further 1.5 miles towards Wareham.
O.S.GR: SY899903. GPS: N50:43.304 W02:09.373

Charges guide

Per person	£ 2.75 - £ 4.50
child (5-15 yrs)	£ 2.00 - £ 3.25
standard pitch incl. electricity	£ 9.50 - £ 16.25
'superior' pitch fully serviced	£ 11.50 - £ 18.25
dog	free - £ 1.50

Couples and families only.

For further details and free colour brochure write or phone:
Tel: (01929) 551393 Fax: (01929) 558321
Tony and Sarah Birch, Wareham Forest Tourist Park, North Trigon, Wareham, Dorset BH20 7NZ
email: holiday@wareham-forest.co.uk
www.wareham-forest.co.uk
Credit cards accepted.

UK2020 Ulwell Cottage Caravan Park

Ulwell, Swanage BH19 3DG (Dorset)

Tel: **01929 422823**. Email: **enq@ulwellcottagepark.co.uk**   **www.alanrogers.com/UK2020**

Nestling under the Purbeck Hills on the edge of Swanage, in the Dorset and East Devon Coast World Heritage Site, Ulwell Cottage is a family run holiday park with an indoor pool and wide range of facilities. A good proportion of the park is taken by caravan holiday homes (140), but an attractive, undulating area accessed by tarmac roads is given over to 77 numbered touring pitches interspersed with trees and shrubs. All have electricity (16A) and 8 are fully serviced. The colourful entrance area is home to the Village Inn with a courtyard adjoining the heated, supervised indoor pool complex (both open all year and open to the public) and modern reception. The hill above the touring area, Nine Barrow Down, is a Site of Special Scientific Interest for butterflies and overlooks Round Down. It is possible to walk to Corfe Castle this way. With Brownsea Island, Studland Bay, Corfe village and the Swanage Railway close by, Ulwell Cottage makes a marvellous centre for holidays.

Facilities

The modern, cheerful toilet block at the top of the site is heated and includes a unit for disabled visitors. An older block in the holiday home section has been converted to family rooms. Both are well equipped. Laundry room and baby sinks in the upper block. Well stocked shop with gas (Easter - mid Sept). Bar snacks and restaurant meals with family room. Takeaway (July/Aug). Indoor pool with lifeguard (times vary acc. to season). Playing fields and play areas. Off site: Beach 1 mile. Fishing and golf 1 mile. Bicycle hire, sailing and riding 2 miles.

Open: 1 March - 7 January.

Directions

From A351 Wareham - Swanage road, turn onto B3351 Studland road just before Corfe Castle. Follow signs to right (southeast) for Swanage and drop down to Ulwell. Park is on right about 100 yards after 40 mph sign. O.S.GR: SZ019809. GPS: N50:37.567 W01:58.267

Charges guide

Per unit incl. up to 6 persons	£ 18.50 - £ 36.70
full services incl. hardstanding	£ 21.00 - £ 39.00
extra tent, car or boat	£ 2.50

Less £2 for two persons only.
Less £1 for three persons.

For a brochure call:
01929 422823
website: **www.ulwellcottagepark.co.uk**
e-mail: **enq@ulwellcottagepark.co.uk**

Find a warm welcome at this family run park in the Isle of Purbeck, an area of outstanding natural beauty and breath taking World Heritage coastline. Nearby sandy beaches, coastal walks and golf.
- **77 Touring Pitches** with hard standings, electric, water and drainage hook-ups and views of the surrounding hills
- **Superb meals at the 'Village Inn'** ● **Heated Indoor Pool** ● **General Shop**

UK2050 Rowlands Wait Touring Park

Rye Hill, Bere Regis BH20 7LP (Dorset)

Tel: **01929 472727**. Email: **enquiries@rowlandswait.co.uk**   **www.alanrogers.com/UK2050**

Rowlands Wait is in a designated area of outstanding natural beauty (AONB) and part of the park is officially of special scientific interest (SSSI). The top of the park, edged by mature woods (full of bluebells in spring) is a haven for tents (and squirrels) with marvellous views and provides 30 places in three descending fields. The rest of the park is a little more formal – and nearer to the central toilet block. Most pitches back on to hedging or trees and they are generally level. There are 71 pitches in total with 23 seasonal pitches. Many walks are possible from the park with information leaflets available from reception. It is also possible to walk into the village of Bere Regis. The owners Ivor and Stevie Cargill are keen to welcome nature lovers who enjoy bird watching, walking, and cycling. Sightings of various owls and two pairs of buzzards have been reported on the park. The park is a member of the Countryside Discovery group and open in winter by arrangement. Rallies welcome.

Facilities

The refurbished toilet block is fully equipped. New family room and facilities for disabled visitors. Laundry room. Recycling bins. Shop (reduced hours in low season) providing basic essentials and a freezer for ice packs. Play area. Games room. Bicycle hire arranged. Torch useful. Off site: Village (10 minute walk) with shops, two pubs, etc. plus a bus service for Dorchester and Poole. Golf 3 miles. Fishing 5 miles. Riding 9 miles.

Open: 16 March - 31 October, winter by arrangement.

Directions

Park is about 0.5 miles south of Bere Regis on the road to Wool. O.S.GR: SY842933. GPS: N50:44.621 W02:13.443

Charges guide

Per unit incl. 2 persons	£ 11.00 - £ 14.00
incl. electricity	£ 13.00 - £ 16.00
extra person	£ 3.00 - £ 4.00
child (under 16 yrs)	£ 1.50 - £ 2.50
dog	£ 1.00 - £ 2.00

UK2070 The Inside Park Touring Caravan & Camping Park

Blandford Forum DT11 9AD (Dorset)

Tel: **01258 453719**. Email: **inspark@aol.com**   www.alanrogers.com/UK2070

The Inside Park is set in the grounds of an 18th century country house that burned down in 1941. Family owned and carefully managed alongside an arable farm, this is a must for those interested in local history or arboriculture and it is a haven for wildlife and birds. The nine acre camping field, a little distant, lies in a sheltered, gently sloping dry valley containing superb tree specimens – notably cedars, with walnuts in one part – and a dog graveyard dating back to the early 1700s under a large Cedar of Lebanon. In total there are 125 spacious pitches, 90 with electricity (10A) and some in wooded glades. The six acres adjoining are the old pleasure gardens of the house. The reception/toilet block and games room block are respectively the coach house and stables of the old house. No vehicle access to the park is allowed after 22.30 (there is a separate late arrivals area and car park). Extensive, marked walks are provided through the farmland and a guide is available in the shop.

Facilities

The toilet block provides some washbasins in cubicles, comfortably sized showers and facilities for disabled visitors or mothers and babies. Laundry room. Shop with basics, gas and camping provisions. Spacious games room. Safe-based adventure play area. Day kennelling facilities for dogs. Mountain bike course. Winter caravan storage. Off site: Blandford leisure and swimming centre (temporary membership possible) 2 miles. Fishing and riding 2 miles. Golf 3 miles. Beach 25 miles.

Open: Easter - 31 October.

Directions

Park is about 2 miles southwest of Blandford and is signed from roundabout junction of the A354 and A350 roads. O.S.GR: ST864045.
GPS: N50:50.480 W02:11.709

Charges guide

Per person	£ 3.00 - £ 3.95
child (5-15 yrs)	free - £ 1.35
pitch	£ 6.00 - £ 7.85
electricity	£ 2.90
dog	£ 0.60 - £ 1.00

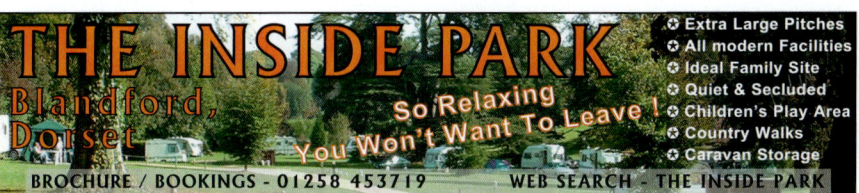

THE INSIDE PARK
Blandford, Dorset
So Relaxing You Won't Want To Leave !
⊕ Extra Large Pitches
⊕ All modern Facilities
⊕ Ideal Family Site
⊕ Quiet & Secluded
⊕ Children's Play Area
⊕ Country Walks
⊕ Caravan Storage
BROCHURE / BOOKINGS - 01258 453719   WEB SEARCH - THE INSIDE PARK

UK2090 Whitemead Caravan Park

East Burton Road, Wool BH20 6HG (Dorset)

Tel: **01929 462241**. Email: **whitemeadcp@aol.com**   www.alanrogers.com/UK2090

The Church family continue to make improvements to this attractive little park which is within walking distance of the village of Wool, between Dorchester and Wareham. Very natural and with open views over the Frome Valley water meadows, it provides 95 numbered pitches on flat grass sloping gently north and is orchard-like in parts. The 76 touring pitches are well spaced, mostly backing onto hedges or fences and all have electrical connections (10A). All roads are now tarmac. There are no caravan holiday homes but 20 pitches are seasonal. There may be some rail noise but this is not intrusive at night. The park is 4.5 miles from the nearest beach at Lulworth and is handily placed for many attractions in this part of Dorset (the railway station and a main route bus stop is within 400 yards of the park).

Facilities

The toilet block provides showers, private cubicles, a baby room, dishwashing and laundry sinks, washing machine and dryer. Shop (limited hours) with off-licence, gas supplies and information room/library. Takeaway with breakfasts at weekends (low season Tuesday, Friday and Sunday, otherwise all 15/3-31/10). Games room with pool table and darts. Playground. Caravan storage. WiFi in games room. Off site: The Ship Inn is 300 yards. Riding, fishing and golf 3 miles. Bicycle hire 2 miles.

Open: 15 March - 31 October.

Directions

Turn off main A352 on eastern edge of Wool, just north of level crossing, onto East Burton road. Site is 350 yards. on right. O.S.GR: SY841871.
GPS: N50:40.898 W02:13.557

Charges guide

Per unit with 2 persons and electricity	£ 11.25 - £ 17.50
extra person (over 5 yrs)	£ 3.00
dog	£ 0.75 - £ 2.00

No credit cards.

UK2080 Merley Court Touring Park

Merley, Wimborne BH21 3AA (Dorset)

Tel: **01590 648331**. Email: **holidays@shorefield.co.uk**   **www.alanrogers.com/UK2080**

Merley Court is the latest addition to the Shorefield Group and all aspects of this well planned, attractively landscaped park are constantly maintained to the highest of standards. Tarmac roads connect 179 touring pitches, 162 of which have 16A electricity, on neat lawns or one of the many hardstandings. This provision includes 20 serviced pitches with water, waste disposal and satellite TV. The entire park is interspersed with a variety of shrubs, plants and the odd ornamental urn. Some attractive tent pitches are to be found in a small wooded valley. A well furnished club complex provides a lounge bar where meals are available. There is also a snack bar, takeaway, large games room with pool tables and a family room leading onto a spacious sheltered patio. This in turn leads to a paved and walled swimming pool area. There are woodland walks (including dog walks) directly from the site connecting to the disused railway line where nature has returned with an abundance of wild flowers, which in turn leads to Delph woods with designated nature trails. A member of the Best of British group.

Facilities

Three heated toilet blocks, two with showers, are of good quality. Separate facilities for disabled visitors and babies. Dishwashing and laundry facilities. Motorcaravan service point. Shop with caravan accessories and gas. Café and takeaway. Bar with food (limited hours in low and mid season). Outdoor pool (30 x 20 ft) with children's section open mid May - mid Sept. Tennis and short tennis courts. Play area. Games room with pool tables. Tourist information. Barrier card £5 deposit. Off site: Fishing, riding and golf all within 2 miles. Bicycle hire 5 miles. Poole 5 miles, Bournemouth 8 miles. Tower Park leisure and entertainment centre is nearby, Kingston Lacy House, Knoll Gardens, Brownsea Island and the Moors Valley Country Park are also near.

Open: All year excl. 2 January - 6 February.

Directions

Site clearly signed at the junction of the A31 and A349 roads (roundabout) on the Wimborne bypass. O.S.GR: ST008984. GPS: N50:47.144 W01:59.115

Charges 2009

Per pitch incl. 2 persons	
and electricity	£ 13.50 - £ 35.00
all service pitch	£ 19.00 - £ 40.00
extra person	£ 4.00

No extra pup tent as well as awning.

UK2060 Wilksworth Farm Caravan Park

Cranborne Road, Wimborne BH21 4HW (Dorset)

Tel: **01202 885467**. Email: **rayandwendy@wilksworthfarmcaravanpark.co.uk**   **www.alanrogers.com/UK2060**

First opened by the parents of the present owners, the careful and sympathetic development of Wilksworth continues with the aim of providing all the 'mod cons' yet remain in keeping with the environment. It is a spacious, quiet park, well suited for families with a heated outdoor pool which has been totally refurbished in a beautiful Spanish style. The rural situation is lovely, just outside Wimborne and around 12 miles from the beaches between Poole and Bournemouth. The park takes 65 caravans and 25 tents mainly on grass. All pitches have electricity and 10 also have water and drainage. There are 77 privately owned caravan holiday homes in a separate area. With a duck pond at the entrance, the park has been well planned on good quality ground with fairly level grass and some views. Facilities are in attractively converted farm buildings designed to be in keeping with the listed status of the other buildings. A heated swimming pool and a tennis court are on the far side of the touring area.

Facilities

The central, well equipped toilet block has under-floor heating, washbasins in cubicles, a family bathroom and a shower/bath for children with baby changing. Facilities for disabled visitors. Laundry room. Modern reception and shop (basics only, limited hours, Easter - 30 Sept). Gas supplies. Freezer for ice packs. Attractive coffee shop serving simple meals with takeaway service (weekends and B.Hs. only outside the main season). Heated 40 x 20 ft. swimming pool (unsupervised, but walled and gated, May-Sept). Small paddling pool with slide. Adventure play area. BMX track. Golf practice net. Two tennis courts, one full and one short size. Games room. Winter caravan storage. Off site: Golf, fishing and riding 3 miles. Kingston Lacy (NT) 3 miles and Wimborne town centre (with its Minster) 1 mile. Beach 12 miles.

Open: Easter/1 April - 30 October.

Directions

Park is 1 mile north of Wimborne, west off the B3078 road to Cranborne. O.S.GR: SU010019. GPS: N50:49.002 W01:59.424

Charges guide

Per unit incl. 2 persons	
and electricity	£ 14.00 - £ 24.00
extra person	£ 3.00
child	£ 2.00
full services	£ 2.00
dog	£ 1.00

No credit cards.

UK2100 Sandford Caravan Park

Organford Road, Holton Heath, Poole BH16 6JZ (Dorset)

Tel: **01202 631600**. Email: **enquiries@parkdeanholidays.co.uk**   www.alanrogers.com/UK2100

Sandford Park is an 'all singing, all dancing' park with a wide range of facilities near the popular coastal areas of Dorset. It has a large permanent section with caravan holiday homes and lodges. However, the touring section is in an attractive secluded area and can accommodate around 354 units of any type. The pitches are mainly on level grass, either with mature evergreen hedging, or in a more open style area broken up by shrubs. All have 10A electrical connections and 13 are fully serviced. Early booking is advisable. Sandford is a large, very busy holiday park with a wide range of entertainment. The central complex, the Plaza, contains a variety of bars and restaurants (book in busy periods) and a large hall with stage and dance floor. The daily entertainment programme caters for different tastes and age groups. There is provision for simple hot meals and takeaways elsewhere on site in peak season. The 25 m. heated and supervised outdoor swimming pool and a very large play pool, ideal for children, are attractively situated with a snack bar and terraced area close by. There is also an impressive, heated and supervised indoor pool.

Facilities

Three toilet blocks also include facilities for disabled visitors and babies. Large launderette. Ladies' hairdresser. Bars, restaurants. TV lounges. Outdoor swimming pool (May - Sept) and indoor pool. Large supermarket and other shops, including well stocked camping accessory shop. Supervised soft indoor play area (April - Oct and Christmas). Playground. Tennis court. Multisport court. Two short mat bowling greens (outdoor). Crazy golf. Bicycle hire. One dog walk. Off site: Beach 9 miles. Golf 3 miles.

Open: March - November.

Directions

From the A351 (Wareham - Poole) road turn west at traffic lights in Holton Heath (signed Organford and Sandford Park). Park is on left after about 50 yards. Touring pitch reception is at the top of the park. O.S.GR: SY940913. GPS: N50:43.204 W02:05.132

Charges guide

Per pitch incl. up to 6 persons	£ 13.00 - £ 31.00
incl. electricity	£ 16.00 - £ 34.00
serviced pitch	£ 18.00 - £ 36.00
dog (max 2)	£ 3.00 - £ 5.00

UK2130 Grove Farm Meadow Holiday Park

Meadowbank Holidays, Stour Way, Christchurch BH23 2PQ (Dorset)

Tel: **01202 483597**. Email: **enquiries@meadowbank-holidays.co.uk**   www.alanrogers.com/UK2130

Grove Farm Meadow is a quiet, traditional park with caravan holiday homes and a small provision for touring units. The grass flood bank which separates the River Stour from this park provides an attractive pathway. The river bank has been kept natural and is well populated by a range of water birds. It is popular with bird watchers and there is fishing in the river. There are just under 200 caravan holiday homes (75 for hire), sited in regular rows. For touring units there are 41 level pitches, all clearly numbered with electricity (10A), backing on to fencing or hedging and accessed by tarmac roads. There are 21 fully serviced with hardstanding, shingle base for awnings and chemical disposal point (the other grass pitches share service points). The impressive, modern reception has a good collection of tourist information. The Littledown Centre, said to be the south coast's premier leisure facility is nearby. Bournemouth is 10 minutes by car, Christchurch 5 minutes.

Facilities

The well kept toilet block provides a bathroom for each sex (50p). Separate toilet and washbasin with ramped access for disabled visitors. Baby room. Spin dryer, iron and board and washing lines provided. Launderette near reception. Well stocked shop (limited hours in low season). Games room with pool table and electronic games. Adventure play area beside the river bank. Fishing (permits from reception). Dogs or other pets are not accepted. Off site: Golf 0.5 miles. Large supermarket 1.5 miles. Beach, boat launching and sailing 2 miles. St Catherine's nature reserve.

Open: 1 March - 31 October.

Directions

From A388 Ringwood - Bournemouth road take B3073 for Christchurch. Turn right at the first roundabout and Stour Way is the third road on the right. O.S.GR: SZ136946. GPS: N50:45.027 W01:48.524

Charges guide

Per 'luxury' pitch incl. 2 persons and electricity	£ 14.00 - £ 27.00
large pitch	£ 11.50 - £ 23.00
standard pitch (no awnings)	£ 8.50 - £ 17.50
extra person over 5 yrs	£ 1.00 - £ 2.00
extra car or boat	£ 1.00 - £ 2.00

UK2120 South Lytchett Manor Caravan & Camping Park

Dorset Road, Lytchett Minster, Poole BH16 6JB (Dorset)

Tel: **01202 622577**. Email: **info@southlytchettmanor.co.uk**　　　**www.alanrogers.com/UK2120**

Close to Poole, the Isle of Purbeck and the Jurassic Coast, Lytchett Manor is a quiet, attractive, rural campsite with views over the surrounding countryside. There are 150 pitches laid out in fields at either end of the site – one for tents, one for tents or caravans – and a long main drive connecting them. It has been extensively renovated by the new owners, Joanne and David Bridgen, with new hardstandings, toilet blocks and electricity system. There are 25 hardstandings (some used by seasonal units). All pitches have electricity (10A) and 78 have TV aerial connections. Water points are plentiful and the three heated toilet blocks have facilities for all needs. This park will suit those who are looking for a quiet holiday or to visit the many attractions in this part of Dorset. Although there are no such facilities on site, there are two pubs within a mile and a local craft centre (300 yards) has some evening events.

Facilities

Three modern, heated toilet blocks include private cabins, en-suite facilities for disabled people, family rooms and dishwashing sinks. Motorcaravan service point. Laundry. Shop in reception for basics, off licence and gas. Takeaway (B.Hs and July/Aug). Games room with TV. Internet. Large grass playing field. New play area. Bicycle hire. Off site: Shops, pubs, ATM 1 mile. Beach and sailing 2 miles. Golf, fishing and riding 3 miles. Ferry port 3 miles.

Open: 24 March - 12 October.

Directions

At the roundabout at the end of the dual carriageway on the A35 to the west of Poole turn north on B3067 to Lytchett Minster. Go through village and site is on the left half a mile past the church, through imposing wrought iron gates. O.S.GR: SY966934. GPS: N50:44.375 W02:03.325

Charges guide

Per person	£ 5.00 - £ 7.00
child (3-14 yrs)	£ 2.50 - £ 3.50
pitch	£ 4.50 - £ 6.00
incl. electricity	£ 6.50 - £ 8.00

UK2150 Woolsbridge Manor Farm Caravan Park

Three Legged Cross, Wimborne BH21 6RA (Dorset)

Tel: **01202 826369**. Email: **woolsbridge@btconnect.com**　　　**www.alanrogers.com/UK2150**

Close to the Moors Valley Country Park, this friendly, family run site is within easy reach of the south coast, the resorts of Christchurch, Bournemouth and Poole, and the ancient market town of Wimborne Minster. Entry is restricted to couples and families. The 7 acre camping meadow has 101 large level pitches (51 seasonal) all with electricity (16A) and arranged on either side of a central tarmac road. Reception has a well stocked shop and a good selection of tourist information. The site is part of a working beef cattle farm, so parents should be aware of moving farm machinery and tractors. A cycleway/footpath crosses the fields to the Country Park – very safe for children – where amenities include coarse fishing, golf, steam railway, bicycle hire, a tea room and a country shop.

Facilities

The neat, refurbished toilet block is well maintained and has ample facilities. Four newly built family rooms each with shower, WC, basin, handrails and ramped access provided for disabled people, babies and toddlers. Washing machine, dryer and ironing facilities. Shop. Gas. Playground. Fishing. American RVs accepted, advance booking appreciated. Torches useful. Caravan storage. Off site: Old Barn Farm inn and restaurant 400 m. Riding, golf and bicycle hire 0.5 miles. Boat launching and sailing 5 miles.

Open: Easter - 31 October.

Directions

From Ringwood take A31 southwest to the large Ashley Heath roundabout (Junction of A31 and A338 to Bournemouth). Take left hand slip road up to roundabout, avoiding underpass, and turn right (north) onto unclassified road signed for Three Legged Cross, Ashley Heath and Moors Valley Country Park. Follow signs to Country Park (2 miles), pass the park entrance on right, continue for another 400 yards to site (well signed on right). O.S.GR: SZ 099052. GPS: N50:50.615 W01:51.450

Charges guide

Per unit incl. 2 persons and electricity	£ 15.50 - £ 20.50
extra person	£ 5.50 - £ 6.00
child (under 16 yrs)	£ 3.50 - £ 4.00
dog	£ 1.50 - £ 2.00

UK2180 Beacon Hill Touring Park

Blandford Road North, Poole BH16 6AB (Dorset)

Tel: **01202 631631**. Email: **bookings@beaconhilltouringpark.co.uk**   **www.alanrogers.com/UK2180**

Beacon Hill is located in a marvellous, natural environment of partly wooded heathland, with certain areas of designated habitation for protected species such as sand lizards and the Dartford Warbler, but there is also easy access to main routes. Wildlife ponds encourage dragonflies and other species but fishing is also possible. Conservation is obviously important in such a special area but one can ramble at will over the 30 acres, with the hilltop walk a must. Grassy open spaces provide 170 pitches, 151 with 10A electricity, on sandy grass which is sometimes uneven. Of these, 50 are for tents only and a few are seasonal. The undulating nature of land and the trees allows for discrete areas to be allocated for varying needs – for young families near the play area, families with teenagers close to the bar/games room, those with dogs near the dog walking area, and for young people further away. The park provides a wide range of facilities, including an open air swimming pool and a tennis court. It is well situated for beaches, Poole harbour and ferries for France or the Channel Isles.

Facilities

Two fully equipped toilet blocks include facilities for disabled people. Laundry facilities. Well stocked shop at reception. Coffee bar and takeaway (main season). Bar (July - Aug, B.Hs, half-terms). Heated swimming pool (mid May - mid Sept). All weather tennis court (charges). Adventure play areas including a hideaway. Games room with pool tables and amusement machines. TV room. Internet (WiFi). Fishing (charges). Off site: Poole harbour and ferries 3 miles. Riding 2 miles. Bicycle hire 3 miles. Brownsea Island, Studland beach with Sandbanks ferry and the Purbecks near.

Open: 17 March - end September.

Directions

Park is about 3 miles north of Poole. Take the A350 (towards Blandford) at roundabout where A350 joins A35. Park signed to the right (northeast) after about 400 yards. O.S.GR: SY977945. GPS: N50:44.972 W02:02.068

Charges guide

Per person	£ 3.50 - £ 6.25
child (under 16 yrs)	£ 2.50
pitch	£ 3.00 - £ 18.00
awning	£ 1.00 - £ 2.50
electricity	£ 2.00

UK2250 Hoburne Bashley

Sway Road, New Milton BH25 5QR (Hampshire)

Tel: **01425 612340**. Email: **enquiries@hoburne.co.uk**   **www.alanrogers.com/UK2250**

This is an attractive, well run park with many holiday homes (380), but it also has a very sizeable tourist section and can take 300 touring units. However, tents, trailer tents and pup tents are not accepted. Spread over three flat meadows the numbered touring pitches are large, divided by hedging or low fencing, and include 20 'super' pitches. These are of mixed grass and hardstanding with electricity. Set in pleasant park-like surroundings not far from beaches, Bournemouth and the New Forest, the park has a good clubhouse with excellent facilities. This overlooks an 18 m. circular outdoor swimming pool and an 18 m. paddling pool, a sensible size and great fun with its geysers, clown and beach effect.

Facilities

Three well constructed toilet blocks, one central to each area, are fully tiled with modern fittings and washbasins in cabins. Showers are pre-set (no dividers, but shower heads are set fairly low). Baby changing facilities. Launderette. Clubhouse with bars, restaurant and takeaway (1/3-30/10). 10-pin bowling. TV room. Video arcade and games room with snooker tables, plus two pool tables, table tennis and darts in other rooms. Children's club. Shop (1/3-30/10). Indoor pool. Outdoor pools (June - mid Sept). Crazy golf. Golf course (9-hole, par 3). Tennis courts (3). Adventure play area. Soft ball play area. Only one dog or pet permitted per unit. American motorhomes accepted. Off site: Fishing and riding 1 mile. Mudeford beach 8 miles.

Open: 10 February - 30 October plus weekends.

Directions

Park is on the B3055 about 400 yards east of the crossroads with the B3058 in Bashley village. O.S.GR: SZ246969. GPS: N50:46.360 W01:39.011

Charges guide

Per unit incl.up to 6 persons and electricity	£ 13.00 - £ 36.50
multi-service pitch	£ 15.00 - £ 38.50
2 car pitch	£ 15.00 - £ 38.50
pet (1 only)	£ 2.00
Weekend breaks available.	

UK2280 Lytton Lawn Touring Park

Lymore Lane, Milford-on-Sea SO41 0TX (Hampshire)

Tel: **01590 648331**. Email: **holidays@shorefield.co.uk**   www.alanrogers.com/UK2280

Lytton Lawn is the touring arm of Shorefield Country Park, a holiday home park and leisure centre. Set in eight acres, Lytton Lawn provides 135 marked pitches. These include 53 'premier' pitches (hardstanding, 16A electricity, pitch light, water and waste water outlet) in a grassy, hedged area – this section with its heated toilet block is open for a longer season. The rest of the pitches, all with electricity, are in the adjoining, but separate, gently sloping field, edged with mature trees and hedges and with a further toilet block. The new larger reception and well stocked shop make this a good, comfortable, self-sufficient site. Visitors to Lytton Lawn are entitled to use the comprehensive leisure facilities at Shorefield itself (2.5 miles away). These include a very attractive indoor pool, solarium, sauna and spa, fitness classes and treatments, all weather tennis courts, outdoor pools, restaurant facilities including a bistro (Easter - 2 Nov), and entertainment and activity programmes. The comprehensive facilities at Shorefield are of a very good standard and are mostly free (extra charges are made for certain activities). These include the 'Reflections' day spa and 'Expressions' hair salon.

Facilities

Two purpose built, modern toilet blocks are tiled and well fitted. Dishwashing, washing machine and dryer in each block. Baby changing facilities in one block and facilities for disabled visitors (Radar key). Motorcaravan service point. New shop (all year). Small fenced play area and hedged field with goal posts. Only one dog per pitch is accepted. Off site: Village pub 10 minutes walk. Golf, riding, coarse fishing (all within 3 miles), sailing, windsurfing and boat launching facilities (1.5 miles). The New Forest, Isle of Wight, Bournemouth, Southampton and the beach at Milford on Sea are near.

Open: All year excl. 2 January - 6 Feburary.

Directions

From M27 follow signs for Lyndhurst and Lymington on A337. Continue towards New Milton and Lytton Lawn is signed at Everton; Shorefield is signed at Downton. O.S.GR: SZ293937. GPS: N50:44.098 W01:37.082

Charges 2009

Per pitch incl. all persons and electricity	£ 11.00 - £ 34.00
premier pitch incl. water, drainage and TV connection	£ 13.50 - £ 37.50
dog (1 only)	£ 1.50 - £ 3.00

Less 40% Monday - Thursday in certain periods. Min. weekly charge at busy times.

See advertisement on page 105

UK2285 Forest Edge Touring Park

229 Ringwood Road, Saint Leonards, Ringwood BH242SD (Hampshire)

Tel: **01590 648331**. Email: **holidays@shorefield.co.uk**   www.alanrogers.com/UK2285

This popular family park is the latest addition to the Shorefield Group. Offering 40 pitches for touring holidays, it is complemented by the leisure facilities available at Oakdene Forest Park (which no longer takes touring units). There is easy access to the level, marked pitches, each with 16A electricity hook-ups. In addition, there are pitches for 20 seasonal units and 140 caravan holiday homes. The cheerful, flowery reception and well stocked shop help create a friendly and relaxed atmosphere. Picnic tables are dotted about the park giving it a country feel. A short walk through Hurn Forest (less than a mile) leads to Oakdene and its new clubhouse and entertainment centre. Visitors at Forest Edge may use the bar, restaurant, large pools, games room and other free entertainment which is ideal for families not wishing to travel too far. The location of Forest Edge is ideal for visiting Bournemouth (beaches, shops and shows), the New Forest and all the attractions of Dorset.

Facilities

The toilet block provides clean but fairly standard facilities. Unit for disabled visitors. Baby area. These facilities may be under pressure in high season. Laundry in a separate room near the play area. Gas supplies. Shop with off-licence. Heated outdoor swimming pool (July - Sept). Off site: Riding 1 mile. Fishing 2 miles. Golf 3 miles. Beach 5 miles.

Open: All year excl. 2 January - 1 February.

Directions

Take the A31 westbound from Ringwood. After 3 miles and two roundabouts, turn left at the second roundabout into Boundary Lane (before you get to Oakdene). Site is signed. O.S.GR: SU105024. GPS: N50:49.282 W01:50.993

Charges 2009

Per unit incl. 6 persons	£ 9.50 - £ 28.00
incl. electricity	£ 11.50 - £ 34.00
dog	£ 1.50 - £ 3.00

See advertisement on page 105

UK2340 Shamba Holidays

Ringwood Road, Saint Leonards, Ringwood BH24 2SB (Hampshire)

Tel: **01202 873302**. Email: **enquiries@shambaholidays.co.uk**   www.alanrogers.com/UK2340

Shamba is a family run, very modern park, although the aim remains to create a relaxed, pleasant atmosphere. There are 150 pitches, most of which are used for touring units, 45 are on a seasonal basis. Surrounded by trees, the camping area is on flat, open grass with electricity (10/16A) available on all pitches. A Scandinavian style building forms the focal point and here you will find reception, a bar/restaurant, takeaway and a shop. The indoor swimming pool has walls and a roof which can be opened in good weather. The park's location is excellent for a short stop-over but well worth a longer stay for a family holiday. Bournemouth with its shops and beaches is 8 miles, while the delights of the New Forest and Dorset are within easy reach.

Facilities

Sanitary facilities with under-floor heating include modern showers, washbasins and toilets and family changing rooms. Baby rooms with bath and facilities for disabled visitors. Launderette. Motorcaravan service point. Bar with meals and takeaway. Indoor pool (12 x 6 m, heated) and children's pool. Large play area. Amusements room. Adjacent field for dog walking and football/sports pitch. Off site: Riding 1 mile. Golf 2 miles. Fishing and bicycle hire 2.5 miles. Ringwood 2.5 miles. Moors Valley Country Park 1 mile. Beach 8 miles.

Open: 1 March - 31 October.

Directions

Take the A31 westbound from Ringwood, after 3 miles, at second roundabout, turn back on yourself and after only 20 m. turn left at the park sign. O.S.GR: SU104026. GPS: N50:49.504 W01:51.187

Charges guide

Per pitch incl. 2 persons and electricity	£ 16.00 - £ 26.00
extra person	£ 3.25
dog	£ 2.25
child (6-11 yrs)	£ 2.25

Minimum advance booking policy applies at peak periods.

Camping Cheques accepted.

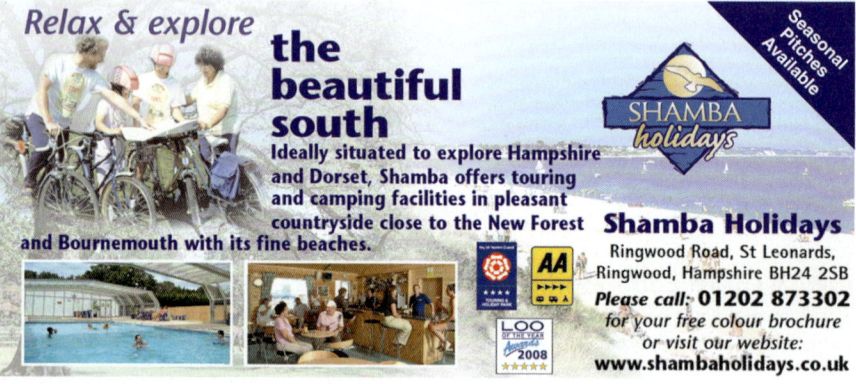

UK2300 Forest Holidays Ashurst

Forest Holidays, Lyndhurst Road, Ashurst SO40 7AR (Hampshire)

Tel: **02380 292097**. Email: **info@forestholidays.co.uk**   www.alanrogers.com/UK2300

An attractive Forest Holidays site on the fringe of the New Forest, Ashurst is set in a mixture of oak woodland and grass heathland which is open to the grazing animals of the Forest. Smaller than the Hollands Wood site (23 acres), it provides 280 pitches, 180 of which have been gravelled to provide semi-hardstanding; otherwise you pitch where you like, applying the 20 ft. rule on ground that can be uneven. There are no electricity connections. Some noise must be expected from the adjacent railway line – the station is just five minutes walk away.

Facilities

The single central toilet block has been refurbished and provides everything necessary, including hairdryers, a well equipped unit for visitors with disabilities (key required) and a good laundry room. It could be under pressure when the site is full in the main season. Motorcaravan service point. Bread and milk to order. Dogs are not accepted. A torch is useful. Off site: Local garage sells gas. Nearby pub by footpath. Shops and local buses within a five minute walk. Guided forest walks. Golf 4 miles.

Open: March - September.

Directions

Site is 2 miles east of Lyndhurst, set back from the A35 Southampton - Bournemouth road, 5 miles southwest of Southampton. O.S.GR: SU344099. GPS: N50:53.286 W01:31.708

Charges guide

Per unit incl. 2 persons	£ 9.40 - £ 19.70
extra person	£ 3.80 - £ 7.90
child	£ 1.90 - £ 4.00

Less 20% all year for disabled guests and outside 7/7-28/8 for senior citizens.

UK2290 Sandy Balls Holiday Centre

Godshill, Fordingbridge SP6 2JZ (Hampshire)

Tel: 0845 2702248. Email: post@sandy-balls.co.uk

www.alanrogers.com/UK2290

Sandy Balls sits high above the sweep of the Avon river near Fordingbridge, amidst woodland which is protected as a nature reserve. It well deserves the entry it has maintained in these guides for over 30 years and continues to improve and develop, with a multi-million pound improvement project currently well under way. This very well run park covers an extensive area of woodland and fields, providing 148 lodges and caravan holiday homes (many for rent), some tent areas with unmarked pitches, and 233 serviced pitches for touring units. These pitches are separated by hedges on part-hardstanding, part-grass, with 16A electricity and TV connections. In winter only 50 pitches are available. The central village area with all the amenities is designed to blend with the forest surroundings. The centre is now a traffic-free, pedestrianised 'piazza' from which all facilities can be easily accessed. New facilities include a drive-through check-in system and Guest Services centre, as well as a Bistro. The Leisure Club provides for all the family and includes a solar heated outdoor pool, a large indoor pool with exercise facilities and Tempus, a mind and body treatment centre with qualified therapists. Here too are bars, restaurants and shops, plus high season entertainment and varied activities. A woodland leisure trail allows wild animals and birds to be observed in their natural surroundings. The attractions of the New Forest are nearby. A member of the Best of British Group.

Facilities

Three modern toilet blocks have under-floor heating and washbasins in cubicles. One 'portacabin' style unit remains as an overflow in the tent field. Baby facilities. Toilets for disabled visitors. Excellent central launderette. Motorcaravan services. Supermarket with bakery. Takeaway. Restaurants, bars and family room. Entertainment (high season). Outdoor pool (25/5-30/8). Indoor pool (66 x 30 ft). Well equipped gym, jacuzzi, steam room, sauna and solarium. Tempus therapy centre. Games room. Adventure playground and play areas. Clay modelling and story telling. River fishing (permit). Riding. Bicycle hire. Archery. Orienteering. Dogs only allowed on certain fields. Off site: Golf 6 miles. Beach 20 miles.

Open: All year.

Directions

Park is northwest off the B3078 (Fordingbridge - Cadnam) road just west of Godshill village, and about 1.5 miles east of Fordingbridge. O.S.GR: SU168147. GPS: N50:55.816 W01:45.612

Charges guide

Per person	free - £ 3.50
child (12-17 yrs)	free - £ 2.00
child (3-11 yrs)	free - £ 1.50
pitch	£ 15.00 - £ 25.00
dog	free - £ 3.00

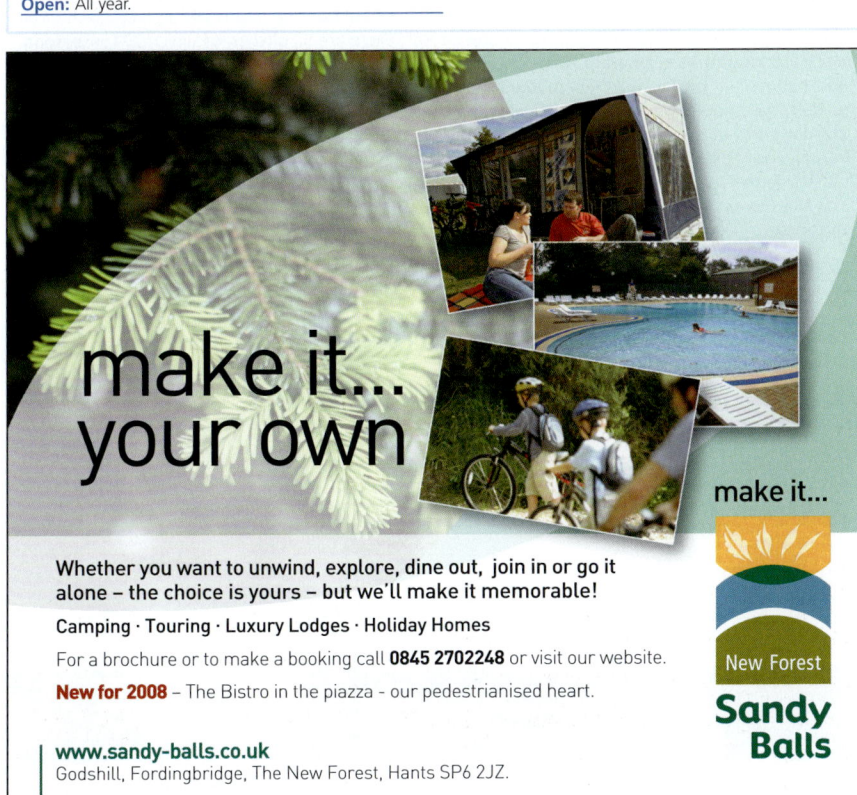

make it...
your own

Whether you want to unwind, explore, dine out, join in or go it alone – the choice is yours – but we'll make it memorable!

Camping · Touring · Luxury Lodges · Holiday Homes

For a brochure or to make a booking call **0845 2702248** or visit our website.

New for 2008 – The Bistro in the piazza - our pedestrianised heart.

make it...

New Forest

Sandy Balls

www.sandy-balls.co.uk
Godshill, Fordingbridge, The New Forest, Hants SP6 2JZ.

111

UK2360 Hill Cottage Farm Camping & Caravan Park

Sandleheath Road, Alderholt, Fordingbridge SP6 3EG (Hampshire)

Tel: **01425 650513**. Email: **hillcottagefarmcaravansite@supanet.com**　　www.alanrogers.com/UK2360

This established, modern site is set in 47 acres of beautiful countryside on the Dorset and Hampshire border. The 35 pitches, all on hardstandings with electric hook-ups (16A), water taps and drainage are arranged around a circular gravel roadway. Secluded and sheltered, they have views across the surrounding countryside. A field, also with electric hook-ups, alongside the camping area is used for tents and rallies, and has space for ball games and a small playground. Also on site there are two lakes for coarse fishing, and there are many woodland walks in the area. Overall this site is more suitable for adults and younger children – it is not really designed for active teenagers.

Facilities

A large modern barn-style building provides excellent heated facilities, including a laundry room with washing machines and dryers, plus facilities for disabled people and babies – in all, a very generous provision. New facilities for tent pitches. The first floor has a games room with a full size snooker table, pool tables and a darts board, plus a separate function room. Shop. Motorcaravan services. Playground. Shepherd's hut for hire. Off site: Village centre with pub, church, Post Office and store is a 20 minute woodland walk. Local attractions include Rockbourne Roman Villa, Cranborne Chase, The Dolls Museum at Fordingbridge, Salisbury, and Ringwood with its Wednesday market.

Open: 1 March - 30 November.

Directions

From Fordingbridge take B3078 westwards for 2 miles to Alderholt. On entering the village, at left hand bend, turn right towards Sandleheath (site signed) and site entrance is about 300 yards on the left. O.S.GR: SU120130. GPS: N50:55.141 W01:49.967

Charges guide

Per unit incl. 2 persons,	
fully serviced	£ 15.00 - £ 19.00
extra person	£ 5.00
child (0-15 yrs)	£ 2.00 - £ 4.00
tent incl. 2 persons and electricity	£ 12.00 - £ 18.00
dog	£ 1.00

UK2380 Hill Farm Caravan Park

Branches Lane, Sherfield English, Romsey SO51 6FH (Hampshire)

Tel: **01794 340402**. Email: **gjb@hillfarmpark.com**　　www.alanrogers.com/UK2380

This 11 acre rural park is ideal for those seeking a quiet base but one that is within easy reach of all the main tourist attractions of Hampshire and Dorset. There are 92 pitches, of which 30 for seasonal units are located in a separate area. The touring area is a large open field surrounded by trees and hedges. All pitches are well marked, numbered and mainly level. All have electric hook-ups (6/10A), 12 pitches are fully serviced and some are available with hardstanding. Adding to the attractiveness of the site is a pitch and putt golf course, set in a sizeable and well landscaped area. For anyone interested in roses, nearby Mottisfont Abbey (National Trust) has a unique collection of old-fashioned varieties and during the summer open-air plays, films and concerts take place here. The New Forest with Beaulieu Estate and National Motor Museum is just a short drive away. A trip to the Isle of Wight makes a good excursion – the ferry terminal is within a 30 minute drive.

Facilities

Two very clean traditionally built toilet blocks include washbasins, both open style and in cubicles, and controllable showers. Facilities for babies and disabled visitors. Motorcaravan service point. Shop in reception for gas supplies and basics. Bread and pasties are cooked on the premises. Snack bar serves breakfast and takeaway meals. Play area. Pitch and putt golf. Off site: Riding and fishing 3 miles. Bicycle hire 15 miles. Bournemouth and Southampton for shopping, leisure and family entertainment nearby.

Open: 1 March - 31 October.

Directions

From Romsey, drive north on the A27 for 3.5 miles, turning right into Branches Lane and site is a further 0.5 miles on right. O.S.GR: SU235300. GPS: N51:00.376 W01:34.609

Charges guide

Per unit incl. 2 persons and 2 dogs	£ 14.00 - £ 36.00
extra person	£ 4.00
child (4-17 yrs)	£ 1.50 - £ 2.50

Minimum booking requirement for B.Hs, July and August weekends. No credit cards.

UK2350 **Red Shoot Camping Park**

Linwood, Ringwood BH24 3QT (Hampshire)

Tel: **01425 473789**. Email: **enquiries@redshoot-campingpark.com**   **www.alanrogers.com/UK2350**

Red Shoot is set on four acres of open, slightly sloping, level grass, in the heart of the New Forest. A simple, rural retreat with panoramic views of the surrounding countryside and forest, it is very popular in high season. There are around 130 good sized pitches, 45 with electrical hook-ups (10A), served by a circular gravel road. There is no site lighting so a torch would be useful. The adjacent Red Shoot Inn (under separate ownership) serves hot or cold meals and brews its own real ales – Forest Gold and Tom's Tipple. There are ample opportunities for walking, cycling and naturalist pursuits in the area, and nearby Ringwood has a market on Wednesday. Local attractions include watersports at the New Forest Water Park near Ringwood, a Doll Museum in Fordingbridge, cider making in Burley, and Breamore House just north of Fordingbridge.

Facilities

The sanitary facilities have been extended and refurbished and, as well as under-floor heating, include a family shower room, baby bath and changing area. Well equipped laundry room. Good unit for disabled visitors. Very well stocked, licensed shop. Fenced adventure style playground. Mountain bike hire. Off site: Fishing 5 miles. Riding 6 miles. Golf 7 miles. Beach 12 miles.

Open: 1 March - 31 October.

Directions

From A338 about 1.75 miles north of Ringwood, turn east (signed Linwood and Moyles Court). Follow signs, over a staggered crossroads, and continue straight on for another 1.75 miles to Red Shoot Inn. O.S.GR: SU188095. GPS: N50:53.035 W01:44.082

Charges guide

Per unit incl. 2 persons	£ 15.00 - £ 24.00
extra person	£ 6.90
child (3-14 yrs)	£ 3.75
electricity	£ 4.00
dog	£ 1.00
Min. pitch charge £11.50.	

UK2310 **Forest Holidays Hollands Wood**

Forest Holidays, Lyndhurst Road, Brockenhurst SO43 7QH (Hampshire)

Tel: **01590 622967**. Email: **info@forestholidays.co.uk**   **www.alanrogers.com/UK2310**

Forest Holidays is a partnership between the Forestry Commission and The Camping & Caravanning Club. This is a large, spacious 168 acre secluded site in a natural woodland setting (mainly oak). It is set in the heart of the New Forest, with an abundance of wildlife. The site is arranged informally with 600 level unmarked pitches but it is stipulated that there must be at least 20 feet between each unit. There are no electrical connections and traffic noise is possible from the A337 which runs alongside one boundary. Brockenhurst village is only about half a mile where there are shops for supplies and gas, plus trains and buses. Reception offers a freezer pack service and sells batteries, maps and guides. Barbecues are not permitted in dry weather. The site can get very busy and we include the smaller Ashurst site as an alternative.

Facilities

Two large utilitarian toilet blocks (and a third smaller, older one) are fully equipped if somewhat basic. Facilities for disabled people and baby changing surfaces. Two laundry rooms with washing machines and dryers. These facilities are under pressure at peak times. Motorcaravan service point. Bread and milk to order. Night security with the barrier closed 22.30-07.30 hrs (overnight area). Torches essential. Off site: Bicycle hire and riding 2 miles. Golf 3 miles.

Open: 29 March - 25 September.

Directions

Site entrance is on east side of A337 Lyndhurst - Lymington road, half a mile north of Brockenhurst. O.S.GR: SU303034. GPS: N50:50.193 W01:34.171

Charges guide

Per unit incl. 2 persons	£ 8.70 - £ 17.40
extra person	£ 3.60 - £ 7.00
child	£ 2.00 - £ 3.60

UK2315 Riverside Holidays

Satchell Lane, Hamble, Southampton SO31 4HR (Hampshire)

Tel: 023 8045 3220. Email: enquiries@riversideholidays.co.uk

www.alanrogers.com/UK2315

What makes Riverside so special is its location; close to the River Hamble, Mecca for the international yachtsman. The site is family-owned and covers five acres surrounded by trees and hedges; it has 125 pitches of which 77 are level for touring caravans and tents with 53 electricity hook-ups (16A). The remaining pitches are used for lodges and residential and static caravans on slightly rising ground, but so well spaced and with plenty of grass they are not too obtrusive. Currently the amenities block comprises an old 'Portacabin', screened by fencing and butterfly shrubs. However, the owners have already received planning permission to replace this with a totally new reception, shop, clubroom, toilet block and a pool in the next two years. A warden-run log cabin reception, with tourist information, including local bus and rail times, is at the entrance. Hamble village, a mile away, with its cobbled streets, pubs and restaurants, is famed the world over for its association with yachting. This is an ideal base for the Southampton Boat Show, Cowes Week and its very own Hamble Week Regatta. On the marina adjacent to the site, a mere two minutes walk, is Oyster Quay with a bar and restaurant overlooking hundreds of yachts worth millions.

Facilities

The old 'Portacabin' unit is clean but not quite up to standard, with a baby changing area but no unit for the disabled. However, an additional amenities block has recently been installed. Small laundry room alongside. All these facilities could be under pressure in high season. Bicycle hire. Caravan storage. Off site: Buses and trains 1 mile. Fishing, sea fishing, sailing, supermarket, 1 mile in village. Riding 3 miles. Golf 4 miles. You can catch a small ferry across to Warsash. The New Forest, Winchester and Portsmouth are nearby.

Open: 1 March - 31 October.

Directions

From the M27 take exit 8 and follow signs for Hamble. Taking B3397 with Tesco on the left, continue 1.9 miles through traffic lights until Hound roundabout. After 50 yds turn left into Satchell Lane (signed Mercury Marina) and site is on left in 1 mile. Q,S. GR: SU484082. GPS: N50:52.200 W01:18.667

Charges guide

Per unit incl. 2 persons	£ 12.00 - £ 30.00
extra person	£ 3.50
child (4-16 yrs)	£ 2.50

Camping Cheques accepted.

UK2320 Chichester Camping & Caravanning Club Site

345 Main Road, Southbourne PO10 8JH (Hampshire)

Tel: 01243 373202

www.alanrogers.com/UK2320

This small, neat site is just to the west of Chichester and north of Bosham harbour. Formerly an orchard, it is rectangular in shape with 58 pitches on flat, well mown lawns on either side of gravel roads. All pitches have 16A electricity, 42 with level hardstanding. Although the A27 takes most of the through traffic, the site is by the main A259 road so there may be traffic noise in some parts (not busy at night). Opposite the park are orchards through which paths lead to the seashore. Unfortunately there is no parking outside or overnight area for late arrivals. Arrive before 20.00.

Facilities

The well designed toilet block is of first class quality. Fully tiled and heated in cool weather, with facilities for people with disabilities (access by key). Laundry facilities. Gas supplies. No ball games permitted. Off site: Shops, restaurants and pubs within walking distance in the village. Chichester has a leisure centre. Bicycle hire 1 mile. Fishing or golf 5 miles, riding 6 miles.

Open: February - November.

Directions

Park is on the A259 Chichester - Havant road at Southbourne, 750 yards west of Chichester Caravans. Coming from the west, it is 2.8 miles from the A27/A259 junction near Havant. O.S.GR: SU774056. GPS: N50:50.699 W00:54.179

Charges guide

Per person	£ 6.30 - £ 8.25
pitch (non-member)	£ 5.65

UK2450 The Orchards Holiday Caravan & Camping Park

Newbridge, Yarmouth PO41 0TS (Isle of Wight)

Tel: **01983 531331.** Email: **info@orchards-holiday-park.co.uk**   **www.alanrogers.com/UK2450**

In a village situation in the quieter western part of the island, The Orchards, 'a park for all seasons', is a busy and lively family holiday park combining 64 caravan holiday homes (in a separate area) with a neat touring area. There are 164 marked touring pitches, arranged on gently sloping meadow, broken up by apple trees, mature hedges and fences. All have electricity and 62 have hardstanding. In addition, there are 22 'all-service' pitches, also with hardstanding. Tents are very welcome. A good place from which to explore the Island; the beaches and Yarmouth are only four miles away. A meeting room (up to 50 persons) is suitable for small rallies. There are walking and cycling routes from the park with leaflets available. There is no evening entertainment on site. A butterfly garden within the holiday home area was opened by David Bellamy. Part of the Caravan Club's affiliated scheme, non-members are also very welcome. The park is also a member of the Best of British group.

Facilities

A new toilet block provides showers and enclosed washbasins. Separate facilities for disabled visitors. Baby and toddler facilities. Family room with bath and shower. Drying area. Launderette. Campers' kitchen. Gas. Shop. Motorcaravan service point. Restaurant (weekday evenings and Sunday lunch), takeaway (both mid March - Oct). Two heated pools (indoor Feb - Dec, outdoor late May - Sept). Licensed coffee shop. Play areas. TV and amusements rooms. Bicycle hire arranged. Off site: Bus stop at entrance. Riding 1 mile. Membership available for the village social club. Small discount at Freshwater golf course (4 miles). Boat launching 4 miles.

Open: All year excl. 3 January - 15 February.

Directions

Park is in Newbridge village, signed north from B3401 (Yarmouth - Newport) road. O.S.GR: SZ411878. GPS: N50:41.278 W01:25.198

Charges guide

Per unit incl. 2 persons and electricity	£ 15.00 - £ 25.00

No pitch fee for hikers or cyclists.
Packages incl. ferry travel – ring park for best deal.
Camping Cheques accepted.

ISLE OF WIGHT · Nr YARMOUTH

the **Orchards**
HOLIDAY CARAVAN & CAMPING PARK

ANWB · CARAVAN CLUB AFFILIATED SITE · Best of British · AA · Premier Park · Gold David Bellamy Conservation Award

- Indoor pool (open all year)
- Outdoor pool
- Excellent touring facilities
- Luxury holiday caravans most with central heating
- Cycling & walking from the park
- Rural situation, excellent views
- Ferry inclusive package

OPEN CHRISTMAS AND NEW YEAR

www.orchards-holiday-park.co.uk   t. 01983 531331

UK2470 Southland Camping Park

Newchurch, Sandown PO36 0LZ (Isle of Wight)

Tel: **01983 865385.** Email: **info@southland.co.uk**   **www.alanrogers.com/UK2470**

Southland was opened in 1981 in the grounds of a former nursery and it has matured nicely with many attractive shrubs and trees. The pleasant surroundings have won many awards. In the peaceful country setting of the Arreton valley, it is a sheltered and well run park with 120 large, level pitches backing on to and separated by high hedging. Comfortable and spacious, all have electricity (10/16A) and some water points. Two acres of land on the western edge of the park overlooking the valley have been developed as a nature area. Nearby are the villages of Arreton and Newchurch.

Facilities

The excellent toilet block is well maintained and includes washbasins in cubicles, en-suite basin and shower cubicles. Bathroom (on payment). Baby room. Good unit for disabled visitors. Two family shower rooms. Motorcaravan service point. Shop. Play area. WiFi. More than one dog by prior arrangement. Off site: Bus stop. Pubs. Walks and bridleways. Beach 2.5 miles. Fishing 1 mile. Riding 2 miles. Bicycle hire and golf 3 miles.

Open: 1 April - end September.

Directions

Park is signed from A3055/6 Newport - Sandown road, southeast of Arreton. O.S.GR: SZ558848. GPS: N50:39.588 W01:12.718

Charges guide

Per person	£ 5.60 - £ 8.50
child (3-15 yrs)	£ 2.00 - £ 4.50
dog	£ 1.20

Packages incl. ferry travel.
Special low season offers.

 www.**alanrogers**.com for latest campsite news

Southern England

UK2495 Whitefield Forest Touring Park

Brading Road, Ryde PO30 1QL (Isle of Wight)

Tel: **01983 617069**. Email: **pat&louise@whitefieldforest.co.uk**   www.alanrogers.com/UK2495

This new, family run park, opened in May 2007, has been sympathetically developed by the owners working closely with the Forestry Commission to maintain the natural beauty of the ancient woodland of Whitefield Forest. There is a mixture of well drained all-weather hardstanding and grass pitches, (70 in total) all with 16A electricity. Varying in size (100-170 sq.m), the pitches are level and sheltered with some on terraces. They are all suitable for tents, caravans and motorcaravans. There is good access to the park and the pitches. Some slight road noise is audible from a few pitches. The park is suitable for families and pre-teen children who want a peaceful relaxing holiday. The nearby towns of Ryde, Shanklin and Sandown provide evening entertainment.

Facilities

The excellent well appointed heated toilet block has private cubicles, hairdryers and razor points. Family shower rooms. Baby changing and facilities for people with disabilities. Laundry room with free ironing (iron from reception). Motorcaravan service point. Paperback book exchange. Adventure type play area with bark surface for children over 5 yrs. Suitable for American style motorhomes and twin axle caravans. Off site: Network of public footpaths from the site. Golf 1 km. Riding, fishing and boat launching 3 km. Bicycle hire 4 km. Beach 3 km. Supermarket 1 km.

Open: Easter - October.

Directions

From Fishbourne and East Cowes follow A3054 to Ryde. Follow the A3055 to Brading. Site is 800 yds. on left (signed) after Tesco roundabout. From Yarmouth follow A3054 to Newport, then to Ryde. Follow the A3055 to Brading and as above. O.S.GR: SZ606894. GPS: N50:42.026 W01:08.743

Charges guide

Per person	£ 5.00 - £ 7.50
child (3-14 yrs)	£ 1.50 - £ 3.75
dog	£ 1.00 - £ 1.50

UK2475 Lower Hyde Holiday Park

Landguard Road, Shanklin PO37 7LL (Isle of Wight)

Tel: **01983 866131**. Email: **holiday.sales@park-resorts.com**   www.alanrogers.com/UK2475

This site is located on the edge of Shanklin, within walking distance of shops and services and only 1.5 miles from the beach. Lower Hyde is a large holiday park complex with around 200 caravan holiday homes for rent and 114 privately owned. The separate touring area has 115 well-spaced and numbered pitches, 85 with electric hook-ups (16A) of which 26 are fully serviced with hardstanding, water, waste-water drain, electricity and TV hook-up. This area is in an elevated position with good views over the surrounding countryside. The pitches are large and flat, easily accessed, with tarmac roads and low level lighting. Landscaping is good, with much wildlife planting throughout. There is a permanent warden for the tourers. This section has a modern toilet block but the rest of the facilities and entertainment are in the holiday home area, near reception, a few minutes walk. This is a lively site with a large dedicated stage area for discos and spectacular cabaret shows. With all the activities, lots of young staff, security personnel and lifeguards, it is excellent for a family holiday.

Facilities

The new toilet block has WCs, open washbasins, showers, a family shower room and two bathrooms. Separate baby room. Suite for disabled persons. Launderette. Shop. Bar. Restaurant and takeaway. Indoor and outdoor pools. Adventure playground. Children's clubs. Entertainment. Multicourt. Soccer. Archery. Fencing. Tennis. ATM. Off site: Fishing and boat launching 1.5 miles. Golf 2.5 miles. Riding and bicycle hire 5 miles.

Open: 2 April - 29 October.

Directions

From East Cowes ferry terminal take A3021 for about 2.5 miles to roundabout and turn right on A3054 to Newport. From Newport take A3020 towards Sandown and Shanklin. After 1.5 miles (at Blackwater) continue straight on joining A3056 to Sandown. Keep on this road until you pass Safeway on the left, and shortly afterwards, turn right into Whitecross Lane. Keep straight on, past Landguard and site is on right after 1 mile. O.S.GR:SZ576817. GPS: N50:37.999 W01:10.859

Charges guide

Per unit incl. up to 6 persons	£ 3.00 - £ 32.00
hardstanding	£ 5.00
dog	£ 1.00 - £ 3.00

UK2480 Appuldurcombe Gardens Holiday Park

Wroxall, Ventnor PO38 3EP (Isle of Wight)

Tel: 01983 852597. Email: info@appuldurcombegardens.co.uk

www.alanrogers.com/UK2480

Originally part of the grounds of an historic house, this pretty family holiday park is situated in 14 acres of beautiful countryside in the valley of Stenbury Downs and St Martin's Downs, close to the sandy beaches at Sandown, Shanklin and Ventnor. The camping field is set in a grassy meadow through which a stream meanders, with a tranquil seating area close by. With hard access roads, there are 100 spacious marked pitches for touring units and tents, 70 of which have electricity hook-ups (10A). The old walled orchard contains 40 good quality caravan holiday homes, the access friendly Orchard Lodge (all accommodation on one level with ramp access to outside), plus two self contained apartments. In an area of outstanding natural beauty, it is an ideal spot for bird watching and horse riding. For walkers and cyclists there is an excellent network of footpaths and cycle paths.

Facilities

Two good toilet blocks (access by key) are fully tiled with free hot water throughout. Facilities for visitors with disabilities. Launderette. Shop (fresh baguettes baked daily) and café. Bar and family entertainment room. All amenities open from Spring B.H. Large outdoor swimming pool and toddlers' pool (May - early Sept). Play area. Pitch and putt. Crazy golf. Off site: Fishing, golf, riding, bicycle hire, boat launching, beach, sailing, all within 2-3 miles.

Open: All year excl. mid December - mid January.

Directions

Do not use Sat Nav instructions, road with restricted access nearby. From Newport take A3020 towards Shanklin and Ventnor. Travel through Blackwater, Rookley, Godshill and Sandford. At Whiteley Bank roundabout turn right towards Wroxhall (B3320). Pass Donkey Sanctuary and turn right into Appuldurcombe Road. Park entrance is second on the right, 150 yards along this road. O.S.GR: SZ548803. GPS: N50:37.135 W01:13.594

Charges guide

Per person	£ 5.00 - £ 7.50
child (3-14 yrs)	£ 1.50 - £ 3.75
serviced pitch	£ 2.50
dog	£ 1.00 - £ 1.50

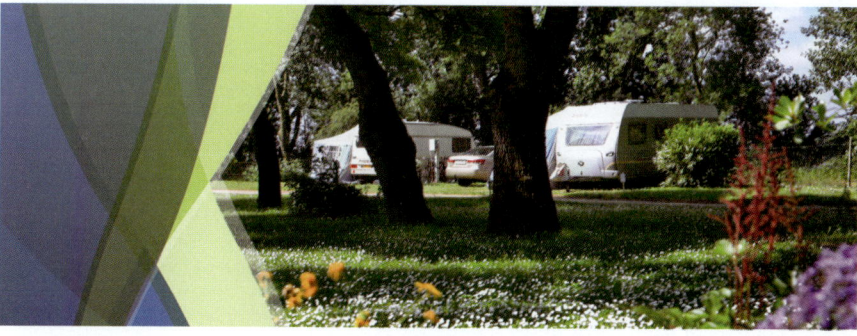

117

UK2515 Nodes Point Holiday Park

Saint Helens, Ryde PO33 1YA (Isle of Wight)

Tel: **01983 872401**. Email: **holiday.sales@park-resorts.com**   **www.alanrogers.com/UK2515**

In a spectacular position, Nodes Point overlooks Bembridge Bay and is set in 65 acres of parkland running down to the beach. This is a park of 200 holiday homes with a separate area for 70 touring caravans. There is a further large dedicated field for up to 200 tents which runs down to the beach. The caravan pitches are large, level and numbered, all with electricity hook-ups (16A) and including 25 fully serviced (hardstanding, water, electricity and TV point). A one-way circular tarmac road leads you round the site which is landscaped and has been cultivated with wildlife in mind. A permanent warden lives in this same area to assist. Alongside are 30 park-owned rented tents, all well sited and maintained. The latest modern toilet block supplements two older ones and a 'portacabin' style unit – together these are ample. The rest of the facilities and entertainment are in the holiday home area, a few minutes walk away. There is a large stage area for discos and spectacular cabaret shows. With these and the park's location by the beach, Nodes Point makes for a good family holiday.

Facilities

Together, the toilet blocks have WCs, open washbasins, showers, a family shower room and two baths. Baby room. Suite for disabled persons. Launderette. Shop. Bar. Restaurant and takeaway. Indoor pool. Adventure playground. Children's clubs. Entertainment. Archery. Riding. ATM. Off site: Fishing and boat launching 2 miles. Golf 3 miles.

Open: Easter - 29 October.

Directions

From Ryde, take the A3055. At Bishop Lovett School (on the left), go straight ahead onto B3330 towards St Helens. After about 2 miles, as road curves right, turn left into signed entrance. O.S.GR:SZ631896. GPS: N50:42.325 W01:06.317

Charges guide

Per unit incl. up to 6 persons	£ 3.00 - £ 29.00
hardstanding pitch	£ 8.00
dog	£ 1.00 - £ 3.00

UK2520 Thorness Bay Holiday Park

Thorness Bay, Cowes PO31 8NJ (Isle of Wight)

Tel: **01983 523109**. Email: **holiday.sales@park-resorts.com**   **www.alanrogers.com/UK2520**

Spread over a large area of rural down and woodland that slopes down to the beach at Thorness Bay, this is a large site with more than 500 holiday homes. The touring area has around 90 pitches, most with electricity (16A) including 27 multi-serviced pitches on gravel hardstandings with electricity, water, drain and TV points. These and some grass pitches are on terraces served by tarmac roads. The remainder are on sloping open grassland either divided by ranch style rails or in an open tent area, and all have views of the surrounding countryside. The main activity centre is located in the holiday home area, a short walk from the touring site. Outdoor sporting activities on-site include a multi-court, soccer, archery, and fencing. The indoor pool provides snorkelling, scuba diving and adult only swimming sessions. There is evening entertainment for all the family.

Facilities

New toilet block providing showers, WCs and washbasins. Suite for disabled visitors. Baby changing. Laundry facilities. Shop. Indoor pool. Indoor playroom for small children. Adventure playground. Multisport court. Children's club. Off site: The beach is easily accessed from the main entertainment complex. All the attractions of the Island are within easy day-trip distances. Riding within 1 mile. Golf 4 miles.

Open: Easter - 29 October.

Directions

Thorness Bay is southwest of Cowes. From East Cowes ferry follow signs to Newport. Follow the A3054 (Yarmouth). Continue for about 2.5 miles to crossroads, turning right (north) to Thorness Bay. After about 2 miles, on sharp right hand bend, turn left, site signed. O.S.GR: SZ452926. GPS: N50:43.868 W01:21.628

Charges guide

Per unit incl. electricity and up to 6 persons	£ 6.00 - £ 30.00
tent pitch	£ 3.00 - £ 27.00
hardstanding pitch, plus	£ 5.00
dog	£ 1.00 - £ 3.00

UK2500 Heathfield Farm Camping

Heathfield Road, Freshwater PO40 9SH (Isle of Wight)

Tel: 01983 756756. Email: web@heathfieldcamping.co.uk   www.alanrogers.com/UK2500

Heathfield is a pleasant contrast to many of the other sites on the Isle of Wight, in that it is a 'no frills' sort of place, very popular with tenters, cyclists and small camper vans. Despite its name, it is no longer a working farm. A large, open meadow provides 60 large, level pitches, 40 with electricity (10A). Two small fenced areas provide traffic free zones for backpackers and cyclists' tents. There is no shop as you are only eight minutes walk from the centre of Freshwater. The site overlooks Colwell Bay and across the Solent towards Milford-on-Sea and Hurst Castle. A play field for ball games also has two picnic tables and two barbecues, and there is a wild flower meadow with the perimeter mown for dog walking. It is ideal for visiting attractions on the western side of the island including Totland and Freshwater Bays, The Needles and Old Battery, Compton Down, and Mottistone Manor Garden. The Military road which runs from Freshwater Bay to St Catherine's Point gives spectacular coastal views.

Facilities

The main toilet unit is housed in a modern, ingeniously customised, 'portacabin' type unit including one washbasin cubicle for ladies and a baby room. Showers have two pushbutton controls, one for pre-mixed hot water, the other for cold only. A second similar unit has WCs and washbasins in cubicles, plus facilities for disabled visitors. Laundry facilities. Motorcaravan service point. Gas supplies. Ice pack service. Play field. Bicycle hire arranged. No commercial vehicles accepted. Gate locked 22.30-07.00. Off site: Bus stop 200 m. Beach 0.5 miles. Fishing 0.5 miles. Golf 1.25 miles. Riding 3 miles.

Open: 1 May - 30 September.

Directions

From A3054 north of Totland and Colwell turn into Heathfield Road where site is signed. Site entrance is on right after a short distance. O.S.GR: SZ336879. GPS: N50:41.364 W01:31.622

Charges guide

Per unit incl. 2 persons	£ 18.00 - £ 25.00
extra person	£ 4.00 - £ 5.00
child (3-15 yrs)	£ 1.75 - £ 2.75

Min. pitch fee July/Aug £12.00
(no fee for backpacker pitches).
One night booking supplement £2.00.
No credit cards.

UK2530 Waverley Park Holiday Centre

51 Old Road, East Cowes PO32 6AW (Isle of Wight)

Tel: 01983 293452. Email: sue@waverley-park.co.uk   www.alanrogers.com/UK2530

This pleasant small family owned site is set in the grounds of an old country house which was once frequently visited by Dr Arnold, the subject of 'Tom Brown's Schooldays'. The owners have now terraced the grass area for touring units. This has created 31 large and level, well spaced, fully serviced hardstanding pitches all with outstanding views over the Solent. The remaining 14 caravan pitches share a sloping grass area with tents – these have no electricity. To one side there are 75 private and rental holiday homes. At the bottom of the park a gate leads onto the promenade and the pebble beach which is popular with sailors and windsurfers. The site, just five minutes from the East Cowes ferry terminal, is an ideal vantage point for Cowes Week, and has good views of the ocean liners sailing in and out of Southampton. A chain ferry across the Medina River operates between East Cowes and West Cowes with its altogether better shops and tourist attractions.

Facilities

At the top of the park, a toilet block provides the usual facilities, including some spacious cubicles with washbasins en-suite. Good suite for disabled people with baby changing. Basic chemical disposal point in the static area. Laundry facilities. Basic shop. Heated outdoor pool and paddling pool with sun terrace. Club with restaurant and bar serving good value meals. Family entertainment in season (all Whitsun - early Sept). Small adventure style playground. Games room. Boats accepted by prior arrangement – public slipway nearby. Off site: Tennis courts nearby (key from reception). East Cowes, with its basic shops and services is within walking distance. Bus stop outside the site entrance.

Open: 29 March - 30 September (statics all year).

Directions

Immediately after leaving Southampton - Cowes ferry, take first left, then right into Old Road, and park entrance is 300 yds on left. O.S.GR: SZ505958. GPS: N50:45.653 W01:17.020

Charges guide

Per person	£ 5.00 - £ 7.50
child (5-13 yrs)	£ 2.50 - £ 4.00
pitch	£ 3.00
dog	£ 0.50 - £ 1.50

During Cowes Week min. pitch fees apply (£12.00 - £14.50). Packages incl. ferry travel and other offers available.

119

UK2570 Lincoln Farm Park

High Street, Standlake, Witney OX29 7RH (Oxfordshire)

Tel: **01865 300239**. Email: **info@lincolnfarmpark.co.uk**   **www.alanrogers.com/UK2570**

From its immaculately tended grounds and quality facilities, to the efficient and friendly staff, this park is a credit to its owner. Situated in a small, quiet village, it is well set back and screened by mature trees, with wide gravel roads, hedged enclosures, brick pathways and good lighting. All 90 numbered, level touring pitches are generously sized and have electrical connections (10/16A), 75 with gravel hardstanding and grass for awnings, and 22 are fully serviced (fresh and waste water, electricity and satellite TV). Gazebos or extra tents are not permitted on pitches. Although only a relatively small site its leisure facilities are quite outstanding. The indoor leisure centre boasts two heated pools plus a pool for toddlers, spa pools, saunas, steam room, sun bed and a fitness suite. Charges for all of these are modest, and outside of the open sessions everything can be hired privately by the hour. Oxford and the Cotswolds are conveniently close. A member of the Best of British group.

Facilities

Two heated toilet blocks are well maintained and exceptionally clean, with showers and washbasins in cubicles. A well equipped, separate unit for disabled people. Two family bathrooms (with baby bath and changing facilities). Laundry facilities, freezers, fridges and microwaves. Motorcaravan service point. Shop (basic supplies). Information kiosk. Outdoor chess/draughts, putting green and adventure play area. Indoor swimming pools. WiFi. Off site: Riding centre and watersports nearby. Fishing (lake and river) 300 yds and 5 miles. Golf 5 miles.

Open: 1 February - mid November.

Directions

Take A415 Witney - Abingdon road and turn into Standlake High Street by garage; park is 300 yds on the right. O.S.GR: SP396029.
GPS: N51:43.392 W01:25.727

Charges guide

Per pitch incl. 2 persons and electricity	£ 13.95 - £ 24.95
extra person	£ 3.00
child (5-14 yrs)	£ 2.00
dog	£ 1.25
Low season offers.	

UK2580 Cotswold View Caravan & Camping Park

Enstone Road, Charlbury OX7 3JH (Oxfordshire)

Tel: **01608 810314**. Email: **bookings@cotswoldview.co.uk**   **www.alanrogers.com/UK2580**

On the edge of the Cotswolds and surrounded by fine views, this well-run family park offers a warm welcome. Originally a working farm, the touring park and self catering country cottages are situated amongst 54 acres of farmland. Wide gravel or tarmac roads ensure easy access to the 125 pitches (all with 10A electricity) in the 10-acre touring area. The park has been thoughtfully separated by hedges into different areas to enable those with children to be close to play areas, and quieter areas for those wanting to enjoy the peaceful surroundings. The small reception also serves as a licensed shop selling freshly baked bread and homemade cakes. Farmhouse breakfasts (ordered the night before) are served in the farmhouse itself with Bed & Breakfast also offered. Extensive tree planting has been undertaken to create well defined and maintained grass trails in the forest. There is also a farm trail where small animals, pigs, sheep and donkeys in enclosures can be observed. Convenient for touring the Cotswolds, there is also a good train service for day trips to London.

Facilities

Two well maintained heated toilet blocks provide washbasins in cubicles, showers, two family shower rooms (free), bathrooms (50p) and hairdryers. Good units for disabled people. Baby changing area. Laundry facilities. Shop and off-licence. Motorcaravan service point. Bar. Play areas. Games room. Tennis. Outdoor chess and draughts. American motorhomes accepted. Security barrier (£5 deposit). Off site: Fishing 1 mile. Golf 7 miles. Riding 10 miles. Boat launching 1 mile.

Open: 1 April (or Easter if earlier) - 31 October.

Directions

From A44 Oxford - Chipping Norton road, take B4022 to Charlbury, just south of Enstone. The park is 2 miles on left. O.S.GR: SP365210.
GPS: N51:53.170 W01:28.248

Charges guide

Per unit incl. 2 persons and electricity	£ 15.00 - £ 19.50
extra person	£ 2.25
child (6-16 yrs)	£ 2.00
dog	free

Southern England

UK2590 Greenhill Farm Caravan & Camping Park

Bletchingdon OX5 3BQ (Oxfordshire)

Tel: **01869 351600**. Email: **info@greenhill-leisure-park.co.uk**   www.alanrogers.com/UK2590

On a working farm in a rural setting, this is a newly established site. The approach is a half mile gravel track down into the valley, past recently planted woodlands, fields and the farm. The reception office with a shop and tourist information is located in the farmhouse. A gravel path continues round the park giving access to 50 pitches, all with 16A electricity and 25 with hardstanding. Growing trees and hedges partition the site and screen the water stands. An adjacent field is available for rallies and there is a second smaller field for tents. Continuing developments include two fishing lakes (carp, roach, bream and tench). One of the farm barns is now a games room and another has been converted into a toilet block. Many trees and hedges have been planted and as these mature the aspect will be less open giving more shade and walks through the woodland. This is a quiet, pleasant park with modern facilities, a variety of animals and convenient for visiting various local attractions including Blenheim Palace and Stratford.

Facilities

Two new toilet blocks, one in a converted barn with ramp access for facilities for disabled visitors and families. Separate laundry room. Shop (April - Sept). Play area with assault course and basketball hoop. Fishing lakes. Games room which can also be used for meetings. Pets are not accepted 1/10-1/3. Off site: Golf 2 miles. Boat launching and canal walks 1 mile.

Open: All year.

Directions

From M40 exit 9 take the A34 to Newbury and Oxford. After 5 miles turn left on the B4027 signed Bletchingdon. After 2.5 miles park is on left just past the village. O.S.GR: SP488177. GPS: N51:51.452 W01:17.485

Charges 2009

Per unit incl. 2 persons	£ 12.00 - £ 15.00
extra person (over 4 yrs)	£ 3.00
electricity	£ 3.00
dog	£ 3.00

No credit cards.

UK2610 Bo Peep Caravan Park

Aynho Road, Adderbury, Banbury OX17 3NP (Oxfordshire)

Tel: **01295 810605**. Email: **warden@bo-peep.co.uk**   www.alanrogers.com/UK2610

Set amongst 85 acres of farmland and woodland, there is an air of spacious informality about this delightful, friendly park which blends perfectly with the surrounding views. Warm Cotswold stone buildings, dovecotes and extensive planting of trees, shrubs and hedges enhance the natural environment of the park. There are 104 numbered pitches all with 16A electricity for caravans and motorhomes in several areas, each with a different character. A separate 4 acre field for tents provides a further 40 pitches, including 4 electricity points. One area near the central buildings provides 8 gravel hardstandings. Gravel roads connect the various touring areas which are screened by hedges and trees. A network of circular walks along well kept grass trails have been developed around the park, including a pleasant river walk. Bench seats and waste bags and bins for dogs are provided. A 15 acre field is available for recreational use. Children are welcome but there is no play area or facilities for babies.

Facilities

The original toilet block has been supplemented by a larger, purpose-built unit, all very clean and heated. Large showers. Hairdryers. Laundry rooms. Motorcaravan service point. Low level lighting. Excellent small shop with off-licence, gas and basic supplies. Information centre with armchairs and internet access. Fishing. Caravan storage. Caravan cleaning area. Off site: Golf 1 mile. Riding 10 miles. Banbury 3 miles. Blenheim Palace 15 miles. Silverstone 16 miles. Day trips to Warwick and Stratford-upon-Avon.

Open: 14 March - 26 October.

Directions

Adderbury village is on the A4260 Banbury - Oxford road. From the north on the M40 use exit 11, the A422 (Banbury) then the A4260. At traffic lights in Adderbury turn on B4100 (Aynho). Park is signed 0.5 miles on the right (0.5 mile drive). From the south on the M40 use exit 10 onto the A43, then the B4100 (Aynho and Adderbury). O.S.GR: SP480348. GPS: N52:00.951 W01:17.966

Charges guide

Per unit incl. 2 persons and electricity	£ 15.00 - £ 28.00
tent incl. 1 or 2 persons	£ 13.00 - £ 15.00
extra person	£ 3.00
child (4-16 yrs)	£ 2.50
dog	£ 1.00

No credit cards.

121

www.**alanrogers**.com for latest campsite news

Southern England

UK2600 Barnstones Caravan & Camping Park

UK2600 Barnstones Caravan & Camping Park

Great Bourton, Banbury OX17 1QU (Oxfordshire)

Tel: **01295 750289**   www.alanrogers.com/UK2600

Three miles from Banbury and open all year round, this small, neat park provides an excellent point from which to explore the Cotswolds, Oxford and Stratford-upon-Avon. There are 49 level pitches of which 44 have gravel hardstanding with a grass area for awnings (no groundsheets are allowed) and 10A electricity; 20 of these are fully serviced. The park provides a pleasant environment for couples and young families, but it is near the main road, so some traffic noise is to be expected.

Facilities

The good toilet block is small, but very clean, heated and well maintained. It is quite adequate for the number of people it serves. Good tiled, adjustable showers. Laundry rooms. Freezer. Gas supplies. Good enclosed play area. Boules. American motorhomes accepted by prior arrangement. Off site: Pub 150 yds. Nearest shop 1 mile. Supermarket, fishing, bicycle hire, golf and riding, all within 3 miles.

Open: All year.

Directions

From M40 take exit 11 for Banbury. Follow signs for Banbury and Southom. On the two small roundabouts follow signs for Southom and Great Bourton. At third roundabout turn right on A423, Southom is 2.5 miles. Turn right (Great Bourton and Crofredy). Site almost immediately on right. O.S.GR: SP454454. GPS: N52:06.321 W01:02.021

Charges guide

Per unit incl. 2 persons and electricity	£ 10.00
extra person	£ 1.50
No credit cards.	

UK2620 Wysdom Touring Park

The Bungalow, Burford School, Burford OX18 4JG (Oxfordshire)

Tel: **01993 823207**   www.alanrogers.com/UK2620

You'll have to go a long way before you find anything else remotely like this site! The land is owned by Burford School and the enterprising caretaker and his wife, caravanners themselves, suggested that they create this wonderful place to raise money for the school (£30,000 raised in 2005/6). Beautifully maintained, it really is like stepping into their own private garden. This 'adults only' park is screened from the main school grounds by trees and provides 25 pitches (6 seasonal), separated by hedges, all with electricity and some with water. Tents are accepted for short stays by arrangement.

Facilities

The older sanitary building is clean and well maintained with two unisex showers (20p token) – there may be a queue at peak times. (Max. 2 dogs per pitch). Tennis courts. Off site: Burford is yards away with its famous hill full of antique shops, old coaching inns and all those 'interesting' shops it is so much fun rooting about in. Burford Golf Club is next door.

Open: All year (excl. 14 December - 5 January).

Directions

From roundabout on A40 at Burford, take A361 towards Lechdale on Thames. Park is a few yards on right signed Burford School. Once in drive watch for narrow entrance to site on right in about 100 yards. O.S.GR: SP250115. GPS: N51:48.119 W01:38.362

Charges guide

Per unit incl. 2 persons and electricity (16A)	£ 9.00 - £ 10.50
extra person	£ 1.50
No credit cards.	

UK2750 Highclere Farm Country Touring Park

Newbarn Lane, Seer Green, Beaconsfield HP9 2QZ (Buckinghamshire)

Tel: **01494 874505**. Email: **highclerepark@aol.com**   www.alanrogers.com/UK2750

Only 25 miles from London and 12 miles from Windsor, this is a peaceful park that backs onto fields and woodland. Originally developed around a working farm, the owners continue to keep chickens. There are 95 level pitches all with 10A electricity. Of these 60 with gravel hardstanding are reserved for caravans and motorcaravans, the remainder being mainly used for tents. The atmosphere is friendly but informal, with reception doubling as a small shop supplying freshly laid eggs.

Facilities

The toilet and shower block is fully equipped and can be heated. Large showers (20p). Unit with toilet and washbasin for disabled people. Baby changing. Two new units (in former stables) provide extra luxury facilities including showers at 50p. Launderette. Fridge and freezer. Basic shop in reception. Play area. Footpath for walks. Off site: Inn serving food 0.25 miles. Golf 0.5 miles. Riding 2 miles. Bicycle hire 3 miles. Fishing 8 miles. Bekonscot Model Village and Milton's Cottage are close.

Open: All year excl. February.

Directions

From M40 exit 2, follow signs for Beaconsfield at first roundabout. Take A355 towards Amersham and after 1 mile turn right (Seer Green and Jordans), following signs to park. From the north on M25 take exit 18 to Little Chalfont, B44442 to Chalfont St Giles. Go through village. Park is 1.25 miles on right. O.S.GR: SU977927. GPS: N51:37.537 W00:35.452

Charges guide

Per pitch	£ 12.00 - £ 19.00
electricity	£ 2.50

UK2690 Wellington Country Park

Riseley, Reading RG7 1SP (Berkshire)

Tel: **01189 326444**. Email: **info@wellington-country-park.co.uk**   **www.alanrogers.com/UK2690**

Wellington Country Park is open to all on payment of an entry fee (entry for campers is included in pitch fees) and many visit it for a day out. It contains play areas for children, nature trails, a deer park, crazy golf and a miniature railway. The camping site is situated in woodland within the 350 acre park. There are 72 pitches, 10 with hardstanding and 56 with electricity hook-ups (10A). A few 'Premium' pitches are larger, more private and have picnic tables. It is a very pleasant setting and once the Country Park closes at 17.30 all is very quiet. You should aim to arrive before 17.30 when the main park reception centre closes. Access to the site is through a locked gate (key from reception). The design of the site with individual pitches and some small groups all within woodland clearings gives a very rustic and relaxed ambience. A warden lives on the site.

Facilities

The central toilet block provides traditional style facilities including washbasins in cubicles and well equipped showers with good dry areas. Ample laundry. Shop stocks basics (from 1/5). Gas supplies. Country Park with fishing, nature walks, crazy golf and play areas. Family events. Torch useful. Off site: Wellington Farm Shop 0.5 miles. Bus service at Risley 2 miles. Legoland and Windsor 30 minutes drive. Riding 1 mile. Golf 6 miles.

Open: 3 March - 9 November.

Directions

Park is signed at Riseley, off the A33 road between Reading and Basingstoke. From M4 exit 11 park is 4 miles south off the second roundabout (signed). From the M3 use exit 8 and follow the A33 for 7 miles towards Reading. Park is signed after the Wellington monument at the next roundabout. O.S.GR: SU727628. GPS: N51:21.552 W00:57.670

Charges guide

Per unit incl. up to 2 persons	£ 13.00 - £ 20.00
extra person	£ 3.00
child (3-15 yrs)	£ 2.50
electricity	£ 2.00 - £ 4.00
dog	£ 1.00

UK2700 Hurley Riverside Park

Hurley, Maidenhead SL6 5NE (Berkshire)

Tel: **01628 824493**. Email: **info@hurleyriversidepark.co.uk**   **www.alanrogers.com/UK2700**

On the banks of the Thames, not far from Henley-on-Thames, you will find the picturesque village of Hurley where some buildings date back to 1086. Just outside the village is Hurley Riverside Park providing facilities for holiday home, touring units and moorings for boats. The touring area is flat and separated into smaller fields. With the pitches arranged around the outside of each field and the centre left free, the park has a spacious feel. There are 138 touring pitches with 10A electricity including 12 fully serviced on long hardstandings. A camping field provides a further 62 pitches including 6 electric hook-ups. A very popular park, there is also a large rally field. You can enjoy walks along the banks of the Thames or visit the various pubs and restaurants in the village for a good meal and a pint. Nearby Windsor has its famous castle or for younger members of the family, Windsor is the home of Legoland. At Henley you can watch the regatta. Alternatively, you can just relax in the peaceful settings of the site.

Facilities

Three wooden toilet blocks (raised on legs) include a very good new unisex block with private bathrooms (shower, washbasin, toilet). The other blocks have been renovated and are well equipped. Separate shower and toilet facilities for disabled visitors. Baby area. Laundry. Motorcaravan service point. Shop at reception. Off site: Golf, riding 3 miles. Bicycle hire 4 miles. Legoland at Windsor.

Open: 1 March - 31 October.

Directions

From M4 exit 8/9 take A404M towards Wycombe. After 3 miles take A4130 (Henley). Go down steep hill (Hurley village signed on right) – ignore this turning and take next right (site signed from here). O.S.GR: SU825838. GPS: N51:32.796 W00:49.488

Charges guide

Per unit incl. 2 persons	£ 9.00 - £ 18.00
full services	£ 12.00 - £ 19.00
extra person	£ 2.00
child (5-17 yrs)	£ 1.50
dog	£ 2.00

MAP 3

Land of 1066, the So
East is brimming w
historical sights as
castles, stately hom
and cathedrals abou
It also boasts miles of
footpaths and cycle rout
through some of the best
landscapes in England, passing
chalk downland, wooded valle
and dramatic white-faced cliff

THE SOUTH EAST COMPRISES: EAST SUSSEX, WEST SUSSEX, SURREY AND KENT

The chalk countryside of golden downland in Sussex offers many opportunities for an active holiday, from walking and cycling to more adventurous pursuits such as rock climbing or ballooning. Once an ancient forest, much of the Weald is now taken up with farmland, but some areas still remain, including Ashdown Forest, a walker's paradise with stunning views of the High Weald and South Downs. The many rivers of the county have cut their way through gaps in the chalk landscape, ending spectacularly in white cliffs on the coast. Here you will find the Regency resorts of Bognor Regis and Brighton, with its Royal Pavilion, famous pier and quirky shops. Often referred to as the 'Garden of England', Kent is a richly fertile region flourishing with hop fields, fruit orchards and flowers. It is also home to the world renowned Canterbury Cathedral, several splendid castles, hidden towns, and quaint villages with oast houses. Surrey too boasts a rich heritage with numerous stately homes and National Trust sites plus large areas of ancient woodland. With a network of rivers, an enjoyable way to explore the beautiful countryside is by boat, stopping off at a riverside pub – or two!

Places of interest

East Sussex: Runnymede; Thorpe Park i
Chertsey; Bexhill; historical towns of
Hastings and St Leonards.

West Sussex: Eastbourne; Chichester;
Bognor Regis; Arundel, with castle;
Littlehampton.

Surrey: Guildford castle and cathedral;
Valley; Royal Horticultural Society's garc
at Wisley; Chessington World of Adven
Dorking, a renowned centre for antiqu

Kent: Leeds Castle and gardens, the ol
stately home in the country; Canterbur
a designated World Heritage Site; Dove
with museum and castle; traditional se
resort of Folkstone; Hever Castle in
Sevenoaks; market town of Maidstone
Isle of Thanet incorporating Margate,
Broadstairs and Ramsgate.

Did you know?

Hastings is home to Britain's first Norm
castle, built by William the Conqueror.

Some of England's finest writers have f
inspiration from living in Sussex – Rudy
Kipling, Sir Arthur Conan Doyle and
A.A.Milne.

Bexhill housed one of the country's firs
cinemas and was the first to permit 'ris
mixed sea bathing.

The world famous Mclaren F1 racing te
has its base in Woking.

Runnymede takes its name from the
meadow where the Magna Carta, the
charter of English liberties, was sealed
King John in 1215.

Winner Alan Rogers Awards 2008

UK2885 **Warner Farm Touring Park**

Warner Lane, Selsey, Chichester PO20 9EL (West Sussex)

Tel: **01243 604499**. Email: **touring@bunnleisure.co.uk**   www.alanrogers.com/UK2885

This site is a member of the Bunn Holiday Villages group, owners of several large holiday home parks which surround the pretty holiday town of Selsey. Warner Farm is a top quality touring park with 250 large grassy pitches, 165 of which have electricity. Pitches have a generally open aspect and there is a large area at the back of the site, the 'Artichoke Field', which offers an unmarked camping area, as well as providing picnic tables and barbecues. There are 35 serviced pitches with electricity, water and waste water. The site is modern and well maintained, and benefits from free access to the extensive leisure facilities on offer at the neighbouring holiday villages. These include the Oasis Pool and Leisure Complex with two indoor pools, a fun fair, a number of bars and restaurants and a lively 'top name' entertainment programme and kid's club. Surprisingly perhaps, the site retains a pleasant rural feel with plenty of space despite its proximity to the sea and the resort of Selsey.

Facilities

Modern toilet block with facilities for disabled visitors. Pre-set showers in large cubicles. Washing machines and dryers. Small shop. Play area. Multisport area. Communal barbecues, picnic area and dog walking area. Free shuttle bus to neighbouring parks. Off site: Nearest beach 900 m. Oasis Pool and Leisure Complex, indoor pools, fun fair, bars, restaurants, entertainment and kid's club. Bicycle hire. Tennis.

Open: 1 March - 30 October.

Directions

Head for Chichester on the A27. At the Whyke roundabout join the B2145 and follow signs to Selsey. At Selsey go across mini-roundabout and continue past entrance to Bunn Leisure. After next mini-roundabout take second right into School Lane, right again into Paddock Lane and then first left into Warner Lane. Follow signs to park.
O.S.GR: SZ846939. GPS: N50:44.289 W00:47.948

Charges guide

Per pitch incl. up to 4 persons and electricity	£ 18.50 - £ 32.00
incl. services	£ 26.00 - £ 42.00
extra child (0-18 yrs)	£ 5.00
dog	£ 3.00

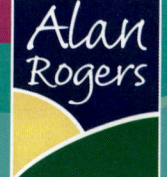
125

UK2950 Washington Caravan & Camping Park

Old London Road, Washington RH20 4AJ (West Sussex)

Tel: **01903 892869**. Email: **washcamp@amserve.com**

www.alanrogers.com/UK2950

Washington is a pleasant campsite to the north of Worthing with a bias towards tenting families. It provides only 21 hardstanding pitches for caravans or motorcaravans, and a large gently sloping grassy field with enough space for 80 tents. The 23 electricity hook-ups (16A) are on slot meters (50p). There is some road noise from the A24. An equestrian centre adjacent to the campsite offers stabling and paddock facilities. There are excellent riding opportunities on the bridle paths of the South Downs Way. Local attractions (all with free admission, check opening times) include Highdown Chalk Gardens at Worthing, Nutbourne Vineyard near Pulborough, and Steyning Museum.

Facilities

A heated wooden chalet style building houses the sanitary facilities including spacious shower rooms (20p) and indoor dishwashing and laundry facilities. No on-site shop but eggs, bread, butter and milk can be obtained from the reception office. Drinks machine and freezer. Off site: Bus stop 200 yds in village. Eating out options include the local pub and a nearby restaurant. Beach 9 miles.

Open: All year.

Directions

Site entrance is just east of the junction of A24 and A283 at Washington, 6 miles north of Worthing. O.S.GR: TQ122134. GPS: N50:54.525 W00:24.336

Charges guide

Per unit incl. 2 persons	£ 19.00
extra person	£ 4.00
tent	£ 6.00
electricity on meter	£ 0.50
car	£ 5.00

Weekly terms acc. to time of year.

Washington
Caravan & Camping
Park

Bring your horse on holiday
01903 892869
* Beautiful landscaped grounds
* Superb Equestrian facilities
* Close to many attractions
@ washcamp@amserve.com: W www.washcamp.com

UK2930 Sheepcote Valley Caravan Club Site

East Brighton Park, Brighton BN2 5TS (East Sussex)

Tel: **01273 626546**

www.alanrogers.com/UK2930

Brighton is without doubt the South of England's most popular seaside resort and the Caravan Club's Sheepcote Valley Site is a first class base from which to enjoy the many and diverse attractions both in the town and this area of the south coast. A wide tarmac road winds its way through the site from reception, with gravel pitches on either side, leading to terraces with grass pitches on the lower slopes of the valley. The 169 pitches all have electricity (16A), 85 have hardstanding and 11 have water, drainage and TV sockets. Three grass terraces are for tents and these have hard parking nearby as a low fence prevents cars being taken onto the camping areas. Although there are trees, many are young so do not yet provide shade. Flower beds add to the attractiveness of the site. It occupies a quiet situation in an almost fully enclosed valley in the South Downs, a mile north of the town's interesting Marina which has a superstore and good variety of shops and restaurants. The site fully lives up to the very high standards expected from the Caravan Club.

Facilities

Two heated sanitary blocks include all washbasins in private cabins. In the main season a third timber-clad building provides additional services near the tent area. Well equipped room for wheelchair users, another one for walking disabled and two baby and toddler wash rooms. Laundry facilities. Motorcaravan service point. Gas available. Milk and bread from reception. Play area with safety base. Off site: Brighton is 2 miles with a bus service from the entry road. Extensive recreation grounds adjacent.

Open: All year.

Directions

From the north (London) on the M23/A23, join the A27 (Lewes). Immediately after passing Sussex University on left, exit via slip road for the B2123 (Falmer/Rottingdean). At roundabout turn right on B2123. Continue for 2 miles then turn right at traffic lights by Downs Hotel into Warren Ave. After 1 mile turn left at traffic lights into Wilson Ave, crossing Racecourse. In 1.75 miles at foot of hill (just before lights) turn left and follow lane to site. O.S.GR: TQ341043. GPS: N50:49.404 W00:07.756

Charges guide

Per person	£ 5.00 - £ 6.50
child (5-16 yrs)	£ 1.50 - £ 3.00
pitch incl. electricity	
(non-member)	£ 10.90 - £ 15.30

UK2940 Honeybridge Park

Honeybridge Lane, Dial Post, Horsham RH13 8NX (West Sussex)

Tel: **01403 710923**. Email: **enquiries@honeybridgepark.co.uk**   www.alanrogers.com/UK2940

This 15 acre park is situated amidst beautiful woodlands and countryside on the edge of the South Downs, within an Area of Outstanding Natural Beauty. Of the 200 pitches, 147 are for touring. Some are on hardstandings and the majority have electricity hook-ups (16A). Some pitches are hedged for privacy, others are on slightly sloping grass, well spaced and generously sized. The reception building houses a licensed shop. A large wooden, adventure-style playground is provided for children away from the pitches, and simple family entertainment is organised on special occasions. A large games room provides darts, table tennis, pool, free use of many board games and a library. The tourist information centre is also here. This site is ideally situated for visiting the South Downs with its many attractive villages and the popular coastal resorts.

Facilities

Modern toilet facilities are heated in cool weather and include spacious facilities for disabled visitors (radar key). Laundry facilities. Motorcaravan service point. Licensed shop. Play area. Games room with library. Security barrier (card access) is locked 23.00-07.00. Barrier pass (£10 deposit). Off site: Bus 0.5 miles. Pub/restaurant in nearby Dial Post village. Old Barn Nurseries serves meals during the day. Billingshurst and Horsham are both 8 miles. Fishing 1 mile. Golf 10 miles. Riding 5 miles. Beach at Worthing 10 miles.

Open: All year.

Directions

Two miles south of the junction of A24 and A272 at Dial Post, turn east by Old Barn Nurseries. Follow signs to site (about 0.5 miles). O.S.GR: TQ153183. GPS: N50:56.918 W00:21.164

Charges guide

Per person	£ 4.00 - £ 6.00
child (5-14 yrs)	£ 2.50
pitch	£ 7.00
incl. electricity	£ 9.00 - £ 11.00
2 man small tent (incl. pitch fee)	£ 9.50

Senior citizen discounts.

Spacious 15 acre Park, within an 'Area Of Outstanding Natural Beauty'. 145 spacious touring pitches, heated amenity block, disabled facilities, licensed shop, children's play area. Seasonal pitches & Storage. Dogs welcome. Open all year. Luxury holiday Lodges and Statics for sale.

Honeybridge Park

★ ★ ★ ★

AA

Honeybridge Lane, Dial Post, Nr Horsham, West Sussex RH13 8NX. Tel/Fax 01403 710923   Web: www.honeybridgepark.co.uk

UK2895 Nunnington Farm Campsite

Rookwood Road, West Wittering PO20 8LZ (West Sussex)

Tel: **01243 514013**. Email: **nunningtonfarm@hotmail.com**   www.alanrogers.com/UK2895

This no-frills, basic, family run farm site for touring units only can be found on the coast a mere seven miles from Chichester. There are 147 touring pitches, 77 with 15A electricity connections. The pitches are large, level and grassy, providing a comfortable feeling, even when the site is full. The safe, sandy beaches of The Witterings, only a mile away, make this an especially good venue for families in the holidays and a quieter one for off-season visitors. The easily accessible pets corner is an attraction for children of all ages. Visitors with tents are very welcome here and a second field is opened in busy periods, but with no electricity.

Facilities

Three rather dated but clean, central toilet blocks provide all facilities including showers in cubicles, open washbasins, baby bath, washing machines and ramped facilities for disabled visitors (key access). Gates closed 23.00-07.00. Off site: Local shops 300 yds. Bus service to Chichester every 30 minutes. Beach and boat mooring 1 mile. Bicycle hire 2 miles. Golf 3 miles.

Open: Easter - 2nd week October.

Directions

From A27 at Chichester, take A286 signed The Witterings and continue to roundabout. Take second exit on B2179 for West Wittering and site is on left after 2 miles. O.S.GR: SZ785988. GPS: N50:47.026 W00:53.153

Charges guide

Per unit incl. 2 persons	£ 13.00 - £ 18.00
extra person	£ 2.00
child (under 17 yrs)	£ 0.50
boat	£ 1.00

No credit cards.

127

UK2900 **Horam Manor Touring Park**

Horam, Heathfield TN21 0YD (East Sussex)

Tel: **01435 813662**. Email: **camp@horam-manor.co.uk**

www.alanrogers.com/UK2900

In the heart of the Sussex countryside, this rural touring park is part of (but under separate management from) Horam Manor which has a farm museum, nature trail and several fishing lakes. The 90 generously sized, numbered pitches, 54 with electricity, are on two open meadows. The area nearer reception has an undulating surface, the second field is flatter but slopes – levelling blocks are needed for motorcaravans. Both areas are ringed with a variety of mainly tall trees. The whole park, back from the main Eastbourne to Tunbridge Wells road, is a haven of peace and tranquillity, although in high season it naturally becomes very busy. The site has no shop but the village is very close, with supermarkets in Heathfield (3 miles). Two inns are within walking distance and the Lakeside cafe at the Farm Centre serves drinks and snacks (9.30 - 17.00). The Craft Centre to the side of the site has some interesting exhibits, farm machinery and riding stables. The nature trail has walks ranging from 30 to 90 minutes in length. Fishing is possible in 10 lakes on the estate.

Facilities

The well built toilet block (unheated) is fully equipped and is said to be cleaned four times daily. Some curtained cubicles. Family room (access by key from reception) with shower, washbasin, toilet and baby bath, suitable also for disabled visitors (not good for wheelchairs). Laundry. Gas supplies. Very simple fenced play area (under 12 yrs). Off site: Horam Manor adjacent with café, fishing and riding. Shops and inns within walking distance. Tennis (small fee) 200 yds. Golf within 1 mile. The coastal towns of Brighton, Hastings and Eastbourne are within easy reach, as is the famous Pantiles at Tunbridge Wells.

Open: 1 March - 31 October.

Directions

Horam is on the A267 between Tunbridge Wells and Eastbourne and entry to the park is signed at the recreation ground at the southern edge of the village. O.S.GR: TQ577169.
GPS: N50:55.907 E00:14.410

Charges guide

Per unit incl. 2 adults and 2 children under 18 yrs	£ 15.50 - £ 16.50
extra person	£ 6.00
extra child	£ 2.50

No credit cards.

UK2920 **Bay View Park**

Old Martello Road, Pevensey Bay BN24 6DX (East Sussex)

Tel: **01323 768688**. Email: **holidays@bay-view.co.uk**

www.alanrogers.com/UK2920

This friendly beachside park is located at the end of a private road right beside the beautiful Sussex coast and its pebble beach and the park's own brand new 9-hole, par 3 golf course. Two separate areas of grass (some areas are a little uneven) are surrounded by low banks and hedges to give shelter if it is windy. Careful use of wooden fencing adds to the attractiveness, whilst also keeping the rabbits off the flowers. The 94 touring pitches (80 sq.m, most with 16A electricity and some with hardstanding) are neatly marked and numbered. Several caravan holiday homes for hire are positioned at the back of the park. The golf course clubhouse provides tea, coffee and snacks. Visitors can enjoy all the attractions of Sussex, as well as swimming, fishing and windsurfing. This is an ideal park for a family beach holiday. A cycle path leads to Pevensey Bay and Eastbourne's new Sovereign Harbour marina with its shops, restaurants and cinema.

Facilities

Each area has toilet facilities, one a new, fully equipped block with private cubicles (shower, washbasin and WC) and facilities for babies and disabled visitors. Heated when required, both blocks are kept very clean. Fully equipped laundry room. Motorcaravan services. Well stocked shop (open long hours as the managers live on site). Golf (9-hole, par 3). Clubhouse for tea, coffee and snacks. Gas. Popular, fenced play area (10 yrs and under). Winter caravan storage. Off site: Sailing club. Sea fishing. Indoor swimming pool 1 mile.

Open: 1 March - 31 October.

Directions

From the A27/A259 roundabout at Pevensey take A259 through Pevensey Bay. Park and golf course are signed after 1 mile (private access road) to the left, 2 miles east of Eastbourne. O.S.GR: TQ648028.
GPS: N50:48.000 E00:20.279

Charges guide

Per unit incl. 1 or 2 persons	£ 14.50 - £ 16.50
incl. electricity	£ 17.50 - £ 19.50
extra person	£ 2.50
child (5-16 yrs)	£ 2.00
dog	£ 1.00

Couples and families only.
No commercial vehicles, large vans or pick-ups.

UK2915 Fairfields Farm Caravan & Camping Park

Eastbourne Road, Westham, Pevensey BN24 5NG (East Sussex)

Tel: **01323 763165**. Email: **enquiries@fairfieldsfarm.com**   www.alanrogers.com/UK2915

Part of a working, family-run farm, this is a simple peaceful park which is ideally located to enjoy the Sussex countryside and coast, just a short distance from Eastbourne. A single, rectangular meadow is split by a line of attractive silver birch trees and provides 66 large pitches, all but 4 with electricity connections. The farm and its rural landscape stretch towards the sea at Pevensey Bay and you can walk through the fields to the beach. Beyond the camping field there is a duck pond with grassy surrounds and picnic benches, pens with numerous small animals and pets and a pleasant walk to a fishing lake. Children are invited to feed the animals (with special food on sale). Within walking distance are the villages of Westham and Pevensey with a choice of pubs and restaurants, as well as Pevensey Castle which has a history spanning 16 centuries. Eastbourne has a promenade and beautiful beaches with a new retail complex and cinema at the Sovereign Centre.

Facilities

The single, central toilet block is traditional in style and very clean. Toilet for disabled visitors. Laundry facilities. Farm shop. Small animals and pets. Fishing lake (licence required). Off site: Pubs, restaurants and fish and chip shop within walking distance. Beach 1.5 miles. Golf 4 miles. Eastbourne 5 miles.

Open: 1 April - 31 October.

Directions

From the roundabout junction of the A27 and A259 (Little Chef and petrol station) take exit to Pevensey and the Castle. Go around the castle walls and into Westham village. At end of high street turn left (B2191), over level crossing and park is on left. O.S.GR: TQ639041. GPS: N50:48.815 E00:19.469

Charges guide

Per unit incl. 2 persons	£ 11.50 - £ 13.00
incl. electricity	£ 15.00 - £ 16.50
extra person	£ 3.00
child (3-13 yrs)	£ 1.50
dog	£ 1.00

UK2955 Kloofs Camping & Caravan Park

Sandhurst Lane, Whydown, Bexhill-on-Sea TN39 4RG (East Sussex)

Tel: **01424 845669**. Email: **camping@kloofs.com**   www.alanrogers.com/UK2955

This peaceful and rural park is situated in a quiet country lane with countryside views yet within easy reach of several well known towns on the East Sussex coast. Set in three acres, Kloofs is owned and run by Terry and Helen Griggs who have taken great care in making this a most attractive and well maintained park. There are 40 level, generously sized touring pitches, divided into two areas, and a combination of grass and hardstanding making them suitable for all-weather touring. It is evident that considerable investment has been made to ensure visitors have a comfortable stay. The lower field, surrounded by hedging and trees offers some landscaped pitches which are divided by their own trellised garden area, complete with picnic table. Pitches for caravans and motorcaravans are terraced, easy to access and surrounded by hedges and mature trees which provide shade. Most pitches have electric hook-ups and a water tap, some also have waste water drainage. This is an ideal location for a quiet and relaxing break and for visiting the attractions of the South Coast. Very large units would find the narrow lanes to the park a challenge.

Facilities

One main, centrally heated toilet block is modern and spotlessly clean. Washbasins in cubicles and spacious hot showers. Large shower room for families and good en-suite facility for disabled visitors (key from reception). A new paddock service block is partially completed and will provide further toilet and shower facilities also suitable for disabled visitors. Heated kitchen area. Washing machine, dryer, iron and board. Small shop in reception for basic requirements and camping gas. Wooden adventure style play area, fenced. Small library. Off site: Footpath from site to local village for pubs and other eating places 1.4 miles. Beach 2 miles. Bexhill-on-Sea 3 miles. Battle 6 miles. Hastings 8 miles. Eastbourne 11 miles. Watersports, golf, riding and fishing all nearby.

Open: All year.

Directions

From the north (Battle, Catsfield, Ninfield), take A269 and turn right into Pear Tree Lane, then right at crossroads. Sandhurst Lane is 300 m. on the left and site is signed a short way down on the right. From east (Hastings), take A259 to Little Common roundabout. Turn off right into Pear Tree Lane, then left at crossroads. Then as above. From the west (Eastbourne), take A259 to Little Common roundabout. Turn left into Pear Tree Lane, left at crossroads, then as above. O.S.GR: TQ708090. GPS: N50:51.361 E00:25.628

Charges guide

Per person	£ 5.50
child (5-17 yrs)	£ 2.50
pitch incl. electricity and water	£ 7.00 - £ 14.00
small tent	£ 6.00

129

UK2960 Crazy Lane Tourist Caravan Park

Crazy Lane, Sedlescombe, Battle TN33 0QT (East Sussex)

Tel: **01424 870147**. Email: **info@crazylane.co.uk**   www.alanrogers.com/UK2960

This simple, neat two acre park has just 36 pitches arranged on grassy terraces, all with electricity (5/10A) and 4 with hardstanding. Many pitches are used by seasonal units so it may be best to phone to make sure space is available before travelling long distances. With easy access from the A21 (some background road noise), the park is set in the heart of '1066 Country' with its historical links. Other local attractions within easy reach include the pretty village of Sedlescombe, a steam railway, an organic vineyard and the seaside at Hastings. This is an ideal park for couples.

Facilities

New solar heated toilet facilities are unisex providing excellent private rooms, each with WC, shower and washbasin. Laundry facilities. Shop at reception. Caravan storage. Off site: Golf 0.5 miles. Riding 2 miles. Fishing 3.5 miles. Bus stop and pub in the village. The fascinating towns of Battle and Rye, plus Hastings (6.5 miles) with its beaches, markets and Heritage Shipwreck Centre.

Open: March - October.

Directions

From the A21, 6 miles north of Hastings and 100 yards south of the junction with the B2244 (to Sedlescombe), turn right into Crazy Lane. Site is immediately on the right. O.S.GR: TQ782170. GPS: N50:55.472 E00:32.097

Charges guide

Per unit incl. 2 persons	£ 13.00 - £ 16.00
incl. electricity	£ 15.00 - £ 18.00
extra person over 8 yrs	£ 1.00
awning	£ 1.50

No credit cards.

UK3030 Tanner Farm Touring Caravan & Camping Park

Goudhurst Road, Marden TN12 9ND (Kent)

Tel: **01622 832399**. Email: **enquiries@tannerfarmpark.co.uk**   www.alanrogers.com/UK3030

Tanner Farm is a top class, quality park, developed as part of a family working farm in the heart of the Weald of Kent. It is surrounded by orchards, oast houses, lovely countryside and delightful small villages and the owners are much concerned with conserving the natural beauty of the environment. The park extends over 15 acres, most of which is level and part a gentle slope. The grass meadowland has been semi-landscaped by planting saplings, etc. which units back onto, as the owners do not wish to regiment pitches into rows. There are 100 pitches, all with 16A electricity, 38 with hardstanding, 27 with water tap and 15 with waste water point also. Places are numbered but not marked, allowing plenty of space between units which, with large open areas, gives a pleasant, comfortable atmosphere. Visitors are welcome to walk around the farm and see the Shire horses and other animals. The farm drive links the park with the B2079 and a group of refurbished oast houses (listed heritage buildings) with a duck pond in front, along with pigs, pygmy goats, lambs, etc. make a focal point. The park is a member of the Caravan Club's 'Affiliated Site' scheme although non-members are also very welcome. Best of British and Countryside Discovery groups.

Facilities

Two heated, well cared for sanitary units include some washbasins in private cubicles in both units. Purpose built facilities for disabled visitors. Bathroom (£1 token) and baby facilities in the newer block (this block is not opened Nov - Easter). Small launderette. Motorcaravan service point. A new reception, shop and tourist information building will be opened for 2009 (opening hours and stock limited in winter). Gas supplies. Off site: Riding and golf within 6 miles, leisure centres and sailing facilities near and good shopping facilities at Maidstone and Tunbridge Wells. Many National Trust attractions in the area (Sissinghurst, Scotney Castle, Bodiam Castle).

Open: All year.

Directions

Park is 2.5 miles south of Marden on B2079 towards Goudhurst. O.S.GR: TQ732417. GPS: N51:08.826 E00:28.489

Charges guide

Per person	£ 3.50 - £ 5.50
child (5-16 yrs)	£ 1.30 - £ 2.15
pitch incl. electricity	£ 5.30 - £ 8.10
tent pitch	£ 4.50 - £ 5.50

Only one car per pitch permitted.

UK3040 Broadhembury Caravan & Camping Park

Steeds Lane, Kingsnorth, Ashford TN26 1NQ (Kent)

Tel: **01233 620859**. Email: **holidaypark@broadhembury.co.uk**   www.alanrogers.com/UK3040

In quiet countryside just outside Ashford and within easy reach of Dover, Folkestone and the Kent coast, this sheltered park is attractively landscaped. It takes 65 touring units of any type with several seasonal units and 25 caravan holiday homes (5 for hire) in separate areas. The well kept pitches are on level grass and backed by tall, neat hedges, with over 50 electricity connections (10A). In addition, 4 pitches are fully serviced including16A electricity and 8 more have double hardstanding plus a grass area for an awning. The welcome is friendly at this popular park and it is often full in the main season, with a good proportion of continental visitors, so reservation is advisable. Thoughtfully considered amenities include a very good toilet block, well equipped campers' kitchen and provision for children of all ages. Security arrangements are excellent – with coded entry through gates and onto park. For those who would like a trip to France, the International railway terminal is at Ashford (Paris in two hours) – take your passport. A member of the Best of British group.

Facilities

The toilet block is well equipped including under-floor heating and is kept very clean. Private cabins. High quality facilities for disabled visitors (can also be used as a family bathroom). Well equipped laundry room. Good campers' kitchen, fully enclosed with dishwashing sinks, microwaves, fridge and freezer, all free of charge. Motorcaravan service point. Well stocked shop (bread and papers to order) and comprehensive tourist information. Internet access. TV and pool room. Games room. Two play areas (one for children under 7 yrs) with woodchip bases. Play field away from the touring area. Dog exercise field – up to two dogs per pitch are accepted. Off site: Fishing 300 m. Golf 1 mile. Riding 2 miles. Bicycle hire 3 miles. Beach 12 miles.

Open: All year.

Directions

From M20 junction 10 take A2070. After 2 miles follow sign for Kingsnorth. Turn left at second crossroads in Kingsnorth village. O.S.GR: TR010382. GPS: N51:06.388 E00:52.085

Charges guide

Per unit incl. 2 persons	£ 18.00 - £ 21.00
incl. services	£ 24.00 - £ 26.00
tent incl. 2 persons	£ 14.00 - £ 18.00
extra person	£ 5.00
child (5-16 yrs)	£ 2.00 - £ 3.50

Less 10% for bookings of 7 nights or more.

UK3060 Yew Tree Park

Stone Street, Petham, Canterbury CT4 5PL (Kent)

Tel: **01227 700306**. Email: **info@yewtreepark.com**   www.alanrogers.com/UK3060

Yew Tree Park is a small, quiet site located in the heart of the Kent countryside overlooking the Chartham Downs. Just 5 miles south of Canterbury and 8 miles north of the M20, it is ideally placed either to explore the delights of the ancient city or the many attractions of eastern and coastal Kent. Its nearness to the Channel ports also makes it useful for a night stop on the way to, or on return from, the continent. If catching a late evening ferry you may remain on site after 12 noon for a small payment. With some caravan holiday homes, the site also has 45 pitches for tourers and tents. The 20 with electricity (10A) are marked on mainly level grass either side of the entrance road, the remainder unmarked on a rather attractive, sloping area, left natural with trees and bushes creating cosy little recesses in which to pitch. There are mobile homes and apartments to rent. This neat, tidy park, created by resident proprietors Derek and Dee Zanders, makes an excellent base away from the hurly-burly of life where you can enjoy the rural scenery and also have the opportunity for walking, riding, visiting local places of interest or for Cross-Channel excursions.

Facilities

Two brick-built sanitary blocks (one for each sex) can be heated. Washbasins (H&C) and four showers (on payment). Extra toilets on the edge of the camping area. Toilet/shower room for families or disabled visitors. Laundry and dishwashing sinks, plus a washing machine, dryer and iron. Gas supplies. Outdoor heated swimming pool (60 x 30 ft; June - Sept). Play area. WiFi. Torches may be useful. Dogs are not accepted. Off site: Riding 4 miles. Golf 6 miles. Bicycle hire 5 miles. The County cricket ground is 4 miles.

Open: Easter - mid October.

Directions

Park is on B2068 Canterbury - Folkestone road. From south, take exit 11 from the M20. From Canterbury, ignore signs to Petham and Waltham on B2068 and continue towards Folkestone. From either direction, turn into road beside the Chequers Inn, turn left into park and follow road to owners' house/reception. O.S.GR: TR138507. GPS: N51:13.008 E01:03.491

Charges guide

Per unit incl. 2 persons	£ 11.80 - £ 16.80
serviced pitch	£ 13.80 - £ 19.20
extra person	£ 4.00 - £ 5.00
child (2-16 yrs)	£ 2.00 - £ 2.75

UK3130 Sandwich Leisure Park

Woodnesborough Road, Sandwich CT13 0AA (Kent)

Tel: **01304 612681**. Email: **info@coastandcountryleisure.com**   **www.alanrogers.com/UK3130**

A pleasant well kept site, with modern facilities, this park is in one of England's historic old Cinque Ports and within walking distance of all its attractions, shops and services. From the entrance barrier by reception, you drive through an area of caravan holiday homes (to rent and privately owned) to reach the two touring fields which have 193 pitches, all on grass with 10A electric hook-ups. There are 81 multi-service pitches with electricity, TV, water and drain, 9 of which have hardstanding. A railway runs along one side of the site and there is a little rail noise at times during the day but it is quiet at night. Wildlife is being encouraged in the newer second field by the planting hedges and trees of native varieties and these will give greater privacy as they develop. The site is well lit at night and all roads are well surfaced. Children will love the large, fenced adventure playground with its tube slides etc. which is on a bark surface.

Facilities

Stylish sanitary building provides washbasins in cubicles, controllable hot showers, plus a room which can be heated with some family suites and a full suite for disabled people (radar key). Laundry in reception building with washing machines, dryers, spin dryer and ironing facility. Adventure playground. Skateboarding, rollerblading, skating, scooters and cycling are not permitted on site. Caravan holiday homes to rent. Off site: Supermarket 5 minutes walk. Sandwich has a market on Thursdays. In and around the town are a folk museum, Roman fort, nature reserve, swing bridge, the old gaol, weavers, a sports and leisure centre and further afield is the Dreamland Fun Park. Fishing 3 miles, golf and beach 2 miles.

Open: 1 March - 31 October.

Directions

Sandwich is midway between Ramsgate and Deal, with access from the A256. The town's streets are narrow and there is a one-way system in operation. Follow the brown campsite signs from anywhere in the town centre, the site is to the west of town, just after a railway level crossing. O.S.GR: TR 330575. GPS: N51:16.443 E01:19.935

Charges guide

Per pitch incl. 2 adults, 2 children and electricity	£ 16.00 - £ 25.00
incl. hardstanding	£ 22.00 - £ 29.00
extra person	£ 2.00
dog	£ 1.50

UK3110 Quex Caravan Park

Park Road, Birchington CT7 0BL (Kent)

Tel: **01843 841273**. Email: **info@keatfarm.co.uk**   **www.alanrogers.com/UK3110**

Although there is a large number of privately owned holiday homes at Quex, they do not intrude on the touring area which is in a sheltered glade under tall trees. Here there are 40 shady touring pitches all with electricity hook-ups (16A). This park does not accept tents. This is an attractive and well maintained park, which is well located for the Thanet coast. Local attractions include Quex House and gardens and, of course, the popular seaside resorts of Margate, Ramsgate and Broadstairs. Reception provides a good selection of tourist information and can provide a map of the local area. A member of the Best of British group.

Facilities

The central sanitary unit is in a heated chalet style building with all the usual facilities. Laundry room with sink, washing machine and dryer. Well stocked shop. Playground. Café. Takeaway. More than one dog per pitch accepted by prior arrangement only. Off site: Fishing, golf and riding 3 miles. Supermarkets close by.

Open: 7 March - 7 November.

Directions

From roundabout at junction of the A28 and A299, take the A28 east towards Birchington and Margate. At Birchington carry straight on at roundabout by church, then take next right, then right again, and left at mini-roundabout. Site is on right in half a mile (well signed). O.S.GR: TR320685. GPS: N51:22.055 E01:19.944

Charges guide

Per unit incl. 2 persons	£ 12.00 - £ 15.25
unit over 7 m. incl. electricity	£ 20.00 - £ 25.00
extra adult	£ 3.00 - £ 3.50
child (5-16 yrs)	£ 1.75 - £ 2.00
dog	£ 1.50
Less 10% for 4 nights booked (and paid for on arrival).	

UK3100 Hawthorn Farm Caravan & Camping Site

Martin Mill, Dover CT15 5LA (Kent)

Tel: **01304 852658**. Email: **info@keatfarm.co.uk**   www.alanrogers.com/UK3100

Hawthorn Farm is a large, well run and relaxed park near Dover. Set in 27 acres, it is an extensive park taking 226 touring units of any type on several large meadows which could accommodate far more, plus 160 privately owned caravan holiday homes in their own areas. Campers not requiring electricity choose their own spot, most staying near the toilet blocks, leaving the farthest fields to those liking solitude. There are 112 pitches with electricity (10/16A), 46 of which are large and separated by hedges, the remainder in glades on either side of tarmac roads. There are 15 new hardstandings available. Mature hedging and trees make an attractive environment. A torch would be useful. Being only 4 miles from Dover docks, it is a very useful park for those using the ferries and is popular with continental visitors. Close to the sea at St Margaret's Bay, it is a fairly quiet situation apart from some rail noise (no trains 23.30 - 05.30). A member of the Best of British group.

Facilities

Two heated toilet blocks are well equipped and of good quality. Facilities for disabled visitors. Baby room. Launderette. Motorcaravan services. Breakfast and other meals are served at the shop (all season). Gates close at 20.00 (22.00 in July and August), £10 deposit for card. Caravan storage. Off site: Riding 0.5 miles. Golf 3 miles. Bicycle hire, fishing and boat launching 4 miles. Martin Mill railway station 500 yds.

Open: 1 March - 31 October.

Directions

Park is north of the A258 road (Dover - Deal), with signs to park and Martin Mill where you turn off about 4 miles from Dover. O.S.GR: TR341464. GPS: N51:10.113 E01:20.780

Charges guide

Per unit incl. 2 persons	£ 12.00 - £ 15.25
unit over 7 m. with electricity	£ 20.00 - £ 25.00
extra person	£ 3.00 - £ 3.50
child (5-16 yrs)	£ 1.75 - £ 2.00
dog	£ 1.50

Less 10% for 4 nights booked (paid for on arrival).

UK3095 Little Satmar Holiday Park

Winehouse Lane, Capel-le-Ferne, Folkestone CT18 7JF (Kent)

Tel: **01303 251188**. Email: **info@keatfarm.co.uk**   www.alanrogers.com/UK3095

Capel-le-Ferne is a relatively little known seaside town midway between Dover and Folkestone. Little Satmar is a quiet site a short walk from the delightful cliff top paths which run between these towns and which offer fine views across the English Channel. The site is a member of the Keat Farm group and is located about a mile from the village. There are 61 touring pitches, 51 of which have electricity (10A). The pitches generally have a sunny, open setting, a few with rather more shade. Privately owned mobile homes occupy 78 pitches between the entrance to the site and reception, but these are quite separate from the touring field.

Facilities

Two toilet blocks (one in a 'Portacabin' style unit) are modern and kept very clean and the main block has now been fitted with heating. Washing and drying machines. Shop (with gas). Play area. For more than 1 dog per unit, contact park. Off site: Bus at end of lane to Dover and Folkestone. Port Lympne Zoo, seafront funpark nearby.

Open: 1 March - 31 October.

Directions

Leave A20 Dover - Folkestone road at Capel-le-Ferne exit and follow signs to the village. Site is clearly signed to right after about 0.75 miles. O.S GR: TR256393. GPS: N51:06.115 E01:13.376

Charges guide

Per pitch incl. 2 persons	£ 14.75 - £ 18.00
unit over 7 m. with electricity	£ 20.00 - £ 25.00
extra person	£ 3.00 - £ 3.50
child (5-16 yrs)	£ 1.75 - £ 2.00

133

UK3070 Canterbury Camping & Caravanning Club Site

Bekesbourne Lane, Canterbury CT3 4AB (Kent)

Tel: **01227 463216**. Email: **canterbury@campingandcaravanningclub.co.uk**   **www.alanrogers.com/UK3070**

Situated just off the A257 Sandwich road, about 1.5 miles from the centre of Canterbury, this site is an ideal base for exploring Canterbury and the north Kent coast, as well as being a good stop-over to and from the Dover ferries, and the Folkestone Channel Tunnel terminal. There are 200 pitches, 86 with electric hook-ups (10A) and, except at the very height of the season, you are likely to find a pitch, although not necessarily with electricity. Most of the pitches are on well kept grass with hundreds of saplings planted, but there are also 21 pitches with hardstanding (more are planned). Some pitches do slope so blocks are advised. A good sized overnight area for late arrivals can be reached even when the barriers are down. The site is adjacent to Bekepond nature reserve and within 3 miles of Howletts Zoo. Although the busy A257 is close, there is minimal noise from the traffic. Power lines cross the site.

Facilities

Two modern toilet blocks, the main one with a laundry room, a room for dishwashing, an outside vegetable preparation area, and recycling bins. Motorcaravan service point. Reception stocks a small range of essential foods, milk and gas. Excellent tourist information room. Children's play area with equipment on bark chippings. Off site: Golf adjacent. Bicycle hire 2 miles.

Open: All year.

Directions

From A2 take Canterbury exit and follow signs for Sandwich - A257. After passing Howe military barracks turn right into Bekesbourne Lane opposite golf course. O.S.GR: TR172577.
GPS: N51:16.614 E01:06.812

Charges guide

Per person	£ 4.90 - £ 7.25
child (6-18 yrs)	£ 2.15 - £ 2.25
pitch (non-member)	£ 5.65

UK3090 Black Horse Farm Caravan Club Site

385 Canterbury Road, Densole, Folkestone CT18 7BG (Kent)

Tel: **01303 892665**   **www.alanrogers.com/UK3090**

This neat, tidy and attractive 6 acre park, owned by the Caravan Club, is situated amidst farming country in the village of Densole on the Downs just 4 miles north of Folkestone, 8 west of Dover and 11 south of Canterbury. This makes it ideal for an overnight stop travelling to or from the continent via the Channel Ports or the Tunnel, or as a base for visiting the many attractions of this part of southeast England. Accessed directly from the A260, the tarmac entrance road leads past reception towards the top field which has gravel hardstanding pitches with a grass area for awnings (possibly some road noise), past hedging to the smaller middle area with 8 hardstandings, then to the large bottom field which has been redeveloped to give 140 large pitches (including 15 for tents and some extra large for American Motorhomes), all with electricity (16A). A late arrivals area and pitches for 'one-nighters' are now located in the top field. Opposite the entrance is a general store and newsagent and within 100 yards, a pub and filling station.

Facilities

The carefully thought out and well constructed toilet blocks, one below reception and the other at the far end of the site, have washbasins in private cabins with curtains, good sized shower compartments, a baby room and facilities for disabled visitors, laundry and dishwashing facilities, all well heated in cool weather. Motorcaravan service point. Gas supplies. Play area. A fish and chip van calls on Thursdays (April - Sept). Caravan storage. Off site: Riding 1 mile. Golf and fishing 5 miles.

Open: All year.

Directions

Directly by the A260 Folkestone - Canterbury road, 2 miles north of junction with A20. Follow signs for Canterbury. O.S.GR: TR211418.
GPS: N51:07.957 E01:09.509

Charges guide

Per person	£ 3.95 - £ 5.50
child (5-16 yrs)	£ 1.30 - £ 2.15
pitch incl. electricity (non-member)	£ 11.30 - £ 14.10

UK3120 Gate House Wood Touring Park

Ford Lane, Wrotham Heath, Sevenoaks TN15 7SD (Kent)

Tel: **01732 843062**. Email: **gatehousewood@btinternet.com**   **www.alanrogers.com/UK3120**

This sheltered park has been created in a former quarry where all the pitches are on well drained grass. A spacious paved entrance with a new reception building and well stocked shop, leads on to the park itself. The 54 pitches are level and open with a few small trees, two brick built barbecue units, and 36 electric hook-ups (10A). A playground has swings, seesaw and a slide, all set on a safety base, and the entire site is enclosed by grassy banks on three sides, with a wild flower walk around the top. Local attractions include Brands Hatch Circuit (4 miles), the International Karting Circuit at Buckmore Park (7 miles), and the nearby Country Park at West Malling.

Facilities

Comprehensive toilet facilities are smart and well maintained, including a well equipped room which is designed for disabled people. The laundry and dishwashing room is at one end of the modern heated building. No dogs or other pets. Caravans/motorcaravans greater than 25 ft overall are not admitted. Commercial vehicles are not accepted. Off site: Within walking distance are three pubs and a good Cantonese restaurant. Trains run to London Victoria from Borough Green (2 miles). Golf 1 mile. Riding 3 miles. Fishing 7 miles.

Open: 1 March - 31 October.

Directions

From M26 junction 2a, take A20 eastwards towards Wrotham Heath and Maidstone. Just past junction with A25, and opposite the Royal Oak pub, turn left into Ford Lane, and park is immediately on left. O.S.GR: TQ630580. GPS: N51:18.008 E00:20.723

Charges guide

Per unit incl. 2 persons	£ 12.50 - £ 14.00
incl. electricity	£ 14.50 - £ 16.00
extra person	£ 2.00
child (3-12 yrs)	£ 1.50
No credit cards.	

UK2820 Horsley Camping & Caravanning Club Site

Ockham Road North, East Horsley KT24 6PE (Surrey)

Tel: **01483 283273**   **www.alanrogers.com/UK2820**

London and all the sights are only 40 minutes away by train, yet Horsley is a delightful, quiet unspoilt site with a good duck and goose population on its part lily covered lake (unfenced). It provides 130 pitches, of which 83 have 10A electrical connections and 42 are all weather pitches (most with electricity). Seventeen pitches are around the bank of the lake, the rest further back in three hedged, grass fields with mostly level ground but with some slope in places. A new area has been developed in woodland. There is a range of mature trees and a woodland dog walk area (may be muddy). The soil is clay based so rain tends to settle – sluice gates remove extra water from the lake area when the rain is heavy. A recreation hall with table tennis (bats to hire) is sometimes used for bingo. Basic provisions, gas and books are kept in reception and resident managers will make you comfortable. Guildford and the R.H.S. gardens at Wisley are close by.

Facilities

Two purpose built, heated toilet blocks with good design and fittings, with some washbasins in cabins, a Belfast sink and parent and child room with vanity style basin, toilet and wide surface area. Laundry room and new drying areas. Well designed facilities for disabled people. Small shop in reception. Play area. Fishing is possible from May (adult £5.20/children £2.60 per day, NRA licence required). Off site: Shops and the station are 1 mile. Pubs 1.5 - 2 miles. Golf 1.5 miles. Riding 2 miles.

Open: March - October.

Directions

From M25 junction 10, in the direction of Guildford, after 0.5 miles take first left B2039 to Ockham and East Horsley, continuing through Ockham towards East Horsley. After 2 miles start to watch for brown site sign - not easy to see - and site is on right in 2.5 miles. O.S.GR: TQ083552. GPS: N51:17.184 W00:26.701

Charges guide

Per person	£ 6.60 - £ 8.60
child (6-18 yrs)	£ 2.25 - £ 2.35
non-member pitch fee	£ 6.00

UK2800 Alderstead Heath Caravan Club Site

Dean Lane, Merstham, Redhill RH1 3AH (Surrey)

Tel: **01737 644629**   www.alanrogers.com/UK2800

Alderstead Heath is a surprisingly rural site given that it lies just 25 minutes from central London by train. It is also well located for exploring the North Downs and is situated on the Pilgrim's Way. There are 240 pitches, of which 79 are reserved for touring, all with 16A electrical connections. There are plans to increase the number of touring pitches in future years. Most pitches are on well kept grass, but there are also 59 hardstandings. An attractive wooded area surrounds the site and concrete tracks there were laid during the war for tanks in preparation for the D-Day landings. Given the proximity of the M25 and M23 motorways, there is a certain amount of background traffic noise in parts of the site.

Facilities

Two well maintained toilet blocks, include a parent and toddler bathroom. The main block houses facilities for disabled visitors. Motorcaravan service point. Reception stocks a small range of essential foods, milk and gas. Small playing field. Good tourist information room. Off site: Golf 2 miles, Fishing 3 miles.

Open: All year.

Directions

Leave M25 at junction 8 and join A217 (signed Reigate). Fork left after 300 yards (signed Merstham). After a further 2.5 miles turn left at T-junction and join the A23. After 500 yards turn right into Shepherd's Hill and after a mile turn left into Dean Lane. Site is on the right after 175 yards.
O.S.GR: TQ290557. GPS: N51:17.189 W00:09.050

Charges guide

Per person	£ 3.90 - £ 5.40
child (5-16 yrs)	£ 1.30 - £ 2.15
non-member pitch fee	£ 10.70 - £ 14.10

UK2810 Chertsey Camping & Caravanning Club Site

Bridge Road, Chertsey KT16 8JX (Surrey)

Tel: **01932 562405**   www.alanrogers.com/UK2810

This long-established site (1926) is splendidly located on the banks of the River Thames, only a few minutes walk from the shops and amenities of Chertsey. A flagship site for the Club, it was totally redeveloped for 2004 at a cost of over £1 million pounds. There are 200 pitches including 50 new serviced pitches with hardstanding and 16A electricity and 15 'super service' pitches which have TV aerial points, water and waste drainage. The work included a new road system, heated toilet blocks with facilities for disabled visitors, recreation hall and much more. There has been extensive landscaping and the existing Thames creek has been extended to flow through the site with marshland areas to support the local wildlife environment. When possible, energy saving devices have been used. Squirrels, rabbits and ducks abound and trees and plants create a pretty site with views across the water and towards Chertsey bridge. Unfortunately there is some road noise and, depending on flight paths, aircraft noise. The rail station for London is at Chertsey or Weybridge. Fishing is possible and canoes can be launched from the site.

Facilities

The well equipped toilet blocks can be heated and include washbasins in cabins and facilities for disabled visitors. Hairdryers. Laundry. Motorcaravan service point. Well stocked shop for essentials and gas (08.00-11.00 and 16.00-18.00). Recreation hall. Play area on bark. Fishing (adults £1.70, NRA licence needed). Short dog walk areas. Caravan storage. Torches are necessary. Off site: Bus service in Chertsey 1.5 miles. Trains in Weybridge 3 miles. Golf and bicycle hire 1 mile.

Open: All year.

Directions

From M25 use exit 11. Turn left at roundabout on A317 towards Shepperton and continue to second set of traffic lights. Turn right then almost immediately left watching for green Club camp sign just before Chertsey bridge; the opening is narrow.
O.S.GR: TQ052667. GPS: N51:23.396 W00:29.380

Charges guide

Per person	£ 6.65 - £ 9.25
child (6-18 yrs)	£ 2.45 - £ 5.30
non-member pitch fee	£ 6.00

MAP 3

The largest city in Europe, covering over 600 square miles, London is jam packed with hundreds of magnificent museums, impressive art galleries, historic buildings and monuments, beautiful parks, bustling shopping centres and markets; it really has something to offer everyone.

WE HAVE CHOSEN FOUR PARKS WHICH HAVE EASY ACCESS TO CENTRAL LONDON, INCLUDING ONE IN HERTFORDSHIRE

Despite its size, London is relatively easy to explore, largely thanks to the efficient underground service. Buses are also very useful and allow you to see the famous sights as you travel, in particular, the open-top tourist buses which ply the streets offer a good introduction to the city. Among London's many landmarks are the Tower of London, Trafalgar Square, Piccadilly Circus, Buckingham Palace, Big Ben and the Houses of Parliament, to name but a few! Running through the heart of London is the River Thames, dividing north and south; over the years many attractions, restaurants and chic bars have appeared along its banks. Being one of the most multicultural cities in the world, there is a huge choice of restaurants offering a diverse variety of cuisine; food markets are dotted all around the capital. Shopping is another major feature of the city, from the famous Harrods store and Harvey Nichols, to commercial Oxford Street and the street markets of Camden town and Portobello Road. If all the crowds become too much then head to one of London's beautiful parks such as St James' Park next to Buckingham Palace, or Hyde Park, where you can take a boat trip along the Serpentine.

Places of interest

London Eye: world's highest observation wheel, reaching 450 feet. With 32 capsules, carrying 25 passengers in each, it offers breathtaking views.

Madame Tussaud's: huge collection of wax figures.

Tate Modern: contemporary art gallery housed in a transformed Bankside Power Station.

Victoria & Albert Museum: decorative art and design from around the world.

Kew Gardens: beautiful botanical gardens, with over 40,000 varieties of plants.

London Dungeon: a grisly house of horrors.

Hampton Court Palace: one the best palaces in Britain, with maze.

British Museum: houses a treasure trove of objects from all over the globe.

Did you know?

One in eight of the UK population live in London and over 200 languages are spoken.

The London Underground dates back to 1863 when the first underground railway was opened, from Paddington to Farringdon Street. Today, 150,000 people an hour enter the Tube network.

Founded in 1753 the British Museum is the oldest public museum in the world.

With 345 steps to the top, the Monument marks the start of the Great Fire of London.

London has over 18,000 Licensed Taxis.

At over 900 years old, the Tower of London has been a palace, prison, treasury, arsenal and even a zoo. It is now home to the Crown Jewels, which have been housed there since the 14th century.

RED TEXT DENOTES ALL-YEAR SITE

UK3250 Lee Valley Campsite

Sewardstone Road, Chingford, London E4 7RA (London)

Tel: 020 8529 5689. Email: scs@leevalleypark.org.uk

www.alanrogers.com/UK3250

This attractive site provides an excellent base from which to visit London, having both easy access to the M25 and excellent public transport links into the centre of London. Close to Epping Forest in the heart of the Lee Valley, this site is on a hillside overlooking the King George reservoir in a very pleasant and relaxed setting. Like its sister sites, it is understandably very popular with foreign tourers. With capacity for 200 units the site is mostly level, with several bush sheltered avenues and plenty of trees throughout providing shade. There are 20 pitches with tarmac hardstanding and 100 with electricity (10A). American motorhomes are not accepted. Just outside the gate is the bus stop (reception have full details of good value Travel Card schemes). The bus (no. 215) will take you to Walthamstow Central Underground station from where a frequent service runs to central London. Alternatively you can park at South Woodford or Chingford stations and use the train for London visits. Staff are very pleasant and helpful.

Facilities

Three blocks offer good facilities (one is heated in low season), all recently totally refurbished. Good en-suite room for disabled visitors. Baby changing area. Dishwashing, Laundry. Motorcaravan service point. Well stocked shop. Gas available. Playground. Off site: Fishing 500 yards. Shops within 2 miles. Riding 1 mile. 9-hole golf 1 mile, 18-hole golf 3 miles. Waltham Abbey 3 miles. River Lee Country Park and Epping Forest nearby.

Open: 1 April - 4 November.

Directions

From M25 take exit 26 on A112 to Chingford and site is on right in 3 miles. From A10 take the A110 (Chingford). After passing between reservoirs, at next traffic lights turn left on A112. Site on left after 2 miles. O.S. GR: TQ378970.
GPS: N51:39.239 W00:00.391

Charges guide

Per person	£ 6.45
child (under 16 yrs)	£ 2.90
electricity	£ 2.80
dog	£ 1.65

Minimum charge £8.60 per unit, per night.

UK3230 Lee Valley Camping & Caravanning Park

Meridian Way, Edmonton, London N9 0AS (London)

Tel: **020 8803 6900**. Email: **leisurecentre@leevalleypark.org.uk**   **www.alanrogers.com/UK3230**

Certainly one of the only sites in this guide with a multiplex cinema just outside the gate, you are greeted here by a very attractive entrance with flower displays. The site offers 140 spacious level pitches, with hardstandings and 100 with electricity hook-ups. The pitches are well laid out around a large field and there is a tent area just behind two grassy mounds. The grass and gardens are well trimmed and kept very tidy. There is a small kitchen facility and eating area with TV, set out under a gazebo. The site also offers hook-up points for tents. The adjacent sports complex is being rebuilt and will be used for the 2012 Olympics. The cinema complex incorporates a pizza restaurant, and from here you can hop on a bus to Edmonton Green or Ponders End station from where there is a regular service into central London (the journey time is around 40 minutes). The friendly site managers have detailed information about the various Travel Card schemes available. Alternatively, historic Waltham Abbey, Epping Forest and the 1,000 acre River Lee Country Park are all within easy access. This is a popular site, very well looked after and kept clean and tidy by site managers, this is a peaceful stop within easy reach of the city.

Facilities

Two modern, heated toilet blocks include spacious showers and two large en-suite units for disabled people. Baby changing area. All facilities are accessed by combination locks. Laundry. Motorcaravan service point. New barbecue area. Kitchen. Shop. Play area. Tennis and badminton. Tents for hire. Off site: Cinema with pizza restaurant at entrance. Supermarket 0.5 miles. Fishing 0.5 miles. Golf adjacent. Riding 4 miles.

Open: All year excl. Christmas, Boxing Day, New Year.

Directions

From M25 take exit 25. Follow signs for the city. At first set of traffic lights turn left (Freezywater). Continue on for about 6 miles. Follow signs for Lee Valley Leisure Complex. After roundabout (where A110 crosses), turn left at second set of traffic lights onto the complex. Follow site signs. O.S.GR: TQ357940. GPS: N51:37.943 W00:02.303

Charges guide

Per person	£ 6.40
child (under 16 yrs)	£ 2.90
electricity	£ 2.70
Minimum charge £ 9.60 per unit, per night.	

139

UK3260 Abbey Wood Caravan Club Site

Federation Road, Abbey Wood, London SE2 0LS (London)

Tel: **020 8311 7708**   www.alanrogers.com/UK3260

Situated close to Abbey Wood, it is hard to believe that this park is in London and the wardens have made every effort to create an attractive environment. There are 120 level caravan pitches all with 16A electricity and TV aerial connections. Of these, 64 have hardstandings. A large tent area provides an additional 100 pitches. Many pitches benefit from shade by mature trees. A secure fence around the perimeter is linked to close circuit TV cameras for security and just outside is a late arrivals area with electric and toilets; also protected by cameras. This park attracts many UK and overseas visitors as it offers a very good base from which to visit central London. A train service runs every 15 minutes from Abbey Wood station (5 minutes walk) to either Charing Cross or Cannon Street.

Facilities

Three modern, fully equipped toilet blocks, two with under-floor heating, one designed to be open all year, include washbasins in cubicles, generous showers, baby/toddler washroom, laundry equipment and dishwashing sinks. Good private facilities for disabled visitors. Motorcaravan service point. Gas. Bread, milk and cold drinks from reception (high season). Play area. Good travel and information centre can provide tickets for travel and tourist attractions. Off site: Sports centre 1 mile. Golf 4 miles.

Open: All year.

Directions

From east on M2/A2 or from central London: on A2 (third exit) turn off at A221 into Danson Road (signed Bexleyheath, Welling and Sidcup). Follow sign Bexleyheath to Crook Log (A207 junction); at traffic lights turn right and immediately left into Brampton Road. In 1.5 miles at traffic lights turn left into Bostal Road (A206); in 0.75 miles at traffic lights turn right into Basildon Road (B213). In 300 yds. turn right into McLeod Road, in about 0.5 miles at roundabout turn right into Knee Hill; in 100 yds. turn right (second right) into Federation Road. Site on left in 50 yds. From M25, north, west or south approach: leave at junction 2 onto A2 (London), then as above. O.S.GR: TQ472785. GPS: N51:29.216 E00:07.054

Charges guide

Per person	£ 4.70 - £ 6.20
child (5-16 yrs)	£ 1.50 - £ 3.00
pitch incl. electricity	
(non-member)	£ 10.90 - £ 15.30
Tent campers apply to site.	

UK3270 Crystal Palace Caravan Club Site

Crystal Palace Parade, London SE19 1UF (London)

Tel: **020 8778 7155**   www.alanrogers.com/UK3270

The Caravan Club's site at Crystal Palace in south London provides easy access to the city centre and all its many attractions. The pitches are pleasantly arranged in terraces overlooking the ruins of the old Crystal Palace, its park and National Sports Centre. It is surprisingly quiet given its location (with the exception of police sirens and over-flying aircraft). In peak season advance booking is always necessary. Most pitches are on gravel hardstanding, so it is particularly useful for out of season stays. There are places for 126 caravans or motorcaravans, all with electricity (16A). Tents are placed on the site's well mown lawns near reception, where there are four additional electric points. The Crystal Palace park is extensive and provides open spaces for strolls or picnics and plenty of activities for children. The Sports Centre has two swimming pools, tennis and squash courts and gym facilities, with national events in a variety of sports to watch at certain times. An area at the site entrance should be used for arrivals after 20.00.

Facilities

The main toilet block can be heated in cool weather with curtained washbasins for ladies. Another block provides basic unisex showers and toilets. Facilities for disabled visitors. Laundry room. Dishwashing sinks and rubbish bins. Motorcaravan service facilities. Gas available. Off site: Shops, pubs, etc. 400 yards. Many buses stop outside the site, including services to central London.

Open: All year.

Directions

On A205 South Circular road travelling east, pass Dulwich College and golf course on right, turn right at traffic lights. Within 400 yards, at traffic lights, turn right into Sydenham Hill. In 350 yds. at roundabout turn left. Site is 1 mile opposite mini-roundabouts. Travelling west on A205 South Circular, immediately after passing under Catford railway bridge, keep left onto A212 (Crystal Palace). After 2.75 miles, site is on left. O.S.GR: TQ341724. GPS: N51:25.552 W00:04.427

Charges guide

Per person	£ 4.70 - £ 6.20
child (5-16 yrs)	£ 1.50 - £ 3.00
pitch incl. electricity	
(non-member)	£ 10.90 - £ 15.30
Tent campers apply to site.	

MAP 4

East of England

The East of England is a perfect mix of soft and gentle countryside, ancient cities, historical towns, and storybook villages. Its coastline is largely untouched and studded with nature reserves, ideal for bird-watching, while the traditional beach resorts offer old-fashioned seaside fun.

THIS REGION INCLUDES THE COUNTIES OF ESSEX, SUFFOLK, NORFOLK, CAMBRIDGESHIRE, HERTFORDSHIRE AND BEDFORDSHIRE

Bedfordshire and Hertfordshire are the smallest counties in the region, with peaceful canals, undulating countryside with chalk downs, and some of the greatest stately homes in the country. Essex is full of quaint villages with a smattering of old towns and traditional seasides resorts, including Colchester and Southend-on-Sea. The river Cam winds its way through Cambridgeshire; punting along the river in Cambridge is a good way to relax and take in the many famous university buildings that dominate the waterfront along the 'Backs'. Further along the river is the ancient cathedral city of Ely, once an island before the Fen drainage. The flat Fenland has a network of rivers and canals, ideal for narrowboat trips, as are the Norfolk Broads. Norfolk itself is very flat, sparsely populated and tranquil, popular with walkers and cyclists, while the numerous nature reserves attract a variety of wildlife. It also has a beautiful coastline; the seaside towns of Great Yarmouth and Hunstanton are major draws. This unspoilt coastline stretches into Suffolk, 'Constable Country'. Full of space, with picturesque villages set amongst lush green countryside, dotted with timbered cottages and ruined abbeys, the county is home to Newmarket, the horse racing capital of the world.

Places of interest

Essex: Clacton-on-Sea; Walton-on-the-Naze, with nature reserve; Colchester, Epping; Chelmsford.

Suffolk: Ipswich; Felixstowe; Lowestoft; Bury St Edmonds; village of Clare with country park.

Norfolk: Norwich, seaside resort of Cromer; old fishing village of Sheringham, Sandringham Palace near King's Lynn; Banham Zoo.

Cambridgeshire: King's College and Chapel in Cambridge plus Fitzwilliam Museum; Peterborough; Imperial War Museum in Duxford; Huntingdon; Wildfowl & Wetland Trust near Wisbech.

Hertfordshire: St Albans; stately homes and gardens of Knebworth House and Hatfield House.

Bedfordshire: Bedford, Woburn with Abbey and safari park; Whipsnade Wild Animal Park; Shuttleworth Collection near Biggleswade.

Did you know?

Newmarket has been recognised as the Headquarters of Racing for over 300 years.

The highest point of the East of England is the Dunstable Downs at 244 metres.

Colchester is Britain's oldest recorded town with Europe's largest Norman Castle keep.

The artist John Constable was born in 1776 in the village of East Bergholt. Nearby Flatford Mill, was portrayed in his most famous scene 'The Haywain'.

Peterhouse is the first Cambridge college, founded in 1284 by the Bishop of Ely.

Epping Forest was the haunt of the renowned highwayman, Dick Turpin.

UK3300 **Homestead Lake Park**

Thorpe Road, Weeley, Clacton on Sea CO16 9JN (Essex)

Tel: **01255 833492**. Email: **lakepark@homesteadcaravans.co.uk**   **www.alanrogers.com/UK3300**

This well laid out, 25 acre park was opened in 2002. It is hidden from the road at the rear of Homestead Caravans sales areas and workshops in the countryside of the Tendring district, at Weeley near Clacton. It offers 50 fully serviced hardstanding pitches on gently sloping ground overlooking a fishing lake and recently built holiday lodge accommodation on the other side of the lake. Tents accepted for short stays only on a limited number of pitches. The park makes an ideal spot to stay, either for fishing or a relaxing weekend, or as a base for touring this part of Essex. A special area has been added to allow wheelchair users to fish. You could even arrange for your caravan to be serviced or repairs to be made while you stay. Homestead also have a large accessories superstore. Breakfast is recommended at the café as a start to your day.

Facilities

The toilet block offers clean and spacious facilities including an en-suite unit for disabled visitors. Baby changing facilities. Shop. Coffee shop and snack bar. Fishing lake. Woodland walks. Caravan sales, workshops and accessory shop.

Open: 1 March - 31 October.

Directions

From Colchester take A120, then A133 signed Clacton. At roundabout, turn left on B1033 into Weeley and site and showrooms are on left just past council offices. O.S GR: TM149225.
GPS: N51:51.593 E01:07.213

Charges guide

Per unit incl. 2 persons and electricity	£ 14.00 - £ 19.00
extra person	£ 3.00
child (under 18 yrs)	£ 1.00
dog	£ 1.00

UK3290 Fen Farm Caravan & Camping Site

East Mersea, Colchester CO5 8FE (Essex)

Tel: **01206 383275**. Email: **fenfarm@talk21.com**   **www.alanrogers.com/UK3290**

Tents were first pitched at Fen Farm in 1923 and since then the park has 'grown rather than developed' – something of which owners Ralph and Wenda Lord are proud. Most of the 90 pitches are unmarked, on grass and within two touring areas, either side of an area for over 80 holiday homes. All pitches have electricity connections and some have hardstanding and are fully serviced. A limited number of touring pitches are available on the smaller field, with outstanding views and direct access to the beach. This is an attractive well laid out site with trees and two ponds.

Facilities

The toilet block in the main touring field includes a family room and shower/toilet for disabled visitors. Laundry room. Another block has facilities for disabled visitors. Mobile shop for papers, bread and milk (weekends in summer). Basics from van (daily high season, weekends low season). Gas supplies. Play area. Caravan and boat storage. Off site: Shop 1.5 miles. 'Pick your own' fruit.

Open: 1 March - 31 October.

Directions

From Colchester, take B1025 to Mersea Island. After crossing causeway bridge, take left fork to East Mersea. Follow road for 2.75 miles to 'Dog and Pheasant' pub. Site entrance is next right. O.S.GR: TM058144. GPS: N51:47.398 E00:59.076

Charges guide

Per pitch	£ 18.00 - £ 20.00
extra car	£ 5.00

UK3285 Martello Beach Holiday Park

Belsize Avenue, Jaywick, Clacton on Sea CO15 2LF (Essex)

Tel: **0871 2501010**   **www.alanrogers.com/UK3285**

Situated on the outskirts of Jaywick and adjacent to a small sandy beach and the Martello tower, this large park is a member of the Park Resorts chain which specialises in caravan holiday home parks. On the far side of the park a large touring field provides 110 unmarked pitches, 70 of which have access to electricity. Tourers have access to the park's entertainment complex providing children's clubs, an arcade and evening entertainment. An outdoor pool is due to be replaced with a new indoor pool. However, facilities for tourers here are very limited indeed, with one toilet block providing showers and toilets, very limited fresh water provision and a very restricted dishwashing area.

Facilities

An older style toilet block provides showers and toilets, restricted dishwashing and a chemical disposal point. The toilet block has two outside fresh water points for tourers. No baby changing or facilities for disabled visitors. Launderette. Shop. Café. Outdoor pool (indoor pool planned). Entertainment complex with clubs for children, entertainment and arcade. Off site: Jaywick is a short drive. Clacton-on-Sea seaside resort is about 4 miles.

Open: 7 April - 27 October.

Directions

From A12 take A133 to Clacton-on-Sea. On outskirts of Clacton, turn right into B1077 (St John's Road). Continue for 1.5 miles, turn left into Jaywick Lane. Continue for 3 miles, then follow road signs for park. O.S.GR: TM138128. GPS: N51:46.361 E01:05.923

Charges guide

Per touring pitch	£ 6.00 - £ 29.00
tent pitch	£ 3.00 - £ 26.00

UK3310 Low House Touring Caravan Centre

Bucklesham Road, Foxhall, Ipswich IP10 0AU (Suffolk)

Tel: **01473 659437**. Email: **low.house@btinternet.com**   **www.alanrogers.com/UK3310**

Set in a sheltered 3.5 acres, this site has 30 level, grass pitches and an abundance of shrubs and flowers. The park has been divided into two areas bordered by mature trees and the grounds are well maintained. There are many different varieties of trees with a tree walk leading round two sides of the park. All the pitches have electrical connections (10/16A) and they back onto trees that provide plenty of shade and the opportunity to observe a range of wildlife. Low House lies between Felixstowe and Ipswich and would be a useful stopover for the Felixstowe port or Harwich.

Facilities

The older style, heated sanitary block is spotlessly clean with hot showers (50p). No on-site provisions but a supermarket is 2 miles (towards Ipswich). Frozen goods can be stored. Calor gas is available. Small, secure play area. Pet area with rabbit, hens and guinea fowl. Off site: Good bus service to Ipswich stops nearby. Pub in Bucklesham village (1.5 miles) and other good pubs nearby. Golf 2 miles.

Open: All year.

Directions

Turn off A14 (was A45) Ipswich ring road (south) via slip road onto A1156 (signed Ipswich East). Follow road over bridge crossing over the A45 and almost immediately turn right (no sign). After 0.5 miles turn right (Bucklesham). Site is on left after 400 yards. O.S.GR: TM225423. GPS: N52:02.041 E01:14.704

Charges guide

Per unit incl. 2 adults and children	£ 13.00
extra person	£ 3.00
child (5-15 yrs)	£ 2.00

No large commercial vehicles. No credit cards.

143

UK3315 Orwell Meadows Leisure Park

Priory Lane, Ipswich IP10 0JS (Suffolk)

Tel: **01473 726666**. Email: **recept@orwellmeadows.co.uk**   www.alanrogers.com/UK3315

This popular, family park is set on the edge of the Orwell Country Park near Ipswich with its many miles of walks and the famous Orwell Bridge with views of the Suffolk countryside. The park is run by David and Sally Miles and offers an ideal spot for a family holiday. Spacious pitches are around the edges of several separate meadows (surrounded on three sides by earth banks), all offering 16A electricity hook-ups. There is lots to see and do in the area, from towns such as Ipswich and Colchester to villages such as Framlingham and Aldeburgh, plus the rest of Constable country.

Facilities

The modern toilet block includes clean and spacious showers. It is kept to a very high standard. En-suite facilities for disabled visitors. Well stocked shop. Good clubhouse with bar and restaurant. Outdoor swimming pool. Play area. TV/family room. Max. two dogs per unit.

Open: March - January.

Directions

From A14 Ipswich bypass take Nacton/Ipswich exit (north of the A14) and follow signs for Orwell Country Park (narrow lane). Cross single track bridge over the A14 to the site entrance 20 yards on left. Follow signs past house/reception up hill and park on the left and walk back to reception.
O.S.GR: TM190408. GPS: N52:01.226 E01:11.497

Charges guide

Per unit incl. 2 persons and electricity	£ 15.00 - £ 17.00
extra person	£ 3.00 - £ 6.00

UK3330 Moat Barn Touring Caravan Park

Dallinghoo Road, Bredfield, Woodbridge IP13 6BD (Suffolk)

Tel: **01473 737520**   www.alanrogers.com/UK3330

Mike Allen opened this small touring park in April 2000 on the Suffolk Heritage Cycle Route, and also the Hull - Harwich National Cycle Route. The main touring area is bordered by established hedging and incorporates a circular roadway. The park currently provides 25 level grass pitches, all with electricity (10A), and there are plans to extend the number of pitches to 34. The park is popular with both walkers and cyclists and provides a tranquil environment to explore nearby Woodbridge and surrounding areas. The park has limited provision for large units. There are no facilities for children.

Facilities

The well equipped sanitary block can be heated. A separate unit houses a dishwashing sink. Motorcaravan service point. Bicycle hire. Laundry and shop planned. Off site: Nearby pub serving food. Public footpath.

Open: 1 March - 15 January.

Directions

Park is midway between Woodbridge and Wickham Market. From A12 take Bredfield turning (left from south, right from north). At village pump turn right. Follow road past church, through S-bends and, after 200 yards, site entrance on left, after farm buildings.
O.S.GR: TM270537. GPS: N52:08.106 E01:19.026

Charges 2009

Per unit incl. 2 persons and electricity	£ 14.00

UK3335 Westwood Park Caravan Park

Old Felixstowe Road, Bucklesham, Ipswich IP10 0BN (Suffolk)

Tel: **01473 659637**. Email: **julie@westwoodcaravanpark.co.uk**   www.alanrogers.com/UK3335

This brand new park opened in Easter 2007 and has been developed on land previously owned by the neighbouring farm. The park is situated between Felixstowe and Ipswich and is within easy reach of the River Deben and Woodbridge. The enthusiastic managers, Justin Rich and Julie Freeland have undertaken extensive planting throughout the park which promises to bring benefits and shade over time. The 90 level grass pitches are of varying size to accommodate both small and large caravans and motorhomes. All have 16A electricity and the hedges, once matured, should ensure separation.

Facilities

A brand new, but traditionally built, toilet block in the centre of the park includes facilities for disabled visitors (£5 deposit for key). Laundry. Purpose built reception provides local information and sells a limited range of provisions e.g. milk (plus bread and papers at B.Hs and high season). Recycling facilities planned. Off site: Free range eggs from a nearby farm. Pubs serving meals in Bucklesham and surrounding villages. Fishing 2 miles. Golf 4 miles. Beach 5 miles. Bus service to Ipswich nearby.

Open: All year excl. 16 January - 28 February.

Directions

Site is near Bucklesham. From the A12 (south) or A14(12) (north) take A14 towards Felixstowe. Continue for 5 miles and turn left signed Kirton, Bucklesham and Brightwell. Continue for about 1 mile: Park is on the right, immediately after Tenth Road on the left. O.S.GR: TN253411. GPS: N52:01.390 E01:17.033

Charges guide

Per unit incl. 2 persons and electricity	£ 15.00
extra person	£ 2.50

UK3322 Run Cottage Touring Park

Alderton Road, Hollesey, Woodbridge IP12 3RQ (Suffolk)

Tel: **01394 411309**. Email: **contact@run-cottage.co.uk**   **www.alanrogers.com/UK3322**

This small and very attractive 20 pitch site in the heart of unspoilt Suffolk countryside offers an opportunity to explore many of the local attractions on Suffolk's 'Heritage Coast'. Facilities on the site are limited but certainly adequate and the resident owners, Michele and Andy Stebbens are always available to ensure that you have an enjoyable stay. The site is open all year round and all pitches have 10A electricity, with 6 on hardstanding. This is a popular site and advance booking is strongly recommended. Local attractions include Sutton Hoo, Orford Castle and Framlingham Castle. The market town of Woodbridge is only 6 miles away. Within a short drive are the pretty coastal towns of Southwold, Dunwich, Orford and Aldeborough.

Facilities

New, well finished sanitary block is easily accessed and is well equipped. Reception contains a comprehensive selection of tourist leaflets and details of local attractions. Off site: Excellent pubs and restaurants within 1 mile. Riding 1 mile. Beach 1.5 miles. Fishing 1.5 miles. Golf and bicycle hire 5 miles.

Open: All year.

Directions

From A12 (Ipswich - Lowestoft) turn right at roundabout at Melton onto A1152 (Bawdsey, Orford). In 1.5 miles, at roundabout, turn right onto B1083 (Bawdsey, Hollesley). Within 0.75 miles take left fork to Hollesley. At Duck Corner cross road, turn right and continue through village to site on the left, 100 yds past Red Brick Bridge. Note: Do not follow SatNav directions. O.S.GR: TM351442.
GPS: N52:02.702 E01:25.610

Charges guide

Per unit incl. 2 persons and electricity	£ 16.00
tent incl. 2 persons	£ 10.00
extra person (over 3 yrs)	£ 2.50
dog (max. 2)	free

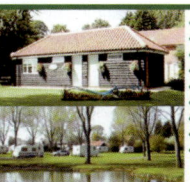

Close to the town of Woodbridge we are a small family run touring park with 20 pitches. Set in a 2.5 acre parkland setting with a large pond and views over open farmland, we offer peace and tranquillity. A place to escape the hustle and bustle of today's busy lifestyle.

Run Cottage Touring Park, Alderton Road, Hollesey, Woodbridge, Suffolk. IP12 3RQ
Tel: 01394 411 309
Website:http://www.run-cottage.co.uk
Email: contact@run-cottage.co.uk

- All electric hook ups
- Six all weather caravan pitches
- Open all year
- Two acre dog exercise area
- Toilet & shower block
- Chemical disposal point
- Tourist information area
- 1.5 miles from shingle beach
- Village shop & pub within easy walking distance

UK3320 The Moon & Sixpence

Newbourne Road, Waldringfield, Woodbridge IP12 4PP (Suffolk)

Tel: **01473 736650**. Email: **info@moonandsixpence.eu**   **www.alanrogers.com/UK3320**

This excellent site offers 60 large touring pitches that are positioned in the centre of an established and very spacious caravan holiday home park. The site is extremely well maintained and all the 60 touring pitches are equipped with 5A electricity, TV point, water tap and a drain. In the centre of the site and easily accessible to all, is a lake with a sandy beach that provides children with a place to swim and play with small inflatable boats. An area at one end of the lake is set aside for 10 pitches for adults only, all with views of the lake. There is an excellent bar and restaurant that offers a good range of dishes, with 'specials' at weekends. The site boasts good leisure facilities with three tennis courts and a nine hole pitch and putt course. These, together with other recreational facilities, are positioned at the rear of the site and do not affect those looking for a peaceful holiday break in the unspoilt Suffolk Countryside.

Facilities

Exceptionally well finished, centrally placed unisex sanitary block consists of 11 fully equipped private rooms containing a selection of WCs, washbasins and showers and baths. No specific facilities for disabled visitors but access to the block is via a ramp. Laundry facilities. Well stocked shop. Bar and restaurant. TV room. Lake swimming. Pitch and putt. Fishing. Off site: Golf (18-hole golf) 0.5 miles. Boat launching 2 miles. Fishing, bicycle hire and riding 5 miles.

Open: 1 April - 31 Ocotber.

Directions

From the A12 (Ipswich - Lowestoft) turn right at roundabout, towards Waldringfield and follow signs to site. Turn left at Waldringfield Golf Club to site on the left. O.S.GR: TM260457.
GPS: N52:03.751 E01:17.915

Charges guide

Per person (over 2 yrs)	£ 8.00 - £ 15.00

Min. charges apply.
Max. length 6.5 m. Max. age of unit 15 yrs.

UK3325 The Oaks Caravan Park

Chapel Road, Bucklesham, Ipswich IP10 0BT (Suffolk)

Tel: **01394 448837**. Email: **oakscaravanpark@aol.com**   www.alanrogers.com/UK3325

Situated between Felixstowe and Ipswich and with views over open farmland, this pleasant adult only touring park provides access to the surrounding countryside and towns, including the River Deben, Woodbridge and the Suffolk Heritage coast. Trees and shrubs planted around the perimeter and across the length of the site are now maturing, creating screening and shade for the 89 marked touring pitches. There are 79 electricity hook-ups and the well maintained grass pitches are laid out either side of an oval gravel path.

Facilities

The single modern sanitary block provides bright and clean toilet and shower facilities. Motorcaravan point. Facilities for disabled people planned. Gas is available at reception. Bicycle hire. Off site: Bus service outside park. Minibus service in the evenings by prior arrangement to nearby local pubs/restaurants, fish and chips Friday evenings. Riding 1 mile. Fishing less than 1 mile. Golf 4 miles. Beach 5 miles.

Open: 1 April - 31 October.

Directions

Site is between Bucklesham and Kirton. From the A12 (south) or A14(12) (north) take the A14 towards Felixstowe. Continue for 5 miles and turn left signed Bucklesham and Brightwell. Continue for 1 mile, past Tenth Road on the left, take next right signed Kirton and Newbourne. Park is on the right in 550 yds. O.S.GR: TM261411. GPS: N52:01.326 E01:17.948

Charges guide

| Per unit incl. 2 persons and electricity | £ 13.00 - £ 15.00 |
| extra person | £ 2.50 |

UK3340 Polstead Touring Park

Holt Road, Bower Housetye, Polstead CO6 5BZ (Suffolk)

Tel: **01787 211969**. Email: **polsteadtouringpark@hotmail.co.uk**   www.alanrogers.com/UK3340

This lovely adult only touring park in the peaceful Suffolk countryside is an ideal base from which to explore many places of interest. These include Flatford Mill, the scene for Constable's famous painting, Sudbury (the birthplace of Gainsborough), Long Melford with its Hall and Colchester, Britain's oldest town. The very neat and well cared for park is attractively presented and offers 30 level pitches all having electricity (10A). Well established hedges separate the pitches, 27 of which have gravel hardstanding. Following a change in ownership, the enthusiastic new owners plan to create an additional 20 pitches, including 4 super pitches. A tent field provides facilities for campers.

Facilities

The toilet block is well cared for with freshly laundered hand towels. Spacious showers. Facilities for disabled visitors are provided in both men's and ladies' rooms (showers large enough for wheelchair access), plus separate toilets. Laundry. Reception sells basic supplies. Fish and chips delivered by arrangement Saturdays. Rally field. Caravan storage. Off site: Fishing and golf nearby. Pub serving food, 3 minutes walk. Farm shop 100 yards.

Open: All year.

Directions

From A1071 Hadleigh - Sudbury road, just past the 'Brewers Arms' pub, turn left just before a water tower towards Polstead; park is 250 yards. O.S.GR: TL985403. GPS: N52:01.719 E00:53.741

Charges guide

Per unit incl. 2 persons	£ 14.00 - £ 17.50
extra person	£ 4.00 - £ 5.00
dog	£ 0.50

No credit cards.

UK3345 The Dell Caravan & Camping Park

Beyton Road, Thurston, Bury Saint Edmunds IP31 3RB (Suffolk)

Tel: **01359 270121**. Email: **thedellcaravanpark@btinternet.com**   www.alanrogers.com/UK3345

Close to the A14 and surrounded by farmland, this small touring site, 4 miles east of Bury St Edmunds, provides a convenient base to explore the nearby town and surrounding villages or as a stopover point. The current owners have created 60 spacious pitches within the main touring area, divided into two sections – one of which is reserved for adults only. All pitches have 10A electricity. A separate field with a further 10 pitches under trees is for contractors working locally, as well as any visitors who prefer shaded areas. The main touring field has some shade.

Facilities

Excellent and ample toilet and spacious shower facilities (free) are provided within a purpose built sanitary block. Ladies' toilets include a private bathroom and toilet. Family bathroom with bath, shower and baby changing facilities (charged). Separate toilet/shower for disabled visitors. Laundry room. Off site: Bus service from outside park. Fishing, golf and riding 3 miles.

Open: All year.

Directions

From the A14 take exit for Thurston and Beyton, 4 miles east of Bury St Edmunds. Follow signs to Thurston. Park is on the left, shortly after arriving at Thurston and signed from Beyton. O.S.GR: TL928640. GPS: N52:14.432 E00:49.462

Charges guide

| Per unit incl. 2 persons | £ 11.00 |
| incl. electricity | £ 13.00 - £ 15.00 |

UK3350 Church Farm Holiday Park

Church Farm Road, Aldeburgh IP15 5DW (Suffolk)

Tel: **01728 453433**. Email: **aldeburgh@amberleisure.com**   **www.alanrogers.com/UK3350**

This area of the Suffolk coast has always been a popular destination for visitors and Church Farm has an enviable location on the outskirts of Aldeburgh. The park includes a large area designated for caravan holiday homes as well as a separate touring area situated to the front of the park. The touring area provides 85 pitches for caravans and motorhomes (tents are not accepted). Pitches are separated by attractive hedging that blends in well with the natural environment. 60 pitches have access to 16A electricity, as well as water taps and a shared waste outlet (one between two pitches).

Facilities

The single toilet block has been fully upgraded with heating, free showers, toilets and washbasins (entry card with deposit). Access to the toilets and showers are via two steps, making it unsuitable for wheelchair users. Laundry room. Gas. Off site: Bus service 0.5 - 1 mile. Shops, pubs, etc. 15 minutes walk. Beach 5 minutes walk. Fishing and bicycle hire 1 mile. Riding 2 miles.

Open: Easter - 31 October.

Directions

On arrival at Aldeburgh, site is signed at roundabout in the direction of Thorpeness. Where road meets seafront, site is on left. From town centre follow road along seafront to site on left at end of town.
O.S.GR: TM465572. GPS: N52:09.496 E01:36.198

Charges guide

Per pitch	£ 20.00 - £ 24.00
incl. services	£ 24.00 - £ 28.00

UK3370 Kessingland Beach Holiday Park

Kessingland, Lowestoft NR33 7RN (Suffolk)

Tel: **01502 740636**. Email: **holidaysales.kessinglandbeach@park-resorts.com www.alanrogers.com/UK3370**

Set near the most easterly point in the UK, this park offers all you need for that total family holiday experience, including, bowling, pool tables, an amusement arcade and indoor and outdoor pools. If you so wish you need never leave Kessingland Beach until your holiday ends. There is evening entertainment, as well as a selection of bars and restaurants. Although mainly a large park for static caravan holiday homes, there is a touring area to the west of the park with quite spacious pitching and electricity. The toilet block is older in style but has been refurbished.

Facilities

The toilet block has been refurbished. Access is not suitable for wheelchairs. Laundry. Shop. Bars, restaurants, fish and chips. Entertainment complex. Indoor and outdoor swimming pools. New all-weather sports court. Adventure play area. Tennis courts. Amusements. Crazy golf. Bicycle hire. Off site: Beach and sea fishing 100 yds. Golf and riding 3 miles.

Open: 20 March - 26 October.

Directions

From Lowestoft, north, on A12 ignore first turning to Kessingland village and continue along A12 to next roundabout. Take left turning on roundabout signed Kessingland Beach. From A12 south, turn right at roundabout signed Kessingland Beach. At beach take sharp right to park entrance (narrow road).
O.S.GR: TM535859. GPS: N52:24.429 E01:43.482

Charges guide

Per caravan or motorcaravan incl. electricity	£ 6.00 - £ 29.00

UK3385 Applewood Caravan & Camping Park

Banham Zoo, The Grove, Banham NR16 2HE (Norfolk)

Tel: **01953 888370**. Email: **info@banhamzoo.co.uk**   **www.alanrogers.com/UK3385**

Applewood is a 13 acre touring park, adjacent to the famous Banham Zoo, the residents of which are the only thing that may disturb your relaxation while on this park (but they do not usually rise until 08.00). Visitors to the park receive a special price for admission to the Zoo. At weekends, one of Norfolk's largest car boot sales is held at the arena area alongside the site. Applewood has 100 pitches, 70 with electric hook-ups (10A). They are spread amongst thirteen areas, each separated by high, established hedges which offer privacy and seclusion. There is a large rally field and a function room. The Appleyard, two minutes walk from the park provides a Spar shop, Huckleberry's restaurant and gift shops. The village with its pub is also within walking distance.

Facilities

Two toilet blocks, one new and one refurbished provide good, clean and spacious facilities. Room for disabled visitors. Laundry. Motorcaravan service point. Accessory shop, rally field and function room. Gas supplies. Off site: Zoo and The Appleyard with shop and restaurant. Snetterton race circuit 3 miles. Norwich 15 miles.

Open: All year.

Directions

From Attleborough on the A11 take B1077 to New Buckenham and Banham Zoo. Follow road to T-junction with B1113 and turn right signed Banham. Follow through village and park is on the left.
O.S.GR: TM058871. GPS: N52:26.782 E01:01.508

Charges guide

Per person (4 yrs and over)	£ 1.50
pitch incl. electricity	£ 15.00
tent	£ 7.75

147

UK3382 Rose Farm Touring Park

Stepshort, Belton, Great Yarmouth NR31 9JS (Norfolk)

Tel: **01493 780896**. Email: **myhra@rosefarmtouringpark.fsnet.co.uk**   **www.alanrogers.com/UK3382**

This part of Norfolk is well known for its seaside attractions and the campsites which combine caravan holiday homes and touring pitches. Rose Farm caters for another type of camping holiday, offering space with the peace and tranquillity that you may not be expecting in this particular area! Spread over eight acres, the park is split into two separate fields. The first is large and open, surrounded by fencing and hedges, with pitches around the edge. It is very spacious with a very good toilet/shower block. The second field is long with pitching on either side. A new shower block here offers top quality facilities. Both blocks are immaculate with thoughtful decor. Several hardstanding pitches are also available. Recent landscaping of the site includes a new walkway along the bank with picnic tables. With nearby attractions such as Fritton Lake Country Park, Pleasure Wood Hills Theme Park and of course Great Yarmouth with its fun fair and amusement arcades, your holiday in Norfolk could be full of busy days. Sue and Tora Myhra are very proud of Rose Farm and what they have achieved in the few years since taking over what was quite a run-down campsite.

Facilities

The two excellent blocks offer super facilities. The newer block is in Norwegian style, with a very modern fresh and spacious interior. Showers are good with changing space, washbasins are open or in cubicles. The laundry is in the first block along with an iron and ironing board. Facilities for disabled visitors (pitching can be arranged in advance). Adventure playground. TV room. Dog walk. Internet access. Off site: Shops nearby. Fishing and golf 3 miles. Riding and bicycle hire 4 miles. Beach 5 miles.

Open: All year.

Directions

From Great Yarmouth and Gorleston take the A143 signed Beccles and Diss. At dual carriageway (Bradwell) take immediate right to Burgh Castle, take next right, site on right in 25 yards.
O.S.GR: TG486033 GPS: N52:34.282 E01:40.126

Charges guide

Per unit incl. 2 persons	£ 11.00 - £ 16.00
incl. electricity	£ 13.50 - £ 19.00
extra person	£ 2.50

Special offers available. No credit cards.

UK3390 The Dower House Touring Park

Thetford Forest, East Harling NR16 2SE (Norfolk)

Tel: **01953 717314**. Email: **info@dowerhouse.co.uk**   **www.alanrogers.com/UK3390**

Set on 20 acres in the heart of Britain's largest forest on the Suffolk and Norfolk borders, The Dower House provides quiet woodland walks and cycle ways, with an abundance of wildlife. David and Karen Bushell, owners for many years, continue to upgrade the facilities without compromising the park's natural features. There are 160 really large pitches with 10A electricity available. Most are level, although given the forest location there are a few tree roots. A fourth field provides 60 pitches for tents. Six pitches for visitors with mobility problems are linked by a path to the main facilities. The Dower House, as well as being the owners' home, houses a pleasant bar serving bar food (weekends only in low season). A pleasant patio area is used for occasional entertainment at weekends. A torch is necessary as there is no site lighting other than at the facilities.

Facilities

Two toilet blocks. A small, refurbished one near the entrance and a larger one with a baby room. A separate building houses the showers (five for each sex) and a unit for disabled people. Dishwashing room, including a lower sink for children or disabled people. Laundry room with washing machine and dryer. Separate licensed shop doubling as reception and open daily in the season, on request at other times. Gas supplies. Information room. TV and quiet rooms (no games machines). New heated outdoor swimming pool (25/5-2/9, under 15s must be with an adult). Paddling pool. Caravan storage. Torches necessary. Off site: Fishing nearby 1.5 miles. Snetterton motor racing circuit and Sunday market 2-3 miles.

Open: 15 March - 29 September.

Directions

From A11 (Thetford - Norwich) road, 7 miles from Thetford, turn right on B1111 towards East Harling. Turn right at church and right at T-junction; park is on right. From A1066 Thetford-Diss road take left fork signed East Harling. Ignore signs for Forestry Commission site and park is next on left. Follow long drive (unmade road) for about 1 mile – keep speed down. O.S GR: TL969853.
GPS: N52:25.697 E00:53.779

Charges guide

Per unit incl. 2 persons	£ 11.50 - £ 19.95
incl. electricity	£ 14.50 - £ 23.25
extra person	£ 3.50 - £ 4.00
child (4-17 yrs)	£ 1.25 - £ 2.00

No charge for awnings or dogs.

UK3400 The Old Brick Kilns Caravan & Camping Park

Little Barney Lane, Barney, Fakenham NR21 0NL (Norfolk)

Tel: 01328 878305. Email: enquiries@old-brick-kilns.co.uk   www.alanrogers.com/UK3400

This is a tranquil, family run park and a friendly, helpful atmosphere prevails. The park's development on the site of old brick kilns has resulted in land on varying levels. This provides areas of level, well drained pitches (e.g. the Dell, the Orchard) all of which are on hardstanding. There are 65 pitches in total, all with electricity (16A), including a newer area with serviced pitches. Banks around the park and a wide range of trees and shrubs provide shelter and are home for a variety of wildlife. There are garden areas, including a butterfly garden, and a conservation pond is the central feature. Drinking water is supplied by a 285 ft. bore and excellent roofed service areas provide water and waste disposal. Amenities include a large, comfortable bar area and restaurant, open at weekends. and as the park is 8 miles from the coast, it is ideally situated to explore North Norfolk. A member of the Best of British group.

Facilities

Smart, heated toilet blocks provide good, clean facilities with washbasins in curtained cubicles. Baby room. Facilities for disabled people (unisex; Radar key). Laundry room. Motorcaravan service point. Good shop with gas supplies. Bar/restaurant (weekends) with patio area outside with barbecue. TV and games room. Giant chess. Small library. Fenced play area. Fishing (purpose-built platforms). Internet access. B&B also available. Strictly no arrivals until after 13.00. Caravan storage. Off site: Riding 6 miles. Golf 5 or 8 miles. Thursford collection 2 miles.

Open: All year excl. 7 January - 1 March.

Directions

From Fakenham take A148 Cromer road. After 6 miles, at Thursford, fork right on B1354 Melton Constable road. In 300 yds, turn right, signed Barney, and then first left along a narrow country lane with passing places, for 0.75 miles. O.S.GR: TG004332. GPS: N52:51.482 E00:58.550

Charges guide

Per unit incl. 2 persons	
and electricity	£ 14.50 - £ 18.50
'super' pitch plus	£ 2.50 - £ 3.50
extra person	£ 3.00
child (up to 15 yrs)	£ 1.00 - £ 2.00
dog (max. 2)	£ 0.75

UK3420 Two Mills Touring Park

Yarmouth Road, North Walsham NR28 9NA (Norfolk)

Tel: 01692 405829. Email: enquiries@twomills.co.uk   www.alanrogers.com/UK3420

Two Mills is a quiet site for adults only. Set in the bowl of a former quarry, the park is a real sun trap, both secluded and sheltered, with bird song to be heard at all times of the day. Neatly maintained with natural areas, varied trees, wild flowers and birds, the owners, Barbara and Ray Barnes, want to add their own touches to this popular park. There are 55 level marked pitches for tourers, 48 all weather gravel, including 12 serviced pitches (hardstanding, patio, water and waste water drainage). All are generously sized and have electricity (10/16A). This is a good centre from which to explore the north Norfolk coast, the Broads or for visiting Norwich. A footpath from the park joins the Weavers Way. A member of the Best of British group.

Facilities

Neat, clean central toilet block can be heated and includes some washbasins in cabins, en-suite facilities for disabled people, laundry and dishwashing rooms. Small shop at reception. TV room with tea and coffee facilities. Dogs are accepted by arrangement only. Only adults are accepted. Off site: Hotel/pub 100 yds. Town 20 minutes walk. Fishing or golf 5 miles. Bicycle hire 1.5 miles. The coast is 5 miles.

Open: All year excl. 2 January - 1 March.

Directions

From A149 Stalham - North Walsham road, watch for caravan sign 1.5 miles before North Walsham (also signed White Horse Common). The road runs parallel to the A149 and site is on right after 1.25 miles. From North Walsham take Old Yarrmouth road past hospital, and park is on left after 1 mile. O.S.GR: TG292287. GPS: N52:48.230 E01:24.216

Charges guide

Per unit incl. 2 persons	£ 13.50 - £ 18.50
'panorama' pitch	£ 15.50 - £ 19.50
extra person	£ 2.50
dog (by arrangement)	£ 0.75
Senior citizen discounts.	

UK3410 **Sandy Gulls Caravan Park**

Cromer Road, Mundesley NR11 8DF (Norfolk)

Tel: **01263 720513**   www.alanrogers.com/UK3410

This is a super, adults only clifftop hideaway on the outskirts of Mundesley-on-Sea. One of the only clifftop parks with space for touring units on this coastline, there are panoramic views from every pitch. All 35 pitches have electricity and TV aerial hook-ups. Some are on hardstanding, others are slightly sloping on grass (chocks advised). Primarily a caravan holiday home park, there are units to rent. Facilities are excellent and well maintained. Access to the Blue Flag beach is via a large tarmac ramp. The village of Mundesley is only a mile away with a 9-hole golf course and a wide variety of shops and pubs, plus an amusement arcade. There is much to see and do in this area of Norfolk with a steam railway further along the coast. North Walsham is within easy reach and has a good array of shops and supermarkets.

Facilities

The toilet block is modern and spacious offering large shower rooms and open washbasins, all kept very clean. Facilities for disabled visitors planned. Shops, pubs and restaurants nearby. Off site: Village 1 mile. Tennis, boat launching, riding and golf nearby.

Open: March - November.

Directions

Site is 1 mile north of Mundesley (4 miles south of Cromer) on the main coast road. O.S.GR: TG302373. GPS: N52:53.074 E01:25.244

Charges guide

Per unit incl. up to 4 peraons	£ 11.00 - £ 20.00
extra person	£ 3.00

UK3450 **Little Haven Caravan & Camping Park**

The Street, Erpingham, Norwich NR11 7QD (Norfolk)

Tel: **01263 768959**. Email: **patl@haven30.fsnet.co.uk**   www.alanrogers.com/UK3450

Within easy reach of the coast and the Broads, this is an attractive, peaceful little site with good facilities. Only adults are accepted. There are 24 grassy pitches, all with electricity (16A) and 6 with hardstanding. They are arranged around the outside of a gravel access road with a central lawn and decorative pergola, a neat little garden and a seating area. There is no shop, but two pubs serving food and traditional ales are within walking distance. This is an ideal base for cycling and walking (the Weavers Way footpath is within half a mile) or just relaxing. Also close by is magnificent Blickling Hall with its superb state rooms, gardens and park, alternatively a short drive takes you to the historic market town of Aylsham.

Facilities

The well maintained toilet unit is heated and includes spacious hot showers and a covered dishwashing and laundry area. Facilities for disabled people are planned. Gas available. Site is unsuitable for American motorhomes. This is an adults only park. Off site: Bus service on the main A140 road. Riding 1 mile. Fishing 3 miles. Bicycle hire 5 miles. Beach 6 miles. Golf 10 miles.

Open: 1 March - 31 October.

Directions

From A140 Cromer - Norwich road, going south towards Aylsham and 3 miles south of Roughton, past the Horseshoes pub and Alby crafts, take first turning right signed Erpingham 2 miles (narrow road). Site is 175 yards on right. O.S.GR: TG190320. GPS: N52:50.525 E01:16.254

Charges guide

Per unit incl. 2 persons, electricity and awning	£ 11.00
No credit cards.	

UK3435 Woodlands Caravan Park

Holt Road, Upper Sheringham NR26 8TU (Norfolk)

Tel: 01263 823802. Email: enquiries@woodlandscaravanpark.co.uk   www.alanrogers.com/UK3435

This pleasantly wooded caravan park is set in the beautiful surroundings of North Norfolk's protected heathland, next to Sheringham Park (National Trust). There are many lovely walks all around the area, including one to the beach (1.5 miles). The park is within easy reach of Holt, Cromer and Sheringham, with the major bird watching areas of Blakeney, Cley and Salthouse also within 30 minutes drive. There are 225 touring pitches in two main areas for caravans and motorcaravans (tents are not accepted). Electricity (10A) is available to most. The excellent Pinewood Park Leisure Club is adjacent to the park offering swimming and other fitness facilities at a discounted rate for those staying at Woodlands.

Facilities

Three well maintained toilet blocks provide good facilities and include facilities for disabled visitors, baby changing and laundry. Well stocked shop. Gas supplies. Lounge bar and family bar with musical entertainment most weekends. Barbecues. Play area (2 acres, fenced and gated). Pinewood Park Leisure Club with indoor pool, gym, sauna. etc (all year). Off site: Golf and bicycle hire 1.5 miles. Fishing and riding 3 miles.

Open: March - October.

Directions

From Cromer on the A148 towards Holt, pass signs for Sheringham Park and site is on right just before Bodham village. From Holt on A148 just after Bodham, site is on left, well signed. O.S.GR: TG130409. GPS: N52:55.418 E01:11.666

Charges guide

Per pitch incl. electricity	£ 15.50 - £ 18.50
awning	£ 2.50

UK3470 Breckland Meadows Touring Park

Lynn Road, Swaffham PE37 7PT (Norfolk)

Tel: 01760 721246. Email: info@brecklandmeadows.co.uk   www.alanrogers.com/UK3470

Within easy reach of the historic market town of Swaffham, this 'adult only' park offers peace and tranquillity and would make a good base to explore East Anglia and the local area. There are just 45 pitches, 25 on hardstanding, the remainder on fairly level, neat grass. All have 16A electricity hook-ups. There are two main roads close to the park but well established hedges and trees help minimise any noise. The Swaefas Way runs alongside the park and from this walkers can access the famous Peddars Way. Many attractions within easy reach include Cockley Cley Medieval Iceni Village and Saxon Church, Castle Acre Priory and Oxburgh Hall. Swaffham has a popular Saturday market.

Facilities

The neat, well cared for toilet block provides all the usual facilities, including spacious showers and a separate toilet and washbasin unit for disabled visitors. Laundry room. Gas supplies. WiFi. Off site: Town 0.5 miles. Bicycle hire 1 mile. Golf 2 miles. Riding 4 miles. Fishing 5 miles.

Open: All year.

Directions

Park is just west of Swaffham on the old A47, about 1 mile from the town centre. O.S.GR: TF809094. GPS: N52:39.069 E00:40.612

Charges guide

Per unit incl. 2 persons and electricity	£ 11.75 - £ 16.00
extra person	£ 3.00
awning	£ 2.00
dog	£ 0.50
No credit cards.	

151

UK3490 The Grange Touring Park

Ormesby Saint Margaret, Great Yarmouth NR29 3QG (Norfolk)

Tel: 01493 730306. Email: info@grangetouring.co.uk   www.alanrogers.com/UK3490

The appealing appearance of this family touring site is that of a garden, with hanging baskets, flower beds, bluebells and daffodils under the trees in spring, with all carefully tended by the resident wardens. There are 60 level pitches with electricity (16A) and 10 for tents, all arranged on well trimmed grass with tarmac access roads. Adjacent to the campsite is The Grange itself – a free house offering a wide range of meals, beers and real ale, plus children's play equipment (open all year). The site owner also has a holiday campsite at Hemsby (4 miles) with its own wide sandy beach, which guests at The Grange are welcome to use. The nearest beach is a mile away and local attractions include Caister Castle and Motor Museum and the Norfolk Rare Breed Centre. Great Yarmouth Centre with many attractions and The Broads are within 5 miles.

Facilities

A modern toilet building is spacious and well maintained, housing all the usual facilities including free showers. Baby room in the ladies'. Laundry room with washing machine and dryer. Washing lines are provided at the rear of the building. Gas supplies. Swings for children. Internet café (£2 per hour) and WiFi. Off site: Bus service 250 yds. Beach, shops and supermarket 1 mile. Riding 2 miles. Golf 3 miles. Fishing 4 miles.

Open: 20 March - 1 October.

Directions

From A149 Great Yarmouth - North Walsham road, on the Caister bypass, at roundabout take the B1159 road signed Hemsby. Park is on left just before next roundabout. O.S.GR: TG515140. GPS: N52:40.087 E01:42.658

Charges guide

Per unit incl. up to 4 persons	£ 8.50 - £ 14.00
extra person	£ 2.50
electricity	£ 3.00

THE GRANGE TOURING PARK

Yarmouth Road, Ormesby St. Margaret, Great Yarmouth, Norfolk NR29 3QG

www.grangetouring.co.uk
info@grangetouring.co.uk

Tel: 01493 730306 - 01493 730023
Fax: 01493 730188

This level grassy park will accommodate seventy touring outfits and tents and adjoins the grounds of the Grange Free House. It is very conveniently situated as a touring centre for Great Yarmouth, the Norfolk Broads and the historic Cathedral City of Norwich. We are approximately one mile from the beach.

UK3455 Deer's Glade Caravan & Camping Park

White Post Road, Hanworth, Norwich NR11 7HN (Norfolk)

Tel: 01263 768633. Email: info@deersglade.co.uk   www.alanrogers.com/UK3455

In 2003, David and Heather Attew decided that they had an area that would make a superb setting for a caravan park and that they could give up farming. In early 2004 after much hard work, they opened this top quality park and it has since developed into a very popular site. Not far from the Norfolk Broads and close to the East Anglian coast, the park is open all year round. There are 125 level pitches (some with hardstandings), all with 16A electricity and 100 with TV aerial points. New hedging between pitches is becoming established.

Facilities

Two spacious new toilet blocks are of a high standard and include vanity style washbasins for ladies, a room for disabled visitors or families, dishwashing room and a laundry. Motorcaravan service point. Licensed shop (all year). Play area. Fishing lake (charge). Bicycle hire. Caravan valet service. Free minibus to local tavern. Off site: Bus service under 1 mile. Pub 1.5 miles. Woodland walks. Riding 2 miles. Beach, golf 5 miles.

Open: All year.

Directions

From Norwich take A140 towards Cromer and 5 miles after Aylsham turn right towards Suffield Park (White Post Road). Park is 0.5 miles on the right. O.S.GR: TG214340. GPS: N52:51.469 E01:17.259

Charges guide

Per person	£ 5.00 - £ 7.50
child	£ 1.75 - £ 2.75
dog	£ 1.00
Family deals available.	

You might also like to consider...

UK3430 Kelling Heath Holiday Park

Weybourne, Holt, Sheringham NR25 7HW (Norfolk)

Tel: **01263 588181**. Email: **info@kellingheath.co.uk**   **www.alanrogers.com/UK3430**

Not many parks can boast their own railway station and Kelling Heath's own halt on the North Norfolk Steam Railway gives access to shopping in Holt or the beach at Sheringham. Set in 250 acres of woodland and heathland overlooking the north Norfolk coast, this spacious holiday park offers freedom and relaxation with 300 touring pitches, all with 16A electricity (some are fully serviced) in four different zones. Pitching is good on quite firm, level grass (no hardstanding). Together with 384 caravan holiday homes (36 to let, the remainder privately owned), they blend easily into the part-wooded, part-open heath. A wide range of facilities provides activities for all ages. 'The Forge' has an entertainment bar, an adult only bar and a family room, with comprehensive entertainment all season. 'Fitness Express' provides an indoor pool, spa pool, sauna, steam rooms and a gym. An adventure playground with assault course is near. The central reception area is attractively paved to provide a 'village store' and an open air bandstand where one can sit and enjoy the atmosphere. The park's natural environment allows for woodland walks, a nature trail and cycling trails, and a small lake for fishing (permit holders only).

Facilities

Three toilet blocks serve the touring pitches, one heated. Facilities for disabled people, baby room. All blocks have a few washbasins in private cubicles, baby baths. Laundry. Shop. Gas. Bar, restaurant and takeaway. Indoor leisure centre with pool (19 x 9 m), gym, etc. with trained staff. Outdoor pool (main season). Adventure play area. Tennis. Fishing. Bicycle hire. Entertainment programme. Environmental 'Acorn Club' for children. Torches useful. Off site: The Norfolk coast and the Broads National Park.

Open: 10 February - 12 December.

Directions

On A148 road from Holt to Cromer, after High Kelling, turn left just before Bodham village (camping sign) signed Weybourne. Follow road for about 1 mile to park O.S.GR: TG117418. GPS: N52:55.708 E01:08.198

Charges guide

Per unit incl. electricity	£ 16.50 - £ 29.50
with full services	£ 21.50 - £ 34.50
dog (max. 2)	£ 3.00 - £ 5.00

Min 7 day stay in high season. No single sex groups.

Escape the normal routine...

UK3480 Little Lakeland Caravan Park

Wortwell, Harleston IP20 0EL (Norfolk)

Tel: **01986 788646**. Email: **information@littlelakeland.co.uk**   **www.alanrogers.com/UK3480**

This peaceful hideaway with its own fishing lake is tucked behind the houses and gardens that border the village main street. It is a traditional, mature little park with just 58 pitches. There are several caravan holiday homes and long stay units, but there should always be around 22 places for tourers. The pitches are mostly individual ones separated by mature hedges and trees. Fishing in the attractive lake is free and solely for campers. A member of the Countryside Discovery group.

Facilities

A modern, heated toilet block provides washbasins all in cubicles for ladies, and one for men. Fully equipped laundry. Separate en-suite room for disabled visitors. A further unit (also heated) by reception provides a shower, WC and basin per sex. Reception stocks gas and some basic essentials. Small play area. Library. Fishing (max. 4 rods per unit). Off site: Bus service 250 yds. Golf 4 miles. Riding 6 miles.

Open: 15 March - 31 October.

Directions

Approaching from Diss, leave A143 at roundabout signed Wortwell. Continue to village, pass 'The Bell' pub then a garage, after which turn right at first bungalow (Little Lakeland Lodge). Site is down lane. O.S.GR: TM270850. GPS: N52:24.977 E01:21.169

Charges guide

Per unit incl. 2 persons	£ 10.80 - £ 13.30
incl. electricity	£ 13.30 - £ 15.80

No credit cards.

153

UK3500 Woodhill Park

Cromer Road, East Runton, Cromer NR27 9PX (Norfolk)

Tel: **01263 512242**. Email: **info@woodhill-park.com**

www.alanrogers.com/UK3500

Woodhill is a seaside site with good views and a traditional atmosphere. It is situated on the cliff top, in a large gently sloping open grassy field, with 300 marked touring pitches. Of these, 210 have electricity (16A), 7 are fully serviced and many have wonderful views over the countryside around the park. A small number of holiday homes which are located nearer to the cliff edge have the best sea views, although perhaps at times a little bracing! Although the site is fenced there is access to the cliff top path (watch young children). Nearby attractions include boat trips to see the seals off Blakeney Point, the Shire Horse Centre at West Runton and the North Norfolk Steam Railway.

Facilities

The three sanitary units are fully equipped but could be a little short of showers at peak times. Laundry with washing machines and dryer (iron from reception). Fully equipped unit for disabled persons. Well stocked shop (19/3-31/8). Good, large adventure playground and plenty of space for ball games. Crazy golf. Giant chess and golf course adjacent to the site. Off site: Beach 0.5 miles. Fishing 1 mile. Bicycle hire, golf and riding 2 miles.

Open: 19 March - 31 October.

Directions

Site is beside the A149 coast road between East and West Runton. O.S.GR: TG190420. GPS: N52:55.984 E01:16.598

Charges guide

Per person	£ 2.50
child (4-16 yrs)	£ 1.00
small pitch (no electricity)	£ 6.20 - £ 8.60
pitch incl. electricity	£ 9.50 - £ 11.80
multi-service pitch	£ 12.75 - £ 15.25

NORTH NORFOLK... *naturally*

Woodhill Park

Relax in your touring caravan or tent enjoying peace and tranquillity with magnificent views of the sea and surrounding North Norfolk countryside. Multi-service, electric pitches and amenity buildings available. Luxurious centrally heated holiday homes for hire.

Bookings or brochure 01263 512242 or online **www.woodhill-park.com** Cromer Road, East Runton, Cromer, Norfolk NR27 9PX

UK3460 The Garden Caravan Site

Barmer Hall, Syderstone, Kings Lynn PE31 8SR (Norfolk)

Tel: **01485 578220**. Email: **nigel@mason96.fsnet.co.uk**

www.alanrogers.com/UK3460

In the quiet Norfolk countryside, this imaginative touring park is set in an enclosed walled garden. Sheltered from the winds by the high walls and a sun trap, visitors can relax in peace and tranquillity. Attractive mature trees, shrubs and climbers provide shade at various times of the day. The Mason family run the site in a relaxed way and the atmosphere is superb. There are 30 pitches, all with electricity (16A) and TV hook-up. Some are slightly slopping and will require blocks. Reception is housed in a small kiosk (not always manned, so pitch yourself and pay later). Barmer Hall is not far from Sandringham, and there are plenty of peaceful lanes to explore on your bicycle or take a woodland walk from the little door in the wall at the rear of the site.

Facilities

The single toilet block (heated when necessary) includes very spacious hot showers and free hot water. Dishwashing sinks are under cover at one end of the building. No shop, but gas, ices, soft drinks and free range fresh eggs are usually available. Off site: Bicycle hire 4 miles. Riding 6 miles. Golf 10 miles. Norfolk Lavender, Langham Glass or the Thursford collection of steam engines and mechanical organs.

Open: 1 March - 1 November.

Directions

About 6 miles west of Fakenham turn off A148 at Fourwinds Garage to Docking and Hunstanton on B1454. After a further 4 miles turn to Barmer Hall (site signed). Road is marked 'unsuitable for motor vehicles' but ignore and follow past and behind the Hall and farm buildings. O.S.GR: TF810330. GPS: N52:51.848 E00:41.470

Charges guide

Per person	£ 6.50 - £ 8.00
child (under 15 yrs)	£ 2.50
pitch incl. electricity	£ 2.50
TV aerial hook-up	£ 1.00
No credit cards.	

UK3485 Clippesby Hall

Clippesby, Great Yarmouth NR29 3BL (Norfolk)

Tel: **01493 367800**. Email: **holidays@clippesby.com**

www.alanrogers.com/UK3485

Set in the heart of the Broads National Park this is an unusual park in the grounds of a private estate where one can wander at will. Clippesby offers the choice of pitching amongst the shady woodland or on the gently sloping lawns of the hall with colourful mature trees and shrubs. The 100 pitches are well spaced and clearly numbered (70 with 10A electricity). 'The Meadow' offers pitches for motorcaravans with hardstandng, 16A electricity, water and drainage. There is a friendly welcome from the Lindsay family who have lived in the single storey Hall for many years and the opportunity to enjoy the mature gardens and facilities. These include a sunken grass tennis court, a small heated pool with mellow flagstone patio area, a timber adventure playground, and family golf with a seaside theme. The Muskett Arms with an attractive, comfortable family bar and a sheltered courtyard outside, provides fresh, home-cooked meals, music nights and other family entertainment and 'Susie's Coffee Shop' has a good selection of food during the day. Children can roam at will and in safety, and parents can relax and unwind at this comfortable park, never mind all the attractions of the Broads and Great Yarmouth on your doorstep and only the peacocks to disturb you!

Facilities

Three timbered heated toilet blocks provide clean and modern facilities. Some washbasins in cabins and 10 showers in total. En-suite room for disabled visitors. Family room with bath and baby changing. Laundry. Gas. Shop (Easter - end Oct). Café and family bar/restaurant (from early May). Pizza takeaway. Swimming pool (end May - end Sept). Adventure play area. Bicycle hire. Dog walk (max. 1 per pitch). Off site: Bus service 1.5 miles. Fishing 2 miles. Riding 3 miles. Golf 5 miles. Great Yarmouth 7 miles. Norwich 15 miles. Beach 5 miles.

Open: 1 April - 31 October.

Directions

From the A47 Norwich - Great Yarmouth road at Acle roundabout take exit for Filby (A1064). After 1.5 miles take left fork on B1152 (Potter Heigham). Take first left and park is 100 yards on the right. O.S.GR: TG423145. GPS: N52:40.370 E01:34.979

Charges guide

Per unit incl. 2 persons	£ 16.00 - £ 23.00
extra person	£ 5.00
child	£ 2.00
dog (max. 1)	£ 3.50
electricity	£ 2.50

Clippesby Hall

The ideal base for exploring Norfolk. From the Broads to the coast. Perfect for a holiday of walking, cycling, fishing, eating, drinking or just putting your feet up!

A wooded country setting with spacious perimeter pitching, mini-golf, cafe, family pub, swimming pool and much more

CALL NOW FOR YOUR FREE BROCHURE

(01493) 367800 www.clippesby.com

UK3510 Breydon Water Holiday Park

Butt Lane, Burgh Castle, Great Yarmouth NR31 9QB (Norfolk)

Tel: **01493 780357**. Email: **breydon.water@park-resorts.com**

www.alanrogers.com/UK3510

Owned by the Park Resorts group, these well established holiday parks (formerly Liffens Holiday Park and Welcome Holiday Centre) are in a semi-rural area on the edge of the Norfolk Broads within easy reach of Great Yarmouth. Breydon Water Holiday Park comprises the two parks, now named Bure Village (caravan holiday homes only) and Yare Village, which are just a short walk apart along a country lane. Visitors at each park may use the facilities at the other. Yare has over 500 pitches which include 211 touring pitches (168 with 16A electricity) on a separate open, level and grassy area. The remaining pitches are used for caravan holiday homes, most privately owned, some for rent.

Facilities

Two toilet blocks offer clean, spacious, but fairly standard facilities. Unit for disabled persons. Baby room. Laundry. Shop. Entertainment complex with restaurant, two bars and takeaway. Swimming and paddling pools (29/5-31/8). Play area. Tennis. Off site: At Bure Village: indoor pool, gym, solarium, amusements and supermarket.

Open: 1 March - 31 October.

Directions

From Great Yarmouth take A143 signed Beccles. At Bradwell turn right (Burgh Castle) into New Road. At mini-roundabout turn right into Butt Lane and park. O.S.GR: TM490050. GPS: N52:35.192 E01:39.577

Charges guide

Per unit with electricity	£ 5.00 - £ 28.00

155

UK3520 Searles Leisure Resort

South Beach Road, Hunstanton PE36 5BB (Norfolk)

Tel: **01485 534211**. Email: **bookings@searles.co.uk**   www.alanrogers.com/UK3520

This 'all-in' family holiday park on the North Norfolk coast offers everything you need for that seaside family holiday. With the beach within walking distance, the covered 'town plaza' including a sports bar, Chinese restaurant and Mediterranean style café, pools, a golf course, fishing lakes and bowling greens, there should be something to entertain everyone. Although now a major caravan holiday home park, for more than fifty years touring pitches have remained important on this site. Spacious pitches separated by hedges, either fully serviced, with electricity or not, are set in seven different areas of the park, with three large toilet blocks providing good facilities. Being such a large site security is important for safety and peace of mind and 24 hour CCTV operates. The seaside resort of Hunstanton is under a mile away providing all the usual ice creams, buckets and spades. The Royal House of Sandringham with its gardens and parts of the house open to the public is within easy reach. For bird watchers a trip further round the coast brings some excellent spots to see some interesting species.

Facilities

Three large toilet blocks offer clean and tidy facilities with background music adding that little extra. Washbasins in cubicles. En-suite rooms in all blocks for disabled visitors. Baby room. Laundry. Dishwashing facilities on the side of each block. Food hall. Restaurants, bars and cafés. Hair and beauty salon. Indoor and outdoor swimming pools. Gym. Tennis. Soft play area. Golf (9-hole course, driving range and putting course). Fishing lake. Bicycle hire. Off site: Nearest beach 200 m. Hunstanton 0.5 miles.

Open: All year.

Directions

On the A149 from Kings Lynn take Hunstanton exit at roundabout. At next roundabout take second exit then immediate left into site. O.S.GR: TF670401. GPS: N52:55.820 E00:28.973

Charges guide

Per pitch	£ 12.00 - £ 34.00
electricity	£ 1.00 - £ 3.00
fully serviced pitch	£ 16.00 - £ 41.00
awning	£ 3.00
dog	£ 2.50

UK3580 Ferry Meadows Caravan Club Site

Ham Lane, Peterborough PE2 5UU (Cambridgeshire)

Tel: **01733 233526**   www.alanrogers.com/UK3580

Three miles from bustling Peterborough and closer still to the East of England Showground, the immaculate Ferry Meadows is an ideal family holiday site occupying 30 acres of the 500 acre Nene Country Park. Meadows, lakes and woodlands provide ample opportunities to sample the facilities. These include watersports, fishing, golf, nature reserves, miniature railway and 60 miles of footpaths, bridleways and cycleways, all off road, even into the town centre. On rainy days Peterborough offers skating, indoor pool, bowling alley, cinema, theatre and ample shopping. Open all year the site provides 254 pitches (16A electricity) – 160 grass pitches on one side of the park, informally laid out in small groups and surrounded by a variety of mature trees, and 94 gravel hardstandings just across the road for caravans and motorcaravans. A very small area (no electricity) is reserved for up to 10 tents. Families with children may prefer the grass area, from where they can keep a watchful eye on the well-equipped playground. Passing by within nostalgic earshot and yielding the occasional tempting aroma of bygone eras is the Nene Valley Steam Railway.

Facilities

Two modern, well appointed and heated toilet blocks are of the usual high standard, with en-suite facilities for disabled visitors in one block. Baby/toddler washroom. Dishwashing sinks under cover, as well as a laundry room. Motorcaravan service point. The office stocks basic provisions. Tourist information room. Good play areas. TV socket and lead. WiFi in one area. Off site: Wheelchair hire in Nene Park. Steam railway 500 yards. Bus Service 800 yards. Pitch and putt 800 yards. Nearest shops 1 mile. Restaurants within 0.5 miles. Peterborough, lido, night clubs and supermarkets 3 miles.

Open: All year.

Directions

From south on A1, do not turn onto A1139, but turn left, 1 mile on, at next junction (signed Showground, Chesterton, Alwalton) and immediately left onto A605, signed Peterborough. Continue straight on at three roundabouts, signed Nene Park. At fourth roundabout turn left into Ham Lane, signed Nene Park and Ferry Meadows. Site is on left 300 yards beyond level crossing. From the east follow the many Nene Park signs around Peterborough onto the A605 and then to the site. O.S.GR: TL151972. GPS: N52:33.473 W00:18.133

Charges guide

Per person	£ 3.90 - £ 5.40
child (5-16 yrs)	£ 1.30 - £ 2.15
pitch incl. electricity (non-member)	£ 10.30 - £ 14.10

UK3560 Highfield Farm Touring Park

Long Road, Comberton, Cambridge CB23 7DG (Cambridgeshire)
Tel: 01223 262308. Email: enquiries@highfieldfarmtouringpark.co.uk   www.alanrogers.com/UK3560

Situated five miles from Cambridge, this eight acre park is set in a delightfully quiet touring location yet close to major routes around Cambridge. The welcome is always warm from the friendly family owners. The facilities are of high quality and the grass and hedges are well cared for. Divided into five enclosures by conifers hedges, there are also shady glades for those who wish to retreat even further; plus one enclosure is reserved for those without children. Offering 60 numbered pitches for caravans or motorcaravans, and 60 for tents, pitching is around the outer edges. As a result, the park never looks crowded even when fully booked (which is frequently the case). All pitches have 10A electricity, 50 have gravel hardstanding and most are level. A good dog walk is provided, which can be extended to a pleasant 1.5 mile walk around the farm perimeter. A member of the Best of British group.

Facilities

Three heated toilet blocks provide more than adequate coverage and good facilities (showers 10p), all very clean and well maintained. Baby room but no dedicated provision for disabled visitors, although one block has extra wide doors and easy access. Laundry room. Small play area. Good shop. Motorcaravan service point. Excellent tourist information. Bicycle hire. Gates closed midnight to 07.30. Off site: Comberton village 0.5 miles. Golf 2 miles. Fishing 3.5 miles. Cambridge 5 miles. Duxford War Museum and National Trust properties.

Open: 23 March - 31 October.

Directions

From M11 exit 12, take A603 towards Sandy. After 0.5 miles turn right, B1046 to Comberton. Turn right just before village signed Madingley (also caravan sign). Site on right just north of village.
O.S GR: TL391571. GPS: N52:11.676 E00:02.020

Charges guide

Per unit incl. 2 persons	£ 9.50 - £ 12.00
hiker or cyclist incl. tent	£ 8.25 - £ 9.75
extra person	£ 3.00
child (5-16 yrs)	£ 2.00
electricity	£ 2.50
No credit cards.	

A warm welcome awaits you at our popular award winning park with its excellent facilities, set in peaceful farming countryside. It is close to the historic University City of Cambridge, the Imperial War Museum, Duxford and ideally suited for touring East Anglia.

Comberton, Cambridge CB23 7DG Tel/Fax: 01223 262308
www.highfieldfarmtouringpark.co.uk

157

UK3575 Stroud Hill Park

Fen Road, Pidley PE28 3DE (Cambridgeshire)

Tel: **01487 741333**. Email: **stroudhillpark@btconnect.com**   www.alanrogers.com/UK3575

Opened in 2003 as an all year round, adult only site, Stroud Hill Park is a well designed, high quality park. It is a credit to its owners, David and Jayne Newman. Developed from existing farmland where David grew up, the park has been landscaped to create a terraced effect and now incorporates a large fishing lake (well stocked with carp, tench, bream, rudd and roach) plus a superb tennis court. The attractive, timber framed barn that dominates the site is all the more impressive when you know that David built most of it; even to the canopy over the open fireplace. There are no half measures here, from the quality of the building itself through to the fittings throughout, everything has been well thought out and it adds up to a gem of new site. The barn is the hub of the site where you will find reception, shop, terrace, bar and a 44 seat restaurant (open Wednesday to Sunday incl.) There are 60 large, slightly sloping pitches, of which 44 are hardstanding, and fully serviced with electricity (16A), fresh water and drainage. The hedges and shrubs around the site are young and need time to mature, but an atmosphere and character has quickly developed and already many return regularly. Affiliated to the Caravan Club, non-members are equally welcome.

Facilities

Toilets and spacious en-suite shower facilities are located in the main building along with a very well equipped room for disabled users. Good size laundry room plus vegetable preparation and dishwashing room, all spotlessly clean. Small, licensed shop stocks basic provisions, home-made cakes, local produce, gas and camping accessories. Attractive bar and café/restaurant. Fishing (£5 per day). All-weather tennis court.
Off site: Golf, ten-pin bowling and paintball adjacent to site. Rding 0.5 miles. Peterborough, Cambridge, Ely, Huntingdon and St Ives all within easy reach.

Open: All year.

Directions

Leave A1 near Huntingdon, take A14 east. Leave A14 at A141, signed March. In Warboys, at roundabout, turn right on B1040 signed Pidley. In Pidley turn left just beyond church, Fen Road. Site is about 1 mile on right. O.S.GR: TL335787. GPS: N52:23.529 W00:02.226

Charges guide

Per unit incl. 2 persons, electricity	£ 21.00
tent incl. 2 persons	£ 15.00
extra person	£ 2.50
dog	£ 1.00

UK3555 Wyton Lakes Holiday Park

Banks End, Wyton, Huntingdon PE28 2AA (Cambridgeshire)

Tel: **01480 412715**. Email: **loupeter@supanet.com**   www.alanrogers.com/UK3555

Wyton Lakes is a family run, adults only park with four well stocked fishing lakes, very close to the River Great Ouse, between Huntingdon and St Ives. There are 52 level pitches of medium size with 40 for caravans and motorhomes and 12 for tents. The tent pitches are on grass and have no electricity. The other pitches are mainly on hardstanding with grass for awnings and all have electricity and a water tap. Most of the pitches border the lakes making fishing possible from the pitch. Well placed as a centre for touring, the park has easy access for large outfits. The old market towns of Huntingdon and St Ives are only three miles away and the delightful village of Houghton with its old mill, pub and riverside walks is just a mile. Just across the road is a large garden centre complete with restaurant and coffee shop.

Facilities

Heated toilet block with all necessary facilities including those for campers with disabilities. Course lake and river fishing (carp, bream, tench, perch, roach and rudd, up to 30 lb). Riverside walks. Off site: Garden centre, restaurant and coffee shop opposite entrance. Interesting old village Houghton, pub, shop, National Trust Mill, riverside walks, 1 mile. St Ives, Huntingdon, 3 miles. Boat hire, golf, 3 miles. Huntingdon Race Course 4 miles. Paxton Pits Nature Reserves, Hinchingbrooke Park.

Open: 4 April - 26 October.

Directions

From the A14 take exit 26 (St Ives). Take A1096 north towards St Ives over four roundabouts. Turn left onto A1123, signed Huntingdon and site entrance is on the left in about 2 miles opposite garden centre. O.S.GR: TL269725. GPS: N52:20.198 W00:08.323

Charges guide

Per unit incl. 2 adults and electricity	£ 15.00
tent pitch incl. 2 adults	£ 12.00 - £ 14.00
extra adult	£ 2.00

Adults only (over 18 yrs). No credit cards.

MAP 4

Spanning central England, from the ancient borders of Wales on the west across to Lincolnshire on the east coast, the Heart of England is rich in glorious rolling countryside, magnificent castles, fine stately houses and beautiful gardens.

THE REGION COMPRISES LINCOLNSHIRE, RUTLAND, NORTHAMPTONSHIRE, NOTTINGHAMSHIRE, WEST MIDLANDS, DERBYSHIRE, STAFFORDSHIRE, LEICESTERSHIRE, WARWICKSHIRE, HEREFORDSHIRE, WORCESTERSHIRE, GLOUCESTERSHIRE & SHROPSHIRE

The charming and diverse countryside of the Heart of England includes: the Lincolnshire Wolds, with the dramatic open landscape of the Fens; the ragged crags, dales and moorland of the Peak District National Park in Derbyshire and Staffordshire; the heathered hilltops of Shropshire; the famous Sherwood Forest, in the heart of Nottinghamshire; and the miles of lush green countryside of Herefordshire, dotted with black and white timber houses. Rutland Water is a mecca for watersports and the whole region offers superb opportunities for walking, cycling and more daring activities such as rock climbing and caving. The Cotswolds to the west of the region is the largest area of Outstanding Natural Beauty in England and Wales. Here you will find many traditional English villages, with charming country pubs and cottage gardens. Another significant feature of the region are the rivers and canals. Passing pretty towns and villages, a large canal network threads its way through the area, weaving through the Lincolnshire Fens, past the waterside bars and restaurants of Birmingham and along to estuaries of the rivers of Severn and Avon.

Places of interest

Lincolnshire: Belvoir Castle near Grantham.

Rutland: market towns of Oakham and Uppingham.

Northamptonshire: Silverstone; Althorp House.

Nottinghamshire: Nottingham Castle.

West Midlands: Birmingham; Cadbury World.

Derbyshire: Bakewell; Buxton; Chatsworth House.

Staffordshire: Alton Towers; Stoke-on-Trent.

Leicestershire: Snibston Discovery Park; Twycross Zoo.

Warwickshire: Warwick Castle; Stratford-upon-Avon.

Herefordshire: Hereford Cathedral.

Worcestershire: West Midland Safari Park.

Gloucestershire: Sudeley Castle; Cheltenham.

Shropshire: Shrewsbury and Whitchurch.

Did you know?

Herefordshire is one of the largest apple cider producers in the world.

The World Toe Wrestling Championship, held every June in Wetton, is a registered international sport.

The hollow trunk of the 'Mighty Tree' in Sherwood Forest is reputedly where Robin Hood and his Merry Men hid from the Sheriff of Nottingham.

Quite different from the more familiar tart, the Bakewell pudding was first created in the 1860s.

Rutland is the smallest county in Britain, measuring just 16 miles by 16 miles.

The Peak District contains over 50 reservoirs, including Ladybower, where the bouncing bomb used in World War II was tested.

UK3660 **Walesby Woodlands Caravan Park**

Walesby, Market Rasen LN8 3UN (Lincolnshire)

Tel: **01673 843285**. Email: **walesbywoodlands@talk21.com**   www.alanrogers.com/UK3660

Surrounded by mature Forestry Commission woodland, this small family owned, touring park is mainly very peaceful (if the wind is in a certain direction trains may be heard in the distance). The owners, Paul and Christine Burrows will make you very welcome. About a mile away is the small town of Market Rasen, but further afield and within easy driving distance, are Lincoln, the east coast including Skegness and, of course, the Lincolnshire Wolds. There are 60 well spaced pitches, 52 with 10A electricity, marked out on a single, mainly flat, grassy field divided by a central gravel road and with a double row of trees providing useful visual screening. The Viking Way passes through Walesby and there are many other shorter walks in the forest and surrounding area.

Facilities

The single, heated toilet block (£5 deposit charged for the key) is spacious and ample for the site. It has toilet facilities for disabled people. Laundry room. Small shop with information section (all season). Coffee shop is planned. Battery charging. Gas supplies. Play area. No kite flying (overhead wires). Winter caravan storage. Off site: Market Rasen racecourse 2 miles. Golf 1.5 miles. Riding 2 miles. Fishing 3 miles.

Open: 1 March - 31 October.

Directions

Market Rasen is on the A46, 17 miles northeast of Lincoln. Park is a mile northeast of the town, just off the B1203, and is signed from all the main approach roads. O.S.GR: TF117907.
GPS: N53:24.081 W00:19.260

Charges guide

Per unit incl. 2 persons	£ 10.00 - £ 12.00
with electricity	£ 12.00 - £ 13.50
extra person	£ 1.50
child (under 12 yrs)	£ 1.25
awning	£ 1.25 - £ 1.50

UK3650 Cherry Tree Site

Huttoft Road, Sutton-on-Sea LN12 2RU (Lincolnshire)

Tel: **01507 441626**. Email: **info@cherrytreesite.co.uk**

www.alanrogers.com/UK3650

This is a delightful, tranquil, adult only site and is a fine example of a small, good value touring park. It is a 15 minute walk from a Blue Flag beach and a short drive from some of the attractive villages of the Lincolnshire Wolds. A very warm welcome awaits from Geoff and Margaret Murray whose attention to detail is evident everywhere. The site is level, the grass is neatly trimmed and well drained, and screening is provided by lines of evergreen hedging. There are 60 good sized pitches of which 40 are for touring, all with 10A electricity and 10 'super pitches' with hardstanding. Buses stop outside hourly, and a shop and pub are within ten minutes walk. Mablethorpe beach is just 4 miles away and Skegness, with all its popular attractions is just down the road.

Facilities

The brick built toilet block, recently extended and refurbished, can be heated and is immaculately kept. Controllable hot showers, hairdryers. En-suite unit for disabled visitors (Radar key required). Combined dishwashing and laundry room with washing machine, spin dryer and tumble dryer. Neat reception and separate tourist information. Gas. Off site: Bicycle hire, tennis, bowls and fishing 1.5 miles. Golf 1 mile. Riding adjacent.

Open: 6 March - 1 November.

Directions

Sutton-on-Sea is 15 miles north of Skegness. The site is 1.5 miles south of the town on A52 coast road, with the entrance leading off a lay-by on the east. O.S.GR: TF518828. GPS: N53:17.568 E00:17.999

Charges guide

Per unit incl. 2 persons and electricity	£ 14.00 - £ 20.00
extra person	£ 3.50
dog	£ 0.50
Min. stay 3 nights at B.Hs.	

UK3675 Willow Holt Camping & Caravan Park

Lodge Road, Tattershall LN4 4JS (Lincolnshire)

Tel: **01526 343111**. Email: **enquiries@willowholt.co.uk**

www.alanrogers.com/UK3675

Willow Holt is a pleasant park with plenty of potential. It will appeal, in particular, to fishing enthusiasts and to those who would like a quiet location from which to explore this interesting corner of Lincolnshire with its RAF associations. It covers some 25 acres of woodland and former gravel pits, with the camping areas on flat land alongside the large lake. There are 60 pitches occupied on a seasonal basis but a further 47 are available for touring units. All have 10A electricity and water taps close by. An area without electricity is available for tents. There are a few privately owned mobile homes along the lakeside. The young owners are working hard to improve the facilities; the roads have been resurfaced with gravel and a new reception building should now be ready. There are plenty of interesting places to visit nearby, including Tattershall Castle, the Battle of Britain Memorial Flight, Woodhall Spa, with its Kinema in the Woods, and Horncastle. Further afield are Lincoln, Boston, Skegness and the Lincolnshire coast.

Facilities

The toilet block is small and must be under considerable pressure at busy times. Showers are pre-set and hot water is free to the open style basins. Motorcaravan service point. Laundry room with washing machines, dryers and iron/ironing board. No facilities for disabled visitors or for babies and young children. Free fishing (permit required). Off site: Golf and riding 2.5 miles. Shops, pubs and restaurants in Tattershall (1.5 miles) and Woodhall Spa (2.5 miles). Beaches 30 miles.

Open: 15 March - 31 October.

Directions

Tattershall is 20 miles southeast of Lincoln on the A153 Sleaford - Horncastle/Louth road. Site is 1.5 miles north of town; from Market Place follow brown campsite sign along Lodge Road. Entrance is on left before junction with B1192 to Woodhall Spa. O.S.GR: TF201592. GPS: N53:07.190 W00:12.474

Charges guide

Per unit incl. 2 persons	£ 10.00 - £ 14.00
incl. electricity	£ 12.00 - £ 16.00
extra person	£ 2.00
child	£ 1.00

UK3680 Ashby Park

West Ashby, Horncastle LN9 5PP (Lincolnshire)

Tel: **01507 527966**. Email: **ashbyparklakes@aol.com**   www.alanrogers.com/UK3680

Ashby Park is a pleasant, well run site located in 70 acres of former gravel pits that now provide seven attractive fishing lakes. There is a series of clearings occupied by privately owned caravan holiday homes and by 77 touring pitches. Most are on grass, but some have hardstanding. All have access to electricity (16A) and 12 super pitches also have hardstanding, water tap and waste water drain. Lakeside pitches will no doubt appeal to anglers, whereas families with young children will probably prefer to be further away from the lakes, which are inevitably unfenced. This is a peaceful site in an interesting area. The market town of Horncastle is just down the road, whilst nearby are Tattershall Castle, the Battle of Britain Memorial Flight and Woodhall Spa with its 'Kinema in the Woods'. Further afield are Lincoln, Boston, Skegness and the Lincolnshire coast.

Facilities

Three toilet blocks are well maintained and equipped, with open style washbasins and controllable showers; all hot water is metered (20p). Good en-suite facilities for disabled visitors. Laundry room with washing machine and dryer. Limited dishwashing (in new block – a long walk from lakeside pitches). Motorcaravan service point. Gas sales. Tourist information. Fishing (day ticket £4.50). Off site: Golf 0.5 miles. Riding 5 miles. Sailing and lakeside beach 6 miles. Seaside beaches 20 miles. Shops, pubs and restaurants in Horncastle 2 miles.

Open: 1 March - 30 November.

Directions

Horncastle is 20 miles east of Lincoln on the A153 Sleaford - Louth road. Turn west 1.6 miles north of the town along Docking Lane and follow signs to site in 0.8 miles. O.S.GR: TF251724. GPS: N53:14.126 W00:07.585

Charges guide

Per unit incl. 2 adults, 2 children	£ 11.50
incl. electricity	£ 15.00
serviced pitch	£ 18.50 - £ 20.00

UK3690 Bainland Country Park

Horncastle Road, Woodhall Spa LN10 6UX (Lincolnshire)

Tel: **01526 352903**. Email: **bookings@bainland.co.uk**   www.alanrogers.com/UK3690

A family park with many amenities, Bainland has 170 spacious, level pitches in hedged bays (120 touring pitches) grouped in circles and islands and linked by curving roads. There are 51 fully serviced pitches with hardstanding, honeycombed for awning, individual water, drainage and chemical disposal, electricity and TV aerial hook-ups. The remainder of the pitches are either on gravel hardstanding or level grass, all with 10/16A electricity. The friendly reception is housed in a pleasant Swiss-style building together with the heated indoor pool and jacuzzi, a bistro and spacious bar area. These overlook an 18-hole, par 3 golf course and outdoor bowls area. Bainland is 1.5 miles from Woodhall Spa, with its old fashioned charm and Dambusters associations, yet deep in the heart of the Lincolnshire Wolds, surrounded by mature trees and with direct access to woods for walking dogs. A member of the Best of British group.

Facilities

Three modern, well equipped, heated toilet blocks including a baby room, unisex en-suite shower rooms, family bathroom, fully equipped unit for disabled people. Laundry room. Motorcaravan service points. Licensed shop (Feb - Dec). Bistro and bar (all year). Indoor pool (under 16s must be accompanied by an adult). Adventure playground. Trampolines. Crazy golf. Croquet. TV and games room. Soft play area. Floodlit tennis dome with 3-4 courts including badminton (the dome comes off in the summer). Leisure activities, including the pool, are individually booked and paid for at reception. Some entertainment in high season. Winter caravan storage. Off site: Fishing 3 miles. Riding 6 miles.

Open: All year (in winter, 'super' pitches only).

Directions

Woodhall Spa is 18 miles southeast of Lincoln. Entrance to park is off B1191 Horncastle road 1.5 miles northeast of the village by 50 mph sign. O.S.GR: TF214637. GPS: N53:09.517 W00:11.011

Charges guide

Per unit incl. electricity	£ 15.00 - £ 22.00
serviced pitch	£ 16.00 - £ 26.00
extra person over 12 yrs	£ 2.00 - £ 5.00
dog	£ 2.00 - £ 4.00
pup tent/awning	free - £ 4.00

Special rate for firework display (min. 2 nights, 4/5 Nov). Discounts for senior citizens.

UK3692 Glen Lodge Touring Park

Glen Lodge, Edlington Moor, Woodhall Spa LN10 6UL (Lincolnshire)

Tel: **01526 353523**   www.alanrogers.com/UK3692

This quiet, modern site is ideal for couples and families who enjoy the rural lifestyle, yet it is only just over a mile from the thriving village of Woodhall Spa which retains much of its old-fashioned charm. All 35 pitches have hardstanding and 10A electricity hook-ups (one or two appeared to need long leads) and are served by shingle roads with some street lighting. The grass and flowerbeds are obviously tended by someone who enjoys gardening. In fact, the whole park has a much-loved feel. Places to visit include the Battle of Britain Memorial Flight, Tattershall Castle, Horncastle with its antiques centre and the city of Lincoln. Skegness is only 26 miles away.

Facilities

The modern heated toilet block (key-pad access) is spotlessly clean with vanity style washbasins and piped music. Facilities for disabled visitors. Washing machine and dryer. Off site: Pub 0.5 miles, golf 2 miles, fishing 5 miles, riding 6 miles.

Open: 1 March - 30 November.

Directions

Woodhall Spa is 18 miles southeast of Lincoln. From mini-roundabout in village turn northeast towards Bardney on B1190 (Stixwould Road) past Petwood Hotel. In about 1 mile at sharp left bend, turn right. Site is 300 yards on left. O.S.GR: TF189647. GPS: N53:09.974 W00:13.200

Charges guide

Per unit incl. 2 adults and electricity	£ 13.00
extra person (over 4 yrs)	£ 2.00
No credit cards.	

GLEN LODGE TOURING PARK

Small family run park within a mile of Woodhall Spa, set in beautiful woodland surroundings. Heated toilet/shower block and utility room with washer, dryer and phone. A great combination of peace and tranquillity and yet within easy reach of the seaside town of Skegness. Discounts available Monday to Thursday for senior citizens.

Edlington Moor, Woodhall Spa, Lincolnshire LN10 6UL ■ Tel/Fax No. 01526 353523

UK3730 Skegness Sands Touring Site

Winthorpe Avenue, Skegness PE25 1QZ (Lincolnshire)

Tel: **01754 761484**. Email: **info@skegness-sands.com**   www.alanrogers.com/UK3730

This very well organised touring site is part of a much larger caravan holiday home park, but has its own entrance. It is a modern, well appointed site adjacent to the promenade and beach. There are 85 pitches, all level and with electricity (16A). 48 are grass (3 tents only) and 37 gravel hardstandings, four of which are fully serviced. Site lighting is good throughout and there are regular security patrols. The gate to the promenade is locked at all times, campers getting a key. Local attractions include Funcoast World, Fantasy Island, Hardy's Animal Farm, a seal sanctuary and Gibraltar Point National Nature Reserve. The site is a member of the Caravan Club's 'managed under contract' scheme, members and non-members are all made very welcome.

Facilities

The good quality, heated toilet block includes washbasins in curtained cubicles plus three family shower rooms with WC and washbasin and a well equipped room for disabled people. Two dishwashing sinks are outside under cover. Laundry room. Gas supplies on site. Hairdressing salon. Indoor heated swimming pool (Spr. B.H - 30 Sept; adult £3, child £2). Small modern playground. Off site: Well stocked shop/post office 200 m. Pubs, fast food outlets and a supermarket are all within easy walking distance. 'Hail and ride' bus service to Skegness and Ingoldmells at 200 m. Fishing 1 mile. Golf 2 miles. Riding 5 miles. Also stock car racing and ten pin bowling.

Open: All year.

Directions

Site is off the A52 Boston - Skegness - Mablethorpe road, 1.75 miles north of Skegness town centre. Turn east opposite 'Garden City' public house into Winthorpe Avenue and site entrance is on the left at far end of road. Note: This entrance is locked from 17.00 - 08.00. At other times, access is by the Roman Bank entrance, a short distance further north on A52. New arrivals please contact site if unable to arrive before 17.00. O.S.GR: TF570640. GPS: N53:10.008 E00:20.970

Charges guide

Per person	£ 4.50 - £ 5.80
child (5-16 yrs)	£ 1.50 - £ 2.50
pitch	£ 4.80 - £ 8.00
'super' pitch supplement	£ 3.00

UK3750 Foreman's Bridge Caravan Park

Sutton Saint James, Spalding PE12 0HU (Lincolnshire)

Tel: **01945 440346**. Email: **foremansbridge@btconnect.com**

www.alanrogers.com/UK3750

Foreman's Bridge is an extremely pleasant and compact park and the new owners are now well established. It makes an excellent base from which to explore the Fens, including Spalding, famous for its annual flower festival held at the beginning of May. Fishing and cycling are popular pastimes in the area, indeed bicycle hire and fishing licences are both available from the site, with fishing possible in the river that runs just past the entrance. Occupying a large, level and grassy meadow surrounded by trees and high hedges which give it a very secluded feel, the park has 40 level pitches, of which 28 are touring pitches, all with electricity (10A) and 20 with gravel hardstanding. There are now holiday homes for sale on site. Fruit trees, flower beds, hanging baskets and planted troughs provide bursts of vibrant colour. At times there can be noise from military aircraft.

Facilities

The modern, brick built toilet unit is spacious and kept very clean, providing really large individual shower rooms with seats and washbasins (showers on payment). Dishwashing room. Laundry room with washing machine, dryer and ironing. Basic provisions and gas are kept. Fishing. Bicycle hire. Site barrier (£5 deposit for card). Winter caravan storage. Off site: Small shop in village 1 mile. Golf 3 miles. Riding 8 miles. Coast 12 miles (The Wash); nearest beach 32 miles.

Open: 1 March - 15 January.

Directions

Sutton St James is 26 miles northeast of Peterborough and 17 miles west of Kings Lynn. From A17 Spalding - Kings Lynn road turn south on the B1390 at Long Sutton towards Sutton St James for about 2 miles. The park entrance is on the left immediately after the bridge. O.S.GR: TF410198. GPS: N52:45.471 E00:05.280

Charges guide

Per unit incl. 2 persons	£ 10.00 - £ 14.00
extra person	£ 3.00
child	£ 2.00
electricity	£ 2.00
dog	£ 1.00
No credit cards.	

UK3760 Tallington Lakes Camping & Caravanning

Barholm Road, Tallington, Stamford PE9 4RJ (Lincolnshire)

Tel: **01778 347000**. Email: **info@tallington.com**

www.alanrogers.com/UK3760

The 160 acre site spreads around a series of lakes that provide for many watersport activities including water-ski (slalom and jump courses), jet-ski, sailing (sailboards and dinghies) and angling. The touring campsite has 118 pitches, of which 106 have electricity hook-ups (10A), and 11 are on hardstandings. Major roads are tarmac, with gravel roads serving the pitches, and maturing hedges and shrubs separate the rows. The complex also has eight mobile homes for hire and there are some 200 privately-owned holiday homes. Local places of interest are Stamford Museum, Burghley House, Sacrewell Farm and Country Centre and the Nene Valley Railway.

Facilities

The heated sanitary unit has facilities for babies, small children and disabled visitors. Additional WCs and showers (also used by the water skiers). Laundry facilities. Motorcaravan service point. Bar and restaurant. Swimming and paddling pools. Climbing wall. Go-karting. Watersports. Fishing. Dry-ski slope, snowboard centre and tennis. Small, well fenced, adventure style playground (age 5-12 yrs). Key-card for toilet unit and barrier (£10 refundable deposit). Off site: Bus stop 1 mile. Golf, riding and bicycle hire 5 miles.

Open: 1 March - 31 January.

Directions

From A16, midway between Stamford and Market Deeping, just east of the railway crossing at Tallington, turn north into Barholm Road and site entrance is on the right. (site is signed). O.S.GR: TF085090. GPS: N52:40.204 W00:22.764

Charges guide

Per person	£ 2.00
pitch	£ 6.00
electricity	£ 2.00
awning or pup tent	£ 1.50
dog (max. 2 per unit)	£ 1.00

UK3765 Woodland Waters

Willoughby Road, Ancaster, Grantham NG32 3RT (Lincolnshire)
Tel: **01400 230888**. Email: **info@woodlandwaters.co.uk**   **www.alanrogers.com/UK3765**

This attractive holiday park occupies 70 acres of woodland, gently sloping grassland and lakes, with the caravan park itself taking up about 20 of them. The site has 120 pitches although only 60 are regularly used (all with 10A electricity and water taps nearby). There is a rally field of 20 pitches with hook-ups, plus areas for camping and those not requiring hook-ups. The land slopes gently down to the 14 acre lake and the pitches nearer the water are more level, although probably not suitable for those with younger children since there is no fencing. Reception is housed in a neat modern building at the entrance to the park. The welcome is warm, fishing tickets are sold and tourist information is available. The pleasant bar and restaurant (open to the public) occupy a chalet-style building near the lake; the menu seemed varied and reasonably priced. There are four fishing lakes (plus a junior pool), with carp, tench, bream, roach, rudd and pike. Walking and bird watching are other featured attractions of the park, while days out could include Nottingham, Lincoln and even Skegness (50 miles). Some aircraft noise is possible.

Facilities

A single, modern, heated toilet block is well maintained and kept clean. Washbasins (in cubicles for ladies) and free showers (controllable for ladies, push-button for men). A second block will provide extra facilities when the additional camping areas are fully occupied. Small laundry room with washing machine, dryer and iron, but no laundry sinks. Motorcaravan service point. Bar and restaurant with takeaway (all year). Play area. Fishing. Off site: Limited bus service from near entrance. Shop and trains in village 1 mile. Go-karting and paintball 1 mile. Golf 3 miles. Riding 6 miles.

Open: All year.

Directions

Ancaster is 8 miles northeast of Grantham and 19 miles south of Lincoln. The park entrance is off the A153 Grantham - Sleaford road, 600 yards west of the junction with the B6403 High Dyke road (Ermine Street). O.S.GR: SK973437. GPS: N52:58.832 W00:32.819

Charges guide

Per unit incl. up to 4 persons	£ 12.00 - £ 14.00
incl. electricity	£ 15.00 - £ 17.00
extra person	£ 2.00
child	£ 1.00
dog	£ 1.00

UK3770 Low Farm Touring & Caravan Park

Spring Lane, Folkingham, Sleaford NG34 0SJ (Lincolnshire)
Tel: **01529 497322**. Email: **info@lowfarmpark.com**   **www.alanrogers.com/UK3770**

This quiet secluded park is a lovely spot either just to relax or to tour the Lincolnshire countryside. Jane and Nigel Stevens continue to work hard to make this site a pleasant place to stay and have a well laid out park offering good quality facilities which are very clean and tidy. The site offers 36 touring pitches with electricity (12A) and a field for tents and small rallies. Some hardstandings are available. The site is on the edge of the village of Folkingham with a pub (currently serving food at lunch time only) and a couple of small shops. There are some pleasant walks around the village which is set in attractive Lincolnshire countryside. Larger shops and places of interest are in and around Bourne (9 miles), Grantham (14 miles), Lincoln and Peterborough (both 26 miles).

Facilities

Central, well maintained toilet block with controllable free showers and open style washbasins. Washing machine. Reception is at the owners' house but nearby is a tourist information room with toilets. Large field where children can play (also sometimes used by tenters). Off site: Fishing 2 miles. Golf 6 miles. Riding 7 miles.

Open: Easter - 30 September.

Directions

Folkingham is 26 miles south of Lincoln on the A15 to Peterborough, 2 miles south of the roundabout junction with the A52 (Nottingham, Grantham - Boston). Park is on southern edge of village; at foot of hill at campsite sign, turn west and site is at end of lane. O.S.GR: TF070333. GPS: N52:53.211 W00:24.670

Charges guide

Per unit incl. 2 persons	£ 9.00 - £ 12.00
extra person	£ 3.00
child (over 5 yrs)	£ 1.50
incl. electricity	£ 12.00 - £ 15.00
awning	£ 1.50
No credit cards.	

165

UK3815 Lickpenny Touring Park

Lickpenny Lane, Tansley, Matlock DE4 5GF (Derbyshire)

Tel: **01629 583040**. Email: **lickpenny@btinternet.com**   **www.alanrogers.com/UK3815**

This spacious caravan park on a hill above Matlock has 122 terraced pitches, all on hardstandings (no tents) and with electricity (16A). Of these, 100 are touring pitches, 27 of which are fully serviced and 22 are seasonal. There are rows of mature trees and pitches are large and separated by shrubs and bushes. The enthusiastic owners have taken full advantage of the fact that this was previously a market garden and are continuing to work very hard to maintain high standards and improve facilities. Recreational grassy areas and attractive flower borders are well tended, whilst the top corner of the park has been kept as woodland. Buildings are of natural stone and well equipped. Reception incorporates a small shop (basics only at present) and tourist information. Local attractions include Matlock Bath and the Heights of Abraham, Chatsworth House, Haddon Hall, Hardwick Hall, Eyam and Castleton.

Facilities

Two well equipped, heated toilet blocks include free controllable showers and some washbasins in cubicles. Good facilities for disabled people. Family room with small bath, toilet and washbasin. Laundry room with washing machines, dryers, irons and ironing boards. Motorcaravan service point. Security barrier with keypad access at all times. Off site: Bus service from end of the road. Riding 1 mile. Fishing 3 miles. Golf 4 miles. Bicycle hire 6 miles. Woodland walk to Garden Centre with restaurant serving snacks and lunches (200 yards).

Open: All year.

Directions

Matlock is 18 miles west of the M1 at exit 28. From motorway, follow signs for Matlock on the A38, A61 and A615. After 5 miles on A615 turn north on Lickpenny Lane to site (signed). From Matlock take A615; after Tansley fork left on B6014 (Clay Cross) and turn right at top of hill after Garden Centre. O.S.GR: SK339598. GPS: N53:08.072 W01:29.429

Charges guide

Per unit incl. 2 persons	£ 18.00 - £ 21.00
extra person	£ 4.00
child (4-14 yrs)	£ 1.50

UK3840 Lime Tree Park

Dukes Drive, Buxton SK17 9RP (Derbyshire)

Tel: **01298 22988**. Email: **info@limetreeparkbuxton.co.uk**   **www.alanrogers.com/UK3840**

A select park with high quality, modern facilities, Lime Tree is in a convenient, edge of town location that makes a very good base for touring the Peak District. There are 99 pitches including 36 seasonal, 28 privately owned mobile homes and 12 mobile homes to rent. The 64 with 10A electricity hook-ups (hardstandings available) and an area for tents (some terracing but mainly sloping ground) are on the two upper terraces which have the best views but are slightly more exposed. Below are areas set aside for late arrivals and the mobile homes. On site there is a small shop for gas, caravan spares and basic groceries. Buxton town centre is a comfortable stroll away and Lime Tree is well placed for exploring the Derbyshire countryside. With good views, the park is situated next to a thickly wooded, limestone gorge and a magnificent old railway viaduct provides a dramatic backdrop.

Facilities

A modern toilet building serves the caravan and motorcaravan area, including some washbasins in cubicles, controllable showers, a baby room with the very latest design of baby bath, and a family room with facilities for disabled people. The refitted original unit serves the tent area. Both units can be heated and have top quality fittings. Laundry room with washing machine and dryer. Motorcaravan service area. Shop. Basic play area. Games/TV room. Off site: The nearest pub serving food is just around the corner. Swimming, riding and golf 1 mile. Fishing, bicycle hire, sailing and boat launching 5 miles. Alton Towers 22 miles. Supermarket in Buxton.

Open: 1 March - 31 October.

Directions

Park is on outskirts of Buxton and is signed from A515 Buxton - Ashbourne road 1 mile south of town. From town, immediately after hospital bear sharp left into Dukes Drive, go under railway viaduct and site is on the right. From south watch out for sharp turn right at foot of hill (signed in advance). O.S.GR: SK069725. GPS: N53:15.014 W01:53.800

Charges guide

Per unit incl. 2 persons and electricity	£ 18.00
extra person	£ 6.00
child (5-15 yrs)	£ 3.00
awning	£ 2.00
dog	£ 2.00

UK3850 Rivendale Caravan & Leisure Park

Holiday homes ▶ page 326

Buxton Road, Alsop-en-le-Dale, Ashbourne DE6 1QU (Derbyshire)
Tel: 01335 310311. Email: enquiries@rivendalecaravanpark.co.uk

www.alanrogers.com/UK3850

This unusual park has been developed in the bowl of a hill quarry which was last worked over 50 years ago. The steep quarry walls shelter three sides with marvellous views over the Peak National Park countryside to the south. A wide access road passes the renovated stone building which houses reception, a shop, bar and a café/restaurant. It gently climbs to a horseshoe shaped area providing 136 pitches some of which are rather small but most are of a generous size, with 16A electricity. The pitches are a mixture of hardstanding and grass, and are divided by shrubs. A further, open, marked grass area is accessed by hardcore roads. All the pitches are within easy reach of the central stone-built toilet block which is in keeping with the environment and thoughtfully provided with under-floor heating. The park takes up about 11 acres and a further 26 acres belong to the owners with certain parts suitable for walking – a must to appreciate the Derbyshire countryside with its dry stone walls, wild flowers and a little more of the quarry history. The park is situated almost on the Tissington Trail for walking or off road cycling and linking with the High Peak and Monsal Dale Trail. Other spectacular walks and cycle rides run along the Manifold, Wye and Dove valleys.

Facilities

First rate toilet facilities include some washbasins in cubicles for ladies, and an excellent en-suite room for disabled visitors. Laundry room. Shop (all essentials). Bar (evenings) and café with home-made and local food (open mornings, lunch and evenings, both with limited opening in low season). Packed lunches from reception. Special events monthly and games in main season. Hot tubs for hire, delivered to your pitch. Off site: Bicycle hire and riding 5 miles. Sailing and boat launching 8 miles. Fishing and golf 10 miles. Alton Towers 35 minutes drive. Chatsworth House and Gardens, Heights of Abraham and Guillivers Kingdom near.

Open: All year excl. 9 January - 2 February.

Directions

Park is 7 miles north of Ashbourne on the A515 to Buxton, on the eastern side of the road. It is well signed between the turnings east to Alsop Moor and Matlock (A5012), but take care as this is a very fast section of the A515. O.S.GR: SK161566.
GPS: N53:06.383 W01:45.634

Charges guide

Per unit incl. 2 persons	
and electricity	£ 14.50 - £ 18.00
extra person	£ 2.50
child (4-15 yrs)	£ 2.00
dog	£ 1.00

Camping Cheques accepted.

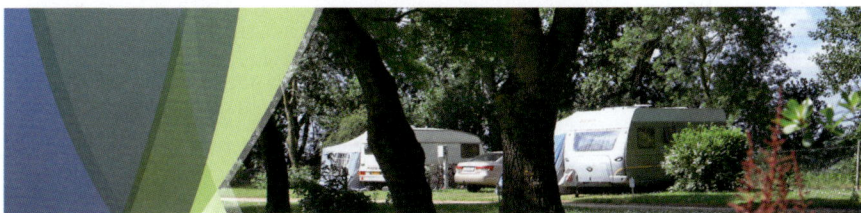

might also like to consider...

www.**alanrogers**.com for latest campsite news

UK3845 Clover Fields Touring Caravan Park

1 Heath View, Harpur Hill, Buxton SK17 9PU (Derbyshire)
Tel: 01298 78731. Email: cloverfields@tiscali.co.uk
www.alanrogers.com/UK3845

Stephen and Jan Redfern are more than happy to welcome you to their family owned park. It is located on the outskirts of the beautiful spa town of Buxton within easy reach of the magnificent Peak District National Park. You will be able to relax here in the 'away from it all' atmosphere. There are just 25 pitches, part hardstanding and part grass, all with 16A electricity, a water tap and a barbecue. They are divided by low hedges which have yet to mature. There is also a large field for tents. There is a little noise from the adjacent road. The site has its own animals which are happy to be spoiled by visitors! As well as a resident donkey and ponies, there are also rabbits, lambs, hens, geese and ducks. An unusual feature of this site is that the owner offers towing and pitching courses.

Facilities

The toilet and shower block is modern and clean. Facilities for disabled visitors. Gas supplies. Laundry room. Motorcaravan service point. Small shop selling essentials, home made jam and chutney and caravan accessories. Newspapers and milk delivered to your pitch. Towing and pitching courses. Plant sales. Small library. Torches recommended. Off site: Supermarket and fish and chip shop in Buxton. Opera House and Pavilion. Golf 3 miles. Riding 6 miles. Bicycle hire 6 miles.

Open: All year.

Directions

From Buxton, at Harpur Hill just to the southeast, turn right off the A515 (Buxton - Ashbourne) onto the B5053. Turn immediately right towards Harpur Hill. Site is 0.5 miles on the left. O.S.GR: SK075704. GPS: N53:13.840 W01:53.268

Charges guide

Per unit incl. 2 persons and electricity	£ 14.00
extra person (over 5 yrs)	£ 4.00
tent (per person)	£ 5.00

No credit cards.

UK3855 Callow Top Holiday Park

Buxton Road, Sandybrook, Ashbourne DE6 2AQ (Derbyshire)
Tel: 01335 344020. Email: enquiry@callowtop.co.uk
www.alanrogers.com/UK3855

Situated just north of the market town of Ashbourne, Callow Top nestles within an elevated country setting. The park's location makes it well placed to allow visitors to explore the picturesque villages, bustling market towns and the many attractions of the Peak District. It is ideal for both walking and cycling holidays. Spread over seven separate areas, there are 200 flat pitches of which 100 are for touring units. Those on hardstanding have 10A electricity, the grass pitches have no power supply. Water points tend to be rather scarce. Some of the pitches are rather small and on these, cars are parked away from the pitch. The focal point of the park is an old farmhouse which has been converted into an 'Olde English' style inn/restaurant serving real ale brewed in its own brewery and a good selection of pub food. The Inn also has a family room and a large beer garden. There are also cottages and caravan holiday homes for rent. Dove Dale, Tissington and High Peak trails and the Manifold Valley are nearby.

Facilities

Three heated toilet blocks (only one open in low season) provide unisex showers (20p). Toilet for disabled visitors. Laundry room. Chemical disposal point but no service point for motorcaravans. Calor gas. Shop. Inn/restaurant. Snack bar and takeaway. Heated swimming and paddling pools (May - Sept). Bicycle hire. Games room. Play area. Entertainment (w/ends and high season). Fishing. Winter caravan storage. Off site: Golf 1.5 miles. Riding 3 miles. Ashbourne (supermarket etc) 1 mile. Carsington Water (boat launching) 4 miles. Alton Towers 10 miles.

Open: 14 March - 9 November.

Directions

At Sandybrook, 0.5 miles north of Ashbourne, turn left off the A515 (Ashbourne - Buxton) into site road. Site is signed. O.S.GR: SK179483. GPS: N53:01.616 W01:44.788

Charges guide

Per unit incl. 2 persons	£ 14.50 - £ 17.50
incl. hardstanding and electricity	£ 18.00 - £ 21.00
extra person	£ 2.50
child (4-16 yrs)	£ 1.50

www.alanrogers.com for latest campsite news

UK3904 Greendale Farm Caravan & Camping Park

Pickwell Lane, Whissendine, Oakham LE15 7LB (Rutland)

Tel: **01664 474516**. Email: **enq@rutlandgreendale.co.uk**   www.alanrogers.com/UK3904

This is a delightful little, adult only park set in rolling countryside, ideal for those seeking peace and tranquillity. It is very eco-friendly and extremely well appointed for such a small site. Reception, the shop and the toilet facilities are housed in a modern building adjoining the owners' house. The shop is well stocked with essentials and local produce. It also has one of the best presented and most comprehensive information displays we have seen on any campsite. This includes charts for visitors to record birds seen on the park – the list is impressive – walking and cycle routes and pub menus. There are weekly meetings for birdwatchers, would-be artists (the office is decorated with the paintings produced by previous visitors) and photographers, all free in April and May. Cooked breakfasts are available on Sundays. There are only 15 pitches, all with 10 or 16A electricity, so it is worth checking availability!

Facilities

Each of the two rooms of the toilet block has a power shower, WCs and two washbasins (cubicles for the ladies). All is beautifully appointed and immaculately kept. Outdoor dishwashing sink plus one in the shop which can also be used for laundry. Washing machine and dryer. Chemical disposal and nearby sluicing point. Small open air swimming pool (6 x 3 m; £1 charge), heated by solar panels, with summer house. Two bicycles for hire. Off site: Village with bus service 0.5 miles. Riding 4 miles. Fishing 6 miles. Golf 8 miles. Sailing, birdwatching, walking, cycling (and bicycle hire) and fishing at Rutland Water 8 miles.

Open: 15 April - 30 September.

Directions

Oakham is 20 miles east of Leicester and Whissendine is just off the A606 Oakham - Melton Mowbray road. Approach park from this road and NOT through the village. From Oakham ignore the first turning to Whissendine, continue 2 miles and turn right at campsite sign. From Melton ignore first two turnings to Whissendine; turn left 0.6 mile after Rutland sign (at campsite sign). Park is on right in 0.6 mile. O.S.GR:SK819133.
GPS: N52:42.710 W00:47.317

Charges guide

Per unit incl. two adults and electricity	£ 16.00 - £ 19.00

UK3980 Longnor Wood Caravan & Camping Park

Longnor, Buxton SK17 0NG (Derbyshire)

Tel: **01298 83648**. Email: **info@longnorwood.co.uk**   www.alanrogers.com/UK3980

A secluded rural location, deep in the heart of the Peak District, Longnor Wood is an adult only park (over 18 yrs) and an ideal environment for a relaxing break from the outside world. It is a good base for walking, red deer and bird watching (barn owls) and serious cycling – the area is very hilly. There are 47 touring pitches plus an additional 14 pitches for holiday homes and 29 seasonal. Pitches are level, some on small terraces, all with 10A electricity hook-ups. There are 17 with multi-services (electricity, water, waste water and TV connections) and 40 on half hardstanding and half grass. The tenting area is at the top of the site with wonderful views over the National Park, but you may have a problem with tent pegs as the topsoil can be rather thin in places. There is a well appointed late arrivals area at the entrance. The approach road is narrow with passing places. Reception has a brochure with the history of the old market town of Longnor (where 'Peak Practice' was filmed), which includes several places worth visiting.

Facilities

The single heated building has modern facilities and includes cubicles with a toilet and washbasin and spacious showers. Freezer for ice packs and a microwave oven (donations to charity). Laundry facilities. Reception stocks basic requirements. Gas supplies. Putting green, badminton and boules courts. Dogs accepted, max. 2 per unit. RVs accepted by appointment. Off site: Markets in Buxton 6 miles (Tues/Sat), Leek (Wed). Sightseeing opportunities include Dove Dale and the Manifold Valley, Arbor Low Stone Circle, and Flash, at 1,580 ft. is the highest village in England. Riding 4 miles. Fishing 5 miles. Bicycle hire 6.5 miles. Golf 8 miles.

Open: All year excl. 11 January - 28 February.

Directions

Longnor village is on the B5053, about 6 miles south of Buxton. At crossroads in village square, turn right. Take left turn after 1.25 miles and then immediately right. Also signed from the A53 between Leek and Buxton, turning next at the Winking Man pub. O.S.GR: SK072640. GPS: N53:10.252 W01:54.025

Charges 2009

Per unit incl. 2 persons and electricity	£ 18.00
serviced pitch incl. 2 persons	£ 20.00
extra person	£ 5.00
tent incl. 2 persons	£ 16.00

169

UK3910 Teversal Camping & Caravanning Club Site

Silverhill Lane, Teversal NG17 3JJ (Nottinghamshire)

Tel: **01623 551838**. Email: **teversal@thefriendlyclub.co.uk**   www.alanrogers.com/UK3910

Formerly known as Shardaroba, this attractive, campsite has 126 pitches. A paradise for walkers and cyclists, it has a peaceful village location, and yet is surprisingly close to the motorway network. The site is beautifully kept and has won recent awards. Many of the spacious touring pitches are on hardstandings, arranged in well spaced rows surrounded by areas of grass and flower beds. All have electric hook-ups (16A), and 16 are multi-serviced. A grassed area for campers has a patio nearby with tables and chairs. Adjacent is an attractive country park – the highest point in Nottinghamshire.

Facilities

Two excellent, well equipped, heated toilet blocks with spacious showers, and family room. Shower room and toilet/wash room for disabled visitors. Separate laundry. Separate building with six full suites (3 male and 3 female with WC, washbasin, shower) and unisex toilet/washbasin next to camping area. Motorcaravan service point. Shop with basics. Calor gas. Playground. Off site: Fishing, bicycle hire, pub, bakery, chip shop and general stores all within 1 mile. Riding 200 yds. Golf 800 yds.

Open: All year.

Directions

Teversal is central in a triangle formed by M1 exits 28 and 29, and Mansfield. Site is signed off B6014 at western end of the village, turning north by the Carnarvon Arms into Silverhill Lane. Site entrance is 300 yds. on left. O.S.GR: SK485625. GPS: N53:08.911 W01:17.750

Charges guide

Per person	£ 6.60 - £ 7.60
child	£ 2.25 - £ 2.35
pitch (non member)	£ 6.00

UK3920 Riverside Caravan Park

Central Avenue, Worksop S80 1ER (Nottinghamshire)

Tel: **01909 474118**   www.alanrogers.com/UK3920

A town centre touring park, adjacent to the Worksop cricket ground, this excellent site is attractive and surprisingly peaceful. Riverside is within easy walking distance of the town centre pedestrian precinct and shops, and the Chesterfield Canal runs close to its northern side offering delightful towpath walks or fishing. For those who cannot resist the thwack of leather on willow, this site is ideal. Of the 60 marked level pitches, 50 are for touring, mainly on gravel hardstanding, others are on grass and some are separated by trees and low rails, and all have electric hook-ups (10A).

Facilities

The modern sanitary unit near reception can be heated and has all the usual facilities, although showers are on payment (20p). No laundry, but a launderette is close by in the town. Off site: Fishing 0.5 miles. Several golf courses 1 mile. Bicycle hire 4 miles. Squash and flat or crown green bowling nearby. Campers are made very welcome at the cricket ground clubhouse. One of Worksop's most interesting buildings, the medieval Priory Gatehouse, is open free of charge.

Open: All year.

Directions

Worksop is 7 miles west of the M1 at exit 30 and 4 miles east of the A1. Easiest approach to Park is from A57/A60 roundabout west of the town – third roundabout from the A1. Turn east (at Little Chef) on B6024 towards Town Centre. Site is well signed: in 400 yds. Site entrance is left of clubhouse. O.S.GR: SK580790. GPS: N53:18.360 W01:07.720

Charges guide

Per pitch incl. 2 persons, electricity	£ 16.00
extra person	£ 4.00

UK3940 Smeaton's Lakes Touring Caravan & Fishing Park

Great North Road, South Muskham, Newark-on-Trent NG23 6ED (Nottinghamshire)

Tel: **01636 605088**. Email: **lesley@smeatonslakes.co.uk**   www.alanrogers.com/UK3940

This 82 acre site is really ideal for anglers, with four fishing lakes (coarse, carp and pike) and river fishing on the Trent. There are 130 pitches of which 100 have electricity (16A). Non-anglers might choose this park if visiting antique fairs or events at nearby Newark Showground, or Newark town (1 mile) with its castle, air museum and various weekly markets. During your stay, you might visit Southwell Cathedral, Sherwood Forest, Clumber Park or Lincoln with its castle and cathedral.

Facilities

Two toilet blocks (with keypad access) are heated and include a good unit for disabled people, but no laundry room. Reception keeps gas, soft drinks, dairy produce, etc. and newspapers can be ordered. On-site concessions for lake and river fishing. Security cameras and night-time height barrier (about 6 ft). Off site: Bus stop at the end of the entry lane – buses run into Newark every hour until 10 pm. Riding and boat launching 2 miles. Golf 3 miles.

Open: All year.

Directions

From south on A1, take A46 west (signed Newark, then Leicester) and turn north on A6065/A616 towards South Muskham. From southwest (M1/A46) turn north off Newark bypass on A6065/A616 as above. From north on A1 leave B6325 (Newark) continue through South Muskham and follow signs for Newark. GPS: N53:05.616 W00:49.240

Charges guide

Per unit incl. 2 persons	£ 12.00 - £ 13.00
with electricity (16A)	£ 15.00 - £ 18.00

UK3945 Milestone Caravan Park

Great North Road, Cromwell, Newark NG23 6JE (Nottinghamshire)

Tel: 01636 821244. Email: enquiries@milestone-park.co.uk

www.alanrogers.com/UK3945

Situated just off the A1 north of Newark, Milestone has a good deal more to offer than simply a stopover option. Its 91 good-sized, level touring pitches all have electricity (16A) and nearby water points. Grass pitches are available, but most are all-weather in a variety of locations. Five are outside the barrier for those in transit (although key access is always available), then comes a pleasantly landscaped area and finally terraces overlooking an attractive fishing lake. An embankment built to muffle traffic noise provides a pleasant grassed walk with views across an adjoining lake and the surrounding countryside. This is a Caravan Club affiliated site. The site is convenient for Newark's Antiques Fairs and showground events and the historic town has a 12th century castle, an Air Museum, two other museums and an art gallery, as well as five markets a week. Southwell with its Minster and its racecourse is only 10 miles away, while Lincoln, Sherwood Forest, Clumber Park and Nottingham are not much further.

Facilities

Two heated toilet blocks provide pushbutton showers and open-style washbasins (may be under pressure at busy times). Excellent en-suite facilities for disabled visitors. Washing machine, dryer and ironing facilities. Motorcaravan service points. WiFi. Comprehensive tourist information, guides and children's quiz sheets on the site's wildlife. Fishing (£3 a day). Lakeside cabin with nature and fishing displays). Off site: Large fishing lake adjacent. Village has shop, small brewery and buses to Newark. Riding and boat launching 3 miles. Golf 5 miles. Bicycle hire at Sherwood Forest 12 miles.

Open: All year.

Directions

From the south on A1, 3.7 miles after A46 junction, take slip road to Cromwell and site is on the left after the village. From the north on the A1, 9 miles after Markham Moor junction, take slip road for Cromwell, turn right over bridge and right again to site. O.S.GR: SK798620.
GPS: N53:08.964 W00:48.462

Charges guide

Per person	£ 4.60 - £ 6.00
child	£ 1.50 - £ 2.50
pitch incl. electricity (16A)	£ 4.80 - £ 7.60

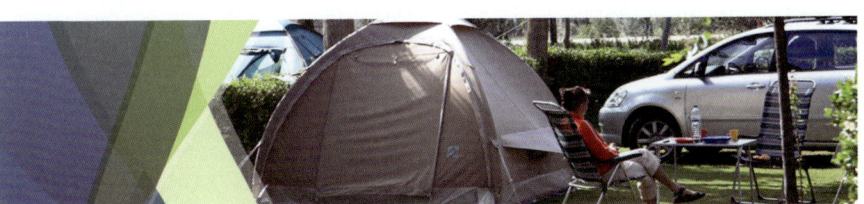

UK3950 Orchard Park

Marnham Road, Tuxford, Newark NG22 0PY (Nottinghamshire)

Tel: 01777 870228. Email: info@orchardcaravanpark.co.uk

www.alanrogers.com/UK3950

This well established family run touring and caravan park has been created in an old fruit orchard in a quiet location, yet is very convenient for the A1. It has a friendly feel, with just 65 pitches, all with electricity (10A), 34 with hardstanding and 20 occupied by seasonal units. There is also a spacious camping field with good views. Reception is at the owner's house with a nearby cabin with tourist information on attractions including Sundown Adventureland, Laxton Medieval village and Victorian Times, Rufford Abbey, Clumber Park, Sherwood Forest and the Robin Hood Centre.

Facilities

The heated toilet block has push button showers, open style washbasins and a well equipped room for disabled visitors. Laundry with washing machines, dryer and free spin dryer, iron and freezer for ice-packs. Small shop with basics and gas. Picnic area. Excellent children's adventure trail and nature walk. Apples, pears and blackberries can be picked in season. WiFi available on most of site (£3 per weekend). Off site: Pub 0.5 miles, shops 1 mile. Riding 3 miles. Fishing 4 miles. Bicycle hire and golf 10 miles.

Open: March - October.

Directions

Tuxford is 15 miles north of Newark and 18 miles west of Lincoln. Park lies to the east of the A1. Leave at signs for Tuxford and turn east on A6075 towards Lincoln (A57), continue through village and turn south towards Marnham for 0.5 miles. Site is on right 0.5 miles after railway bridge (well signed). O.S.GR: SK750710. GPS: N53:13.776 W00:52.170

Charges guide

Per unit incl. 2 persons and electricity	£ 15.00 - £ 36.00
extra person	£ 3.00
child (4-12 yrs)	£ 1.00
Book for 7 nights, pay for 6.	

UK3970 Glencote Caravan Park

Station Road, Cheddleton, Leek ST13 7EE (Staffordshire)

Tel: **01538 360745**. Email: **canistay@glencote.co.uk**

www.alanrogers.com/UK3970

At the entrance to the Churnet Valley, three miles south of the market town of Leek, Glencote is a pleasant, family run park of six acres. It has 88 numbered touring pitches set on flat grass, all have patio style hardstandings with tarmac access roads, electrical connections (16A) and a dedicated water supply. Pretty flowerbeds and trees make a very pleasant environment. An attractive, sunken play area, on grass and bark with an abundance of shrubs and flowers, sits alongside the small (fenced) coarse fishing pool. There is also a refurbished barbecue area complete with gazebo.

Facilities

The toilet block is centrally situated and can be heated. Facilities include one private cabin for ladies, a combined shower and toilet for disabled visitors, a small laundry room, and dishwashing sinks under cover. Mobile shop visits (except Sunday). Gas. Max. 2 dogs per unit. Internet. Off site: Small supermarket and post office in Cheddleton 0.5 miles. Variety of inns within walking distance. Golf 4 miles. Bicycle hire 5 miles. Riding 10 miles.

Open: 1 February - end December.

Directions

Park is signed off A520 Leek - Stone road, 3.5 miles south of Leek on northern edge of Cheddleton Village. O.S.GR: SJ982524. GPS: N53:04.243 W02:02.033

Charges guide

Per unit incl. 2 persons and awning	£ 18.00
extra person	£ 5.00
child (5-16 yrs)	£ 2.50
electricity	£ 2.50

UK4040 Clent Hills Camping & Caravanning Club Site

Fieldhouse Lane, Romsley, Halesowen B62 0NH (West Midlands)

Tel: **01562 710015**

www.alanrogers.com/UK4040

Conveniently close to Birmingham and only a couple of miles or so off the M5/M42 intersection, this site is a real surprise in terms of being quiet and peaceful and very pretty with good views. Its only disadvantage is that it is on sloping ground, but the present, helpful holiday site managers are happy to assist in pitching anyone who has a problem in getting level (mainly motorcaravanners); in fact, there are some level pitches and these are all earmarked for motorcaravans. The 95 pitches are all of a good size, 74 with electrical connections (10/16A) and 17 with hardstanding. Generally this is a well run and attractive site, very usefully situated.

Facilities

The central sanitary toilet block can be heated and provides the latest facilities, including washbasins in cabins, hairdryers, baby room and a toilet and shower for disabled people. It was spotless when last visited. Washing machine, dryer and ironing facilities. Small play area with safety surface. Gas supplies. Caravan storage. Off site: Riding 1 mile. Fishing 3 miles. Golf 7 miles.

Open: March - November.

Directions

From M5 exit 4 take A491, branch right to Romsley on B4551 and watch for site signs in Romsley village by shops. Site is on left. O.S.GR: SO955795. GPS: N52:24.881 W02:04.088

Charges guide

Per person	£ 4.90 - £ 7.25
child (6-18 yrs)	£ 2.15 - £ 2.15
non-member pitch fee	£ 5.65

UK4070 Somers Wood Caravan Park

Somers Road, Meriden CV7 7PL (Warwickshire)

Tel: **01676 522978**. Email: **enquiries@somerswood.co.uk**

www.alanrogers.com/UK4070

Somers Wood is a quiet, peaceful park, attractively situated amongst pine trees. It is beside an 18-hole golf course and a fishing lake, both of which may be used by visitors and next to a bridle path which can be used to exercise dogs. From the reception building at the entrance, an oval gravel road provides access to 48 pitches, all on hardstanding and with 10A electricity hook-ups. There are also wooden table and chairs. This is a very pleasant park which only accepts adults and does not take tents. It is useful for those visiting the various shows at the NEC when it can get very busy.

Facilities

The central, heated sanitary block is fully equipped. Shower cubicles are especially large. Two dishwashing sinks on the veranda area. Laundry service at reception. WiFi on payment. Off site: Local shops and restaurant less than 1 mile and visitors also welcome to use the bar and restaurant at the golf club next door.

Open: 1 February - 3 January.

Directions

From M42 exit 6 (NEC) take A45 towards Coventry. Keep in left lane down to roundabout and exit on A452 (signed Leamington/Meriden), then turn left into Hampton Lane at the next roundabout. Site is signed with golf and fishing centres on the left. O.S.GR: SP228819. GPS: N52:26.358 W01:40.168

Charges guide

Per pitch incl. 2 persons and electricity	£ 18.00 - £ 20.00
extra person	£ 3.00

Special offers for some weeks.

UK4075 Hollyfast Caravan Park

Wall Hill Road, Allesley, Coventry CV5 9EL (Warwickshire)

Tel: 02476 336411. Email: sales@hollyfastcaravanpark.co.uk   www.alanrogers.com/UK4075

Hollyfast is situated in beautiful countryside on the outskirts of Coventry, part of the park being set within a lovely woodland area giving peace and tranquillity all year round. Located on the Birmingham side of Coventry, this means a five minute drive into the centre of Coventry and just a ten minute drive to Birmingham's National Exhibition Centre. You will receive a friendly welcome and be directed to a very clean and well spaced site with 35 pitches of varying sizes with 16A electricity connections. You may be asked to park your car on a nearby car park. A new toilet block provides very clean facilities, along with a games room. Rallies are welcome and a club house is provided with a stage, television and kitchen areas for these groups. Under the same ownership, a motorcaravan sales centre with caravan and motorhome storage, LPG and a children's play area are reached through the site.

Facilities

The modern toilet block provides simple clean facilities with good sized showers (3 per sex) and open washbasins. Toilet and shower for disabled campers. Laundry. Games room. Club house for rallies. Deposit for barrier (£25). Off site: The local area has shops, three pubs (hot and cold food), a golf course and a riding centre. Bus stop 1 mile for Coventry. Interesting British Road Transport museum. Birmingham, Stratford upon Avon, Leamington Spa and Warwick are within driving distance.

Open: All year.

Directions

From M1/M45 (or the M40/A46, or M69/A46) take A45 towards Birmingham. Turn right on A4114 and follow brown and white caravan signs. After turning by the White Lion pub, site is 0.5 miles on the left. From the north take M6 north of Birmingham or the M1 north (Nottingham) follow M42 to NEC, A45 towards Coventry and onto A4114 and as above. O.S.GR: SP303831. GPS: N52:26.753 W01:33.343

Charges guide

Per unit incl. 2 persons	
and electricity	£ 12.50 - £ 17.00
extra person	£ 2.50
child (5-15 yrs)	£ 1.50
dog	£ 1.00

UK4080 Riverside Caravan Park

Tiddington Road, Tiddington, Stratford-upon-Avon CV37 7AB (Warwickshire)

Tel: 01789 292312. Email: info@stratfordcaravans.co.uk   www.alanrogers.com/UK4080

On the bank of the River Avon, this spacious site has 250 pitches in total, and about 100 privately owned mobile homes. The 125 touring pitches (no tents) are on level grass, all with electric hook-ups (16A). There is a small shop and cafe on site, which serves breakfasts and takeaways in addition to stocking a selection of basic supplies. A clubhouse that incorporates a bar, playground, games room and TV room is on the adjacent Rayford Park which is under the same management. There is a possible flood risk during periods of inclement weather. A river taxi runs to Stratford.

Facilities

The main toilet unit has been re-fitted to modern standards and is bright and comfortable with central heating. Spacious pre-set showers, some washbasins in cubicles, with a child-size toilet and shower in the ladies. Facilities for disabled guests. Utility room with dishwashing and laundry facilities. Slipway and fishing. Courtesy river launch to Stratford. Gas supplies. No commercial vehicles are accepted. Off site: Shakespeare.

Open: 1 April - 31 October.

Directions

From Stratford take B4086 towards Wellesbourne. Site entrance is on left, after 1 mile, just before Tiddington village (ignore entrance to Rayford Park C.P.). O.S.GR: SP219559. GPS: N52:12.014 W01:40.928

Charges guide

Per unit incl. 4 persons	£ 20.00
extra person	£ 5.00
dog	free

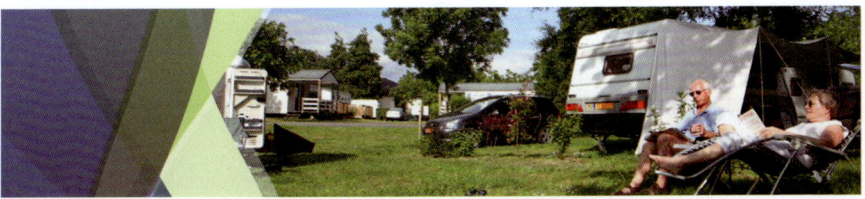

UK4090 Island Meadow Caravan Park

The Mill House, Aston Cantlow B95 6JP (Warwickshire)

Tel: **01789 488273**. Email: **holiday@islandmeadowcaravanpark.co.uk**   **www.alanrogers.com/UK4090**

This peaceful, traditional, family run site is in a rural location, surrounded by the River Alne and its mill race. A good base for walking, cycling and birdwatching, it has 80 pitches in total, with 56 holiday homes (4 for rent) located around the perimeter. The 24 touring pitches are on the spacious, central grassy area of the site, all have 10A electric hook-ups. Only environmentally friendly groundsheets are permitted. The small shop has an adequate stock of basic requirements and gas supplies, and a good stock of local visitor information. Note: The site is on an island with obvious hazards for small children. There is an excellent playground in the village centre (five minutes walk via footpath across Mill Meadow).

Facilities

Two sanitary units, both heated. The original provides adequate WCs and washbasins for men, and the more modern unit has been provided for women, with a separate access shower unit for the men, and a suite for disabled people on one end. Laundry with washing machine, sink and ironing facility. The millpond and its weir offer good coarse fishing. Off site: The village has its own 'club' (campers welcome) and the local pub serves good meals. Golf 3 miles, riding 4.5 miles, bicycle hire 6 miles. Warwick Castle. Stratford-upon-Avon. Mary Arden's house in Wilmcote is only 1 mile from the site. Buses from village to Alcester and Stratford, including a late night service.

Open: 1 March - 31 October.

Directions

From A46 (Stratford - Alcester) follow signs for Mary Arden's House. At Wilmcote follow signs to Aston Cantlow and site. O.S.GR: SP136598. GPS: N52:14.129 W01:48.159

Charges guide

Per unit incl. 2 persons and electricity	£ 16.50
extra person	£ 1.00
child (5-10 yrs)	£ 0.50
tent (2 man)	£ 12.50

Gazebos only by prior arrangement.
No credit cards.

UK4100 Hoburne Cotswold

Broadway Lane, South Cerney, Cirencester GL7 5UQ (Gloucestershire)

Tel: **01285 860216**. Email: **enquiries@hoburne.co.uk**   **www.alanrogers.com/UK4100**

Since this park is adjacent to the Cotswold Water Park, those staying here will have easy access to the varied watersports available. On the park itself there is a lake with pedaloes and canoes for hire. Its wide range of other amenities includes outdoor and indoor heated swimming pools and an impressive, large indoor leisure complex. There are 200 well marked touring pitches for any type of unit, all with hardstanding (only fairly level) and a grass surround for awning or tent; 90 are serviced 'super' pitches. Of good size but with nothing between them, all have electricity (some need long leads). There are also 210 holiday units, mainly for letting. The large, refurbished clubhouse has a big general lounge with giant TV screen, entertainment at times, food service (or food bar in lounge), big games room and a lounge bar which overlooks the outdoor pool and lake with a patio. This is a very secure park which is being continually updated. Part of the Hoburne group.

Facilities

Six small toilet blocks are clean and well maintained with pre-set showers and background heating. Baby facilities. Basic facilities for disabled visitors. The site has heavy weekend trade. Launderette. Supermarket. Indoor leisure complex including pool with flume, spa bath, sauna, steam room and sun bed. Outdoor pool (Whitsun - early Sept). Clubhouse with bar, food and entertainment. Football field. Tennis. Adventure playground. Crazy golf. Fishing lake. Dogs or pets are not accepted.

Open: March - October.

Directions

Three miles southeast of Cirencester on A419, turn west towards Cotswold Water Park at new roundabout on bypass onto B4696. Take second right and follow signs. O.S.GR: SU055957. GPS: N51:39.611 W01:55.146

Charges guide

Per pitch incl. max. 6 persons and electricity	£ 12.50 - £ 30.00
serviced 'super' pitch	£ 13.50 - £ 32.00

Weekly rates and weekend breaks available.

UK4150 Croft Farm Water & Leisure Park

Bredon's Hardwick, Tewkesbury GL20 7EE (Gloucestershire)

Tel: **01684 772321**. Email: **enquiries@croftfarmleisure.co.uk**   www.alanrogers.com/UK4150

Croft Farm is an AALA licensed Watersports Centre with Royal Yachting Association approved tuition available for windsurfing, sailing, kayaking and canoeing. The lakeside campsite has around 96 level pitches, with 80 electric hook-ups (10A), but there are many seasonal units, leaving around 36 pitches for tourists, plus some tent pitches. There are 36 gravel hardstandings but very little shade or shelter. 'Gym and Tonic' is a fully equipped gymnasium with qualified instructors, sunbed and sauna. Sports massage, aromatherapy and beauty treatments are available by appointment. Activity holidays for families and groups are organised. Campers can use their own non-powered boats on the lake with reduced launch fees and there is free fishing. Climb Bredon Hill (2 miles) for a panoramic view of the Severn and Avon Valleys. Places of interest include Bredon Barn, pottery and church, Beckford Silk Mill and Tewkesbury Abbey.

Facilities

A new building (open in summer) has excellent facilities with spacious hot showers, plus some dishwashing sinks. A heated unit in the main building is always open and best for cooler months; this provides further WCs, washbasins and showers, laundry and facilities for disabled persons. Gas. Cafe/bar (Fri-Sun low season, daily at other times). Takeaway. Gym. Playground. Fishing. Barrier and toilet block key (£5 deposit). Off site: Pub opposite. Tewkesbury 1.5 miles. Golf 3 miles. Riding 8 miles.

Open: All year, excl. January and February.

Directions

Bredon's Hardwick is midway between Tewkesbury and Bredon on B4080. Site entrance opposite 'Cross Keys Inn'. From M5 exit 9 take A438 (Tewkesbury), at first traffic lights turn right into Shannon Way. Turn right at next lights, cross motorway bridge. Turn left (housing estate) and cross second motorway bridge. At T-junction turn right on B4080, site is immediately on left. O.S.GR: SO912353.
GPS: N52:00.958 W02:07.816

Charges guide

Per unit incl. 2 persons and awning	£ 14.00
extra person (over 3 yrs)	£ 3.00
electricity	£ 2.00
dog	£ 0.75
Discount 10% for 8 nights or more (excl. July, August and B.Hs).	

CROFT FARM WATER PARK

BREDONS HARDWICK, TEWKESBURY, GLOS. GL20 7EE
TEL 01684 772321
www.croftfarmleisure.co.uk
Lakeside caravan and camping park - water sports centre
log cabin clubhouse - modern facilities

UK4130 Moreton-in-Marsh Caravan Club Site

Bourton Road, Moreton-in-Marsh GL56 0BT (Gloucestershire)

Tel: **01608 650519**   www.alanrogers.com/UK4130

This excellent, busy, but rural site in the heart of the Cotswolds offers most one would hope for from a camping holiday. Only 250 yards from the town, there is plenty of choice for food and pubs. Surrounded by trees, the site has 182 pitches, all with electricity (16A) and TV sockets, 172 with hardstanding. Milk and ice-cream are available from reception. Adjacent to a dog exercise field is a recently updated play area, crazy golf and a boules pitch. In an adjoining field there is plenty of room for ball games. Kite flying is not allowed because of low power cables. Moreton-in-Marsh is famous for its Tuesday street market and is always a busy town, being only a few miles from the pretty villages of Bourton-on-the-Water and Stow-on-the-Wold, just two of the many interesting Cotswold villages worthy of a visit in this lovely area of England. Tents are not accepted.

Facilities

The two toilet blocks have been completely renovated and offer excellent facilities. Both have a large room for disabled people and babies. Small toilet and bath with seat for children. Large laundry. Play area. Boules. Internet access. Off site: Shops, pubs and restaurants 400 yards. Golf 7 miles. Nearby are the Cotswold Falconry Centre, Hidcote Manor Gardens and the Rollright Stones.

Open: All year.

Directions

From Evesham on A44, site on left after Bourton-on-the-Hill village, 150 yards before town sign. From Moreton-in-Marsh take A44 towards Evesham and site is on right, 150 yards past the Wellington museum. O.S.GR: SP200323.
GPS: N51:59.325 W01:42.650

Charges guide

Per person	£ 4.70 - £ 6.20
child (5-16 yrs)	£ 1.50 - £ 3.00
pitch incl. electricity (non-member)	£ 10.90 - £ 15.30

175

UK4170 Tudor Caravan & Camping Park

Shepherds Patch, Slimbridge GL2 7BP (Gloucestershire)

Tel: **01453 890483**. Email: **info@tudorcaravanpark.co.uk**

www.alanrogers.com/UK4170

This traditional style campsite is adjacent to the Gloucester - Sharpness Canal. Located behind the Tudor Arms public house, a gate clearly identifies the entrance and reception is up a short path on the left. There are many trees and hedges, particularly surrounding the site, so the canal is not visible. Attractively laid out on two separate fields, there are 75 pitches, all with electric hook-ups (16A), and 35 with hardstanding. The old orchard is for long stay or 'adult only' units, with some concrete wheel track hardstands, and a more open grassy meadow is for family touring units. The adjacent pub has a restaurant and bar (2007 CAMRA award winner) and just across the road, beside the canal, is a café and shop where boats can be hired. This is a delightful, peaceful park with plenty to offer: walking, fishing and boating, not to mention ornithology as the Wildfowl and Wetlands Centre founded by Sir Peter Scott at Slimbridge is only 800 yards away.

Facilities

The toilet building located to one side of the orchard, provides all the usual facilities including push-button hot showers and it can be heated in cool weather. No facilities for disabled persons at present but a new block is planned in the meadow which will include facilities for disabled people and babies. Gas available. Some site lighting but a torch would be useful. Gate is locked 22.30-07.00. Off site: Meals at the Tudor Arms pub. Shop and cafe in boatyard opposite the site (Easter-Sept), also serves breakfasts. Fishing adjacent. Towpath walks. Berkeley Castle, Frampton and Stroud.

Open: All year.

Directions

From A38 by the junction with A4135 (Dursley), turn west, signed WWT Wetlands Centre Slimbridge. Continue for 1.5 miles turning left into car park of the Tudor Arms. Site entrance is at rear of car park. O.S.GR: SO728042. GPS: N51:44.132 W02:23.749

Charges guide

Per unit incl. 2 persons	£ 11.00 - £ 15.00
extra person	£ 2.00
child (under 12 yrs)	£ 1.00
electricity	£ 2.25 - £ 2.50

No credit cards.

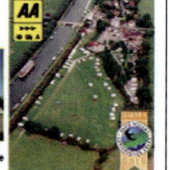

UK4140 Winchcombe Camping & Caravanning Club Site

Brooklands Farm, Alderton, Tewkesbury GL20 8NX (Gloucestershire)

Tel: **01242 620259**

www.alanrogers.com/UK4140

This is a popular, quiet site in a rural location, close to the Cotswold attractions. Some pitches surround a small coarse fishing lake, with others in a more recently developed area with open views over the surrounding countryside. In total there are 80 pitches, 53 with electric hook-ups (10A) and 42 with gravel hardstanding. The reception building flanks a small gravel courtyard car park and late arrivals area approached from a tarmac drive. Future plans include the addition of lodges, an extended camping area and a new toilet block. Places to visit include Gloucester Docks and the National Waterways Museum, whilst south of Gloucester are Owlpen Manor near Uley, and the Painswick Rococo Garden. The Wildfowl and Wetlands Trust at Slimbridge, first opened in 1946 by Sir Peter Scott is also well worth a visit. Much closer to the site is the GWR (Gloucester Warwickshire Railway) at Toddington or Winchcombe.

Facilities

The main, heated sanitary unit, kept very clean and tidy by the wardens, is well equipped. To the rear of the site is a small, 'portacabin' style sanitary unit (also heated). Well equipped unit for disabled people. Laundry facilities. Gas supplies. Large games room with bowling alley. Small outdoor play area. Off site: Several pubs and restaurants in the area. Golf 7 miles.

Open: 16 March - 15 January.

Directions

From M5 exit 9, take A46 Evesham road for 3 miles to Toddington roundabout, then the B4077 towards Stow-on-the-Wold for a further 3 miles to the site entrance. Ignore signs for Alderton village. O.S.GR: SP 007324. GPS: N51:59.424 W01:59.441

Charges guide

Per person	£ 6.30 - £ 7.25
child (5-16 yrs)	£ 2.15 - £ 2.25
non-member pitch fee	£ 5.65

UK4180 **Ranch Caravan Park**

Honeybourne, Evesham WR11 7PR (Worcestershire)

Tel: **01386 830744**. Email: **enquiries@ranch.co.uk**   **www.alanrogers.com/UK4180**

Set in the Vale of Evesham, Ranch lies not far from both Evesham and Broadway in quiet rural surroundings of 50 acres and just half an hour's drive from Stratford-on-Avon. The park takes 120 touring units – caravans, motorcaravans or trailer tents, but not other tents – on flat, partly undulating, hedged meadows with well mown grass and a spacious feel. The pitches are not marked but the staff position units. All have electrical connections (10A) and there are 20 hardstandings including 8 fully serviced pitches (electricity, TV, water and drainage). There are 169 caravan holiday homes in their own section. The Vale of Evesham is noted for being a sheltered area growing fruit and other produce from early spring through to late autumn.

Facilities

Two very well appointed, modern sanitary blocks with free hot showers and heating. Motorcaravan service point. Shop. Clubhouse (weekends only in the early and late seasons) offering wide range of good value meals and entertainment is arranged at B.H weekends and Saturdays in school holidays. Heated pool (55 x 30 ft; June - Sept). Gym and sauna. Games room with TV, video machines and pool table. Playground. Off site: Riding and bicycle hire 2 miles. Fishing 4 miles. Golf 6 miles.

Open: 1 March - 30 November.

Directions

From A46 Evesham take B4035 towards Chipping Campden. After Badsey and Bretforton follow signs for Honeybourne down unclassified road (Ryknild Street, Roman road). Park is through village on left by station. O.S.GR: SP112444.
GPS: N52:05.833 W01:49.874

Charges guide

Per unit incl. 2 persons and electricity	£ 18.00 - £ 23.00
incl. water and drainage	£ 21.50 - £ 26.50
extra person (over 5 yrs)	free - £ 4.00
dog	free - £ 2.50
One free night for every 7 booked.	

UK4160 **Forest Holidays Christchurch**

Bracelands Drive, Christchurch, Coleford GL16 7NN (Gloucestershire)

Tel: **01594 837258**. Email: **info@forestholidays.co.uk**   **www.alanrogers.com/UK4160**

Forest Holidays is a partnership between the Forestry Commission and The Camping & Caravanning Club. With 280 unmarked pitches, this 20 acre site occupies an undulating, open grassy area in the heart of the Forest of Dean. There are around 60 seasonal units, seven hardstandings and 95 pitches with 10A electricity. Reception houses a well stocked shop and good tourist information, including a leaflet about the forest trails (55p). Tenters will appreciate the large pavilion in the centre of the site, a large room with a stove, tables and chairs – an ideal retreat if the weather proves inclement.

Facilities

Four sanitary units, two fairly modern with spacious well equipped showers, some vanity style basins with dividers, plus two much older units with WCs and washbasins only. The central block has a laundry and dishwashing room. Units for disabled people and baby changing in two blocks. Adventure playground on bark. Dogs are not accepted. Off site: Fishing and swimming 1 mile. Coleford 1.5 miles. Golf 2 miles. Bicycle hire 3 miles. Ross-on-Wye 8 miles. Riding 10 miles.

Open: All year excl. 14 Jan - 28 Feb.

Directions

From Monmouth take A4136 east for 5 miles and turn north at Pike House Inn, site is 0.5 miles. From Coleford take road towards Monmouth, turning right to Symonds Yat and Berry Hill (site signed). O.S.GR: SO569129. GPS: N51:48.800 W02:37.641

Charges guide

Per unit incl. 2 persons	£ 7.60 - £ 14.60
extra person	£ 3.10 - £ 5.90
child (5-14 yrs)	£ 1.60 - £ 3.00
Discounts for disabled guests and senior citizens.	

177

UK4185 Weir Meadow Holiday Park

Lower Leys, Evesham WR11 3AA (Worcestershire)

Tel: **01386 442417**

www.alanrogers.com/UK4185

On entering this park you drive through neat caravan holiday homes surrounded by flowers and shrubs, but this does not prepare you for the view which opens in front of you of touring pitches set out on the banks of the river Avon with splendid vistas of the narrow boats on the river and of the weir itself. The park has 130 caravan holiday homes, 8 caravans for hire and 27 touring pitches. Pitches are clearly marked off the tarmac roads and all have electricity. Units over 9 m. may have access problems. A central barbecue area is provided beside the river.

Facilities

A well kept toilet block includes provision for disabled visitors. Excellent laundry area. Barbecue area. Fishing is available (in season with the necessary licence) at £5 per day. Off site: All town centre facilities nearby. River walks.

Open: 1 March - 31 October.

Directions

From the A44 follow signs for Evesham town centre. Go straight across two roundabouts, turn right at second set of traffic lights, then in 80 m. turn left. Site is clearly marked from the A44.
O.S.GR: SP041438. GPS: N52:05.629 W01:56.342

Charges guide

Per unit incl. 2 persons	£ 16.00 - £ 21.00
extra person	£ 2.00

UK4190 Kingsgreen Caravan Park

Kingsgreen, Berrow, Malvern WR13 6AQ (Worcestershire)

Tel: **01531 650272**

www.alanrogers.com/UK4190

A friendly and extremely well kept site with views of the Malvern Hills, Kingsgreen has an attractive rural location. An ideal site for adults who like the quiet life, there are no amusements for children. The surrounding countryside is ideal for walking or cycling, and the small, fenced fishing lakes on the site are well stocked (£4 per day). There are 45 level, grass and gravel pitches, all with 16A electricity, plus an additional area for tents. Some old orchard trees provide a little shade in parts. The site is 7 miles from the market town of Ledbury with its half timbered buildings and within easy driving distance of Malvern, the Cotswolds, Forest of Dean or Tewkesbury with its 12th century Abbey.

Facilities

Modern heated toilet facilities (key on deposit) provide hot showers (25p token from reception) and a separate unit for disabled people (WC and washbasin). Laundry room with washing machine, dryer, sink and iron and board (all metered). Gas and barbecue fuels are stocked and a milkman calls daily with milk, eggs, bread, soft drinks, etc. Off site: Nearest shop and pub 1.5 miles. Bicycle hire 2 miles. Riding 3 miles. Golf 5 miles.

Open: 1 March - 31 October.

Directions

From M50 exit 2, take A417 towards Gloucester, then first left, where site is signed, also signed the Malverns, back over the motorway. Site is 2 miles from the M50. O.S.GR: SO767338. GPS: N52:00.157 W02:20.309

Charges guide

Per unit incl. 2 persons and electricity	£ 14.50 - £ 17.50

No credit cards. VAT not included.

UK4210 Lickhill Manor Caravan Park

Lower Lickhill Road, Stourport-on-Severn DY13 8RL (Worcestershire)

Tel: **01299 871041**. Email: **excellent@lickhillmanor.co.uk**

www.alanrogers.com/UK4210

Lickhill Manor is a well managed touring and holiday site within easy walking distance of the town centre via a footpath along the River Severn which lies a short distance below the site. There are opportunities for fishing and boating. The touring area has 70 marked, level, pitches accessed via tarmac roads, all with electricity (10/16A). The 124 holiday homes, well screened from the touring area, are not visually intrusive, and there is a separate rally field (with 64 hook-ups). There is an excellent play area for children and the park has recently created wildlife ponds and planted over 1,000 native trees and shrubs. This park has matured into one of the best in the area.

Facilities

A second sanitary building serves the touring pitches and complements the older unit at the other end of the park. This heated building provides good, modern facilities including a well equipped suite for disabled guests which doubles as a family washroom with facilities for baby changing. Motorcaravan service point. Gas. Children's play park in separate family area. Off site: Riding 1 mile. Bicycle hire 3 miles. Golf 5 miles.

Open: All year.

Directions

From the A451 in Stourport take B4195 northwest towards Bewdley. After 1 mile turn left at crossroads into Lickhill Road North where site is signed.
O.S.GR: SO790730. GPS: N52:20.616 W02:17.879

Charges guide

Per unit incl. 4 persons and electricity	£ 13.00 - £ 19.50
extra person over 2 yrs	£ 2.00

Weekly rates available. Senior citizen discounts.

UK4300 Poston Mill Caravan Park

Peterchurch, Golden Valley HR2 0SF (Herefordshire)

Tel: **01981 550225**. Email: **enquiries@poston-mill.co.uk**   **www.alanrogers.com/UK4300**

Set in the heart of the Golden Valley, Poston Mill Park is a pleasant, neat park in farmland a mile from the delightful village of Peterchurch. It is an ideal location for relaxation or exploring. There are currently 43 touring pitches set on level grass or hardstanding with mature trees and conifers around the perimeter of the park. All the pitches are fully serviced with electricity (16A), water and TV connections (leads to hire). An attractive walk along one side of the park, edging the River Dore (fishing available), follows the line of the old Golden Valley railway. Adjoining the park is 'The Mill' restaurant and Fraser's Farm Shop. There is a footpath from the park over the fields. Peterchurch village is only 1 mile. Holiday cottages and caravan holiday homes are available to rent. A member of the Best of British group.

Facilities

One central sanitary block with a smaller, refurbished block near the holiday home area which includes private cubicles. Both are fully equipped and include units for disabled people and families. Laundry rooms. Motorcaravan service point. Play area. Pitch and putt. Tennis, petanque and croquet. Golf driving range. Games room. Winter caravan storage. Off site: Riding 3 miles. Bicycle hire 10 miles. Fishing and walking.

Open: All year.

Directions

Park is 1 mile southeast of Peterchurch on the B4348 road. O.S.GR: SO356371. GPS: N52:02.111 W02:56.782

Charges guide

Per unit incl. 2 persons	
and electricity	£ 15.00 - £ 20.00
extra person	£ 3.00
child (4-10 yrs)	£ 1.50
awning	£ 2.00
dog	£ 1.00

Min. charge at B.Hs. 5 nights.

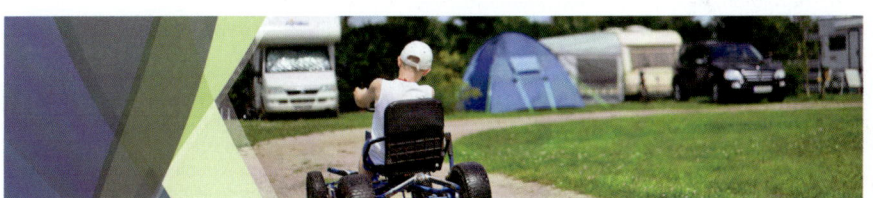

UK4310 Lucksall Caravan & Camping Park

Mordiford, Hereford HR1 4LP (Herefordshire)

Tel: **01432 870213**. Email: **karen@lucksallpark.co.uk**   **www.alanrogers.com/UK4310**

Set in around 17 acres on the bank of the River Wye and benefiting from improvements by the new owners, Lucksall has 80 large, well spaced and level touring pitches, of which 80 have 16A electricity and 30 have hardstanding. The river is open to the site but lifebelts and safety messages are in evidence. Canoes are available for hire – or bring your own – and fishing permits may be obtained from reception. A large, fenced new playground and a large grassy area for games are provided. The site shop is well stocked with a variety of goods and gas (a mini-market is within 1.5 miles). Amongst the local places worthy of a visit are the Cider Museum and King Offa Distillery in Hereford, Belmont Abbey and Queenswood Country Park. The park is also a good base for touring the Wye Valley. A member of the Countryside Discovery group.

Facilities

The main sanitary facilities provide showers (20p) and a separate unit for disabled visitors with ramped entrance, WC, washbasin, shower, hairdryers and hand-dryer. New laundry room. A smaller, refurbished, now c/heated open all times shop (basics only). Fishing. Canoeing. Site barrier (2.13 m. height limit) locked 21.00-09.00 hrs. Only 'breathable' groundsheets are permitted. Off site: Golf 5 miles. Bicycle hire 9 miles.

Open: 1 March - 30 November.

Directions

Between Mordiford and Fownhope, 5 miles southeast of Hereford on B4224, the park is well signed. O.S.GR: SO571355. GPS: N52:01.422 W02:37.832

Charges guide

Per unit incl. 2 persons	£ 11.00 - £ 14.50
extra person (over 5 yrs)	£ 2.00 - £ 3.00
awning	£ 1.50 - £ 2.00

179

UK4320 Broadmeadow Caravan & Camping Park

Broadmeadows, Ross-on-Wye HR9 7BW (Herefordshire)

Tel: **01989 768076**. Email: **broadm4811@aol.com** www.alanrogers.com/UK4320

This modern, spacious park with open views and its own fishing lake, is conveniently located for the town of Ross-on-Wye. The town centre is within easy walking distance. The approach to the site is unusual, but persevere and you will find one of the best laid out, immaculately maintained sites with facilities of the very highest quality. There are 150 large pitches on level, open grass, and the site is especially good for tents. Each set of four pitches has a service post with water, drain, electricity points (16A) and lighting. Although the A40 relief road is at the eastern end of the site, the traffic noise should not be too intrusive (but tenters be aware). This is a good base for touring Herefordshire, the Wye Valley or the Forest of Dean.

Facilities

Two superb modern sanitary buildings are fully equipped, including hairdryers, baby rooms, family bathrooms each with WC, basin and bath, and a comprehensive unit for disabled visitors. Dishwashing room and laundry at each building. Basic motorcaravan service point. Entrance barrier and keypad entry system. Small part-fenced playground. Well fenced fishing lake (coarse fishing £5.50 per day). Off site: Supermarket 200 m. Bicycle hire in town. Golf 3 miles. Riding 8 miles.

Open: Easter/1 April - 30 September.

Directions

From A40 relief road turn into Ross at roundabout, take first right into industrial estate, then right in 0.5 miles before supermarket, where site is signed. O.S.GR: SO610240. GPS: N51:54.994 W02:34.493

Charges guide

Per person	£ 4.00
child (2-9 yrs)	£ 2.50
pitch	£ 8.00 - £ 9.50
incl. electricity	£ 11.00 - £ 12.50
dog	£ 1.50

UK4330 The Millpond Touring Caravans & Camping

Little Tarrington, Hereford HR1 4JA (Herefordshire)

Tel: **01432 890243**. Email: **enquiries@millpond.co.uk** www.alanrogers.com/UK4330

This peaceful little site with its own fishing lake is set in 30 acres of countryside. Opened for the first time in 1997, it has 40 large pitches on open grassland, all with electricity hook-ups (10A) and 15 pitches for tents in an adjacent field. Special attention has been made to providing good facilities for disabled visitors. The large fishing lake (unfenced) is well stocked with coarse fish, has facilities for disabled fishermen and offers reduced rates for campers. Site lighting is minimal (local authority regulations) so a torch might be useful for tents. There may be a little noise at times from a railway track nearby. The large acreage surrounding the campsite has a variety of well established trees that have been supplemented with many new plantings, and well-mowed paths encourage you to wander and enjoy the many trees, wild flowers, birds and the peaceful surroundings. The site is just seven miles from Hereford with its cathedral, the fascinating Mappa Mundi and chained library, seven miles from Ledbury and close to the Black and White Village Trail.

Facilities

A modern building houses heated sanitary facilities, laundry and dishwashing sinks, baby changing surface, an upgraded unit for disabled persons (with wet room shower) and a common room with a massive supply of tourist information, wildlife charts and walking guides. Site is currently not really suitable for American motorhomes. Off site: The local pub is a 10 minute walk, but there is no shop in the village.

Open: 1 March - 31 October.

Directions

Little Tarrington is midway between Hereford and Ledbury. The site is just north of the A438 on the eastern edge of Tarrington village (signed). O.S.GR: SO627409. GPS: N52:04.061 W02:32.914

Charges guide

Per unit incl. 2 persons, awning, electricity and 1 pet	£ 13.00 - £ 16.00
extra person	£ 3.00

www.**alanrogers**.com for latest campsite news

UK4345 Townsend Touring & Caravan Park

Townsend Farm, Pembridge, Leominster HR6 9HB (Herefordshire)

Tel: **01544 388527**. Email: **info@townsend-farm.co.uk**   **www.alanrogers.com/UK4345**

Opened in 2002, this is a modern, family run park. It provides tarmac roads, good site lighting, well spaced pitches and a drive-over motorcaravan service point, with plenty of open space and a small fishing lake (with ducks and unfenced). There are 60 pitches, 20 with gravel hardstanding, the remainder on grass, and all have access to 16A electricity, water and drainage. Reception is at the Farm Shop by the entrance. This is a real treat as it stocks a wide variety of fruit and vegetables, eggs and has a butchery section with farm produced meats. A member of the Best of British group.

Facilities

A modern building with blown air heating, accessed through a foyer with public telephone and tourist information. It is surrounded by wide decking with ramps giving good access for wheelchairs to all facilities including the dishwashing area, laundry room and chemical disposal point. Inside are spacious controllable showers, some washbasins in cubicles, a suite for disabled guests, family bathroom and baby changing facilities. Off site: Riding and bicycle hire 0.5 miles. Kington 5 miles, Leominster 7 miles. Golf 7 miles.

Open: 1 March - 15 January.

Directions

Site is beside the A44, 7 miles west of Leominster. Site is just inside the 30 mph. speed limit on the eastern edge of Pembridge village. O.S.GR: SO385580. GPS: N52:13.108 W02:53.427

Charges guide

Per unit incl. 2 persons incl. electricity, water and drainage	£ 9.00 - £ 15.00
	£ 12.00 - £ 18.00
extra person	£ 3.00
child (5-15 yrs)	£ 1.50
awning or pup tent	£ 2.00

UK4360 Doward Park Camp Site

Great Doward, Symonds Yat West HR9 6BP (Herefordshire)

Tel: **01600 890438**. Email: **enquiries@dowardpark.co.uk**   **www.alanrogers.com/UK4360**

Created around 1997 in a disused quarry, this is a very pleasant, peaceful little site, partially terraced, and in a sheltered location. The access roads and the physical proportions of the site make it suitable only for tents, trailer tents and campervans. This site is popular with couples and young families, but possibly has nothing to offer teenagers. The 33 pitches are mostly on grass (with 6 hardstandings used by seasonal units when we visited) and there are 11 electric hook-ups (16A) for touring units. There are two hardstanding pitches for motorcaravan up to 23 feet in length.

Facilities

A neat central building provides the usual facilities including refurbished hot showers, dishwashing sinks and a freezer for ice packs. Small shop selling basic supplies. Torches are advisable. Only tents, trailer tents and motorcaravans are accepted. Off site: Variety of inns at both Symonds Yat West and East all offering meals. Shops and services in Monmouth 4 miles. Fishing 1 miles. Golf 4 miles. Bicycle hire 10 miles.

Open: 15 March - 31 October.

Directions

From A40 between Ross-on-Wye and Monmouth, turn for Symonds Yat West, and follow signs for Doward Park and Biblins. Turn into narrow lane for 1 mile and site is on right on sharp left hand bend. O.S.GR: SO548157. GPS: N51:50.311 W02:39.420

Charges guide

Per unit incl. 2 persons	£ 14.50 - £ 16.50
extra person	£ 2.50
child (4-15 yrs)	£ 1.75

UK4390 Westbrook Park

Little Hereford, Ludlow SY8 4AU (Shropshire)

Tel: **01584 711280**   **www.alanrogers.com/UK4390**

A beautifully kept, traditional, quiet touring campsite in a 'working' cider apple orchard, Westbrook Park is bordered on one side by the River Teme and within walking distance of the village and pub. There are 52 level pitches with 16A electric hook-ups, some on well mown grass, and 35 on gravel or concrete/gravel all-weather hardstandings with water and waste water drain. Some pitches have semi-shade, other have none. Satellite TV hook-ups are available to all pitches. A footpath along the river bank in one direction leads to the Temeside Inn which serves hot meals.

Facilities

A modern, timber clad, heated toilet block provides spacious hot showers (20p for 5 minutes), washbasins in curtained cubicles, a basic laundry room and dishwashing sinks. Limited facilities for disabled people (WC and basin) – the current steps need to be replaced with a ramp. Gas supplies. Playground. Fishing (£4 per day). Riverside walks. No gazebos. No cycling. Off site: Golf 3 miles. Riding and bicycle hire 5 miles.

Open: 1 March - 30 November.

Directions

From A49 between Ludlow and Leominster, turn east at Woofferton on A456 (Tenbury Wells). In 2 miles turn right just before river bridge and Temeside Inn. Turn left after 150 yds. Park is on left. O.S.GR: SU547679. GPS: N52:13.440 W02:39.955

Charges guide

Per unit incl. 2 persons	£ 14.00 - £ 18.00
extra person	£ 3.00
child (4-10 yrs)	£ 1.50

181

UK4400 Stanmore Hall Touring Park

Stourbridge Road, Bridgnorth WV15 6DT (Shropshire)

Tel: **01746 761761**. Email: **stanmore@morris-leisure.co.uk**

www.alanrogers.com/UK4400

This good quality park is situated in the former grounds of Stanmore Hall, where the huge lily pond, fine mature trees and beautifully manicured lawns give a mark of quality. There are 135 generously sized pitches, 130 with 16A electricity including 30 hardstanding 'super' pitches with TV connections. A limited number of 'standard' hardstanding pitches are also available, but the majority are on grass. Some pitches are reserved for adult only use (over 18 years). Access and internal roads are tarmac; site lighting is adequate and reassuring. Reception is within the shop. The adjacent conservatory and patio overlook the lake, accommodating everything from humbler ducks to the resident peacocks who strut proudly around their domain. But there's something else too; this is a peaceful site with personality. Little wonder it needs advance booking and people keep returning to enjoy its atmosphere. Open all year round, there are even groups who spend Christmas and New Year at Stanmore Hall. The Severn Valley is full of interest – Bridgnorth nearby, the Clee Hills and Ironbridge Gorge Museum are just a few suggestions. The site is a member of the Caravan Club's affiliated site scheme but non-members are also very welcome.

Facilities

Access to the centrally heated sanitary block is by key. Facilities are excellent and provide washbasins in cubicles and a room for disabled people and baby care. Full laundry facilities. Motorcaravan service points. Shop, including caravan accessories and repair items. Play area. Dogs are limited to two per unit. Off site: Fishing at Bridgnorth 1.5 miles. Golf and Riding 2 miles.

Open: All year.

Directions

Site is 1.5 miles from Bridgnorth on the A458 (signed Stourbridge). O.S.GR: SO744922. GPS: N52:31.629 W02:22.717

Charges guide

Per unit with 2 persons and electricity	£ 19.60 - £ 22.30
full services, plus	£ 2.50 - £ 3.00
extra person	£ 6.00 - £ 6.40
child (5-15 yrs)	£ 2.20
dog (max. 2)	£ 1.00

UK4410 Beaconsfield Farm Caravan Park

Battlefield, Shrewsbury SY4 4AA (Shropshire)

Tel: **01939 210370**. Email: **mail@beaconsfield-farm.co.uk**

www.alanrogers.com/UK4410

Just north of the historic market town, a drive of half a mile through open fields lead to this purpose-designed park for adults only (21 yrs). It is neatly laid out in a rural situation, with a well stocked trout fishing lake and a small coarse pool forming the main feature. The ground has been levelled and grassed to provide 80 well spaced pitches, 50 are 'de-luxe' hardstanding pitches. All have electricity connections (10A). Two further areas accommodate 36 caravan holiday homes. The park is well lit with a circular tarmac access road. A large timber chalet-style building provides reception and a coffee shop that is open during reception hours. Recent additions are the bowling green and the popular 'Bothy' a la carte restaurant. Limousins and pedigree Suffolk sheep graze in neighbouring fields and a 'park and ride' scheme operates nearby for those interested in Shrewsbury and its medieval past, bought to life by the Brother Cadfael novels. This is a top class park, maturing by the year. A member of the Best of British Group.

Facilities

Heated toilet facilities (£2 key deposit) are of excellent quality, with roomy, pre-set showers and hairdryers. Excellent unit for disabled visitors. Dishwashing and laundry facilities. Motorcaravan services. A la carte Restaurant. Indoor heated swimming pool with daily open sessions (£3.00 inc. steam room per person) and to hire privately at other times. Small library. Security barrier and CCTV. WiFi. Car hire. Only two dogs per unit are accepted. Only adults are accepted. Off site: Bicycle hire and golf 2 miles. Riding 7 miles.

Open: All year.

Directions

Site is north of Shrewsbury and off the A49 Whitchurch road just before Hadnall. Turn opposite the New Inn at camping sign towards Astley and park entrance is 400 m. on right. O.S.GR: SJ525195. GPS: N52:46.255 W02:42.289

Charges guide

Per grass pitch incl. 2 persons and electricity	£ 15.00 - £ 18.00
hardstanding pitch	£ 18.00 - £ 20.00
extra person	£ 4.00
awning	£ 1.50

No credit cards.
Last arrivals 7 pm. (8 pm. Fridays).

UK4380 Fernwood Caravan Park

Lyneal, Ellesmere SY12 0QF (Shropshire)

Tel: **01948 710221**. Email: **enquiries@fernwoodpark.co.uk**   www.alanrogers.com/UK4380

Fernwood is set in an area known as the Shropshire 'Lake District' – the mere at Ellesmere is the largest of nine meres – and the picturesque Shropshire Union Canal is only a few minutes walk. The park itself is a real oasis of calm and rural tranquillity with its floral landscaping, the setting and the attention to detail, all of a very high standard with planted and natural vegetation blending harmoniously. In addition to 165 caravan holiday homes, used normally only by their owners, the park takes 30 caravans, motorcaravans or trailer tents (but not other tents) in several well cut, grassy enclosures (including 30 seasonal long stay). Some are in light woodland, others in more open, but still relatively sheltered situations. All pitches have electricity (10A) and six also have water and drainage. One area is set aside for units with adults only. Siting is carried out by the management and there is always generous spacing, even when the site is full.

Facilities

The small toilet block for tourers has background heating for cooler days and includes some washbasins in cabins and limited facilities for disabled people. No dishwashing sinks. Basic motorcaravan services. Laundry room near shop and adjacent are WCs for ladies and men. Shop doubles as reception (from 1/4, hours vary). Coarse fishing lake. Forty acres of woodland for walking. Play area on grass.

Open: 1 March - 30 November.

Directions

Park is just northeast of Lyneal village, signed southwest off the B5063 Ellesmere - Wem road, about 1.5 miles from junction of the B5063 with the A495. O.S.GR: SJ452338.
GPS: N52:53.950 W02:48.961

Charges guide

Per unit incl. electricity	£ 18.00 - £ 23.00
multi-service pitch	£ 3.50
awning	free - £ 3.00

One night free for every 7 booked in advance.

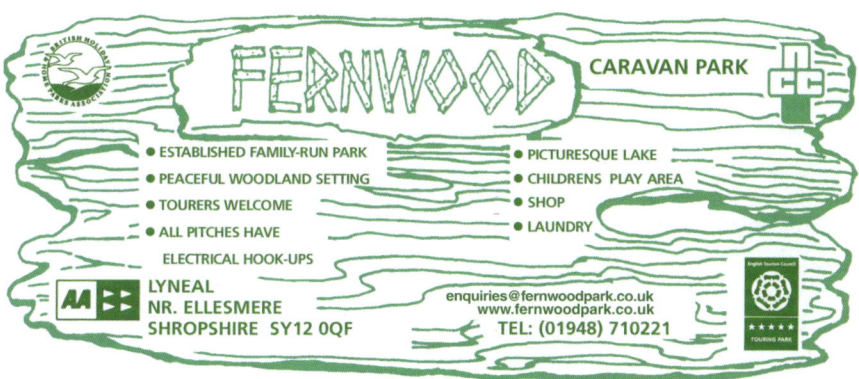

UK4415 Green Lane Farm Caravan & Campsite

Green Lane, Prees, Whitchurch SY13 2AH (Shropshire)

Tel: **01948 840460**. Email: **greenlanefarm@tiscali.co.uk**   www.alanrogers.com/UK4415

Green Lane Farm is a small family run site in the heart of the countryside. Pitches are set on a flat open field, surrounded by trees and hedges and provide a relaxing and really quiet place to stay with no traffic noise to disturb the tranquillity. A gravel track leads into the site and after 30 yards becomes grass encircling the field. The 20 grass pitches are situated around the outside with an attractive group of shrubs beside each electric hook-up stand. There is space for tents in the central area together with play equipment and picnic tables. On site facilities are limited but can be found in the nearby village or in the town of Whitchurch 5 miles away.

Facilities

The recently built sanitary block provides washbasins and showers (only one toilet for men and two for ladies). Large separate toilet and shower for disabled visitors. Play area. Tourist information. Torches useful. Off site: Pubs, shop, garage, takeaway, and club in Prees village, just over a mile away. The site is central to many attractions and activities. Fishing and golf 2 miles. Ironbridge, Telford, Shrewsbury and RAF Cosford are nearby.

Open: April - October.

Directions

The easiest route is from the A41. 4 miles south of Whitchurch turn west signed Prees. In 200 yards turn right. The site is on the right in 200 yards. On the A49 turn east to Prees. In Prees turn right towards the church. Turn left at the church. Site is 1 mile on the left. GPS: N52:54.167 W02:39.548

Charges guide

Per pitch	£ 10.00
electricity	£ 2.00

No credit cards.

183

UK4430 Oxon Hall Touring Park

Welshpool Road, Shrewsbury SY3 5FB (Shropshire)

Tel: **01743 340868**. Email: **oxon@morris-leisure.co.uk**   www.alanrogers.com/UK4430

Oxon Hall is a purpose-built park, well situated for visiting Shrewsbury. It is under the same ownership as Stanmore Hall (no. UK4400) and has been developed from a green field site by an experienced park operator to a very high standard. The site has matured well and the trees and shrubs now provide some shade and shelter. Of the 120 pitches, half are all weather, full service pitches (fresh and waste water facilities, TV hook-up), the others being either grass or with hardstanding. An area is set aside as an 'adults only' section. Most pitches have 16A electricity, some pitches for large units have 32A. Some extra long hardstandings are provided for American motorhomes. Entry to the park is controlled by electronic barriers. Virtually adjacent to the park is the Oxon 'park and ride' which makes a trip into Shrewsbury some 2 miles away very simple. The famous Ironbridge Gorge Museum and the mysteries of the Welsh Borders are all easy day trips from this excellent base. A member of the Best of British group.

Facilities

Toilet facilities here are first rate with washbasins in cubicles, ample showers, baby room, facilities for disabled visitors, dishwashing room and laundry, all at the entrance in a centrally heated building which also houses reception and the shop – perhaps a hike from some of the pitches. Motorcaravan service point. Up to two dogs per pitch. Deposit for toilet block key £5. Off site: Supermarket within walking distance. Golf, riding and fishing nearby.

Open: All year.

Directions

From junction of A5 and A458, west of Shrewsbury, follow signs for Oxon 'park and ride'. Park is signed just 0.5 miles from junction. O.S.GR: SJ457134. GPS: N52:42.924 W02:48.295

Charges guide

Per person	£ 5.50 - £ 5.90
child (5-15 yrs)	£ 2.20
standard grass pitch	£ 7.60 - £ 9.50
dog (max. 2)	£ 1.00

UK4440 The Green Caravan Park

Wentnor, Bishop's Castle SY9 5EF (Shropshire)

Tel: **01588 650605**. Email: **info@greencaravanpark.co.uk**   www.alanrogers.com/UK4440

Remotely situated in a pleasant valley, in a designated 'area of outstanding natural beauty', and sandwiched between the Stipperstones and The Long Mynd, the Green would make an ideal base for some serious walking or cycling. The 15 acre site is very natural, and is divided into several fields. There are 160 pitches, taking 40 seasonal units, and around 20 holiday homes, with approximately 140 pitches for tourists (42 with 16A electric hook-ups). The main field has some hardstandings. The East Onny is a small, shallow river which runs through the site, much enjoyed by the youngsters, who can spend many hours catching minnows. Adults might be more interested in the wildlife with many species of birds, bats and moths to watch out for.

Facilities

One main sanitary block, rather austere in appearance, built into the side of a large barn. However it provides adequate and plentiful facilities with spacious new hot showers (on payment), dishwashing and laundry facilities, but there is no dedicated unit for disabled people. Small shop with reception. Playground. Off site: Four pubs within 3 miles. Fishing 3 miles. Riding 4 miles. Bishops Castle with museums. Leisure Centre. Stapely Hill historic trail. Gliding club.

Open: Easter - 31 October.

Directions

Wentnor lies southwest of Shrewsbury, and to the west of Church Stretton. From Shrewsbury take A488 south for 21 miles. At Lydham Heath turn east on A489 for 0.75 miles, then north on minor road (Wentnor and campsite). Follow signs for 3 miles. Site immediately after The Inn on the Green. O.S.GR: SO381933. GPS: N52:32.025 W02:54.825

Charges guide

Per unit incl. 2 persons	£ 10.00 - £ 12.00
extra person	£ 2.50
child (3-14 yrs)	£ 2.00
dog	£ 2.50
electricity	£ 2.25
Discount for 7 nights.	
Gazebos by prior arrangement only.	

MAP 5

A beautiful and varied region of rolling hills and undulating moors, Yorkshire has an historic past with a wealth of new attractions. Its landscape has inspired famous authors and been the setting for some of Britain's best-loved television programmes.

Yorkshire

THE REGION IS DIVIDED INTO NORTH, SOUTH, EAST AND WEST YORKSHIRE

The major attractions of this region are the parks: the Yorkshire Dales National Park is comprised of 680 square miles of unspoilt countryside with high fells, winding rivers, ancient castles and outstanding views of the surrounding landscapes; the Peak District is noted for its rocky peaks and limestone plateau; while the North York Moors National Park has miles of open, heather covered moorland and pretty villages in its valleys. These areas are ideal places for walking, cycling, horse riding and climbing. Or if you prefer to relax and take in the scenery, the North Yorkshire Moors Railway, starting at Pickering, is one of the many steam railways in the region. On the coast, traditional family resorts like Scarborough, Bridlington and Cleethorpes offer the holidaymaker a wide range of activities. Also by the sea is Kingston Upon Hull, a maritime city with powerful links to Britain's proud seafaring tradition, and the picturesque fishing port of Whitby, once home to Captain James Cook. Elsewhere in the region are the vibrant cities of York, with its wealth of ancient sites including the Minster, Leeds and Sheffield plus the busy market town of Doncaster.

Places of interest

North: Harrogate; Wensleydale Creamery in Hawes; Jorvik Viking Centre in York; Lightwater Valley Theme Park, near Ripon; Castle Howard near York: Flamingo Land Theme Park and Zoo in Malton; Skipton Castle.

South: Hatfield Waterpark near Doncaster; Tropical Butterfly House and Wildlife Centre in Anston; Sheffield Ski Village, Europe's biggest artificial ski resort; Magna science adventure centre in Rotherham.

East: Bempton Cliffs RSPB Nature Reserve near Bridlington, England's largest seabird colony; market town of Beverly; Captain Cook Museum in Whitby; Scarborough Millennium.

West: Bolling Hall in Bradford; Royal Armouries Museum in Leeds; 'Brontë Country' and village of Haworth; Pontefract.

Did you know?

The comedy series Last of the Summer Wine is filmed in the Pennine town of Holmfirth and its surrounding countryside.

York is the oldest city in Yorkshire, founded in AD71. The Minster is the largest Gothic Cathedral in Northern Europe.

Pontefract has been growing liquorice since medieval times, it is believed that Pontefract cakes were made by the monks for medicinal purposes.

The Tan Hill Inn is the highest pub in England at 528 metres above sea level.

Dick Turpin, the notorious 17th century highwayman, lived in Pontefract.

Rudston is said to be the oldest inhabited village in England, named after the Rood Stone, a mysterious 4000 year old monolith.

185

RED TEXT DENOTES ALL YEAR SITE

UK4496 ## Skipsea Sands Holiday Park

Mill Lane, Skipsea YO25 8TZ (East Yorkshire)

Tel: **0871 664 9812**. Email: **skipsea.sands@parkresorts.com**   www.alanrogers.com/UK4496

This well established holiday park is now owned by Park Resorts and is primarily dedicated to caravan holiday homes, of which there are 600 privately owned and 61 to rent. There is however a pleasantly laid out touring park occupying its own corner of the site and bordered by an attractive duck pond and a large playing area (both well fenced). The 91 marked, level pitches are separated by hedges and all have electricity (16A), water and waste water points; 18 also have sewage connections. The leisure facilities are outstanding and a full daily programme of activities and entertainment is offered for children and adults. Situated on the cliffs on the Yorkshire coast south of Bridlington, beaches are either a good walk or a short drive away. There is a wide choice of possible days out: Beverley with its Minster and its horse racing; Spurn Point or Bempton Cliffs (RSPB); Cruckley Animal Farm or Bondville Miniature Village; Bridlington's beaches and its Harbour Heritage Museum; even Pickering and the North York Moors are within easy reach.

Facilities

Two heated toilet blocks are fairly basic, with pushbutton showers and open washbasins. En-suite facilities for disabled visitors are rather stark. Basic chemical disposal and motorhome service point. Washing machines and dryers. Well stocked shop. Bar, coffee shop and restaurant with takeaway. Leisure centre with sports hall, ten-pin bowling, heated indoor swimming pool, jacuzzi, sauna and steam room. Fitness centre with gym and sun bed. Games 'Kingdom' with electronic games and 'Kids Zone'. Off site: Beach 0.25 m (on foot) or 4 miles (by car). Fishing 2 miles. Golf 3 miles. Boat launching 6 miles. Riding and sailing 9 miles. Buses from park gates. Village with shops, pub, restaurant 1 mile.

Open: Easter - 31 October.

Directions

Skipsea is 20 miles northeast of Hull and 10 miles south of Bridlington. From the Humber Bridge or from the M62/A63 west of Hull, head north on the A164 to Beverley. Then take the A165 towards Bridlington and turn east on B1249 to Skipsea. In village, turn right then left to site (signed). O.S.GR: TA175565. GPS: N53:59.374 W00:12.430

Charges guide

Per unit incl. all services	£ 14.00 - £ 33.00
tent pitch	£ 3.00 - £ 24.00
dog	£ 1.00 - £ 3.00

UK4498 South Cliff Caravan Park

Wilsthorpe, Bridlington YO15 3QN (East Yorkshire)

Tel: **01262 671051**. Email: **southcliff@eastriding.gov.uk**   **www.alanrogers.com/UK4498**

This traditional style caravan park is part of a large complex owned and operated by the East Riding of Yorkshire Council. There are 184 touring pitches, each with an electricity post (16A); 20 for tents, the remainder with hardstanding surrounded by grass or, in a few cases, extended to the road. Many of them lie back from the road, so access for larger units can be tricky when the site is full. Direct access to the seafront is through the vast caravan holiday home park and from there a 'land train' runs a mile along the shore to Bridlington. Here you can visit the historic old town, the harbour with its heritage museum, the Spa Theatre and Ballroom, Sewerby Hall and Gardens, or Leisure World. Further afield are Beverley with its Minster and racecourse, Flamborough Head, Spurn Point, Scarborough and even Pickering and the North York Moors.

Facilities

Two toilet blocks (one traditional, one new) provide push button showers, open washbasins (a few in cubicles for ladies). Excellent en-suite units for disabled visitors. Three bathrooms with washbasins and baby changing facilities. No motorcaravan service point. Franchised facilities: launderette (washing machines and dryers). Well stocked shop (1/3-8/10); fish and chip shop (busy at times). Leisure complex (bar, restaurant, clubroom, games room) offering entertainment evenings in high season and monthly themed weekends (outside August). Off site: Golf 0.5 m. Beach (by car), riding, sailing, boat launching and bicycle hire 1 mile. Shops, pubs and restaurants within 2 miles.

Open: 1 March - 30 November.

Directions

Bridlington is 40 miles east of York via the A166 and A614. From M62 exit 37, take A614 to Bridlington. Before Carnaby turn east to join the A165 to Bridlington South. From the Humber Bridge take A164 to Beverley, then A165 to Bridlington. Site is signed from A165 at Wilsthorpe.
O.S.GR: TA166648. GPS: N54:03.850 W00:12.794

Charges guide

Per unit incl. up to 5 persons	£ 17.00 - £ 20.00
extra person	£ 1.00

Discounts in low season and mid seasons.

UK4500 Burton Constable Holiday Park & Arboretum

The Old Lodges, Sproatley, Hull HU11 4LN (East Yorkshire)

Tel: **01964 562508**. Email: **info@burtonconstable.co.uk**   **www.alanrogers.com/UK4500**

This park is in the grounds of the stately home of Burton Constable, and consequently the entrance is most impressive – one of the gatehouses acts as reception and tourist information room. The 40 acre campsite is part of the 300 acre park which was landscaped by Capability Brown in the 18th century and with well trimmed grass and hedges, it has a spacious feel. All 180 touring pitches have 10A electricity, there is a separate field for tents and a large hardstanding area providing electricity, water and drainage for 6 motorcaravans. All the pitches overlook two small lakes (unfenced), both of which are used for fishing (permits at reception), one for boating (bring your own, but no engines). Privately owned caravan holiday homes are quite separate and do not intrude.

Facilities

Two heated toilet blocks – one older and small with unisex showers, the central newer block including a laundry room with baby changing. Well equipped room for disabled visitors (Radar key). Shop in the mobile home area. Bar with family room and tables outside overlooking the lakes. Good adventure play area. Off site: Sproatley (1 mile) has pubs, a shop and the occasional bus. Hull 7 miles. Golf 4 miles. Riding 3 miles.

Open: 1 March - 31 October.

Directions

From south via the M62 or Humber Bridge, take the A63 into Hull, then follow signs to A165 Bridlington. On eastern outskirts of Hull follow B1238 signed Aldborough. At Sproatley, site is signed to left. From the north and Beverley, take A1035 to Hornsea. At roundabout with A165 (Hull - Bridlington) follow signs to Burton Constable for about 8 miles. Pass the Hall to Sproatley, then follow caravan signs.
O.S.GR: TA186357. GPS: N53:48.159 W00:11.948

Charges guide

Per unit incl. 2 persons and electricity	£ 13.00 - £ 24.00
extra person	£ 1.50
awning	£ 2.00

187

UK4520 **Flower of May Holiday Park**

Lebberston Cliff, Scarborough YO11 3NU (North Yorkshire)

Tel: **01723 584311**. Email: **info@flowerofmay.com**   **www.alanrogers.com/UK4520**

Situated on the cliff tops, 4.5 miles from Scarborough and 2.5 miles from Filey, Flower of May is a large, family owned park for both touring caravans and caravan holiday homes. There is a cliff walk to the beach but it is only suitable for the reasonably active – there is an easier walk down from a car park a mile away. The entrance to the park is very colourful and the reception office is light and airy. The park is licensed for 300 touring units and 184 caravan holiday homes (45 to hire, the remainder privately owned). The touring pitches are pretty level, arranged in wide avenues, mainly on grass and divided by shrubs. There are 223 with electricity (10A), including 200 'star pitches' with water and drainage also. The range of leisure facilities grouped around reception includes an indoor pool with areas for both adults and children, a water flume and a jacuzzi. In the same building are two squash courts, 10 pin bowling, table tennis and amusement machines. The leisure centre is also open to the public (concessionary rates for campers) but during high season is only available to local regulars and the caravanners and campers on the park. Riverside Meadows at Ripon and Rosedale Country Caravan Park near Pickering are under the same ownership.

Facilities

Three toilet blocks, all refurbished in a light and colourful style, are fully tiled with washbasins in both cabins and vanity style. Baby rooms. Facilities for disabled visitors. Well stocked and licensed shop near the leisure centre, as is the laundry room. Two modern bar lounges, one for families and one for adults only, with discos in season. Café and takeaway fish and chips. Games room with TV. Large adventure playground. Pay and play golf course (£5 a round). Indoor swimming pool. Skateboard ramps. Basketball. Dog exercise area, but numbers and breeds are limited (one per pitch) and not allowed at all at B.Hs and the six week summer holiday. Off site: The Plough Inn near the park entrance offers good bar meals. Fishing, boat slipway or riding 2 miles. Bicycle hire 4 miles.

Open: Easter - 28 October.

Directions

Park is signed from roundabout at junction of the A165 and B1261 from where it is 600 yds. O.S.GR: TA088836. GPS: N54:13.752 W00:20.550

Charges guide

Per unit incl. up to 4 persons and electricity	£ 14.00 - £ 19.00
tent (no electricity)	£ 11.50 - £ 15.50
extra person (over 3 yrs)	£ 3.00
awning	£ 4.00
dog (see above)	£ 1.00

10% discount on pitch fee for weekly advance bookings.

UK4770 **Rosedale Caravan & Camping Park**

Rosedale Abbey, Pickering YO18 8SA (North Yorkshire)

Tel: **01751 417272**. Email: **info@flowerofmay.com**   **www.alanrogers.com/UK4770**

In a beautiful location below Rosedale Moor and on the edge of a popular village, this is a campsite that is highly suitable for walkers. The surrounding hillsides are a maze of public footpaths and these and nearby Cropton Forest can all be reached without using your car. The site itself has a wide entrance on the edge of the village and as it is within the National Park, the buildings are in the local stone and in keeping with the area. The site is reasonably level, with 200 pitches, a few with hardstanding and with 28 electricity connections (10A). There are some caravan holiday homes (private) and seasonal touring pitches in their own areas, with the remainder for touring caravans and motorcaravans. The majority have superb views of the surrounding hills. One field is set aside for tents only and many are sited near the river which runs along the edge of the park. In summer the Dales bus runs through the village, connecting several of the popular villages. The 13 mile Rosedale circuit follows the route of the old iron ore railway, giving magnificent views and reminders of bygone industries. There is a glass blower at the village blacksmith's and the Ryedale Folk Museum at Hutton-le-Hole is 3.5 miles.

Facilities

Fully refurbished sanitary facilities with under-floor heating include free showers and hairdressing units. Facilities for disabled visitors and baby changing. Dishwashing and laundry facilities. Reception provides maps and a small selection of camping accessories, plus gas supplies. Games room with pool and video games. Large play area with space for ball games. Entrance barrier controlled by card (£10 deposit). Off site: The village has a general store with daily papers, a post office, bakery, pubs and a restaurant. Nine 9-hole golf course (set on a picturesque hillside) 200 yards.

Open: Easter - 28 October.

Directions

Rosedale is signed from the A170, 2 miles west of Pickering. Site is in the village of Rosedale Abbey, 8 miles north of the A170. O.S.GR: SE725958. GPS: N54:21.220 W00:53.277

Charges guide

Per unit incl. electricity and up to 4 persons	£ 14.00 - £ 19.00
tent incl. up to 4 persons	£ 11.50 - £ 15.50

10% discount on pitch fee for weekly bookings.

Yorkshire

UK4510 Thorpe Hall Caravan & Camping Site

Rudston, Driffield YO25 4JE (East Yorkshire)

Tel: **01262 420393**. Email: **caravansite@thorpehall.co.uk**   www.alanrogers.com/UK4510

Just outside the village of Rudston, in the grounds of Thorpe Hall, this pleasant small touring park is 4.5 miles from the sea at Bridlington. Enthusiastically managed by Jayne Chatterton, it is set on flat grass, largely enclosed by the old kitchen garden wall. The 90 pitches are numbered and well spaced with 78 electrical hook-ups (16A) and TV connections. A separate area takes tents and there are no caravan holiday homes. There is always a chance of finding space, though it is best to book for Bank Holidays and peak weeks. Information sheets on a range of local walks are provided and Sir Ian Macdonald takes visitors on walks around the estate.

Facilities

The solid, central toilet block has been completely refurbished and can be heated. Some washbasins are in cabins. Refurbished bathroom for disabled visitors and families with children (deposit for key). Launderette. Large recycling area. Small shop with gas, essentials and local produce. Games room. TV room. Coarse fishing lake. Off site: Bicycle hire, golf and boat launching at Bridlington 4.5 miles. Riding 2 miles. Footpath to the village with a shop, post office, garage, pub and restaurant, plus a twice weekly bus service to Bridlington.

Open: 1 March - 31 October.

Directions

Site is by the B1253 road, 4.5 miles from Bridlington, on east side of Rudston. O.S.GR: TA105676. GPS: N54:05.629 W00:18.750

Charges guide

Per unit incl. all persons and electricity	£ 13.50 - £ 26.00
tent pitch incl. 2 persons	£ 9.50 - £ 22.00

Less 25% on booked stays of 7 days or more. Other discounts available.

UK4528 Sandfield House Farm Caravan Park

Sandsend Road, Whitby YO21 3SR (North Yorkshire)

Tel: **01947 602660**. Email: **info@sandfieldhousefarm.co.uk**   www.alanrogers.com/UK4528

Although it is set on a hill in undulating countryside on the low cliffs near Whitby, this park provides 200 level pitches, all with electricity. There are 60 pitches for touring caravans, all on hardstanding, and these are mainly set to the front of the park giving wonderful views over the golf course and the sea. Tents are not accepted here. Whitby is only a mile away and a quarter of a mile walk down a gently sloping track from the park brings you to a two mile long sandy beach. From here it is a gentle stroll along the new promenade to Whitby harbour.

Facilities

Two toilet blocks (one older, one new and very good) have free hot showers. Laundry room with washing machines, dryers and iron. No facilities for disabled visitors. Tents are not accepted. Off site: Shops 800 yards. Hourly bus service to town centre. Fishing 400 yds. Golf 200 yds. Boat launching 800 yds.

Open: 18 March - 30 October.

Directions

From Whitby follow signs for Sandsend on the A174. The park is on the landward side of the road, opposite the golf course and well signed. O.S.GR: NZ872117. GPS: N54:29.503 W00:38.566

Charges guide

Per unit incl. up to 4 persons and electricity	£ 13.00 - £ 15.50

No credit cards.

UK4540 Saint Helens in the Park

Wykeham, Scarborough YO13 9QD (North Yorkshire)

Tel: **01723 862771**. Email: **caravans@wykeham.co.uk**   www.alanrogers.com/UK4540

St Helens is a high quality touring park with pleasant views, set within 30 acres of parkland. The site is divided into terraces with trees screening each area (one of which is set aside for adults only) and the 250 mainly level pitches have a spacious feel. Electricity (16A) is available on 240 pitches, also in the late arrivals area. Set on a hillside, the park's buildings are built in local stone and all is maintained to a high standard. The Downe Arms, a short stroll away, is known for its good food and family-friendly atmosphere. Scarborough is only 5 miles with its beaches and summer shows .

Facilities

Four heated toilet blocks are well equipped and maintained to a high standard. Some washbasins in cabins, free showers and baby baths. Unit for disabled visitors. Good laundry room. Well stocked shop. Café and takeaway. Internet café. WiFi. Bicycle hire. Small games room. Caravan storage. Off site: Nearby Wykeham Lakes offer fishing, scuba diving, windsurfing and sailing (in your own boat), 1 mile. Golf and riding 2 miles.

Open: All year excl. 15 January - 13 February.

Directions

Park access road leads off the A170 (Pickering - Scarborough) road in Wykeham village 2 miles west of junction with B1262. O.S.GR: SE963835. GPS: N54:14.282 W00:30.028

Charges guide

Per unit incl. 2 persons	£ 10.30 - £ 13.00
electricity	£ 3.50
extra person (over 3 yrs)	£ 1.50

UK4532 Middlewood Farm Holiday Park

Middlewood Lane, Fylingthorpe, Robin Hood's Bay YO22 4UF (North Yorkshire)

Tel: **01947 880414**. Email: **info@middlewoodfarm.com**   **www.alanrogers.com/UK4532**

Middlewood Farm is a level park, surrounded by hills and with views of the sea from some of the pitches. A short walk through the farm fields and wild flower conservation areas leads to the picturesque old fishing village of Robin Hood's Bay and the sea. The park has 22 touring pitches for caravans and motorcaravans with 10A electricity, 17 with hardstanding and the remainder on grass. There is space for around 130 tents in two areas with 12 electricity connections (10A) and 30 caravan holiday homes to rent. A good beach is only ten minutes walk through the fields and the nearby village of Fylingthorpe with a post office, stores and a pub is a level walk. This is a very tidy farm park.

Facilities

The central toilet block has clean facilities and is modern, heated and tiled with free showers. Another new block is planned. Fully equipped laundry room including iron and board. Facilities for babies and disabled persons. Two private family shower rooms to rent. Play area with bark base set amongst the tents. Off site: Sandy beach with fishing 0.5 miles. Boat launching 2 miles. Golf 7 miles. Shop in village 5 minutes walk.

Open: Easter - early November.

Directions

From the A171 Scarborough - Whitby road turn right signed Robin Hood's Bay and Fylingthorpe (site signed). Just past the 30 mph sign bear right and after 100 yds. turn right into Middlewood Lane (site signed). From Whitby on the A171 turn left on B1447 signed Robin Hood's Bay and Fylingthorpe. After 1.5 miles turn right signed Fylingthorpe. Follow for 1 mile to crossroads and shops and straight on to Middlewood Lane (site signed). O.S.GR: NZ945045. GPS: N54:25.807 W00:32.802

Charges guide

Per unit incl. 2 persons and electricity	£ 12.50 - £ 20.00
extra person	£ 3.00
awning	£ 3.00
dog	£ 1.50

**ROBIN HOOD'S BAY, WHITBY, N. Yorks.
YO22 4UF Tel: 01947 880414**
www.middlewoodfarm.com
Email: info@middlewoodfarm.com

- 2 x SUPERB heated facilities (inc. BATH)
- FREE HOT SHOWERS/dishwashing
- Electric hook-ups for Tourers, Tents & M Homes.
- Children's adventure play area
- SUPERIOR luxury caravans for HIRE
- Village PUB & SHOP - 5 minutes walk
- BEACH — 10 minutes walk

A walkers, artists and wildlife paradise. Small, peaceful family Park. Magnificent panoramic views of sea, moors and "Heartbeat Country"

We're waiting to make you welcome!

UK4534 Overbrook Caravan Park

Maltongate, Thornton-le-Dale, Pickering YO18 7SE (North Yorkshire)

Tel: **01751 474417**. Email: **enquiry@overbrookcaravanpark.co.uk**   **www.alanrogers.com/UK4534**

Situated in the very pretty village of Thornton-le-Dale, Overbrook has been developed on the site of the old railway station. With the line dismantled, the station building now provides holiday cottages and the caravan park toilet facilities. This is a level site with 50 pitches (20 for tourers, the remainder used for seasonal units) arranged either side of a tarmac access road and backed by trees. All are on hardstanding and all have electricity connections (16A). Neither children nor tents are accepted at this 'adult only' park. The owners will do all they can to assist you during your stay. A half mile, level walk brings you to the village. This is very convenient for shops, pubs, tearooms and even a chocolate factory. There is a good bus service to York, Pickering and Scarborough. The beck which runs through the village and down under the railway property is home to kingfishers, herons, ducks and trout. There are plenty of footpaths for walking in this lovely area.

Facilities

The toilet facilities and reception are situated in the old station house. Laundry facilities. Gas supplies. Battery charging (£1). No tents accepted. Children are not admitted. Off site: Village with bus stop, shops, pubs, fish and chips 800 yds. Bicycle hire 800 yds. Fishing 3 miles. Golf courses within 10 miles.

Open: 1 March - 31 October.

Directions

Thornton-le-Dale is on the A170 Pickering - Scarborough road. In the village follow sign for Malton and park is 800 yds. on the left (follow the stream on the left). O.S.GR: SE833821. GPS: N54:13.712 W00:43.374

Charges guide

Per unit incl. 2 persons and electricity	£ 13.50 - £ 14.50
incl. awning	£ 15.00 - £ 16.00
extra person	£ 2.50
dog (max. 2)	free
No credit cards.	

191

UK4550 Cayton Village Caravan Park

Mill Lane, Cayton Bay, Scarborough YO11 3NN (North Yorkshire)

Tel: **01723 583171**. Email: **info@caytontouring.co.uk**   **www.alanrogers.com/UK4550**

Cayton Village Caravan Park can only be described as a gem. Just three miles from the hustle and bustle of Scarborough, it is a peaceful, attractive haven. Originally just a flat field with caravans around the perimeter, years of hard work have produced a park which is very pleasing to the eye and of which the owner, Carol, can be justly proud. The entrance is a mass of flowers. The 200 pitches are numbered and everyone is taken to their pitch. All of the 190 for touring units have electricity (many with hardstanding) and there are 91 fully serviced pitches. The late arrivals area here also has electrical hook-ups. This is useful as the gates are locked at night and anyone leaving early is also expected to use it, so as not to disturb others. A short walk across a field takes you to Cayton Village which has a popular pub providing excellent meals, a post office stores and a church, and Cayton Bay is half a mile. The North York Moors are a short distance away, as is the Forestry Commission's Dalby Forest with its scenic drive, mountain bike trails and way-marked walks.

Facilities

Three toilet blocks (key code locks) can be heated and have high quality tiling and fittings. Some showers are pre-set, others controllable. Two family shower rooms, family bathroom and baby facilities. Reception and shop with comprehensive range including gas and caravan spares. Adventure playground. Nature walk. Caravan storage. Off site: Fishing and bicycle hire 0.5 miles. Riding 4 miles. Golf 3 miles. Regular bus service from the village to Scarborough or Filey.

Open: 1 March - 31 October.

Directions

From A64 Malton - Scarborough road turn right at roundabout (with MacDonald's and pub) signed B1261 Filey. Follow signs for Cayton, in Cayton Village take second left after Blacksmiths Arms down Mill Lane (at brown tourism sign) and park is 200 yds. on left. From roundabout to park is 2.25 miles. From A165 turn inland at Cayton Bay roundabout and park is 0.5 miles on right. O.S.GR: TA057837. GPS: N54:14.144 W00:22.567

Charges guide

Per unit incl. 2 persons, electricity and awning	£ 13.00 - £ 25.00
incl. services and hardstanding	£ 18.00 - £ 28.00
tent pitch without electricity	£ 10.00 - £ 20.00
extra person	£ 1.00
dog	£ 1.00
Special offers available.	

UK4560 Golden Square Caravan & Camping Park

Oswaldkirk, Helmsley, York YO62 5YQ (North Yorkshire)

Tel: **01439 788269**. Email: **reception@goldensquarecaravanpark.com**   **www.alanrogers.com/UK4560**

Golden Square is a popular, high quality, family owned touring park. Mr and Mrs Armstrong are local farmers who have worked hard to turn an old quarry into a very attractive caravan park with a number of level bays that have superb views over the North York Moors. The 130 pitches are not separated but they do have markers set into the ground and mainly back on to grass banks. In very dry weather the ground can be hard, steel pegs would be needed (even in wet weather the park is well drained). All pitches have electricity (10A), 24 have drainage and 6 are 'deluxe' pitches (with waste water, sewage, electricity, water and TV aerial connection). The licensed shop is very well stocked, selling home-made fresh bread and cakes, dairy produce, fresh vegetables and groceries, newspapers, gas and gifts. Visitors may use the Ampleforth College sports centre (charged), with its indoor pool, tennis and gym, etc. The area abounds with footpaths and three well known long distance footpaths are near. Dog owners are well catered for with two or three enormous fields for exercising alongside the park.

Facilities

Two heated toilet blocks have been refurbished and are of excellent quality, with some washbasins in private cabins. Showers are free. Bathroom (£1) also houses facilities for babies. Both ladies and men have full facilities for disabled visitors. Laundry with washing machines, dryers, spin dryer and iron and board. Motorcaravan service point. Tourist information room also houses a microwave and an extra iron and board. Shop. Two excellent play areas. Games field and a barn with games. Bicycle hire. All year caravan storage. Off site: Riding 2 miles. Golf 3 miles. Fishing 5 miles. Outdoor pool at Helmsley, sports centre at Ampleforth with indoor pool, both have shops and pubs with food.

Open: 1 March - 31 October.

Directions

From York take B1363 to Helmsley. At Oswaldkirk Bank Top turn left on B1257 to Helmsley. Take second left turn signed Ampleforth to site. O.S.GR: SE605797. GPS: N54:12.560 W01:04.427

Charges guide

Per unit incl. 2 persons and electricity	£ 13.50 - £ 19.00
No credit cards.	

UK4545 Wolds Way Caravan Park

West Farm, West Knapton, Malton YO17 8JE (North Yorkshire)

Tel: **01944 728463**. Email: **info@ryedalesbest.co.uk**   www.alanrogers.com/UK4545

This new park, opened in 2004, is located along the top of the Yorkshire Wolds with super panoramic views across the Vale of Pickering to the North Yorks Moors. The one and a half mile gravel track from the road to the park is well worth while to reach this peaceful location set amongst glorious countryside. There are 80 level pitches (50 for touring units), most with 16A electricity and some with water points. There are 34 pitches with hardstanding. Seating areas, picnic benches and barbecues are provided on the park. As well as the obvious attractions of walking the Wolds Way national trail and the many other footpaths and cycle ways the area has to offer, the park is well placed for visiting all the local attractions which include Scarborough, Bridlington, Sledmere House and Scampston Hall.

Facilities

A brand new toilet block is very well appointed and heated. Family bathrooms. Laundry facilities. Very large heated room with dishwashing sinks and tourist information. Room for disabled visitors. Reception also provides a small shop selling basic supplies. Play area and football field for children and many places to walk dogs. Caravan storage. Off site: Fishing 3 miles. Golf and riding 5 miles. Beach 15 miles.

Open: 1 March - 31 October.

Directions

Park entrance is on the south side of the A64 York - Scarborough road, just past the B1258 turn off and it is well signed. O.S.GR: SE896744. GPS: N54:09.969 W00:39.242

Charges guide

Per unit incl. 2 persons and electricity	£ 11.00 - £ 15.50
tent incl. 2 persons and car	£ 9.00 - £ 12.00
extra person (over 14 yrs)	£ 2.00
awning	£ 1.50
dog	free

The park is peacefully located adjacent to Wolds farmland and large areas of woodland providing peace and tranquillity, meaning visitors are able to relax amidst wildlife, flora and fauna.

Yorkshire
WOLDS WAY
CARAVAN & CAMPING

West Farm, West Knapton, Malton,
North Yorkshire, YO17 8JE
Telephone/Fax 01944 728 463

www.ryedalesbest.co.uk

Landscaped site situated on a working farm with outstanding views over the Vale of Ryedale and North Yorkshire Moors.
Full Facilities including:-
Fantastic Shower/Toilet block with Family Bathroom
Miles of scenic walks and cycle tracks over adjoining farm and woodland
Electric Hook-Ups and Water to all pitches
Laundry Facilities
Shop

UK4590 Jacobs Mount Caravan Park

Stepney Road, Scarborough YO12 5NL (North Yorkshire)

Tel: **01723 361178**. Email: **jacobsmount@yahoo.co.uk**   www.alanrogers.com/UK4590

Situated just two miles from the centre of Scarborough, on the edge of the Forge Valley National Park, Jacobs Mount is well placed to meet many holiday needs. The sea and the sand are the main attractions, but this is also on the doorstep of the North York moors and the Dalby Forest Drive. In addition to caravan holiday homes in separate areas of the park, there are 142 touring pitches, all with electricity. Of these 131 are fully serviced (water, drainage) on well spaced gravel hardstandings. In sunny locations, some pitches have good views. There is a bar with a pleasant lounge (no children), plus a family room and a games/TV room. Bar meals and a quite extensive range of takeaways can be purchased. There is an activity centre and play area for children.

Facilities

The heated toilet block is new and of a high standard. Washbasins in cubicles with WCs, large shower cubicles (free) and a family bathroom (metered hot water) and baby changing facilities. Separate unisex cubicles contain WC, washbasin and shower. Motorcaravan service point. Small shop in reception for basic needs. Bar with bar meals and takeaway. Two play areas (CCTV monitored) for different ages. Caravan storage. No gazebo style tents allowed. Up to two dogs per pitch are accepted. Off site: Scarborough centre and beach 2 miles. Golf, fishing and bicycle hire 2 miles. Riding 5 miles.

Open: 1 March - 6 November.

Directions

Site entrance is on the A170 Pickering - Scarborough road, about 2 miles west of Scarborough (on the right as you start to drop down into the town). O.S.GR: TA021877. GPS: N54:16.037 W00:26.073

Charges guide

Per unit incl. 4 persons and electricity (16A)	£ 10.50 - £ 18.50
extra person (3 yrs and over)	£ 2.00
awning	£ 2.50
dog (max. 2)	£ 2.50

No single sex parties.

UK4580 Foxholme Touring Caravan & Camping Park

Harome, Helmsley YO62 5JG (North Yorkshire)

Tel: **01439 771696**   www.alanrogers.com/UK4580

Foxholme is now an 'adult only' park. With only 60 pitches for caravans and a large field for tents, it is unusual in that nearly all the pitches are individual ones in clearings in the quite dense coniferous plantation. The trees give much shade and quite a lot of privacy (manoeuvring may be difficult on some of the pitches). All pitches have electricity (6A, a few need long leads) and six places have hardstanding. Some picnic tables are provided. There are 30 pitches for tourers, the remainder being taken by seasonal units. The site is managed by a warden, with limited reception opening times. Very basic provisions are kept. The park is set in quiet countryside and would be a good base for touring, being within striking distance of the moors, the coast and York. There are no on site activities but campers may use the indoor pool at the Pheasant Hotel in Harome. There is lighting, but a torch would be useful.

Facilities

The toilet block is an older style building and is clean but basic. Laundry facilities and a washing up area. Two further small blocks provide WCs only in other parts of the park. Motorcaravan service point. Caravan storage. Off site: The nearest shops are at Helmsley and Kirkbymoorside, both about 4 miles away, where there is also bicycle hire. Riding and golf also 4 miles.

Open: Easter - 31 October.

Directions

Turn south off the A170 between adjoining villages of Beadlam (to west) and Nawton (to east) at sign to Ryedale School, then 1 mile to park on left (passing another park on right). From east ignore first site sign at turning before Nawton. From west turn right 400 yards east of Helmsley, signed Harome, turn left at church, go through village and follow camp signs. O.S.GR: SE661831. GPS: N54:14.247 W00:59.420

Charges 2009

Per unit incl. 2 persons	£ 15.50 - £ 17.50
No credit cards.	

FOXHOLME TOURING CARAVAN PARK

HAROME, HELMSLEY, NORTH YORKSHIRE YO62 5JG

Telephone: (01439) 771241, 770416 or 771696   Fax: (01439) 771744

AA 3 PENNANT - CARAVAN CLUB APPROVED - CAMPING CLUB APPROVED

A quiet, rural site for touring vans, motor caravans and some tents. All pitches in well sheltered clearings in the 6 acres of 40 year old woodland. All weather roads, some hardstandings, luxury toilet block graded excellent by the AA, washbasins in cubicles, H&C showers, laundry room, small shop, gas exchange and mains electric hook-ups available.

ADULTS ONLY   BEAUTIFUL COUNTRYSIDE
CLOSE TO THE NORTH YORK MOORS NATIONAL PARK
Please send stamp for brochure to G.C. Binks

UK4570 Forest Holidays Spiers House

Cropton Forest, Cropton, Pickering YO18 8ES (North Yorkshire)

Tel: **01751 417591**. Email: **info@forestholidays.co.uk**   www.alanrogers.com/UK4570

Forest Holidays is a partnership between the Forestry Commission and The Camping & Caravanning Club. The Spiers House site is set in a sunny clearing in the middle of Cropton Forest. It is an ideal location for a cycling or walking holiday without having to move your car. The site buildings, built in local stone, are set around a central courtyard with a pedestrian archway leading to the pitches. The welcoming reception also incorporates a well stocked shop. Sloping fields provide for 150 pitches, which include 74 with 10A electricity and 19 with hardstanding.

Facilities

The tiled toilet block is spacious, if a little Spartan, with open plan washbasins and roomy, pre-set showers (refurbishment is planned). Unit for disabled campers. Dishwashing sinks under cover with free hot water, laundry room with washing machine, dryer and sinks (hot water charged). Well stocked shop. Large adventure playground and games field set under tall pines. Raised barbecues are permitted. Off site: Pub with home-brewed beer 1 mile. Riding 5 miles. Fishing 7 miles. Golf 12 miles.

Open: All year excl. 14 January - 28 February.

Directions

From A170 Pickering head west towards Helmsley. Turn right signed Cropton and Rosedale (avoid Cropton village). Park is signed after 4 miles. Entrance is a 500 m. single track with passing places. O.S.GR: SE758918. GPS: N54:18.459 W00:50.776

Charges guide

Per unit incl. 2 persons	£ 8.70 - £ 13.50
extra person over 15 yrs	£ 3.50 - £ 5.40
electricity	£ 3.00
Prices are higher at weekends.	

UK4610 Moorside Caravan Park

Lords Moor Lane, Strensall, York YO32 5XJ (North Yorkshire)

Tel: **01904 491208**   www.alanrogers.com/UK4610

Strensall is only a few miles from York, one of England's most attractive cities and Moorside, an adults only park, will provide a peaceful haven after a day's sightseeing. It will impress you with its pretty fishing lake, masses of flowers and the tranquillity (except for the odd passing daytime train). There are 57 marked pitches on neat well trimmed grass, most with electricity (5/10A) and 18 with paved hardstanding. The whole park is very well maintained making it a very pleasant environment. The small lake is well stocked for coarse fishing and the pitches bordering the lake are the most popular. York golf course is almost opposite the site entrance. Children under 16 years are not accepted.

Facilities

The purpose built toilet block can be heated and houses immaculately kept facilities with washbasins in cubicles for ladies. One WC is suitable for use by disabled visitors. Fully equipped laundry room. Tourist information and books to borrow. Coarse fishing (£3 per day). Caravan storage. Off site: Strensall village with shops and places to eat is less than a mile. Golf 0.5 miles. Riding 3 miles.

Open: March - end October.

Directions

From A1237 York outer ring road follow signs for Earswick and Strensall. At Strensall follow Flaxton road. The park entrance is on the left past signs to Strensall village and York Golf Club.
O.S.GR: SE647614. GPS: N54:02.564 W01:00.701

Charges guide

Per unit incl. 2 adults and electricity	£ 11.00 - £ 14.50

No credit cards.

UK4620 Upper Carr Chalet & Touring Park

Upper Carr Lane, Malton Road, Pickering YO18 7JP (North Yorkshire)

Tel: **01751 473115**. Email: **info@uppercarrchaletandtouringpark.co.uk**   www.alanrogers.com/UK4620

With a central location in the Vale of Pickering, Upper Carr is well placed for the many attractions the area has to offer. Now under new ownership, the enthusiastic manager is keen to develop it into a family friendly park, introducing themed weekends and nature trails. The park is surrounded by a high, well trimmed hedge which protects it from the wind and deadens the road noise. Upper Carr's six acres provide 80 level pitches, 75 with 10A electricity and some with hardstanding. Seasonal units use 25 pitches. The picturesque village of Thornton Dale can be reached on foot or by cycle.

Facilities

The heated toilet blocks are dated (in a 'chalet' style building) but clean and there are plans for these to be updated. Showers are charged for. Baby facilities. Separate room with WC and washbasin for disabled visitors. Laundry room. Motorcaravan service point. Small shop in reception supplies basic needs and gas. Good play area. Bicycle hire. Nature trail. Off site: Pub 100 yards. Golf (9-hole) or tennis adjacent. Pickering 2 miles. Riding 6 miles. Fishing 5 miles. Bus service passes entrance.

Open: 1 March - 31 October.

Directions

Travelling on the Pickering - Malton A169 road, park is on the left about 1.5 miles south of Pickering.
O.S.GR: SE804815. GPS: N54:13.378 W00:46.140

Charges guide

Per unit incl. 2 adults, 2 children and electricity	£ 13.00 - £ 18.90
extra adult	£ 2.50
extra child	£ 1.50

UK4638 Alders Caravan Park

Home Farm, Alne, York YO61 1RY (North Yorkshire)

Tel: **01347 838722**. Email: **enquiries@homefarmalne.co.uk**   www.alanrogers.com/UK4638

The Alders is located in the village of Alne, only nine miles from the centre of the ancient city of York. Carefully developed on a working farm in historic parkland, the drive to reach the pitches gives a real feeling of space. On reaching the 87 level pitches (25 for tourers, the rest for seasonal units), you will find an area of well trimmed grass and a pitch layout designed to give as much privacy and space as possible. Arranged in small bays, each group is named after a Yorkshire Abbey or Dale. Newly planted woodland with woodland walks and a water meadow with wild flowers enhance the wonderful peace and tranquillity.

Facilities

The central toilet block is heated with family sized shower rooms, one also has a bath (£1 charge). A new block includes en-suite bathrooms with bath or shower, laundry and dishwashing facilities. Provision for disabled visitors. Gas is sold at reception (shop in the village). Off site: Floodlit tennis courts in the village. Fishing 2 miles. Golf 3 miles. Riding 4 miles.

Open: 1 March - 31 October.

Directions

From the north on the A19: after leaving Easingwold bypass take next right turn signed Alne. From the south (A19), 5 miles north of Shipton turn left at sign for Alne. In 1.5 miles at T-junction turn left and in about 0.5 miles, site is signed in the village.
O.S.GR: SE496651. GPS: N54:04.911 W01:14.463

Charges guide

Per unit incl. 2 persons, electricity	£ 14.00

UK4640 Goose Wood Caravan Park

Sutton-on-the-Forest, York YO61 1ET (North Yorkshire)

Tel: **01347 810829**. Email: **edward@goosewood.co.uk**   **www.alanrogers.com/UK4640**

A family owned park in a natural woodland setting, Goose Wood provides a quiet, relaxed atmosphere from which to explore York itself or the surrounding Yorkshire Dales, Wolds or Moors. The park has a well kept air and a rural atmosphere, with 100 well spaced and marked pitches, all with electricity (16A) on hardstanding (4 also have water and drainage). Tents are not accepted. For children, there is a 'super plus' adventure playground in the trees at one side of the park and for adults, a small coarse fishing lake and attractive, natural woodland for walking, plus a large scale chess set. A new health suite has been added with pool, sauna, hot tub and exercise machines. The park is popular with families in high season when it can be busy at weekends. A 'park and ride' scheme for York operates from nearby all year, six days a week or there is a local bus every two hours. The park is just over a mile from Sutton village. A member of the Best of British group.

Facilities

Tiled and heated, the modern toilet block is well maintained. Bathroom (£1). An additional unit provides shower rooms, WC and washbasins in cubicles and extra dishwashing sinks. Full facilities for disabled visitors. Laundry room. Motorcaravan service point. Small shop (with gas). Health Suite (can be hired for 45 minutes, max. 8 people at a time). Fishing lake. Large adventure playground. Games room with pool and TV. Outdoor table tennis. Dogs (max. two per pitch), to be exercised in nearby woodland. No tents are accepted. Off site: Riding or golf 1 mile. Bicycle hire 6 miles. York 6 miles.

Open: All year excl. 15 - 31 January.

Directions

Park is 6 miles north of York; from the A1237 York outer ring-road take the B1363 for Sutton-on-the-Forest and Stillington, taking the first right after the Haxby and Wigginton junction and follow park signs. O.S.GR: SE595636. GPS: N54:03.557 W01:05.644

Charges guide

Per unit incl. 1 or 2 persons,	
car and electricity	£ 17.50 - £ 20.50
extra person	£ 2.50
awning or extra pup tent (1 only)	£ 2.50
fully serviced pitch plus	£ 5.00

UK4630 Ripley Caravan Park

Ripley, Harrogate HG3 3AU (North Yorkshire)

Tel: **01423 770050**. Email: **ripleycaravanpark@talk21.com**   **www.alanrogers.com/UK4630**

Peter and Valerie House are the friendly, resident owners of Ripley Park, an 18 acre grass caravan park with an indoor heated pool. It accommodates 100 touring units and 40 caravan holiday homes on fairly level grass which undulates in parts. Connected by a circular gravel road, some pitches are marked, others carefully spaced (allowing the grass to recover). There are 130 electricity connections (10A) and 20 hardstandings. The owners have planted 2,000 trees and these are developing well to provide individual areas and shelter. A pond with ducks provides an attractive feature. The park is situated at the gateway to the Yorkshire Dales National Park and almost midway between the spa town of Harrogate and historic Knaresborough. The village of Ripley, dominated by its castle, is within walking distance.

Facilities

The central, attractively designed toilet block can be heated and provides smart facilities including washbasins in curtained cubicles, 4 new individual wash facilities, a baby bath and a separate unit with a shower for disabled people. Small laundry. Motorcaravan service point. Recycling bins. Shop with gas (limited hours in low seasons). Games room with TV. Nursery playroom. Adventure play equipment and football area. Heated indoor pool (75p per person) and sauna. Up to two dogs per unit are welcome unless by prior arrangement. Winter caravan storage. Off site: Fishing, riding and golf 3 miles. Bus service 150 yds.

Open: Easter - 31 October.

Directions

About 4 miles north of Harrogate, park access is 150 yds. down the B6165 Knaresborough road from its roundabout junction with the A61. O.S.GR: SE291601. GPS: N54:02.214 W01:33.530

Charges guide

Per unit incl. 2 persons	
and electricity	£ 13.00 - £ 15.00

UK4645 The Ranch Caravan Park

Cliffe Common, Cliffe, Selby YO8 6EF (North Yorkshire)
Tel: 01757 638984. Email: contact@theranchcaravanpark.co.uk   www.alanrogers.com/UK4645

The Ranch is a small, family run caravan park set in six acres of woodland. There are 55 pitches in total, with 39 for touring units on well draining land with some hardstandings available. All have electricity (10/16A) and 4 also have water and a drain. Several pitches are most suitable for American style motorhomes and these are welcomed. The reception has a tiny shop that stocks UHT milk. This is a well maintained park with two areas of open grass, one surrounded by a gravel road. Most of the site is surrounded by trees. There is a security gate at the entrance. A slightly overgrown wooded area (when we visited) had some adventure playground equipment amongst it. A large function hall is attached to the toilet block with a small bar, lounge area, tables and a dance floor. Light meals and takeaways are offered on Friday and Saturday evenings only during the season and at the owner's discretion at other times.

Facilities

Heated toilet block has free showers (with dividing curtains). Facilities for disabled visitors that doubles as a family bathroom and baby room. Motorcaravan service point. Small laundry. Function hall with bar and lounge area. Light meals and takeaway (Friday and Saturday evenings). Off site: Selby 4 miles. York 12 miles. Fishing 2 miles. Golf and riding 15 miles.

Open: All year excl. 5 January - 5 February.

Directions

Leave M62 at exit 37 (Goole) and take A63 towards Selby. At Cliffe turn right and after 1 mile, turn left at crossroads. Park is 80 yards on the right. O.S.GR: SE663338. GPS: N53:47.893 W00:59.438

Charges guide

Per unit incl. 2 persons and electricity	£ 14.50
extra person	£ 1.50
child (5-16 yrs)	£ 1.00

UK4670 Wood Nook Caravan Park

Skirethorns, Threshfield, Skipton BD23 5NU (North Yorkshire)
Tel: 01756 752412. Email: enquiries@woodnook.net   www.alanrogers.com/UK4670

Wood Nook is a family run park in the heart of Wharfedale, part of the Yorkshire Dales National Park. The access road is narrow for a short distance, so care should be taken. The site includes six acres of woodland with quite rare flora and wildlife. Reception is in the farmhouse, as is the small shop. The gently sloping fields have gravel roads and provide 20 touring pitches with gravel hardstanding. All have electricity (10A) and nearby water and chemical disposal points. There is also room for 24 tents and there are some caravan holiday homes to let. The Thompson family are very friendly, always willing to have a chat, although Wood Nook is still a working farm producing beef cattle. The park itself adjoins the fells, with direct access from the top of the site. Nearby is the village of Grassington, with its cobbled main street and quaint gift shops. This is a delightful and peaceful base from which to explore the Yorkshire Dales.

Facilities

Converted farm buildings provide modern, clean sanitary facilities which can be heated. Washbasins in cubicles for ladies. Roomy showers (coin-operated) in another building. Laundry facilities. Motorcaravan service points. Licensed shop for basics and gifts (from Easter). Gas. Small play area. American motorhomes are taken by prior arrangement. Internet access. WiFi coverage (charged). Off site: Fishing and bicycle hire 2 miles. Riding 3 miles. Golf 9 miles. Leisure centre.

Open: 1 March - 31 October.

Directions

Threshfield is 9 miles north of Skipton on the B6265. Continue through village onto B6160 and after garage turn left into Skirethorns Lane. Follow signs for 600 yds, keeping left up narrow lane, then turn right up track for 300 yds. The last 900 yds. is single track – on arrival you could phone ahead to make sure it is clear. O.S.GR: SD974641. GPS: N54:04.360 W02:02.519

Charges guide

Per person	£ 3.00
child (5-15 yrs)	£ 1.50
serviced pitch incl. electricity	£ 8.00
hiker or cyclist incl. tent	£ 5.00
Payment also accepted in euros.	

197

UK4660 Woodhouse Farm Caravan & Camping Park

Winksley, Ripon HG4 3PG (North Yorkshire)

Tel: 01765 658309. Email: woodhouse.farm@talk21.com   www.alanrogers.com/UK4660

This secluded family park on a former working farm, is only six miles from Ripon and about four from the World Heritage site of Fountains Abbey. It is a very rural park with a spacious feel and various pitching areas are tucked away in woodland areas or around the edges of hedged fields with the centres left clear for children. There are hard roads and most of the 160 pitches have 16A electricity. There are 56 acres in total, 17.5 devoted to the site and 20 acres of woodland for walking, with a good area where dogs can run free. The 2.5 acre fishing lake (day tickets from reception) is a big attraction and provides a pleasant area for picnics or walks. The tastefully developed bar (daily) and restaurant (weekends only) offers reasonably priced menus. Woodhouse Farm has a quiet, secluded location from which many excursions can be made – the Yorkshire Dales of Nidderdale, Wharfedale, Wensleydale and Swaledale are all within easy reach.

Facilities

The clean toilet block near the touring pitches has been upgraded and includes heating, roomy showers (20p) and some washbasins in cabins. Two bathrooms. Facilities for disabled visitors. Extra facilities are in the farm buildings along with a well equipped laundry, reception and shop. Gas supplies. Motorcaravan services. Bar (daily) and restaurant (weekends). Takeaway on request. Games room and TV. Play equipment. Fishing. Mountain bike hire. Caravan storage. Deposit for amenity block key £10. Off site: Twice daily bus passes gate.Attractive villages with inns with food. Historic city of Ripon with beautiful cathedral. Riding 3 miles. Golf 6 miles.

Open: 1 March - 31 October.

Directions

From Ripon take Fountains Abbey - Pateley Bridge road (B6265). After about 3.5 miles turn right to Grantley and then follow campsite signs for further 1-2 miles. O.S.GR: SE241715.
GPS: N54:08.245 W01:38.080

Charges guide

Per unit incl. 2 persons	£ 11.00 - £ 14.00
incl. electricity	£ 12.50 - £ 15.50
extra person	£ 2.50
child (5-16 yrs)	£ 0.75
small tent incl. 2 persons	£ 9.50 - £ 12.50

Woodhouse Farm Caravan Park

Set in glorious tranquil woodland and meadows with its own private coarse fishing lakes. The ideal base for exploring the specular countryside of North Yorkshire

- **Fishing**
- **Laundrette**
- **Licensed shop**
- **Games Room**
- **Dogs welcome**
- **Bar/Meals available**
- **Easy access to Ripon, Fountains Abbey, Brimham Rocks**

Winksley, Ripon, North Yorkshire, HG4 3PG   Tel: 01765 658309
Email: woodhouse.farm@talk21.com   Website: www.woodhousewinksley.com

UK4710 Rudding Holiday Park

Follifoot, Harrogate HG3 1JH (North Yorkshire)

Tel: 01423 870439. Email: holiday-park@ruddingpark.com   www.alanrogers.com/UK4710

The extensive part wooded, part open grounds of Rudding Park are very attractive, peaceful and well laid out. One camping area is sloping but terraces provide level pitches and further pitches are in the very sheltered old walled garden. All 141 touring pitches have electricity (10/16A) and 49 'super pitches' are fully serviced. Further pitches are let on a seasonal basis and a separate area contains 96 owner-occupied caravan holiday homes and chalets. On the outer edge of the park is 'The Deer House', a family pub serving bar meals. There is also an 18-hole golf course and driving range. This is an attractive park with something for all the family.

Facilities

Two toilet blocks (heated when necessary and may be under pressure at peak times), some washbasins in cabins, baby room and bathroom. Laundry. Facilities for disabled visitors. Motorcaravan service point. Shop (1/3-4/11). Gas. Restaurant and bar. Heated swimming and paddling pools (25/5-30/8), supervised and with extra charge. Adventure playground. Games room. Golf. Off site: Riding 1 mile.

Open: 1 March - 31 January.

Directions

Park is 3 miles southeast of Harrogate, clearly signed north of the A658 and west of the A661.
O.S.GR: SE333528. GPS: N53:58.384 W01:29.832

Charges guide

Per pitch incl. electricity	£ 15.00 - £ 30.00

Special offers - contact park.

198

UK4690 Constable Burton Hall Caravan Park

Constable Burton Hall, Leyburn DL8 5LJ (North Yorkshire)

Tel: 01677 450428   www.alanrogers.com/UK4690

This tranquil park is in beautiful Wensleydale and the emphasis is on peace and quiet, the wardens working to provide a relaxing environment. In the grounds of Constable Burton Hall, it has a spacious, park-like feel to it. On part level, part sloping, well trimmed grass, the 120 pitches (40 for touring units) are of a good size and all have 10A electricity (10A). There are no pitches for tents. Ideally placed for visiting the Northern Dales, the gardens of the Hall are open to the public, with a collection of maples and terraced gardens developed by Mrs Vida Burton.

Facilities

Two toilet blocks built of local stone and blending in with the local surroundings are well tiled, kept immaculately clean, and can be heated. New facility for disabled visitors and baby room. The former deer barn has been adapted for use as a laundry room and extra washrooms with basins for both men and women. Gas supplies. Off site:Pub with meals opposite. Irregular bus service from site gate. Fishing and golf within 5 miles.

Open: Late March - 31 October.

Directions

Park is by the A684 between Bedale and Leyburn, 0.5 miles from the village of Constable Burton on the Leyburn side. O.S.GR: SE152907. GPS: N54:18.750 W01:45.250

Charges guide

Per unit incl. 2 persons	£ 15.00 - £ 18.00
extra person	£ 5.00 - £ 7.00
child (5-16 yrs)	£ 3.00
No commercial vehicles.	

UK4700 Nostell Priory Holiday Park

Nostell, Wakefield WF4 1QE (West Yorkshire)

Tel: 01924 863938. Email: info@nostellprioryholidaypark.co.uk   www.alanrogers.com/UK4700

This tranquil, secluded woodland park is within the Nostell Priory estate and provides 40 touring pitches, in addition to 84 caravan holiday homes in a separate area. In a grassy, flat and sheltered area edged with mature trees, all the touring pitches have electricity (5A) and hardstanding. The park's amenities are designed to blend into the environment and are built in rustic wood, including the sanitary block. The park is well cared for and the natural environment is encouraged. Nostell Priory itself, with its collection of Chippendale furniture and attractive gardens, is well worth a visit.

Facilities

The toilet block, although older in style, has been refurbished and includes some washbasins in cubicles (coded entry). Laundry with two washing machines and a dryer (opening times on the door). Gas supplies. Milk and papers can be ordered at reception. Play area (no ball games on site). Fishing. Up to two dogs are accepted. Off site: Nearest shops 2 miles. Golf 5 miles. Boat launching 8 miles.

Open: 1 March - 31 October.

Directions

Park entrance is off A638 Wakefield - Doncaster road, 5 miles southeast of Wakefield. Follow drive for 0.5 miles (rose nursery on left). Approaching from the south on A638, the site entrance is almost a mile past the entry to the Priory, on the right. O.S.GR: SE394181. GPS: N53:39.297 W01:23.910

Charges guide

Per unit incl. 2 persons	£ 12.50 - £ 19.00
extra person (over 5 yrs)	£ 2.00
dog (max. 2)	£ 1.00

UK4760 Riverside Meadows Country Caravan Park

Ure Bank Top, Ripon HG4 1JD (North Yorkshire)

Tel: 01765 602964. Email: info@flowerofmay.com   www.alanrogers.com/UK4760

Riverside Meadows is a rural park, although the approach to it belies that fact. The short approach from the main road passes a row of houses and a factory, but once they are passed, the park opens up before you and you are once again back in the countryside. There are plenty of caravan holiday homes here but they are, on the whole, quite separate from the 64 touring pitches. These pitches, practically all with electricity, are mainly on gently sloping grass with just a few hardstandings. A meadow separates the park from the River Ure, a favourite place for strolling and fishing (licences available). There is lots to see and do on and off the park for both families and couples.

Facilities

The tiled toilet block is quite new and includes a baby room, dishwashing room, a fully fitted shower room for disabled visitors. Laundry facilities. Shop. Bar with snacks. Games room. Well equipped play area. An indoor pool is planned. Off site: Fishing, bicycle hire and riding 800 yds. Golf 1.25 miles. Ripon is 20 minutes walk.

Open: Easter - 31 October.

See advertisement on page 189

Directions

At the most northern roundabout on the Ripon bypass (A61), turn onto the A6108 signed Ripon, Masham and Leyburn. Go straight on at mini-roundabout and park is signed on right. O.S.GR: SE317727. GPS: N54:09.027 W01:30.900

Charges guide

Per unit incl. up to 4 persons	£ 11.50 - £ 19.00
extra person (over 3 yrs)	£ 3.00
dog (max. 2)	£ 1.00

199

UK4715 Riverside Caravan Park

High Bentham LA2 7FJ (North Yorkshire)
Tel: 01524 261272. Email: info@riversidecaravanpark.co.uk   www.alanrogers.com/UK4715

The pretty, tree lined approach to Riverside leads into an attractive park, owned by the Marshall family for over 30 years. Nestling in beautiful countryside, alongside the River Wenning, the park has easy access to the Yorkshire Dales and the Lake District. There are 49 marked, level grass touring pitches with 10A electricity and TV hook-ups. In addition there are 12 'super' pitches on tarmac. An area has been developed for 50 seasonal pitches on gravel. Located away from the touring area are 206 privately owned holiday homes. Tents are not accepted. The smart reception building includes a small shop selling caravan accessories. A new building opposite houses an excellent laundry, and a library containing internet access plus WiFi, a wide variety of books and local tourist literature. The Forest of Bowland is on the doorstep providing endless opportunities for walking and sightseeing in pretty villages. The small town of High Bentham is an easy walk from the park, and the local railway station links to the very scenic Settle to Carlisle railway.

Facilities

The modern toilet block with underfloor heating is centrally situated. Washbasin cubicles. Unisex showers in a separate area. Toilet and shower room for disabled visitors (radar key) also doubles as a family shower room (charged). Motorcaravan services. Caravan storage. Outdoor play area for younger children, large field for ball games. Family games room. The river can be used for fishing (permit from reception) swimming, and small boats. Off site: Golf nearby.

Open: 1 March - 31 October.

Directions

From M6 exit 34, head east on the A683 towards Kirkby Lonsdale. After about 5 miles take B6480 signed to High Bentham. At the Black Bull Hotel follow the caravan signs. The park entrance is on the right after crossing the river bridge.
O.S.GR: SD662687. GPS: N54:06.787 W02:30.640

Charges guide

Per unit incl. 2 persons	£ 15.90 - £ 19.00
extra person	£ 4.50
child (2-16 yrs)	£ 2.50
dog	£ 1.50

Min. charge per night £ 15.90.
Less 10% for bookings over 7 nights.

UK4740 Jasmine Park

Cross Lane, Snainton, Scarborough YO13 9BE (North Yorkshire)
Tel: 01723 859240. Email: info@jasminepark.co.uk   www.alanrogers.com/UK4740

Jasmine is a very attractive, quiet and well manicured park with owners who go to much trouble to produce many plants to decorate a very colourful entrance. Set in the Vale of Pickering, the park is level, well drained and protected by a coniferous hedge. The 106 pitches (54 for touring units) are on grass, with electricity connections (10A) for all caravans and some tents. There is no play equipment for children, although a field is provided for games. Much tourist information is provided in a log cabin and the owners are only too happy to advise. The market town of Pickering and the seaside town of Scarborough are both 8 miles. Many local attractions are within easy reach, including Castle Howard, Dalby Forest, Sledmere House, Nunington Hall, Goathland (the setting for ITV's 'Heartbeat') and the North York Moors Railway. Some privately owned log cabins and seasonal tourers are also on the site. This is an award-winning, peaceful park for a restful holiday. A member of the Countryside Discovery group.

Facilities

The heated toilet block has been refurbished to a high standard and is kept very clean. It includes a large room for families or disabled visitors containing a bath, shower, WC and washbasin (access by key). Laundry room with dishwashing sinks, washing machine, dryer and iron (hot water metered). Motorcaravan service point. Licensed shop selling essentials and gas. Dogs are welcome but there is no dog walk. Caravan storage. Off site: Bus service in village 0.5 miles. Riding 2 miles. Golf driving range and 9-hole course 2 miles. Fishing and bicycle hire 5 miles.

Open: 1 March - 31 December.

Directions

Snainton is on the A170 Pickering - Scarborough road and park is signed at eastern end of the village. Follow Barker GPS: N54:13.115 W00:34.534

Charges guide

Per unit incl. 4 persons	£ 14.00 - £ 20.00
extra person	£ 1.50
child (5-14 yrs)	£ 1.00
awning	£ 2.00

Min. stay at Easter 4 nights, other B.Hs 3 nights.

UK4765 Otterington Park

Station Farm, South Otterington, Northallerton DL7 9JB (North Yorkshire)

Tel: 01609 780656. Email: info@otteringtonpark.com   www.alanrogers.com/UK4765

This family owned, five acre park is located near a farm and the entrance to the park is via stables, paddocks and the farm itself. Between Thirsk and Northallerton, in the Vale of York, it is ideally placed to visit the moors and dales of Yorkshire along with local market towns, theme parks and stately homes. Predominantly it is a flat grass site with pebble hardstanding providing 40 touring pitches, each with 16A electricity. There is a separate paddock for tents or visitors not needing electricity. The park is shared with seasonal caravans and some privately owned luxury chalets. At present, landscaping offers limited shade. Unmade roads throughout may cause dust problems. A family oriented park, there is a children's playground and grassy play areas. The owners have supplied good tourist information and local nature walks for visitors. There is course fishing in a well stocked, spring fed, one acre lake located 200 m. from the site. The main London - Edinburgh railway line runs to the rear of the park, so some train noise may be experienced.

Facilities

One purpose built, clean block in a heated building. Unisex en-suite style shower rooms with free showers. Laundry. Facilities for disabled visitors incorporating a baby area. Small shop in reception. Play areas. Fishing. Off site: Large supermarket 3 miles. Local bus service to Thirsk and Northallerton run every 2 hours from park entrance (not Sunday) Several local country pubs serving meals within 1 mile. Riding 1 mile. Golf 3 miles.

Open: 1 March - 31 October.

Directions

From A1M join A684 for Leeming Bar and Morton-on-Swale. At roundabout bear right on A167 signed South Otterington and Topcliffe. At South Otterington crossroads (pub) turn left signed Thornton-le-Dale to park in 500 yards.
GPS: N54:17.263 W01:25.228

Charges guide

Per unit incl. 4 persons
and electricity   £ 15.00 - £ 19.00

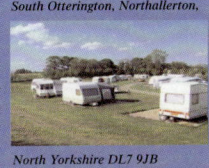

UK4720 Knight Stainforth Hall Caravan & Camping Park

Little Stainforth, Settle BD24 0DP (North Yorkshire)

Tel: 01729 822200. Email: info@knightstainforth.co.uk   www.alanrogers.com/UK4720

In a very attractive setting, this park is located in the heart of the Yorkshire Dales, the whole area a paradise for hill-walking, fishing and pot-holing and with outstanding scenery. The camping area is on slightly sloping grass, sheltered by mature woodland. There are 100 touring pitches, 50 with electricity (10A) and 10 with hardstanding, and a separate area contains 60 privately owned caravan holiday homes. Buildings near the farmhouse provide reception, a games/TV room and a shop (for basics). A gate leads from the bottom of the camping field giving access to the river bank where the Ribble bubbles over small waterfalls and rocks and whirls around deep pools where campers swim in warm weather. This is not fenced and children should be supervised, although it is a super location for a family picnic. Fishing permits and licences are available from reception and one can fish for trout (or salmon when available). Settle is only 2 miles away, as is Giggleswick and its well known school. Train buffs will want to travel on the Settle - Carlisle railway over the famous Ribblehead Viaduct. The magic of the Dales National Park is on the doorstep.

Facilities

A new building provides all new facilities including some washbasins in cubicles. Dishwashing sinks. Laundry room with washing machine and dryers. Shop. Games/TV room. Play area with safety base. Fishing. Security barrier at entrance. Deposit for key to toilet block and barrier £10. Off site: Bicycle hire and golf 3 miles. Riding 6 miles. The Dales Falconry and Conservation Centre at Felzor.

Open: 1 March - 31 October.

Directions

From Settle town centre, drive west towards Giggleswick. Ignore turning marked Stainforth and Horton, and after 200 yards turn right into Stackhouse Lane (signed Knight Stainforth). After 2 miles turn right at crossroads. O.S.GR: SD815671.
GPS: N54:06.015 W02:17.090

Charges guide

Per unit incl. 2 persons	£ 12.00 - £ 17.00
extra person	£ 2.50
child (5-16 yrs)	£ 1.50
backpacker	£ 4.25

Min. stay at B.Hs 3 nights. Special offers.

201

UK4750 Howgill Lodge Caravan & Camping Park

Barden, Skipton BD23 6DJ (North Yorkshire)

Tel: 01756 720655. Email: info@howgill-lodge.co.uk

www.alanrogers.com/UK4750

Howgill Lodge is a traditional family site set in the heart of the Dales. Arranged on a sloping hillside, the terraced pitches have fantastic views. It is a small park catering for the needs of walkers, tourers and the people who like to just relax. The whole area is a haven for both experienced walkers or the casual rambler, without having to move your car. All the pitches at the upper part of the park are on hardstanding and have electricity connections (10A), the lower ones are mainly on grass (40 in total). Picnic tables and chairs are provided. Reception also houses a small shop which sells most of the basics including fresh foods. Pretty villages abound in the area, all with attractive inns and nearby Embsay has the Dales Railway with steam trains. This very pleasant park, with clean facilities, has a very relaxing feel to it.

Facilities

Heated toilet facilities are at the entrance, close to reception, with dishwashing sinks outside, under cover. Showers are large and adjustable (on payment). Fully equipped laundry room with washing machine, dryer and iron and four unisex showers also here. Outdoor washing lines are provided. Two small blocks housing WCs are lower down the site for the convenience of tent campers. Shop. No play area. Fishing licences are available from reception. B&B is available. Off site: Bus service within walking distance (3 per day). Skipton 8 miles. Bolton Abbey with its beautiful riverside walks is 3 miles. Fishing 1 mile. Golf, riding and bicycle hire 7 miles.

Open: 1 April - 31 October.

Directions

Turn off A59 Skipton - Harrogate road at roundabout onto B6160 Bolton Abbey, Burnsall road. Three miles past Bolton Abbey at Barden Towers, bear right signed Appletreewick and Pateley Bridge. This road is fairly narrow for 1.25 miles (with passing places). Park is signed on right at phone box. O.S.GR: SE065593. GPS: N54:01.546 W01:54.590

Charges guide

Per unit, 2 persons and electricity	£ 15.00
family unit incl. electricity	£ 21.00
awning	£ 2.00
hiker	£ 5.00
tent incl. car and 2 persons	£ 15.00

UK4755 Maustin Caravan Park

Kearby with Netherby, Wetherby LS22 4DA (North Yorkshire)

Tel: 01132 886234. Email: judith@maustin.co.uk

www.alanrogers.com/UK4755

A tranquil site for couples only, this well manicured park is set within the North Yorkshire National Park. It offers 25 well spaced pitches sited on grass, all with peaceful, scenic views of the surrounding area. Caravan holiday homes are in a separate area. A bowling club on the site offers membership to all visitors and competitions are held throughout the season. Relax in the comfortable lounge or in the tasteful bar and restaurant area. A covered terrace overlooks the bowling green. There is a information building providing a books, DVDs, videos and games which you may borrow free of charge. Local wildlife and tourist information is also available, along with internet services. Close to Harewood House and Harrogate, you can enjoy country walks or scenic drives throughout 'Emmerdale country' and the surrounding villages. The attentive park managers ensure that the luxury facilities are spotlessly clean so that you have a pleasant stay.

Facilities

One heated, purpose built toilet block has luxury showers, free hairdryers and roomy toilet and washing cubicles, all with non slip flooring. Designated facility for disabled visitors. Laundry room. Kitchen area with freezer. Milk, newspapers, etc. to order. Internet facilities. Off site: Riding 2 miles. Golf 4 miles.

Open: All year excl. February.

Directions

From A1 North take exit 47 for Harrogate (A59), then after three roundabouts (9 miles) turn left on A61 (Leeds). In 2 miles turn left (Kirkby Overblow) then right to Kearby and park. From A1 South follow Harewood House signs through Collingham (A61). At lights turn right over River Wharfe, right for Kirkby Overblow, then as above. O.S.GR: SE331468. GPS: N53:55.091 W01:29.711

Charges guide

Per unit incl. 2 persons	£ 15.50
incl. services	£ 17.50
extra person	£ 2.00
dog	free

UK4780 Lebberston Touring Park

Filey Road, Lebberston, Scarborough YO11 3PE (North Yorkshire)

Tel: 01723 585723. Email: info@lebberstontouring.co.uk   www.alanrogers.com/UK4780

Lebberston Touring Park is a quiet, spacious touring site and is highly suitable for anyone seeking a quiet relaxing break, such as mature couples or young families (although tents are not accepted). There is no play area or games room, the only concession to children being a large central area with goal posts, so teenagers may get bored. The park itself has a very spacious feel – it is gently sloping and south facing and the views are superb. There are 125 numbered pitches with 75 for touring units. All have 10A electricity and 25 are on hardstanding. The circular access road is tarmac, the grass is well manicured and the entrance a mass of flowers. Reception is part of a farmhouse style new build, also the home of the owners and their young family. The resorts of Filey, Bridlington, Scarborough and Hornsea provide something for everyone, the moors and the Dalby forest are also within a short distance. This being such a popular area, we feel justified in adding another site to this guide, especially one of such quality.

Facilities

Recently upgraded toilet blocks are of high quality and kept very clean. Large shower cubicles and washbasins in cubicles with curtains. Both blocks have dishwashing sinks and one has a family bathroom (20p). Good room for disabled visitors. Laundry with washing machine, dryer, spin dryer, iron and board. A key is supplied for the laundry and bathroom, with radar key access to the disabled shower room. Reception sells a few supplies, plus papers, ice cream and gas. Only 'breathable' groundsheets are permitted. WiFi. Off site: Hourly bus 5 minutes walk. Local pub 5 minutes walk. All new arrivals are given details of parking in Scarborough including a parking disc.

Open: 1 March - 31 October.

Directions

From A64 Malton - Scarborough road turn right at roundabout (MacDonald's, pub and superstore) signed B1261 Filey. Go through Cayton, Killerby and in 4.5 miles, the park is signed on the right. O.S.GR: TA082823. GPS: N54:13.590 W00:20.825

Charges guide

Per unit incl. 2 persons and electricity	£ 13.00 - £ 21.00
extra person	£ 1.50
child (5-14 yrs)	£ 1.00
trailer tent over 8 sq.m.	£ 2.00
full awning	£ 2.00

UK4775 Cote Ghyll Caravan & Camping Park

Osmotherley, Northallerton DL6 3AH (North Yorkshire)

Tel: 01609 883425. Email: hills@coteghyll.com   www.alanrogers.com/UK4775

Jon and Helen Hill are working hard to maintain the good standard and make improvements to their park, and their efforts are evident. The site is set on a secluded hillside with the higher pitches terraced and the lower ones on a level grassy area, bordered by the small Cod Beck stream. Of the 80 pitches, 50 are for tourers. There are also 18 pitches used for caravan holiday homes and 30 are seasonal. All pitches have 10A electricity hook-ups, 12 are fully serviced. A simple site, Cote Ghyll is highly suited for lovers of peace and quiet, for bird watching or for more energetic hobbies such as cycling and walking. On the western edge of the North York Moors, cycle paths and footpaths lead almost from the site entrance and the three main long distance footpaths, the Lyke Wake walk, the Cleveland Way and the Coast to Coast, all pass close by.

Facilities

Two heated toilet blocks, one new, provide free power showers, vanity style washbasins and hairdryers. Bathroom and facilities for babies and disabled visitors. Laundry room with washing machine, dryer, iron and board. Drying room. Motorcaravan service point. New reception and larger shop. Gas supplies. Play area. Caravan storage. Off site: Shops and pubs 10 minutes walk. Fishing 1 mile. Bicycle hire 6 miles. Golf and riding 8 miles. Mount Grace Priory 4 miles. Swimming pool and leisure centre 6 miles. Beach 18 miles.

Open: 1 March - 31 October.

Directions

Osmotherley is east of the A19. Leave the A19 at A684 exit signed Northallerton and Osmotherely. Go to Osmotherley and site is at the northern end of the village, well signed. O.S.GR: SE460983. GPS: N54:22.586 W01:17.500

Charges guide

Per unit incl. 2 persons	£ 14.00 - £ 17.50
incl. electricity	£ 16.00 - £ 19.50
incl. full services plus	£ 4.50
extra person	£ 2.50
child (5-12 yrs, max. 4)	£ 1.00

MAP 5

The northwest regio
boasts a wealth of
industrial heritage
with undiscovered
countryside, the vibr
cities of Manchester
and Liverpool, the seasid
resorts of Blackpool and
Morecambe Bay, plus miles of
glorious coastline, home to
a wide variety of bird species.

THIS REGION INCLUDES: CHESHIRE, LANCASHIRE, MERSEYSIDE, GREATER MANCHESTER AND THE HIGH PEAKS OF DERBYSHIRE

The miles of beautiful, North West countryside offers endless opportunities for recreation. For the more active, the peaceful plains of Cheshire are a walker's haven with endless trails to choose from. Lancashire is also good walking country, with way marked paths passing through the outstanding forest of Bowland, which affords marvellous views over the Lake District in Cumbria and the Yorkshire Dales. Birdwatchers are catered for too, with the coast offering some of the best bird spotting activitiy in the country, most notably along the Sefton coast and around the Wirral Peninsula. The region's cities have their own charm. Manchester, with its fabulous shopping centres and vibrant nightlife, boasts a rich Victorian heritage; the maritime city of Liverpool has more museums and galleries than any other UK city outside London; Lancaster features fine Georgian buildings and an imposing Norman castle; while Chester is renowned for its medieval architecture and shopping galleries. And offering good, old-fashioned seaside fun is Blackpool. England's most popular seaside resort is packed full of lively entertainment and attractions, such as the white knuckle rides at the pleasure beach, amusement games on the pier and the observation decks in the famous Tower.

Places of interest

Cheshire: Tatton Park in Knutsford; Ches
Cathedral and Zoo; Cheshire Military
Museum; Lyme Park stately home in
Macclesfield; Beeston Castle; Boat Muse
at Ellesmere Port.

Lancashire: Williamson Park, Castle and
Leisure Park in Lancaster; Camelot Them
Park; Museum of Football in Preston;
Morecambe Bay; Hoghton Tower and
National Museum of Football in Preston.

Merseyside: Liverpool Football Club Mus
and Tour Centre; The Beatles Story Muse
Speke Hall Garden and Estate; The Wirra
Country Park; Williamson Tunnels Herita
Centre.

Greater Manchester: Imperial War Muse
North; Manchester United Football Club
Museum; The Lowry; Corgi Heritage Cen
in Rochdale; Stockport Air Raid Shelter.

Did you know?

The first public gallery to open in Englan
was in Liverpool in 1877.

Lancaster Castle is infamous as host to
the Pendle Witch trials in 1612.

The first passenger railway station was
built in Manchester.

Hoghton Tower is where King James I
knighted a loin of beef in 1617 – hence
the name Sirloin.

To date 300 bird species have been recor
within the boundaries of Sefton.

Chester has the most complete set of cit
walls in Britain.

Opened in 1894, the Blackpool Tower w
copied from the Eiffel Tower; the height
the top of the flagpole is 518 feet 9 inch

RED TEXT DENOTES ALL YEAR SITE

5605
5350
CARNFORTH
5270
5271
INGLETON
4715
4720
MORECAMBE
LANCASTER
SETTLE
MALHAM
4670
4750
YORKSHIRE
North Yorkshire
SKIPTON
FLEETWOOD
5272
M6
Lancashire
A59
BINGLEY
5300
A629
BLACKPOOL
5330
M55
PRESTON
BRADFORD
5295
West Yorkshire
5290
SOUTHPORT
A59
NORTH WEST
M62
A62
5360
5280
M61
Greater Manchester
M6
MANCHESTER
Merseyside
M62
LIVERPOOL
Derbyshire
RUNCORN
M56
A34
A6
A55
NORTHWICH
MACCLESFIELD
BUXTON
3840
3845
5240
HEART
CHESTER
Cheshire
CONGLETON
3980
WALES
LEEK
3850
North Wales
3970

UK5240 Lamb Cottage Caravan Park

Dalefords Lane, Whitegate, Northwich CW8 2BN (Cheshire)

Tel: **01606 882302**. Email: **lynn@lccp.fsworld.co.uk**   www.alanrogers.com/UK5240

This quiet, family run 'adult only' park is set in the midst of the lovely Vale Royal area of Cheshire. The entrance road is flanked by 22 privately owned caravan holiday homes which are not unduly obtrusive, and a second area beyond has 15 landscaped seasonal caravan pitches. Beyond this again is the touring area which has 25 large pitches, all with 16A electric hook-ups, gravel hardstandings, water and drainage. Only 'breathable' groundsheets are permitted and tents are not accepted. Nearby are Delamere Forest with its walking and mountain biking trails, Whitegate Way walking trail, Oulton Park Motor Racing Circuit and the city of Chester, which is 12 miles.

Facilities

Toilet and shower facilities are housed in a new custom built 'park home' style unit which includes washbasins in cubicles and facilities for disabled guests. Laundry room. Calor gas stocked. Max. 2 dogs per unit. Off site: Pub serving food under 1 mile. Riding 1.5 miles. Golf 2 miles. Supermarket 3 miles. Fishing 3 miles. Bicycle hire 4 miles.

Open: 1 March - 31 October.

Directions

From M6 exit 19 take A556 towards Chester. After 12 miles turn left at lights (Winsford and Whitegate) into Dalefords Lane. Continue for 1 mile and site is on right between white house and bungalow. O.S.GR: SJ614693. GPS: N53:13.074 W02:34.834

Charges guide

Per pitch incl. 2 persons and electricity	£ 18.00
extra person	£ 5.00

205

UK5360
Willowbank Touring Park

Coastal Road, Ainsdale, Southport PR8 3ST (Mersey)

Tel: **01704 571566**. Email: **info@willowbankcp.co.uk**

www.alanrogers.com/UK5360

Well situated for the Sefton coast and Southport, Willowbank is a fairly new park. The touring park is set on the edge of sand dunes amongst mature, wind swept trees. Entrance to the park is controlled by a barrier, with a pass-key issued at the excellent reception building which doubles as a sales office for the substantial, high quality caravan holiday home development. There are now 87 touring pitches, 30 on gravel hardstandings, 24 on grass (these all with 10A electricity) and a further 33 pitches with 16A electricity. These are on grass hardstanding using an environmentally friendly reinforcement system. Large units (longer than 8 m) and caravans of foreign manufacture are not accepted. The owners are very well supported on the touring side by the reception team which has considerable experience in managing the touring park. There could be some noise from the nearby main road. This is a good area for cycling and walking and the attractions of Southport with its parks, gardens, funfair and shopping are 4 miles away.

Facilities

The purpose built, heated toilet block is of a high standard including an excellent bathroom for disabled visitors, although the showers are rather compact. Baby room. Laundry. Motorcaravan service point. Play area. Units over 8 m. long and caravans of foreign manufacture are not accepted. Off site: Beach 1.5 miles. Golf and riding 0.5 miles. Fishing 4 miles. Bicycle hire 4.5 miles. Martin Mere nature reserve nearby.

Open: All year excl. 11 January - 28 February.

Directions

Park is 4 miles south of Southport. From Ainsdale on A565 travel south for 1.5 miles to second traffic lights (Woodvale) and turn right into Coastal Road to site on right in 150 yds. From south pass RAF Woodvale and turn left at second set of lights. O.S.GR: SD308108. GPS: N53:35.328 W03:02.640

Charges guide

Per unit incl. 2 persons and electricity	£ 12.00 - £ 22.00
hardstanding	£ 1.50
extra person	£ 2.80
child (5-16 yrs)	£ 2.20
dog (max. 2)	£ 1.10

Latest arrival time 21.00 hrs.

You might also like to consider...

www.**alanrogers**.com for latest campsite news

UK5272 Moss Wood Caravan Park

Crimbles Lane, Cockerham, Lancaster LA2 0ES (Lancashire)

Tel: **01524 791041**. Email: **info@mosswood.co.uk**   **www.alanrogers.com/UK5272**

Moss Wood is a well established park set in a secluded rural location near the village of Cockerham. A sheltered field has 25 touring pitches on level hardstandings (steel pegs may be required) with 16A electricity. Most also have water and drainage. Screened from the touring area by a high fence so not visually intrusive are 175 privately owned holiday homes. There is a large adventure playground on site and, although well screened by mature trees, it could be lively and noisy at busy times. A purpose built log cabin houses reception and a shop which sells basic supplies. Although there are passing places, the approach road to the park is narrow so care should be taken.

Facilities

New centrally located sanitary block (key entry) is kept spotlessly clean and provides vanity style washbasins and roomy, pre-set showers. Fully equipped facilities for disabled visitors. Undercover food preparation area, dishwashing and laundry facilities. Play area. Large sports field and woodland dog walking. Off site: Pubs at Cockerham 1 mile. Garstang, historic Lancaster, seaside Morecambe and the Lune Valley all within easy reach. Fishing nearby. Riding 3 miles. Golf 4 miles. Beach 5 miles.

Open: 1 March - 31 October.

Directions

Park is 1 mile west of Cockerham on the A588 road. Leave M6 at exit 33 and follow signs for Cockerham. A588 is about 4 miles. Site is signed on the left. O.S.GR: SD456498. GPS: N53:56.273 W02:49.252

Charges guide

Per unit incl. 2 adults,	
2 children and electricity	£ 16.00 - £ 20.00
extra person	£ 3.00
awning	£ 3.00

UK5270 Bolton Holmes & Detrongate Holiday Park

A6, Main Road, Bolton Le Sands, Carnforth LA5 8ES (Lancashire)

Tel: **01524 732854**. Email: **info@holgatesleisureparks.co.uk**   **www.alanrogers.com/UK5270**

Previously two adjacent parks, Bolton Holmes and Detrongate is being developed by the Holgate family into an excellent addition to their group. Situated on the coast north of Lancaster, the park is an ideal base for exploring the Lake District, North Yorkshire and the Forest of Bowland. The park is divided into several grassy, sloping fields and many of the pitches have stunning views over Morecambe Bay, others look towards the Lakeland Fells. It is a very open park with little shade. Of the 240 touring pitches, 135 have 10A electricity and 6 are fully serviced. There are also 100 pitches for caravan holiday homes. From the park there is direct access to the salt marshes and eventually the sea, although care must be taken in Morecambe Bay because of the quicksands. A safe way of crossing the bay is to join am organised walk led by the Queen's Guide, Cedric Robinson. These take place on many weekends during the summer, and a list of dates is posted in reception.

Facilities

Three toilet blocks, one refurbished the others to follow. Facilities for disabled visitors. Good laundry. Motorcaravan service point. Small shop. Playground for younger children, large field for ball games. Games room. Future plans include a bar/restaurant. Off site: Fishing 200 yds. Golf and riding 3 miles. Canal cruises on Lancaster Canal. Leighton Moss RSPB nature reserve. Good shopping in nearby Lancaster and Kendal 15 miles.

Open: 1 March - 31 October.

Directions

From M6 exit 35 take the A601M to roundabout and follow signs to Morecambe. Continue through Carnforth and after mini-roundabout look for site sign in 500 yds on the right. O.S.GR: SD480692. GPS: N54:06.961 W02:47.275

Charges guide

Per unit with 2 persons,	
car and electricity	£ 10.00 - £ 14.00
extra person	£ 3.00
child	£ 2.00

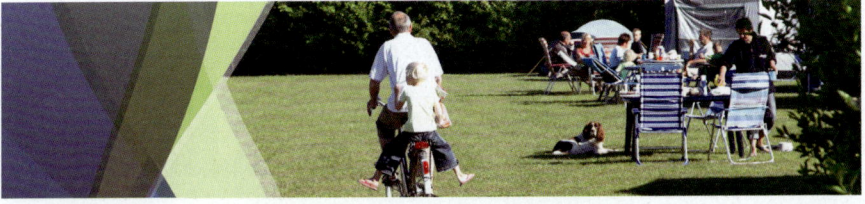

UK5350 Holgates Caravan Park

Middlebarrow Plain, Cove Road, Silverdale, Carnforth LA5 0SH (Lancashire)

Tel: **01524 701508**. Email: **caravan@holgates.co.uk**   www.alanrogers.com/UK5350

This attractive, very high quality park is in an outstanding craggy, part-wooded, hillside location with fine views over Morecambe Bay. It takes 70 touring units, with 339 privately owned caravan holiday homes and 11 to rent located in woodland away from the touring pitches. With just 5 grassy pitches for tents, the remaining 65 large touring pitches are on gravel hardstandings, all with electricity (16A), free TV connection, individual drainage and water points. The main complex with reception and the entrance barrier, provides a well stocked supermarket, lounge bar, restaurant with good value meals and a terrace with views over the bay. There is also an indoor leisure centre. Children have a choice of two adventure playgrounds and plenty of space for ball games. Also on site is a small but challenging 'pitch and putt' course. Everything is completed to the highest standards.

Facilities

Two modern, heated toilet buildings are fully equipped with top quality fittings and including some private cubicles with WC and washbasin. Dishwashing sinks at each block. Excellent provision for disabled visitors with a reserved pitch and parking bay adjacent. Launderette. Shop. Gas supplies. Bar and restaurant. Indoor pool (17 x 17 m; with lifeguard) with spa pool, steam room and sauna (no unaccompanied under 10s). Playgrounds. Games room with pool table and video games. Pitch and putt course (£2 per person). Facilities are limited mid week in January and early February. Admission restrictions include no unaccompanied under 18s or single sex groups, certain breeds of dog or commercial vehicles. Off site: Riding, cycling and fishing within 9 miles. Morecambe or Lancaster 12 miles. Kendal 15 miles.

Open: All year excl. 6 November - 21 December.

Directions

From traffic lights in centre of Carnforth take road to Silverdale under low bridge. After 1 mile turn left signed Silverdale and after 2.5 miles over level crossing, carry on and turn right at T-junction. Follow Holgates sign from here watching for left then right forks (narrow roads). O.S.GR: SD460755.
GPS: N54:10.569 W02:50.154

Charges guide

Per unit incl. 2 adults and 2 children	£ 32.50 - £ 33.00
extra person	£ 7.00
extra child (5-17 yrs)	£ 4.00
awning or pup tent	£ 3.00

Minimum stays apply for all B.H weekends.

UK5290 Royal Umpire Caravan Park

Southport Road, Croston, Preston PR26 9JB (Lancashire)

Tel: **01772 600257**. Email: **reception@royalumpire.co.uk**   www.alanrogers.com/UK5290

Royal Umpire is a spacious park near the coast and the M6 for overnight or longer stays. The entrance to the park is past a large grass area leading to the security barrier with the shop and reception immediately to the left, and slightly ahead, an unusual sunken garden area that is a pleasing feature. Comprising 58 acres, the park has 200 pitches, almost all with 10A electricity, but a few with 16A. About 75% of the pitches now have gravel hardstanding, some with TV and water connections. Tarmac and gravel roads connect the various pitch areas. A good choice of pubs serving bar or restaurant meals is nearby. The gates are closed 23.00 - 07.00.

Facilities

The two tiled toilet blocks, one beside reception, the other centrally situated. Fully equipped laundry. Very good facilities for disabled visitors that are shared with baby facilities (entrance with key, £5 deposit). Motorcaravan services. Adventure playground. Field area for ball games. Rally field. Off site: A short walk takes you to the nearby river for fishing. Riding 2 miles.

Open: All year.

Directions

From north use M6 exit 28 joining A49 going south (parallel to M6) for 2 miles. Then right across M6 on A581 to Croston (4 miles). From the south use exit 27 onto A5209 but immediately right on B5250 and follow towards Eccleston, joining A581 at Newtown (about 5 miles). Site is clearly signed with wide entrance east of Croston. O.S.GR: SD505189.

Charges -guide

Per grass pitch incl. 2 persons, electricity and awning	£ 8.50 - £ 13.00
hardstanding pitch	£ 9.50 - £ 17.40
extra adult	£ 2.50

Less 10% for 7 nights pre-booked.

 www.**alanrogers**.com for latest campsite news

UK5280 Abbey Farm Caravan Park

Dark Lane, Ormskirk L40 5TX (Lancashire)

Tel: **01695 572686**. Email: **abbeyfarm@yahoo.com**   **www.alanrogers.com/UK5280**

This quiet, well equipped, family park beside the Abbey ruins has views over open farmland. It is an ideal base for a longer stay with plenty of interest in the local area, including Ormskirk parish church, unusual for having both a tower and a spire. Market days are on Thursday and Saturday. The park is divided into small paddocks, one of which is for 30 privately owned seasonal units, one for tents, the others for touring units, plus a rally field for special events. The 60 touring pitches, all with electricity (10/16A), are on neatly mown level grass, separated by small shrubs and colourful flower borders. Some mature trees provide shade in parts. Amenities include a farm walk and a small, free lending library with good tourist information. The owners organise two annual events – a barbecue in early June and a Bonfire Night in November. They have planned plenty of routes for walkers from the park. Southport with its beach and Pleasureland is 10 miles. Wigan Pier, Aintree for the Grand National, the annual Beatles Festival or Southport Flower Show and Martin Mere Nature reserve are some of the attractions within easy reach. A member of the Countryside Discovery group.

Facilities

The main toilet block is modern, heated and spotless, providing controllable hot showers. Dual purpose family bathroom that includes facilities for disabled people. A second smaller unit has individual shower, WC and washbasin cubicles. Laundry room with washing machine, dryer, spinner, ironing board and airing cupboard. Small well stocked shop shares space with reception, with a butcher calling twice weekly. Indoor games room with table tennis and football games machine. Small adventure playground and large field for ball games. Fishing lake (£2 per rod, per day).

Open: All year.

Directions

From M6 junction 27 take A5209 (Parbold) road. After 5 miles turn left (just before garage) onto B5240, and then first right into Hob Cross Lane, following signs to site. O.S.GR: SD433099. GPS: N53:34.188 W02:51.399

Charges guide

Per unit incl. 2 persons	£ 7.00 - £ 16.60
serviced pitch	£ 15.60 - £ 15.90
extra person	£ 2.50
child (5-15 yrs)	£ 1.50

Less 10% for 7 nights booked on or before arrival.

UK5295 Eastham Hall Caravan Park

Saltcotes Road, Lytham Saint Annes FY8 4LS (Lancashire)

Tel: **01253 737907**. Email: **info@easthamhall.co.uk**   **www.alanrogers.com/UK5295**

Eastham Hall is a well established, family run park set in rural Lancashire between the Victorian town of Lytham and the pretty village of Wrea Green. Entering by an electronic barrier system, one sees an area of 150 caravan holiday homes. Quite separate are around 150 pitches for touring units and seasonal rental on open plan, mostly level grass, with 10A electricity throughout. Tents are not accepted. Recent additions include 11 large 'super' pitches on hardstanding and grass with full services including 16A electricity, A further 5 extra large pitches are on grass (units up to 28 feet can be taken). Mature trees border the park and shrubs and bushes separate the various areas. The reception is spacious with lots of tourist information and, at one end, is a large well stocked shop. The park has no bar or clubhouse, but Lytham is just five minutes by car or a pleasant twenty minute walk. The flat terrain is also ideal for cycling.

Facilities

Four toilet blocks are old and fairly basic, but are kept clean. New laundry. New facilities for disabled visitors. Gas supplies. Well stocked shop. Adventure play area and large sports field. Barrier (£10 deposit). Off site: Excellent pub in Wrea Green. Shops and restaurants in Lytham 2.5 miles. Blackpool 6 miles. Golf and riding 1 mile. Fishing 2.5 miles. Boat launching 2 miles. Local bus stops at entrance to park.

Open: 1 March - 31 October.

Directions

From M55 take exit 3 and turn left for Kirkham. At roundabouts follow signs for Wrea Green and Lytham. Continue on B5259 passing Grapes pub and village green. After 1.5 miles cross level crossing (Moss Side) and park is 1 mile on left. O.S.GR: SD377290. GPS: N53:45.225 W02:56.535

Charges guide

Per unit incl. 1-4 persons	£ 10.00 - £ 15.00
incl. electricity	£ 15.00 - £ 22.00
serviced pitch	£ 18.00 - £ 25.00
dog	£ 1.00

209

UK5271 Old Hall Caravan Park

Capernwray, Carnforth LA6 1AD (Lancashire)

Tel: **01524 733276**. Email: **info@oldhallcaravanpark.co.uk**   www.alanrogers.com/UK5271

In a woodland clearing, just five minutes drive from junction 35 of the M6, Old Hall Caravan Park is a gem. Approached along a tree-lined road, this secluded park offers peace and tranquillity. There are 38 touring pitches which are accessed from a circular roadway,. They are all on marked and level hardstandings and with 15A electricity, water and drainage (shared between two pitches). TV aerial hook-ups are also available for hire. Tents are not accepted on this park. There are 220 privately owned holiday homes which are quite separate from the touring pitches.

Facilities

The central sanitary block (combination lock) is very clean and is heated during cooler months. Vanity style washbasins and large controllable showers. Separate unit for disabled visitors doubles as a family room. Laundry facilities. Gas supplies. Off site: Canal fishing 100 yds. Over Kellet 2 miles. Carnforth 3 miles. Historic Lancaster and the seaside town of Morecambe (15 minutes drive).

Open: 1 March - 10 January.

Directions

From M6 exit 35 take link road signed Over Kellet. Turn left on B6254. At Over Kellet village green turn left signed Capernwray and follow for 1.5 miles. Park is on the right at the end of a 0.5 mile drive. O.S.GR: SD538718. GPS: N54:08.375 W02:42.814

Charges guide

Per unit incl. electricicy	£ 16.50 - £ 18.50
awning	£ 1.00 - £ 2.00

UK5300 Kneps Farm Holiday Park

River Road, Stanah, Thornton-Cleveleys FY5 5LR (Lancashire)

Tel: **01253 823632**. Email: **enquiries@knepsfarm.co.uk**   www.alanrogers.com/UK5300

A well established park with top class modern facilities, Kneps Farm is still operated by the family who opened it in 1967. Next to Wyre Country Park, it makes an excellent base from which to explore the area. A VNPR operated barrier system flanks the reception building which also houses a well stocked shop. The 60 marked and numbered touring pitches are generally on hardstandings with electricity (16A) available to most, and all are accessed from tarmac roads. There are also some grassy pitches and a separate area with 70 caravan holiday homes (most privately owned).

Facilities

The excellent, large, centrally heated sanitary building is warm and inviting with ten individual family bathrooms, each providing a WC, basin and bath/shower. Separate toilet facilities with electric hand-wash units for men and women. Well equipped room for disabled visitors. Combined baby care/first aid room. Laundry room. Shop. Small, fenced playground. Up to two dogs are accepted per unit. Off site: Fishing 0.25 miles. Golf 2.5 miles.

Open: 1 March - 15 November.

Directions

From M55 exit 3, take A585 towards Fleetwood. Turn left at traffic lights, then turn right at traffic lights (Thornton-Cleveleys), straight across next lights, then right at the roundabout by River Wyre Hotel. After 1 mile turn right at roundabout into Stanah Road, continue into River Road with site ahead O.S.GR: SD350430. GPS: N53:52.742 W02:59.104

Charges guide

Per unit incl. 2 adults, 2 children and electricity	£ 22.50 - £ 25.00
Special Senior Citizen rates.	

UK5330 Marton Mere Holiday Village

Mythop Road, Blackpool FY4 4NX (Lancashire)

Tel: **01253 767544**. Email: **sarah.corlett@bourne-leisure.co.uk**   www.alanrogers.com/UK5330

If Blackpool is your holiday destination and your family are looking for lots to do then this Haven Holidays park may well be a suitable choice. Although mainly used for static caravan holiday homes, there are 148 touring pitches with hardstanding, of which 60 are fully serviced. All have electricity hook ups (10/16A). A few trees give a small amount of shade, but as with a lot of coastal sites, it can be a little windy. On site there is plenty of entertainment including three licensed bars, discos and the Rainbow room where children are entertained.

Facilities

Two heated toilet blocks (key pad entry system) have piped music playing and although of older design are clean and well kept with large pre-set showers and hairdryers. EWell stocked supermarket, bars, fast food outlets and restaurants. Outdoor splash pool and heated indoor pool with flume, jacuzzi and sauna. Amusement arcades, multisport court, crazy golf and bowling. Two children's clubs with full entertainment schedule. Off site: Martin Mere nature reserve. Blackpool.

Open: 24 March - 30 October.

Directions

From M55 junction 4, turn right at roundabout taking A583 towards Blackpool. Pass the windmill, then right at the traffic lights by the Clifton Arms into Mythop Road. Park is on the left O.S.GR: SD344351. GPS: N53:48.171 W02:59.488

Charges guide

Per unit incl. up to 4 persons and electricity	£ 11.00 - £ 13.00
extra person	£ 2.00 - £ 3.00
Variety of special offers available.	

www.**alanrogers**.com for latest campsite news

MAP 5

Cumbria

With spectacular lakes, undulating fells, impressive mountains and lush green valleys, Cumbria is ideal for those who wish to get away from it all and unwind in peaceful, natural surroundings, or for the more active who want to participate in a range of outdoor pursuits.

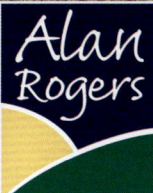

Cumbria is best known for the beautiful Lake District National Park, with the picturesque valleys and lakes of Windermere, Ullswater and Derwentwater, each with its own distinctive character. Windermere offers no shortage of watersports, whereas Ullswater mainly attracts peaceful sailing boats. While the Lake District is well known, there are also many quiet, undiscovered areas in the region including the wild, rugged moors of the north Pennines and the beautiful Eden Valley, an ideal place for a casual stroll along the riverside footpaths. The Western Lakes and Fells offer more tranquillity. Here the fells drop down to a long and spectacular coastline, with many undiscovered, quiet corners from Ennerdale and Esdale to the sandstone cliffs of St Bees Head, now part of a designated Heritage Coast. The Lake District Peninsulas along the southern coast of Cumbria also display beautiful scenery and are home to a cluster of ancient ruins such as Furness Abbey and the medieval castle, built by monks, on Piel Island. Rich in heritage, the historic city of Carlisle, which was sited on the Roman built Hadrian's wall, boasts an impressive castle, Cumbria's only cathedral, a superb Victorian covered market and an array of speciality shops.

Places of interest

Barrow-in-Furness: South Lakes Wild Animal Park; Dalton Castle; Furness Abbey; Piel Island.

Carlisle: 11th century castle; Birdoswald Roman fort; Lanercost Priory.

Ravenglass: Muncaster Castle, an historic haunted castle and Headquarters of the World Owl Trust.

Ulverston: the world's only Laurel and Hardy museum.

Kendal: historic riverside town situated between the Lakes and Dales, famous for its mint cake and castle ruins.

Lake Derwentwater: lakeside theatre open all year hosting plays, music, dance, comedy and film.

Windermere: Steamboat Centre, a collection of Windermere's nautical heritage with boats on display; World of Beatrix Potter.

Grasmere: Dove Cottage and Wordsworth Museum.

Did you know?

Cumbria has the steepest road in England, called the Hardknott Pass.

The Lake District was the inspiration for many poets, writers and artists, including William Wordsworth, Beatrix Potter and John Ruskin.

Ulverston is the birthplace of Quakerism and pole vaulting.

Bassenthwaite is the only real lake in the Lake District! All the others are either meres, (Windermere) or waters (Derwentwater, Coniston Water and Ullswater).

Stretching 73 miles, Hadrian's Wall was built by Romans in the second century.

RED TEXT DENOTES ALL YEAR SITE

UK5506 Hylton Caravan Park

Eden Street, Silloth, Wigton CA7 4AY (Cumbria)

Tel: 01697 332666. Email: ericstanwix@stanwix.com

www.alanrogers.com/UK5506

Hylton Caravan Park is owned and managed by the Stanwix family and although it is only a short walk away from the livelier Stanwix Leisure Park, it is a peaceful haven for people who prefer the 'quiet life'. The only activity is an adventure park for children which is not visible from the touring area. Divided by a circular road, the 170 privately owned caravan holiday homes are visible but not intrusive. There are 90 open plan, mostly level touring and tent pitches, all fully serviced and with 10A electricity. There is no shop on site as the town and Stanwix Holiday Park are both within walking distance. Club membership for the extensive leisure and entertainment amenities at Stanwix Park is free of charge for the duration of your stay. Local attractions include the Ravenglass - Eskdale Miniature Railway where, the nearby World Owl Centre at Muncaster is a must.

Facilities

A high quality toilet block is superbly fitted out and includes toilets, showers, vanity style washbasins, extra large bathrooms and a separate cubicle for disabled people. Dishwashing under cover. Fully equipped laundry. Gas sales. Off site: Bus stop 1 mile. Entertainment and amenities at Stanwix Park. Silloth golf course. Bowling. Windsurfing and boat launching 1 mile. Riding 7 miles.

Open: 1 March - 15 November.

Directions

On entering Silloth, turn left following signs to Hylton Caravan Park. O.S.GR: NY114534.
GPS: N54:52.100 W03:23.901

Charges guide

Per person	£ 3.60 - £ 4.30
child (under 5 yrs)	£ 2.30 - £ 2.75
pitch	£ 8.90 - £ 11.05

UK5505 Stanwix Park Holiday Centre

Greenrow, Silloth, Wigton CA7 4HH (Cumbria)

Tel: 01697 332666. Email: enquiries@stanwix.com

www.alanrogers.com/UK5505

Stanwix Park is a family run holiday park with absolutely everything anyone could want for a memorable holiday all year round. The park has 83 caravan holiday homes and 28 chalets for rent, together with 212 which are privately owned. These are mostly located around the central complex. In addition at either end of the park, there are 121 fully serviced (10A electricity) pitches for touring units and tents, some on grass, some with hardstanding. The central complex holds all the indoor and outdoor amenities (many of which are included in the nightly fees). A warm welcome awaits in the main reception. The indoor tropical leisure centre contains a 29 m. fun pool with slides, a steam room, sauna, spa, fitness gym and vertical sun shower (charge). The upper floor has the Sky Bar and Dunes Cabaret Bar (adults only) with the Sunset Inn licensed family club, all enjoying nightly entertainment and special themed weekends from November to March. A giant TV and snooker room are in the Gallery observation area with a state-of-the-art, newly refurbished Astro Bowling Centre (charged) and amusement arcade, with a soft play area and ball pond to one side. Outside are a large, terraced swimming pool, an adventure play area and minigolf, all screened by plants and shrubs, Tennis courts and bicycle hire are also available (charge).

Facilities

The two heated sanitary blocks have been recently refurbished to a high standard and are adjacent to the pitches, kept spotlessly clean and opened by combination lock. Large en-suite bathrooms, showers, vanity style washbasins and a unit in each for disabled visitors. Campers kitchen. Fully equipped laundry. Gas sales. Well stocked shop (6/3-15/11). Restaurant with takeaway (all year). Bars (adults only and family) with evening entertainment (6/3-15/11). TV and snooker room. Indoor leisure centre. Outdoor swimming pool (31/5-1/9). Ten-pin bowling centre. Amusement arcade. Soft play area. Minigolf. Tennis. Bicycle hire. Off site: Bus service 1 mile in Silloth (easy walk). Silloth golf club, bowling club and sports ground a short walk. Beach 1 mile.

Open: All year.

Directions

From the south, take exit 41 from the M6 and follow B5305 through Wigton to Silloth. From north on A74/M6 take exit 44 and the A595 and A596 to Wigton. On entering Silloth, turn left following signs for park. Entrance is on the right. O.S.GR: NY108525. GPS: N54:51.684 W03:23.300

Charges guide

Per person	£ 3.60 - £ 4.80
child (under 5 yrs)	£ 2.30 - £ 2.75
pitch	£ 11.15 - £ 13.80
dog (max. 2)	£ 3.00

Many special offers and short break prices.

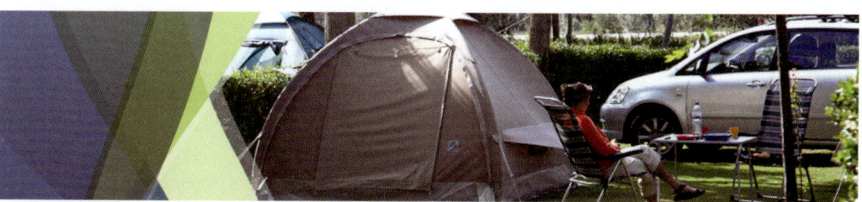

UK5510 The Larches Caravan Park

Mealsgate, Wigton CA7 1LQ (Cumbria)

Tel: **01697 371379**. Email: **info@larchescaravanpark.co.uk**   www.alanrogers.com/UK5510

Mealsgate and The Larches lie on the Carlisle - Cockermouth road, a little removed from the hectic centre of the Lake District, yet with easy access to it (and good views towards it) and to other attractions nearby – the Western Borders, Northumberland, etc. It is a quality, family run park which takes 73 touring units of any type and also accommodates 100 privately owned holiday homes. Touring pitches are in different grassy areas with tall, mature trees, shrubs and accompanying wildlife. Some are sloping and irregular, others on marked hardstandings, with 10A electricity, water and drainage. Events in the surrounding district each day displayed prominently in the window of the shop. On arrival visitors are loaned very comprehensive tourist information brochures. There are bus routes to Carlisle and Keswick, walks from the park and good restaurants nearby. The Elliott family provide a warm welcome at this peaceful, well organised park which is undergoing some redevelopment. This is an ideal haven for couples – only adult visitors are accepted.

Facilities

Toilet facilities, in two purpose designed blocks, are of good quality providing en-suite facilities for both sexes. Washbasins for ladies are in cubicles, those for men set in flat surfaces. Separate unit for disabled visitors can be heated. Campers' kitchen with cooker and microwave (metered). Laundry room. Well stocked shop incl. camping accessories, gas and off-licence. Small indoor heated pool. Table tennis. Wildlife pond. Caravan storage. Off site: Golf 3.5 miles. Bicycle hire 7 miles. Fishing 8 miles. Riding 10 miles.

Open: 1 March - 31 October.

Directions

Park entrance is south off the A595 (Carlisle - Cockermouth) road just southwest of Mealsgate. O.S.GR: NY206415. GPS: N54:45.796 W03:14.148

Charges guide

Per unit incl. 2 adults	£ 11.50 - £ 13.90
incl. electricity	£ 13.50 - £ 15.90
extra person	£ 2.00 - £ 2.50
awning or extra car	£ 1.00 - £ 2.00
backpacker	£ 6.00 - £ 7.50

Discounts for senior citizens and bookings over 7 nights. No credit cards.

UK5520 Skelwith Fold Caravan Park

Ambleside LA22 0HX (Cumbria)

Tel: **01539 432277**. Email: **info@skelwith.com**   www.alanrogers.com/UK5520

Skelwith Fold has been developed in the extensive grounds of a country estate taking advantage of the wealth of mature trees and shrubs. The 300 privately owned caravan holiday homes and 150 touring pitches are absorbed into this unspoilt natural environment, sharing it with red squirrels and other wildlife in several discrete areas branching off the central, mile long main driveway. Touring pitches (no tents) are on gravel hardstanding and metal pegs will be necessary for awnings. Electricity hook-ups (10A) and basic amenities are available in all areas. Youngsters and indeed their parents will find endless pleasure exploring over 90 acres of wild woodland and, if early risers, it is possible to see deer, foxes, etc. at the almost hidden tarn deep in the woods. This is a fascinating site where you feel at home with nature at any time of the year, but it is particularly beautiful in the spring with wild daffodils, bluebells and later in the season, rhododendrons and azaleas. Only caravans, motorcaravans and trailer tents are accepted.

Facilities

Eight toilet blocks, well situated to serve all areas, have the usual facilities including laundry, drying and ironing rooms. Some blocks have facilities for disabled visitors. Well stocked, licensed shop. Battery charging, gas and caravan spares and accessories. Adventure play area. Family recreation area with picnic tables and goal posts in the Lower Glade. Bicycle hire. Off site: Ambleside village 1.5 miles. Pubs within walking distance. Fishing 200 m. Riding 3 miles.

Open: 1 March - 15 November.

Directions

From Ambleside take the A593 towards Coniston. Pass through Clappergate and on the far outskirts watch for the B5286 to Hawkshead on the left. Park is clearly signed 1 mile down this road on the right. O.S.GR: NY358028. GPS: N54:25:029 W02:59.717

Charges guide

Per pitch	£ 17.50 - £ 20.00
incl. electricity	£ 20.50 - £ 23.00
awning	£ 3.00

Discounts for weekly or monthly stays.

UK5570 **Wild Rose Park**

Ormside, Appleby-in-Westmorland CA16 6EJ (Cumbria)

Tel: **01768 351077**. Email: **reception@wildrose.co.uk**   **www.alanrogers.com/UK5570**

Set in the Eden Valley within easy reach of the Lake District and the Yorkshire Dales, Wild Rose is a well known park. The entrance is inviting with its well mown grass, trim borders and colourful flower displays. It is immediately apparent that this is a much loved park, and this is reflected throughout the site in the care and attention to detail. There are 226 touring pitches with on-site wardens to ensure that everything is always neat and tidy. Wild Rose deserves its excellent reputation, which the owners strive to maintain and improve. There are five distinct areas on the park providing a variety of pitches and services. Hazel Heights and Egglestone Tiers provide fully serviced 'super' pitches with hardstanding, Braithwaite Fold and the Chesters have pitches with electricity and shared water points. The grass area of Donkey's Nest provides pitches with shared electricity and water. There are also 268 privately owned caravan holiday homes and lodges and 4 wooden 'wigwams' to rent providing all year round luxurious camping. Nothing is overlooked here, from recycling bins, electric buggies to keep the noise down, 'sac-o-mat' special bags and bins in the dog walk to cycle racks placed around the park. A member of the Best of British group.

Facilities

Three toilet blocks (two heated) of excellent quality and kept spotlessly clean. Most washbasins are in cubicles. Facilities for babies and for disabled visitors. Fully equipped laundry with washing lines and drying rooms. Motorcaravan service point. Exceptionally well stocked shop incl. gas (1/3-1/11). Licensed restaurant with takeaway and conservatory/coffee lounge (weekends only in low seasons). Outdoor pool (late May - Sept and open 10.00 -18.00). Indoor playroom for under fives. Games room. TV room. Cinema room. Tennis. Off site: Fishing 2 miles. Golf and riding 3 miles.

Open: All year.

Directions

Park is signed south off B6260 road 1.5 miles southwest of Appleby. Follow signs to park, in the direction of Ormside. O.S.GR: NY697165. GPS: N54:32.644 W02:28.197

Charges guide

Per unit incl. 2 persons	£ 17.00 - £ 25.50
'super' pitch incl. mains services	£ 22.00 - £ 31.50
extra person (over 4 yrs)	£ 3.00 - £ 4.00
walker or cyclist	£ 7.00
dog	£ 1.50

Less 10% for 7 nights or more and for over 60s. Special long-stay rates.

215

UK5540 Fallbarrow Park

Rayrigg Road, Bowness, Windermere LA23 3DL (Cumbria)

Tel: 01539 444422. Email: enquiries@southlakeland-caravans.co.uk   www.alanrogers.com/UK5540

Fallbarrow Park is most attractively situated alongside Lake Windermere with a lake frontage of about 600 yards; one can stroll among the lawns and gardens near the lake. The major part of the park is occupied by around 225 caravan holiday homes, with about 57 for letting, the remainder privately owned. In the 'Lake' area (not actually by the lake, but some pitches have lake views), there are 38 fenced or hedged touring pitches, all with hardstanding, fresh and waste water points, electric hook-up (10/16A) and TV aerial connection. The Boathouse pub has a spacious and comfortable lounge with bar meals and snacks, ideal for relaxation as the sun sets. Fallbarrow has launched a new 'Deli and Café' (The Barn) where a varied menu includes fresh, local produce. With direct access to the lake, a slipway and jetty make boat launching easy. The site has a boat park with winter storage facilities and can cater for craft up to 18 ft. in length. Amenities for children include a multi-activity play area and outdoor fun and games. Reception is smart and comfortable, with plenty of tourist information. The centre of Bowness is only a short walk and facilities for pony trekking and numerous visitor attractions are nearby.

Facilities

Two excellent toilet blocks serve the touring sections (combination locks) with top quality fittings and heating when required, controllable showers, make-up and hairdressing areas and a baby washroom. Very well equipped laundry. Motorcaravan service point. Well stocked supermarket. Gas. Bar and 'eatery'. Café bar. Fishing. Adventure play area and sports field. Entertainment (dates vary). Internet access. Boat launching and marina. American motorhomes are accepted by prior arrangement. Only one dog per booking. Off site: Bicycle hire 1 mile. Riding 2 miles. Golf 3 miles. Indoor pool at UK5555 White Cross (charged).

Open: 1 March - 14 January.

Directions

Park is beside the A592 road just north of Bowness town centre. O.S.GR: SD401971.
GPS: N54:22.007 W02:55.246

Charges guide

Per unit incl. 2 adults and 2 children	£ 18.00 - £ 27.00
extra person	£ 2.00
child	£ 1.00 - £ 1.50
awning	£ 3.50
dog	£ 3.00

UK5550 Limefitt Park

Windermere LA23 1PA (Cumbria)

Tel: 01539 432300. Email: enquiries@southlakelandparks,co.uk   www.alanrogers.com/UK5550

Part of the South Lakeland Holiday Group, Limefitt Park is located in a really beautiful Lakeland valley with fine views and ideal for walking and cycling. Four miles from Windermere, it is also centrally located for the attractions of the southern Lake District. Of the 151 pitches, 73 are for touring units. These include 38 on hardstanding with direct connections for electricity, TV, fresh water and waste water, and a further 85 hardstanding pitches are fully serviced. Pitches for tents are in a separate area. The ground by the beck has been developed for 65 log cabins (for private sale) in addition to some caravan holiday homes (a few for hire). With various active pursuits on offer nearby and some evening entertainment, this park is designed for families and couples. Activities available from the park include fell walking and pony trekking. Away from the camping area by the river are a play field and an adventure playground on grass and a small riverside area with picnic tables. The park is popular throughout the season so advance reservation is recommended.

Facilities

Sanitary facilities are of excellent quality, well equipped with modern fittings, with one large, central block for the tenting area and a smaller block for the caravan area (combination locks). Toddler rooms with half-size bath and changing facilities. Campers' kitchen. Launderette. Motorcaravan service point. Gas supplies. Supermarket. Bar (real ales), bar meals and takeaway, all open all season. Weekly entertainment. Games room with many machines. Play area. Riding. Play area. Dogs are not accepted. Off site: Fishing 2 miles. Bicycle hire 4 miles. Golf 5 miles. Swimming pool at nearby UK5555 White Cross Bay (charged).

Open: 1 March - 15 November.

Directions

Limefitt is 2.5 miles north up the A592 from its junction with the A591 north of Windermere.
O.S.GR: NY416030. GPS: N54:25.210 W02:54.210

Charges guide

Per unit incl. 2 adults, 2 children and electricity	£ 16.50 - £ 27.00
tent incl. 2 adults, 2 children	£ 18.50 - £ 27.00
extra person	£ 2.00
child (2-14 yrs)	£ 1.00

UK5555 White Cross Bay Leisure Park & Marina

Ambleside Road, Windermere LA23 1LF (Cumbria)

Tel: **01539 443937**. Email: **enquiries@southlakeland-caravans.co.uk**   www.alanrogers.com/UK5555

On the shores of Lake Windernere, White Cross Bay Leisure Park and Marina has a scenic location in a perfect holiday destination for watersports enthusiasts. A large part of the park is occupied by privately owned chalets and holiday homes of which 100 are to let. These are near or overlooking the lake. The Woodside area provides just 26 pitches for touring units, a short walk from the shores of the lake. These are located on large hardstanding areas (steel pegs required), together with many seasonal pitches. The busy main road is close by so noise could be a problem in this area. Electricity (10A) is available via a £1 meter card. We are told that the touring area and its toilet block are to be upgraded. The park's amenities otherwise are really first class. In addition to an excellent marina, there is an indoor pool with sauna, solarium and a gym (charged) and a large games room. There are tennis courts, an adventure play park, picnic areas and woodland walks near the lake. The main complex provides a large reception, a good shop, an attractive restaurant and a comfortable bar.

Facilities

Two toilet blocks serve the park (combination locks). The one adjacent to the touring area is heated and clean, but rather old (renovation planned). Open style washbasins and preset showers with curtains only. Baby changing. Laundry room. The other block (Marina) is a purpose built chalet type building quite close to the lake. It provides facilities for disabled visitors. Shop. Restaurant. Bar and games room. Indoor pool complex (charged). Tennis. Play area. Fishing. Internet access. Marina and boat launching. Off site: Golf, riding and bicycle hire 5 miles.

Open: 1 March - 14 November.

Directions

From M6 exit 36, take A591 to Windermere. Continue on the A591 towards Ambleside and park is 2 miles on the left. O.S.GR: NY395004. GPS: N54:23.788 W02:55.891

Charges guide

Per unit incl. 2 adults and 2 children	£ 16.50 - £ 23.00
extra person	£ 2.00
child	£ 1.00
dog	£ 3.00

UK5545 Park Cliffe Camping & Caravan Estate

Birks Road, Windermere LA23 3PG (Cumbria)

Tel: **01539 531344**. Email: **info@parkcliffe.co.uk**   www.alanrogers.com/UK5545

Set in the heart of the Lake District National Park, this attractive park has been recently acquired by the Holgates family. Sitting high in open countryside it has spectacular views over the Lakeland Fells and Lake Windermere. Well managed and maintained, the park is neat and tidy with attractive shrubs and plants in local, stone-built troughs set around the entrance. The touring pitches here have been redeveloped into numbered gravel hardstandings with electricity (10A), water and drainage services. There are also 24 seasonal pitches positioned high on the hillside with commanding views.

Facilities

The central main building includes two blocks of toilets and showers. These are tiled, heated and very clean with vanity style washbasins, full facilities for disabled visitors and excellent baby room. Laundry. Motorcaravan service point. Bar. Restaurant and takeaway. Small well stocked shop. Freezer (20p). Games room. Large adventure play area. Off site: Fellfoot Park with boat launching.

Open: 1 March - 14 November.

Directions

From M6 exit 36 take A590 to Newby Bridge. Turn right on A592 for 3.6 miles and turn right. Site is signed shortly on the right. Caravans and trailers must approach this way on the A592. O.S.GR: SD391911. GPS: N54:18.751 W02:56.250

Charges guide

Per unit incl. 2 persons and electricity	£ 23.00 - £ 25.00

217

UK5560 Sykeside Camping Park

Brotherswater, Patterdale, Penrith CA11 0NZ (Cumbria)

Tel: 01768 482239. Email: info@sykeside.co.uk   www.alanrogers.com/UK5560

This small touring park is located in a really beautiful, quiet spot in the northern Lakes area (it is just 400 yards from Brotherswater). The site is surrounded by the fells and is ideal for active outdoor holidays with walking or climbing on the high hills. With views up the Dovedale valley, the park has 100 pitches in the valley floor, including several hardstandings. Caravans are now permitted and the access road has been improved. Pitches are not marked and campers arrange themselves to best enjoy the superb views. There are 19 electrical connections (5/10A). The stone-built building, an original barn, near the entrance just 200 yards from the field, houses all the facilities. These include the recently extended and refurbished Barn End bar where meals are served.

Facilities

The toilet block includes hot showers and has been refurbished, with a chemical disposal point added. Small launderette and dishwashing room. Self-service shop with camping equipment, gas and an ice-pack service, doubles as reception. Cosy licensed bar and restaurant (daily in summer, weekends only in winter). Bunkhouse for 30 persons in various groupings. Fishing nearby. Off site: Bicycle hire 3 miles. Riding 8 miles. Golf 10 miles. The Brotherswater Inn is adjacent (open all year).

Open: All year.

Directions

Site is on the west side of the A592 road, about 2 miles south of Patterdale, which lies at the southwestern end of Ullswater. Entrance is just behind the Brotherswater Inn. O.S.GR: NY396005. GPS: N54:29.910 W02:55.530

Charges guide

Per tent incl. 2 persons and car caravan or motorcaravan	£ 12.00 - £ 20.00
incl. 2 persons and electricity	£ 16.00 - £ 22.00
child (5-16 yrs)	£ 2.00
dog	£ 1.50
Min. charge for motorcaravan £15 per night.	

UK5590 Westmorland Caravan Park

Tebay, Orton, Penrith CA10 3SB (Cumbria)

Tel: 01539 711322. Email: caravans@westmorland.com   www.alanrogers.com/UK5590

For caravans, motorhomes and trailer tents only, this is the ideal stopover for anyone heading either north or south, near the M6 motorway, but far enough away for the traffic noise not to be too disturbing. There are 83 level pitches on gravel, divided into bays of about six or seven units (29 are for touring units). All touring pitches have electricity (10/16A). The bays are backed by grassy banks alive with rabbits and birds – a long list in the office describes the large variety of birds to be seen on the site. There is good site lighting and a late arrivals area.

Facilities

The heated toilet block is kept very clean. Showers. Facilities for disabled visitors planned. Sinks for laundry and dishwashing. Laundry. Reception sells gas. Off site: Shops and restaurants five minutes walk away at the motorway service area.

Open: 5 March - 2 November.

Directions

From the M6, just north of junction 38, exit for Tebay Services (site signed). Site is accessible from the services travelling north or south. O.S.GR: NY607060. GPS: N54:26.862 W02:36.388

Charges guide

Per unit incl. 4 persons and electricity	£ 15.50 - £ 18.50

UK5600 Pennine View Caravan & Camping Park

Station Road, Kirkby Stephen CA17 4SZ (Cumbria)

Tel: 01768 371717   www.alanrogers.com/UK5600

Suitable for night halts or longer breaks to visit the Lake District or the Yorkshire Dales, Pennine View is a super small park, well managed and well maintained. With a very attractive rockery at the entrance, the whole site is very neat and tidy. Level, numbered pitches with gravel hardstanding are arranged around the perimeter with grass pitches in the centre. The pitches are of a good size (some being especially large) and are all are supplied with electricity (16A). One end of the park adjoins the River Eden with steps leading down huge projecting stone slabs on the river bank.

Facilities

Built of local stone, the modern toilet block is accessed by a digital keypad and includes individual wash cubicles and deep sink for a baby bath. Both ladies and men have large en-suite units for disabled visitors. Well equipped laundry room. Gas available. Play area. Off site: Nearby hotel offers bar meals. Kirkby Stephen 1 mile. Bicycle hire 300 m. Golf 4 miles.

Open: 1 March - 31 October.

Directions

Park is on the A685 on the southerly outskirts of Kirkby Stephen. Turn left opposite the Croglin Castle hotel. Site is 50 yds. on right. O.S.GR: NY772075. GPS: N54:27.700 W02:21.202

Charges guide

Per person	£ 5.10 - £ 5.50
child (4-15 yrs)	£ 2.00 - £ 2.50
pitch	£ 5.00 - £ 6.00

UK5620 Cove Camping Park

Ullswater, Watermillock, Penrith CA11 0LS (Cumbria)

Tel: **01768 486549**. Email: **info@cove-park.co.uk**   www.alanrogers.com/UK5620

Cove Camping is a delightful small site, some of the 50 pitches having great views over Lake Ullswater. A separate area behind the camping field holds 39 privately owned caravan holiday homes. The grass is well trimmed, there are ramps to keep speeds down to 5 mph. and the site is well lit. At the top of the park are 17 level pitches with electric hook-ups and hardstanding suitable for touring caravans and motorcaravans. The rest of the park is quite sloping. Rubbish bins are hidden behind wooden fencing, as are recycling bins. The park is well situated for walking, boating, fishing and pony trekking activities. The road up from the A592 is narrow, but a self imposed one way system is generally adhered to and the warden will advise on a different way to leave the site.

Facilities

The tiled toilet block is immaculate and heated in cooler months, providing adjustable showers, some washbasins in cabins and, for ladies, a hairdressing area with stool and a baby changing unit. Foyer containing a freezer (free), and tourist information. Laundry with washing machine, dryer and an iron. Gas supplies. Small, grass based play area. Off site: Shop nearby. Fishing 1.5 miles. Riding 3 miles. Golf 6 mile. Bicycle hire 7 miles (will deliver).

Open: March - 31 October.

Directions

We would advise using the following directions rather than GPS. From A66 Penrith - Keswick road, take A592 south, signed Ullswater. Turn right at Brackenrigg Inn (site signed) and follow road uphill for about 1.5 miles to park on left. This road is narrow so if you have a larger unit, telephone the park for advice about an alternative route.
O.S.GR: NY431236. GPS: N54:36.257 W02:52.913

Charges guide

Per unit incl. 2 persons and electricity	£ 15.00 - £ 25.00
tent incl. 2 persons	£ 10.00 - £ 22.00
extra person (5 yrs and over)	£ 2.00
dog	£ 1.00

No credit cards.

UK5625 Lowther Holiday Park

Eamont Bridge, Penrith CA10 2JB (Cumbria)

Tel: **01768 863631**. Email: **alan@lowther-holidaypark.co.uk**   www.alanrogers.com/UK5625

Sitting on the banks of the River Lowther this holiday park occupies 50 acres of rural, wooded parkland, home to the rare red squirrel. There are 400 caravan holiday homes and lodges around the park, together with 200 touring pitches. A proportion of these are taken by seasonal lets. Marked and numbered, on mostly level ground between mature trees, they have 10A electricity and hardstanding. A separate elevated grass area is available for tents. There is a small touring office with 24 hour security adjacent to the holiday home sales office. Here too is a well stocked, licensed shop also selling some caravan accessories. The Squirrel Inn is open all season and serves restaurant meals and takeaways. Outside is a large paved seating area with a play area to one side. A lovely riverside walk has been created with many benches to rest and enjoy the birds and other wildlife.

Facilities

Two toilet blocks are central to the touring areas (key entry). Very clean, they provide large, preset showers. Fully equipped bathroom with baby changing. Drive through motorcaravan service. Well equipped laundry. Full facilities for disabled visitors (Radar key). Licensed shop. Squirrel Inn with restaurant, terrace and games room. Play areas. Fly fishing on river (permit from office). Activity weekends. Live entertainment and children's parties. Max. two dogs per unit. Off site: Market town of Penrith 3 miles. Golf, riding and bicycle hire 2 miles. Boat launching 4 miles.

Open: March - November.

Directions

From M6 exit 40 take A66 towards Scotch Corner for 1 mile. At roundabout take A6 south for 1 mile towards Shap. Lowther is on the right as you pass through village of Eamont Bridge.
O.S.GR: NY527264. GPS: N54:38.860 W02:44.221

Charges guide

Per unit incl. 1-6 persons and electricity	£ 18.00 - £ 22.00

UK5605 Woodclose Caravan Park

Kirkby Lonsdale LA6 2SE (Cumbria)

Tel: 01524 271597. Email: info@woodcloseentre.com   www.alanrogers.com/UK5605

Woodclose is an established, nine acre park with new owners. Situated in the Lune Valley and just one mile from the market town of Kirkby Lonsdale, this park offers a peaceful and secluded setting catering for walkers, tourers and people who just want to relax. Access to the park is narrow, so care should be taken. The whole park has a very well cared for appearance with well mown grass, flowering tubs and neat hedges. The upper part contains many privately owned holiday homes with neat terraces built from local stone. Screened by a hedge and placed around the perimeter are several seasonal pitches with touring units being placed in the centre. These pitches are numbered and mostly level, some on hardstanding, some on grass, with 16A electricity and digital TV hook-ups. More seasonal pitches and holiday homes on the lower part of the park, again most attractively terraced with stone walling and paths. Reception is part of the well stocked shop which includes local produce and fresh baked bread; an information room is adjoining with tables and chairs and internet access (£1 per half an hour).

Facilities

Two toilet blocks, the main one central to the touring area. These facilities are all unisex in large, heated, individual rooms with toilets, washbasin and toilet or washbasin and shower, all well equipped and very clean. Indoor dishwashing, well equipped laundry and chemical disposal within the same building. The second block is in the lower part, again all unisex in cubicles together with an indoor dishwashing area. No motorcaravan service point, but facilities for disabled visitors have been installed. Shop. Small adventure play area. Bicycle hire. Internet access. American style motorhomes accepted (limited space). Gates locked 24.00-07.30, warden and telephone on site for emergencies. Off site: Golf 1 mile. Fishing 7 miles. Beach 20 miles.

Open: 1 March - 1 November.

Directions

From M6 exit 36 take A65 to Kirkby Lonsdale. Site is off the A65 in 6 miles. O.S.GR: SD620781. GPS: N54:11.901 W02:35.101

Charges guide

Per unit incl. 2 persons	
and electricity	£ 10.00 - £ 20.00
tent incl. 2 persons	£ 12.00 - £ 14.00
extra person	£ 3.75
child (5-16 yrs)	£ 2.00
awning	£ 2.00

Book for 7 nights and receive 1 night free (high season only).

UK5615 Hill of Oaks Caravan Park

Tower Wood, Windermere LA12 8NR (Cumbria)

Tel: 01539 531578. Email: enquiries@hillofoaks.co.uk   www.alanrogers.com/UK5615

This park on the banks of Lake Windermere lives up to its name 'Hill of Oaks'. Set on a hillside in mature woodland, the park offers families a safe natural environment with nature walks through the managed ancient woodlands, as well as six jetties for boat launching and access to watersport activities (jet skis are not allowed). The road into the park passing the farmhouse is long, winding and narrow, so care should be taken especially with long outfits, reception being about half a mile from the entrance. The entrance barrier is open from 08.00 until dusk with a security code being provided for exit. The reception and shop selling basics with a tourist information room adjacent are on the lakeside in wooden chalet-type buildings with an abundance of hanging baskets and flowers. Privately owned caravan holiday homes have been built into the hillside on terraces and are quite unobtrusive, screened by hedges and trees. Although the park is situated on Lake Windermere the touring pitches nestle within the trees, not actually by the lake. All 43 have electricity (16A), digital TV hook-up and hardstanding, most large enough to take a car and boat. Three large super pitches, all hardstanding, have 16A electricity, drain, water and digital TV. Tents are not accepted.

Facilities

The central tiled toilet block, recently refurbished, is very clean and heated. Vanity style washbasins, controllable showers and free hairdryers. Baby changing areas. Fully equipped laundry. Dishwashing area under cover. New unit for disabled visitors (combination lock). Recycling bins. Motorcaravan service point. Shop for basics. Two fenced play areas, one for toddlers and adventure type for over 5s. Picnic areas and nature trails. Fishing (licence required). Off site: Fell Foot Park and Gardens 1 mile, with rowing boat hire or ferry rides to Lakeside or Ambleside. Aquarium of the Lakes (3.5 miles) at Newby Bridge. Golf 4 miles. Riding and bicycle hire 6 miles.

Open: 1 March - 14 November.

Directions

From M6 exit 36 head west on A590 towards Barrow and Newby Bridge. Follow the A590 to roundabout signed Bowness and turn right on the A592 for about 3 miles. Site is signed on left. O.S.GR: SD384903. GPS: N54:18.453 W02:56.724

Charges guide

Per pitch	£ 10.00 - £ 24.00
car	£ 1.00
awning	£ 3.00
boat	£ 5.00 - £ 10.50

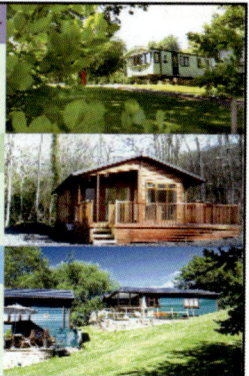
UK5610 Waterfoot Caravan Park

Pooley Bridge, Penrith CA11 0JF (Cumbria)

Tel: **01768 486302**. Email: **enquiries@waterfootpark.co.uk**   **www.alanrogers.com/UK5610**

Waterfoot is a quiet family park for caravans and motorcaravans only. It is set in 22 acres of partially wooded land, developed in the fifties from a private estate. The 146 private caravan holiday homes are quite separate from the 34 touring pitches. Lake Ullswater is only about 400 yards away and a half mile stroll through bluebell woods brings you to the village of Pooley Bridge. Waterfoot's touring pitches are arranged very informally in a large clearing. Most are level, there are some hardstandings and all have 10A electricity. The park no longer accepts American RVs. There is a bar in a large, imposing mansion, in the past a family home then a golf hotel. Public footpaths lead straight from the park. The regular lake steamer service calls at Pooley Bridge, the Ullswater yacht club is only 10 minutes drive and the market town of Penrith is 5 miles. The historic house and gardens of Dalemain are a short walk.

Facilities

The heated toilet block includes washbasins and preset showers in cubicles. New facilities for disabled visitors. Large, light and airy dishwashing room and fully equipped laundry. Small shop selling basics, gas and newspapers. Bar with strictly enforced, separate family room open weekend evenings in low season and every evening in high season. Large fenced field with play equipment to suit all ages and goal posts for football and a new play park. Off site: Fishing 0.5 miles. Riding 1.5 miles. Golf 5 miles. Pooley Bridge has a post office/general store, hotels and restaurants.

Open: 1 March - 14 November.

Directions

Do not use GPS here – it directs outfits the wrong way, finishing up on farm tracks. Please use the following directions. From M6 junction 40, take the A66 signed Keswick. After 0.5 miles at roundabout take A592 signed Ullswater and site is on right after 4 miles. O.S.GR: NY460245.
GPS: N54:36.841 W02:49.869

Charges guide

Per unit incl. all persons and electricity	£ 16.00 - £ 23.00

Pay for 7 nights in one payment and receive 1 night free.

UK5640 Green Acres Caravan Park

High Knells, Houghton, Carlisle CA6 4JW (Cumbria)

Tel: **01228 675418**   **www.alanrogers.com/UK5640**

Green Acres is a small, family run park which from 2009 accepts only adults. Situated in beautiful, rural surroundings, yet only two miles from the M6/A74 it is perfect for an overnight stop or a longer stay to enjoy Cumbria, Hadrian's Wall and the delights of Carlisle city (4 miles away). The Browns have developed Green Acres into an attractive, well maintained and level touring park. There are 30 numbered pitches, all on large hardstandings. Arranged in a semi-circle, there are 19 electricity connections (10A). Divided by a long beech hedge is a large camping field including on one side 12 new hardstanding 'super' pitches for seasonal letting.

Facilities

Small, very clean toilet block with open style washbasins and coin operated showers (50p for 10 minutes). No facilities for disabled people. Laundry room in farm building. Car wash area. No shop but ices, drinks and sweets from reception. Caravan storage. Off site: Golf 3 miles. Fishing 8 miles. Riding and bicycle hire 10 miles.

Open: 1 April - end October.

Directions

Leave M6/A74 at exit 44 and take the A689 for 1 mile. Turn left towards Scaleby (site signed) and site is 1 mile on the left. O.S.GR: NY419615.
GPS: N54:56.656 W02:54.572

Charges guide

Per unit incl. 2 persons and electricity	£ 11.00
extra person	£ 2.00

UK5630 The Quiet Site Caravan & Camping Park

Watermillock, Penrith CA11 0LS (Cumbria)

Tel: **07768 727016**. Email: **info@thequietsite.co.uk**   www.alanrogers.com/UK5630

The Quiet Site is a secluded, family run park, operating as a carbon neutral company. It is situated on a hillside in the National Park with views over the fells and just 1.5 miles from Lake Ullswater. There are 100 unmarked touring pitches, most with hardstanding and 50 with electricity. Most have been terraced to provide level surfaces, but a few are very sloping. The camping area is very undulating. In a separate part of the park, screened by mature trees, are 23 privately owned caravan holiday homes. There are two cottages to rent and recent additions are timber built 'camping pods' as an alternative to bringing your own tent. In converted old farm buildings, the amenities are centred around the reception and shop and include a comfortable first floor bar with oak beams and barrel seats. Many beautiful walks start from right outside the park and the numerous activities and attractions of the Lake District are within a short drive. The owners, the Holder family, continue to develop this attractive, well maintained park with an emphasis on green principles. A member of the Best of British group.

Facilities

The toilet block provides pre-set showers and open style washbasins. Three bathrooms and two private shower rooms. Bathroom with facilities for disabled visitors. Baby area. Laundry facilities. Motorcaravan services. Well stocked shop at reception. Gas supplies. Bar (weekends only in low season). TV and games room. Excellent adventure play area. Caravan storage. American motorhomes would find access very difficult.
Off site: Fishing 1.5 miles. Riding and bicycle hire 3 miles. Golf 8 miles.

Open: All year excl. 17 January - 28 February.

Directions

We advise using the following directions, rather than GPS. From M6, exit 40, take A66 (Keswick) for 1 mile, then A592 signed Ullswater for 4 miles. Turn right at Lake junction, still on A592 signed Windermere. After 1 miles turn right (at Brackenrigg Inn) and follow for 1.5 miles to site on right (large units should phone for an alternative route).
O.S.GR: NY431236. GPS: N54:36.281 W02:52.967

Charges guide

Per unit incl. 2 persons, awning and electricity	£ 17.00 - £ 27.00
tent incl. 2 persons	£ 12.00 - £ 27.00
extra person	free - £ 4.00
Camping Cheques accepted.	

The Quiet Site Ullswater
Award winning park in idyllic setting. Carbon neutral company.
Also caravan storage in the heart of the lakes.
www.thequietsite.co.uk   *07768 727016*

UK5635 Ullswater Caravan, Camping & Marine Park

Watermillock, Penrith CA11 0LR (Cumbria)

Tel: **017684 86666**. Email: **info@uccmp.co.uk**   www.alanrogers.com/UK5635

Located within the Lake District National Park, Ullswater Caravan Park is centrally situated for touring the many attractions of this glorious area. It has 220 pitches, 58 for touring units, the rest used for holiday homes. All have 10A electricity, 50 also have water and drains. Some are situated very close to the bar and are also overlooked by mobile homes with little privacy. At the far end of the park other pitches are in a more wooded area. In between is a large grassy space for tents. There are occasional glimpses of the lake through the trees. The park is owned by the Dobinson family who also have a Marina a mile away where boats can be launched and moorings are available. This is probably the closest place to the park where access can be gained to the lake because of the busy main road which runs along this side of the lake.

Facilities

Two toilet blocks, one refurbished the other a little dated and unheated. Facilities for babies and disabled visitors. Laundry. Shop with off-licence. Bar and games room open 8pm at busy times. Well equipped playground for younger children. Attractive holiday cottages to rent.
Off site: Walks in the hills above the park. Steamer rides on the lake from Pooley Bridge 2 miles.

Open: 1 March - 14 November.

Directions

From M6 exit 40 take the A66 west signed Keswick. At first roundabout (Rheged) take second exit signed Ullswater on the A592. At T-junction turn right still on the A592 and after Breckenrigg Inn on the right, carry on downhill to phone box on right, and sign for church. Turn right and up to entrance in 800 yds.
O.S.GR: NY436229. GPS: N54:35.868 W02:52.489

Charges guide

Per unit incl. 2 persons	£ 15.50 - £ 21.00
extra person	£ 3.50
child (2-13 yrs)	£ 2.50

UK5645 Waters Edge Caravan Park

Crooklands, Kendal LA7 7NN (Cumbria)

Tel: **015395 67708**. Email: **info@watersedgecaravanpark.co.uk**   www.alanrogers.com/UK5645

Being close to the M6 motorway, Waters Edge makes an ideal stop-over. However, it also well worth a longer stay, being centrally situated for visiting the Lake District and the Yorkshire Dales. Surrounded by farmland the park is long and narrow, with one road running down the centre and the pitches on either side. There are 26 level touring pitches, all with hardstanding. These are open and a little on the small side. At each end of the park there are 6 privately owned caravan holiday homes. There are no play areas for children and parents of young children would need to be vigilant here, as there is a well signed but unfenced fast flowing stream. The attractive reception building contains a small but well stocked shop, lounge bar with TV and pool table, The bar opens on to a lovely lawned area with picnic tables and a duck pond. A corner of this grassed area is used for tents. The nearby Crooklands Hotel serves good food, and across the road is the picturesque Lancaster canal where free boat rides can be enjoyed on Sundays during the summer. The busy market town of Kendal is 15 minutes drive with good shopping, a cinema and a swimming pool.

Facilities

Centrally located toilet block, although a little dated, is spotlessly clean with showers and washbasins in cubicles. Facilities for disabled visitors. Laundry. No motorcaravan service point. Shop. Bar with TV. Off site: Hotel serving food. Canal and boat trips. Kendal 15 minutes drive.

Open: March - November.

Directions

From M6 exit 36 take the A65 (east) signed Kirkby Lonsdale for 300 yds. At next roundabout take first exit signed Crooklands and Endmoor. Park entrance is about 1 mile on the right at Crooklands Motor Co. O.S.GR: SD536836. GPS: N54:14.818 W02:42.972

Charges guide

Per unit incl. electricity	£ 13.50 - £ 19.50
tent pitch	£ 10.00

UK5650 Ashes Exclusively Adult Caravan Park

New Hutton, Kendal LA8 0AS (Cumbria)

Tel: **01539 731833**. Email: **info@ashescaravanpark.co.uk**   www.alanrogers.com/UK5650

The Ashes is a friendly, small, adult only park in an extremely peaceful setting in the rolling Cumbrian countryside, yet less than three miles from the M6 motorway, and only slightly further from Kendal. It is therefore not only a convenient night stop, but also a useful base from which to explore the Lake District and the Yorkshire Dales. A very tidy park, the central grass area is attractively planted with shrubs and bushes and there is an open vista (with little shade). There are 25 hardstanding gravel pitches, all with electrical connections (10A). These are neatly placed around the perimeter, with an oval access road. The whole area slopes gently down from the entrance, with some pitches fairly level and others with a little more slope. No tents are accepted other than trailer tents.

Facilities

A small, purpose built stone building with a slate roof houses two unisex, heated shower rooms and the washing and toilet facilities. New facilities for disabled visitors. Laundry service. No shop. New electronic barrier. TV signal booster. Off site: Mr and Mrs Mason have prepared a full information sheet with details of shopping, eating and many other local venues. Fishing 2 miles. Golf and riding 3 miles. Bicycle hire 4 miles. Kendal 4 miles.

Open: 1 March - 9 November.

Directions

From M6 exit 37 follow the A684 towards Kendal for 2 miles. Just past a white cottage turn sharp left at crossroads signed New Hutton. Site is on right in 0.75 miles at a left bend. Only approach and depart using this road. O.S.GR: SD560908. GPS: N54:18.788 W02:40.500

Charges guide

Per unit incl. 2 persons and electricity	£ 13.00 - £ 16.00
extra person (over 18s only)	£ 4.50
awning	£ 3.00

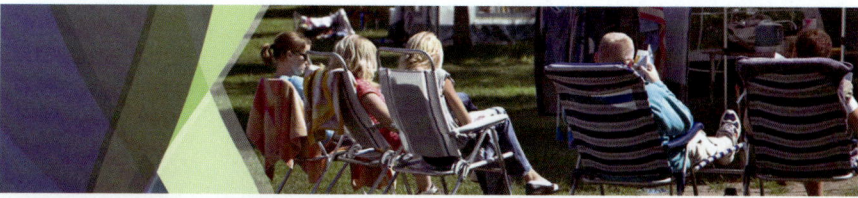

UK5660 Castlerigg Hall Caravan & Camping Park

Keswick CA12 4TE (Cumbria)

Tel: **01768 774499**. Email: **info@castlerigg.co.uk**   www.alanrogers.com/UK5660

This well laid out park was started in the late 1950s by the Jackson family, who over the years have developed and improved the site whilst maintaining its character. Good use has been made of the traditional stone buildings to house the reception and shop, whilst another building houses a modern amenity block along with a really excellent campers' kitchen. Tarmac roads wend their way around the site to the separate tent area of 110 pitches. Gently sloping with some shelter, these pitches have fine views across Keswick, Derwentwater and the western Fells. The 45 caravan pitches tend to be on terraces, again overlooking the lake. Each terrace has a maximum of eight pitches, all on hardstanding and with 10A electricity and nearly all with a water tap and grey water drain. Places to visit include Keswick (about 20 minutes walk), Derwentwater, Ullswater, Penrith, Carlisle, Hadrian's Wall, Rhegad (the village in the hill) and, quite close to the site, Castlerigg stone circle which is believed to be some 4,000 years old, and of course as much walking as you might want. The Jacksons are committed to conservation.

Facilities

The main toilet block is beautifully fitted out, fully tiled and heated, with showers, vanity style washbasins (two in cabins) and hair care areas. Unit for disabled visitors (key). Baby area. Fully equipped laundry. Games room and campers' kitchen complete with microwave, toasters, kettle and hot plates. Two other toilet blocks are older in style but newly decorated and clean. Reception houses tourist information, internet point and a well stocked shop (with gas). Off site: Hotel/pub for meals adjacent to site. Fishing, golf, riding. bicycle hire and boat launching, all 1.5 miles.

Open: mid March - November.

Directions

From Penrith take A66 towards Keswick and Cockermouth. Leave at first sign for Keswick (A591) and follow to junction (A5271). Turn left on A591 signed Windermere and after 1 mile, take small road on right signed Castlerigg and Rakefoot. Park entrance is on right after 400 yards. O.S.GR: NY282227. GPS: N54:35.586 W03:06.755

Charges guide

Per caravan incl. 2 persons	£ 13.50 - £ 15.95
motorcaravan incl. 2 persons	£ 12.00 - £ 14.50
awning (steel pegs required)	£ 1.90 - £ 2.30

UK5670 Flusco Wood Touring Caravan Park

Flusco, Penrith CA11 0JB (Cumbria)

Tel: **01768 480020**. Email: **admin@fluscowood.co.uk**   www.alanrogers.com/UK5670

Flusco Wood Caravan Park is still being developed but everything is to a very high standard. Set amongst woodland with the touring pitches in bays, this park will meet the needs of those requiring a quiet holiday (with plenty of walks from the site) and also those travelling up or down the M6 looking for a quiet night's rest. All pitches are on hardstanding, with an area near reception with hardstandings for motorcaravans. Recent additions here include new log cabins (privately owned), with a further planned. The area abounds with wildlife including deer and red squirrels, as well as many breeds of birds (we watched a woodpecker taking food from a bird feeder). For a wet day you are about 2.5 miles from Rheged, the 'village in the hill' and, if the weather improves, a short drive from Ullswater, Keswick, Penrith and Carlisle. Member of the Countryside Discovery group.

Facilities

A log cabin style building houses very clean, heated facilities including pre-set showers and vanity style washbasins (1 cubicle). Large en-suite shower rooms for families or disabled visitors, one in the ladies' and one in the men's. Dishwashing sinks under cover. Laundry, drying room and boot washing sink. Second log cabin serves as reception/shop with basic supplies, gas and daily papers. Play equipment on bark. Grass area for ball games. Off site: Pub and P.O. stores 2 miles. Fishing, bicycle hire and golf 4 miles. Riding 5 miles.

Open: Easter or 1 April - 29 October.

Directions

From M6 take A66 towards Keswick. Go straight on at first roundabout, then third right at top of hill (signed Flusco, Recycling Centre, Pottery and caravan sign). After 0.5 miles road turns right up hill (narrow, so take care in large units), site is on left at the top. Site is 4 miles from the M6. O.S.GR: NY457293. GPS: N54:39.381 W02:50.537

Charges 2009

Per unit incl. 2 persons and electricity	£ 17.50 - £ 20.50
extra person (over 3 yrs)	£ 3.00
dog	£ 1.00

MAP 5

The most northerly region of England, Northumbria is steeped in history, full of ancient forts and fairytale castles. The great outdoors offers limitless walking with plenty of trails stretching across moorlands and beaches, encompassing views of the beautiful scenery.

Northumbria

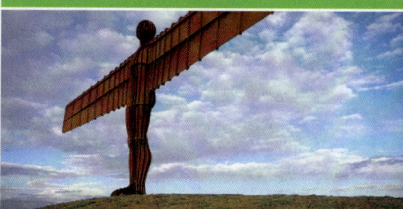

THE REGION COMPRISES: NORTHUMBERLAND, DURHAM, TYNE AND WEAR, AND TEESIDE

The 400 square mile Northumberland National Park is one of the most peaceful, remote places in England. With endless walks across moorlands and hills, it stretches south from the Cheviot Hills, through the Simonside Hills, to the crags of Whin Sill, where it engulfs a section of the historic Hadrian's Wall, built by the Romans to mark the northern limit of their empire. The Pennine Way was the country's first official long-distance path and is still the longest. At 268 miles, it stretches from the Peak National Park to the border. The coastline is not to be forgotten, with mile upon mile of deserted, sandy beaches, with resorts that still have an old fashioned feel to them, such as Whitley Bay, South Shields and Seaton Carew. The majestic castles of Bamburgh, and Dunstanburgh can be seen for miles along the Northumberland coast. Surrounded on three sides by the river Wear, the small, historic city of Durham is dominated by England's greatest Norman Cathedral. With cobbled medieval streets and restricted car access it is a popular place with visitors. Further north is the bustling city of Newcastle. Home to an array of cosmopolitan restaurants and bars, music venues, and fabulous architecture, it also boasts a lively nightlife.

Places of interest

Northumberland: Bamburgh Castle; Alnwick Castle and gardens; Berwick-upon-Tweed; bird reserve on Farne Islands, home to large colony of grey seals; Hauxley Nature Reserve; Dunstanburgh Castle; Corbridge Roman sites at Hadrian's Wall.

Durham: Durham Castle and Cathedral; Barnard Castle, a ruined castle overlooking the River Tees; Diggerland at Langley Park; Harperley POW Camp.

Tyne and Wear: New Metroland, Europe's only indoor theme park within a large shopping complex; Newcastle with Life Science Centre, Discovery Museum and Castle Keep; Whitley Bay.

Teeside: Kirkleatham Owl Centre; Darlington Railway Centre and Museum; Guisborough Hall; Hartlepool Historic Quay and HMS Trinacomalee; Butterfly World in Stockton-on-Tees.

Did you know?

Alnwick Castle is used as the setting of Hogwarts in the Harry Potter films.

Stretching from Wallsend to Bowness-on-Solway, Hadrian's Wall is 81 miles long; it is possible to walk the entire length.

Born in Northumbria in 1825, George Stephenson was the first person to design the steam engine that ran on wheels.

In the past 300 years Berwick has changed hands between the Scottish and the English no less than 13 times.

The Angel of The North is made up of 200 tonnes of steel and rises 20 metres. from the ground.

Built in 1817, HMS Trinacomalee is the oldest ship afloat in the UK.

225

RED TEXT DENOTES ALL YEAR SITE

BERWICK-UPON-TWEED
5800

SCOTLAND

MELROSE
7030
SELKIRK
KELSO
5755 5750
WOOLER

JEDBURGH
Scottish Lowlands
5770

ALNWICK

Northumberland

MORPETH

Tyne and Wear
HALTWHISTLE
5810
HEXHAM
NEWCASTLE
UPON TYNE
5640
CARLISLE
NORTHUMBRIA
SUNDERLAND
CONSETT
CHESTER-LE-STREET
A1(M)
M6
DURHAM
5705
5700
PETERLEE
CUMBRIA
Durham
HARTLEPOOL
5670
PENRITH
5625
BISHOP AUCKLAND
MIDDLETON-IN-TEESDALE
5620
5610
5630
5635
APPLEBY-IN-WESTMORLAND
5570
5710
5720 BARNARD CASTLE
5740
MIDDLESBROUGH
5560
BROUGH
BOWES
DARLINGTON
GUISBOROUGH
KIRKBY STEPHEN
5600
YORKSHIRE
AMBLESIDE 5590
5550
North Yorkshire

UK5740 White Water Caravan Club Park

Tees Barrage, Stockton-on-Tees TS18 2QW (Teeside)

Tel: **01642 634880**   www.alanrogers.com/UK5740

Being part of the multimillion pound development at the Tees Barrage, this pleasantly landscaped club site caters for all tastes, especially water sports enthusiasts. The Tees Barrage has transformed 11 miles of the Tees, providing clean, non-tidal water for many activities. The adjoining White Water Course (Britain's largest purpose-built canoe course) provides facilities for both advanced and beginner canoeists, and hosts major national and international events. Close to the site are wetlands that provide a home for a variety of birds. The site itself provides 115 pitches, hedged with bushes, all with 16A electricity connections, and includes 21 fully serviced pitches set within bays and hedges (fresh water and waste disposal). The site is well lit, with a security barrier.

Facilities

The central, heated toilet block of high quality includes washbasins in cubicles, baby changing facilities and a well appointed unit for disabled visitors. Laundry room. Motorcaravan service point. Play area on fine gravel. Heated family room with TV and pool table for wet weather. Off site: Supermarket 6 minutes. Hotel near the entrance. Retail and leisure park, just across barrage bridge, with 14-screen cinema, 10-pin bowling, shops and fast food outlets. North Yorkshire Moors.

Open: All year.

Directions

From A1(M1) take A66 for Darlington and follow until you pick up signs for Teeside Retail Park and the Tees Barrage. Cross railway bridge and the Barrage bridge, then first right to site on left in 400 yards. O.S.GR: NZ463194. GPS: N54:34.064 W01:17.194

Charges guide

Per person	£ 3.30 - £ 4.60
pitch incl. electricity (non-member)	£ 9.80 - £ 13.20

Tent campers apply to site.

UK5700 Strawberry Hill Caravan Park

Running Waters, Old Cassop, Durham DH6 4QA (Co. Durham)

Tel: **01913 723457**. Email: **info@strawberryhf.co.uk**   **www.alanrogers.com/UK5700**

This park is owned and managed by Howard and Elizabeth who are experienced caravanners. They have terraced their site to offer panoramic views over the fields and woodland from all the pitches. The park is licensed to accommodate more units but the owners prefer to offer space to visitors by providing generous pitches on either grass or hardstanding. There are 44 touring pitches with 16A electricity hook-ups, including 10 on hardstanding, plus a separate terrace for tents. At present the fairly new landscaping on the park offers limited shade. Nature corridors and the surrounding countryside make this a haven for nature lovers and visitors are encouraged to enjoy the tranquillity of the area. The owners supply good tourist information and details of local nature walks. The easy access to the A1M and the proximity of the historic cathedral city of Durham (3 miles) make this an ideal location for visiting local attractions. These include Beamish museum, Gateshead Metro centre and the historic Hartlepool Quays.

Facilities

The single toilet block can be heated and is kept immaculately clean. Free showers. Laundry. Facilities for disabled visitors incorporating a baby care area. Small but well stocked shop in reception. Gas. Off site: Country pub with meals 1 mile. Large hypermarket 3 miles. Riding 5 miles. Park and ride (07.00 - 19.00) into Durham city centre operates nearby. Buses (Durham - Hartlepool) from site entrance.

Open: 1 March - 30 December.

Directions

From A1M exit 61 follow signs for the 177 signed Bowburn and Peterlee. After 200 m. turn right (Peterlee, Sherburn) and watch for brown sign to Bowburn Hall Hotel. Follow this twisting road for 3 miles to crossroads and turn right on A181 Wheatley Hill, Peterlee road. About 1 mile to dual carriageway, entrance to park is 200 m. up the hill (this site can only be approached from the eastbound carriageway). O.S.GR: NZ338399.
GPS: N54:45.196 W01:28.685

Charges 2009

Per unit incl. 2 persons	£ 14.50 - £ 16.50
extra person	£ 3.50
child	£ 1.50

UK5710 Doe Park Touring Caravan Park

Cotherstone, Barnard Castle DL12 9UQ (Co. Durham)

Tel: **01833 650302**   **www.alanrogers.com/UK5710**

This is Hannah Hauxwell country and the Dales, less frequented than other upland areas, provide wonderful walking country; indeed part of the Pennine Way runs near this peaceful site. The farm and park are close to where the River Balder joins the Tees at Cotherstone and the ancient oak wood beside the river is an SSSI (Site of Special Scientific Interest) for its insects and flowers, but is also a haven for birdwatchers. The park's reception is in a log cabin at the entrance to the pitch area and is well stocked with tourist information guides. The farmhouse, formerly Leadgard Hall, is a mellow three storey, Grade II listed building with a history of its own. The Lamb family will make you very welcome and personally take you to your pitch. The camping fields have a lovely open aspect with wonderful views and the 70 pitches are spacious with well mown grass, all with 10A electricity, over 40 with hardstanding (no tents are taken). A bus service passes the park from Barnard Castle to Middleton and the village of Cotherstone is only half a mile with post office and a restaurant with bar meals, a pleasant walk by road or river bank.

Facilities

With toilet facilities at the farmhouse, two well kept blocks are closer to the pitches. Built in local stone, these are fully tiled with the newest one heated. Washbasins in cabins and adjustable showers. Well appointed unisex unit for disabled visitors. Small laundry. Eggs and milk are available from the farmhouse, plus gas supplies and battery charging. No play area but a large grass area in front of some of the pitches can be used for ball games. River fishing on site. Dogs and pets are accepted by arrangement only. Off site: Reservoirs (sailing, water skiing and fishing) 3 miles. Bicycle hire and golf 4 miles. Riding 2 miles. Local leisure centre with pool 4 miles.

Open: 1 March - 31 October.

Directions

Follow B6277 from Barnard Castle in direction of Middleton in Teesdale. The farm is signed on the left just after Cotherstone village (there is no need to go into Barnard Castle). O.S.GR: NZ005204.
GPS: N54:34.693 W01:59.541

Charges guide

Per unit incl. 2 persons	£ 8.25 - £ 10.50
incl. electricity (10A)	£ 11.00 - £ 13.25
extra person (over 6 yrs)	£ 1.50
full awning	£ 1.00
family rate (2 adults, 2 children)	£ 14.00 - £ 16.25
No credit cards.	

227

UK5705 Grange Caravan Club Site

Meadow Lane, Durham DH1 1TL (Co. Durham)

Tel: **01913 844778**

www.alanrogers.com/UK5705

Fully refurbished and landscaped, this park offers 77 flat spacious pitches suitable for all units. Easy access to the A1M and the A690 make it an ideal stop-over for those travelling north or south or for visiting the historic cathedral city of Durham, Beamish museum or Gateshead Metro centre. A coppice of mature trees and newly planted shrubs mask road noise and make an attractive dog walking area. The park has been redesigned with attention to detail in all areas offering pockets of privacy or a central area with picnic tables and benches. A purpose built central block offers spacious, heated, modern and clean facilities with ample free showers and private washing cubicles.

Facilities

The single toilet block is a heated building with free showers, hairdryers, and private cubicles. Laundry and food preparation area. Separate baby area and facilities for disabled visitors are available via a key entry system. Shop in reception with limited supplies, bread, milk and newspapers to order. Gas. Secure caravan storage. Off site: Large supermarket 2 miles. Park and ride (07.00-19.00) into Durham city centre 800 yds. Local service buses run from Belmont and Carville.

Open: All year.

Directions

From A1M exit 62 follow signs for Durham (A690). At roundabout take first exit left and after 20 yds. turn right (across dual carriageway A690) – large units continue along A690 to next roundabout about 2 miles and return. Left turn (signed before A1M). O.S.GR: NZ302446. GPS: N54:47.708 W01:31.761

Charges guide

Per person	£ 4.40 - £ 5.50
pitch incl. electricity	
(non-member)	£ 10.80 - £ 14.60

UK5720 Barnard Castle Camping & Caravanning Club Site

Dockenflatts Lane, Lartington, Barnard Castle DL12 9DG (Co. Durham)

Tel: **01833 630228**

www.alanrogers.com/UK5720

Welcoming non-members and tents, the Camping & Caravanning Club site at Barnard Castle was opened in 1996. One side of the site is bordered by mature trees and further planting now gives privacy to individual pitches. There are 90 flat pitches, most on grass but including 12 hardstanding pitches (gravel base with room for both car and caravan and space for an awning on grass). There are 56 electrical hook-ups (16A). There is an attractive woodland dog walking area leading to a riverside footpath which takes you into Barnard Castle.

Facilities

The centrally located toilet facilities are of good quality and kept spotlessly clean. Washbasins are in cubicles and free, controllable showers are roomy. Baby room. Fully equipped unisex unit for visitors with disabilities. Large laundry with washing machine, dryer, iron and sink, with outside lines provided. Well stocked shop. Motorcaravan service point. Gas. Central play area. Caravan storage. Off site: Riding 200 m. Fishing 4 miles. Golf 2.5 miles. Bus service from end of lane.

Open: 30 March - 30 October.

Directions

Follow B6277 from Barnard Castle (towards Middleton in Teesdale) for 1 mile to Lartington. Turn left at club sign into narrow lane with passing places to site entrance on left (there is no need to go into Barnard Castle). O.S.GR: NZ025168. GPS: N54:32.813 W01:57.755

Charges guide

Per person	£ 4.90 - £ 7.25
child (6-18 yrs)	£ 2.15 - £ 2.25
non-member pitch fee	£ 5.65

UK5770 Dunstan Hill Camping & Caravanning Club Site

Dunstan Hill, Dunstan, Alnwick NE66 3TQ (Northumberland)

Tel: **01665 576310**

www.alanrogers.com/UK5770

Off a quiet lane between Embleton and Craster this is a rural site with a tree belt to shelter it from the north wind and access to the beach by a level footpath through the fields, across the golf course and past the ruins of Dunstanburgh Castle. This is just over a mile by car. With gravel access roads, the peaceful site has 150 level, well spaced pitches, 80 with 16A electricity. Reception is manned by very helpful managers and there is an area for outside parking and late arrivals at the entrance. The site is not suitable for large American motorhomes.

Facilities

Two very clean and well maintained toilet blocks have some washbasins in cubicles. Fully equipped facility for disabled visitors in one block, a laundry in the other. Small shop for gas and basic provisions. Bread and milk to order. Small play area. Torches are useful. Off site: Buses pass the entrance. Fishing 1.5 miles. Golf 1.5 miles. Beach 1.5 miles. Riding 8 miles. Bicycle hire 10 miles.

Open: March - October.

Directions

From A1 just north of Alnwick take the B1340 or B6347 (further north) for Embleton. Site is signed in Embleton village – follow signs for Craster. Site is (south) on the left after about 0.5 miles. O.S.GR: NU236214. GPS: N55:29.130 W01:37.746

Charges guide

Per person	£ 4.90 - £ 7.25
non-member pitch fee	£ 5.65

UK5755 South Meadows Caravan Park

South Meadows, Belford NE70 7DP (Northumberland)
Tel: **01668 213326**. Email: **g.mcl@btinternet.com**   www.alanrogers.com/UK5755

South Meadows is set in the north Northumberland countryside, within walking distance of the village of Belford with its market cross and old coaching inn. Covering 6 acres of level grass, there are 100 hardstanding pitches, most with electricity (13A), water and TV aerial point. At present 20 pitches are available for touring units. A further area can accommodate 50 tents. The manager is environmentally aware and encourages recycling. Determined that visitors have a relaxing holiday, he will site your caravan using his own towing equipment. There is an area especially for disabled visitors with wider paths and safety features including a 24 hour telephone directly to the manager's home on site. The park is pleasantly landscaped and two short walks lead into the adjacent Blue Bell woods with streams, wildlife and spring flowers. Just off the A1 road, this would be a convenient stopover but Northumberland is an undiscovered county with castles and stately homes, the Farne Islands, Holy Island and long golden beaches, and you would be made most welcome here for a longer stay. This attractive, well maintained park is already popular with couples and young families and booking is advised.

Facilities

The fully tiled toilet block is excellent, heated in cool weather, with washbasins in cabins and roomy showers (free). Hairdryers. Full facilities for disabled visitors. Laundry with washing machines, dryers and iron plus a baby unit. Food preparation and cooking area. Coffee shop (weekends, incl. Sunday roast) and takeaway (daily until 16.00). Play area. Caravan storage and servicing. Off-site: Village with pub and shops 0.5 miles. Golf 0.5 miles. Riding 3 miles. Beach 3 miles. Alnwick Castle of Harry Potter fame.

Open: All year.

Directions

Turn off A1 about 15 miles from Alnwick to Belford village and park is signed at the southern end. O.S.GR: NU115331. GPS: N55:35.458 W01:49.355

Charges guide

Per unit incl. 2 persons	£ 17.00 - £ 30.00
extra person	£ 7.50 - £ 10.00
tent per person	£ 8.00 - £ 10.00
child (2-16 yrs)	£ 2.00

UK5750 Waren Caravan & Camping Park

Waren Mill, Bamburgh NE70 7EE (Northumberland)
Tel: **01668 214366**. Email: **waren@meadowhead.co.uk**   www.alanrogers.com/UK5750

Developed from 100 acres of undulating privately owned heath and woodland, Waren Park is a large, spacious family site with marvellous views over Northumberland's golden beaches and the sea. A large section of caravan holiday homes is separate from a self contained four acre touring area. Enclosed by sheltering banks, this provides 170 reasonably level pitches, 100 with electrical connections (10A). Wooden wigwams are also available. As well as the spacious grounds to wander in, there is much to see nearby from historic castles and the Farne Islands to the Cheviot Hills and miles and miles of sandy beaches.

Facilities

The older toilet facilities are poor and in need of refurbishment, whilst a newer block situated in a separate static holiday home section provides good facilities. Laundry room. Motorcaravan service point. Licensed shop. Bar with terrace serving bar meals (all season). Gaming machine room with pool table. Patio area. Children's play park and playing fields. Splash pool (June - Sept). WiFi internet access. Off site: Beach 500 yds. excellent for birdwatching, unsuitable for bathing. Safe bathing beach 4 miles (Bamburgh). Golf or bicycle hire 2 miles. Riding 5 miles. Birdwatching opportunities nearby.

Open: 14 March - 31 October.

Directions

Follow B1342 from the A1 to Waren Mill towards Bamburgh. After Budle Bay turn right and follow signs. O.S.GR: NU154342. GPS: N55:36.027 W01:45.292

Charges 2009

Per unit incl. 2 persons	£ 13.00 - £ 23.00
extra person (over 5 yrs)	£ 3.00
1-man tent (no car)	£ 9.50 - £ 12.00
dog	£ 2.50
Less 10% for bookings of 7 days or over.	

229

UK5800 Ord House Country Park

East Ord, Berwick-upon-Tweed TD15 2NS (Northumberland)
Tel: **01289 305288**. Email: **enquiries@ordhouse.co.uk**   www.alanrogers.com/UK5800

Ord House is 40 acre park for 287 privately owned holiday homes and 74 touring caravan and tent pitches. The park has a very well cared for appearance throughout with well mown grass and colourful arrays of flowering bushes. The touring pitches, all with electricity (10/16A), are in small sections, from the secluded, walled orchard to the more open areas nearer the toilet blocks. There are 39 hardstanding pitches, each with electricity, water and drainage, 12 in the walled garden separated by shrubs and camomile lawns. At the entrance to the park an area with a few pitches is suitable for wheelchair users and close by is a small sanitary unit with WCs and showers plus a large, unisex, well appointed unit (Radar key). The whole site is 'wheelchair friendly' with good access to the airy reception. Ord House itself, an 18th century mansion, has been tastefully converted to provide a bar, lounge bar and family room. Although there are many caravan holiday homes, they are not overwhelming and their presence does mean that other amenities can remain open all season. A member of the Best of British group.

Facilities

The main, modern toilet building is of excellent quality and cleanliness, very well maintained and can be heated. Two good large family bathrooms (with two showers, a bath, WC and washbasin). Two rooms for disabled visitors. Large well equipped laundry. Motorcaravan service point. Gas supplies. Bar, bar food and family room (1/3-10/1). Crazy golf. Draughts. Play area. No commercial vehicles are accepted. Dogs are only accepted by prior arrangement. Off site: Post office stores 50 yards from the entrance. Leisure centre with a pool 15 minutes walk. Fishing 1.5 miles. Riding 8 miles. Golf 2 miles. Sea fishing can be booked in Berwick. Beach 1.5 miles.

Open: All year.

Directions

From A1 Berwick bypass take East Ord exit and follow signs. O.S.GR: NT982515. GPS: N55:45.250 W02:02.009

Charges guide

Per unit incl. up to 4 persons and electricity	£ 15.00 - £ 24.00
extra person over 5 yrs	£ 2.50
tent pitch	£ 10.00 - £ 24.00
dog	free - £ 1.50

Discounts for 1- and 2-man tents and for longer stays.

UK5810 Fallowfield Dene Caravan & Camping Park

Acomb, Hexham NE46 4RP (Northumberland)
Tel: **01434 603553**. Email: **info@fallowfielddene.co.uk**   www.alanrogers.com/UK5810

Although only 2.5 miles from Hexham, Fallowfield Dene Caravan Park is very secluded, situated in mature woodland at the end of a no-through road. Set in woodland glades (formerly a Victorian lead mine), each with a Roman name (Hadrian's Wall is close), are 118 seasonal pitches and 32 touring pitches, all with 16A electricity. A further 10 tent pitches have been added, suitable for smaller tents, and a barbecue area with views of woodland and fields. The park entrance, with reception and a small shop, is neat, tidy and very colourful. There is no play area or games field, but the surrounding woods are a paradise for children. Fallowfield Dene itself is a network of tracks and there are footpaths from the site entrance. The site is a haven for wildlife with red squirrels, foxes and badgers to be seen. Hadrian's Wall is only a mile away, with Roman forts such as Housesteads Fort and Chesters, being great attractions. The whole area abounds with well preserved Roman remains. Nearby, Hexham market town has its Border History museum, housed in the oldest purpose built gaol in England, where one can learn about the Border Reivers. This site has a friendly atmosphere.

Facilities

Brick built toilet blocks (one for each sex) are central and heated in cool weather. Well tiled and kept very clean, there are washbasins in cabins and free hairdryers. Separate, fully equipped room for disabled people. Laundry room. Baby bath. Motorcaravan service point. Small shop for necessities, including gas. Barrier card £5 deposit. Off site: Supermarkets and other shops at Hexham or Corbridge. Good restaurant five minutes walk. Fishing or riding 3 miles. Golf 5 miles.

Open: 17 March - 29 October.

Directions

From the A69 Newcastle - Carlisle road, take the A6079 north signed Bellingham and Rothbury. At village of Acomb, site is signed to right. Follow site signs for about 1.5 miles. The last 0.5 miles is single track with passing places. O.S.GR: NY938676. GPS: N55:00.100 W02:05.682

Charges guide

Per unit incl. 2 persons and electricity	£ 15.50 - £ 16.50
extra person	£ 3.00
child (5-15 yrs)	£ 1.25
dog	£ 0.50

MAP 6

Land of ancient myths and Celtic legends, Wales is a small and compact country boasting a diverse landscape, from lakes and mountains, rivers and valleys to beautiful coastlines and rolling wooded countryside. It offers superb opportunities for an active holiday.

Alan Rogers

WE HAVE DIVIDED OUR LIST OF CAMPSITES IN WALES INTO NORTH, WEST, MID AND SOUTH REGIONS

Wales' biggest asset is undoubtedly its countryside, home to three National Parks that make up almost a quarter of the country's total area. Snowdonia National Park in the north combines dramatic mountain scenery with glacial valleys, lakes and streams, while in the south the Brecon Beacons boast mountains, moorlands, forests and wooded gorges with deep caves. The surrounding area of the Wye Valley on the borders with England is a designated Area of Outstanding Beauty; as is the Gower Peninsula, the Lleyn Peninsula, the Anglesey Coast and the Clwydian Range. The endless miles of largely unspoilt and beautiful Pembrokeshire coastline in the west has some of the finest long beaches in Europe, with pretty little bays plus the lively traditional seaside resorts of Tenby and Whitesand. Further inland is the secluded and pretty Gwaun Valley. The capital of Wales, Cardiff, has many attractions, including its newly developed waterfront, the Millennium Stadium. Castles can be seen all over Wales, ranging from tiny stone keeps to huge medieval fortresses; some of the best preserved are Caernarfon, Conwy and Harlech, all built by Edward I.

Places of interest

North: Isle of Anglesey; Victorian School of 3Rs and Motor Museum at Llangollen; Victorian seaside resort of Llandudno; Colwyn Bay; Caernarfon Castle; Snowdon Mountain Railway at Llanberis.

West: Oakwood Park, Wales' only theme park; the National Botanic Gardens at Aberglasney; Dolaucothi Goldmines; historic, stone-walled Aberaeron.

Mid: Brecon Beacons National Park; the lakes of the Elan Valley; entertaining events all summer at Llanwrtyd Wells; the Centre for Alternative Technology near Machynllleth.

South: Merthyr Tydfil, the Iron Capital of the World; Caerphilly's truly massive medieval castle; Cardiff, capital of Wales; the Wye Valley and the Vale of Usk of the Welsh borderlands with Tintern Abbey.

Did you know?

The origins of the Red Dragon flag may date back to the Roman period, when the dragon was used by military cohorts.

St David's in Pembrokeshire is Britain's smallest city by virtue of its Cathedral to the patron saint of Wales.

There are many sites in Wales linked to the legend of King Arthur: Castell Dinas Brân, near Llangollen, is reputed to be the resting-place of the Holy Grail.

Towering at 1085 metres Mount Snowdon is the highest mountain in England and Wales.

'The Dam Busters' was filmed on location in the Elan Valley.

The Welsh language is one of Europe's oldest languages and shares its roots with Breton, Gaelic and Cornish.

RED TEXT DENOTES ALL YEAR SITE

UK5890 Glen Trothy Caravan & Camping Park

Mitchel Troy, Monmouth NP25 4BD (Monmouthshire)

Tel: 01600 712295. Email: enquiries@glentrothy.co.uk   www.alanrogers.com/UK5890

Glen Trothy is a pretty park on the banks of the river Trothy and visitors are greeted by an array of colourful flowerbeds and tubs around the entrance and reception area. The owners, Horace and Merle Price, are working hard on their site bringing its facilities up-to-date, recently adding a security gate to the new reception office. Three fields provide 40 level touring pitches. The first and largest field has a circular gravel road with seasonal pitches arranged on the outer side of the road and touring pitches on the inner side. These have slabs for vehicle wheels and electricity hook-ups. The second field, just past the toilet block, has pitches for trailer tents and tents only.

Facilities

The sanitary block is old and a little tired (possibly stretched at peak times). Facilities for disabled visitors. Laundry. Tourist information in reception. Bicycle hire. Fishing in the River Trothy (WWA licence required). Dogs are not accepted. Only purpose built barbecues are allowed. Play area. Off site: Golf 2 miles. Shopping and supermarkets at Monmouth. The Wye Valley and the Forest of Dean are nearby for outings.

Open: 1 March - 31 October.

Directions

At Monmouth, take A40 east to Abergavenny. Exit at first junction and at T-junction, where site is signed, turn left onto B4284. Follow signs for Mitchel Troy. Site is on right just past village sign. O.S.GR: SO495105. GPS: N51:47.458 W02:44.046

Charges guide

Per unit incl. 2 persons	£ 8.00 - £ 13.00
extra person	£ 2.50
electricity	£ 2.50

UK5925 Cardiff Caravan Park

Pontcanna Fields, via Sophia Close, Cardiff CF11 9LB (Cardiff)

Tel: **02920 398362**

www.alanrogers.com/UK5925

Run by the city council, this popular site is set within acres of parkland, one mile from the city centre, ideal for visiting the many attractions of the City of Cardiff. The campsite has 73 pitches which are on a fairly open area, with 43 on a grassed grid surface with electric hook-ups (16A), the remainder are on grass. There is a public right of way through the site. Security is good with an on-site warden 24 hours a day, and security cameras (infra red) constantly scanning the whole area. Remember though that you are in a city centre environment, so lock up your valuables.

Facilities

Two heated buildings each with key code entry systems, the one by reception has a laundry with washer and dryer, and facilities for disabled campers. Both have controllable hot showers. Baby facilities. Bicycle hire (the site specialises in cycles adapted for disabled people). Riding can be arranged. Off site: The Millennium Stadium, Glamorgan County Cricket Ground, Cardiff Bay. Local shops and services within easy walking distance. Fishing 0.25 mile, golf 4 miles.

Open: All year.

Directions

From the A48 turn south on A4119 (Cardiff Road). Follow signs for Institute of Sport and at next traffic lights turn into Sophia Close and Gardens. Turn left at Institute of Sport and pass County Cricket Ground on right to site. For satnav use postcode CF11 9XR. O.S.GR: ST171772. GPS: N51:29.493 W03:12.188

Charges guide

Per person	£ 5.50
child (4-14 yrs)	£ 3.00
pitch incl. electricity	£ 7.50

UK5930 Cwmcarn Forest Drive Campsite

Cwmcarn, Crosskeys, Newport NP11 7FA (Newport)

Tel: **01495 272001**. Email: **cwmcarn-vc@caerphilly.gov.uk**

www.alanrogers.com/UK5930

This forest site, run by Caerphilly Council, is set in a narrow, sheltered valley with magnificent wooded slopes. The park is not only central for the many attractions of this part of Wales, but there is also much of the natural environment to enjoy including a small fishing lake and the seven mile forest drive. The site has a slightly wild feel, but is well located and has 27 well spaced, flat pitches, most with 15A electricity (3 with concrete hardstanding), spread over three small fields between the new Visitor Centre and the small lake. Wardens are on hand daily.

Facilities

The single, heated toilet block includes toilet facilities for disabled visitors, laundry facilities, small cooker and fridge. Visitor Centre has a coffee shop selling snacks. Guided walks and the popular Twrch (9 miles) mountain bike trail. Dogs accepted by prior arrangement. Off site: Shops, leisure centre and takeaway food in village less than 1 mile. Riding 2 miles. Golf 3 miles.

Open: All year excl. 23 December - 2 January.

Directions

Cwmcarn Forest Drive is well signed from junction 28 on the M4. From the Midlands and the 'Heads of the Valleys' road (A465), take A467 south to Cwmcarn. O.S.GR: ST230935. GPS: N51:38.263 W03:07.126

Charges guide

Per pitch	£ 7.00 - £ 13.00
electricity	£ 2.50

UK6060 Tredegar House Country Park Caravan Club Site

Coedkernen, Newport NP10 8TW (Newport)

Tel: **01633 815600**

www.alanrogers.com/UK6060

This immaculate Caravan Club site is ideally situated for breaking a journey or for longer stays. It can accommodate 80 caravans, all with 16A electricity and 47 with gravel hardstanding. A further grass area is allocated for 20 tents, with its use limited to families and couples – no single sex groups are accepted. The site itself is set within the gardens and park of Tredegar House, a 17th century house and country park which is open to the public to discover what life was like 'above and below stairs'. The park entrance gates are locked at dusk so contact the site reception for details of latest arrival times. Some road noise may be expected at times, but otherwise this is an excellent site.

Facilities

The sanitary block is of an excellent standard with a digital lock system. It includes washbasins in cubicles. Facilities for disabled visitors. Baby and toddler bathroom. Laundry. Good motorcaravan service point. Calor gas available. Tredegar House visitor centre with tea rooms, gift shop and craft workshops (open Easter - Sept). Adventure play area in the park. Off site: Large supermarket 0.5 miles. Newport 3 miles. Cardiff 9 miles.

Open: All year.

Directions

From M4 take exit 28 or from A48 junction with the M4 follow brown signs for Tredegar House. The caravan park is indicated to the left at the house entrance. O.S.GR: ST299855. GPS: N51:33.048 W03:01.670

Charges guide

Per person	£ 3.90 - £ 5.40
pitch incl. electricity (non-member)	£ 10.30 - £ 14.10

233

UK5927 Acorn Camping & Caravanning

Ham Lane South, Llantwit Major CF61 1RP (Vale of Glamorgan)

Tel: **01446 794024**. Email: **info@acorncamping.co.uk**   **www.alanrogers.com/UK5927**

A peaceful, family owned, rural site, Acorn is situated on the Heritage Coast, one mile from the beach and the historic town of Llantwit Major. The 105 pitches are mostly on grass, with a few private and rental mobile homes at the far end, leaving around 90 pitches for tourers. These include 10 serviced pitches and 4 gravel hardstandings with 74 electric hook-ups (10A), and a separate area for tents. Reception houses a very well stocked shop which includes groceries and essentials, souvenirs, children's toys, camping gear, a delicatessen, and takeaway meals cooked to order. There is occasional aircraft noise. Site lighting is kept to a minimum to allow guests to enjoy the night sky – a torch might be useful. The Glamorgan Heritage Coastal footpath is a short walk from the site and Llantwit Major is also worth a visit, particularly St Illtud's Church for its wall paintings, medieval altar, and collection of Celtic stones.

Facilities

A warm, modern building houses spacious shower cubicles with washbasins, ample WCs, a family/baby room, and a suite for disabled campers. Dishwashing sinks and laundry facilities. Drinks machine. Shop. Gas. Recycling. Snooker room. Games room (charged). Play area with free trampoline. Off site: Glamorgan Heritage Coastal footpath. Llanerch Vineyard. Cosmeston Lakes Country Park at Penarth. Sea fishing 1 mile. Riding 2 miles. Lake 4 miles. Golf, boat launching 9 miles.

Open: 1 February - 8 December.

Directions

From east from M4 exit 33 follow signs to Cardiff airport, take B4265 for Llantwit Major. Turn left at traffic lights, through Broverton and left into Ham Lane East, finally turning left into Ham Manor Park and follow signs to site. From west: M4 exit 35, turn south on A473 for 3 miles, then left on A48, turning right at Pentre Meyrick towards Llantwit Major on B4268/70. Left at roundabout on B4265, over mini-roundabout, right at traffic lights into Llanmaes Road, left at mini-roundabout, continue around back of the town, left at mini-roundabout, and right into Ham Lane East and continue as above.
O.S.GR: SS974678. GPS: N51:24.245 W03:28.909

Charges guide

Per unit incl. 2 persons and electricity	£ 12.85 - £ 14.00
extra person (over 2 yrs)	£ 4.25
dog	£ 0.60

UK5940 Pembrey Country Park Caravan Club Site

Pembrey, Llanelli SA16 0EJ (Carmarthenshire)

Tel: **01554 834369**   **www.alanrogers.com/UK5940**

This very popular Caravan Club site has a wonderful location on the edge of a 520 acre Country Park with a vast range of outdoor activities, including the use of an eight mile stretch of safe, sandy beach a mile away. This well sheltered site is set in 12 acre grounds and provides 50 large hardstanding pitches and 80 level, grass pitches for caravans and motorcaravans, all with 16A electricity. Tents are not accepted. Thoughtful landscaping has included the planting of many species of tree and a circular, one-way tarmac road provides easy access. Sensibly placed service points provide fresh water and waste disposal of all types. RAF jets do practise in this area (although becoming less frequent and generally not flying at the weekend). There may be occasional noise from the nearby motor racing circuit. However, the real plus for this site is its proximity to the Country Park – access to this is free on foot or cycle direct from the site, or the site can organise a special weekly car pass for around £12. Within the parkland are delightful walks, cycle trails, unlimited flora and fauna, bird hides, an equestrian centre, adventure play area, dry ski slope and toboggan run, crazy golf and pitch and putt, miniature railway, bicycle hire and picnic areas, all fronted by Cefn Sidan, an eight mile stretch of golden sands. The nearest section of beach is a 20 minute walk.

Facilities

The toilet block is of an excellent standard including washbasins in cubicles, facilities for disabled visitors and a baby room. Fully equipped laundry room. Dishwashing room and further sinks under cover. Motorcaravan service point. Gas available. Local tradesmen visit each morning selling milk, bread and newspapers. Play area. Late arrivals area (with electricity). Off site: Dogs are restricted on the beach May - Sept (follow signs).

Open: March - January.

Directions

Leave M4 at exit 48 onto A4138 (signed Llanelli). After 4 miles turn right onto A484 at roundabout signed Carmarthen. Continue for 7 miles to Pembrey. The Country Park is signed off the A484 in Pembrey village; site entrance is on right 100 yds before park gates. O.S.GR: SN413006.
GPS: N51:40.909 W04:17.845

Charges guide

Per person	£ 4.40 - £ 5.50
child (5-16 yrs)	£ 1.50 - £ 2.50
pitch incl. electricity (non-member)	£ 10.80 - £ 14.60

UK5880 Springwater Lakes

Harford, Llanwrda SA19 8DT (Carmarthenshire)

Tel: **01558 650788**. Email: **bookings@springwaterlakes.com**

www.alanrogers.com/UK5880

Set in 20 acres of Welsh countryside, Springwater offers a selection of fishing lakes to keep even the keenest of anglers occupied. However, it is not just anglers who will enjoy this site – it is a lovely base to enjoy the peace and tranquillity of this part of Wales. Springwater offers 30 spacious, flat pitches either on grass or gravel hardstanding, all with electricity hook-ups (16A). Malcolm and Shirley Bexon are very proud of their site and welcome all visitors with a smile. This is not a site for children unless they enjoy fishing (no play areas). If you want to learn about fishing Malcolm will be happy to help.

Facilities

The modern toilet block is very clean and includes facilities for disabled visitors (there is also access to the lakes for wheelchairs). Fishing; tackle/bait shop. Off site: Spar shop and garage 500 yards, other shops 5 miles. Bicycle hire and riding 2 miles. Golf 4 miles.

Open: 1 March - 31 October.

Directions

From A40 at Llanwrda take A482 to Lampeter. After 6 miles go through village of Pumsaint and site is 2 miles further on the left, just before garage shop. O.S.GR: SN642429. GPS: N52:04.045 W03:58.935

Charges guide

Per unit incl. 2 persons	£ 13.00
extra person (over 2 yrs)	£ 4.00
electricity	£ 2.75
No credit cards.	

UK5960 Abermarlais Caravan Park

Llangadog SA19 9NG (Carmarthenshire)

Tel: **01550 777868**. Email: **aberma@tiscali.co.uk**

www.alanrogers.com/UK5960

Apart from the attractions of south or mid Wales for a stay, this sheltered, family run park could also double as a useful transit stop close to the main holiday route for those travelling to Pembrokeshire. In a natural setting, up to 88 touring units are accommodated in one fairly flat, tapering five acre grass field edged by mature trees and a stream. Pitches are numbered, and generously spaced around the perimeter or on either side of a central, hedged spine at the wider end, with 48 electrical hook-ups (10A) and some hardstanding. Backpackers have a small, separate area.

Facilities

The one small toilet block is older in style, but is clean, bright, cheerful and adequate with controllable showers. Two external, covered dishwashing sinks but no laundry facilities (nearest about 5 miles). Motorcaravan service point. Shop doubling as reception. Gas supplies. Play area with tennis and volleyball nets and play equipment. Winter caravan storage. Off site: Restaurants nearby. Pubs, shops, etc. at Llangadog. Fishing 2 miles.

Open: 14 March - 14 November.

Directions

Park is on the A40, between the junctions with the A4069 and A482, between Llandovery and Llandeilo. O.S.GR: SN695298. GPS: N51:57.095 W03:54.018

Charges guide

Per person	£ 1.50
child (over 5 yrs)	£ 1.00
pitch	£ 6.00
electricity	£ 2.00

UK6070 Rhandirmwyn Camping & Caravanning Club Site

Rhandirmwyn, Llandovery SA20 0NT (Carmarthenshire)

Tel: **01550 760257**

www.alanrogers.com/UK6070

This is a popular site with those who like a peaceful life with no on-site entertainment, just fresh air and beautiful countryside. The site is only a short drive from the magnificent Llyn Brianne reservoir and close to the Dinas RSPB nature reserve, where a two mile trail runs through oak and alder woodland alongside the River Tywi and the wildlife includes many species of birds including red kites. The site is in a sheltered valley with 90 pitches on level grass, 51 electricity hook-ups (16A) and 17 hardstandings. The village is within walking distance although there is a fairly steep hill to negotiate (but the return is much easier).

Facilities

The single heated sanitary block is kept very clean and tidy. Some washbasins in cubicles, dishwashing sinks and fully equipped laundry. Drive-over motorcaravan service point. Small playground with rubber base. Off site: The village has a Post Office and general store and the Royal Oak Inn serves good value meals. Farmers' market in Llandovery twice a month. Fishing 6 miles. Golf 7 miles. Riding 11 miles.

Open: March - October.

Directions

From centre of Llandovery take A483 towards Builth Wells, after a short distance turn left by the fire station, signed Rhandirmwyn, continue for 7 miles along country lanes. O.S.GR: SN779436. GPS: N52:04.621 W03:47.030

Charges guide

Per person	£ 4.90 - £ 7.25
child (6-18 yrs)	£ 2.15 - £ 2.25
non-member pitch fee	£ 5.65

UK5945 River View Touring Park

The Dingle, Llanedi, Pontarddulais SA4 0FH (Carmarthenshire)

Tel: **01269 844876**. Email: **info@riverviewtouringpark.com**   **www.alanrogers.com/UK5945**

Keith and Kath Brasnett with their warm welcome and helpful efficiency ensure that this park remains attractive, quiet and friendly. Nestling in the valley of the River Gwili, it is made up of three fields: one by the river which is kept mainly for adults and two on a plateau up a steep slope on the opposite side of the lane. Particular care has been taken to protect the natural environment. There are 60 level, generously sized pitches of which 45 are touring pitches, the remainder seasonal. All have electricity (16A), 20 have hardstandings and 5 are fully serviced. This is a popular rural retreat for young families and older couples. The park is close to the end of the M4, allowing easy access and there is plenty to do or see in the near vicinity, castles, gardens, beaches, wildfowl reserves and a water park, and there is an SSSI immediately at the back of the site. The bird life visible from the site is varied and includes buzzards and red kites, and dippers on the river. The toilet block, including an en-suite family room with baby changing facilities and one for the disabled, is modern and equipped to a very high standard, including under floor heating and automatic lighting.

Facilities

The modern, heated, toilet block is spotless with spacious showers, family room and suite for disabled visitors. New laundry with sinks, washing machine, tumble dryer, iron and ironing board. Small shop for basics and local fresh produce. Large grassy recreation area on main field. Fishing. Off site: Shop, bar and restaurant 1 mile. Bicycle hire and golf 5 miles. Beach 12 miles.

Open: 1 March - 6 December.

Directions

From the M4 exit 49 take A483 signed Llandeilo. Take the first turn left (after layby) and park is on the left after 300 yds. O.S.GR: SN578086. GPS: N51:45.490 W04:03.773

Charges guide

Per unit incl. 2 persons and electricity	£ 13.00 - £ 17.00
incl. services	£ 15.50 - £ 19.50
extra person	£ 2.50 - £ 3.00
infant (under 4 yrs)	£ 1.00
dog	free - £ 1.00

No credit cards.

UK5955 Erwlon Caravan & Camping Park

Brecon Road, Llandovery SA20 0RD (Carmarthenshire)

Tel: **01550 721021**. Email: **peter@erwlon.fsnet.co.uk**   **www.alanrogers.com/UK5955**

Just outside Llandovery, on the edge of the Brecon Beacons National Park, Erwlon is an attractive and welcoming campsite. Of the 110 pitches, 7 are used for privately owned caravan holiday homes, 40 have seasonal caravans and 53 are for tourers. Most are on hardstanding with electricity and 11 have water and a drain as well. There is a flat field for tents at the bottom of the park with some electrical outlets, an open-sided, covered area for eating, food preparation and bicycle storage. The site has a relaxed atmosphere where consideration for others minimises the need for formal rules. It is ideal for young families, walkers, cyclists and fishermen. Gold mines and the National Showcaves Centre for Wales (including dinosaur park) are within an easy drive

Facilities

New heated toilet block with washbasins in cabins, 4 family rooms (basin, shower, toilet) and a room for families and disabled visitors which includes a baby unit. Combined, well equipped laundry and dishwashing room. Motorcaravan service point. Fridge freezer. Fishing. Bicycle hire. Off site: Supermarket 500 m. Town amenities (shops, pubs, restaurants and indoor pool) within 1 mile. Riding 1 mile. Fishing 1 mile. Golf 1.5 miles. Beaches 25 miles.

Open: All year.

Directions

Park is about half a mile outside the town boundary of Llandovery on the A40 to Brecon. O.S.GR: SN778344. GPS: N51:59.695 W03:46.846

Charges guide

Per unit incl. up to 4 persons	£ 11.00
incl. services	£ 13.50
extra person	£ 1.00

No credit cards.

UK5974 Pantglas Farm Caravan Park

Tavernspite, Amroth SA34 0NS (Pembrokeshire)

Tel: 01834 831618. Email: pantglasfarm@btinternet.com   www.alanrogers.com/UK5974

A secluded, rural, family run park with a nice atmosphere, Pantglas Farm is four miles from the coast with extensive views over rolling countryside and down to the sea. Set in three gently sloping paddocks spread over 14 acres, there are 86 generously sized, fairly level pitches most with electricity (10A), 70 on gravel hardstanding. Around 86 are available for touring units. This is a popular and attractive site close to the main resorts but enjoying a more tranquil atmosphere. An on-site clubhouse also has a lounge with TV and a games room, with some simple entertainment activities arranged at Bank Holidays, weekends and in high season. Amenities on site include a well equipped, partially fenced play area and activity centre which includes an aerial ropeway. A football field is located at the very end of the site. No kite flying or washing lines are allowed on the site and single sex groups are not accepted.

Facilities

Two toilet blocks (one can be heated) are of a good standard including large controllable showers and some washbasins in cubicles. Facilities for disabled campers. Wet room. Laundry with washing machine, dryer, indoor washing lines and a baby deck. Gas supplies. Battery charging and freezer pack services. Licensed clubhouse (evenings only every day for B.Hs and peak season, weekends only low season). Updated play area. Games field. Games room. TV lounge. Caravan and boat storage. Off site: Supermarket and ATM at Whitland 3 miles. Beaches at Amroth or Pendine 4 miles. Fishing 1 mile. Golf 10 miles.

Open: March - 3rd weekend in October.

Directions

Site is 3 miles southwest of Whitland. From the A477 Tenby - Pembroke road turn right at Red Roses crossroads to Tavernspite for 1.25 miles. At the village pump take the middle road and site is about 0.5 miles on left. O.S.GR: SN 176122.
GPS: N51:46.699 W04:38.725

Charges guide

Per unit incl. 2 persons and electricity	£ 14.00 - £ 16.00
tent incl. 2 persons	£ 10.00 - £ 12.00
extra person	£ 3.00
child (2-15 yrs)	£ 1.50
dog	£ 1.50

UK6005 Brynawelon Touring & Camping Park

Sarnau, Llandysul SA44 6RE (Ceredigion)

Tel: 01239 654584. Email: info@brynawlon.co.uk   www.alanrogers.com/UK6005

Paul and Liz Cowton have turned Brynawelon into a friendly, attractive and well appointed campsite. It is in a stunning rural location within two miles of the Ceredigion coast with its beaches, and close to the River Teifi with plenty of water based activities. All the 40 pitches have electricity hook-ups and of these 26 are serviced pitches (water and waste) on hardstanding. The remainder are on level grass. The park has ample room for children to play, an enclosed play area, an indoor games room with TV, and a sauna next to reception. Buzzards, red kites, owls and the occasional eagle can be seen from the park. There is also a wide variety of small birds. A wide choice of beaches can be found along the coast, there are dolphin trips from Newquay ten miles away and white water rafting on the Teifi at Llandysul. The Teifi is also a well known canoeing and fishing river.

Facilities

New modern toilet block with toilets, showers, washbasins in cabins, two full suites in each side and a separate room for families and disabled visitors. Laundry/kitchen with washing machine, tumble dryer, ironing board and iron, fridge/freezer, microwave, kettle and toaster. Small shop in reception selling basics (July - Sept). Enclosed play area. Games room with pool, electronic games, TV and library. Sauna. Dog walking area and daytime dog care (charged). Off site: Shops and pub 1 mile. Beaches, fishing, sailing and riding 3 miles. Dolphin trips at Newquay 10 miles. White water rafting and canoeing at Llandysul 10 miles.

Open: 15 March - 31 October.

Directions

Travelling north on the A487 from Cardigan turn right (southeast) at the crossroads in Sarnau village, signed Rhydlewis. Site is on the left after 650 yards. Note: the country roads from the south are not suitable for caravans and motorcaravans.
O.S.GR: SN322508. GPS: N52:07.801 W04:27.241

Charges guide

Per unit incl. 2 adults, 2 children and electricity	£ 18.50
incl. services, hardstanding	£ 15.00 - £ 20.00
No credit cards.	

UK6010 Cenarth Falls Holiday Park

Cenarth, Newcastle Emlyn SA38 9JS (Ceredigion)

Tel: 01239 710345. Email: enquiries@cenarth-holipark.co.uk

www.alanrogers.com/UK6010

The Davies family has developed an attractively landscaped, part wooded holiday home park with 86 privately owned units and 3 for hire. However, a neat well cared for, sheltered grassy area at the top of the park provides 30 touring pitches, accessed via a semicircular tarmac road, and all with sunken grass grid hardstanding and electricity (16A). A sunken, kidney shaped outdoor pool with landscaped surrounds and sun beds is a focal point. The Coracles Health and Country Club provides an indoor pool, spa, sauna and steam rooms and a fitness suite (there are reduced rates for campers). It also provides a bar, restaurant area, adult-only lounge and a large function room where live entertainment is organised weekly all season. Everything is of a high quality. A footpath leads to the village and the famous Cenarth Falls. The National Coracle Centre is well worth a visit. A member of the Best of British group.

Facilities

The excellent, heated sanitary block has easy ramped access, even to the chemical disposal unit. Accessed by key, it uses a 'P.I.R.' system that controls heating, lighting, water and air freshener. Provision for disabled visitors (doubling as a family room), spacious well equipped showers and one of the washbasins in a roomy private cabin. Laundry room and ironing facilities (used by the whole park). Gas supplies. Outdoor pool (mid May - mid Sept). Coracles Health and Country Club (see above). Play area. Games room. No dogs on touring field (16/7-3/9). Off site: Shop within 0.5 miles. Fishing 0.25 miles. Riding 7 miles. Bicycle hire 8 miles. Golf 10 miles.

Open: 1 March - 9 January.

Directions

Follow A484 Cardigan - Newcastle Emlyn road and park is signed before Cenarth village.
O.S.GR: SN265421. GPS: N52:02.994 W04:31.903

Charges guide

Per unit incl. up to 4 people	£ 14.00 - £ 24.00
extra person	£ 2.00
awning	£ 2.00
dog	£ 2.00

UK5992 Creampots Touring Caravan & Camping Park

Broadway, Broad Haven, Haverfordwest SA62 3TU (Pembrokeshire)

Tel: 01437 781776

www.alanrogers.com/UK5992

This peacefully located and beautifully manicured, garden-like park is ideal for couples and families with very young children, and is a convenient base within easy reach of beaches or for touring the local area. Creampots has 72 spacious, level pitches all with 10A electric hook-ups, including 12 with gravel hardstanding, and 10 pitches for tents. These are in two neat well hedged and sheltered paddocks. Around 40 seasonal units and one caravan holiday home for rent are also accommodated, and there is a separate rally field and an overflow area taking 30 touring units for the August peak holiday time. American RVs are accepted (maximum 36 ft – book in advance). There is a grassy games area for children. Nearby there are bird sanctuaries and the Pembrokeshire Coastal Path.

Facilities

The single small white-washed sanitary unit is a modern building which can be heated. Two free hot showers per sex, open style washbasins. Washbasin and WC for disabled campers. These facilities were clean and tidy but may come under pressure at peak times. Tiny laundry room with just about space for one person at a time but with washing machine, dryer and sink. Outside are 2 covered dishwashing sinks at each end of the block. Gas supplies. Bread, milk, newspapers to order. Off site: Summer bus service (May - Sept) 400 yds. Shop, post office, pub with hot food in Broad Haven 1 mile. Fishing and boat launching 1 mile. Beach 1.5 miles. Riding 4 miles. Sailing 6 miles. Golf 7 miles.

Open: March - October.

Directions

Site is 5 miles west of Haverfordwest. From Haverfordwest take B4341 to Broad Haven, at Broadway turn left (signed Milford Haven) and park is second entrance on right in under half a mile.
O.S.GR: SM882132. GPS: N51:46.640 W05:04.337

Charges guide

Per unit incl. 2 persons	£ 14.50 - £ 18.50
up to 4 persons	£ 16.50 - £ 20.00
electricity (10A)	£ 3.50
dog	free

UK5975 Little Kings Park

Ludchurch, Amroth SA67 8PG (Pembrokeshire)

Tel: 01834 831330. Email: littlekingspark@btconnect.com   www.alanrogers.com/UK5975

This superb family run park has a number of attributes to make your stay both comfortable and memorable. There are stunning views over Carmarthen Bay to the Gower and on beyond to the coast of Somerset and North Devon. At night no fewer than seven lighthouses can be seen blinking out their warnings. A touring field provides 49 well spaced, large touring pitches all with 10A electricity, 21 with gravel hardstanding and 14 fully serviced. An attractive playground is in the central open grass area. A further 7 pitches are in a different area. There are 40 pitches for tents in an adjoining paddock with 31 electricity hook-ups. A separate well hedged and screened paddock contains 20 caravan holiday homes (13 for hire). The excellent amenities include a restaurant and bar, which has a conservatory overlooking a well presented, covered, heated swimming pool. The restaurant serves a good range of evening meals and has a children's menu. Last, but by no means least, is the comprehensively stocked shop which has just about everything you might need, including reception, tourist information and a bakery offering fresh bread daily and hot snacks (pasties, sausage rolls, etc.) cooked to order. This is an ideal site for a family holiday or for touring the area.

Facilities

The two toilet blocks are modern and well equipped, including controllable hot showers (20p for 6 minutes, 30p for 9), open style washbasins, a family shower room and a full suite for disabled campers. Extras include paper towel and soap dispensers, air fresheners, and hand and hairdryers. Laundry rooms. Shop with bakery, Takeaway, bar and restaurant with conservatory (evenings only; low season at B.Hs and weekends only). Covered swimming pool. Games rooms. Playground. Ball games area. Gas supplies. Off site: Nearest supermarket and ATM at Kilgetty 2.5 miles. Tenby and Pendine Sands both 7 miles.

Open: 1 March - January.

Directions

Site is 5 miles southeast of Narberth. From the A477 Carmarthen to Pembroke road turn left towards Amroth and Wiseman's Bridge. Take first right (signed Ludchurch) and park is 300 m. on left. O.S.GR: SN146093. GPS: N51:45.091 W04:41.274

Charges 2009

Per unit incl. 2 persons and electricity	£ 14.00 - £ 23.00
extra person (over 3 yrs)	£ 2.00
awning	£ 2.00
dog (max. 2)	£ 2.00 - £ 3.00

LITTLE KINGS PARK Quiet family run 5-star Holiday Park offering a high standard of facilities and a warm welcome. Set in an ideal location to explore all that Pembrokeshire has to offer.
- Holiday Homes and Bungalow
- Tourers and Motorhomes
- Tents and Trailer Tents
- Family Bar/Restaurant
- Covered, heated Pool
- Shop and Public Phone
- Games Room
- 2 Amenity Blocks
- 2 Play areas
- Dog walk
- Staff present 24 hrs
Open: March to January (Touring) Easter to September (Holiday Homes)
Tel: 01834 831330   www.littlekings.co.uk
email: littlekingspark@btconnect.com
We look forward to welcoming you to our park - we love it here and hope that you will too.

UK6280 Aeron Coast Caravan Park

North Road, Aberaeron SA46 0JF (Ceredigion)

Tel: 01545 570349. Email: enquiries@aeroncoast.co.uk   www.alanrogers.com/UK6280

Aeron Coast is a family holiday park with a wide range of recreational facilities, on the west coast of Wales. Although it has a high proportion of caravan holiday homes (200 privately owned), touring units of all types are provided for in two fields separated from the beach and sea by a high bank (although the best beach is on the south side of this traditional fishing village). Pitches are on level grass with all units regularly and well spaced in lines in traditional style. The main attraction of the park is its excellent provision for families, both in and out of doors. This includes two outdoor pools (one new) and a toddlers' pool (unsupervised) in a paved, walled area good for sunbathing.

Facilities

Two modern toilet blocks offer excellent facilities including large family showers. Facilities for disabled people and babies are in one block. Basic motorcaravan service point. Swimming pools (heated 24/5-15/9). Club house and bar (from Easter, 12.00-14.00 and from 19.00) with family room serving bar meals and takeaway in school holiday periods. New entertainments room. Shop at the petrol station at the entrance. Only one dog per unit is accepted. Off site: Beach, fishing and boat launching 0.5 miles. A steam railway, craft centre, woollen mills and potteries can be visited locally.

Open: 1 March - 31 October.

Directions

Park is on northern outskirts of Aberaeron village with entrance on the right beside a petrol station. Brown sigpost. O.S.GR: SN461631. GPS: N52:14.670 W04:15.295

Charges 2009

Per unit incl. 4 persons and electricity	£ 15.00 - £ 24.00
extra person (over 2 yrs)	£ 3.00

239

UK6290 Glan-y-Mor Leisure Park

Clarach Bay, Aberystwyth SY23 3DT (Ceredigion)

Tel: **01970 828900**. Email: **glanymor@sunbourne.co.uk**　　　　www.alanrogers.com/UK6290

Follow the road to Clarach Bay and on the seafront is Glan-y-Mor, a busy, holiday park with an enviable situation. On a wet day you may not wish to go far with the comprehensive leisure centre on site – with reduced entry fee for campers. Although the balance of pitches is very much in favour of caravan holiday homes (3:1) which dominate the open park and bay, there are 60 touring pitches, 45 with electricity (10A) and 4 new 'super' pitches. They are rather small and are pressed together in two small sections on the lower part of the park. In high season, tents, tourers or motorcaravans can opt for space and fine views (but maybe winds) on a ridge of higher ground above the park.

Facilities

The heated toilet block is on the lower touring area with dishwashing facilities and laundry room, plus a toilet for disabled people. A 'portacabin' type block (high season only) is on the ridge ground. A unit for disabled people is in a block in the upper static area, with further facilities at the leisure centre (RADAR key). Motorcaravan service point. Supermarket. Play area. Swimming pool. Licensed restaurant and takeaway (from Easter). Freezer service and gas. Off site: Reduced rates are at local golf courses.

Open: 1 March - 31 October.

Directions

Clarach is signed west from the A487 (Aberystwyth - Machynlleth) in village of Bow Street (take care at narrow bridge). Follow signs over crossroads to beach and park. Access for caravans from Aberystwyth on B4572 is difficult.
O.S.GR: SN587841. GPS: N52:26.175 W04:04.815

Charges guide

Per unit incl. 6 persons and electricity	£ 15.00 - £ 27.00
'super' pitch	£ 16.00 - £ 30.00

UK5980 Moreton Farm Leisure Park

Moreton, Saundersfoot SA69 9EA (Pembrokeshire)

Tel: **01834 812016**. Email: **moretonfarm@btconnect.com**　　　　www.alanrogers.com/UK5980

Moreton Farm has been developed in a secluded valley, a 10-20 minute walk from Saundersfoot and four miles from Tenby. It provides 30 caravan (all with 16A electricity, and 17 with hardstanding) and 30 tent pitches on two sloping, neatly cut grass fields, with 12 pine holiday lodges and four cottages for letting occupying another field. The site is approached under a railway bridge (height 10 ft 9 ins, width across the top 6 ft 6 ins), although there is alternative access over the railway line for slightly larger vehicles. There are a few trains during the day, none at night. This is a quiet family site.

Facilities

The toilet blocks (which can be heated) are light and airy, providing pre-set hot showers (on payment). Unit for disabled visitors with ramp (shower, toilet and washbasin). Baby bath. Laundry facilities. Fenced, outside clothes drying area. Small shop for basics and gas. Playground. Bicycle hire can be arranged. No dogs or other pets are accepted. Off site: Fishing and riding 1 mile. Golf 4 miles.

Open: 1 March - 31 October.

Directions

From A477 Carmarthen - Pembroke road take the A478 for Tenby at Kilgetty. Park is signed on left after 1.5 miles. Watch carefully for sign and park is 0.5 miles up poorly made-up road and under bridge.
O.S.GR: SN116050. GPS: N51:42.719 W04:43.661

Charges guide

Per unit incl. 2 persons	£ 12.00 - £ 15.00
electricity	£ 3.00

UK5982 Trefalun Park

Devonshire Drive, Saint Florence, Tenby SA70 8RD (Pembrokeshire)

Tel: **01646 657514**. Email: **trefalun@aol.com**　　　　www.alanrogers.com/UK5982

Only four miles from Tenby and the beaches of Carmarthen Bay, Trefalun Park is an open, well laid out campsite with a friendly atmosphere engendered by the owners. The 100 pitches, including 10 occupied by caravan holiday homes in their own enclave and 22 seasonal units, are mainly level, although the park has gentle slopes. There are 34 hardstandings, of which 12 are serviced pitches. Except for the tent area, pitches are generously sized and have electricity (10/16A). This park will suit those, particularly families, looking for a quiet holiday and also the more active who favour walking, cycling or watersports.

Facilities

Modern heated toilet block, with some washbasins in cabins. Water to showers and laundry and dishwashing sinks is metered (20p). Separate, fully equipped suite for disabled visitors and families. Separate baby room. Laundry. Play area. Gas sold. Off site: Shop, pub (with food) and outdoor pool 1.5 miles. Fishing, riding and wildlife park 600 yds. Golf 3 miles. Tenby 4 miles.

Open: 16 March - 31 October.

Directions

From the A477 at Sageston (4 miles east of Pembroke) turn southeast just to the east of the village on B4318 signed Wildlife Park. Trefalun Park is signed to the left after 2.5 miles, opposite entrance to the Wildlife Park. GPS: N51:41.596 W04:45.204

Charges guide

Per pitch	£ 9.50 - £ 15.00
incl. services	£ 11.00 - £ 19.50

UK5995 Caerfai Bay Caravan & Tent Park

Caerfai Road, Saint Davids SA62 6QT (Pembrokeshire)

Tel: **01437 720274**. Email: **info@caerfaibay.co.uk**   **www.alanrogers.com/UK5995**

About as far west as one can get in Wales, Saint David's is Britain's smallest city, noted for its Cathedral and Bishops Palace. This cliff-top park in West Wales has direct access to the Pembrokeshire Coastal Path and a magnificent sandy beach is just a few minutes away, down the path from the car park by the site entrance. The camping area is spread over three open and sloping fields, all with magnificent views over Saint Brides Bay. The caravan field also has a small number of holiday homes and is closest to reception. The second and third fields are for tents and motorcaravans, almost all on grass with a few hardstandings. Altogether there are 105 touring pitches and 45 electricity hook-ups (10A). Main access roads are tarmac. Caerfai Farm Shop is just across the lane (opens end of May), and other shops and services are just 1 mile. Site lighting is deliberately minimal, so torches are useful.

Facilities

Three main buildings house the sanitary facilities, one by reception which is heated, contains facilities for disabled visitors and families and a room with sinks, microwave and hot drinks machine. Adjacent a small new block offers 3 unisex cubicles (WC and basin). The third in the tent fields (extensively refurbished) includes 4 family rooms. Motorcaravan services. Bicycle storage. Wet suit washing facility and enclosed drying area. Gas. Barbecue stands for hire. Off site: Walk the Pembrokeshire coastal path, visit Ramsey Island Bird and Grey Seal Reserve. Sea fishing 400 yds. Indoor pool and bicycle hire 1 mile. Golf 2 miles. Riding 10 miles. Boat launching 1.5 or 3 miles.

Open: 1 March - 14 November.

Directions

From Haverfordwest take the A487 to St David's. On passing the city boundary, turn left into lane immediately before the National Park Visitor Centre (site signed), and continue on for 0.75 mile to site entrance on right. O.S.GR: SM759244.
GPS: N51:52.379 W05:15.414

Charges guide

Per unit incl. 2 persons	£ 11.00 - £ 15.50
tent incl. 2 persons	£ 9.50 - £ 13.00
extra person	£ 4.25
child (3-12 yrs)	£ 3.00
electricity	£ 4.00

Discounts for early payment,
and for senior citizens in low season.

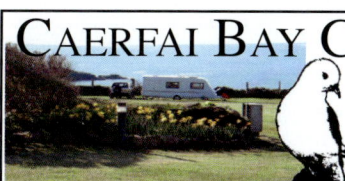

UK5994 Redlands Touring Caravan & Camping Park

Hasguard Cross, Little Haven, Haverfordwest SA62 3SJ (Pembrokeshire)

Tel: **01437 781300**. Email: **info@redlandscamping.co.uk**   **www.alanrogers.com/UK5994**

This peaceful, family run site is located in the heart of the Pembrokeshire countryside, close to many lovely sandy beaches. Redlands takes around 80 touring units in three areas divided by banks topped with pine trees, 64 with 10A electricity. The first two areas take 60 caravans or motorcaravans and include 20 hardstandings, the third takes 19 tents on a level grassy meadow. There are fine views across rolling countryside to St Brides Bay. Reception has a small shop which is open only in peak periods. Breathable groundsheets must be used. American RVs – advance booking only. A sandy beach and the Pembrokeshire Coastal Path are 1.5 miles away.

Facilities

The traditional style toilet block is well kept and heated early and late season. It has all the usual requirements including two extra shower, basin and WC suites. Large utility room with washing machine, dryer and spin dryer. Ironing is free, and there are sinks for laundry and dishes. Shop. Freezers. Wet suit washing area. Off site: Shops and ATM in Broadhaven 2 miles. Summer bus service. Fishing and boat launching 1.5 miles. Riding and sailing 5 miles. Golf 6 miles.

Open: 1 March - mid December.

Directions

Site 6.5 miles southwest of Haverfordwest. From Haverfordwest take the B4327 road towards Dale and site is on the right at Hasguard Cross. Do not approach via Broad Haven. O.S.GR: SM853109.
GPS: N51:45.334 W05:06.743

Charges guide

Per unit incl. up to 4 persons	£ 12.50 - £ 31.00
extra person	£ 4.50
electricity	£ 3.25
dog	£ 0.80

No credit cards.

241

UK5985 Manorbier Country Park

Station Road, Manorbier, Tenby SA70 7SN (Pembrokeshire)

Tel: **01834 871952**. Email: **enquiries@countrypark.co.uk**   www.alanrogers.com/UK5985

This area of southwest Wales is quite attractive, with a variety of historic buildings, sandy beaches and an extensive coastal footpath. This campsite is has 103 caravan holiday homes and 28 seasonal units, which leaves only around 22 pitches for tourists. There are seven orderly rows of concrete and gravel hardstanding pitches set into a level grass field; 32 pitches have electric hook-ups (16A), cable TV and a shared water tap, and 4 are multi-service pitches. Additionally, 10 grass pitches are on the opposite side of the car park with electric hook-ups, and 4 grass pitches at the front of the main field with no services. Cars park away from the caravans on a wide tarmac parking area.

Facilities

A single building at one end of the car parking area provides all toilet facilities, it can be heated, and has controllable showers (on payment), a multi-purpose room suitable for families, babies and disabled campers. Small laundry room. Shop. Bar and restaurant. Indoor heated pools. Jacuzzi. Sauna and steam room, solarium, gym and tennis (all charged). Adventure play area. Dogs are not accepted. Off site: Bicycle hire, boat launching, sailing and beach 1.5 miles. Golf and riding 3 miles. Tenby 6 miles.

Open: 1 March - 31 October.

Directions

From Tenby take A4139 towards Pembroke, passing through Penally and Lydstep. At crossroads (Manorbier signed to left) continue straight on following signs to the station. Turn right by Baptist Chapel into Station Road, and continue to site entrance (do not go into Manorbier village). O.S.GR: SS068991. GPS: N51:39.475 W04:47.657

Charges guide

Per unit incl. up to 4 persons	£ 16.50 - £ 23.50
extra person	£ 2.00

UK5990 Freshwater East Caravan Club Site

Trewent Hill, Freshwater East, Pembroke SA71 5LJ (Pembrokeshire)

Tel: **01646 672341**   www.alanrogers.com/UK5990

This Caravan Club site in the Pembrokeshire Coast National Park is open to non-members (for all units). At the foot of a hill, it has 130 mainly level pitches bounded by trees, 128 with 16A electrical hook-ups and around half on hardstanding. There are a further 12 pitches for tents. The beach and the Pembroke Coastal Path are about a five minute walk. This is an excellent area for walking with magnificent cliff views and birdwatching. Note: TV aerial connections are available.

Facilities

The two heated toilet blocks are modern and clean with washbasins in cubicles, and free hairdryers or sockets for your own. Facilities for disabled visitors. Fully equipped laundry rooms. Gas supplies. Reception keeps basic food items. Information kiosk. Small play area. Off site: Shop 0.5 miles. Fishing within 5 miles.

Open: 7 March - 7 October.

Directions

From the east on A477, fork left 1.25 miles past Milton onto A4075 Pembroke road. After 2 miles in Pembroke immediately (after bridge) sharp left on A4139 (Tenby). In 1.75 miles in Lamphey turn right (B4584). In 1.75 miles turn right (Stackpole, Trewent) and after 400 yds right at Club sign. O.S.GR: SS014980. GPS: N51:38.875 W04:52.136

Charges guide

Per person	£ 4.10 - £ 5.40
pitch (non-member)	£ 10.70 - £ 14.10

UK6240 Cringoed Caravan Park

Cringoed, Llanbrynmair, Newtown SY19 7DR (Powys)

Tel: **01650 521237**   www.alanrogers.com/UK6240

Cringoed is a pleasant, peaceful, small park with a river to one side, hills on the other and trees at either end. There are 30 spacious pitches available for touring and these are in a level open field. Some of these have hardstanding and all have electricity (16A). The 31 caravan holiday homes are at both ends of the site, some amongst trees and some in a newer, more open area. There are also 10 tent pitches. This is a relaxing base where you can sit and listen to the river and watch the wildlife, but it is also within easy reach of some of mid-Wales' best scenery and not far from the coast.

Facilities

The single toilet block is neat, modern and quite adequate. Laundry and dishwashing. Adventure play area. Small tourist information room. Off site: Shops 1 mile. ATM at Spar in Carno 6 miles. Bicycle hire 1 mile. Fishing 5 miles. Golf 8 miles. Riding 12 miles.

Open: 7 March - 7 January (ring first in low season).

Directions

From the A470 between Newton and Machynlleth in village of Llanbrynmair take B4518 signed Staylittle (caravan signs). After 1 mile just before bridge turn right, go over site bridge and turn right into site. O.S.GR: SH887013. GPS: N52:35.900 W03:38.663

Charges guide

Per unit incl. 2 persons and electricity	£ 14.50 - £ 18.00
No credit cards.	

UK6040 Pencelli Castle Caravan & Camping Park

Pencelli, Brecon LD3 7LX (Powys)

Tel: 01874 665451. Email: pencelli@tiscali.co.uk   www.alanrogers.com/UK6040

Open all year round, this is a quality park with atmosphere and character which continues to improve. Set amidst the Brecon scenery, it offers excellent facilities in peaceful, rural tranquillity. The owners, Liz and Gerwyn Rees, have retained the country charm but have added an all embracing range of spacious, heated, luxury facilities, attractively enhanced by potted plants, etc. There are three touring fields. The 'Orchard' incorporates 15 fully serviced pitches with hardstanding, amongst shrubs, fruit trees and a stone cider mill. The 'Oaks' taking 20 caravans and tents and the 'Meadow' for 40 tents (with boot and bike wash) are bordered by majestic trees and the Monmouthshire and Brecon Canal, where gaily painted barges slip past. All the fields are level with neatly mown grass and tarmac access roads. The historic manor house, that dates back to 1583, is adjacent to arched barns that house an increasing collection of vintage farm machinery including carts and rare tractors. For mountain bikers and walkers, a path leaves the village to reach the top of the Brecon Beacons or there is an easy towpath ramble to Tal-y-Bont where there are pubs, tea rooms and a post office.

Facilities

The toilet block is very well designed and includes some private cubicles, two large fully equipped rooms for families or disabled visitors incorporating double showers, baby changing and bath facilities, all humorously decorated for the young at heart. Laundry. Drying room with lockers. Information and planning room. Internet access and WiFi. Motorcaravan service point. Small shop at reception (basics). Playground and nature trail for children. Bicycle hire. Dogs are not accepted (except 'assistance dogs'). Off site: The Royal Oak Inn with meals 100 m. Buses pass regularly for Brecon, Abergavenny. Riding 2 miles. Golf and bicycle hire 5 miles.

Open: All year excl. 3-30 December.

Directions

From A40 south after Brecon bypass take the B4558 at signs for Llanfrynach and later Pencelli (narrow bridge). If travelling north on A40, approach via Tal-y-Bont. Site at south end of Pencelli. O.S.GR: SO095249. GPS: N51:54.887 W03:19.072

Charges guide

Per unit incl. 2 persons and electricity	£ 19.25 - £ 22.25
extra person	£ 6.00 - £ 9.00
child (5-15 yrs)	£ 4.50 - £ 5.50
tent – per person	£ 8.00 - £ 9.50

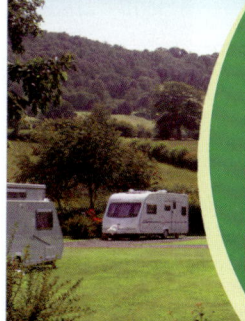

Pencelli Castle Caravan & Camping Park

Peacefully set at the foothills of the Brecon Beacons and within walking distance of the highest peaks. Adjoining Brecon Canal and the Taff Cycle Trail. Village pub 150 yds. Shop, hardstandings, serviced pitches and luxurious shower block. Red deer, vintage farm machinery, and children's play area. On bus route. WiFi and internet access. Closed 3rd to 30th December. **Assistance Dogs Only**

Wales Cymru
Touring & Camping Park
Parc Teithio a Gwersylla
★★★★★

- 2008, 6, 5, 3 & 2 Loo of the Year - National Winner Wales
- 2007, 06, 05 & 4 Wales In Bloom Winner
- 2006 & 02 AA - Best Campsite in Wales
- 2005 WTB Wales Tourism Awards - Winner Best Place to Stay
- 2007 to 01 Gold - David Bellamy Conservation Award
- 2005 Practical Caravan Top 100 Family Park - Winner Wales
- 2003 WTB Wales Tourism Awards - Winner Best Place to Stay
- 2001 Calor Gas - Best Park in Wales

Campsite of the Year
AA
Wales 2006

Pencelli • Brecon • Powys • Wales • UK • LD3 7LX • Tel: 01874 665 451
email: pencelli@tiscali.co.uk • www.pencelli-castle.com

UK6250 Dolswydd Caravan Park

Dolswydd, Pen-y-Bont, Llandrindod Wells LD1 5UB (Powys)

Tel: 01597 851267. Email: Hughes@dolswydd.freeserve.co.uk   www.alanrogers.com/UK6250

Dolswydd is on the edge of a pretty, traditional working farm. Peaceful and tranquil, with fine views of the Welsh hills and surrounding area, it has modern facilities and 25 good spacious pitches mainly on hardstandings, all with electrical connections (16A). The Hughes family extends a warm and friendly welcome to their little park, surrounded by hills and wandering sheep, which is ideal as a touring base or for a one night stop, but booking is recommended, especially at peak times.

Facilities

Modern facilities include lots of hot water, dishwashing, laundry, and a WC/washroom for disabled people. Fishing in the river alongside the site (free, but licence required). Off site: Within walking distance are the local pub and garage. Riding 1 mile. Golf and bicycle hire 5 miles.

Open: Easter - end October.

Directions

Pen-y-bont is 2 miles east of the junction of the A44 and A483 roads at Crossgates. Take the A44 (Kington). Go through Pen-y-bont and immediately after crossing cattle grid, site is on right. O.S.GR: SO117639. GPS: N52:15.793 W03:16.852

Charges 2009

Per unit incl. 2 persons and 2 children	£ 10.00
electricity	£ 2.00

UK6245 Morben Isaf Touring & Holiday Home Park

Derwenlas, Machynlleth SY20 8SR (Powys)

Tel: **01654 781473**. Email: **manager@morbenisaf.co.uk**   www.alanrogers.com/UK6245

Morben Isaf provides 13 touring pitches with multi-services, all with electricity (16A), water tap, waste water drain and a satellite TV hook-up. There is further grassy space below the touring pitches beyond the fishing lake which is normally used as a play field and football pitch but can take around 30 tents who do not need any services. On a lower level, behind the site manager's bungalow, and barely visible from the touring site, are 87 privately owned caravan holiday homes. Also on the site is an unfenced coarse fishing lake which campers are free to use. Machynlleth is a market town, home of Owain Glyndwr's fifteenth century Welsh Parliament building and the Celtica Centre, and is also close to the Tal-y-Llyn Steam Railway, the Centre for Alternative Technology, Corris Craft Centre and King Arthur's Labyrinth. This site is in a convenient location for an overnight halt, or a short stay whilst visiting all these attractions.

Facilities

Small but well equipped, heated modern toilet block includes spacious controllable showers, baby changing and child seats in both ladies' and men's. Facilities for disabled campers. Well equipped laundry. Powered motorcaravan service point suitable for American RVs. Off site: Pub serving hot food 1.5 miles. Leisure Centre, shops and services in Machynlleth 3 miles (market on Wednesday). Centre for Alternative Technology 6 miles.

Open: Mid March - 31 October.

Directions

Site is 2.5 miles southwest of Machynlleth beside the A487. O.S.GR: SN706986. GPS: N52:34.204 W03:54.687

Charges guide

Per unit incl. 2 adults, 2 children and electricity	£ 15.50 - £ 17.50
tent on field	£ 7.50 - £ 12.50

Morben Isaf Caravan Park

Morben Isaf Caravan Park, Machynlleth, Powys. SY20 8SR

Set in a peaceful location, we are ideally located near the historic town of Machynlleth. Fishing is available in the park and golf nearby. Our facilities include a fully serviced laundry room and a first class toilet/shower block. A selection of holiday homes are also available for purchase.
For more details please contact us on **01654 781473**

UK6045 Gilestone Camping & Caravan Park

On A40, Talybont on Usk LD3 7JE (Powys)

Tel: **01874 676236**. Email: **gilestonefarm@aol.com**   www.alanrogers.com/UK6045

Only opened in 2006, Gilestone is situated in the Usk valley within a 300 acre arable and beef farm in the Brecon Beacons National Park. It has 100 pitches, 50 for caravans and 50 for tents, all with electricity, plus 22 fully serviced pitches suitable for large units. Unusually the park can provide horse B&B facilities for those who wish to take their horses and ponies on holiday and has direct access to large areas of trekking country. There is a dedicated area for those with tents which has its own toilet facilities. This rural park caters for all ages and has a four acre play area for children, a well stocked Farm Shop selling local fresh produce and hot tubs to relax in after all those strenuous activities. The owners Chris and Geraint Thomas are extremely knowledgeable about the area and can arrange most requests (with a little advance warning). Ready erected tents can be rented on the site, as can bicycles. Llangorse Lake is only three miles away where windsurfing, sailing and scuba lessons are all on offer. Alternatively, you can just enjoy the peace and tranquillity of the 300 acres where red kite, herons, buzzards, swans and lapwings are readily seen from the lanes.

Facilities

Toilet and shower facilities in the single new main block also housing reception, the Farm Shop and café, should now be available. Hot tubs to rent. Facilities for disabled visitors. Laundry room. Motorcaravan service area. Shop with local produce (all year). Play area. Fishing. Bicycle hire. Horse B&B. Teepee hire for woodland camping. Nature trail. Rallies welcome. Off site: Four pubs with meals within 5 minutes walk. Lake for watersports 3 miles. Riding 2 miles. Golf 5 miles. Two local Play Barns for children.

Open: All year.

Directions

From Brecon on the A40 follow brown tourism signs along the 40 to new junction. Site is on right after bridge over the river. O.S.GR: SO120231. GPS: N51:54.104 W03:17.197

Charges guide

Per unit incl. 2 persons and electricity	£ 16.00 - £ 18.00
incl. services	£ 21.00 - £ 25.00
extra person	£ 6.00 - £ 7.00
child (0-8 yrs)	free

UK6320 Fforest Fields Caravan & Camping Park

Hundred House, Builth Wells LD1 5RT (Powys)

Tel: **01982 570406**. Email: **office@fforestfields.co.uk**   **www.alanrogers.com/UK6320**

This secluded 'different' park is set on a family hill farm in the heart of Radnorshire. Truly rural, there are glorious views and a distinctly family atmosphere. This is simple country camping and caravanning at its best, without man-made distractions or intrusions. The facilities include 80 large pitches on level grass on a spacious and peaceful, carefully landscaped field by a stream. Electrical connections (mostly 16A) are available and there are 17 hardstanding pitches, also with electricity. Several additional areas without electricity are provided for tents. There are two new lakes, one for boating and fly fishing, the other for coarse fishing. A new reception and toilet block are planned. George and Kate, the enthusiastic owners, have opened up much of the farm for moderate or ample woodland and moorland trails which can be enjoyed with much wildlife to see. Indeed wildlife is actively encouraged with nesting boxes for owls, songbirds and bats, by leaving field margins wild to encourage small mammals and by yearly tree planting.

Facilities

The toilet facilities are acceptable with baby bath, dishwashing and laundry facilities including washing machines and a dryer. Milk, eggs and orange juice are sold in reception and gas, otherwise there are few other on site facilities. The village of Hundred House, one mile away, has a pub. Fishing. Torches are useful.
Off site: Bicycle hire and golf 5 miles. Riding 10 miles.

Open: Easter - 17 November.

Directions

Park is 4 miles east of Builth Wells near the village of Hundred House on the A481. Follow brown signs.
O.S.GR: SO098535. GPS: N52:10.273 W03:18.973

Charges guide

Per person	£ 3.50
child	£ 2.50
pitch	£ 4.50
electricity	£ 2.50

Special low season rates for senior citizens.
No credit cards.

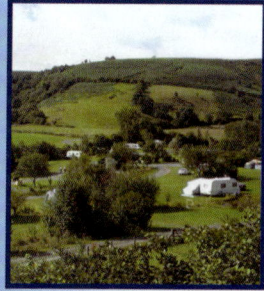

Wonderful walks lead up into the hills from Fforest Fields

UK6330 Daisy Bank Touring Caravan Park

Snead, Montgomery SY15 6EB (Powys)

Tel: **01588 620471**. Email: **enquiries@daisy-bank.co.uk**   **www.alanrogers.com/UK6330**

For adults only, this pretty, tranquil park in the Camlad Valley has panoramic views, and is an ideal base for walkers. Attractively landscaped with 'old English' flower beds and many different trees and shrubs, this small park has been carefully developed. The Welsh hills to the north and the Shropshire hills to the south overlook the three fields which provide a total of 55 pitches. The field nearer to the road (perhaps a little noisy) is slightly sloping but there are hardstandings for motorcaravans, while the second field is more level. All pitches have 16A electricity, water and waste water drainage and TV hook up. With many walks in the area, a series of walk leaflets is available. Although technically in Wales, the park is 500 yards from the Shropshire border, an area rich in history.

Facilities

The well equipped, heated toilet block has modern, en-suite units (6 with shower, WC and washbasin, 2 with WC and washbasin and facilities for disabled visitors). Laundry facilities. Shop in reception (honesty policy at certain times). Gas. Small putting green. Bicycle hire. Small library. WiFi (charged). Off site: Supermarket 2 miles. Fishing 3 miles. Golf and riding 10 miles.

Open: All year.

Directions

Site is by the A489 road 2 miles east of Churchstoke in the direction of Craven Arms. O.S.GR: SO302930. GPS: N52:31.795 W03:01.782

Charges guide

Per unit incl. 2 persons and all services	£ 17.00 - £ 22.00
extra person	£ 5.00
dog	£ 1.00

UK6305 Smithy Park

Abermule, Montgomery SY15 6ND (Powys)

Tel: 01584 711280. Email: info@bestparks.co.uk

www.alanrogers.com/UK6305

Smithy Caravan Park is set in four acres of landscaped ground bordered by the River Severn and the Shropshire Union Canal in the tranquil rolling countryside of central Wales. It does have 60 privately owned caravan holiday homes, but the touring area is separate and also has the benefit of being closest to the river with the best views and a small picnic and seating area on the bank. This area has 26 fully serviced hardstanding pitches (16A electricity, water, waste water and satellite TV hook-ups). A newly installed timber chalet provides all the sanitary facilities, and is located in one corner of the touring area. This is a well run site, which is under the same ownership as Westbrook Park, with a resident manager on-site here. The village has two local pubs, a shop and Post Office, and a bus service – all within easy walking distance. American RVs are accepted with prior notice. Kite flying or cycling on the park are not permitted.

Facilities

The new timber clad chalet building provides two good sized showers per sex, washbasins in cubicles, a family room suitable for the less able (there is a step up to the building). Utility room housing a laundry with washing machine, dryer and dishwashing sink. Fishing in the river Severn. Fenced playground. Gas stocked. Off site: Bus stop in village opposite end of site access road. Supermarkets and all other services in Newtown 3 miles. Golf 3 miles. Riding 5 miles.

Open: 1 March - 30 October.

Directions

Site is 3 miles north of Newtown in the village of Abermule. Turn off the A483 into village, and turn down the lane beside the Waterloo Arms, opposite the village shop and Post Office. Site is at the end of the lane. O.S.GR: SO161948.
GPS: N52:32.653 W03:14.323

Charges guide

Per unit incl. 2 persons and electricity	£ 14.00 - £ 18.00
extra person	£ 3.00
child (4-10 yrs)	£ 1.50
awning	£ 2.00
dog	£ 1.00

UK6310 Bacheldre Watermill Caravan Park

Churchstoke, Montgomery SY15 6TE (Powys)

Tel: 01588 620489. Email: info@bacheldremill.co.uk

www.alanrogers.com/UK6310

A delightful little site, Bacheldre has just 25 pitches arranged around the perimeter of a grass meadow, with no site road. There is just one lamp on the outside of the toilet block and three small lights on the perimeter so torches are useful. However, there are 18 electricity hook-ups (10A) and 10 hardstandings. Ideal for tenters and small units, it is not really suitable for larger units (20 ft. plus) and American RVs. The watermill is fully operational, producing high quality organic wheat flour, which can be purchased from reception, together with eggs and bread. The mill is not normally accessible, although guided tours can be arranged. Note: there are obvious hazards for small children – a deep, partially fenced millpond, moving waterwheel and the stream.

Facilities

A portacabin provides the usual facilities including one controllable hot shower per sex with dishwashing sinks in a separate room. Calor gas stocked. Off site: Walking and cycling along Offa's Dyke 800 yards from site. Clun Castle ruins are worth a visit. Steam enthusiasts are well catered for with the Welshpool and Llanfair light railway. Supermarket at Churchstoke 2 miles.

Open: All year.

Directions

Bacheldre is just off the A489 between Newtown and Churchstoke, about 9 miles east of Newtown and 2 miles west of Churchstoke. Turn into narrow lane (signed Bacheldre Mill), over the bridge and site entrance is almost immediately on your right. O.S.GR: SO243929. GPS: N52:31.649 W03:07.127

Charges guide

Per unit incl. 2 persons	£ 10.00 - £ 13.00
extra person	£ 2.00
awning	£ 2.50

UK6650 Hunters Hamlet Caravan Park

Sirior Goch Farm, Betws-yn-Rhos, Abergele LL22 8PL (Conwy)

Tel: 01745 832237. Email: huntershamlet@aol.com

www.alanrogers.com/UK6650

This small, family owned park is licensed for all units except tents (trailer tents allowed). On a gently sloping hillside providing beautiful panoramic views, one area provides 15 well spaced pitches with hardstanding and 10A electricity hook-ups, with access from a circular, hardcore road. A more recent area has been developed next to this of a similar design but with 8 fully serviced 'super pitches' (water, waste water, sewage, TV and electricity). Shrubs and bushes at various stages of growth enhance both areas. A natural play area incorporating rustic adventure equipment set amongst mature beech trees with a small bubbling stream is a children's paradise. Milk and papers can be ordered and the Hunters will do their best to meet your needs, even to survival rations! The park is well situated to tour Snowdonia and Anglesey and is within easy reach of Llandudno and Rhyl.

Facilities

The tiny heated toilet block has fully tiled facilities including showers en-suite with toilets for both sexes. A sunroom to the rear houses laundry and dishwashing (hot and cold), washing machine and dryer, iron and board, freezer and fridge. Family bathroom (metered) and basic toilet and shower facilities for disabled visitors. Play area. All year caravan storage. Max. 2 dogs per pitch. Off site: Fishing and golf 2 miles. Riding 10 miles.

Open: 21 March - 31 October.

Directions

From Abergele take A548 south for almost 3 miles; turn onto B5381 in direction of Betws-yn-Rhos and park is on left after 0.5 miles. O.S.GR: SH929736. GPS: N53:14.930 W03:36.408

Charges guide

Per unit incl. 2 persons and electricity	£ 15.00 - £ 20.00
super pitch (fully incl.)	£ 20.00 - £ 26.00
extra person	£ 3.00
child	£ 1.00
Less £5 on weekly bookings.	

UK6690 Bron-Y-Wendon Touring Caravan Park

Wern Road, Llanddulas, Colwyn Bay LL22 8HG (Conwy)

Tel: 01492 512903. Email: stay@northwales-holidays.co.uk

www.alanrogers.com/UK6690

Bron-Y-Wendon is right by the sea between Abergele and Colwyn Bay on the beautiful North Wales coast road. This is a quiet park which, by its own admission, is not really geared up for the family unit – there is no playground here, although there is a games room with table tennis and a TV room. The park is manicured to the highest standards and caters for a large number of seasonal caravans on pitches with gravel bases which are kept very tidy. There are a further 65 grass and 20 hardstanding touring pitches, all with electrical hook ups (16A) and tarmac access roads. All pitches have coastal views and the sea and beach are just a short walk away. Trailer tents are accepted, but not other tents. Colwyn Bay, Conwy, Anglesey, Llandudno, Snowdonia and Chester are all within easy reach, so there is lots to do. Having said how peaceful and quiet everything is (particularly for a seaside park in this area), there is some road noise from the adjacent A55 and during our visit a small train passed on the tracks between the park and the sea (just a few yards) and at night with little else going on it could be just noticeable.

Facilities

Two toilet blocks, both with heating, provide excellent facilities including men's and women's shower rooms separate from the toilets and washbasins. Good facilities for disabled visitors. Laundry with washing machines and dryers. Mobile shop visits daily. Gas supplies. Off site: Llanddulas village with shops and several good pubs is very near. Fishing 1 mile. Golf 4 miles. Riding 6 miles. Bicycle hire 15 miles.

Open: All year.

Directions

From A55 Chester - Conwy road turn at Llanddulas interchange (A547), junction 23. Turn right opposite Shell garage and park is 400 yards, signed on coast side of the road. O.S.GR: SH903785. GPS: N53:17.511 W03:38.670

Charges guide

Per unit incl. 2 persons and electricity	£ 18.00 - £ 21.00
extra person	£ 2.00
child (2-12 yrs)	£ 1.00
awning	£ 2.00 - £ 3.00

247

UK6655 Ty Mawr Holiday Park

Towyn Road, Towyn, Abergele LL22 9HG (Conwy)

Tel: 01745 832079. Email: nikkie.lawrence@park-resorts.com

www.alanrogers.com/UK6655

Ty Mawr Holiday Park is located close to the many attractions of the North Wales Coast and the Snowdonia National Park. There are two areas for touring units, one on open meadows with facilities provided in excellent 'portacabin' style units, the other in a more well established area with older, more traditional amenities near the playgrounds and entertainment complex. Both areas are flat with views of open countryside. There is some traffic noise from the road adjacent to the meadow. There is a large proportion of privately owned and rental caravan holiday homes which are neatly sited on well manicured grass pitches. It is an easy walk into the town of Towyn with seaside facilities and Rhyl, some three miles along the coast is a busy resort with a fun fair and holiday amusements. Ty Mawr is ideal for families seeking plenty of holiday park type activities, with organised children's clubs for 5-16 year olds. The outdoor all-weather multisport courts and the playground are excellent facilities for younger family members and the whole family are catered for in the entertainment complex which provides mini ten-pin bowling, pool and darts. In the evening there are discos and live spectaculars. The heated indoor pool complete with flume is the venue for organised water-based activities.

Facilities

Two well maintained, functional blocks which can be heated serve the main touring area with 'portacabin' style units on the open meadows. They are regularly cleaned. Washbasins are open style, preset showers have curtains and hooks, but no seats. Baby rooms. Facilities for disabled visitors (key). Launderette. Ice pack service. Shop. Bar with meals, cafeteria and takeaway. Indoor pool. Multisport courts. Excellent play areas and children's clubs. Evening family entertainment. Off site: Beach 0.25 miles. Bicycle hire 0.5 miles. Golf, riding and boat launching 3 miles. Fishing 6 miles.

Open: Easter - 30 October.

Directions

Take the A55 in a westerly direction into North Wales and take exit for Abergele. Follow signs for the A548 Rhyl towards Towyn. Shortly after Towyn turn right into site. O.S.GR: SH965791 GPS: N53:17.920 W03:33.265

Charges guide

Per pitch	£ 5.00 - £ 33.00
incl. electricity	£ 8.00 - £ 36.00
dog	£ 1.00 - £ 3.00

Units over 6 metres in length are charged for 2 pitches.

UK6355 Woodlands Caravan Park

Harlech LL46 2UE (Gwynedd)

Tel: 01766 780419. Email: grace@woodlandscp.fsnet.co.uk

www.alanrogers.com/UK6355

This delightful little site is lovingly tended by its owners and has just 18 pitches for tourists, all with gravel hardstanding and electric hook-up (10A) for caravans and motorcaravans only. Tents are not accepted. There are also 21 privately owned holiday homes, one for rent and a holiday cottage. However, the location of this site certainly makes up for its diminutive size, nestling under the massive rock topped by Harlech Castle, now a designated World Heritage Site. The narrow lane running alongside the site up to the old town above, is the steepest hill in Britain – no wonder the town is considering installing a funicular railway in the future. The coastal railway runs close to the site and the station is just 100 yards away. Railway noise should not be a problem (the small 'Sprinter' trains do not run at night). The 'Blue Flag' beach is only 500 yards, and the Leisure Centre with its indoor pool is 250 yards.

Facilities

The modern stone built toilet facilities are heated, clean and tidy with controllable showers (50p), vanity style washbasins, a small laundry with a baby changing area, but with no dedicated facilities for disabled visitors (£5 deposit for the key to the facilities). Chemical disposal point but no motorcaravan service point. Off site: Harlech Castle. The town also has a theatre and cinema. Nearby is Portmeirion, location of the cult TV series 'The Prisoner', 8 miles. Barmouth (market Thursday and Sunday) 10 miles. Golf 0.25 mile. Fishing 3 miles. Riding 3 miles.

Open: 1 March - 31 October.

Directions

From Barmouth take A496 to Harlech and continue downhill past Royal St David's Golf Course. Fork right immediately before railway crossing, and site is 200 yards on right. DO NOT turn towards town centre which lies on B4573, it is very narrow and congested. O.S.GR: SH582314. GPS: N52:51.693 W04:06.458

Charges guide

Per unit incl. 2 persons and electricity	£ 14.00 - £ 16.00
extra person	£ 2.50
awning	£ 2.50

No credit cards.

UK6340 Pen-y-Bont Touring & Camping Park

Llangynog Road, Bala LL23 7PH (Gwynedd)

Tel: **01678 520549**. Email: **penybont-bala@btconnect.co.uk**   www.alanrogers.com/UK6340

This is a pretty little park with 59 touring pitches, 42 of which have hardstanding. Connected by circular gravel roads, they are intermingled with trees and further tall trees edge the site. Electricity connections (16A) are available, including 11 for tents, and there are 24 serviced pitches with hardstanding, electricity, water and drainage. There are also pitches for 25 seasonal units. The park entrance and the stone building that houses reception and the well stocked shop provide quite a smart image. With views of the Berwyn mountains, Pen-y-bont has a peaceful, attractive and useful location being the closest park to Bala town, 100 yards from Bala Lake with Snowdonia on hand.

Facilities

The toilet block includes washbasins in cubicles and spacious hot showers. Two new cubicles with washbasin and WC. Separate laundry room and an en-suite unit for disabled visitors, that doubles as a baby room, operated by key (£2 deposit). Motorcaravan service point. Shop. Bicycle hire. Caravan storage. WiFi. Off site: Fishing 200 yds. Boat launching, golf and riding 2 miles.

Open: 1 April - 31 October.

Directions

Park is 0.5 miles southeast of Bala village on the B4391. Bala is between Dolgellau and Conwen on the A494. O.S.GR: SH932350.
GPS: N52:54.103 W03:35.407

Charges guide

Per unit incl. 2 persons	£ 16.00 - £ 20.00
extra person	£ 6.00
child (4-16 yrs)	£ 4.00
tent pitch with 3-6 persons	£ 13.00 - £ 17.00

UK6345 Glanllyn Lakeside Caravan & Camping Park

Llanuwchllyn, Bala LL23 7ST (Gwynedd)

Tel: **01678 540227**. Email: **info@glanllyn.com**   www.alanrogers.com/UK6345

This 16 acre site lying alongside the southern end of Bala lake has 204 pitches. With around 40 seasonal units, this leaves 164 tourist pitches, 94 of which have electric hook-ups. In this location, virtually all the pitches have wonderful views of the lake or the surrounding mountain sides. The terrain is grassy, fairly open and level, but with natural terraces. There are around 19 individual hardstandings and a further hardstanding area by the beach is a favourite with motorcaravanners. The site is served by main tarmac access roads with speed bumps.

Facilities

A complex of three modern buildings (one can be heated and is used in low season) is located centrally at the rear of the site. Facilities for babies and a suite for disabled people (key code access). Laundry. Motorcaravan service point. Well stocked shop at reception (Easter - Oct) and plenty of tourist information. Freezer service. Gas supplies. Splendid, well fenced adventure style playground on bark. Off site: Bus stops outside site gate. Ideal for exploring the southern part of Snowdonia National Park. Bicycle hire, indoor pool and golf in Bala 3 miles. Riding 18 miles.

Open: Easter - mid October.

Directions

From Bala take A494 southwest towards Dolgellau for about 3 miles, entrance is on left, on a right hand bend. O.S.GR: SH893324.
GPS: N52:52.660 W03:38.799

Charges guide

Per unit incl. 2 persons and electricity	£ 16.00
tent pitch incl. 2 persons	£ 12.00 - £ 14.00
child	£ 3.00
dog (max .2)	£ 2.00

UK6580 Llanystumdwy Camping & Caravanning Club Site

Tyddyn Sianel, Llanystumdwy, Criccieth LL52 0LS (Gwynedd)

Tel: **01766 522855**   www.alanrogers.com/UK6580

Overlooking mountains and sea, Llanystumdwy is one of the earliest Camping & Caravanning Club sites. Well maintained with good facilities, it is on sloping grass. However, the managers are very helpful and know their site and can advise on the most suitable pitch and even have a supply of chocks. There are 70 pitches in total (20 ft. spacing), 45 with 10A electricity connections, spaced over two hedged fields with mainly caravans in the top field with four hardstandings for motorcaravans, and with tents lower down. A shop and pub are in the village.

Facilities

A purpose-built toilet block to one side includes excellent, full facilities for disabled visitors including access ramp, one washbasin each in a cubicle for male and female and extra large sinks. Facilities for babies. Laundry (taps with fitting for disabled people). Gas supplies. Off site: Riding or fishing 0.5 miles. Golf 2.5 miles. Beach 3 miles.

Open: March - October.

Directions

Follow the A497 from Criccieth west and take second right to Llanystumdwy. Site is on the right. O.S.GR: SH469384. GPS: N52:55.252 W04:16.731

Charges guide

Per person	£ 4.90 - £ 7.25
child (6-18 yrs)	£ 2.15 - £ 2.25
non-member pitch fee	£ 5.65

249

UK6370 Hendre Mynach Touring Caravan & Camping Park

Llanaber, Barmouth LL42 1YR (Gwynedd)

Tel: **01341 280262**. Email: **mynach@lineone.net**

www.alanrogers.com/UK6370

A neat and tidy family park, colourful flowers and top rate facilities make an instant impression on arrival down the steep entrance to this park (help is available to get out if you are worried). The 240 pitches are allocated in various areas, with substantial tenting areas identified. 40 gravel hardstandings are available and around the park there are 110 electricity hook-ups (10A), 20 fully serviced pitches and ample water taps. The quaint old seaside and fishing town of Barmouth is less than a mile away, a 15-20 minute walk along the prom. Here you will find 'everything'. The beach is only 100 yards away but a railway line runs between this and the park. It can be crossed by pedestrian operated gates which could be a worry for those with young children. Reception will provide leaflets with maps of local walks. Snowdonia National Park and mountain railway, the famous Ffestiniog railway, castles and lakes provide plenty to see and do – this is a classic park in a classic area.

Facilities

Two toilet blocks, one modern and one traditional, both offer excellent facilities including spacious showers (free) and washbasins in cubicles. An extension to the traditional block has added a good unit for disabled visitors with ramp access. Motorcaravan service point. Well stocked shop incorporating a snack bar and takeaway (Easter - 1/11). WiFi. Off site: Beach 100 m. Fishing, boat launching and bicycle hire within 0.5 miles. Riding 5 miles. Golf 9 miles.

Open: All year excl. 10 January - 28 February.

Directions

Park is off the A496 road north of Barmouth in village of Llanaber with entrance down a steep drive. O.S.GR: SH606171. GPS: N52:43.980 W04:03.971

Charges guide

Per caravan or motorcaravan incl. 2 persons and electricity	£ 16.00 - £ 26.00
extra person	£ 4.00
child (2-14 yrs)	£ 2.00
dog	free - £ 1.00

Plus £2 per night for certain weekends.
Mid-season and Christmas/New Year offers.

UK6585 Bolmynydd Camping Park

Llanbedrog, Pwllheli LL53 7UP (Gwynedd)

Tel: **01758 740224**. Email: **bolmynydd@btinternet.com**

www.alanrogers.com/UK6585

The drive to Bolymynydd is not for the faint hearted. The roads are extremely narrow with plenty of bends, and are not recommended for large units. However, those who do make the drive are rewarded with spectacular views and a campsite which is ideal for tents and those who wish for peace and quiet in a wonderful rural setting. Two fields are available for tents, and other fields offer safe play areas for young children. With 10 seasonal caravan pitches and only 8 touring pitches (all with 10/16A electricity), the owners request that you phone ahead to discuss access and availability. The one modern, well maintained utility block, serves both the camping fields and caravan pitches. There is no games room or swimming pool; just beautiful Welsh scenery and nature.

Facilities

One clean sanitary block, maintained to a high standard (may be under pressure in peak season). Separate modern showers, toilets and open style washbasins. Baby bath in well equipped laundry room. No motorcaravan service point. Off site: Five minute walk to small supermarket and pub. Riding, beach and sailing 400 yds. Fishing 1 mile. Golf 3 miles.

Open: Easter - 31 October.

Directions

From Pwllheli take the A499 toward Abersoch. After 4 miles pass through Llanbedrog and at the campsite sign turn sharp left. Continue for about half a mile, site is on the left. O.S.GR: SH325530. GPS: N52:51.139 W04:29.307

Charges guide

Per unit incl. 2 persons	£ 15.00 - £ 16.00
incl. electricity	£ 18.50 - £ 19.50
extra person	£ 5.00
child (3-16 yrs)	£ 2.50

No credit cards.
Visitos must phone prior to arrival to discuss access and availability.

UK6600 Bryn Gloch Caravan & Camping Park

Betws Garmon, Caernarfon LL54 7YY (Gwynedd)

Tel: **01286 650216**. Email: **eurig@bryngloch.co.uk**   www.alanrogers.com/UK6600

Bryn Gloch is a well kept, family owned touring park in the impressive Snowdonia area – an unusual feature is the mountain railway which passes through the park. Neat and quiet, it takes some 160 units on five flat, wide meadows with some breathtaking views. With tarmac access roads and free areas allowed in the centre for play, of the 152 touring pitches, 80 have hardstanding, electricity (10A), water and drainage. In addition, there are 15 caravan holiday homes. Fishing is possible on the river bordering the park with a barbecue and picnic area, adventure play area and field for games. Tourist information is provided in the complex by the reception/shop and the park is very popular with walkers and cyclists. Caernarfon with its famous castle is 5 miles.

Facilities

The two very clean and modern main toilet blocks include washbasins in cabins, large showers, a family bathroom (hot water £1), baby room and complete facilities for visitors with disabilities (coded access). The far field has a 'portacabin' style unit containing all facilities, for use in peak season. Well equipped laundry and separate drying room. Motorcaravan service point and car wash. Shop (1/3-30/10). TV and games rooms with pool tables and amusement machines. Minigolf. Entrance barrier with coded access. Off site: Pub 1 mile. ATM at garage in Ceathro 3 miles. Riding 2.5 miles, bicycle hire or golf 5 miles.

Open: All year, limited facilities 1 November - 1 March.

Directions

From Caernarfon take A4085 signed Beddgelert. Park is just beyond Waunfawr, 5.6 miles southeast of Caernarfon. After crossing river bridge, the entrance is immediately on the right, opposite St Garmon church. O.S.GR: SH536576.
GPS: N53:05.711 W04:11.304

Charges guide

Per unit incl. 2 persons	£ 15.00 - £ 23.00
incl. electricity	£ 18.00 - £ 26.00
fully serviced pitch	£ 20.00 - £ 28.00
extra person	£ 4.00
child (3-16 yrs)	£ 2.00

UK6590 Forest Holidays Beddgelert

Caernarfon Road, Beddgelert LL55 4UU (Gwynedd)

Tel: **01766 890288**. Email: **info@forestholidays.co.uk**   www.alanrogers.com/UK6590

Forest Holidays is a partnership between the Forestry Commission and The Camping & Caravanning Club. This well equipped site is in the heart of Snowdonia. Set in a marvellous, natural, wooded environment on the slopes of Snowdon there is abundant fauna and flora, tumbling streams and always something to watch from the cheeky squirrels to the smallest bird in Britain. Well equipped and well managed, the site provides 280 pitches – tents in a semi-wooded field area and caravans amongst the trees with numbered hardstandings, and 105 places with 10A electricity. Tents may pitch where they like in their areas leaving 6 m. between units or there are 6 new grass pitches with electrical hook-ups for tents. Metal tent pegs may be best (available from the shop). Free maps of the forest walks are provided in reception and orienteering and fishing are possible. A bus service stops at the top of the entrance lane (two hourly for Caernarfon and Porthmadog).

Facilities

Two fully equipped modern sanitary toilet blocks clad in natural wood provide large, free hot showers (with good dry areas). Laundry equipment in one block. A small unit provides extra washbasins and toilets in peak season and there is a toilet and washbasin for disabled visitors. Excellent drive-through motorcaravan service point. Reception is central, as is a well provisioned shop (Easter - end Sept). Well equipped adventure playground. Log cabin common room. Off site: Pub within walking distance (under a mile) and other eating places nearby. Bicycle hire within 500 yds. in forest.

Open: All year.

Directions

Site is clearly signed to the left 1 mile north of Beddgelert on A4085 Caernarfon road.
O.S.GR: SH579492. GPS: N53:01.245 W04:07.186

Charges guide

Per unit incl. 2 persons	£ 8.30 - £ 14.00
extra person	£ 3.40 - £ 5.60
child (5-14 yrs)	£ 1.70 - £ 2.80

Less 20% all year for disabled guests and outside 23/7-31/8 for the over 60s.

Wales

UK6605 Tafarn Snowdonia Parc Brewpub & Campsite

Waunfawr, Caernarfon LL55 4AQ (Gwynedd)

Tel: **01286 650409**. Email: **info@snowdonia-park.co.uk**　　www.alanrogers.com/UK6605

Set on the banks of the River Gwyrfai and amongst spectacular scenery, this no frills campsite is adjacent to the station for the Welsh Highland Railway. The site provides 32 grass pitches, (20 with 16A electricity) of variable size. They are set in an open field and serviced by two small, basic, clean shower and toilet blocks. Enjoy riverside walks and free fishing (licence required) before calling in at the adjoining pub with its own microbrewery (listed in the CAMRA Good Beer guide) and home cooked food. Children are well catered for with a family room in the pub, two gardens (one safe for toddlers) and a playground. The campsite is located between Beddgelert and Caernarfon and 4 miles from the foot of Snowdon. It is an ideal location for walking, climbing, fishing and pony trekking.

Facilities

One small toilet block in main camping field. A second block with separate showers and toilets for men and ladies, is reached via a footbridge over the railway. These may become stretched when site is full. Bar, restaurant and takeaway facilities. TV. Games room. Playground. Free fishing (licence required). Off site: Riding 800 yds. Golf 3 miles. Beach and sailing 5 miles.

Open: All year.

Directions

From Caernarfon take the A4085 for around 4 miles and campsite is on the left. The entrance is at the far end of pub/railway station car park.
O.S.GR: SH526587. GPS: N53:06.367 W04:12.106

Charges guide

Per unit incl. 2 persons	£ 12.00 - £ 16.00
electricity	£ 2.00
children and dogs	free

UK6620 Plas Gwyn Caravan & Camping Park

Llanrug, Caernarfon LL55 2AQ (Gwynedd)

Tel: **01286 672619**. Email: **info@plasgwyn.co.uk**　　www.alanrogers.com/UK6620

In a beautiful location, this traditional, family run touring site is within the grounds of a house that was built in 1785 in the Georgian style with a colonial style veranda. The 37 touring caravan pitches are set around the perimeter of a slightly sloping grass field, and there are 8 hardstandings. The separate tent field has 10 pitches. There are 30 electric hook-ups (16A), and with minimal site lighting on the caravan field and none on the tent field, a torch could be very useful. The site is just 2.5 miles from the Llanberis Pass and this is good walking country. Large motorhomes are accepted but it is essential to telephone ahead to check availability. A member of the Countryside Discovery Group.

Facilities

An older style building houses the toilet facilities, although the fittings inside are modern and are kept neat and tidy. Controllable free hot showers, a good laundry room (by reception), but no facilities for babies or disabled campers. Motorcaravan service point. Gas. Reception stocks basic food items. Breakfast 'butties' made to order and delivered. Internet access. Off site: Golf 1 mile. Riding 2.5 miles. Bicycle hire 3 miles. Fishing 4 miles.

Open: 1 March - 31 October.

Directions

Site is on the A4086, 3 miles from Caernarfon, and 2.5 miles from Llanberis, well signed with easy access. O.S.GR: SH522634.
GPS: N53:08.804 W04:12.734

Charges guide

Per person	£ 2.00
child (0-15 yrs)	£ 1.00 - £ 1.50
pitch incl. awning and electricity	£ 7.50 - £ 12.50
tent pitch	£ 2.50 - £ 10.50

UK6635 Fron Caravan & Camping Park

Brynsiencyn, Anglesey LL61 6TX (Isle of Anglesey)

Tel: **01248 430310**. Email: **mail@froncaravanpark.co.uk**　　www.alanrogers.com/UK6635

A traditional, all touring campsite in a peaceful rural location, Fron has panoramic views over the surrounding countryside. From the entrance gate a tarmac drive passes through a two acre grass paddock, which is reserved for 35 large sized tent and trailer tent pitches. The drive leads up to the old farmhouse which houses reception and a well stocked shop. Behind the farmhouse is another two acre sloping paddock with 40 caravan and motorcaravan pitches with electricity hook-ups (10A).

Facilities

Toilet facilities are in three units of varying ages and designs located at both sides of the farmhouse. These include a unit for ladies with some washbasins in cubicles, good hot showers with dividers (20p), hairdryers, a baby area. Suite for disabled campers. Laundry. Motorcaravan services. Heated swimming pool (30 x 14 ft; May - Sept). Gas. Max. 2 dogs. Torches useful. Off site: Fishing 1.5 miles. Riding 3 miles. Golf 4 miles.

Open: Easter - end September.

Directions

Cross the Britannia Bridge and take first slip road signed Llanfairpwll A4080, then next left signed Newborough and Brynsiencyn. Continue for 5 miles, turning right in village at the Groeslon Hotel.
O.S.GR: SH472668. GPS: N53:10.573 W04:17.271

Charges guide

Per unit incl. 2 adults and 2 children	£ 16.00
electricity	£ 3.00

No credit cards.

UK6636 Plas Uchaf Caravan & Camping Park

Benllech Bay, Benllech LL74 8NU (Isle of Anglesey)

Tel: **01407 763012**   www.alanrogers.com/UK6636

This spacious, family run, park is set in 16 acres of flat, well mown grass with some hardstandings. Within the park there are woodland walks and a play route for children to explore, an attractive play area with robust play equipment and a dog walk. All in an open, rural setting this park offers a safe haven for young families to enjoy. The pitches are set around the perimeter of six individual areas, each with picnic tables for communal use and all 110 touring pitches offer electricity (10/16A). Motorcaravans over 26 ft are not accepted. With five privately owned mobile homes in a separate field, this popular campsite is ideally located with a safe sandy beach a mile away and well positioned for exploring the island. Motor bikes, boats and jet skis cannot be accommodated.

Facilities

Three clean, traditional style sanitary blocks have separate facilities for men and women, with hot showers (charge), open style washbasins, hairdryers and small baths. Baby areas. No facilities for disabled visitors. Limited laundry. Large playing field, play equipment and dog walk. Freezer facilities. Off site: Shops, bars, restaurants, fishing, golf, sandy beach, horse riding and sailing all within 1 mile.

Open: 14 March - 14 October.

Directions

From the Britannia Bridge take the A5025. In Benllech turn left onto the B5108. After the fire station on left, turn first right and the park is signed. O.S.GR: SH509832. GPS: N53:19.606 W04:14.374

Charges guide

Per unit incl. 2 persons	£ 9.00 - £ 14.00
extra person (over 3 yrs)	£ 2.00
electricity	£ 3.00

No credit cards.

PLAS UCHAF CARAVAN CAMPING PARK

Benllech Bay, Anglesey, Evans Partnership   Telephone: 01407 763012

½ mile from Benllech signposted B5108. Level, well sheltered, safe family park, 10 acres, Tarmacadan roads, street lights, close mown, all pitches are perimeter parking, near beach, dog walk, play areas, swings, 30+ picnic tables, 2 wc blocks, hot showers, pot and pan rooms, family rooms, ample sinks, toilets, hairdryers, 100 electric hook-ups, 60 water points, freezers etc.

UK6640 Home Farm Caravan Park

Marianglas, Anglesey LL73 8PH (Isle of Anglesey)

Tel: **01248 410614**. Email: **enq@homefarm-anglesey.co.uk**   www.alanrogers.com/UK6640

A tarmac drive through an open field leads to this neatly laid out quality park, with caravan holiday homes to one side. Nestling below what was once a Celtic hill fort, later decimated as a quarry, the park is edged with mature trees and farmland. A circular, tarmac access road leads to the 102 well spaced and numbered touring pitches. With five types available, there are pitches for everyone; ranging from grass with no electricity, to oversized, deluxe hardstandings with electricity, water tanks/taps, waste water drain and TV hook-ups. All electricity is 16A and there are separate well maintained grass fields/areas for tents. Some areas are slightly sloping. The 'piece de resistance' must be the children's indoor play area, large super adventure play equipment, complete with tunnels and bridges on safe rubber matting, not to mention an outside fenced play area and fields available for sports, football, etc. and walking. Various beaches, sandy or rocky, are within a mile. A member of the Best of British group.

Facilities

Two purpose built toilet blocks, one part of the reception building, are of similar design, can be heated and are maintained to a high standard. En-suite provision for people with disabilities (with key). Excellent small bathroom for children with baby bath and curtain for privacy. Family room (with key). Laundry room. Motorcaravan service point. Ice pack service. Reception provides basic essentials, gas and some caravan accessories. Indoor and outdoor play areas. TV and pool table. Small library. Hard tennis (extra charge) with racquet hire. Off site: Restaurants, shops and ATM at Benllech 2 miles. Beach 1 mile. Fishing and golf 2 miles. Riding 8 miles.

Open: April - October.

Directions

From the Britannia Bridge take second exit left signed Benllech and Amlwch on the A5025. Two miles after Benllech keep left at roundabout and park entrance is 300 yards on the left beyond the church. O.S.GR: SH499850. GPS: N53:20.433 W04:15.382

Charges guide

Per unit incl. 2 persons	£ 13.00 - £ 19.00
incl. electricity	£ 15.50 - £ 22.00
incl. hardstanding	£ 16.50 - £ 26.50
extra person	£ 3.00 - £ 5.25
child (5-16 yrs)	£ 1.75 - £ 3.00

UK6660 Nant Mill Family Touring Caravan & Tenting Park

Gronant Road, Prestatyn LL19 9LY (Denbighshire)

Tel: 01745 852360. Email: nantmilltouring@aol.com   www.alanrogers.com/UK6660

This traditional style, family owned and run park of around five acres, takes some 150 units arranged over four fields. There are some distant sea views to be had from many pitches. These are carefully allocated to ensure that the largest, central, sloping field is reserved for families. A smaller more intimate field for tents only is to one side of this and two small paddocks on the other side are for couples who might prefer a quieter, more level location. There are 96 electrical connections (10/16A) but tents are not permitted on pitches with hook-ups. The immaculate sanitary buildings are located in the central field and reception is at the farmhouse. Fresh milk and eggs can be purchased. Lighting is fairly minimal, being located at the service points and around the toilet block, therefore a torch is useful. Children have a designated ball games area and a very good, enclosed adventure playground on a bark surface. Small children might like to visit the duck pond at the rear of the farmhouse. The best beach is the Blue Flag Prestatyn central beach which is about half a mile from the site. The main site gate is locked at night generally around dusk until 08.00 each morning. An alternative entry point is available during these hours. There is a length restriction of 26 ft for touring vehicles.

Facilities

The main toilet block is older in style but very well kept, with showers, an ample number of open style washbasins and baby changing in both ladies' and men's rooms. Extra showers are in a small modern 'portacabin' style unit alongside. Showers are charged (50p), with a £1 deposit for the cubicle key (return after each shower). A separate 'portacabin' unit with ramp provides a full suite of services for disabled visitors. Large utility room with washing machines, dryers, spin dryer, ironing facilities, together with sinks for washing and dishes plus a hairdressing station. Playground and play field. Off site: Beach 0.5 mile. Town with supermarkets, shops, services and gas supplies 0.5 mile. Sea fishing 0.5 mile.

Open: Easter - mid October.

Directions

Site entrance is 0.5 miles east of Prestatyn on the A548 coast road. O.S.GR: SJ073832. GPS: N53:20.259 W03:23.592

Charges guide

Per unit incl. 2 persons	£ 14.00 - £ 17.00
extra person (over 3 yrs)	£ 1.00
electricity	£ 2.50
No credit/debit cards.	

UK6695 Tyddyn Du Touring Park

Conwy Old Road, Penmaenmawr LL34 6RE (Conwy)

Tel: 01492 622300. Email: stay@tyddyndutouringpark.co.uk   www.alanrogers.com/UK6695

This attractively landscaped campsite for adults only is conveniently situated close to the A55 and positioned on a hillside with panoramic views across Conwy Bay to The Great Orme at Llandudno and Puffin Island. Offering peace and quiet in a superb location between mountains and the sea and being within easy reach of Conwy, Snowdonia National Park and many historic regions of North Wales, this is an ideal base for exploring the area. Tarmac roads connect the three levels which are tiered to maximise the views for everyone. There are 92 touring pitches on either grass or hardstanding and all have 16A electricity. One modern, roomy and well equipped utility building houses separate facilities for men and women, whilst an additional, older, more traditional sanitary block is located at the top of the site. Some traffic noise from the A55 can be heard but this should not spoil the enjoyment of this pretty campsite. Units over 26 ft. in length are not accepted No arrivals before 14.00 please and visitors under the age of 18 are not allowed on site.

Facilities

Two well maintained sanitary blocks provide showers, open style washbasins and hairdryers. En-suite facilities for disabled visitors (Radar key). Motorcaravan service point (care needed to access). Well equipped laundry room. Small library. £5 (cash only) refundable deposit for entry card. Off site: Shops and restaurants within 1 mile. Pub at entrance to park. Sandy beach 10-15 minutes walk. Fishing and sailing 1 mile. Golf 0.5 miles. Conwy 4 miles. Llandudno 9 miles.

Open: 22 March - 31 October.

Directions

From the A55 take exit 16 and at roundabout signed Penmaenmawr turn immediately sharp left into Ysguborwen Road. Entrance to park is 300 yards on the right. O.S.GR: SH728768. GPS: N53:16.455 W03:54.379

Charges guide

Per unit incl. 2 persons and electricity	£ 16.00 - £ 18.00
extra person (over 16 yrs)	£ 2.00
awning	£ 1.00 - £ 2.00

UK6700 Ty-Ucha Farm Caravan Park

Maesmawr Road, Llangollen LL20 7PP (Denbighshire)

Tel: **01978 860677**   www.alanrogers.com/UK6700

Only a mile from Llangollen, Ty Ucha has a rather dramatic setting, nestling under its own mountain and with views across the valley to craggy Dinas Bran castle. It is a neat, ordered park, carefully managed by the owners and providing 40 pitches (30 with 10A electrical hook-up) for caravans and motorcaravans only (tents are not accepted). They are well spaced round a large, grassy field with an open centre for play. One side slopes gently and is bounded by a stream and wood in which a Nature Trail has been made. Because of overhead cables, kite flying is forbidden; no bike riding either. A path leads to various mountain walks, depending on your energy and ability. The world famous Eisteddfod is an international festival of music and dance held for six days starting on the first Tuesday of the first full week in July every year – it is a very busy time for the area.

Facilities

The single toilet block, although of 'portacabin' style, is clean and well maintained and can be heated. It includes two metered showers for each sex (a little cramped). Dishwashing sink with cold water outside. No laundry facilities but there is a launderette in Llangollen. Gas supplies. Games room with table tennis. Late arrivals area. Tents are not accepted. Off site: Hotel 0.5 miles with reasonably priced meals. Fishing 1 mile, golf 0.5 miles.

Open: Easter - October.

Directions

Park is signed off A5 road, 1 mile east of Llangollen (250 yds). O.S.GR: SJ228411.
GPS: N52:57.928 W03:08.741

Charges guide

Per unit incl. 2 persons	£ 9.00 - £ 10.00
extra person	£ 2.00
electricity	£ 3.00

Reductions for OAPs for weekly stays.
No credit cards.

UK6670 The Plassey Leisure Park

Eyton, Wrexham LL13 0SP (Wrexham)

Tel: **01978 780277**. Email: **enquiries@theplassey.co.uk**   www.alanrogers.com/UK6670

The Plassey has been carefully developed over the past 45 years. Originally a dairy farm, the park is set in 247 acres of the Dee Valley and offers an extensive range of activities. It has been divided into discreet areas with pitches around the edges. There are 120 touring pitches with 16A electricity, including 30 new fully serviced pitches with hardstanding. Five further areas accommodate 120 seasonal caravans. There is much to do and to look at in the rural setting at the Plassey but it is probably best enjoyed midweek, avoiding the busy Bank Holidays. The Edwardian farm buildings have been tastefully converted to provide a restaurant, coffee shop, health, beauty and hair studio, a small garden centre and 16 different craft and retail units, open all year. Unusually there is also a small brewery on site, producing its own unique Plassey Bitter! In addition to recent landscaping to the park, the pool and the golf clubhouse have been refurbished to provide improved facilities. A member of the Best of British group.

Facilities

Some refurbished toilet facilities are supplemented by a new heated block with individual washbasin cubicles, a room for disabled visitors or families. Laundry. Motorcaravan services. Shop (with gas). Club room with games room for children. Heated indoor pool with sun bed, sauna and new viewing area (charged). Adventure play area. 9-hole golf course. Fishing lakes. Wildlife meadow and countryside footpaths. No bicycles, skateboards or footballs permitted. Winter caravan storage. Off site: Riding 2 miles. Bicycle hire 5 miles.

Open: January - November.

Directions

Follow brown and cream signs for The Plassey from the A483 Chester - Oswestry bypass onto the B5426 and park is 2.5 miles. Also signed from the A528 Marchwiel - Overton road. O.S.GR: SJ349452. GPS: N53:00.154 W02:57.725

Charges guide

Per unit incl. 2 persons	
and electricity	£ 12.50 - £ 21.50
incl. services	£ 16.00 - £ 28.50
extra person (over 5 yrs)	£ 3.75
dog	£ 2.00

Includes club membership, coarse fishing, badminton and table tennis (own racquets and bats required).

www.alanrogers.com for latest campsite news

UK6680 James' Caravan Park

Ruabon, Wrexham LL14 6DW (Wrexham)
Tel: 01978 820148. Email: ray@carastay.demon.co.uk   www.alanrogers.com/UK6680

Open all year, this park has attractive, park-like surroundings with mature trees and neat, short grass. However, edged by two main roads it is subject to some road noise. The old farm buildings and owner's collection of original farm machinery, carefully restored and maintained, add interest. The park has over 40 pitches, some level and some on a slope, with informal siting giving either a view or shade. Electricity (6/10A) is available all over, although a long lead may be useful. A free freezer for ice packs and tourist information are available in the foyer of the toilet block. This is a useful park with easy access from the A483 Wrexham - Oswestry road.

Facilities

The heated toilet block offers roomy showers with a useful rail to help those of advancing age with feet washing. En-suite facilities for visitors with disabilities complete with special 'clos-o-mat' toilet! Motorcaravan service point. Gas available. Off site: The village is 10 minutes walk with a Spar shop, fish and chips, a restaurant, launderette and four pubs. Golf 3 miles.

Open: All year.

Directions

Park is at junction of A483/A539 Llangollen road and is accessible from the westbound A539.
O.S.GR: SJ302434. GPS: N52:58.972 W03:02.456

Charges guide

Per unit incl. 2 persons and electricity	£ 12.00
extra person	£ 2.00
awning	£ 2.00 - £ 5.00
dog	£ 1.00

No credit cards.

James Caravan Park

Idyllic Park with mature trees, well cared for grass, renovated buildings and all modern facilities

ray@carastay.demon.co.uk • Tel: 01978 820148 • Ruabon, LL14 6DW

From gentle rolling hills and rugged coastlines, to dramatic peaks, punctuated with beautiful lochs, Scotland is a land steeped in history that provides superb opportunities to enjoy wild, untamed and spectacular scenery.

WE HAVE DIVIDED THE CAMPSITES IN SCOTLAND INTO THE FOLLOWING REGIONS: LOWLANDS, HEART OF SCOTLAND, GRAMPIANS, AND HIGHLANDS AND ISLANDS

Probably the most striking thing about Scotland is the vast areas of uninhabited landscape. Southern Scotland boasts beautiful fertile plains, woodlands and wild sea coasts. It also has a rich heritage with ancient castles, abbeys and grand houses. Further north are the Trossachs with their heather-clad hills, home of Rob Roy, the folk hero. The Highlands and Islands, including Skye, Mull and Islay, have some of the most dramatic landscapes in Europe, dominated by breathtaking mountain ranges, such as Ben Nevis and the Grampians, plus deep glistening lochs: the largest being Loch Ness, where the monster reputedly lives. And lying at the very edge of Europe, the islands of the Inner and Outer Hebrides share a rugged natural beauty, with unspoilt beaches and an abundance of wildlife. The two largest cities, Edinburgh and Glasgow, have their own unique attractions. The capital, Edinburgh, with magnificent architecture, comprises the medieval Old Town and the Georgian New Town, with the ancient castle standing proud in the middle. A short distance to the west, Glasgow has more parks and over 20 museums and galleries, with works by Charles Rennie Mackintosh scattered around the city.

Places of interest

Lowlands: Floors Castle near Kelso; Museum of Scotland and Balmoral Castle in Edinburgh; People's Palace, Burrell Collection in Pollock Park, Glasgow; Sweetheart Abbey near Dumfries; New Lanark World Heritage Site; Melrose Abbey.

Heart of Scotland: fishing town of Oban; Stirling Castle and Wallace Monument; Loch Lomond; Pitlochry; university town of St Andrews; Aberdeen; Dunfermline Abbey; fishing villages of Crail and Anstruther; Famous Grouse Experience in Crieff.

Highlands and Islands: Fort William; Eilean Donan Castle near Dornie; the Cairngorms; Highland Wildlife Part at Kingussie; Inverness; Aviemore; Urquhart Castle near Drumnadrochit; Jacobite Steam Train, operates between Fort William and Mallaig; Dunvegan Castle on the Isle of Skye.

Did you know?

Dunfermline Abbey is the final resting place of 22 kings, queens, princes and princesses of Scotland, including Robert the Bruce.

Whales can be seen off the west coast of the Highlands, and the Moray Firth is home to bottle-nosed dolphins.

Arbroath Abbey is the site where Scotland's nobles swore independence from England in 1320.

Since 1861, every day (except on Sundays), the one o'clock gun has boomed out from Edinburgh castle.

Charles Rennie Mackintosh, famous architect and designer, was born in Glasgow in 1868.

Eas Coul Aulin near Kylesku in Sutherland is Britain's highest waterfall at 200 metres – four times the height of Niagara.

Ben Nevis is the highest mountain in the UK.

257

Scotland

RED TEXT DENOTES ALL YEAR ROUND SITE

Miles		
0	20	40
0	32	64	96

Kms

Shetland
Islands
Lerwick
80 miles

Shetland
Islands

LERWICK
7980

Orkney Islands

7950   KIRKWALL

7735

THURSO

7730

WICK

7920

7720

HELMSDALE

A9

7710
ULLAPOOL

7700

7750

A835

DINGWALL

FRASERBURGH

A98   ELGIN

7740

Highlands and Islands

7690   INVERNESS

7540

7550

7530

A96

KYLE OF LOCHALSH   7760

7670

ABERDEEN

A87

A82

A9   7680

Grampian

MALLAIG

NEWTONMORE

BRAEMAR

7850
FORT WILLIAM   7830

7800

7790

7300   7295
7305   PITLOCHRY

7280

7810

SCOTLAND

Heart of Scotland

A9

DUNDEE   7410

OBAN

CRIANLARICH

7310   A85   PERTH

A90

7270

7290

INVERARAY

A82

7260

7220

7230   7320

STIRLING

7860

7240

7060

GREENOCK

7050   7065
EDINBURGH   7045   6980   A1
6990
7035

GLASGOW
7000

A702

BERWICK-UPON-TWEED   5800

IRVINE   KILMARNOCK

6960

5750

MELROSE   7030   KELSO   5755

M74

SELKIRK   A1

7025

AYR

JEDBURGH   A68

ALNWICK

CAMPBELTOWN

7010   7015

Scottish Lowlands

A76

MOFFAT

A7   A68

NORTHUMBRIA

A77

LOCKERBIE

MORPETH

Northumberland

DUMFRIES

6940   6930   6910

NEWTON
STEWART

6870

ANNAN   GRETNA GREEN
5640

5810

HEXHAM

BALLYMENA   LARNE   STRANRAER   7020

A75   CASTLE
DOUGLAS   6880   6875   CARLISLE   A69

6945   5506   CONSETT

6890   KIRKCUDBRIGHT   5505   CUMBRIA

6885   6950   6900   5510   A68

ANTRIM

258

www.alanrogers.com for latest campsite news

UK6960 Crossburn Caravan Park

Edinburgh Road, Peebles EH45 8ED (Borders)

Tel: **01721 720501**. Email: **enquiries@crossburncaravans.co.uk**   **www.alanrogers.com/UK6960**

A peaceful, friendly small park, suitable as a night stop, Crossburn is on the south side of the A703 road, half a mile north of the town centre. The entrance has a fairly steep slope down to reception and the shop which also sells a very large selection of caravan and camping accessories. Passing the caravans for sale and the holiday homes you might think that this is not the site for you, but persevere as the touring area is very pleasant. Of the 50 pitches, 46 have electricity (16A), 20 have hardstanding and 8 are fully serviced. There is also a sheltered area for tents.

Facilities

Two toilet blocks, the smaller one (which can be heated) with fairly basic facilities, the other more modern with washbasins in cubicles, hairdryers and spacious, controllable free showers. Campers' kitchen. Shop. Games room with games machines. Good play area. Riverside dog walk. Card operated barrier (£10 deposit). Off site: Buses from site gate or in Peebles (a short walk).

Open: Easter/1 April - end October.

Directions

Park is by the A703 road, about 0.5 miles north of Peebles. O.S.GR: NT248417.
GPS: N55:39.730 W03:11.600

Charges guide

Per unit incl. 2 persons	£ 14.00 - £ 16.00
incl. services	£ 18.00

UK7030 Gibson Park Caravan Club Site

High Street, Melrose TD6 9RY (Borders)

Tel: **01896 822969**   **www.alanrogers.com/UK7030**

This is an ideal transit park, being so close to the A68, but is also a perfect base for exploring this Southern Scotland area or indeed a trip to Edinburgh, as this is only 35 miles away by car or one of the regular buses which run from the park entrance. This small, three acre park has only 60 touring pitches plus, unusually, an extra 12 tent pitches (summer only) next to the adjacent rugby pitch. All touring pitches have electricity (16A) and TV connections (otherwise it is a bad signal here), 57 have hardstanding and 10 are serviced with water and drainage. One-way system on the tarmac roads.

Facilities

First rate toilet facilities are in a new building with spacious showers, washbasins in cabins, centrally heated and all fitted out with purpose made faced boarding giving a very pleasing finish. Laundry facilities. Separate room with shower and WC for disabled visitors. Motorcaravan service point. Gas is available. Security barrier (operated by card). Off site: Situated on the edge of the little town of Melrose, a five minute walk, shops, pubs and restaurants are all in easy reach. Play area next to site.

Open: All year.

Directions

Turn left off A68 Jedburgh - Lauder road at roundabout about 2.5 miles past Newton St Boswell onto A6091 Galashiels road. In about 3.25 miles at roundabout turn right onto B6374 to Melrose. Site is on right at filling station opposite Melrose Rugby Club, just before entering town centre.
O.S.GR: NT545340. GPS: N55:35.881 W02:43.454

Charges guide

Per person	£ 4.40 - £ 5.50
pitch incl. electricity (non-members)	£ 10.80 - £ 14.60

UK6875 Southerness Holiday Village

Southerness, Dumfries DG2 8AZ (Dumfries and Galloway)

Tel: **01387 880256**. Email: **enquiries@parkdeanholidays.co.uk**   **www.alanrogers.com/UK6875**

Set beside a two mile stretch of sandy beach, at the foot of the beautiful Galloway Hills, is Southerness Holiday Village. Part of the Parkdean Group, it is a large park with the main emphasis on caravan holiday homes. However, there are also 100 open plan pitches for caravans, motorcaravans and tents. Set away from the static units, these are divided into two areas, some on level hardstanding with water connection, others on grass and all with 16A electrical connections. The light and airy reception office displays local information including a weekly 'What's On' programme as the main leisure complex is located a short walk from the touring area.

Facilities

A modern and very clean toilet block provides en-suite facilities throughout (key entry). Excellent unit for disabled visitors. Laundry. Shop. Bar with large TV. Bistro, takeaway and coffee shop. Indoor swimming pool. Indoor soft play area. Amusement arcade. Evening entertainment. Bowling. Adventure play area. Crazy golf. Nature trails. Off site: Golf course adjacent. Fishing 2 miles. Coastal drive to Rockcliffe and Kippford. Bus from outside gate.

Open: Before Easter - 31 October.

Directions

From Dumfries take A710 Solway Coast road for about 10 miles. Sign for Holiday Village is on the left. O.S.GR: NX974545. GPS: N54:52.568 W03:36.022

Charges guide

Per pitch incl. 8 persons	£ 8.00 - £ 22.00
incl. services	£ 10.00 - £ 26.00
dog	£ 2.00

UK6950 Brighouse Bay Holiday Park

Brighouse Bay, Borgue, Kirkcudbright DG6 4TS (Dumfries and Galloway)

Tel: **01557 870267**. Email: **info@gillespie-leisure.co.uk**   **www.alanrogers.com/UK6950**

Hidden away within 1,200 exclusive acres, on a quiet, unspoilt peninsula, this spacious family park is only some 200 yards through bluebell woods from a lovely sheltered bay. It has exceptional all weather facilities, as well as golf and pony trekking. Over 90% of the 210 touring caravan pitches have electricity (10/16A), some with hardstanding and some with water, drainage and TV aerial. The three tent areas are on fairly flat, undulating ground and some pitches have electricity. There are 120 self-contained holiday caravans and lodges of which about 30 are let, the rest privately owned. On site leisure facilities include a golf and leisure club with 16.5 m. pool, water features, jacuzzi, steam room, fitness room, games room (all on payment), golf driving range, bowling green and clubhouse bar and bistro. The 18-hole golf course extends onto the headland with superb views over the Irish Sea to the Isle of Man and Cumbria. A 9-hole family golf course is a popular attraction. Like the park, these facilities are open all year. The TRSS Approved Pony Trekking Centre, also open all year, offers treks for complete beginners and a range of hacks for the more experienced. Also available are 'weenie rides' for under 5s, riding lessons and stable management sessions for adults and children. This is a well run park of high standards and a member of the Best of British group.

Facilities

The large, well maintained main toilet block includes 10 unisex cabins with shower, basin and WC, and 12 with washbasin and WC. A second, excellent block next to the tent areas has en-suite shower rooms (one for disabled people) and bathroom, separate washing cubicles, showers and baby room. One section is heated in winter. Laundry facilities. Motorcaravan service point. Gas supplies. Licensed supermarket. Bar, restaurant and takeaway (all year). Golf (new practice area) and Leisure Club with indoor pool (all year). Play area (incl. new one for under 5s). Riding centre. Mountain bike hire. Quad bikes, boating pond, 10 pin bowling, playgrounds, putting. Nature trails. Coarse fishing ponds plus sea angling and an all-tide slipway for boating enthusiasts. Caravan storage. New purpose built chalet for tourist information and leisure facility bookings.

Open: All year.

Directions

In Kirkcudbright turn onto A755 and cross river bridge. In 400 yards turn left onto B727 at international camping sign. Or follow Brighouse Bay signs off A75 just east of Gatehouse of Fleet. O.S.GR: NX630455. GPS: N54:47.250 W04:07.746

Charges guide

Per unit incl. 2 persons	£ 13.25 - £ 18.65
extra person	£ 2.25
child (4-15 yrs)	£ 1.50
electricity	£ 3.80
fully serviced pitch	£ 4.90 - £ 5.40

Contact site for full charges.
Golf packages in low season.
Camping Cheques accepted.

UK6880 Sandyhills Bay Leisure Park

Sandyhills, Dalbeattie DG5 4NY (Dumfries and Galloway)

Tel: **01387 780257**. Email: **info@sandyhills-bay.co.uk**   **www.alanrogers.com/UK6880**

Sandyhills Bay is a small, quiet park beside a sheltered, sandy beach. Reception is on the left through a car park used by visitors either walking the hills or enjoying the beach. Beyond is a large flat camping area, above which, divided by a tree lined hedge, are 60 pitches, half taken by mobile homes situated around the perimeter. The 30 touring pitches, 28 with electrical connection (16A) are in the centre of the all grassed flat area and wigwams are available to hire. This is an excellent family park, with the beach and a children's play area at the site, whilst up the hill next to the park is an 18-hole golf course where you can enjoy a bar meal in the clubhouse. Within walking distance, at Barend, is an approved riding centre suitable for all the family. There is a well stocked licensed shop and a takeaway with table and chairs outside from where you can enjoy the well kept garden and splendid views across the Solway.

Facilities

The sanitary facilities are of traditional design, situated in one central block to the side of the touring area. Laundry room (tokens from reception). Shop and small takeaway. New adventure play area by the beach. Visitors can also use the facilities at Brighouse Bay, the largest park in the Gillespie Group. Barrier at entrance and beach car park (returnable deposit). Off site: Clifftop walk from Sandyhills to Rockcliffe approx. 10 miles. Pleasant drive to Rockcliffe and Kippford, a well known sailing centre.

Open: Easter - 31 October.

Directions

From Dumfries take A710 Solway coast road (about 16 miles). Site is on left just after signs for Sandyhills. O.S.GR: NX890549. GPS: N54:52.741 W03:43.862

Charges guide

Per unit incl. 2 persons	£ 10.85 - £ 15.60
extra person	£ 1.70
child (4-15 yrs)	£ 1.15
electricity	£ 3.80

UK6945 Barlochan Caravan Park

Palnackie, Castle Douglas DG7 1PF (Dumfries and Galloway)
Tel: **01557 870267**. Email: **info@barlochan.co.uk**   www.alanrogers.com/UK6945

Barlochan Caravan Park is situated on a hillside overlooking the Urr Estuary on the Solway Coast close to Dalbeattie and Castle Douglas, with the small village of Palnackie being a short walk away. Set on terraces, level, marked and numbered, most of the touring and tent pitches are on grass with a limited number of hardstandings available. There are 12 with electrical connections (16A). In addition, 55 mobile homes (5 for rent) are positioned on terraces high above the touring areas and screened by mature shrubs and trees. Just to the left of the entrance there is a minigolf course and an adventure play area screened from the park with mature trees. Through the village, under a mile from the park, there is a course fishing lake which is free for visitors to the park. Castle Douglas is just 9 miles away and gardeners will enjoy an afternoon at the well known Threave Gardens.

Facilities

The refurbished sanitary facilities are kept spotlessly clean. Shower cubicles have recently been made larger suitable for wheelchair entry, but if required there is also a separate unit with WC and basin. Fully equipped laundry with outside drying area. Dishwashing under cover. Reception and well stocked shop. Large games/TV room. On site: Fishing 400 yds. Bicycle hire 6 miles. Golf 7 miles. Riding 10 miles. Beach 10 miles.

Open: Easter - end October.

Directions

From Dumfries take A711 west to Dalbeattie. Continue through Dalbeattie for 0.5 miles, bear left at T-junction (Auchencairn). Site is 2 miles on right. O.S.GR: NX819571. GPS: N54:53.757 W03:50.601

Charges guide

Per unit incl. 2 persons	£ 10.25 - £ 14.70
extra person	£ 1.60
child (4-15 yrs)	£ 1.10
electricity	£ 3.60
dog	£ 2.00

UK6900 Seaward Caravan Park

Dhoon Bay, Kirkcudbright DG6 4TJ (Dumfries and Galloway)
Tel: **01557 870267**. Email: **info@seaward-park.co.uk**   www.alanrogers.com/UK6900

Seaward Caravan Park is little sister to the much larger Brighouse Bay Holiday Park, 3.5 miles away. Set in an idyllic location overlooking the bay, this park is suitable for all units. The terrain is slightly undulating, but most of the numbered pitches are flat and of a good size. There are 35 pitches (21 hardstandings) for caravans and motorcaravans, a further 14 for tents, plus 43 caravan holiday homes (6 for hire). Electric hook-ups (16A) are on 32 of the touring pitches and 12 are serviced with water and drain. This is a quiet park ideally suited for that relaxing holiday or for touring the region.

Facilities

The principal, fully equipped toilet block is to the rear of the park. Four rooms with en-suite facilities are also suitable for disabled campers. Well equipped baby room. Laundry facilities. No motorcaravan service point but the manager can lift a manhole cover to empty waste tanks. The reception/shop stocks basic provisions, books, gifts and gas. Unsupervised heated outdoor swimming pool (15/5-15/9). Central play area with bark surface and picnic tables. Excellent games room. Pitch and putt. Off site: Beach and sea angling nearby. Riding and bicycle hire 3.5 miles. Kirkcudbright 2.5 miles.

Open: 1 March - 31 October.

Directions

In Kirkcudbright turn onto A755 signed Borgue. Go over river bridge and after 400 yards turn left onto B727 at international camping sign. Proceed with caution when turning right into site as turn is tight. O.S.GR: NX680510. GPS: N54:49.186 W04:04.927

Charges guide

Per unit incl. 2 persons	£ 11.40 - £ 16.30
extra person	£ 1.80
child (4-15 yrs)	£ 1.15
electricity	£ 3.80
serviced pitch	£ 4.90 - £ 5.40

UK6870 Glenearly Caravan Park

Dalbeattie DG5 4NE (Dumfries and Galloway)

Tel: **01556 611393**

www.alanrogers.com/UK6870

Glenearly is a fairly new park (opened in 2000), owned and managed by Mr and Mrs Jardine. Rurally located, it has been tastefully developed from farmland into a touring and mobile home, all year park. There are 39 marked, open pitches, all with 16A electrical connections (and TV), most on hardstandings. Seasonal units use some pitches. Walls and shrubs divide the touring section from the caravan holiday homes (two for rent), with mature trees around the perimeter. There are attractive views over the hills and forest of Barhill and buzzards, yellow wagtails, woodpeckers and goldfinch are some of the birds that can be seen, along with the park's own donkeys, ponies and sheep. The large games room, converted from an old barn, is excellent – heated and with plenty of chairs and tables for parents to supervise the activities. A super play area suitable for all ages is conveniently situated behind the touring area. A ten minute stroll brings you into the small town of Dalbeattie. Just 6 miles from the park along the Solway coast is Kippford, a well known sailing centre from which you can walk the Jubilee Path (1 mile) to Rockcliffe. Set in a bay, Rockcliffe has a small sandy beach, an excellent tea room and gift shop.

Facilities

Situated in the centre of the touring area, the toilets and showers are fitted out to a high standard. Unit for disabled visitors or families. Laundry room with washing machines and dryer and an outside drying area. Large games room. Play area. Off site: Shops, pubs, restaurants, etc. at Dalbeattie. Bicycle hire at Mabie Forest just 3 miles from Dumfries on the A710.

Open: All year.

Directions

From Dumfries take A711 towards Dalbeattie. Six miles beyond Beeswing, after passing sign for Edingham Farm, park is signed with entrance on right (beside a bungalow). O.S.GR: NX834626. GPS: N54:56.692 W03:49.337

Charges 2009

Per unit incl. 2 persons	£ 13.00 - £ 15.00
extra person over 5 yrs	£ 2.00
electricity	£ 2.00 - £ 2.50

UK6885 Kings Green Caravan Park

South Street, Port William DG8 9SG (Dumfries and Galloway)

Tel: **07988 700880**. Email: **enquiries@portwilliam.com**

www.alanrogers.com/UK6885

Kings Green Caravan Park is now owned and run by the Port William Community Association. Kept very natural and situated beside the sea overlooking Luce Bay and the Mull of Galloway, it is within walking distance of Port William, well known for its harbour and fishing community. The all grass, open site provides 30 marked and numbered pitches for caravans, motorcaravans and tents (21 with 10A electricity). On arrival visitors are given a welcome pack which includes a guide on the history of the area and local information. Second Sands at the northern end of the village is perfect for the launching and recovery of boats at any stage of the tide and provides wheelchair and pushchair access to the beach. When we inspected the park, volunteers were in charge. Reception may not therefore always be open. You are invited to park and details of reserved pitches are placed on the notice board.

Facilities

The small toilet block (key entry) is kept very clean and has vanity style washbasins, free electric showers and hair dryers. Facilities for disabled visitors include WC and washbasin (Radar key). Small basic outdoor dishwashing. No laundry, motorcaravan point or gas sales. Large play and ball game area adjacent. Off site: Shops, restaurants and bars in Port William. Local walks and cycle routes. Fishing 50 yds. Golf 2 miles. Sailing and boat launching 600 yds. Riding 3 miles. Bladnoch distillery and the Isle of Whithorn just a short drive away or further to Stranraer with boats to Ireland.

Open: 30 March - 31 October.

Directions

From Dumfries, take A75 to Newton Stewart. Follow A714 to Wigtown, then B7085 to Port William. O.S.GR: NX337433. GPS: N54:45.358 W04:34.892

Charges guide

Per pitch	£ 8.00 - £ 9.00
incl. electricity	£ 10.00 - £ 11.00

UK6910 Hoddom Castle Caravan Park

Hoddom, Lockerbie DG11 1AS (Dumfries and Galloway)

Tel: **01576 300251**. Email: **hoddomcastle@aol.com**   **www.alanrogers.com/UK6910**

The park around Hoddom Castle is landscaped, spacious and well laid out on mainly sloping ground with many mature and beautiful trees, originally part of an arboretum. The drive to the site is just under a mile long with a one way system. Many of the 120 numbered pitches have good views of the castle and have gravel hardstanding with grass for awnings. Most have electrical connections (16A). In front of the castle are flat fields used for tents and caravans with a limited number of electricity hook-ups. The oldest part of Hoddom Castle itself is a 16th century Borders Pele Tower, or fortified Keep. This was extended to form a residence for a Lancashire cotton magnate, became a youth hostel and was then taken over by the army during WW2. Since then parts have been demolished but the original 'Border Keep' still survives, unfortunately in a semi-derelict state. The site's bar and restaurant have been developed in the courtyard area from the coach houses, and the main ladies' toilet block was the stables. Amenities include a comfortable bar lounge with a TV. The park's 9-hole golf course is in an attractive setting alongside the Annan river, where fishing is possible for salmon and trout (tickets available). Coarse fishing is also possible elsewhere on the estate. This is a peaceful base from which to explore historic southwest Scotland.

Facilities

The main toilet block can be heated and very well appointed. Washbasins in cubicles, 3 en-suite cubicles with WC and basin (one with baby facilities) and an en-suite shower unit for disabled visitors. Two further tiled blocks, kept very clean, provide washbasins and WCs only. Well equipped laundry room at the castle. Motorcaravan service point. Licensed shop at reception (gas available). Bar, restaurant and takeaway (restricted opening outside high season). Games room. Large, grass play area. Crazy golf. Mountain bike trail. Fishing. Golf. Guided walks (high season). Caravan storage. Off site: Tennis nearby.

Open: 1 April - 30 October.

Directions

Leave A74M at junction 19 (Ecclefechan) and follow signs to park. Leave A75 at Annan junction (west end of Annan by-pass) and follow signs. O.S.GR: NY155725. GPS: N55:02.482 W03:18.660

Charges guide

Per unit incl. 2 persons	£ 9.00 - £ 16.00
incl. electricity	£ 12.00 - £ 19.00
extra person	£ 3.00
child (7-16 yrs)	£ 1.00

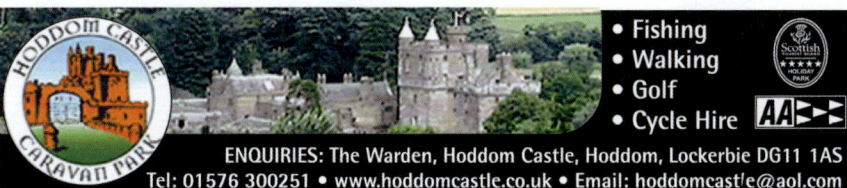

UK7020 Aird Donald Caravan Park

London Road, Stranraer DG9 8RN (Dumfries and Galloway)

Tel: **01776 702025**. Email: **enquiries@aird-donald.co.uk**   **www.alanrogers.com/UK7020**

Aird Donald is a good stopping off place when travelling to and from the Irish ferries, but it is also useful for seeing the sights around Stranraer. This tidy park comprises 12 acres surrounded by conifers, flowering trees and shrubs and the 300 yard drive is lit and lined with well trimmed conifers. There are grass areas for caravans or tents and hardstandings with electricity hook-up (these are very handy for hardy winter tourers). A small play area caters for young children, but the local leisure centre is only a walk away and provides swimming, table tennis, gym, etc, and a theatre that hosts everything from country and western to opera. It also has bar facilities. The area has three world famous gardens to visit, numerous golf courses, fishing, riding and watersports.

Facilities

Two toilet blocks, the new block modern and heated. Kept very clean with excellent, tiled facilities, this one is kept locked with a key deposit of £5. There are two types of shower, an electric one which is metered (20p) and two others which are free. Washbasins are in vanity units, ladies having one in a cubicle. Unit for visitors with disabilities with washbasin and WC. The original block is being renovated but is more basic with free showers and open all the time. Small laundry with sinks, dryer, washing machine, an old fashioned mangle and clothes lines. Motorcaravan services. Play area.

Open: All year.

Directions

Enter Stranraer on A75 road. Watch for narrow site entrance on left entering town, opposite school. O.S.GR: NX075605. GPS: N54:54.111 W05:00.373

Charges guide

Per unit incl. 2 persons and electricity	£ 15.80
tent	£ 12.00
No credit cards.	

263

UK6930 Park of Brandedleys

Crocketford, Dumfries DG2 8RG (Dumfries and Galloway)

Tel: **01387 266700**. Email: **brandedleys@holgates.com**

www.alanrogers.com/UK6930

Brandedleys is a first class park providing pitches for some 75 caravans and a limited number of tents, plus 55 self-contained caravan holiday homes in three or four flat and variably sloping fields with tarmac access roads, 15 for rent. It has excellent facilities and amenities. Caravan pitches are on lawns or terraced hardstandings, many with a pleasant outlook across a loch. All have electrical connections (10A) and 21 pitches also have water and drainage. Improvements continue with more serviced pitches. A heated outdoor swimming pool is open when the weather is suitable and the heated indoor pool adjacent to the bar/restaurant is open all season with changing room (both pools free) and a sauna. The bar and licensed restaurant are open for lunch and dinner with full menus at reasonable prices and a patio area overlooking Auchenreoch Loch. Walks on the open moors or forest and beautiful sandy beaches 12 miles away from this popular, quality park.

Facilities

The main heated toilet block has been extensively modernised with clean, well appointed shower cubicles with toilet and washbasin (just one for men), in addition to the normal provision. Bathroom for disabled visitors. Laundry room, baby and hair care room. Covered dishwashing sinks. A second block of equal size and standard is in the lower field, also with laundry and dishwashing facilities. Bar and restaurant. Takeaway food to order (18.00-21.30 hrs). Swimming pool. All-weather tennis courts, outdoor badminton court. Play area. Games room, pool table and air-hockey table. Off site: Riding, fishing 1.5 miles. Golf 6 miles. Bicycle hire 9 miles. Beach 12 miles.

Open: All year.

Directions

Park is 9 miles from Dumfries on the south side of the A75 Dumfries - Stranraer road, just west of the village of Crocketford. O.S.GR: NX830725. GPS: N55:01.966 W03:49.898

Charges guide

Per unit incl. 2 persons and electricity	£ 15.50 - £ 21.00
family (2 adults, 3 children)	£ 19.00 - £ 24.50
serviced pitch	£ 3.50
dog	£ 2.50

No single sex groups.

The Park of BRANDEDLEYS

Peaceful.
Exhilarating.
Inspiring.
Breathtaking.
Invigorating.

A panoramic position, a peaceful Loch and miles of rolling countryside - relax, be inspired and just drink in the views.

The Park of Brandedleys, Crocketford, Dumfries DG3 8RG
T. 01387 266 700   www.holgates.com

UK6940 Loch Ken Holiday Park

Parton, Castle Douglas DG7 3NE (Dumfries and Galloway)

Tel: **01644 470282**. Email: **penny@lochkenholidaypark.co.uk**

www.alanrogers.com/UK6940

Loch Ken Holiday Park sits right on the shore of the loch, adjacent to the RSPB bird reserve and the Galloway Forest Park – it is a peaceful haven in an area of outstanding beauty. This is a family owned park with 52 touring pitches and 33 caravan holiday homes, 10 of which are for rent. The touring pitches, all with 10A electricity, are quite separate and are arranged in a mostly open-plan way on a large, neatly mown grass area beside the water. Some of this area is gently undulating. Mature trees border the park and provide an area for walking dogs. The toilet block is a little walk from some pitches, although there are pitches nearby. Site lighting is minimal so torches are advised. The spacious reception and well stocked shop are at the site entrance with a separate tourist information area. There are facilities for launching small boats, but these must be registered with the local council (at reception). This park is probably mostly suited to couples and families with older children who enjoy outdoor pursuits.

Facilities

The toilet block is old and fairly basic, but is kept clean. Showers 50p. Facilities for disabled visitors, a laundry and dishwashing are also old and in need of refurbishment (planned). Gas supplies. Well stocked shop. Small play area. Bicycles, canoes and dinghies for hire. Boat launching (permit from reception). Fishing (permit). Off site: Bars and restaurants in Castle Douglas, 9 miles. Kirkcudbright 15 miles. Golf and riding 7 miles. Skiing 0.5 miles. Buses stop at the entrance, but are limited.

Open: 1 March - 31 October.

Directions

From Castle Douglas take the A713 north for 7 miles. Site entrance is on left in Parton. O.S.GR: NX688701. GPS: N55:00.624 W04:03.341

Charges guide

Per unit incl. 2 persons, 2 children under 10 yrs and electricity	£ 14.00 - £ 18.00
tent, no electricity	£ 11.00 - £ 13.00
extra person over 10 yrs	£ 2.00
dog	£ 2.00

264

UK6890 Mossyard Caravan Park

Gatehouse of Fleet, Castle Douglas DG7 2ET (Dumfries and Galloway)

Tel: **01557 840226**. Email: **enquiry@mossyard.co.uk**   **www.alanrogers.com/UK6890**

Mossyard is a family run park set within a working farm right beside the sea in a sheltered bay. The park and farmhouse appear together suddenly over the horizon and in the distance as you approach, with some breathtaking views across the Solway where the Galloway Hills and the waters of Wigtown Bay meet. There are 37 grass pitches, 12 for caravans and motorcaravans on an elevated area that slopes in parts. The remaining 25 pitches for any unit are on a level camping field which adjoins the beach but is a little way from the sanitary facilities. Electrical connections (10A) are available. On arrival you pass through the farm buildings into the park which is divided into two sections by stone walls. Around the perimeter are several new wooden chalets and holiday homes and self catering holiday cottages. This is a wonderful park for outdoor activities such as watersports and fishing where small craft can be launched from site. Although some of the beaches and tides around the Solway Coast are dangerous, the one around this bay is very safe.

Facilities

Some of the farm buildings around the main farmhouse have been utilised for the toilet facilities, which are of traditional design. Showers are coin-operated (20p). Roomy facilities for disabled visitors can also be used as a family bathroom. Purpose built building with laundry, dishwashing area and information room with freezer and fridge for visitors' use. No shop. Off site: Gatehouse of Fleet with shops, pubs and restaurants 4 miles.

Open: 28 March - 31 October.

Directions

Take A75 road from Dumfries towards Stranraer and park is signed to the left, 4 miles west of Gatehouse of Fleet, about 1 mile down a single track farm road. O.S.GR: NX547518. GPS: N54:50.411 W04:15.609

Charges 2009

Per caravan or motorcaravan	£ 13.00 - £ 15.00
tent	£ 12.00 - £ 15.00
electricity	£ 2.00
awning	£ 1.00 - £ 2.00

UK7015 The Ranch Holiday Park

Culzean Road, Maybole KA19 8DU (South Ayrshire)

Tel: **01655 882446**   **www.alanrogers.com/UK7015**

This holiday park is situated in the Ayrshire countryside, four miles from the small town of Maybole. The Ranch, a Caravan Club affiliated site, is managed by the McAuley family. Barrier controlled, the park is beautifully set out with 60 spacious touring pitches, all with 16A electricity connections and including 8 super pitches. Most are on level hardstanding with a few level, all grass pitches arranged open plan facing a huge playing field. There are also 65 caravan holiday homes, 1 for rent. There are plans to extend the number of touring pitches and holiday homes. The superb facilities include a private Leisure Centre with an indoor heated pool, sauna, solarium and well equipped gym, complete with changing room, toilets, shower and free hair dryers. To the rear is a small unfenced play park adjacent to the small camping area which has undercover seating for rainy days. A 'Wee Honesty Shop' offers exchange books and magazines and a 'kiddies' corner for children under 5 years old. This is an excellent park for relaxing and enjoying the amenities or for touring the area with nearby sandy beaches at Maybole Shore and Croy Bay plus the wonderful freak of nature, where the laws of gravity are turned upside down at the Electric Brae, where you can see water run uphill.

Facilities

The sanitary facilities are away from the touring area and older in style, but kept spotlessly clean, (there are plans for a new block). Washbasins in vanity units, four in cubicles with WCs for ladies. Large pre-set showers. Individual unit with WC and basin for disabled visitors. Purpose built wooden building housing a well equipped laundry with dishwashing area on the end. No shop on site but reception has a good information area. Off site: Golf at Turnberry and fishing at Mochram Loch.

Open: March - October (and weekends).

Directions

From Maybole turn onto B7023 (signed Culzean Maidens) for 1 mile and site is signed on left. O.S.GR: NS286102 GPS: N55:21.358 W04:42.368

Charges guide

Per unit incl. 2 persons	£ 10.60 - £ 16.60
extra person	£ 3.30 - £ 4.80
child	£ 1.10 - £ 1.60

Scotland

UK7010 Culzean Castle Camping & Caravanning Club Site

Maybole KA19 8JJ (South Ayrshire)

Tel: **01655 760627**

www.alanrogers.com/UK7010

With wonderful views of the Firth of Clyde and over to the Isle of Arran, this quiet Camping & Caravanning Club site is next door to Culzean Castle (pronounced Kullayne). Visitors are given a pass to walk in the grounds (when open) with their 17 miles of footpaths as many times as they wish. The 18th century, clifftop castle is built on the site of a former ancient castle and its armoury exhibition is superb. Besides the woodland walks, deer park and aviary, there are three miles of rocky shore and small sandy beaches. A full programme of events is staged at the castle over the season, including special children's weeks, sheepdog trials, bands, battle re-enactments, ranger walks and craft fairs. The campsite has 90 pitches, some level others slightly sloping, and 60 have 10A electricity connections. A few level pitches are suitable for motorcaravans and 20 pitches have hardstanding. American style motorhomes (more than 25 ft.) must contact the site prior to arrival as large pitches are limited. Should you have your fill of the castle and its grounds, Maybole with shops, etc. is only four miles and the area has a wealth of places to visit.

Facilities

The toilet blocks, kept very clean, can be heated and include some washbasins in cubicles. Unit for disabled visitors has a WC, washbasin and shower – an excellent facility. Dishwashing sinks. Well equipped laundry. Small shop for basics opens for short periods morning and evening. Adventure playground. Units over 25 ft. long only accepted by prior arrangement. Off site: Golf or bicycle hire 4 miles. Fishing 8 miles. Buses pass the gate.

Open: 30 March - 30 October.

Directions

From Maybole follow signs for Culzean Castle and Country Park, turning in the town on B7023 which runs into the A719. Country Park entrance is clearly signed on right after 3.75 miles; entrance to caravan park is on the right in Country Park drive. O.S.GR: NS247103. GPS: N55:21.207 W04:46.167

Charges guide

Per person	£ 4.90 - £ 7.25
child (6-18 yrs)	£ 2.15 - £ 2.25
non-member pitch fee	£ 5.65

UK7410 Riverview Holiday Park

Marine Drive, Monifieth DD5 4NN (Angus)

Tel: **01382 535471**. Email: **info@riverview.co.uk**

www.alanrogers.com/UK7410

A quiet, family park, Riverview overlooks a long sandy beach and has magnificent views over the River Tay towards the Kingdom of Fife and yet is within walking distance of Monifieth town. The park is neatly set out with flowering shrubs and bushes dividing 40 numbered touring pitches. Some enjoying river views, they are grassy and level, each with 16A electricity and two also with water and drainage. Bordering the park are 46 privately owned caravan holiday homes and 4 to rent. At the entrance to the park is a small reception office and separate tourist information room and a leisure suite with sauna, steam baths and gym (charge). For children, there is an indoor games room with a pool table and a play area for the under 5s, and a small outdoor adventure play area for under 12s with seats alongside for supervision. A member of the Best of British group.

Facilities

The spotlessly clean amenity block (key entry) has open washbasins, one in a cabin with WC, and pre-set showers. Baby bath. Full facility for disabled visitors. Well equipped laundry. Leisure suite. Games room and play area. Adventure play area. Off site: Picnic areas and small boat slipway adjacent. Opposite the Riverview recreation park offers football pitches, putting, crazy golf, tennis, bowling as well as a well equipped adventure play park. Golf 800 yds. Fishing 2 miles. Riding 3 miles. Dundee city 5 miles. Bus service nearby.

Open: 1 April - 31 October.

Directions

From Dundee follow signs for Monifieth on A930, after passing Tesco. Turn right at sign for golf course and right again under railway bridge. Park is signed on the left. O.S.GR: NO501322. GPS: N56:28.797 W02:48.692

Charges guide

Per unit incl. 2 adults and 2 children	£ 13.00 - £ 15.00
extra person	£ 2.00
awning	£ 2.00

UK7790 Invercoe Caravan & Camping Park

Invercoe, Glencoe PH49 4HP (Argyll and Bute)

Tel: **01855 811210**. Email: **holidays@invercoe.co.uk**   www.alanrogers.com/UK7790

On the edge of Loch Leven, surrounded by mountains and forest, Iain and Lynn Brown are continually developing this attractively located park in its magnificent historical setting. It provides 63 pitches for caravans, motorcaravans or tents on level grass (can be a bit wet in bad weather) with gravel access roads (some hardstandings). You choose your own numbered pitch, those at the loch side being very popular. The only rules imposed are necessary for safety because the owners prefer their guests to feel free and enjoy themselves. There is much to do for the active visitor with hill walking, climbing, boating, pony riding and sea loch or fresh water fishing in this area of outstanding natural beauty. This is a park you will want to return to again and again.

Facilities

The well refurbished toilet block can be heated. Dishwashing under-cover, excellent laundry facilities with a drying room. New large under-cover eating area. Motorcaravan service point comprising multi-drainage point, fresh water, dustbins, and chemical disposal point. Shop (Easter - end Oct). Play area with swings. Fishing. Off site: The village with pub and restaurant is within walking distance. Visitors' Centre at Glencoe 2 miles. Bicycle hire 2 miles. Golf 3 miles.

Open: All year.

Directions

Follow A82 Crianlarich - Fort William road to Glencoe village and turn onto the B863; park is 0.5 miles along, well signed. O.S.GR: NN098594. GPS: N56:41.194 W05:06.359

Charges guide

Per unit incl. 2 persons and electricity	£ 18.00
extra person	£ 3.00
child (3-15 yrs)	£ 1.00
awning	£ 2.00
Senior citizens less £1 per person outside July/Aug.	

UK7860 Glendaruel Caravan Park

Glendaruel PA22 3AB (Argyll and Bute)

Tel: **01369 820267**. Email: **mail@glendaruelcaravanpark.co.uk**   www.alanrogers.com/UK7860

Glendaruel is in South Argyll, in the area of Scotland bounded by the Kyles of Bute and Loch Fyne, yet is less than two hours by road from Glasgow and serviced by ferries from Gourock and the Isle of Bute. There is also a service between Tarbert and Portavadie. Set in the peaceful wooded gardens of the former Glendaruel House in a secluded glen surrounded by the Cowal hills, it makes an ideal centre for touring this beautiful area. The park takes 35 units on numbered hardstandings with electricity connections (10A), plus 15 tents, on flat oval meadows bordered by over 50 different varieties of mature trees. In a separate area are 28 privately owned holiday homes and 2 for rent. The converted stables of the original house provide an attractive little shop selling basics, local produce, venison, salmon, wines (some Scottish!) and tourist gifts. Glendaruel is a park for families with young children or for older couples to relax and to enjoy the beautiful views across the Sound of Bute from Tighnabruaich or the botanical gardens which flourish in the climate. The Craig family provides a warm welcome and will advise you where to eat and what to do – they are justifiably proud of their park and its beautiful environment.

Facilities

The toilet block is ageing but it is kept very neat and tidy and can be heated. Washing machine and dryer. A covered area has picnic tables for use in bad weather. Shop (hours may be limited in low season). Gas available. Games room. Behind the laundry is a children's play centre for under 12s and additional play field. Fishing. Torches advised. Off site: Sea fishing and boat slipway 5 miles, adventure centre (assault courses, abseiling and rafting) and sailing school close. Golf 12 miles.

Open: 28 March - 26 October.

Directions

Entrance is off A886 road 13 miles south of Strachur. Alternatively there are two ferry services from Gourock to Dunoon, then on B836 which joins the A886 about 4 miles south of the park - this route not recommended for touring caravans. Note: the park has discount arrangements with Western Ferries so contact the park before making arrangements (allow 7 days for postage of tickets). O.S.GR: NS001865. GPS: N56:02.038 W05:12.770

Charges guide

Per person	£ 3.00
pitch incl. electricity	£ 10.00
Special weekly rates and senior citizen discount outside July/Aug.	

Scotland

UK7025 Seal Shore Camping & Touring Site

Kildonan KA27 8SE (North Ayrshire)

Tel: **01770 820320**. Email: **mdeighton@seashore.fsnet.co.uk**   www.alanrogers.com/UK7025

A warm welcome awaits here on the Island of Arran from the resident owners, Sylvia and Maurice Deighton. Located on the southernmost point of the island, this is a quiet and peaceful park situated along its own private beach with wonderful sea views. The open, grassy area, sloping in parts, takes caravans, motorcaravans and tents with 8 electrical connections (16A). The reception doubles as a shop selling basics with a TV room adjacent. There are picnic and barbecue areas. The Kildonan Hotel is next door serving restaurant and bar meals. Permits are available for loch fishing and charters provided by the owner, a registered fisherman. Golfers can choose from seven courses.

Facilities

The good toilet block is clean and tidy and includes full facilities for disabled visitors that double as a baby room. No laundry but you may use the owner's washing machine and iron. Indoor dishwashing with fridge and freezer for campers use. Shop. Camping gas. Fishing. Sailing. Off site: Golf 4 miles. Heritage Museum in Brodick. North of the Island Lochranza castle and distillery.

Open: March - October.

Directions

From Brodick take A841 south for 12 miles to sign for Kildonan. Site is downhill, on the seashore, next to the Kildonan Hotel. O.S.GR: NS022209. GPS: N55:26.460 W05:06.838

Charges guide

Per person	£ 6.00
pitch	£ 1.00 - £ 2.00
electricity	£ 2.00

UK7260 Forest Holidays Ardgartan

Ardgartan, Arrochar G83 7AR (Dunbartonshire)

Tel: **01301 702293**. Email: **fe.holidays@forestry.gsi.gov.uk**   www.alanrogers.com/UK7260

Forest Holidays is a partnership between the Forestry Commission and The Camping & Caravanning Club. Ardgartan is a rugged site in the Argyll Forest Park. At the northern end of the Cowal Peninsula, the site is on a promontory on the shores of Loch Long, with good sea fishing and facilities for launching small boats. The 70 touring pitches are in sections which are well divided by grass giving an uncrowded air. Most with hardstanding and marked by numbered posts, they are accessed from hard surfaced roads and 54 have electrical hook-ups. There are additional grass areas for tents. Midges can be a problem in this area of Scotland. The site gate is locked 22.00 - 07.30.

Facilities

The main toilet block is opposite the reception and shop. It is a basic, but clean provision with facilities for disabled visitors and a launderette. These facilities may be quite stretched when the park is busy. Play equipment (bark surfaces). Raised barbecues are allowed. Off site: Arrochar village (2 miles) has fuel, general stores and a restaurant.

Open: All year excl. 14 January - 28 February.

Directions

From A82 Glasgow - Crianlarich road take A83 at Tarbet signed Arrochar and Cambletown. Site is 2 miles past Arrochar, the entrance on a bend. O.S.GR: NN275030. GPS: N56:11.327 W04:46.900

Charges guide

Per unit incl. 2 persons	£ 9.00 - £ 13.70

Less 20% all year for disabled guests and outside 22/7-30/8 for senior citizens.

UK7810 Oban Camping & Caravanning Club Site

Barcaldine, By Connel PA37 1SG (Argyll and Bute)

Tel: **01631 720348**   www.alanrogers.com/UK7810

Owned by the Camping & Caravanning Club, this site at Barcaldine, 12 miles north of Oban, is a small, intimate site taking 75 units. Arranged within the old walled garden of Barcaldine House, the walls give it some protection from the wind and make it quite a sun trap. There are 23 level, fairly small pitches with hardstanding and 52 electrical hook-ups (16A). (It can be wet underfoot in bad weather). Being a small site, it has a very cosy feel to it, due no doubt to the friendly welcome new arrivals receive. Through the garden gate, one is immediately in the Barcaldine forest with its miles of forest tracks, absolutely perfect for both dog walking and mountain biking.

Facilities

The central toilet block can be heated and is kept very clean with free hot showers, hair dryers and plenty of washbasins and WCs. Excellent unit for disabled visitors. Laundry. Motorcaravan service point. Small shop open a few hours each day for basic provisions and gas. Bar serving bar meals. Small play area with effective safety base. Off site: Sea Life Centre 2 miles. Bus every hour outside gate.

Open: April - end October.

Directions

Entrance is off the A828 road on south side of Loch Creran, 6 miles north of Connel Bridge. From the south, go past Barcaldine House and site is 300 yards on right. O.S.GR: NM966420. GPS: N56:31.590 W05:18.596

Charges guide

Per person	£ 4.20 - £ 6.60
child (6-18 yrs)	£ 2.05 - £ 2.15
non-member pitch fee	£ 5.65

UK6980 Drum Mohr Caravan Park

Levenhall, Musselburgh EH21 8JS (East Lothian)

Tel: **01316 656867**. Email: **bookings@drummohr.org**

www.alanrogers.com/UK6980

This family owned, attractively laid out touring park is on the east side of Edinburgh. It is a secluded, well kept modern park, conveniently situated for visits to Edinburgh, the Lothian and Borders regions. It has been carefully landscaped and there are many attractive plants, flowers and hedging. There are 120 individual pitches, 40 with hardstanding, for touring units of any type, well spaced out on gently sloping grass in groups of 12 or more, marked with white posts. Most have electric hook-ups and 13 are fully serviced with water and waste water connections. Free space is left for play and recreation.

Facilities

The two toilet blocks are clean, attractive, of ample size and can be heated. Free hot water to washbasins (one cabin for men, two for ladies in each block) and to four external dishwashing sinks, but hot water is on payment for the showers (outside the cubicle) and laundry sinks. Laundry facilities in each block. Motorcaravan service point. Well stocked, licensed shop (gas available, bread and papers to order). Playground on sand. Excellent dog walk. Caravan storage. Security barrier with code access. No late night arrivals area. Off site: Golf course adjacent.

Open: 1 March - 31 October.

Directions

From Edinburgh follow A1 signs for Berwick on Tweed for 6-7 miles. Turn off for Wallyford and follow camp and Mining Museum signs. From south follow A1 taking junction after Tranent village (A199 Musselburgh) and follow signs. O.S.GR: NT371732. GPS: N55:57.002 W03:00.700

Charges guide

Per unit incl. 2 persons	£ 14.00 - £ 17.00
serviced pitch	£ 17.00 - £ 20.00
awning	£ 2.00
extra person (over 5 yrs)	£ 2.00
dog	£ 1.00

UK7050 Edinburgh Caravan Club Site

35-37 Marine Drive, Edinburgh EH4 5EN (Edinburgh)

Tel: **01313 126874**

www.alanrogers.com/UK7050

Situated as it is on the northern outskirts and within easy reach of the city of Edinburgh, this large, busy Caravan Club site (open to non-members) provides an ideal base for touring. Enter the site through rather grand gates to find the visitors' car park and reception to the left. There are 147 large flat pitches (103 hardstandings, 12 with water tap and waste water disposal) with electric hook-ups (16A) and TV aerial and provision for 50 tents in a separate field (hook-ups available) with a covered cooking shelter and bicycle stands close by. As the bushes planted around the site mature, there will be shade. The nearest hotel/restaurant is under a mile away, Royal Yacht Britannia and many other attractions in the city, Firth of Forth bridge about 2 miles. Bus (number 42) stops just outside the gates) and takes you right into the centre of the city and within walking distance of many of its attractions. A day saver ticket can be used on other Lothian buses.

Facilities

Two heated, well kept toilet blocks provide washbasins in cubicles, hair and hand dryers, an en-suite room for campers with disabilities, plus a baby and toddler room with child-size facilities. Each block houses a dishwashing and vegetable preparation area, and a laundry. Drying room. No shop, but milk, bread, and newspapers can be ordered, with ice creams and gas from reception. Fenced play area. Boules. Dog walk in the only natural wood in Edinburgh (part of the site). WiFi internet access. Off site: Bicycle hire nearby. Health club (with internet access) 400 yds – ask at site for introduction card.

Open: All year.

Directions

Turn right off A720 at Gogar roundabout at end of bypass signed City Centre, A8). Shortly turn left on to A902 (Forth Road Bridge), then right onto the A90. At Blackhall junction traffic lights fork left into Telford Road (A902). At Crewe Toll roundabout turn left (B9085) and at T-junction (after bridge) turn right at traffic lights towards Leith, A901. Turn left at traffic lights (Silverknowes, Davidson's Mains). In half a mile at roundabout turn right into Marine Drive. Site is half a mile on the left. O.S.GR: NT212768. GPS: N55:58.653 W03:15.870

Charges guide

Per person	£ 4.60 - £ 6.00
child (5-16 yrs)	£ 1.50 - £ 2.50
pitch incl. electricity (non-member)	£ 11.80 - £ 14.60
Tent campers apply to site.	

UK7060 Tantallon Caravan & Camping Park

Tantallon Road, North Berwick EH39 5NJ (East Lothian)
Tel: **01620 893348**. Email: **tantallon@meadowhead.co.uk**

www.alanrogers.com/UK7060

Tantallon is a large park with views over the Firth of Forth and the Bass Rock. The park has 147 quite large, grass touring pitches in two lower, more sheltered areas (Law Park), with the rest having good views at the top (Bass Park). Many have some degree of slope. There are 75 electrical connections (10A) and 10 pitches also with water and waste water. Each area has its own sanitary facilities, the top block a little way from the end pitches. About 55 caravan holiday homes for sale or hire are in their own areas. Wooden wigwams are also available. This a mature, well managed park with good facilities. This area is a popular venue for bird-watchers with its world famous gannet colony. Tantallon and Dirleton Castles are also nearby. Access to the beach is through the golf course and then down the road or via cliff paths.

Facilities

Bass Park has 8 unisex units with shower, washbasin and toilet. The other areas have open washbasins. Two heated units for disabled visitors. Good launderette with spin dryer and free iron. Motorcaravan service point. Reception sells a few ices, chocolate bars, cold drink and papers at weekends. Games room with pool table and TV. Internet access in reception and WiFi. Good playground and better than average putting green. Dogs are only accepted by prior arrangement. Off site: Tesco supermarket within walking distance. Golf next door, sea fishing, safe sandy beaches in walking distance. Town (with footpath) 1 mile. Riding 5 miles. Bicycle hire 1 mile.

Open: 13 March - 31 October.

Directions

Park is beside the A198 just to the east of North Berwick, which lies between Edinburgh and Dunbar. It is easily accessible from the A1.
O.S.GR: NT567850. GPS: N56:03.345 W02:41.450

Charges 2009

Per unit incl. 2 persons	£ 13.50 - £ 26.00
extra person (over 5 yrs)	£ 2.50
dog	£ 3.00

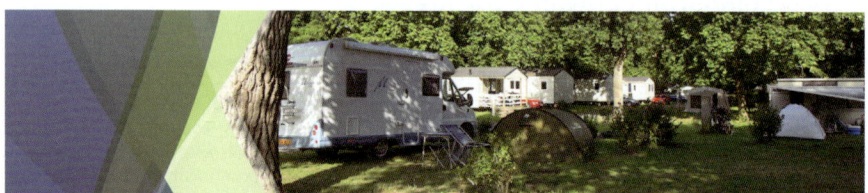

UK7065 Belhaven Bay Caravan & Camping Park

Belhaven Bay, West Barns, Dunbar EH42 1TU (East Lothian)
Tel: **01368 865956**. Email: **belhaven@meadowhead.co.uk**

www.alanrogers.com/UK7065

Located in the John Muir Country Park, Belhaven Bay Caravan Park is just one mile from the historic town of Dunbar, where the ancient castle ruin stands guard over the town's twin harbours. This is an excellent family park with easy access to the beach and to the clifftop trail which has spectacular views capturing the beauty of the countryside and seascapes. The park's 67 caravan holiday homes (7 for rent) are located quite separately from the touring and tent areas. These are surrounded by mature trees and are arranged in large open bays. There are 27 reasonably level, mostly grass touring pitches with 10A electricity connections. Two separate areas accommodate 25 pitches for tents.

Facilities

Facilities are central and include a unit for disabled visitors. Laundry room. Motorcaravan service point. Reception also has a small shop and tourist information. Cyber Café and WiFi internet access. Play area and ball game area. Off site: Golf 1 mile. Riding and boat launching 2 miles. Bus stop at entrance.

Open: 13 March - 31 October.

Directions

From the A1 (north or south) exit at the Thistley Cross roundabout west of Dunbar. Park is 1 mile down the A1087 towards Dunbar.
O.S.GR: NT655784. GPS: N55:59.806 W02:32.707

Charges 2009

Per unit incl. 2 persons	£ 13.75 - £ 23.50
extra person (over 5 yrs)	£ 2.00
tent, 2 persons with car	£ 7.00 - £ 9.00
dog	£ 2.50

UK6990 Mortonhall Caravan & Camping Park

38 Mortonhall Gate, Frogston Road East, Edinburgh EH16 6TJ (Edinburgh)
Tel: **01316 641533**. Email: **mortonhall@meadowhead.co.uk**   www.alanrogers.com/UK6990

Mortonhall Park makes a good base to see the historic city of Edinburgh and buses to the city leave from the park entrance every ten minutes (parking in Edinburgh is not easy). Although only four miles from the city centre, Mortonhall is in quiet mature parkland, in the grounds of the Mortonhall estate, and easy to find with access off the bypass. There is room for 250 units mostly on numbered pitches on a slight slope with nothing to separate them, but marked by jockey wheel points. Over 180 places have electricity (10/16A), several with hardstanding, water and drainage as well, and there are many places for tents. The park is very popular but only part is reserved and tourists arriving early may find space. An attractive courtyard development houses a lounge bar and restaurant, open all year and to all, with good value meals in pleasant surroundings. There are mobile homes (20) and wooden family camping cabins (wigwams) for rent.

Facilities

Two modern toilet blocks with outside, but covered dishwashing sinks, but the only cabins are in the third excellent facility at the top of the park, which has 8 unisex units incorporating shower, washbasin and WC. The courtyard area provides further basic facilities and 'portacabin' type units are added for the high season to serve the large number of tents. Facilities for disabled visitors. Laundry room with washing machines and dryer. Motorcaravan services. Bar/restaurant. Self-service shop (15/3-31/10). Games and TV rooms. Play area. Internet access. Late arrivals area with hook-ups. Torches useful in early and late season. Security lockers. Internet access at reception (£1 per half an hour). WiFi internet access (£5 per day). Off site: Bus from site gate. Golf courses and driving range 2 miles. Riding 2 miles. Bicycle hire 4 miles.

Open: 13 March - 4 January.

Directions

Park is well signed south of the city, 5 minutes from A720 city bypass. Take the Mortonhall exit from the Straiton junction and follow camping signs. Entrance road is alongside the Klondyke Garden Centre.
O.S.GR: NT262686. GPS: N55:54.200 W03:10.800

Charges 2009

Per unit incl. 2 persons	£ 13.00 - £ 28.50
extra person (5 yrs and over)	£ 2.50
dog	£ 3.00

UK7045 Linwater Caravan Park

West Clifton, East Calder, Edinburgh EH53 0HT (West Lothian)

Tel: 0131 333 3326. Email: linwater@supanet.com

www.alanrogers.com/UK7045

This delightful small family run park is set in the countryside but is still close to the city of Edinburgh. The park is level and the 60 large touring pitches are a mixture of grass and hardstanding; 49 have 16A electricity connections. Parts of the park are screened off by trees and fences. Two sides are sheltered by trees and shrubs and one side is open with views over fields. With just the occasional sound of aircraft from the airport, it is difficult to believe that you are so close to a major city. Linwater is a useful park for visiting Edinburgh and areas outside the city. The reception area has a wealth of information on places to visit. Just 4 miles down the road is a 'park and ride' scheme and the purchase of a Day Saver ticket is a cheap way to get into Edinburgh and to explore the area. The Falkirk Wheel, houses, castles and gardens are all within easy reach.

Facilities

The modern and well maintained heated sanitary block has private cabins. Facilities for disabled visitors. Laundry. Gas supplies. Milk, bread and newspapers to order (by 21.00 for the next morning). Home produced, free range eggs and bacon from reception (and strawberries in season). Sand pit. Three timbertents for hire. Off site: Fishing 1 mile.

Open: 13 March - 1 November.

Directions

From the A720 Edinburgh bypass, leave at sign for Wilkieston on the A7. In Wilkieston turn right at traffic lights (park signed). Continue to next sign indicating left and site 1 mile further on the right. O.S.GR: NT102697. GPS: N55:54.662 W03:26.153

Charges guide

Per unit incl. 2 persons	£ 12.00 - £ 15.00
tent incl. 2 persons	£ 10.00 - £ 13.00
extra person	£ 3.00
child (5-18 yrs)	£ 1.50

Linwater Caravan Park,
West Clifton, East Calder,
West Lothian, EH53 0HT
Tel: 0131 333 3326
queries@linwater.co.uk
www.linwater.co.uk

A family-run touring park just west of Edinburgh with easy access to Edinburgh, Royal Highland Showground and Falkirk Wheel. Excellent amenities and lovely walks to Canal and Country Park. Call in on your way north or south, or stay awhile, you will be most welcome.

UK7035 Lothianbridge Caravan Park

Craigesk, Newtongrange EH22 4TP (Mid Lothian)

Tel: 0131 663 6120. Email: lothianbridge@tiscali.co.uk

www.alanrogers.com/UK7035

You will receive a warm welcome at this small, family run park. It is situated beside the A7, a major road into Edinburgh, and the entrance is through a disused but very grand railway viaduct which crosses one side. The park is level with hardstanding and grass pitches, 45 of which are for touring. The central area is grassed with some electrical points (long leads useful for some) and newly planted trees. A key controls access to the park and the sanitary facilities. There are several picnic tables for visitors to use and tall trees and shrubs provide a green perimeter. The family live on site so they are able to see and let in late arrivals. It is very easy to get into Edinburgh from here and to visit other places of interest. There is public transport 450 yards from the entrance.

Facilities

A modern toilet block also housing a well equipped en-suite for disabled visitors. Laundry facilities, iron (from reception) and microwave. No shop but a few items are available in peak season. Motorcaravan service point. Play area. Free WiFi internet access. Two bungalows available to rent. Off site: Supermarket (24 hour) 2 miles with ATM. Golf, riding and fishing all within 5 miles. Beach 8 miles.

Open: 1 April - 6 January.

Directions

Travelling on the A7, just southeast of Edinburgh and due west of Newtongrange, the site is clearly marked by brown camping signs. A large viaduct marks the entrance. O.S.GR: NT326648. GPS: N55:52.279 W03:04.580

Charges guide

Per unit incl. 2 persons	£ 14.00 - £ 16.00
electricity	£ 2.00
extra person	£ 2.00
child (5-17 yrs)	£ 1.00

UK7290 Craigtoun Meadows Holiday Park

Mount Melville, Saint Andrews KY16 8PQ (Fife)

Tel: **01334 475959**. Email: **craigtoun@aol.com**   **www.alanrogers.com/UK7290**

This attractively laid out, quality park has individual pitches and good facilities and although outnumbered by caravan holiday homes, the touring section is an important subsidiary. Its facilities are both well designed and comprehensive. With 67 units taken on gently sloping land, caravans go on individual hardstandings with grass alongside for awnings on most pitches. All caravan pitches are large (130 sq.m) and are equipped with electricity (16A), water and drainage. There are 15 larger 'patio pitches' with summer house, barbecue patio, picnic table and chairs, partially screened. Tents are taken on a grassy meadow at one end, also with electricity available. The 157 caravan holiday homes stand round the outer parts of the site; 27 are owned and let by the park. Buses pass the entrance and Craigtoun park with boating pond and miniature railway, etc. is within walking distance. This is a well run park, two miles from St Andrews with its golf courses and long, sandy beaches, from where there is a picturesque view of St Andrews and its ruined Abbey and Castle.

Facilities

An excellent, de-luxe, centrally heated sanitary building serves the touring area. All washbasins are in cabins and each toilet has its own basin. Showers are unisex, as are two bathrooms, with hand and hair dryers. Facilities for disabled people and babies. Launderette. Shop and licensed restaurant (both restricted hours in low seasons), also providing takeaway. Games room. Well equipped playground, play field and 8 acres of woodland. Barbecue area. Tennis. Information room. Dogs and other pets are not accepted. Off site: Golf or bicycle hire 1.5 miles. Fishing 5 miles. Riding 6 miles.

Open: 15 March - 15 November.

Directions

From M90 junction 8 take A91 to St Andrews. Just after sign for Guardbridge (to left, A919), turn right at site sign and sign for Strathkinness. Go through village, over crossroads at end of village, left at next crossroads, then 0.75 miles to park. O.S.GR: NO482151. GPS: N56:19.477 W02:50.247

Charges guide

Per caravan or motorcaravan	£ 18.00 - £ 24.50
tent	£ 18.00

Only 'breathable' type groundsheets may be used in awnings.

UK7000 Strathclyde Country Park Caravan Site

Strathclyde Country Park, 366 Hamilton Road, Motherwell ML1 3ED (North Lanarkshire)

Tel: **01698 266155**. Email: **strathclydepark@northlan.gov.uk**   **www.alanrogers.com/UK7000**

The 1,200 acre Country Park is a large green area less than 15 miles from the centre of Glasgow. Well kept and open to all, it provides nature trails, children's adventure play area, sandy beaches and coarse fishing, with an 18-hole golf course two miles away. In addition there is a large water sports centre offering sailing, water skiing, windsurfing, canoeing, rowing (all with craft for hire), a water bus, a selection of family 'fun boats' and bicycle hire, plus Scotland's own theme park nearby. The touring site, part of the park, is suitable for both overnight or longer stays (max. 14 days) and has 80 numbered pitches for caravans or tents, 70 with electrical connections (10A). Arranged in semicircular groups on flat grass they are served by made-up access roads and the site is well lit. As it is close to the motorway, there may be some traffic noise.

Facilities

Four solidly built toilet blocks make a good provision. Enclosed sinks for dishwashing or food preparation. Laundry in two blocks (irons from reception). Block 4 has facilities for visitors with disabilities, block 3 has a baby changing room. Motorcaravan services. Shop within reception sells basic provisions. Play equipment. Bicycle hire. American motorhomes accepted up to 22 ft. Barrier card and toilet block key £10 deposit. Off site: Bar and restaurant facilities (100 yds) in the Country Park. Fishing 400 yards. Bus 1 mile.

Open: Easter - 18 October.

Directions

Take exit 5 from the M74 and follow sign for Strathclyde Country Park. Turn first left for site. O.S.GR: NS720584. GPS: N55:48.235 W04:02.804

Charges guide

Per caravan pitch incl. 2 persons and electricity	£ 13.00
tent pitch (4 persons)	£ 8.70
extra person	£ 1.25
child	£ 1.00

No credit cards.

273

UK7220 The Gart Caravan Park

Stirling Road, Callander FK17 8LE (Perth and Kinross)

Tel: **01877 330002**. Email: **enquiries@theholidaypark.co.uk**   www.alanrogers.com/UK7220

Gart Caravan Park is situated within the Loch Lomond and Trossachs National Park, just a mile from the centre of Callander. Surrounded by mature trees, this attractive, family run park is peaceful and spacious. All is kept in a pristine condition and a very warm welcome awaits on arrival with a superb information pack given to all. The 128 all grass touring pitches are reasonably level, open plan and marked, with electricity (16A), water and drain. Tents or pup tents are not accepted, groundsheets are not permitted. Privately owned caravan holiday homes are located away from the touring section near the river which runs for 200 m. along the park boundary.

Facilities

Modern heated central facilities are immaculate, with toilets and showers, plus extra areas with showers, baby changing and hair washing basins. Facilities for disabled visitors. Laundry. Motorcaravan service point. Gas sales. No shop but a breakfast car arrives at 09.00 with papers and basic provisions. Adventure play area. Field for ball games. Free fishing (not Sundays). Max. two dogs. Off site: Golf and bicycle hire 1 mile. Riding 6 miles.

Open: 1 April - 15 October.

Directions

From the south take M9. Near Stirling, leave at exit 10 and follow A84 through Doune. Park is on the left, 1 mile before Callander town centre. O.S.GR: NN643070. GPS: N56:14.190 W04:11.346

Charges 2009

Per pitch incl. services	£ 19.50
awning	£ 1.50
Reduced rates for the over 50s.	

UK7230 Trossachs Holiday Park

Aberfoyle FK8 3SA (Perth and Kinross)

Tel: **01877 382614**. Email: **info@trossachsholidays.co.uk**   www.alanrogers.com/UK7230

Nestling on the side of a hill, three miles south of Aberfoyle, this is an excellent base for touring this famously beautiful area. Lochs Lomond, Ard, Venachar and others are within easy reach, as are the Queen Elizabeth Forest Park and, of course, the Trossachs. This park specialises in the sale and hire of top class mountain bikes. Very neat and tidy, there are 45 well laid out and marked pitches arranged on terraces with hardstanding. All have electricity and TV connections and most also have water and drainage. There is also a large area for tents. You will receive a warm welcome from Joe and Hazel Norman at this well run, family park. A member of the Best of British group.

Facilities

A modern building houses sanitary facilities providing toilets, showers and washbasins. Two private cabins for ladies. Laundry. Well stocked shop and bike shop. Games room with TV. Play equipment. Off site: Golf, boat launching and fishing. A passport scheme arranged with a local leisure centre (10 miles, 8 passes) provides a sauna solarium, swimming, badminton, tennis, windsurfing, etc.

Open: 1 March - 31 October.

Directions

Park is 3 miles south of Aberfoyle on the A81 road, well signed. O.S.GR: NS544976. GPS: N56:08.408 W04:21.330

Charges guide

Per unit incl. 2 persons	
and electricity	£ 14.00 - £ 18.00
incl. all services	£ 16.00 - £ 20.00
tent pitch incl. 2 persons	£ 12.00 - £ 18.00

UK7270 Auchterarder Caravan Park

Nether Coul, Auchterarder PH3 1ET (Perth and Kinross)

Tel: **01764 663119**. Email: **info@prestonpark.co.uk**   www.alanrogers.com/UK7270

This is a charming small park, purpose designed and landscaped by the owners Stuart and Susie Robertson. In a sheltered position, it is conveniently situated for exploring central Scotland and the Highlands with many leisure activities close at hand (particularly golf) and within walking distance of the village (1 mile). The 21 original pitches, all with electricity (6A) and hardstanding, 12 with drainage, are well spaced around the edge of the elongated, level grass park. Marked pitches with grass frontage back on to raised banks with trees. Further pitches have been developed to one side of the site, along with a trout fishing pond (exclusively for campers) and a woodland walk.

Facilities

Toilet facilities (with key system) include controllable, well equipped hot showers. A toilet for disabled people is provided in both the male and female units. Laundry room with sink and washing machine; an iron can be provided. Fishing. Caravan storage. Off site: Village 1 mile. Golf 1 mile. Bicycle hire and riding 4 miles. The historic cities of Perth and Stirling are less than half an hour's drive away.

Open: All year.

Directions

Park is between the A9 and A824 roads east of Auchterarder village, only 2 miles from the main road. It is reached by turning on to the B8062 (Dunning) road from the A824. O.S.GR: NN964138. GPS: N56:18.260 W03:40.570

Charges guide

Per unit incl. up to 4 persons	
and electricity	£ 14.50
No credit cards.	

UK7280 Nether Craig Caravan Park

By Alyth, Blairgowrie PH11 8HN (Perth and Kinross)

Tel: **01575 560204**. Email: **nethercraig@lineone.net**   **www.alanrogers.com/UK7280**

Nether Craig is a family run touring park, attractively designed and beautifully landscaped, with views across the Strathmore valley to the long range of the Sidlaw hills. The 40 large pitches are accessed from a circular, gravel road; 26 have hardstanding (for awnings too) and 10A electrical connections. The majority are level and there are 9 large tent pitches on flat grass. There is a personal welcome for all visitors at the attractive wooden chalet beside the entrance (with a slope for wheelchairs) which doubles as reception and shop providing the necessary essentials, gas and tourist information. A one mile circular woodland walk from the park has picnic benches and a leaflet guide is provided. Otherwise you can just enjoy the peace of the Angus Glens by hill walking, bird watching, fishing or pony trekking. Alyth with its Arthurian connections is only 4 miles away and Glamis Castle, the childhood home of the Queen Mother, is nearby, as is the beautiful Glenshee and Braemar with its castle.

Facilities

The central, purpose built toilet block is modern, well equipped and maintained, and can be heated. Unit for disabled visitors (entry by key). Separate sinks for dishwashing and clothes are in the laundry room (metered hot water), plus a washing machine, dryer and iron, and clothes line. Shop. Play area. Small football field. Bicycle hire. Caravan storage. Off site: Fishing 2 miles. Riding 4 miles. Golf within 4 miles. Boat launching 6 miles.

Open: 15 March - 31 October.

Directions

From A926 Blairgowrie - Kirriemuir road, at the roundabout south of Alyth join B954 (Glenisla). Follow caravan signs for 4 miles and turn right onto unclassified road (Nether Craig). Park is on left after 0.5 miles. O.S.GR: NO265528. GPS: N56:39.684 W03:11.988

Charges guide

Per unit incl. 2 persons and electricity	£ 14.00 - £ 16.00
tent per person	£ 7.00
extra person	£ 1.50 - £ 5.00

UK7295 The River Tilt Park

Golf Course Road, Blair Atholl, Pitlochry PH18 5TB (Perth and Kinross)

Tel: **01796 481467**. Email: **stuart@rivertilt.co.uk**   **www.alanrogers.com/UK7295**

This good quality, family owned park is set on the banks of the River Tilt, a short walk from the village of Blair Atholl, where the 16th Century Blair Castle stands proud. There are 51 caravan holiday homes including 3 for rent. Two central areas have been set aside for touring caravans, motorcaravans and tents, with 31 pitches mostly with hardstanding. Divided by mature shrubs and hedges, all have 10A electricity connections, 18 have water and a drain. One of the areas is reserved for dog owners and their pets. The Steadings Spa provides an indoor pool, solarium, steam room, spa pool and multigym, plus Waves hair salon. Also open to the public, there are charges for these facilities. The park also has an award winning restaurant. Adjacent are a riverside walk and a golf course. There may be some noise from the railway line that runs alongside the park.

Facilities

The purpose built toilet block is centrally situated (with key entry) and provides en-suite toilet and washbasin cabins and individual large pre-set showers, one suitable for disabled visitors. Baby facilities. Well equipped laundry. Motorcaravan service point. Bar and restaurant. Leisure spa complex with indoor pool, etc. Hair salon. Tennis. Max. 2 dogs per pitch. No ball games. Off site: Private fishing and golf adjacent. Bicycle hire and riding 1 mile. Pitlochry with its famous salmon leap 6 miles. Bus or train from Blair Atholl.

Open: 17 March - 13 November.

Directions

From the A9 just north of Pitlochry, take B8079 into Blair Atholl and follow signs for River Tilt. O.S.GR: NN874655. GPS: N56:45.923 W03:50.377

Charges guide

Per unit incl. 2 persons	£ 10.00 - £ 16.00
incl. electricity	£ 12.00 - £ 18.00
extra person	£ 1.00
dog	£ 2.00

275

UK7300 Blair Castle Caravan Park

Blair Atholl, Pitlochry PH18 5SR (Perth and Kinross)

Tel: **01796 481263**. Email: **mail@blaircastlecaravanpark.co.uk**   **www.alanrogers.com/UK7300**

This attractive, well kept park is set in the grounds of Blair Castle, the traditional home of the Dukes of Atholl. It has a wonderful feeling of spaciousness with a large central area left free for children's play or for general use. There is space for 277 touring units with 190 electricity connections (10/16A), 144 hardstandings and 44 fully serviced pitches with water and waste water facilities also. Caravan holiday homes, 83 privately owned and 27 for hire, are in separate areas. A quality park, quiet at night and well managed. The castle is open to the public, its 32 fully furnished rooms showing a picture of Scottish life from the 16th century to the present day, while the beautiful grounds and gardens are free to those staying on site. The castle grounds provide many walking trails and the village is within walking distance with hotels, shops, a water mill craft centre and folk museum.

Facilities

The five toilet blocks can be heated and are of excellent quality and very clean. Large hot showers, some incorporating WC and washbasin, and further cubicles with WC and washbasin. Facilities for disabled visitors with bath or shower, WCs and washbasins. Baby changing mats. Motorcaravan service point. Reception, shop, games room, laundry and internet gallery. Gas supplies. American motorhomes accepted (max. 30 feet or 5 tons). Off site: Mountain bike hire, riding, golf and fishing within 1 mile.

Open: 1 March - 27 November.

Directions

From A9 just north of Pitlochry take B8079 into Blair Atholl. Park is in grounds of Blair Castle, well signed. O.S.GR: NN868659. GPS: N56:46.050 W03:50.644

Charges guide

Per unit incl. 2 persons	£ 13.50 - £ 16.00
tent (no car)	£ 13.50 - £ 16.00
child (6-14 yrs)	£ 1.20 - £ 1.50
electricity	£ 3.00
dog (max. 2)	£ 1.00

UK7305 Tummel Valley Holiday Park

Tummel Bridge, Pitlochry PH16 5SA (Perth and Kinross)

Tel: **01882 634221**. Email: **enquiries@parkdeanholidays.co.uk**   **www.alanrogers.com/UK7305**

Set in the Tay Forest Park on the banks of the River Tummel, this large family holiday park is part of the Parkdean Group. Divided into two areas by the roadway, the main emphasis is on chalets to let on the side that overlooks the river. Privately owned caravan holiday homes and touring pitches are on the other, quieter side. The 36 touring pitches, open plan with hardstanding, electricity hook-up and a shared water point, overlook a small fishing lake which is an added attraction for all the family. The leisure complex with indoor and outdoor activities is on the river side, as is the reception office. On arrival, you should turn right and park, then cross back to book in.

Facilities

The very clean toilet block has vanity style washbasins, pre-set showers and a bathroom in each section. Good facilities for disabled visitors. Well equipped laundry. Chemical disposal but no motorcaravan service point. Shop. Riverside entertainment complex with bar with terrace, restaurant and takeaway. Indoor heated pool and toddlers' splash pool. Solarium and sauna. Amusements. Separate area with pool tables. All weather sports court. Adventure play area. Crazy golf. Nature trails. Bicycle hire. Fishing. Note: all venues are non-smoking. Max. 2 dogs per unit. Off site: Golf and riding 10 miles. Buses leave near park entrance.

Open: 24 March - 1 November.

Directions

Travel through Pitlochry. After 2 miles turn left on B8019 to Tummel Bridge (10 miles). Park is on both the left and right. Tourers should turn right and park, then return to reception on the left. O.S.GR: NN764590. GPS: N56:42.445 W04:01.201

Charges guide

Per pitch	£ 12.50 - £ 29.50

www.**alanrogers**.com for latest campsite news

UK7310 Twenty Shilling Wood Caravan Park

Comrie PH6 2JY (Perth and Kinross)

Tel: **01764 670411**. Email: **alowe20@aol.com**   **www.alanrogers.com/UK7310**

Everyone gets a warm welcome from the Lowe family when they arrive at Twenty Shilling Wood. Set amongst 10.5 acres of wooded hillside, this unusual park has a few touring pitches for caravans and motorcaravans (no tents), plus a number of owner occupied caravan holiday homes. However, with terracing and landscaping, not many of these are visible and flowering trees and shrubs help to hide them. The lowest level is the entrance where there is a late arrivals area and visitor car park. You will be escorted to your pitch. There are just 12 level touring pitches on gravel with grass bays between them, all with electricity hook-ups (10A). Television reception is poor.

Facilities

The clean and spacious toilet blocks have some washbasins in cubicles. Laundry. No shop but rolls, milk and papers can be ordered at reception. Games room and lounge area. Fenced adventure playground for all ages. Only two dogs per pitch are accepted. Off site: Buses pass the gate. Comrie 1 mile. Golf or fishing within 1 mile, riding or bicycle hire 6 miles.

Open: 1 April - 17 October.

Directions

Park is on north side of A85 Crieff - Lochearnhead road, about 0.75 miles west of B827 junction, 0.5 miles west of Comrie. O.S.GR: NN762222. GPS: N56:22.513 W04:00.390

Charges guide

Per unit incl. 2 persons, electricity and TV hook-up	£ 16.00
extra person (over 2 yrs)	£ 1.75

UK7320 Witches Craig Caravan Park

Blairlogie, Stirling FK9 5PX (Stirling)

Tel: **01786 474947**. Email: **info@witchescraig.co.uk**   **www.alanrogers.com/UK7320**

Witches Craig is a neat and tidy park, nestling under the Ochil Hills and the friendly Stephen family take each visitor to their pitch to make sure that they are happy. All 60 pitches have 10A electricity and 26 have hardstanding, 7 of these being large (taking American style motorhomes easily). Reasonably level, the park covers five well maintained acres with the grass beautifully manicured. Seven residential park homes are well kept and surrounded by flowering shrubs. The area has a wealth of historic attractions, starting with the Wallace Monument which practically overlooks the park. Being by the A91, there is some day-time road noise.

Facilities

The modern, heated toilet block is well maintained, and includes one cubicle with washbasin and WC each for ladies and men. Free controllable showers. Baby bath and mat. Good unit for disabled campers. Laundry. Bread, milk, drinks and papers daily (supermarket 2.5 miles). Large play area. Off site: Riding or bicycle hire 2 miles, fishing 3 miles, golf 1 mile. Buses stop at the entrance.

Open: 1 April - 31 October.

Directions

Park is on the A91, 2 miles northeast of Stirling. O.S.GR: NS822968. GPS: N56:08.882 W03:53.920

Charges guide

Per unit incl. 2 persons	£ 12.50 - £ 14.50
incl. electricity	£ 14.50 - £ 16.50
extra person	£ 2.00
child (2-13 yrs)	£ 1.00

£5 deposit for key to facilities. No credit cards.

UK7240 Lomond Woods Holiday Park

Tullichewan, Old Luss Road, Balloch G83 8QP (West Dunbartonshire)

Tel: **01389 755000**. Email: **lomondwoods@holiday-parks.co.uk**   **www.alanrogers.com/UK7240**

A series of improvements over the last few years has made this one of the top parks in Scotland. Almost, but not quite, on the banks of Loch Lomond, this landscaped, well planned park is suitable for both transit or longer stays. Formerly known as Tullichewan Holiday Park, it takes 110 touring units on well spaced, numbered pitches on flat or gently sloping grass. Most have hardstanding, all have electrical connections (10A) and 27 have water and waste water too. Watersport activities and boat trips are possible on Loch Lomond, with a visitor attraction, 'Lomond Shores' opened nearby. This is a well run park, open all year, with very helpful wardens and reception staff.

Facilities

The single large heated, well kept toilet block includes some showers with WCs, baths for ladies, a shower room for disabled visitors and two baby baths. Launderette. Motorcaravan service points. Games room with TV. Playground. Caravan storage. American motorhomes accepted with prior notice. Off site: Fishing and boat launching 400 yards. Riding 4 miles. Golf 5 miles. Restaurants, bar meals and buses in Balloch.

Open: All year.

Directions

Turn off A82 road 17 miles northwest of Glasgow on A811 Stirling road. Site is in Balloch at southern end of Loch Lomond and is well signed. O.S.GR: NS389816. GPS: N56:00.093 W04:35.534

Charges guide

Per unit incl. up to 2 persons and electricity	£ 15.00 - £ 20.00
incl. mains services and awning	£ 17.00 - £ 22.00
extra person	£ 2.00

UK7530 Aden Country Park Caravan Park

Station Road, Mintlaw AB42 8FQ (Aberdeenshire)

Tel: **01771 623460**   www.alanrogers.com/UK7530

Aden Country Park is owned by the local authority and is open to the public. The caravan and camping site is on one side of the park. Beautifully landscaped and well laid out with trees, bushes and hedges, it is kept very neat and tidy. It provides 48 numbered pitches for touring units, with varying degrees of slope (some level) and all with electrical hook-ups (16A), plus an area for tents. There are also 12 caravan holiday homes. The park is in a most attractive area and one could spend plenty of time enjoying all it has to offer. Attractions for visitors include an Agricultural Heritage Centre, Wildlife Centre, Nature Trail and restaurant, as well as open and woodland areas with a lake, for walking and recreation.

Facilities

The modern toilet block is clean, with good facilities for disabled visitors. It can be heated and provides free, pre-set hot showers, hairdryer for ladies, and a baby bath, but no private cabins. Dishwashing and laundry facilities (metered). Motorcaravan service point. Gas supplies. Small shop in reception area. Restaurant in the Heritage Centre. Games areas. Play equipment (safety surfaces). Dog exercise area. Off site: Shops in Mintlaw 0.5 miles. Fishing 1 mile. Riding 2 miles.

Open: Easter - 25 October.

Directions

Approaching Mintlaw from west on A950 road, park is shortly after sign for Mintlaw station. From east, go to the western outskirts of village and entrance is on left – Aden Country Park and Farm Heritage Centre. O.S.GR: NJ985484.
GPS: N57:31.485 W02:01.567

Charges guide

Per unit incl. electricity	£ 13.40 - £ 15.00
tent (2 persons)	£ 6.40 - £ 7.10
awning	£ 2.00

UK7550 Huntly Castle Caravan Park

The Meadow, Huntly AB54 4UJ (Aberdeenshire)

Tel: **01466 794999**. Email: **enquiries@huntlycastle.co.uk**   www.alanrogers.com/UK7550

Huntly Caravan Park's hard-working owners, the Ballantynes, are justly proud of their neat, well landscaped 15 acre site that is managed under contract for the Caravan Club (non-members are very welcome). The 11 level grass and 41 hardstanding touring pitches are separated and numbered, with everyone shown to their pitch. Arranged in three bays with banks of heathers and flowering shrubs separating them, most pitches have electric hook-ups (16A) and 15 are fully serviced with water and waste water. Two bays have central play areas and all three have easy access to a toilet block, as has the camping area. Campers are provided with a covered cooking shelter (with work tops) should the weather turn inclement. The park also has 33 privately owned caravan holiday homes (3 to hire). An Activity Centre near the entrance contains two indoor safe play areas (one for up to 2 yrs old, the other up to height 1.37 metres). There are snooker and pool tables, table tennis, badminton and short tennis. The area abounds with things to do, from forest trails to walk or cycle, a falconry centre, malt whisky distilleries and an all year Nordic ski track. A member of the Best of British group.

Facilities

The three heated toilet blocks are well designed and maintained, with washbasins (in cubicles for ladies) and large showers. Each block also has a family shower room, dishwashing sinks and a room for disabled visitors. Laundry room. Milk and papers may be ordered at reception. Activity centre (charged and facilities are also open to the public; open weekends and all local school holidays). Off site: Huntly is 10 minutes walk. Fishing, golf or bicycle hire within 1 mile. Riding 5 miles.

Open: 1 April - 1 November.

Directions

Site is well signed from A96 Keith - Aberdeen road. O.S.GR: NJ526402. GPS: N57:27.123 W02:47.496

Charges guide

Per unit incl. 2 persons and electricity	£ 15.25 - £ 18.90
extra person	£ 4.50
child (5-16 yrs)	£ 1.30 - £ 2.15
awning/pup tent	£ 1.95

UK7540 Aberlour Gardens Caravan & Camping Park

Aberlour-on-Spey AB38 9LD (Moray)

Tel: **01340 871586**. Email: **Aberlourgardens@aol.com**   **www.alanrogers.com/UK7540**

This pleasant park is within the large walled garden of the Aberlour Estate on Speyside. The owners have made many improvements to the sheltered, five acre, family run park which provides a very natural setting amidst spruce and Scots pine. Of the 73 level pitches, 35 are for touring units leaving the remainder for holiday homes (2 for rent) and seasonal units. All pitches have electrical connections (10A) and 9 are 'all-weather' pitches. This is an ideal area for walking, birdwatching, salmon fishing and pony trekking or for following the only 'Malt Whisky Trail' in the world, while Aberlour has a fascinating old village shop – a time capsule.

Facilities

The ladies toilet block has been refurbished. The men's is traditional in style (there are plans for refurbishment) with four large showers. Facilities for visitors with disabilities can also be used as family or baby changing room. Laundry facilities. Motorcaravan service point. Small licensed shop stocking basics and with an information area. Play area. Caravan storage. Off site: Riding 0.5 miles. Swimming and bicycle hire 1 mile. Fishing 1 or 5 miles. Golf 4 miles.

Open: 1 March - 28 December.

Directions

Turn off A95 midway between Aberlour and Craigellachie onto unclassified road. Site signed in 500 yds. Vehicles over 10'6" high should use the A941 Dufftown road (site signed). O.S.GR: NJ282432. GPS: N57:28.491 W03:11.916

Charges 2009

Per unit incl. 2 persons	£ 14.70 - £ 18.40
tent	£ 11.65 - £ 18.40
extra person (over 5 yrs)	£ 2.00
backpacker and tent (per person)	£ 6.70 - £ 7.80
dog	free

UK7670 Grantown-on-Spey Caravan Park

Seafield Avenue, Grantown-on-Spey PH26 3JQ (Highland)

Tel: **01479 872474**. Email: **warden@caravanscotland.com**   **www.alanrogers.com/UK7670**

John Fleming takes care of this excellent park. Peacefully situated on the outskirts of the town, with views of the mountains in the distance, the park consists of well-tended gravel (raked so that it is perfect for each occupant) and grass pitches. Trees and flowers are a feature of this landscaped location. There are 136 pitches for caravans or motorcaravans, of which 14 offer fresh and waste water facilities and 16 have individual fresh water taps. A further 12 pitches are used for seasonal occupation, and there is space for 50 or more tents. More than 71 pitches have 10A electrical hook-ups, WiFi internet for small charge on every pitch. There are a further 53 super pitches with individual water and waste hook up, 16A electric and individual Sky TV box. The wardens escort visitors to their pitch and will help to site caravans if necessary. Caravan holiday homes are located in a separate area of the park.

Facilities

New toilet and shower block complete with laundry and drying room. A further block provides good, clean toilet facilities, with new wash cabins for ladies. Facilities for disabled visitors. Laundry room. Motorcaravan service point. Gas cylinders, ice creams, cold drinks and camping accessories available at reception. Games room. Touring and motorcaravan secure storage. Off site: Fishing, golf and mountain bike hire within 1 mile. Riding 3 miles.

Open: 15 December - 31 October.

Directions

Go into the town. Turn north at Bank of Scotland. Park straight ahead half a mile. O.S.GR: NJ028283. GPS: N57:20.088 W03:37.117

Charges guide

Per pitch incl. 2 persons and 10A electricity	£ 14.50 - £ 18.50
small 2-man tent	£ 9.50 - £ 14.00
extra person	£ 1.50 - £ 3.00

279

UK7690 Torvean Caravan Park

Glenurquhart Road, Inverness IV3 6JL (Highland)

Tel: 01463 220582   www.alanrogers.com/UK7690

Torvean is a small and neat, select touring park for caravans and motorhomes only. It is situated on the outskirts of Inverness beside the Caledonian Canal and is within easy reach of the town's amenities which include an ice rink, theatre and leisure sports centre. The pitches on level grass are clearly marked with a tarmac access road and street lighting giving a very neat appearance. There are 47 touring pitches (27 with 10A electricity connections, 18 fully serviced with fresh water tap, waste water disposal and electricity). Excursions to the coast and Highlands are possible.

Facilities

Two heated toilet blocks are of good quality – ladies have two cubicles with washbasin and toilet and a hair washing cubicle. Controllable hot showers on payment. Suite for disabled people with toilet and shower over a bath. Launderette. Motorcaravan service point. Gas supplies. Play area. Only one dog per unit is accepted. Off site: Golf adjacent, bicycle hire or fishing 3 miles.

Open: Easter - end October.

Directions

Park is off the main A82 road on the southwest outskirts of the town on the west side of the Tomnahurich Canal Bridge (looks like a railway crossing rather than a bridge). O.S.GR: NH638438. GPS: N57:27.924 W04:14.731

Charges guide

Per unit incl. 2 persons	£ 9.00 - £ 9.50
de-luxe pitch incl. electricity	£ 12.50 - £ 13.00
extra person	£ 1.00 - £ 2.00

No credit cards.

UK7700 Pitgrudy Caravan Park

Poles Road, Dornoch IV25 3HY (Highland)

Tel: 01862 821253   www.alanrogers.com/UK7700

In a rural situation, Pitgrudy has superb views over the Dornoch Firth and the surrounding Ross-shire hills. There are 40 touring pitches for caravans, motorcaravans or tents, mostly on slightly sloping grass and with electrical connections (10A). A few have hardstanding (unfortunately still on a slope) and six are fully serviced (drinking water, waste water disposal point and electricity). Located at the top of the park are 35 caravan holiday homes, of which 25 are privately owned. The whole park is on immaculately tended grass with tarmac roads. The pleasant little town of Dornoch is less than a mile away with shops, restaurants, plus the cathedral.

Facilities

Sanitary facilities are in a modern, superior 'portacabin' style unit which is very clean and well equipped. Laundry with washing machine, dryer and iron. Dishwashing sinks. Gas supplies. Off site: Safe sandy beach 1 mile. The area is good for walking and golf (there are 7 courses within 15 miles of the park). Fishing 1 mile, bicycle hire or boat launching 3 miles, riding 5 miles.

Open: 25 April - 30 September.

Directions

At the war memorial in Dornoch, turn north (park signed) on the B9168. Park is 0.5 miles on the right (45 miles north of Inverness). O.S.GR: NH795911. GPS: N57:53.045 W04:02.379

Charges guide

Per unit incl. 2 persons	£ 7.50 - £ 9.00
full service pitch	£ 11.00 - £ 12.00
extra person	£ 0.75 - £ 1.50

No credit cards.

UK7710 Ardmair Point Caravan Park

Ardmair Point, Ullapool IV26 2TN (Highland)

Tel: 01854 612054. Email: sales@ardmair.com   www.alanrogers.com/UK7710

This spectacularly situated park, overlooking the little Loch Kanaird, just round the corner from Loch Broom, has splendid views all round. The 68 touring pitches are arranged mainly on grass around the edge of the bay, in front of the shingle beach. Electrical hook-ups (10A) are available and some gravel hardstandings are on the other side of the access road, just past the second toilet block. Tent pitches, together with cheaper pitches for some tourers are in a large field behind the other sanitary facilities. Scuba diving is popular at Loch Kanaird because the water is so clear. Seals and otters are regularly seen in the bay and the whole area is full of interest

Facilities

Two toilet blocks, both with good facilities. One block has wonderful views from the large windows in the laundery area. Large en-suite rooms for disabled people. Motorcaravan service point. Shop. Play area. Fishing. Sailing and boating (with your own boat). Off site: Ullapool for shops, golf and bicycle hire 3 miles.

Open: 1 April - late September (depends on weather).

Directions

Park is off the A835 road, 3 miles north of Ullapool. O.S.GR: NH109983. GPS: N57:56.038 W05:11.821

Charges guide

| Per unit incl. 2 persons | £ 11.00 - £ 18.00 |
| backpacker tent incl. 1 person | £ 7.00 |

Less for 7 or more nights pre-paid.

UK7720 Woodend Camping & Caravan Park

Achnairn, Lairg IV27 4DN (Highland)

Tel: **01549 402248**

www.alanrogers.com/UK7720

Woodend is a delightful, small park overlooking Loch Shin and perfect for hill walkers and backpackers. Peaceful and simple, it is owned and run single-handedly by Mrs Cathie Ross, who provides a wonderfully warm Scottish welcome to visitors. On a hill with open, panoramic views across the Loch to the hills beyond and all around, the large camping field is undulating and gently sloping with some reasonably flat areas. The park is licensed to take 55 units and most of the 22 electrical hook-ups (16A) are in a line near the top of the field, close to the large, fenced play area which has several items of equipment on grass. There are opportunities for fishing and hill walking. The famous Falls of Shin with a Visitor Centre is an ideal place to see the salmon leap (about 10 miles).

Facilities

The sanitary facilities are of old design but kept very clean and are quite satisfactory. Laundry with two machines and a dryer. Kitchen with dishwashing sinks and eating room for tent campers. Reception is at the house, Sunday papers, daily milk and bread may be ordered. Fishing licences for the Loch (your catch will be frozen for you). Off site: Mountain bikes can be hired in Lairg, 5 miles. Several scenic golf courses within 20-30 miles.

Open: 1 April - 30 September.

Directions

Achnairn is near the southern end of Loch Shin. Turn off the A838 single track road at signs for Woodend. From the A9 coming north take the A836 at Bonar Bridge, 11 miles northwest of Tain. O.S.GR: NC558127. GPS: N58:04.816 W04:26.823

Charges guide

Per unit incl. electricity	£ 10.00
tent	£ 8.00

No credit cards.

UK7680 Forest Holidays Glenmore

Aviemore PH22 1QU (Highland)

Tel: **01479 861271**. Email: **info@forestholidays.co.uk**

www.alanrogers.com/UK7680

Forest Holidays is a partnership between the Forestry Commission and The Camping & Caravanning Club. This site is attractively laid out in a fairly informal style in several adjoining areas connected by narrow part gravel, part tarmac roads, with access to the lochside. One of these areas, the Pinewood Area, is very popular and has 32 hardstandings (some distance from the toilet block). Of the 220 marked pitches on fairly level, firm grass, 122 have electricity (16A). This site with something for everyone would be great for family holidays. The Glenmore Forest Park lies close to the sandy shore of Loch Morlich amidst conifer woods and surrounded on three sides by the impressive Cairngorm mountains. It is conveniently situated for a range of activities, including skiing (extensive lift system), orienteering, hill and mountain walking (there are way-marked walks), fishing (trout and pike) and non-motorized watersports on the Loch.

Facilities

New toilet and shower blocks. Next to the site is a range of amenities including a well stocked shop (open all year), a café serving a variety of meals and snacks, and a Forestry Commission visitor centre and souvenir shop. Barbecues are not permitted in dry weather. Off site: The Aviemore centre with a wide range of indoor and outdoor recreations 7 miles. Golf within 15 miles. Fishing and boat trips.

Open: All year.

Directions

Immediately south of Aviemore on the B9152 road (not the A9 bypass) take the B970 then follow sign for Cairngorm and Loch Morlich. Site entrance is on right past the loch. O.S.GR: NH976097. GPS: N57:10.022 W03:41.683

Charges guide

Per unit incl. 2 persons	
(fee for 3 nights)	£ 33.40 - £ 49.90
premium pitch	£ 42.40 - £ 58.90

Less 20% all year for disabled guests and outside 7/7-28/8 for senior citizens.

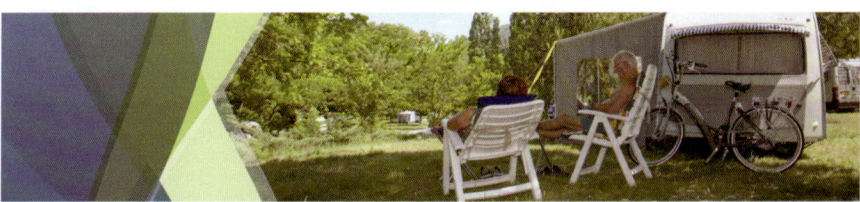

UK7730 Scourie Caravan & Camping Park

Harbour Road, Scourie IV27 4TG (Highland)

Tel: **01971 502060**   www.alanrogers.com/UK7730

Mr Mackenzie has carefully nurtured this park over many years, developing a number of firm terraces with 60 pitches which gives it an attractive layout – there is nothing regimented here. Perched on the edge of the bay in an elevated position, practically everyone has a view of the sea and a short walk along the shore footpath leads to a small sandy beach. The park has tarmac and gravel access roads, with well drained grass and hardstanding pitches, some with 10A electric hook-ups. A few are on an area which is unfenced from the rocks (young children would need to be supervised here).

Facilities

The toilet facilities can be heated. Showers have no divider or seat. Laundry. Motorcaravan service point. The 'Anchorage' restaurant at the entrance to the park (used as reception at quiet times) serves meals at reasonable prices, cooked to order (l/4-30/9). Boat launching. Fishing permits can be arranged. Off site: Village with shop and post office, and mobile banks visit regularly.

Open: Easter - 30 September, but phone first to check.

Directions

Park is by Scourie village on A894 road in northwest Sutherland. O.S.GR: NC153446.
GPS: N58:21.085 W05:09.406

Charges guide

Per unit incl. 1-2 persons	£ 11.00 - £ 12.00
extra person	£ 1.50 - £ 2.50
electricity	£ 2.00
No credit cards.	

UK7735 Sango Sands Oasis Caravan & Camping Site

Durness via Lairg IV27 4QB (Highland)

Tel: **01971 511726**. Email: **keith.durness@btinternet.com**   www.alanrogers.com/UK7735

Sango Sands Oasis is a quiet, ten acre site overlooking the beautiful Sango Bay, a Blue Flag beach. The site was established by the family in 1978 and they have worked hard improving the facilities over the years. There are 82 pitches for tents and touring caravans, 46 with electricity hook-ups (16A). The land is well drained and fairly level. It is possible to see whales, porpoise, dolphins and seals from the site plus a variety of sea birds which nest nearby. An ideal area for walkers with numerous marked paths and there is an excellent variety of angling, from rivers to the sea.

Facilities

Traditional toilet and shower blocks are lit at night but a torch may be useful. Free showers with curtains. Showers and toilets are separate. With the beach so close don't be surprised to find sand in the showers. En-suite facilities for disabled visitors. Laundry with sinks, washing machines, dryers, irons and boards. Campers kitchen with cooking rings. Café, bar and licensed restaurant. TV. Games room with pool and darts. Off site: Two grocery stores, post office, ATM, petrol, diesel and gas supplies in the village. Nearby Visitor Centre with extensive information on the area.

Open: All year.

Directions

From Thurso take the North Coast road (A836 as far as Tongue, where it continues on as the A838 to Durness). Site on right as you go through village. From Ullapool follow A835 north to Ledmore Junction and turn left on the A837. After 8 miles turn right onto the A894 and continue to Laxford Bridge. Turn left on A838. Durness is 19 miles further on this road. Site on left going through the village. O.S.GR: NC420668. GPS: N58:33.869 W04:44.533

Charges guide

Per person	£ 5.25
electricity	£ 2.75
No credit cards.	

UK7760 Reraig Caravan Site

Balmacara, Kyle of Lochalsh IV40 8DH (Highland)

Tel: **01599 566215**. Email: **warden@reraig.com**   www.alanrogers.com/UK7760

This is a small, level park close to Loch Alsh with a wooded hillside behind (criss-crossed with woodland walks). Set mainly on well cut grass, it is sheltered from the prevailing winds by the hill and provides just 45 numbered pitches. There are electrical connections (10A) and 35 hardstandings (2 without electricity). Large tents and trailer tents are not accepted at all. Small tents are permitted at the discretion of the owner, so it would be advisable to telephone first if this affects you. Reservations are not taken so it may be best to arrive before late afternoon in July and August.

Facilities

The single sanitary block has been extensively refurbished and is kept immaculately clean. Children have their own low basins. Controllable hot showers are on payment (10p for 2 minutes). Laundry sinks and spin dryer. A slope replaces the small step into the ladies and sink rooms. Motorcaravan drainage point. Off site: The Balmacara Hotel with bar, shop, sub-post office and off-licence.

Open: 1 May - 30 September.

Directions

On A87, park is 2 miles west of the junction with the A890, beside the Balmacara hotel. O.S.GR: NG815272. GPS: N57:16.988 W05:37.591

Charges guide

Per unit incl. 2 persons	£ 11.50
extra person (13 yrs or over)	£ 2.00
awning (May, June, Sept only)	£ 3.00
electric hook-up (10A)	£ 1.30

UK7830 Glen Nevis Caravan & Camping Park

Glen Nevis, Fort William PH33 6SX (Highland)

Tel: **01397 702191**. Email: **camping@glen-nevis.co.uk**   **www.alanrogers.com/UK7830**

Just outside Fort William in a most attractive and quiet situation with views of Ben Nevis, this spacious park is used by those on active pursuits as well as sightseeing tourists. It comprises eight quite spacious fields, divided between caravans, motorcaravans and tents (steel pegs required). It is licensed for 250 touring caravans but with no specific tent limits. The large touring pitches, many with hardstanding, are marked with wooden fence dividers, 174 with electricity (13A) and 100 also have water and drainage. The park becomes full in the peak months but there are vacancies each day. If reception is closed (possible in low season) you site yourself. There are regular security patrols at night in busy periods. The park's own modern restaurant and bar with good value bar meals is a short stroll from the park, open to all. A well managed park with bustling, but pleasing ambience, watched over by Ben Nevis. Around 1,000 acres of the Glen Nevis estate are open to campers to see the wildlife and explore this lovely area.

Facilities

The four modern toilet blocks with showers (extra showers in two blocks); and units for visitors with disabilities. An excellent block in Nevis Park (one of the eight camping fields) has some washbasins in cubicles, showers, further facilities for disabled visitors, a second large laundry room and dishwashing sinks. Motorcaravan service point. Shop (Easter - mid Oct), barbecue area and snack bar (May - mid Sept). Play area on bark. Off site: Pony trekking, golf and fishing near.

Open: 15 March - 31 October.

Directions

Turn off A82 to east at roundabout just north of Fort William following camp sign. O.S.GR: NN124723. GPS: N56:48.271 W05:04.435

Charges guide

Per person	£ 1.60 - £ 2.50
child (5-15 yrs)	£ 0.80 - £ 1.30
pitch incl. awning	£ 4.40 - £ 12.00
serviced pitch plus	£ 2.00 - £ 3.00

Glen Nevis **Caravan and Camping Park**

AA Campsite of the Year for Scotland 2006

Glen Nevis, Fort William, PH33 6SX - 01397 702 191 - glen-nevis.co.uk

UK7800 Resipole Farm Caravan & Camping Park

Loch Sunart, Acharacle PH36 4HX (Highland)

Tel: **01967 431235**. Email: **info@resipole.co.uk**   **www.alanrogers.com/UK7800**

This quiet, open park is marvellously set on the banks of Loch Sunart, 8 miles from Strontian, on the Ardnamurchan peninsula. It is a must for anyone seeking peace and tranquillity and really worth the journey. With views across the water and regularly visited by wild deer, Resipole Farm offers a good base for exploring the whole of this scenic area or, more locally, for fishing, boating (launching from the site's own slipway) and walking in the unspoilt countryside. There are 48 level and well drained touring pitches here, 40 with electric hook-ups (10/16A). Tents are sited by the hedges.

Facilities

The central, modern sanitary block can be heated and is kept very clean. Good dishwashing facilities. Excellent provision for visitors with disabilities. Laundry facilities. Motorcaravan service point. Caravan storage. Art gallery and studios. Off site: Riding 5 miles.

Open: Easter or 1 April - 31 October.

Directions

From A82 Fort William road, take Corran ferry located 5 miles north of Ballachulish and 8 miles south of Fort William. Leaving ferry, turn south along the A861. Park is on the north bank of Loch Sunart, 8 miles west of Strontian. Single track road for 8 miles approaching Resipole – care is needed. O.S.GR: NM676740. GPS: N56:42.656 W05:43.213

Charges guide

Per unit incl. 2 persons	£ 11.00 - £ 13.00
incl. electricity (10A)	£ 13.00 - £ 15.00
extra person	£ 1.00 - £ 3.00

283

UK7850 Linnhe Lochside Holidays

Corpach, Fort William PH33 7NL (Highland)

Tel: **01397 772376**. Email: relax@linnhe-lochside-holidays.co.uk   www.alanrogers.com/UK7850

This quiet well run park has a very peaceful situation overlooking Loch Eil, and it is beautifully landscaped with wonderful views. There are individual pitches with hardstanding for 65 touring units (12 seasonal) on terraces leading down to the water's edge. They include 32 with electricity connection (16A), water and drainage, plus 30 with electricity only (10A). A separate area on the lochside takes 15 small tents (no reservation). There are also 60 caravan holiday homes and 14 centrally heated pine chalets for hire. Fishing is free on Loch Eil and you are welcome to fish from the park's private beach or bring your own boat and use the slipway and dinghy park.

Facilities

Toilet facilities are excellent, heated in the cooler months and include baths (£1). First class laundry and outdoor clothing drying room (charged per night). Self-service, licensed shop (end May - end Sept). Gas supplies. Barbecue area. Toddlers' play room and two play areas. Large motorhomes are accepted but it is best to book first. Caravan storage. Max. two dogs per pitch. Off site: Bicycle hire 2.5 miles. Riding and golf 5 miles.

Open: 20 March - 31 October.

Directions

Park entrance is off A830 Fort William - Mallaig road, 1 mile west of Corpach. O.S.GR: NN072772. GPS: N56:50.869 W05:09.615

Charges guide

Per person	£ 2.00
pitch	£ 7.50 - £ 14.50
dog (max. 2, not on tent pitches)	£ 1.00

UK7920 Laxdale Holiday Park

6 Laxdale Lane, Stornoway HS2 0DR (Isle of Lewis)

Tel: **01851 706966**. Email: info@laxdaleholidaypark.com   www.alanrogers.com/UK7920

Whilst not in the most scenic of locations, this good park is well placed for touring. Surrounded by trees, it is on the edge of Stornaway (ferry port) and is well laid out with a tarmac road running through the centre. A level hardstanding area for touring caravans has 14 electricity hook-ups plus 2 for tents and a grassy area for the tents gently slopes away to the trees and boundary. There are 5 holiday caravans and a self catering holiday bungalow available for rent on the site, plus a bunkhouse. The site is centrally situated in an ideal spot for touring the Isle of Lewis with easy access to all parts of the island.

Facilities

The well maintained and modern toilet block is heated and raised above the hardstanding area. Access is via steps or a gravel path to the ramp. Good (but narrow) showers with dividing curtain (50p). Well equipped laundry. Telephone. WiFi in reception. Off site: Bus stop 200 m. The fishing port of Stornoway with shops and restaurants. New sports centre with swimming pool.

Open: 1 April - 31 October.

Directions

From Stornoway take the A857 for 1 mile then take the second turning on the left past the hospital. O.S.GR: NB420348. GPS: N58:13.643 W06:23.552

Charges guide

Per person	£ 2.00 - £ 3.00
pitch	£ 5.00 - £ 8.00
electricity	£ 2.00
Credit cards accepted over £50.	

UK7950 Point of Ness Caravan & Camping Site

Well Park, Ness Road, Stromness KW16 3DN (Orkney)

Tel: **01856 873535**. Email: recreation@orkney.gov.uk   www.alanrogers.com/UK7950

This quiet site is in an idyllic position bounded by the sea one side (an entrance to the harbour). It is sheltered by the land from the open sea and has views to the mountains and the island of Hoy. There is a rocky beach close by and walks from the site. It is a level, firm grassy site, protected from the small drop to the sea by a low fence. Access to the steps to the sea is gained by a gate in the fence. Whilst being located at one end of Orkney, it is still easy to visit the Churchill Barriers and the Italian Chapel as well as the closer Maes Howe and Skara Brae sites.

Facilities

The well maintained traditional style toilet block has good-sized showers (20p) with curtains separating the changing area. Well equipped laundry. Telephone and tourist information. Lounge for campers is at one end of the block. Off site: Fishing, golf and bicycle hire all nearby.

Open: 28 April - 30 September.

Directions

Site is just west of Stromness. Campers can walk along the narrow high street to the site on the edge of the town. Caravans and motorcaravans are advised to take the road at the back of the town (about 2 miles) that is clearly marked. O.S.GR: HY256079. GPS: N58:57.266 W03:18.025

Charges guide

Per caravan pitch	£ 8.30
tent	£ 4.40 - £ 7.95
No credit cards.	

UK7980 Clickimin Caravan & Camp Site

Clickimin Leisure Complex, Lochside, Lerwick ZE1 0PJ (Shetlands)

Tel: **01595 741000**. Email: **clickimin.centre@srt.org.uk**   **www.alanrogers.com/UK7980**

The caravan and camping site is in the grounds of the Clickimin leisure complex, but it is not dominated by the building with its swimming pool and restaurant, etc. The site is arranged in two tiers which are well laid out with a tarmac road in the centre of each tier. The lower grass tier is separated into areas by shrubs and provides a camping area for 30 tents. The upper tier has 50 touring pitches, each with a large gravel area and divided from its neighbour by a wide impressed concrete section for sitting out. Electricity, water and waste disposal is provided at each pitch.

Facilities

The modern toilet block is clean and includes a toilet and shower cubicle for disabled visitors. Large, warm and well equipped laundry and drying room with an area for food preparation. Bar (evenings). Café and takeaway. Heated indoor and outdoor swimming pools. Off site: Shop and bicycle hire within 1 mile. Golf 3 miles. Riding 12 miles.

Open: May - September.

Directions

Site is on the west side of Lerwick and is signed as you start to leave Lerwick. Take the A969 north or south. Just before leaving the town is the road North Lochside (turn south) or South Lochside (turn north). Clickimin Leisure Centre is on this road. O.S.GR: HU464413. GPS: N60:09.209 W01:09.560

Charges guide

Per unit incl. electricity	£ 11.10
tent pitch	£ 5.30 - £ 9.90

UK7740 Loch Greshornish Camping Site

Arnisort, Edinbane IV51 9PS (Isle of Skye)

Tel: **01470 582230**. Email: **info@skyecamp.com**   **www.alanrogers.com/UK7740**

Mr and Mrs Palmer took over this simple, spacious site with simple facilities in 1999. In a beautiful, peaceful setting with views over the loch to the low hills to the northwest of Skye, it is suitable for long or short stays. There are 30 level grass pitches for motorcaravans and caravans, 28 with 10A electric hook-ups. There are also places for up to 100 tents (but numbers never reach that level). A new building houses reception and a small, licensed shop selling basic essentials. A launderette will be completed this year.

Facilities

The refurbished toilet facilities are light, airy and spotlessly clean. The showers are a little cramped. Dishwashing sink in the ladies' and another in the men's. Launderette. Camper's shelter with seating, cooking and eating area. Small shop. Bicycle hire (with safety helmets). Canoe hire. Off site: The local village has two hotels for drinks and meals; Portree, the nearest town, is 15 miles. Riding 2 miles. Golf 3 miles.

Open: Easter - 30 September.

Directions

Site is 15 miles west of Portree on the A850 Dunvegan road by Edinbane. O.S.GR: NG343524. GPS: N57:29.113 W06:26.097

Charges guide

Per person	£ 3.50
child (5-15 yrs)	£ 1.25 - £ 2.25
pitch	£ 1.50 - £ 2.00
electricity	£ 2.00
No credit cards.	

UK7750 Staffin Caravan & Camping Site

Staffin IV51 9JX (Isle of Skye)

Tel: **01470 562213**. Email: **staffincampsite@btinternet.com**   **www.alanrogers.com/UK7750**

This simple camping site is on the side of a hill just outside Staffin, where the broad sweep of the bay is dotted with working crofts running down to the sea. A marked walk from the site leads to the seashore and slipway (good for walking dogs but too far to be taking a boat). With 50 pitches, the site is quite sloping but there are 18 reasonably level pitches with improved hardstanding for caravans and motorcaravans, all with 16A electricity. Skye has many activities to offer and for the truly dedicated walker the Cuillins are the big attraction but the hills above Staffin look demanding!

Facilities

The sanitary block includes large, controllable showers. Dishwashing sinks are unfortunately not under cover and have only cold water. An older block is only opened at very busy times. Motorcaravan service point. Gas available. Off site: Fishing or boat launching 1 mile. Bicycle hire 5 miles. Riding 9 miles. Staffin village is 400 yards and has a large shop, a restaurant and a launderette (useful as the site has no laundry). The Columbia Centre in the village provides internet access.

Open: 1 April - 30 September.

Directions

Site is 15 miles north of Portree on A855 (2 miles of single track at the start), just before 40 mph signs on the right. O.S.GR: NG496668. GPS: N57:37.321 W06:11.760

Charges guide

Per caravan or motorcaravan incl. 2 persons	£ 11.50
tent incl. 2 persons	£ 10.50
extra person	£ 1.50
No credit cards.	

MAP 8

With a diversity of unspoilt landscapes, ranging from wild coastlines to green valleys, rugged mour and shimmering lakes, the natural phenomenon the Giant's Causeway, Norther Ireland, though small, is cramm full of sights offering somethin for everyone.

NORTHERN IRELAND COMPRISES THE FOLLOWING COUNTIES: ANTRIM, ARMAGH, DOWN, FERMANAGH, LONDONDERRY AND TYRONE

The rugged coastline of the Causeway Coast and the nine Glens of Antrim, in the north, is an area of outstanding natural beauty, with white sandy shores and little bays, tranquil forests and romantic ruins and castles, full of tales of the ancient Irish Giants and other myths and legends. At over 60 million years old, with a mass of 4,000 tightly packed basalt columns, each a polygon shape, the Giant's Causeway is a popular attraction. One of the most beautiful regions is in the west around Londonderry, a delightful walled city set on a hill on the banks of the Foyle estuary. Further south is the beautiful region of Fermanagh, with glistening lakes and little islands all surrounded by lush green fields, hillsides and forests. The large lake of Lough Erne is to be found here: made up of two channels, the lower and upper Loughs, the meeting point of these channels is Enniskillen, a town steeped in history, boasting numerous preserved buildings including a castle. Across to the eastern shores lies the ancient Kingdom of Down, with its endless miles of spectacular coastline, little fishing villages, country parks and the Mountains of Mourne. And ringed by hills, sea lough and river valley is Belfast, a bustling city full of theatres, concert halls, art galleries and restaurants.

Places of interest

Antrim: Antrim Lough Shore Park; Rathl Island; Giant's Causeway; Dunluce Castl near Portrush.

Belfast & environs: Belfast zoo and castl Irish Linen Centre in Lisburn; Carrickferg Castle.

Armagh: Gosford Forest Park near Markethill; Lough Neagh Discovery Cent on Oxford Island.

Down: County Museum and Downpatri Cathedral; Mourne Mountains; Castlew forest park; Ballycopeland Windmill nea Millisle.

Fermanagh: Enniskillen Castle and Castl Coole; village of Belleek; Marble Arch C near Lough Macnean; Devenish Island c Lough Erne.

Londonderry: St Columb's Cathedral, Harbour Museum, Foyle Valley Railway Centre in Derry.

Tyrone: Omagh; Beaghmore stone circle near Cookstown; Dungannon; Sperrin Mountains.

Did you know?

Northern Ireland measures 85 miles fro north to south and is about 110 miles v

The world's most famous ship the Titan was built in Belfast.

Legend has it that the rugged Giant's Causeway was built by Finn McCool, th legendary Irish Giant, when he travelled Scotland to bring back his sweetheart.

At 2,240 yards an Irish Mile is 480 yard longer than a standard English mile.

Mountsandel near Coleraine is where Ireland's first known house was built 9,000 years ago.

UK8340 Drumaheglis Caravan Park

36 Glenstall Road, Ballymoney BT53 7QN (Co. Antrim)
Tel: **028 2766 0280**. Email: **info@ballymoney.gov.uk**   **www.alanrogers.com/UK8340**

A caravan park which continually maintains high standards, Drumaheglis is popular throughout the season. Situated on the banks of the lower River Bann, approximately 4 miles from the town of Ballymoney, it appeals to watersports enthusiasts or makes an ideal base for exploring this scenic corner of Northern Ireland. This attractive site is well laid out with trees, shrubs, flower beds and tarmac roads. There are 35 serviced pitches for touring units with hardstanding, electricity (5/16A) and water points. The marina offers superb facilities for boat launching, waterskiing, cruising, canoeing or fishing. Getting out and about can take you to the Giant's Causeway, seaside resorts such as Portrush or Portstewart, the sands of Whitepark Bay, the Glens of Antrim or the picturesque villages of the Antrim coast road. Ballymoney is a popular shopping town and the Joey Dunlop Leisure Centre provides a high-tech fitness studio, sports hall, etc. There is much to see and do within this Borough and of interest is the Ballymoney museum in Townhead Street.

Facilities

Modern toilet blocks were very clean when we visited. Individual wash cubicles. Facilities for disabled visitors. Baby room and four family shower rooms. Washing machine and dryer. Play area. Barbecue and picnic areas. Barrier with key system. Off site: Marina. Bus service from park entrance. Bicycle hire and golf 4 miles. Riding 6 miles. Beach 10 miles.

Open: 19 March - end October.

Directions

From A26/B62 Portrush - Ballymoney roundabout continue for about 2 miles on the A26 towards Coleraine. Site is clearly signed – follow International camping signs. GPS: N55:04.327 W06:35.449

Charges 2009

Per unit incl. electricity	£ 18.00
tent pitch	£ 13.50

UK8330 Six Mile Water Caravan & Camping Park

Lough Road, Antrim BT41 4DG (Co. Antrim)

Tel: 028 9446 4963. Email: sixmilewater@antrim.gov.uk   www.alanrogers.com/UK8330

Six Mile Water is located at the Lough Shore Park and is adjacent to the Antrim Forum leisure complex, a major amenity area that includes swimming pools, a bowling green, an adventure playground for children, fitness and health gyms and sports fields. Managed by Antrim Borough Council, the park is easily accessible when travelling to and from the ports of Belfast and Larne making it perfect for stop overs. There are 20 pitches with electricity, arranged in a herringbone layout of hardstandings with grass for awnings, and 24 pitches for tents to one side, plus picnic and barbecue areas. Advance booking is advisable. Six Mile Water is central for sightseeing in the area including the Antrim Castle Gardens and Clotworthy Arts Centre or for shopping in Antrim town. The Lough Shore Park offers visitors boating and water activities and boat launching on the beautiful Lough Neagh, as well as walking and cycling the Lough Shore Trail which takes in 25 places of interest along its 128 mile cycle route. The nearby golf club also offers a 20 bay driving range.

Facilities

The small, modern toilet block provides bright facilities including toilets, washbasins and showers. Facilities for disabled campers. Baby changing unit. Laundry room. TV lounge and games room. Fishing and boat launching. Off site: The facilities of Lough Shore Park including a café open all year round. Antrim Forum leisure centre. Bus service 1 mile. Shops, pubs and restaurants within 1.5 miles. Golf 1.5 miles. Riding 6 miles.

Open: 27 February - 2 November.

Directions

Site is 1 mile south of the city centre. Follow signs for Antrim Forum and Lough Shore Park. On the Dublin road, turn off into Lough Road. Pass Antrim Forum and park is at the end of the road.
GPS: N54:42.920 W06:14.025

Charges guide

Per unit incl. electricity	£ 16.00
tent pitch	£ 10.00 - £ 16.00

UK8320 Curran Court Caravan Park

131 Curran Road, Larne BT40 1XB (Co. Antrim)

Tel: 028 2827 3797. Email: curran.court-hotel@virgin.net   www.alanrogers.com/UK8320

Formerly run by the local borough council, this park is now managed by the Curran Court Hotel (opposite the park). Attractive garden areas add to the charm of this small, neat site which is very conveniently situated for the ferry terminal and only a few minutes walk from the sea. The 29 pitches, all with hardstanding and electricity connections (14A), give reasonable space off the tarmac road and there is a separate tent area of 1.5 acres. Larne market is on Wednesdays. You may consider using this site as a short term base for discovering the area as well as an ideal overnight stop. The warden can usually find room for touring units so reservations are not normally necessary.

Facilities

The toilet block is clean and adequate without being luxurious. Laundry room with dishwashing facilities. Play area with good equipment and safety surfaces. Bowls and putting on site. Late arrivals can call at the hotel. Off site: Train station and bus stop within a few minutes walk. Bicycle hire 0.5 miles. Golf 2 miles. Boat launching 500 yds. Many other amenities are very close including a shop (100 yards), the hotel for food and drink, tennis and a leisure centre with swimming pool (300 yards).

Open: Easter - 30 September.

Directions

Immediately after leaving the ferry terminal, turn right and follow camping signs. Site is 400 yards on the left. GPS: N54:50.997 W05:48.491

Charges guide

Per caravan, motorcaravan or large tent	£ 11.00
tent	£ 5.00 - £ 10.00
electricity	£ 1.00

UK8360 Ballyness Caravan Park

40 Castlecatt Road, Bushmills BT57 8TN (Co. Antrim)
Tel: **028 2073 2393**. Email: **info@ballynesscaravanpark.com**   **www.alanrogers.com/UK8360**

Ballyness is immaculately cared for and is designed with conservation in mind. In keeping with the surrounding countryside, it is extensively planted with native trees and shrubs which attract local wildlife and birds and there are ponds with ducks and swans. The overall appearance of this site, with its entrance gate, white stone pillars and broad tarmac drive is attractive. The drive leads to 46 hardstanding pitches with electricity hook-ups, water and drainage. There is a dedicated area for tents and several caravan holiday homes, but these are placed away from the touring pitches. From the site you can enjoy a relaxing walk by way of the meadow ponds and winding pathway alongside the stream known as St Columb's Rill. The village of Bushmills, with its famous Whiskey Distillery, is within walking distance and the Causeway Coast a short drive.

Facilities

One spotlessly clean and well decorated, cottage style heated sanitary block (key coded). Facilities for disabled visitors (toilet and shower). New family room with bath. Laundry room. Play area. Play field. Nature trail. Off site: Bus service 0.5 miles. Bicycle hire 0.5 miles. Beach and fishing 1 mile. Golf and boat launching 1.5 miles. Riding 5 miles.

Open: 17 March - 31 October.

Directions

From M2 follow A26. At Ballymoney turn right on the B66 towards Dervock and turn left. Stay on the B66 and site is 5.5 miles on right.
GPS: N55:12.073 W06:31.258

Charges guide

Per unit incl. 2 persons, electricity, water and drainage	£ 17.00
extra person (over 5 yrs)	£ 1.00
awning or pup tent	£ 2.00

UK8310 Carnfunnock Country Park Caravan Park & Campsite

Coast Road, Drain's Bay, Larne BT40 2QG (Co. Antrim)
Tel: **028 2827 0541**. Email: **carnfunnock@larne-gov.uk**   **www.alanrogers.com/UK8310**

In a magnificent parkland setting overlooking the sea, what makes this touring site popular is its scenic surroundings and convenient location. It is 3.5 miles north of the market town of Larne on the famed Antrim Coast Road and offers 28 level 'super' pitches, all with hardstanding, water, electricity (15A), drainage, individual pitch lighting and ample space for an awning. The site has a neat appearance with a tarmac road following through to the rear where a number of pitches are placed in a circular position with allocated space for tents. Run by the Borough Council and supervised by a manager, the surrounding Country Park is immaculately kept. The Visitor Centre includes a gift shop and information about local attractions and the restaurant/coffee shop is pleasant and looks towards the sea. Spending time around the parkland, you find a walled time garden with historic sundials, a maze, forest walk, children's adventure playground, putting green, 9-hole golf course, wildlife garden and miniature railway. There is also a summer events programme.

Facilities

A small building beside the entrance gates houses toilet facilities (entry by key) which are kept clean, but are now starting to show signs of wear. There are shower units, facilities for disabled people and dishwashing. Motorcaravan service point. Off site: Larne with bus services 3.5 miles. Fishing and boat launching 400 yds.

Open: Easter - 31 October.

Directions

From ferry terminal in Larne, follow signs for Coast Road and Carnfunnock Country Park; well signed 3.5 miles on A2 coast road.
GPS: N54:52.998 W05:05.000

Charges guide

Per caravan or motorcaravan	£ 12.50 - £ 14.00
serviced hardstanding	£ 14.00 - £ 16.00
tent (2 persons)	£ 8.00 - £ 9.00
tent (3 or more persons)	£ 12.50 - £ 14.00

289

UK8350 Bush Caravan Park

97 Priestland Road, Bushmills BT57 8UJ (Co. Antrim)

Tel: **028 2073 1678**   www.alanrogers.com/UK8350

An ideal base for touring the North Antrim Coast, this family run, recently extended park is only minutes away from two renowned attractions, the Giant's Causeway and the Old Bushmills Distillery. This fact alone makes Bush popular, but its fast growing reputation for friendliness and top class facilities makes it equally appealing. Located just off the main Ballymoney - Portrush Road (B62), it is approached by a short drive. The site is partly surrounded by mature trees and hedging, but views across the countryside can still be appreciated. Tarmac roads lead to 47 well laid out and spacious pitches with hardstanding and 16A electricity or to a grass area for tents. Unique features on site are murals depicting the famed scenery, sights and legends of the Causeway Coast. The enthusiastic owners organise tours to the Distillery and coastal trips – a musical evening cannot be ruled out.

Facilities

The toilet block (opened by key-pad) is modern, clean and equipped to a high standard. Facilities include controllable showers with excellent provision for people with disabilities (can also be used by families). Washing machine and dryer. Central play area. Recreation room for all ages. Off site: Riding 2 miles. Golf and fishing 3 miles. Bicycle hire and boat launching 4 miles. Beach 3 miles.

Open: Easter - 31 October.

Directions

From the A26 turn onto the B62 road for 7 miles. Turn onto the B17 Priestlands Road and the site is immediately on the left.
GPS: N55:10.262 W06:34.268

Charges guide

Per unit incl. all persons	
and electricity	£ 12.50
tent	£ 5.00 - £ 10.00
awning	£ 1.50

UK8405 Cranfield Caravan Park

123 Cranfield Road, Cranfield West, Kilkeel BT34 4LJ (Co. Down)

Tel: **028 417 62572**. Email: **jimchestnut@btconnect.com**   www.alanrogers.com/UK8405

On the shores of Carlingford Lough with direct access to a blue flag beach, this friendly family run park immediately impresses with its well cared for flower beds, neat hedging, cordyline trees and the elegant building which incorporates the family home and reception. Situated at Northern Ireland's most southerly point, the surrounding scenery of the Mourne Mountains, the Lough and distant vistas is stunning. A focal point is the Haulbowline lighthouse, built in the 1800s, which sits in the middle of the sea. Despite the many privately owned caravan holiday homes on site, touring pitches are kept separate and situated towards the park entrance. Each pitch has a sea view, has hardstanding and all have tower units providing an electricity hook up (16A), water, waste water point and TV outlet; 19 have a main sewerage connection.

Facilities

A modern, heated toilet block (entrance by key) is well maintained with tiled walls/floors, pre-set showers (50p token) and open style washbasins. Excellent suite for disabled visitors doubles as a family room, also a night WC (by key). Dishwashing sinks and well equipped laundry in a separate building. Play area (outside park). Sea fishing, boat launching and beach (with lifeguard). Off site: Kilkeel town (3.5 miles). Golf, hill walking in the Mournes, Anglo Norman castle.

Open: 17 March - 31 October.

Directions

Travelling southeast on A2 Newry - Kilkeel Road turn right about 5.5 miles after passing through Rostrevor onto local road, signed Cranfield and Greencastle. Site signed at end of road.
GPS: N54:01.796 W06:04.098

Charges guide

Per unit incl. all persons and electricity	£ 15.00

UK8420 Tollymore Forest Caravan Park

178 Tullybrannigan Road, Newcastle BT33 6PW (Co. Down)

Tel: **028 4372 2428**   www.alanrogers.com/UK8420

This popular park, for touring units only, is located within the parkland of Tollymore Forest. It is situated away from the public footpaths and is noted for its scenic surroundings. The forest park, which is approached by way of an ornate gateway and majestic avenue of Himalayan cedars, covers an area of almost 500 hectares. It is backed by the Mourne mountains and situated two miles from the beaches and resort of Newcastle. The site is attractively laid out with hardstanding pitches, 72 of which have electricity (6A). The Head Ranger at Tollymore is helpful and ensures that the caravan site is efficiently run and quiet, even when full. Exploring the forest park is part of the pleasure of staying here, and of note are the stone follies, bridges and entrance gates. The Shimna and Spinkwee rivers flow through the park adding a refreshing touch and tree lovers appreciate the arboretum with its many rare species.

Facilities

Toilet blocks, timbered in keeping with the setting, are clean and modern with wash cubicles and facilities for disabled people. Dishwashing and laundry area. Off site: Confectionery shop and tea room nearby. Small grocery shop a few yards from the exit gate of the park with gas available.

Open: All year.

Directions

Approach Newcastle on the A24. Before entering the town, at roundabout, turn right on to A50 signed Castlewellan and follow signs for Tollymore Forest Park. GPS: N54:13.578 W05:56.069

Charges guide

Per unit incl. all persons	£ 9.00 - £ 13.00
electricity	£ 1.50

Low season mid-week special rates.

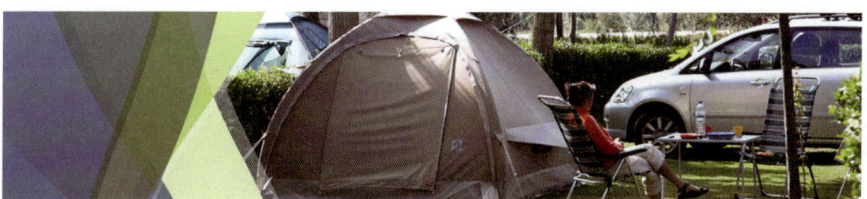

UK8460 Delamont Country Park Camping & Caravanning Club Site

Delamont Country Park, Downpatrick Road, Killyleagh BT30 9TZ (Co. Down)

Tel: **028 4482 1833**   www.alanrogers.com/UK8460

This is Northern Ireland's first Camping & Caravanning Club site and although not long in existence, it is proving to be one of the country's most popular sites. Within the boundaries of Delamont Country Park, it is an idyllic location for those seeking an away from it all feel, yet wanting to be within easy reach of major attractions. The country park is a designated area of outstanding natural beauty and commands from its highest point, breathtaking vistas of Strangford Lough and surrounding countryside. Facilities on the campsite itself are excellent and it has an orderly, neat and tidy appearance. Reception stands to the fore of the site and the sanitary block towards the rear. The 64 all weather pitches on level terrain all have electricity, plus water and waste hook-ups. Although the site is surrounded by trees and the rich vegetation of the country park, the young shrubs and trees around the pitches will take time to mature.

Facilities

The single modern toilet block, with heating, has wash cubicles and a baby bath. En-suite facilities for disabled visitors. Laundry sinks, washing machine and dryer; dishwashing inside. Small shop area selling basics. Adventure playground and miniature railway in country park. Free admittance to country park for campers. Off site: Tyrella beach 7 miles. Fishing and riding 1 mile. Golf 4 miles.

Open: March - October.

Directions

From Belfast follow A22 southeast to village of Killyleagh. Pass through village and site entrance is on left after 1 mile. GPS: N54:23.194 W05:40.594

Charges guide

Per person	£ 4.90 - £ 7.25
child	£ 2.15 - £ 2.25
non-member pitch fee	£ 5.65

UK8510 Mullynascarthy Caravan Park

Lisnaskea BT92 0NZ (Co. Fermanagh)

Tel: **028 6772 1040**

www.alanrogers.com/UK8510

This is a well kept touring site situated on the banks of the Colebrooke River. It has instant appeal, for the setting at Mullynascarthy is more like a mature garden. The pitches to the right of reception, which are grass on hardstanding, are mostly angled between the many tree varieties, also separated by low hedging and flowering shrubs. To the left of the facility block additional pitches are spread over meadow-like terrain and all have electric hook-ups. Sanitary facilities, although not ultra modern, are kept very clean and housed alongside reception, which doubles up as a sub-post office. The attention and care this site obviously receives is due to the warden who also extends a friendly warm welcome to her guests. Lisnaskea makes an ideal base for exploring this lakeland county which abounds in historic treasures, stately homes, and is excellent for watersports enthusiasts. The county town of Enniskillen is within a short drive and the Marble Arch caves are an experience not to be missed.

Facilities

The toilet block (key operated) has showers, open style washbasins, facilities for people with disabilities (washbasin/WC), laundry room and dishwashing sinks. Games and sports area. Play area. River fishing (licences and permits available). Off site: Bus service 1.5 miles. Golf and bicycle hire 10 miles.

Open: 17 March - 31 October.

Directions

From Enniskillen take the A4 towards Dungannon for 8 miles, then turn right on A34 signed Lisnaskea. Continue on A34 for 2.5 miles and turn right onto B514 where site is signed Mullynascarthy. GPS: N54:16.105 W07:29.006

Charges guide

Per unit incl. 2 persons and electricity	£ 15.00
tent	£ 8.00 - £ 14.00

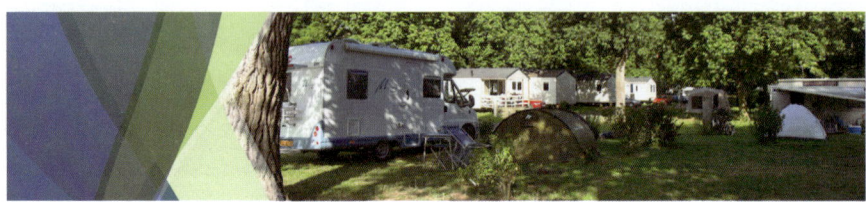

UK8550 Dungannon Park

Moy Road, Dungannon BT71 6DY (Co. Tyrone)

Tel: **028 8772 8690**. Email: dpreception@dungannon.gov.uk

www.alanrogers.com/UK8550

This small touring park nestles in the midst of a 70 acre park with a multitude of tree varieties, brightly coloured flower beds and a 12 acre fishing lake. The 12 pitches, which are discreetly sited, some with lake views, are on hardstanding with water, waste and 16A electricity connections. There is also an unmarked grass area for tents. Run by Dungannon Council the park, which also incorporates tennis courts, football and cricket pitches, lies about one mile south of Dungannon town. Walkers can enjoy three miles of parkland walks which command from the high ground, views of the surrounding countryside and Lough Neagh. A modern Visitor Amenity Centre houses the reception, sanitary facilities, a TV area and vending machines.

Facilities

Sanitary facilities which include showers (by token), washbasins, baby changing mat and spacious unit for disabled visitors are to the rear of the Amenity Centre. Laundry room with washing machine and dryer, dishwashing area and chemical disposal unit. Night watchman (until 06.00). Excellent play area. Tennis, fishing and walking, orienteering. Off site: Bus stop and shop at main entrance to park. Restaurants, shops, leisure facilities in Dungannon. Tyrone Crystal (guided tours), walking and cycling in Clogher Valley, local markets.

Open: 1 March - 31 October.

Directions

Leave M1 motorway at junction 15 to join the A29 towards Dungannon. Turn left at second traffic lights signed Dungannon Park. GPS: N54:23.413 W06:45.478

Charges guide

Per pitch with electricity	£ 12.00
tent	£ 8.00

UK8590 Tullans Farm Holiday Park

46 Newmills Road, Coleraine BT52 2JB (Co. Londonderry)

Tel: **028 7034 2309**. Email: **tullansfarm@hotmail.com**   **www.alanrogers.com/UK8590**

A high quality, well run family park convenient for the Causeway coast, Tullans Farm is one of the most popular in the area. It has a quiet, heart of the country feel, yet the University town of Coleraine is within a mile, the seaside resort Portrush and Portstewart five miles and a shopping centre a five minute drive. Tullans Farm has earned a reputation for its spotlessly clean toilet block, attractive flower displays and its well cared for appearance. Around the park roads are gravel and the 32 pitches are on hardstanding; all with electric hook-ups (10A), water and drainage. In season the owners organise barbecues, barn dances and line dancing (raising funds for charity). In a central position, fronted by a parking space, stands a long white building housing the sanitary facilities and reception.

Facilities

The toilet and shower rooms, including a family shower unit, are spacious, modern and include facilities for people with disabilities. Laundry and washing up room with sinks, washing machine, dryers and a large fridge. Play areas. TV lounge. Games room. Barn used for indoor recreation. Caravan storage. Off site: Public transport in Coleraine 1 mile. Fishing and riding 1.5 miles. Golf and bicycle hire 5 miles. Beach 5 miles.

Open: March - 30 September.

Directions

From the Lodge Road roundabout (south end of Coleraine) turn east onto A29 Portrush ring road and proceed for 0.5 miles. Turn right at sign for park and Windy Hall. Park is clearly signed on left. GPS: N55:07.534 W06:38.354

Charges guide

Per unit incl. all persons, electricity and awning	£ 17.00
tent pitch	£ 8.00 - £ 12.00

No credit cards.

UK8600 Bellemont Caravan Park

10 Islandtasserty Road, Coleraine BT52 2PN (Co. Londonderry)

Tel: **028 7082 3872**   **www.alanrogers.com/UK8600**

Close to Coleraine and Portstewart, this well kept park makes an immediately favourable impression with its white concrete roads, its perfect grass areas and well laid out appearance. The gently sloping ground rises at the far right of the park to give views over Portstewart and towards the sea. To the left of the entrance and security gate are five privately owned caravan holiday homes. There are 30 touring pitches, all with hardstanding, electric hook-up and water. These are spacious and well distributed around this open, parkland style setting. In a central position stands a gleaming white building, with flower tubs decorating the forecourt, which houses reception and heated sanitary facilities. Bellemont makes a good base for visiting the university town of Coleraine, the resorts and beaches of Portstewart and Portrush, or famous sights such as Dunluce Castle, Carrick-a-Rede rope bridge and the Giant's Causeway.

Facilities

Toilet facilities with good sized showers (token operated). En-suite unit for disabled visitors. Laundry room with two washing machines, two dryers and iron (token operated), plus dishwashing sink and drainer to the outside. Play area with swings and slide on a bark surface. Dogs are not accepted. Off site: Bus service 0.5 miles. Fishing, bicycle hire, riding and golf 2 miles. Beach 2.5 miles.

Open: Easter - 30 September.

Directions

From Lodge Road roundabout on eastern outskirts of Coleraine follow A29 north to fourth roundabout. Continue towards Portrush and site is clearly signed on left after 400 yards. GPS: N55:10.318 W06:40.528

Charges guide

Per unit incl. all persons and electricity	£ 15.00
awning	£ 1.50

No credit cards.

MAP 8

Famed for its folklore, traditional music, and friendly, hospitable people, the Republic of Ireland offers spectacular scenery contained within a relatively compact area. With plenty of beautiful areas to discover, and a decidedly relaxed pace of life, it is an ideal place to unwind.

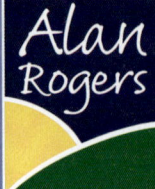

Alan Rogers

IRELAND IS MADE UP OF FOUR PROVINCES: CONNAUGHT, LEINSTER, MUNSTER AND ULSTER, COMPRISING 32 COUNTIES, 26 OF WHICH FALL IN THE REPUBLIC OF IRELAND

Ireland is the perfect place to indulge in a variety of outdoor pursuits while taking in the glorious scenery. There are plenty of way-marked footpaths, which lead through woodlands, across cliffs, past historical monuments and over rolling hills. The dramatic coastline, with its headlands, secluded coves and sandy beaches, is fantastic for watersports: from sailing to windsurfing, scuba diving and swimming; or for just simply relaxing and watching the variety of seabirds that nest on the shores. The Cliffs of Moher, in particular, is a prime location for birdwatching and Goat Island, just offshore, is where puffins make their nesting burrows. Fishing is another popular activity; the country is full of pretty streams, rivers, hidden lakes and canals, which can all be explored by hiring a boat. In the south the beautiful Ring of Kerry is one of the most visited regions. This 110-mile route encircles the Inveragh Peninsula, and is surrounded by mountains and lakes. Other sights include: the Aran Islands, home to some of the most ancient Christian and pre-Christian remains in Ireland, and the Rock of Cashel, with its spectacular group of medieval buildings; not to mention the bustling cities of Dublin, Galway and Cork.

Places of interest

Connaught: Boyle Abbey; Connemara National Park; Céide Fields at Ballycastle; Kylemore Abbey; Aran Islands; Galway city; Westport; Sligo Abbey; megalithic tombs at Carrowmore.

Leinster: Wicklow Mountains National Park; Rock of Cashel; Killkenny Castle; Guinness brewery, Trinity College and National Museum in Dublin; Dunmore Cave at Ballyfoyle; Wexford Wildfowl Reserve.

Munster: harbour towns of Kinsale and Clonakilty; Blarney Castle in Cork; historic city of Limerick with 13th century castle fortress and old town; Ring of Kerry; Bunratty Castle; Cliffs of Moher; Killarney National Park.

Ulster: Glenveagh National Park; Slieve League, the highest sea cliffs in Europe; Donegal Castle; Newmills Corn and Flax Mills in Letterkenny.

Did you know?

The official currency of the Republic of Ireland is the Euro.

The international dialling code for the Republic of Ireland is 00 353 (then drop the first '0' of the number).

The Blarney Stone, reputedly cast with a spell by a witch to reward a king who saved her from drowning, is said to bestow the gift of eloquence on all those who kiss it.

The harp is a symbol of the Irish people's love of music: since mediaeval times it has been the official emblem for Ireland.

Hurling is the oldest native sport.

On display in Trinity College, the Book of Kells is one of the oldest books in the world written around the year 800 AD.

RED TEXT DENOTES ALL YEAR ROUND SITE

Miles
0   20   40   60
0   32 9   64   6
Kms

8600
8360
COLERAINE
8350
8590
8340
LONDONDERRY
A2
STRABANE   A6
BALLYMENA   A36

NORTHERN
IRELAND
8330
ANTRIM

DONEGAL
OMAGH   COOKSTOWN
A32
8550
ENNISKILLEN   ARMAGH
8510

8690
8695
SLIGO   N16

NEWRY

8750
N17
8825
CAVAN   DUNDALK   8405
8730
N5
8810   8815
8770   8790   8780
N17
8740

ATHLONE   8960   8965
GALWAY   N6

IRELAND

9100   DUBLIN
NAAS
9140
9460   N18
9130
PORTLAOISE   9160
9420   9080
WICKLOW
N7
9150
N8
LIMERICK   N9
N24   KILKENNY   N11
9240
TIPPERARY   9230
9400
TRALEE   9370
9550   9650   9410
N20   CLONMEL   WEXFORD
KILLARNEY   N8
9600   9590   9620   9470   ROSSLARE
9640   9630   9170
9610
N22   9330   9340
9480
9560   9580   CORK   N25
9570
9510

9505   9500

IR8690 Greenlands Caravan & Camping Park

Rosses Point (Co. Sligo)

Tel: **071 917 7113**. Email: **noelineha@eircom.net**   **www.alanrogers.com/IR8690**

Just off the N15 road and 8 km. from Sligo town, this is a well run park at Rosses Point, in the sand hills adjoining a championship golf course. It is thoughtfully laid out with small tents placed to the front of reception and the hardstanding touring pitches separated from the trailer tent pitches which occupy the rear. The ground is undulating and adds interest to the overall appearance. Your view depends on where you are pitched – look towards Coney Island and the Blackrock lighthouse which guards the bay, take in the sight of Benbulben Mountain or appreciate the seascape and the water lapping the resort's two bathing beaches. Electricity hook-ups (10A) are available for touring units. This is an excellent base from which to explore the 'Yeats Country' and discover the beauty spots immortalised in his poems, such places as Lissadell, Dooney Rock, the Isle of Innisfree and the poet's burial place at Drumcliffe.

Facilities

Modern toilet facilities, recently extended and refitted, are kept exceptionally clean, with hot showers (€ 1 token). Washing machine, dryer and iron. Motorcaravan service point. Campers' kitchen. Information point and TV room beside reception. Play area and sand pit for children. Outdoor chess and draughts sets. Night security. Off site: Shop, restaurant and evening entertainment in the village. Fishing and boat launching 100 m. Golf 50 m. Bicycle hire 8 km. Riding 14 km.

Open: 30 April - 14 September.

Directions

From Sligo city travel about 800 m. north on N15 road, turn left onto R291 signed Rosses Point. Continue for 6.5 km. and park is on right after village. GPS: N54:18.424 W08:34.161

Charges guide

Per unit incl. 2 persons	€ 19.00 - € 21.00
extra person	€ 5.00
child	€ 3.00
electricity (10A)	€ 4.00
hiker/cyclist incl. small tent	€ 11.00 - € 16.00
Weekly rates available.	

IR8695 Strandhill Caravan & Camping Park

Strandhill (Co. Sligo)

Tel: **071 916 8111**. Email: **sxi@iol.ie**   **www.alanrogers.com/IR8695**

This seaside park is located on 20 acres of undulating grass with a sandy base with natural protection from the onshore breezes of the famous Strandhill beach. There are 55 hardstanding pitches for caravans and motorcaravans, with electricity and ample water points, and two camping areas for tents, one with views of the sea and the second more sheltered. Throughout the site many hollows provide ideal pitches for tents. Strandhill, world recognised as a surfing Mecca, also provides activities for all the family. There are miles of sandy beach and dunes and the Knocknarea Mountain provides walkers with choice. The Megalithic Tombs at Carrowmore, older than the Pyramids at Giza, are 5 km. away and the flat beach at Culleenmore is 2 km. Strandhill provides an excellent touring base for the Benbulban, Yeat's Country and Lough Gill's 'Isle of Inisfree' combining nature, heritage, and fable. There are two flights daily into nearby Sligo airport.

Facilities

The toilet block (keys provided on deposit) is clean and fresh with hot showers (token € 1), electric hand dryers and hairdryer. Laundry including ironing facilities. TV and games room. Book swapping. Security on site all season. Off site: Public transport from village. Shops, restaurants, takeaway, pubs and ATM are just beyond the park's boundary in the village. Strandhill golf course 500 m. Riding 2 km. Swimming pool and sports centre in Sligo 8 km.

Open: Easter - 30 September.

Directions

Strandhill is 8 km. west of Sligo city on the R292. Site is on the airport road. GPS: N54:16.345 W08:36.269

Charges guide

Per unit incl. 2 persons	€ 19.00
plus 2 children	€ 21.00
electricity (10A)	€ 4.00
extra person	€ 3.00 - € 5.00

IR8730 Keel Sandybanks Caravan & Camping Park

Keel, Achill Island (Co. Mayo)

Tel: **098 432 11**. Email: **info@achillcamping.com**   www.alanrogers.com/IR8730

This is a park offering a taste of island life and the opportunity to relax in dramatic, scenic surroundings. Achill, Ireland's largest island, is 24 km. long and 19 km. wide and is connected to the mainland by a bridge. The site is situated beside Keel village and approached by the R319 from the swivel bridge at Achill Sound. Although there are static holiday mobile homes on this site, the 42 pitches for caravans and 42 for tents are kept separate. Some with hardstanding are located at the perimeter fence overlooking the beach. Although sand based, the ground is firm and level. Roads are tarmac and there is direct access to the beach which is supervised by lifeguards. Occasionally a traditional music evening is organised on the site. Whilst a treat in store is the natural beauty of Achill, worth seeing are Kildownet Castle, the Slievemore deserted village and the Seal Caves.

Facilities

Two modern toilet blocks serve the site, one at the entrance gate beside reception and the other in a central position. Heated facilities include WCs (one for disabled visitors), washbasins and hot showers (on payment). Hair and hand dryers. Play area. TV room. Watersports enthusiasts can enjoy surfing, canoeing and board sailing on Keel Strand and Lough. Fishing trips can be arranged. Off site: Bicycle hire and golf 200 m. Riding 6 km. In the village there is a food shop, takeaway, restaurants and music at night in the pubs.

Open: 27 May - 4 September.

Directions

From Achill Sound follow the R319 for 16 km. Site is on the left before Keel village. GPS: N53:58.521 W10:04.674

Charges guide

Per pitch	€ 16.00 - € 18.00
electricity (6A)	€ 3.00
cyclist/hiker incl tent	€ 10.00 - € 12.00

IR8740 Cong Caravan & Camping Park

Lisloughrey, Quay Road, Cong (Co. Mayo)

Tel: **094 954 6089**. Email: **info@quietman-cong.com**   www.alanrogers.com/IR8740

It would be difficult to find a more idyllic and famous spot for a caravan park than Cong. Situated close to the shores of Lough Corrib, Cong's scenic beauty was immortalised in the film 'The Quiet Man'. This well kept park is 1.6 km. from the village of Cong, near the grounds of the magnificent and renowned Ashford Castle. The owner's house that incorporates reception, shop and the hostel, stands to the fore of the site. Toilet facilities and the holiday hostel accommodation are entered from the courtyard area. The 40 grass pitches, 36 with electricity, are placed at a higher level to the rear, with the sheltered tent areas below and to the side. The park can be crowded and busy in high season. When not spending time around the village of Cong with its picturesque river setting and Monastic relics, there is much to keep the active camper happy. Watersports, cycling, walking, climbing, caving and scenic drives can all be pursued. Not least of the on-site attractions at this park is a mini cinema showing 'The Quiet Man' film nightly all season and associated museum guided tours can be arranged.

Facilities

Toilet facilities are tastefully decorated, kept clean and are heated when necessary. Hot showers with curtains (€ 1 charge). Campers' kitchen. Launderette service. Shop. Catering is a feature – full Irish or continental breakfast, dinner or packed lunch may be ordered, or home baked bread and scones purchased in the shop. Barbecue, games room and extensive play area. TV lounge. Bicycle hire. Off site: Riding and golf within 2 km. Fishing and boat slipway 500 m.

Open: All year.

Directions

Leave N84 road at Ballinrobe to join the R334/345 signed Cong. Turn left at end of the R345 (opposite entrance to Ashford Castle), slow down take next road on right (about 300 m) and the park is on right (200 m). GPS: N53:32.357 W09:16.253

Charges guide

Per unit incl. 2 persons	€ 21.00
exttra person	€ 3.00
child	€ 2.50
electricity	€ 5.00

IR8750 Belleek Caravan & Camping Park

Belleek, Ballina (Co. Mayo)

Tel: **096 715 33**. Email: **lenahan@belleekpark.com**

www.alanrogers.com/IR8750

Belleek has a quiet woodland setting, only minutes from Ballina, a famed salmon fishing centre. With excellent pitches and toilet block, the family owners are committed to ensuring that it is immaculate at all times. From the entrance gate, the park is approached by a drive that passes reception and leads to 58 well spaced pitches. With a very neat overall appearance, 32 pitches have hardstanding, 45 have electricity hook-ups, and you may choose your pitch. Sports facilities within a short distance of the park include a swimming pool, tennis and bicycle hire. There is a Blue Flag beach at Ross. Other local attractions are Ceide Fields (Neolithic farm), Down Patrick Head, Mayo North Heritage Centre or a seaweed bath at Kilcullen's Bath House, Enniscrone.

Facilities

Spotlessly clean, tastefully decorated toilet block providing showers (€ 1 token). Baby bath. Facilities for disabled people. Laundry facilities. Reception includes a shop (June - Sept) and a tea room also serving breakfast. Campers' kitchen and emergency accommodation with beds provided. TV room. Games room. Play area. Ball game area. Tennis. Barbecue area. Off site: Fishing 1 km. Bicycle hire 2 km. Golf 3.5 km. Beach 10 km.

Open: 15 March - 1 November, by arrangement all year.

Directions

Take R314 Ballina - Killala road. The park is signed on the right after about 3 km.
GPS: N54:06.840 W09:09.240

Charges guide

Per unit incl. 2 persons	€ 19.00
extra person	€ 5.00
child	€ 2.50
electricity (10A)	€ 4.00
hiker/cyclist and tent	€ 9.00

Low season discounts for stays of 3 or more nights when pre-paid.

IR8770 Parkland Caravan & Camping Park

Westport House Country Park, Westport (Co. Mayo)

Tel: **098 277 66**. Email: **camping@westporthouse.ie**

www.alanrogers.com/IR8770

Located in the grounds of an elegant country estate, this is a popular park. From Westport Quay, you enter the grounds of the estate by way of a tree lined road that crosses the river and leads to the site. In an attractive, sheltered area of the parkland, set in the trees, are 155 pitches. There are 65 with hardstanding and 76 electric hook-ups. Early in the season the site may not be fully prepared, and only minimal facilities may be available. There is the choice of a 'pitch only' booking, or a 'special deal' (min. stay three nights). This includes free admission to Westport House and many of the activities of the adjoining leisure park. There is a children's animal and bird park, boating and fishing on the lake and river, pitch and putt, 'slippery dip', ball pond and 'supabounce', a play adventure world, hillside train rides and a flume ride. Stay one week or more and all the above are free, plus tennis, a par 3 golf course and 20% discount on bar food in the Horse and Wagon bar on the site. Westport is an attractive town with splendid Georgian houses and traditional shop fronts. There are many good restaurants and pubs.

Facilities

Toilet facilities are provided at various points on the site, plus a 'super-loo' located in the farmyard buildings. Facilities for disabled people. Laundry facilities. Fifties style function room and bar with food and musical entertainment (all 1/6-31/8). Westport House and Country Park. Off site: Within 5 km. of the estate are an 18-hole golf course and deep sea angling on Clew Bay.

Open: 14 May - 5 September.

Directions

Take the R335 Westport - Louisburgh road and follow signs for Westport Quay, then turn in through gates of Westport House and continue through estate following signs for camping.
GPS: N53:48.320 W09:32.369

Charges guide

Per unit incl. 2 persons and electricity	€ 28.00 - € 33.00
hiker or cyclist	€ 25.00 - € 27.50

Family weekend rates in June.

IR8780 Knock Caravan & Camping Park

Claremorris Road, Knock (Co. Mayo)

Tel: **094 938 8100**. Email: **caravanpark@knock-shrine.ie**

www.alanrogers.com/IR8780

This park is immediately south of the world famous shrine that receives many visitors. Comfortable and clean, the square shaped campsite is kept very neat with tarmac roads and surrounded by clipped trees. The pitches are of a decent size accommodating 50 caravans or motorcaravans, 20 tents and 18 caravan holiday homes (for rent). All pitches have hardstanding (5 doubles) and there are 52 electrical connections (13A), with an adequate number of water points. There is also an overflow field. Because of the religious connections of the area, the site is very busy in August and indeed there are unlikely to be any vacancies at all for 14-16 August. Besides visiting the shrine and Knock Folk Museum, it is also a good centre for exploring scenic Co. Mayo.

Facilities

Two heated toilet blocks have good facilities for disabled visitors and a nice sized rest room attached, hot showers (on payment) and adequate washing and toilet facilities. Laundry room. Gas supplies. Playground. Off site: Fishing 4.5 km. Golf and riding 11 km.

Open: 1 March - 31 October.

Directions

Exit from the N17 at the Knock bypass and from the roundabout follow signs to the site which is just south of the village. GPS: N53:47.262 W08:55.165

Charges 2009

Per person	€ 2.00 - € 2.50
child	€ 1.00
pitch	€ 16.00 - € 17.00
electricity (13A)	€ 3.50
hiker or cyclist incl. tent	€ 10.50 - € 11.50

No credit cards.

IR8790 Carra Caravan & Camping Park

Belcarra, Castlebar (Co. Mayo)

Tel: **094 903 2054**. Email: **post@mayoholidays.com**

www.alanrogers.com/IR8790

This is an ideal location for those seeking a real Irish village experience in a 'value for money' park. Small, unpretentious and family run, it is located in Belcarra, a regular winner of the 'Tidiest Mayo Village' award. Nestling at the foot of a wooded drumlin, it is surrounded by rolling hills and quiet roads which offer an away from it all feeling, yet Castlebar the county's largest town is only an 8 km. drive. On the pleasant 1.5 acre park, the 20 unmarked touring pitches, 7 with electric hook-up (13A), are on flat ground enclosed by ranch fencing and shaded in parts by trees. An additional novel idea at Carra are eight horse-drawn caravans for hire. Also of interest are the talks on the area that are given by the owner Sean and daughter Deirdre. There are recommended walks and maps provided. New to the area is the Museum of Country Life at Turlough (8 km) which is now a super attraction.

Facilities

The basic toilet block has adequate, well equipped showers (€ 0.50). Combined kitchen with dishwashing, laundry area with fridge/freezer, sink, table, chairs, washing machine and dryer. Comfortable lounge with TV, books and magazines located at reception. Off site: Village shops, a post office and 'Flukies' cosy bar which serves Irish breakfast and where Irish stew is a speciality. Leisure centre and tennis courts. Free fishing area and special walkway to the river. Golf 8 km.

Open: 2 May - 22 September.

Directions

From Castlebar take N60 Claremorris road for 8.5 km. southeast and turn right at sign for Belcarra. Continue for 4.5 km. to village and site on left at end of village. GPS: N53:47.974 W09:12.989

Charges guide

Per unit incl. all persons	€ 12.00
electricity	€ 2.00

No credit cards.

299

IR8810 Lough Lannagh Caravan Park

Old Westport Road, Castlebar (Co. Mayo)

Tel: **094 902 7111**. Email: **llv@eircom.net**   **www.alanrogers.com/IR8810**

Lough Lannagh is an attractive holiday village on the shores of the lake which comprises quality accommodation, self catering cottages and a caravan park. It is within walking distance of Castlebar with its many restaurants, pubs theatres and shops. County Mayo's main attractions are also within a short drive. The caravan park has 20 touring pitches, well laid out in a separate dedicated corner of the village, all on hardstanding with electric connections. One reception area serves all and is situated to the right of the security barrier. When not out and about, there are many on site activities for all the family. The main attraction is the fitness suite, sauna and steam room, plus reflexology and therapies available (over 18s only admitted to the gym). Popular with the young is the three times weekly club held in July/August. Anglers need only travel 500 metres, or if you prefer cycling, bicycles can be hired.

Facilities

One modern heated sanitary block provides washbasins and well equipped, pre-set showers. En-suite unit for disabled people. Laundry room with sink, washing machines and dryers. Café (serving breakfast). Fitness suite. Tennis. Bicycle hire.

Open: 10 April - 31 October.

Directions

To get to Castlebar take the N5, N60 or N84. At Castlebar ring road follow directions for Westport. Site is signed on all approach roads to the Westport roundabout. GPS: N53:50.950 W09:18.713

Charges 2009

Per unit incl. 2 persons, electricity and hardstanding	€ 21.00 - € 28.00
tent incl. 2 persons	€ 16.00 - € 18.00
child	€ 1.50

IR8960 Lough Ree (East) Caravan & Camping Park

Ballykeeran, Athlone (Co. Westmeath)

Tel: **090 647 8561**. Email: **athlonecamping@eircom.net**   **www.alanrogers.com/IR8960**

This touring park is alongside the river, screened by trees but reaching the water's edge. Drive into the small village of Ballykeeran and the park is discreetly located behind the main street. The top half of the site is in a woodland situation and after the reception and sanitary block, Lough Ree comes into view and the remaining pitches run down to the shoreline. There are 60 pitches, 20 with hardstanding and 52 with electricity. With fishing right on the doorstep there are boats for hire and the site has its own private mooring buoys, plus a dinghy slip and harbour. A restaurant and 'singing' pub are close.

Facilities

The toilet block is clean without being luxurious. Hot showers (€ 1). Dishwashing sinks outside. Laundry room (wash and dry € 8). A wooden chalet houses a pool room with open fire and campers' kitchen (no cooking facilities). Off site: Riding 4 km. Golf 8 km.

Open: 1 April - 30 September.

Directions

From Athlone take N55 towards Longford for 4.8 km. Park is in the village of Ballykeeran, clearly signed. GPS: N53:26.915 W07:53.460

Charges guide

Per unit incl. 2 persons	€ 18.00
extra person	€ 4.00
child (under 14 yrs)	€ 2.00
electricity (10A)	€ 3.00
No credit cards.	

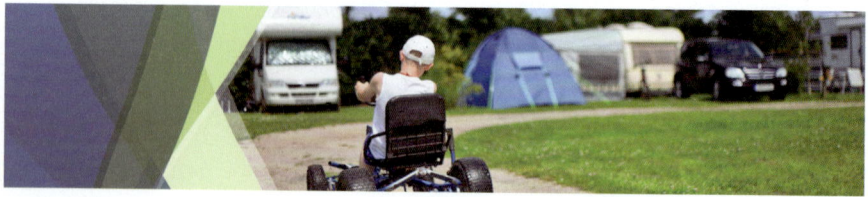

IR8825 Lough Key Caravan & Camping Park

Lough Key Forest Park, Boyle (Co. Roscommon)

Tel: 071 966 2212

www.alanrogers.com/IR8825

This caravan and camping park is set deep in the 320 hectares of the Lough Key Forest Park. Comprising mixed woodland including giant red cedar, beech, ash and oak trees, the forest is bounded by Lough Key and incorporates several of its islands. The rustic design of the main building on the park (which houses reception, a camper's kitchen, a TV room, and the sanitary and laundry facilities) blends well with the wooded environment. The well landscaped, 5 hectare site provides space for 52 touring units with electricity connections and ample water points. There is a separate area for tents. The history of the parkland goes back to 1184. A visit to the Lough offers views of islands inhabited by monks and hermits in days gone by, ring forts and tunnels, and natural and historical features including the Temple, the Wishing Chair, the Bog Gardens and Rockingham House and harbour. The location in Lough Key Forest Park offers a base for visiting Strokestown House, Boyle Abbey, Famine Museum and Garden, and the Elphin 18th century windmill. A fisherman's dream, there are pike, bream, roach and perch in Lough Key and brown trout at nearby Lough Arrow. Walks combine the historical and the legend with wildlife, flora and fauna. Boat tours of the lake and boat hire are also available. Coillte, the Irish Forestry Board, who manage the amenity, strictly enforces the forest code.

Facilities

The main toilet block includes metered hot showers. Facilities for disabled campers (key required). Campers' kitchen and sheltered eating area. Laundry. TV room. Play area in the centre of the park with adventure type play equipment in a hedged area, plus seating for parents. Forest walks and trails. Boat tours and boat hire. Security barrier closed at night. Off site: Restaurant at Rockingham harbour. Nearby town of Boyle for bars, restaurants and entertainment 3 km. Bicycle hire and golf 5 km.

Open: Easter - mid September.

Directions

The Forest Park and the site are 4 km. east of Boyle on the A4 Carrick-on-Shannon road.
GPS: N53:58.875 W08:14.110

Charges guide

Per unit incl. 2 persons	€ 16.00 - € 20.00
hiker or cyclist	€ 8.00 - € 10.00
electricity	€ 2.00
small tent	€ 8.00 - € 10.00

No credit cards.

IR8815 Willowbrook Camping & Caravan Park

Kiltybranks, Ballaghaderreen (Co. Roscommon)

Tel: 094 986 1307. Email: info@willowbrookpark.com

www.alanrogers.com/IR8815

This is a campsite with a difference. Willowbrook is a small family run caravan and camping park, which offers a unique holiday in an unspoiled part of Ireland. It has 8 hardstanding pitches with electricity and a central level grass area without power, all with ample water points. An additional tenting area is available in the adjoining field. The main difference is that meditation, Tai Chi and other relaxation techniques, all adding to the tranquillity of the setting, are organised by Dave and Lin Whitefield whose aim is to ensure their guests relax and unwind in this idyllic hideaway. Archery, guided walks on the Suck Valley Way and in the Ox and Curlieu mountains, and coarse fishing for more active relaxation are also provided. A bunkhouse (for up to twelve), a library and reading room with a TV in a renovated 100 year old cottage add to the ambiance of the park. The camper's kitchen is spotless and homely. This clean and well cared for park is located in an area rich with archaeology and heritage, about 20 minutes from Knock airport. It is ideal as a holiday base or as a stop over on the Dublin - Mayo route to the west of Ireland.

Facilities

The toilet block is immaculate and lit at night, with separate shower cubicles and facilities for disabled campers. Laundry room. Campers' kitchen with microwave, kettle and toaster. Library and reading room with TV. Fishing. Torches useful. Off site: Local sporting activities available include tennis, golf and fishing.

Open: All year.

Directions

Park is 6 km. from Ballaghaderreen. Take the R293 from Ballaghaderreen towards Castlerea and Ballyhaunis, then the R325 over the bridge. Bear left, still towards Castlerea and Ballyhaunis for 1.5 km. Turn right at sign to site in 500 m.
GPS: N53:52.003 W08:36.128

Charges guide

Per unit incl. 2 persons	€ 16.00
family tent incl. 2 adults and 2 children	€ 20.00

No credit cards.

IR8965 Lough Ennell Camping & Caravan Park

Tudenham Shore, Mullingar (Co. Westmeath)

Tel: **044 934 8101**. Email: **eamon@caravanparksireland.com**   www.alanrogers.com/IR8965

Nature and rustic charm is the visitor's first reaction on arrival at Lough Ennell Caravan Park. Set in 18 acres of mature woodland beside a Blue Flag lake, Eamon and Geraldine O'Malley run this sheltered and tranquil park with their family who live on the site. They receive a blend of visitors – seasonal residents in camping holiday homes (private and to rent), caravanners and motorcaravanners and there are ample areas for tents. Pitches are varied, sheltered with trees and natural shrubbery, and spacious with gravel or gravel and grass combinations. Electricity is available on 44 hardstanding and grass pitches and there are water points on or near all the pitches. Just an hour from Dublin, it provides a good holiday base or a useful stop over en-route to the West of Ireland. The watersports permitted on the lake include canoeing, sailing, windsurfing, boating, fishing and safe swimming. The woodlands offer ample opportunities for walking and cycling. Numerous other lakes in the area provide fishing for all varieties especially wild trout. Other activities might include tennis, horse riding, golf, dog racing and of course forest walks. Belvedere House and Tullynally Castle are nearby and the large town of Mullingar is just 6 km.

Facilities

The toilet block provides toilets, washbasins and hot showers (€ 1 coin). Additional dishwashing areas are around the park. Laundry. Small shop. Café and coffee shop with takeaway. TV and games room. Play areas and area for ball games. Small lakeside beach. Fishing. Late arrivals area outside. Security including CCTV. Some breeds of dog are not accepted. Off site: Bus service 8 km. Golf 1.5 km. Riding 4 km. Bicycle hire 6 km.

Open: Easter/1 April - 30 September.

Directions

From N4 take the N52. Follow signs for Belvedere House and take turn 300 m. south of Belvedere House (signed for site). Continue to the shores of Lough Ennell and turn left.

Charges guide

Per person	€ 5.00
child	€ 3.00
pitch	€ 10.00
electricity	€ 3.00
No credit cards.	

Lough Ennell Caravan & Camping Park

Tel: +353 - 44 - 9348101
Fax: +353 - 44 - 9342676

Tudenham Shore, Mullingar, County Westmeath. Republic of Ireland.

Beautiful family run park with 18 acres of of matured woodland. Facilities include service block, showers/toilets, kitchen, wash-up area, laundry room, TV room, games room, restaurant & coffee dock, take away and mini mart.

www.caravanparksireland.com

IR9080 Forest Farm Caravan & Camping Park

Dublin Road, Athy (Co. Kildare)

Tel: **059 863 1231**. Email: **forestfarm@eircom.net**   www.alanrogers.com/IR9080

This site makes an excellent stop over if travelling from Dublin to the southeast counties. It is also ideally placed to visit local places of interest including the Shackleton exhibition, the Japanese Gardens and the Irish National Stud. Part of a working farm, the campsite spreads to the right of the modern farmhouse, which also provides B&B and holiday apartments. The owners have cleverly utilised their land to create a site which offers 64 unmarked touring pitches on level ground. Of these, 32 are for caravans, all with electricity and 10 with hardstanding, and 32 places are available for tents. Full Irish breakfasts are served at the farmhouse and farm tours are arranged on request. The park is signed on the N78 and approached by a 500 m. avenue of tall pines.

Facilities

The centrally located, red brick toilet block is heated and double glazed, providing quality amenities. Spacious shower unit for disabled visitors. Family room with shower and WC. Laundry room. Campers' kitchen with fridge/freezer, cooker, table and chairs. Comfortable, large lounge/games room (a TV can be provided). Sand pit and picnic tables. Off site: Shop, bar and restaurant 3 km. Golf courses nearby. Course and game fishing 4 km.

Open: All year.

Directions

Site is 4.8 km. northeast of Athy town off the main N78 Athy - Kilcullen road.
GPS: N53:00.835 W06:55.534

Charges guide

Per unit incl. electricity	€ 12.00
person	€ 4.00
child	€ 2.00
hiker, cyclist or motorcyclist incl. tent	€ 6.00

IR9100 **Camac Valley Tourist Caravan & Camping Park**

Green Isle Road, Clondalkin Dublin 22 (Co. Dublin)

Tel: **014 640 644**. Email: **reservations@camacvalley.com**   **www.alanrogers.com/IR9100**

Opened in 1996, this campsite is not only well placed for Dublin, but also offers a welcome stopover if travelling to the more southern counties from the north of the country, or vice versa. Despite its close proximity to the city, being located in the 300 acre Corkagh Park gives it a 'heart of the country' atmosphere. There are 163 pitches, 48 for tents placed to the fore and hardstandings for caravans laid out in bays and avenues with electricity, drainage and water points. Maturing trees and shrubs separate pitches and roads are of tarmac. Beyond the gate and forecourt stands an attractive timber fronted building housing the site amenities. Its design includes various roof levels and spacious interior layout, with large windows offering a view of the site. Housed here are reception, reading, TV and locker rooms plus a shop and the sanitary facilities. After a day of sightseeing in Dublin, which can be reached by bus from the site, Camac Valley offers an evening of relaxation with woodland and river walks in the park or a number of first class restaurants and pubs nearby. The entrance and sign are distinctive and can be spotted in time when approaching on the busy N7.

Facilities

Heated sanitary facilities include good sized showers (token). Facilities for disabled people. Baby room. Laundry. Shop and coffee bar. Playground with wooden play frames and safety base. Fishing. Electronic gate controlled from reception and 24 hour security. Off site: Bicycle hire 1.5 km. Golf 6 km. Riding 9 km.

Open: All year.

Directions

From north follow signs for West Link and M50 motorway. Exit M50 at junction 9 onto N7 Cork road. Site is on right of dual-carriageway (beside Green Isle Hotel) after 2 km. and is clearly signed. At City West business park, cross over bridge and return on dual-carriageway following site signs - site is on left after 800 m. GPS: N53:18.285 W06:24.931

Charges guide

Per unit incl. 2 persons	€ 19.00 - € 24.00
incl. up to 4 children	€ 26.00
extra person	€ 5.00
electricity (10A)	€ 5.00

IR9130 **Roundwood Caravan & Camping Park**

Roundwood (Co. Wicklow)

Tel: **012 818 163**. Email: **info@dublinwicklowcamping.com**   **www.alanrogers.com/IR9130**

In the heart of the Wicklow mountains, the hospitable owner of this park maintains high standards. It is neatly laid out with rows of trees dividing the different areas and giving an attractive appearance. There are 46 hardstanding pitches for caravans and motorcaravans, all with electricity (5A), plus 33 pitches for tents, arranged off tarmac access roads. There are excellent walks around the Varty Lakes and a daily bus service to Dublin city. Close by are many places of natural beauty.

Facilities

The renovated sanitary block is kept clean, with adequate washing and toilet facilities, plus spacious showers on payment (€ 1). Good laundry facilities, but ask at reception as machines are not self-service. Motorcaravan service point. Campers' kitchen and dining room. TV room. Adventure playground. Bicycle hire. Off site: Roundwood village has shops, pubs, restaurants, and a Sunday market. Fishing 1 km. Riding, golf 3 km.

Open: 1 May - 31 August.

Directions

Turn off N11 Dublin - Wexford road at Kilmacanogue towards Glendalough and then 15 km. to Roundwood. Park is on the north side of the village. GPS: N53:04.149 W06:13.355

Charges guide

Per unit incl. 2 persons	€ 26.00
extra person	€ 4.00 - € 8.00
electricity	€ 4.00
No credit cards.	

303

IR9140 Valley Stopover & Caravan Park

Killough, Kilmacanogue (Co. Wicklow)

Tel: **012 829 565**. Email: **rowanbb@eircom.net**   www.alanrogers.com/IR9140

In a quiet, idyllic setting in the picturesque Rocky Valley, this small, neat, family run park is convenient for the Dublin ferries. Situated in the grounds of the family home, covering under an acre, it can be used either as a transit site or for a longer stay. It will appeal to those who prefer the more basic 'CL' type site. There are 15 grassy pitches, 11 with electric hook-ups, 8 hardstandings, 2 water points, night lighting and a security gate. Staying put here you are only minutes from Enniskerry which lies in the glen of the Glencullen river.

Facilities

Toilet facilities, clean when we visited, are housed in one unit and consist of two WCs with washbasins, mirrors, etc. and a shower. Laundry sink, spin dryer. Campers' kitchen. Full cooked Irish breakfast in the family guest house. Off site: Riding 3 km. Golf 7 km. Fishing 16 km.

Open: Easter - 31 October.

Directions

Turn off N11 Dublin - Wexford road at Kilmacanogue, following signs for Glendalough. Continue for 1.6 km. and take right fork signed 'Waterfall'. Park is first opening on the left in about 200 m. GPS: N53:10.023 W06:09.803

Charges guide

Per person	€ 1.25
pitch incl. electricity	€ 17.50

IR9150 River Valley Caravan & Camping Park

Redcross Village (Co. Wicklow)

Tel: **040 441 647**. Email: **info@rivervalleypark.com**   www.alanrogers.com/IR9150

In the small country village of Redcross, in the heart of County Wicklow, you will find this popular, family run park. Based here you are within easy reach of beauty spots such as the Vale of Avoca (Ballykissangel), Glendalough and Powerscourt, plus the safe beach of Brittas Bay. The 145 touring pitches at River Valley are mostly together in a dedicated area, all have electricity connections (6A) and offer a choice of hardstanding or grass – you select your pitch. A late arrivals area has electricity hook-ups, water and night lighting. Within this 16 acre site children can find day long amusement.

Facilities

A luxurious new sanitary block is modern and well designed. Excellent facilities for disabled visitors. Showers are on payment (€ 0.50). Laundry area. Campers' kitchen. Motorcaravan service points. Gas supplies. Wine/coffee bar and restaurant (1/6-31/8). TV and games room. Three tennis courts. Par 3 golf course. Bowling green. Sports complex. Adventure and toddlers' playgrounds. Caravan storage. No dogs in July/Aug. Off site: Riding 2 km.

Open: 13 March - 1 November.

Directions

From Dublin follow N11 Wexford road south, bypassing Ashford and Rathnew. Pass The Beehive pub, look for Doyle's pub on the right. Turn right at pub and continue for 5 km. to the park at the top of Redcross village. GPS: N52:53.351 W06:08.664

Charges guide

Per caravan, motorcaravan incl. 2 persons and electricity	€ 24.00
extra person	€ 4.00 - € 6.00

IR9160 Moat Farm Caravan & Camping Park

Donard (Co. Wicklow)

Tel: **045 404 727**. Email: **moatfarm@ireland.com**   www.alanrogers.com/IR9160

Providing a true feel of the countryside, this park is part of a working sheep farm. It offers incredible vistas across a scenic landscape, yet is within driving distance of Dublin and Rosslare. Driving into the village of Donard you little suspect that alongside the main street lies a pleasant, well cared for and tranquil five acre campsite. The entrance is approached by way of a short road where the ruins of a Medieval church sit high overlooking the forecourt and reception. There are 40 pitches for caravans and tents. Spacious pitches with hardstanding line both sides of a broad avenue, incorporating ample space for awnings and all with electricity and drainage.

Facilities

The toilet block is kept very clean and includes spacious showers. Facilities for visitors with disabilities. Well equipped laundry room. Good quality campers' kitchen. Large recreation/entertainment room with open fire. Three large barbecues and patio area. Caravan storage. Off site: Mountain climbing. Sites of archaeological interest. Fishing 3 km. Bicycle hire 15 km. Golf 13 km.

Open: 15 March - 30 September.

Directions

Park is 16.5 km. south of Blessington. Leave the M50 Dublin ring motorway, exit 10 to join the N81 southwest for 19 km. to Blessington. Continue on N81 for a further 16.5 km. and turn left at Old Toll House pub. Follow signs to park in Donard village (3.5 km). GPS: N53:01.262 W06:36.881

Charges guide

Per unit incl. 2 persons	€ 18.00
extra person	€ 4.00 - € 5.00
electricity (10A)	€ 4.00
No credit cards.	

IR9170 Saint Margaret's Beach Caravan & Camping Park

Lady's Island, Rosslare Harbour, Rosslare (Co Wexford)

Tel: 053 913 1169. Email: stmarg@eircom.net

www.alanrogers.com/IR9170

'This park is loved' was how a Swedish visitor described this family run, environmentally friendly caravan and camping park, the first the visitor meets near the Rosslare ferry port. Landscaping with flowering containers and maze-like sheltered camping areas and a pretty sanitary block all demonstrate the Traynor family's attention to detail. Most pitches give shelter from the fresh sea breeze and ferries can be seen crossing the Irish sea. Just metres away, the safe, sandy beach (part of the Wexford coastal path) curves around in a horseshoe shape ending in a small pier and slipway. Tourist information on the area is provided in the well stocked shop. The immediate area boasts of thatched roof cottages and cottage gardens. The park is an ideal base from which to explore the sunny southeast or as an overnight stop to prepare for touring Ireland or for departure. Local lakes and the Saltee Islands, various locations of ornithological interest, deep sea and shore fishing, and award-winning pubs and restaurants provide something for everyone.

Facilities

The toilet block is spotless. Laundry room. Campers' kitchen including toaster, microwave and TV. Shop (June - Aug). Fresh milk and bread daily. Mobile homes for rent. Off site: Walking, beach and fishing. Boat slipway 2.5 km. Pitch and putt 2 km. Riding 6 km. Pubs and restaurants. The JFK Arboretum, Johnstown Castle and Gardens, the Irish National Heritage Park, Kilmore Quay and Marina, and Curracloe beach (featured in the film 'Saving Private Ryan').

Open: Mid March - October.

Directions

From the N25 south of Wexford town, outside village of Tagoat, follow signs for Lady's Island and Carne. After 3 km. pass Butlers Bar and take next left and continue for 2.5 km. Site is well signed.
GPS: N52:12.393 W06:21.355

Charges guide

Per unit incl. 2 persons	€ 14.00 - € 22.00
extra person	€ 2.50
child (2-16 yrs)	€ 1.50
electricity	€ 2.00

IR9230 Nore Valley Park

Annamult, Bennettsbridge (Co. Kilkenny)

Tel: 056 772 7229. Email: norevalleypark@eircom.net

www.alanrogers.com/IR9230

This lovely site is set on a grassy hillock overlooking the valley and the river Nore, with a woodland setting behind. Situated on a working farm, it offers 70 touring pitches, 50 of which have 6A electricity. There is an additional area for tents and 4 mobile homes for rent. The owners, Samuel and Isabel, are proud of their park and Isabel's baking and jams must be sampled. An attractive courtyard houses several unusual facilities including a sand pit and a straw loft play area for wet weather. There is outdoor chess and tractor rides and go-karts in the fields. This is an ideal park for families, especially in school holidays, offering children and adults alike the opportunity to feed the animals (goats, lambs, ducks, chickens and donkey). It is a peaceful holiday base from which to explore the sunny southeast, including the historic city of Kilkenny, renowned for its history and craftwork, Kells Abbey and Dumoe Caves. The village of Bennettsbridge is 3 km. with shops and eating places. There is easy access to Waterford city, famous for its crystal.

Facilities

The modern toilet block is kept very clean and can be heated. Two units suitable for disabled visitors. Laundry room with washing machine and dryer. Motorcaravan services. The original block in the courtyard is used mainly in the low season. Shop (basic items such as milk, bread and camping gaz) and café (June - Aug). Comfortable lounge. Games room. Play area. Minigolf. Bicycle hire. Off site: Bennettsbridge 3 km. Outdoor pursuits nearby such as canoeing, walking or fishing (4 km). Riding 6 km. Golf 10 km.

Open: 1 March - 31 October.

Directions

From Kilkenny take the R700 to Bennettsbridge. Just before the bridge turn right at sign for Stoneyford and after about 3 km. site is signed Nore Valley Park.
GPS: N52:33.777 W07:11.698

Charges guide

Per person (over 2 yrs)	€ 4.00
pitch	€ 8.00 - € 12.00
electricity (6A)	€ 3.00

305

IR9240 Tree Grove Caravan & Camping Park

Danville House, Kilkenny (Co. Kilkenny)

Tel: **056 777 0302**. Email: **treecc@iol.ie**

www.alanrogers.com/IR9240

The entrance gate to this small family run site is easily spotted off the R700 road. An orderly, neat park, it appeals because its young owners are friendly and have designed a logical layout to suit both the terrain and campers needs. It is terraced with the lower terrace to the right of the wide sweeping driveway laid out with 11 hardstanding pitches for caravans. All 30 pitches have electrical hook-ups (10A) and plenty of water points are to be found. On a higher level, is a grass area for hikers and cyclists with further caravan and tent pitches sited near the elevated sanitary block. If needed more grass pitches face reception, which is housed in a modern wooden chalet. Whilst there are mature trees at the entrance and around the site perimeter, many shrubs have been effectively placed together with flower troughs. On the patio there are bench seats with tables and umbrellas. Tree Grove is within walking distance of medieval Kilkenny, known for its elegance and famed for its beer and cats. There is much to see and do around the ancient city (1.5 km) with its cobbled streets and castle. County Touring Routes are worth following.

Facilities

House plants add decoration inside the toilet block giving a cared for look to this modern building. Family room with shower, WC and washbasin which can be used by disabled people. Laundry room. Open, covered kitchen for campers with fridge, worktop, sink and electric kettle adjoins a comfortable games/TV room with pool table, and easy chairs. Bicycle hire. Tents to rent. Off site: Fishing 500 m. Riding 1 km. Golf 2 or 15 km.

Open: 1 March - 15 November.

Directions

Travelling north on the N10 Waterford - Kilkenny Road turn right at roundabout on ring road. Continue to 2nd roundabout and turn right onto R700. Site is 150 m. on right.
GPS: N52:38.400 W07:13.780

Charges guide

Per unit incl. 2 persons and electricity	€ 17.00 - € 22.00
with 2 children	€ 22.00 - € 27.00
tent (per person)	€ 6.50 - € 7.50
extra person	€ 6.50

No credit cards.

IR9340 Newtown Cove Camping & Caravan Park

Newtown Road, Tramore (Co. Waterford)

Tel: **051 381 979**. Email: **info@newtowncove.com**

www.alanrogers.com/IR9340

Well run and friendly, this very attractive small park is only five minutes walk from the beautiful Newton Cove. It offers views of the famous and historic Metal Man and is 2.5 km. from Tramore beach and 11 km. from Waterford. Neatly set out on gently sloping grass are 40 pitches, with the abundance of shrubs and bushes reflecting the efforts of the owners. All pitches have electrical connections (10A), some with hardstanding also, and access is by well lit, tarmac roads. There are around 50 privately owned caravan holiday homes. A modern building at the entrance houses reception, the amenities and additional sanitary facilities. The village of Tramore, with a wide range of shops and eating houses, is close and there is a choice of many delightful cliff walks in the immediate vicinity.

Facilities

The main sanitary block at the bottom end of the site is not very modern but provides good, clean facilities including a bathroom. Showers on payment (token from reception). Facilities for disabled visitors. Motorcaravan services. Campers' kitchen with cooking facilities, sheltered eating area, lounge and small laundry. Small shop (1/7-30/8). TV room. Games room. Small play area. Off site: Beach 400 m. Fishing 400 m. Golf 800 m. Riding 3 km.

Open: 9 April - 27 September.

Directions

From Tramore on R675 coast road to Dungarvan. Turn left 2 km. from town centre, following signs.
GPS: N52:08.877 W07:10.358

Charges 2009

Per person	€ 6.00
child (3-15 yrs)	€ 3.00
pitch	€ 8.00 - € 13.00
hiker, cyclist or motorcyclist	€ 8.00 - € 11.00
electricity (10A)	€ 4.00

No single sex groups.

IR9330 Casey's Caravan & Camping Park

Clonea, Dungarvan (Co. Waterford)

Tel: **058 419 19**   www.alanrogers.com/IR9330

Set on 20 acres of flat grass, edged by mature trees, this family run park is well managed and offers 284 pitches which include 110 touring pitches all with electrical hook-ups and 39 with hardstanding. The remainder are occupied by caravan holiday homes. There is direct access from the park to a sandy, 'Blue Flag' beach with a resident lifeguard during July and August. A highly recommended leisure centre is adjacent should the weather be inclement. The park is 5.5 km. from Dungarvan, a popular town for deep sea angling, from where charter boats can be hired and three 18-hole golf courses are within easy driving distance. Suggested drives include the scenic Vee, the Comeragh Drive and the coast road to Tramore.

Facilities

The central toilet block (key system), has good facilities kept spotlessly clean. Showers on payment (€ 1). Small laundry with washing machine and dryer. A further modern block provides an excellent campers' kitchen, laundry room and toilet for disabled visitors. Large adventure play area. Games room. TV lounge. Minigolf. Gas supplies. Full time security staff in high season. Off site: Two village stores near the beach. Golf 5 km. Fishing 4 km. Riding 20 km.

Open: 21 March - 7 September.

Directions

From Dungarvan centre follow R675 east for 3.5 km. Look for signs on the right to Clonea Bay and site. Site is about 1.5 km. GPS: N52:05.686 W07:32.770

Charges guide

Per unit incl. 2 persons	€ 23.00 - € 26.00
extra person	€ 7.00
child	€ 3.00
electricity (10A)	€ 4.00
No credit cards.	

CASEY'S CARAVAN & CAMPING PARK

Grade Category 4★ • Bord Failte Registered • Bord Failte / ICC Park Awards
Best 4★ 2004 • 2000 & 2002 Overall Winner Best Park
2001 & 2002 Personal Choice Awards • Merit Award 4★ 2003

Top class facilities including; playground, electric sites for tents & tourers (10A), crazy golf, games & TV rooms and also laundry & kitchen facilities. The park is situated next to EU Blue Flag beach. 2 shops with takeaway are also nearby.

Ambience Award 2006
Best Seaside Park Award 2007

Dungarvan town is 5.5km away and there's a choice of scenic views to visit. Adjacent hotel with 19 metre pool and leisure centre with bowling alley. Other activities can include deep sea and river angling and an 18 hole golf course which are all within easy reach.

Clonea, Dungarvan, Co Waterford   Tel: +353 (0)58 41919

IR9370 Ballinacourty House Caravan & Camping Park

Glen of Aherlow, Tipperary (Co. Tipperary)

Tel: **062 565 59**. Email: **info@camping.ie**   www.alanrogers.com/IR9370

Ballinacourty House and its cobble-stoned courtyard form the centrepiece of this south-facing park with views of the Galtee Mountains. Accessed by a tree-lined lane, the reception area is in part of the renovated 18th century building, as is the adjoining restaurant. The park is level with 26 touring pitches with 6A electricity and 25 grassy pitches for tents. Some areas are shaded areas and there are open spaces to accommodate rallies and larger groups. Self-catering cottages and B&B are also available. This tranquil site is an ideal base from which to tour the Rock of Cashel, the Mitchelstown Caves, Swiss Cottage and the towns of Tipperary, Cahir and Cashel. Activities in the area include horse riding and trekking, fishing for perch and brown trout, cycling, forest walks, three 18-hole golf courses, leisure centre with swimming pool, cinema, theatre and pottery shop.

Facilities

Sanitary facilities provide free hot water and showers. Baby room. Facilities for disabled visitors are planned. Laundry with ironing facilities. Campers' kitchen. Ice pack freezing. Licensed restaurant (early booking advised). Motorcaravan services. Gas supplies. Minigolf. TV and games rooms. Picnic benches. Tennis. Play area. Off site: Riding, fishing, golf.

Open: 1 May - 21 September.

Directions

From the N24 Tipperary - Cahir road, take Glen of Aherlow scenic route 6.5 km. from Cahir and follow signs. GPS: N52:24.590 W08:12.630

Charges guide

Per unit	€ 8.00 - € 10.00
extra person	€ 5.00
child	€ 2.00
electricity	€ 3.00

IR9400 The Glen of Aherlow Caravan & Camping Park

Newtown, Glen of Aherlow (Co. Tipperary)

Tel: **062 565 55**. Email: **rdrew@eircom.net**

www.alanrogers.com/IR9400

The owners of one of Ireland's newest parks, George and Rosalind Drew, are campers themselves and have set about creating an idyllic park in an idyllic location. This five acre park is set in one of Ireland's most picturesque valleys and is open all year. There are beautiful views of the wooded and hilly areas of Slievenamuck and the Galtee Mountains. There are 42 large and level pitches, with both hardstanding and grass places, each with a 10A electricity connection and water point. The Drew family is happy to welcome large groups and rallies and large units can be accommodated. The excellent facilities are located in a purpose built building.

Facilities

The modern toilet block includes free showers and facilities for disabled visitors. Motorcaravan service point. Laundry room with ironing. Campers' kitchen. Recreation and TV rooms. Off site: Holiday homes to rent 300 m. Restaurant 300 m. Outdoor activities. Fishing. Golf and riding 7 km.

Open: All year.

Directions

From Tipperary town take N24 via Bansha, then R663 to Newtown. Continue through village and pass Coach Road Inn to park in 300 m.
GPS: N52:24.966 W08:12.630

Charges guide

Per unit incl. 2 persons	€ 20.00
extra person	€ 4.00
child (2-14 yrs)	€ 2.00
electricity	€ 4.00

IR9420 Streamstown Caravan & Camping Park

Streamstown, Roscrea (Co. Tipperary)

Tel: **050 521 519**. Email: **streamstowncaravanpark@eircom.net**

www.alanrogers.com/IR9420

This family run site, set on a dairy farm in the centre of Ireland, has been open for over 30 years. It is conveniently situated off the N7 Dublin - Limerick road and makes a good overnight halt or for a longer stay if you are seeking a quiet, restful location with little to disturb the peace. There are 27 touring pitches, 10 with hardstanding and separated by low hedges. The remainder are on grass and more suitable for units with awnings. This is a working farm and the owners, who are friendly and welcoming, are in the process of improving and developing their site.

Facilities

The sanitary facilities, very clean when we visited, are housed in a modern block. Showers (free), toilets and washbasins are older in style but a couple of washbasins are in cubicles. Facilities for disabled visitors in family shower room. Good laundry room. Good campers' kitchen with fridge/freezer, electric cooker and TV. Play area. TV and games room. Caravan storage. Off site: Fishing 1.8 km. Golf 5 km. Riding 8 km.

Open: 12 April - 8 October.

Directions

From Roscrea centre follow signs for R491 Shirone. Continue towards Shirone following site signs for about 2.5 km. and site entrance is on left.
GPS: N52:57.432 W07:50.362

Charges guide

Per person	€ 4.50
child (under 14 yrs)	€ 2.00
pitch	€ 10.00
electricity (10A)	€ 4.00
5 nights for the price of 4.	

IR9460 Corofin Village Camping & Caravan Park

Main Street, Corofin (Co. Clare)

Tel: **065 683 7683**. Email: **corohost@iol.ie**

www.alanrogers.com/IR9460

This compact green oasis in the centre of the village of Corofin occupies one acre and adjoins the family's hostel. The owners, Jude and Marie Neylon live on the site and have a policy of always having a family member on hand at all times. They are very environmentally aware and have excellent recycling facilities. The 20 pitches all have electricity and there are ample water points. A campers' kitchen, laundry room and the TV and games room are separate to the hostel facilities. This little site is neat and well maintained and makes an ideal base for sightseeing throughout Clare.

Facilities

The sanitary block is bright and clean with free hot showers. Separate facilities for disabled campers. Laundry room with washing machine and dryer. CCTV security. Torches useful. Site is not suitable for large units. Off site: Fishing and boat launching 2 km. Riding 8 km. Bicycle hire 10 km. Golf 20 km. Beach 20 km.

Open: 1 April - 30 September.

Directions

Corofin village is 12 km. from Ennis. Take the N85 to Ennistymon and after 2 km. (well signed) turn on R476. Site is in the centre of the village.
GPS: N52:56.442 W09:03.536

Charges 2009

Per unit with 2 persons	€ 25.00
plus 2 children	€ 30.00
electricity	€ 5.00

IR9410 The Apple Camping & Caravan Park

Moorstown, Cahir (Co. Tipperary)

Tel: **052 74 414 59**. Email: **con@theapplefarm.com**

www.alanrogers.com/IR9410

This fruit farm and campsite combination offers an idyllic country holiday venue in one of the most delightful situations imaginable. For tourers only, it is located off the N24, midway between Clonmel and Cahir. The park has 32 pitches in a secluded situation behind the barns and are mostly grass with a few hardstandings, with electricity connections to 25. Entrance is by way of a 300 m. drive which follows straight through the heart of the farm. Apple trees guard the route, as do various non-fruit tree species, which are named and of interest to guests who are free to spend time walking the paths around the farm. When we visited, strawberries were being gathered – the best we had tasted all season – and award winning apple juice, cordials, jams, etc. are also sold by Con and Noreen in the farm shop. Reception is housed with the other site facilities in a large farmyard barn. Although a rather unusual arrangement, it is central and effective. The towns of Cahir and Clonmel are of historic interest and the countryside around boasts rivers, mountains, Celtic culture and scenic drives.

Facilities

Toilet facilities, kept very clean, quite modern in design and with heating, comprise showers, washbasins with mirrors, electric points, etc. in functional units occupying two corners of the large floor space. Facilities for disabled visitors. Also in the barn are dishwashing sinks, washing machine and a fridge/freezer for campers to use. Motorcaravan service point. Tennis. Play area. Dogs are not accepted. Off site: Fishing, golf, bicycle hire and riding within 6 km.

Open: 1 May - 30 September.

Directions

Park is 300 m. off main N24, 9.6 km. west of Clonmel, 6.4 km. east of Cahir.
GPS: N52:22.719 W07:50.509

Charges 2009

Per person	€ 6.50
child (0-12 yrs)	€ 4.50
electricity (13A)	€ 2.50

No charge per pitch.
Less 20% for groups of 4 or more.

IR9480 Blarney Caravan & Camping Park

Stone View, Blarney (Co. Cork)

Tel: **021 451 6519**. Email: **con.quill@camping-ireland.ie**

www.alanrogers.com/IR9480

There is a heart of the country feel about this 'on the farm' site, yet the city of Cork is only an 8 km. drive. What makes this friendly, family run park so appealing is its secluded location and neatly laid out, open appearance. The terrain on the three acre park is elevated and gently sloping, commanding views towards Blarney Castle and the surrounding mountainous countryside. The 80 pitches, 39 of which have hardstanding and 10A electrical connections, are with caravans sited to the centre and left and tents pitched to the right. There are gravel roads, well tended young shrubs and a screen of mature trees and hedging marks the park's perimeter. In the Blarney area, apart from Blarney Castle, house and gardens, there are shops, restaurants, pubs with traditional music and an abundance of outdoor pursuits such as walking, riding and fishing, and easy access to sightseeing in Cork city.

Facilities

Excellent toilet areas, one new, are housed in converted farm buildings with reception and small shop. Facilities for disabled visitors. Laundry room. Campers' kitchen. Motorcaravan service point. Shop (1/6-31/8). TV lounge. 18-hole golf and pitch and putt course. Off site: Bar and restaurant 100 m. serving food all day. Within easy reach of the ports of Cork and Rosslare.

Open: 1 April - 31 October.

Directions

Site is 8 km. northwest of Cork, just off the N20. Take the N20 from Cork for about 6 km. and then left on R617 to Blarney. Site clearly signed at Top Filling station in village, in 2 km.
GPS: N51:56.872 W08:32.776

Charges guide

Per person	€ 6.00
child	€ 3.00
pitch	€ 8.00 - € 10.00
electricity (10A)	€ 4.00

309

IR9500 The Meadow Camping Park

Glandore (Co. Cork)

Tel: 028 332 80. Email: the_meadow@oceanfree.net

www.alanrogers.com/IR9500

The stretch of coast from Cork to Skibbereen reminds British visitors of Devon before the era of mass tourism. This is rich dairy country, the green of the meadows matching the emerald colours of the travel posters. Thanks to the warm and wet Gulf Stream climate, it is also a county of gardens and keen gardeners. The Meadows is best described not as a site, but as a one acre garden surrounded, appropriately, by lush meadows. The owners, who live on the park, have cunningly arranged accommodation for 19 pitches among the flower beds and shrubberies of their extended garden. There are 10 hardstandings for motorcaravans with 6A electric hook-ups. Among the homely features are a sitting room and a well equipped kitchen. The Meadow lies 1.5 km. east of the fishing village of Glandore, a haven in the summer for sailing. A further 5 km. west is the regional centre, Skibbereen, beyond which the landscape moves from 'unspoilt Devon' to 'unspoilt Cornwall'. West Cork has myriad small coastal villages and scenic routes.

Facilities

Facilities are limited but well designed and immaculately maintained. Showers on payment. Washing machine and dryer. Larger units may be accepted depending on length and available space; contact park before arrival. Football and cycling are not permitted on the park. Off site: Riding 5 km. Fishing, swimming, boat launching and sailing at Glandore 2 km. Bicycle hire 10 km. Golf 19 km.

Open: 1 May - 15 September.

Directions

Park is 1.5 km. east of Glandore, off N71 road, on R597 midway between Leap and Rosscarbery (coast road). GPS: N51:34.009 W09:05.818

Charges 2009

Per unit incl. 2 persons	€ 20.00
incl. electricity	€ 23.00
extra person	€ 6.00
child (under 16 yrs)	€ 3.00
No credit cards.	

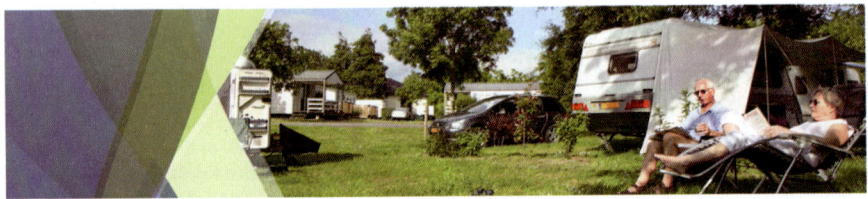

IR9550 Anchor Caravan Park

Castlegregory (Co. Kerry)

Tel: 066 713 9157. Email: anchorcaravanpark@eircom.net

www.alanrogers.com/IR9550

Of County Kerry's three long, finger-like peninsulas which jut into the sea, Dingle is the most northerly. Tralee is the main town and Anchor Caravan Park is 20 km. west of this famed town and under 4 km. south of Castlegregory on Tralee Bay. A secluded and mature, five acre park, it is enclosed by shrubs and trees that give excellent shelter. A gateway leads to a beautiful, sandy beach which is safe for bathing, boating and shore fishing. There are 30 pitches, all with electric hook-ups and some also with drainage and water points. Although there are holiday homes for hire, these are well apart from the touring pitches. In this area of great beauty, miles of sand abound and taking in the panorama of mountain scenery from the top of the Conor Pass is a wonderful experience.

Facilities

Toilet facilities (entry by key) are kept very clean and provide showers on payment (€ 0,50), two private cabins, some low level basins and a toilet with handrail. No facilities for disabled campers. Laundry facilities (incl. drying room, clothes lines and ironing). Campers' kitchen with fridges, freezers and seating. Motorcaravan services. Two play areas. Games and TV rooms. Off site: Beautiful sandy beach 2 minutes. Fishing 2 km. Riding or bicycle hire 3 km. Golf 4 km.

Open: Easter - 30 September.

Directions

From Tralee follow the Dingle coast road for 19 km. Park is signed from Camp junction. GPS: N52:14.646 W09:59.141

Charges 2009

Per unit incl. 2 persons	€ 18.00 - € 20.00
incl. 2 children	€ 22.00 - € 25.00
extra person	€ 2.00 - € 5.00
electricity	€ 2.00
awning	€ 3.00
No credit cards.	

IR9470 Blackwater Valley Caravan & Camping Park

Mallow-Killarney Road, Fermoy (Co. Cork)

Tel: **025 321 47**

www.alanrogers.com/IR9470

The location of this park provides the best of both worlds, as it backs onto green fields adjacent to the Blackwater river, yet is within 200 m. of Fermoy town. Pat and Nora Ryan live overlooking the park which ensures supervision and attention to detail. Ideal for touring, there are 25 pitches with hardstanding and electricity connections (13A) and water supply nearby, and considerable additional space for tents towards the rear of the park. There are five caravan holiday homes to rent. Fermoy provides local amenities, such as a cinema and the town park with a leisure centre with pool and a play area. There are restaurants and pubs, many providing traditional music.

Facilities

Modern, tiled toilet block provides the usual facilities including for disabled visitors. Laundry room with ironing facilities. Campers' kitchen with cooking facilities and dining area. TV and games room. Motorcaravan service point. Off site: Fishing adjacent to park. Bicycle hire 500 m. Golf 3.5 km. Beach 35 km. Internet access 100 m. Petrol station with gas across the road.

Open: 15 March - 31 October.

Directions

In Fermoy town take the N72 for Mallow. The park is 200 m. from the junction.
GPS: N52:08.460 W08:16.700

Charges guide

Per unit incl. 2 persons	€ 17.00
extra person	€ 2.00 - € 5.00
electricity	€ 3.50

No credit cards.

IR9505 The Hideaway Camping & Caravan Park

Skibbereen (Co. Cork)

Tel: **028 222 54**. Email: **skibbereencamping@eircom.net**

www.alanrogers.com/IR9505

A sister park to The Meadow at Glandore, the Hideaway is ideally situated as a touring base for the southwest of Ireland. It is a well run site under the constant supervision of the owners and although it enjoys tranquil surroundings, including preserved marshland, it is only ten minutes walk from the busy market town of Skibbereen. The Hideaway is a touring only park with 60 pitches, including 50 with hardstanding and 6A electric hook-up. The remainder are for tents. Shrubs and low hedges divide the park giving an open feel overall and commanding views across the fields and hills. One long building houses reception, the toilet facilities and a games room.

Facilities

The modern toilet block has non slip floors, well equipped showers (on payment). Baby room with bath. En-suite unit for disabled visitors. Laundry. Campers' dining room. Motorcaravan service point. Adventure play area. Football and cycling not permitted on the park. Off site: Fishing 1.6 km. Golf 2 km. Riding 4 km. Bicycle hire 1 km.

Open: 10 - 19 April, then 1 May - 15 September.

Directions

From Skibbereen town centre take R596 (signed Casteltownsend). Site is on the left after 1 km.
GPS: N51:32.500 W09:15.605

Charges 2009

Per unit incl. 2 persons	€ 20.00
incl. electricity	€ 23.00
extra person	€ 3.00 - € 6.00

No credit cards.

IR9510 Eagle Point Caravan & Camping Park

Ballylickey, Bantry (Co. Cork)

Tel: **027 506 30**. Email: **eaglepointcamping@eircom.net**

www.alanrogers.com/IR9510

Midway between the towns of Bantry and Glengarriff, the spectacular peninsula of Eagle Point juts into Bantry Bay. The first impression is of a spacious country park rather than a campsite. As far as the eye can see this 20 acre, landscaped, part-terraced park, with its vast manicured grass areas separated by mature trees, shrubs and hedges, runs parallel with the shoreline providing lovely views. Suitable for all ages, this is a well run park devoted to touring units, with campers pitched mostly towards the shore. It provides 125 pitches (60 caravans, 65 tents), and electric hook-ups, thus avoiding overcrowding during peak periods.

Facilities

Three well maintained, well designed toilet blocks are above expected standards. Laundry. Motorcaravan services. Play area. Tennis. Football field to the far right, well away from the pitches. Fishing. Supermarket at park entrance. Dogs are not accepted. Off site: Bicycle hire 6 km. Riding 10 km. Golf 2 km.

Open: 24 April - 27 September.

Directions

Take N71 to Bandon, then R586 Bandon to Bantry. From Bantry take N71 to Glengarriif. 6.4 km. from Bantry; park entrance is opposite EMO petrol station.
GPS: N51:43.207 W09:26.977

Charges 2009

Per unit incl. 2 persons	€ 26.00 - € 28.00
child	€ 3.00
motorcyclist, hiker or cyclist (per person)	€ 12.00
electricity (6A)	€ 4.00

Republic of Ireland

311

IR9570 Creveen Lodge Caravan & Camping Park

Healy Pass, Lauragh (Co. Kerry)

Tel: **064 831 31**. Email: **info@creveenlodge.com**

www.alanrogers.com/IR9570

The address of this park is rather confusing, but Healy Pass is the well known scenic summit of the road (R574) crossing the Beara Peninsula, which lies between Kenmare Bay to the north and Bantry Bay to the south. Several kilometres inland from the north coast road (R571), the R574 starts to climb steeply southward towards the Healy Pass. Here, on the mountain foothills, is Creveen Lodge, a working hill farm with a quiet, homely atmosphere. There are 20 pitches, with 16 for tents, 4 for caravans, plus an area of hardstanding for motorcaravans. Electrical connections (5A) are available. To allow easy access, the steep farm track is divided into a simple one-way system. Creveen Lodge, commanding views across Kenmare Bay, is divided among three gently sloping fields separated by trees. The park is carefully tended with neat rubbish bins and rustic picnic tables informally placed. Although not so famed as the Iveragh Peninsula, around which runs the Ring of Kerry, the northern Beara is a scenically striking area of County Kerry. This is walking and climbing countryside or, of interest close by, is Derreen Gardens.

Facilities

Well appointed and immaculately maintained, the small toilet block provides showers on payment (€ 0.65). Communal room with very good cooking facilities, a fridge, freezer, TV, ironing board, fireplace, tables and chairs. Reception is in the farmhouse. Play area. Off site: Water sports, riding, 'Seafare' cruises, shops and a restaurant nearby. Fishing 2 km. Bicycle hire and boat launching 9 km.

Open: Easter - 31 October.

Directions

Park is on the Healy Pass road (R574) 1.5 km. southeast of Lauragh. GPS: N51:45.312 W09:45.615

Charges guide

Per unit incl. 2 persons	€ 16.00
extra person	€ 3.00
child	€ 1.00
electricity (5A)	€ 4.00
No credit cards.	

Creveen Lodge • Caravan & Camping Park

Set in the heart of beautiful scenery of the Ring of Beara

Ideal for walkers, cyclists, climbers and for those who want to relax. Cottage sleeping up to 6 also available. Dogs welcome.

Tel: +353 64 83 131 Web: www.creveenlodge.com

IR9560 Wave Crest Caravan & Camping Park

Caherdaniel (Co. Kerry)

Tel: **066 947 5188**. Email: **wavecrest@eircom.net**

www.alanrogers.com/IR9560

It would be difficult to imagine a more dramatic location than Wave Crest's on the Ring of Kerry coast. Huge boulders and rocky outcrops tumble from the park entrance on the N70 down to the seashore which forms the most southern promontory on the Ring of Kerry. There are spectacular southward views from the park across Kenmare Bay to the Beara peninsula. Sheltering on grass patches in small coves that nestle between the rocks and shrubbery, are 65 hardstanding pitches and 20 on grass offering seclusion. Electricity connections are available (13A). This park would suit older people looking for a quiet, relaxed atmosphere. A unique feature is the TV room, an old stone farm building with a thatched roof. Its comfortable interior includes a stone fireplace heated by a converted cast iron marker buoy. Caherdaniel is known for its cheerful little pubs and distinguished restaurant. The Derrynane National Park Nature Reserve is only a few kilometres away, as is Derrynane Cove and Bay.

Facilities

Two blocks house the sanitary facilities and include hot showers on payment (⇔1). Toilet for disabled people. Laundry service. Small shop and takeaway service (May - Sept). Play area. Fishing and boat launching. Off site: Riding 1 km. Bicycle hire and golf 10 km. Small beach near and Derrynane Hotel with bar and restaurant.

Open: 27 April - 30 September.

Directions

On the N70 (Ring of Kerry), 1.5 km. east of Caherdaniel. GPS: N51:45.496 W10:05.325

Charges guide

Per person	€ 2.00
child	€ 1.00
pitch	€ 12.00 - € 13.00
electricity (13A)	€ 2.00

IR9610 Mannix Point Camping & Caravan Park

Cahirciveen (Co. Kerry)

Tel: 066 947 2806. Email: mortimer@campinginkerry.com   www.alanrogers.com/IR9610

A tranquil, beautifully located seashore park, it is no exaggeration to describe Mannix Point as a nature lovers' paradise. Situated in one of the most spectacular parts of the Ring of Kerry, overlooking the bay and Valentia Island, the seven acre park commands splendid views in all directions. The park road meanders through the level site and offers 42 pitches of various sizes and shape, many with shelter and seclusion. There are 36 electrical connections (13A) available. A charming, flower bedecked old fisherman's cottage has been converted to provide facilities including reception, a cosy sitting room with turf fire, and an 'emergency' dormitory for campers is a feature. There is no television, but compensation comes in the form of a knowledgeable, hospitable owner who is a Bord Fáilte registered local tour guide. A keen gardener, Mortimer Moriarty laid out the site over 20 years ago and his intention to cause as little disruption to nature as possible has succeeded. The site opens directly onto marshland which teems with wildlife (a two acre nature reserve) with direct access to the beach and seashore. This park retains a wonderful air of Irish charm aided by occasional impromptu musical evenings. A viewing platform allows observation of seals and birdlife and to consider the secrets of the park sculpture, 'the pinicle'. This is also an ideal resting place for people walking the Kerry Way.

Facilities

Toilet and shower facilities were immaculate when we visited. Modern and well equipped campers' kitchen and dining area. Laundry facilities with washing machines and dryer. Motorcaravan service point. Picnic and barbecue facilities. Off site: Bicycle hire 800 m. Riding 3 km. Golf 14 km. Pubs, restaurants and shops 15 minutes walk. Watersports, bird watching, walking and photography. Local cruises to Skelligs Rock with free transport to and from the port for walkers and cyclists.

Open: 15 March - 1 October.

Directions

Park is 300 m. off the N70 Ring of Kerry road, 800 m. southwest of Cahirciveen (or Cahersiveen) on the road towards Waterville.
GPS: N51:56.571 W10:14.607

Charges guide

Per person	€ 6.00
child (1 or 2 children)	€ 2.00

Reductions for activity groups and rallies if pre-paid. No credit cards.

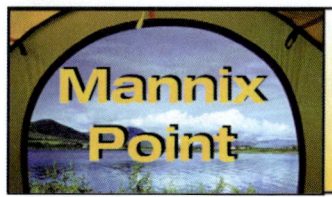

Would you like to wake up in the morning and have a view like this without getting out of your bed?

Mannix Point is a special place. Stay with us and discover why.

Telephone: **00353 66 9472806**

www.campinginkerry.com   mortimer@campinginkerry.com

IR9580 Beara Camping The Peacock

Coornagillagh, Tuosist, Post Killarney (Co. Kerry)

Tel: 064 842 87. Email: campingthepeacock@eircom.net   www.alanrogers.com/IR9580

Five minutes from Kenmare Bay, The Peacock is a unique location for campers who would appreciate the natural surroundings of a campsite where disturbance to nature is kept to a minimum. This five acre site offers simple, clean and imaginative camping facilities. Located on the Ring of Beara, bordering the counties of Cork and Kerry, visitors will be treated with hospitality by a Dutch couple, almost more Irish than the Irish, who have made Ireland their home and run the site with their family and Kleintje, the pot-bellied Vietnamese pig. The variety of accommodation at Beara Camping includes the hostel, caravan holiday homes, secluded hardstanding pitches with electricity and level grass areas for tenting. Bert and Klaske are only too anxious to share with visitors the unspoiled natural terrain, the local wildlife, the opportunity of a cosy sheltered campfire and advice on the walking and hiking routes in the area aided by maps provided on loan.

Facilities

Three small blocks, plus facilities at the restaurant provide toilets, washbasins and free hot showers. Laundry service for a small fee. Campers' kitchens and sheltered eating area. Small shop (May - Oct). Restaurant and takeaway (May - Oct). Bicycle hire. Off site: Public transport from the gate during the summer months. Pub 900 m. Riding 6 km. Golf 12 km. Boating, fishing and sea angling 200 m. Beach (pebble) 500 m.

Open: All year.

Directions

From the A22, 17 km. east of Killarney, take the R569 south to Kenmare. In Kenmare take the R571 Castletownbere road and site is 12 km.

Charges guide

Per unit incl. 2 persons	€ 12.50 - € 17.50
extra person	€ 3.00
child (4-10 yrs)	€ 1.75
electricity	€ 2.50

IR9590 Fossa Caravan & Camping Park

Fossa, Killarney (Co. Kerry)

Tel: **064 663 1497**. Email: fossaholidays@eircom.net   www.alanrogers.com/IR9590

This mature, well equipped park is in a scenic location, ten minutes drive from the town centre. Fossa Caravan Park is recognisable by its forecourt on which stands a distinctive building with reception area and shop. The well laid out park is divided in two – the touring area lies to the right, tucked behind the main building and to the left is an open grass area mainly for campers. Touring pitches, with electricity and drainage, have hardstanding and are angled between shrubs and trees in a tranquil, well cared for garden setting. To the rear at a higher level and discreetly placed are 30 caravan holiday homes. Sheltered by the thick foliage of the wooded slopes which climb high behind the park, these are unobtrusive. Not only is Fossa convenient for Killarney (5.5 km), it is also en-route for the famed Ring of Kerry, and makes an ideal base for walkers and golfers.

Facilities

Modern toilet facilities kept spotlessly clean include showers on payment. Laundry room. Campers' kitchen. Shop. Takeaway (8/7-25/8). TV lounge. Tennis. Play area. Picnic area. Games room. Security patrol. Off site: Fishing and golf 2 km. Riding 3 km. Bicycle hire 5 km.

Open: 1 April - 30 September.

Directions

Approaching Killarney from all directions, follow signs for N72 Ring of Kerry/Killorglin. At last roundabout join R562/N72. Continue for 5.5 km. and Fossa is the second park to the right. GPS: N52:04.246 W09:35.147

Charges 2009

Per person	€ 6.00
child (under 14 yrs)	€ 2.50
pitch	€ 8.00 - € 10.00
electricity (10/15A)	€ 4.00

IR9620 Fleming's White Bridge

Ballycasheen Road, Killarney (Co. Kerry)

Tel: **064 663 1590**. Email: info@killarneycamping.com   www.alanrogers.com/IR9620

Once past the county border, the main road from Cork to Killarney (N22) runs down the valley of the Flesk river. On the final approach to Killarney off the N22 Cork road, the river veers away from the road to enter the Lower Lake. On this prime rural position, between the road and the river, and within comfortable walking distance of the town, is Fleming's White Bridge, a nine acre woodland park. The ground is flat, landscaped and generously adorned with flowers, shrubs and trees. There are now 92 pitches (46 caravans and 46 tents) that extend beyond a wooden bridge to an area surrounded by mature trees. A new toilet block, one of three, is sited in this area.

Facilities

Three toilet blocks are maintained to high standards. Motorcaravan service point. Campers' drying room and two laundries. Shop (1/6-1/9). Two TV rooms and a games room. Fishing (advice and permits provided). Canoeing (own canoes). Bicycle hire. Woodland walks. Off site: Riding 3 km. Golf 2 km.

Open: 9 April - 5 October, 23-26 October.

Directions

From Cork and Mallow: at N72/N22 junction continue towards Killarney and take first turn left (signed Ballycasheen Road). Proceed for 300 m. to archway entrance on left. From Limerick: follow N22 Cork road. Pass Super Valu and The Heights Hotel take first right (signed Ballycasheen Road) and continue as above. From Kenmare: On N71, pass Gleneagles Hotel and Flesk Bridge. Turn right at traffic lights into Woodlawn Road and Ballycasheen Road and continue 2 km. to archway. GPS: N52:03.372 W09:28.463

Charges 2009

Per unit incl. 2 persons	€ 27.00 - € 28.00
child (under 14 yrs)	€ 3.00
hiker, cyclist and tent	€ 10.00 - € 11.00
electricity (10A)	€ 5.00
No credit cards.	

IR9650 Woodlands Park Touring Caravan & Camping Park

Dan Spring Road, Tralee (Co. Kerry)

Tel: **066 712 1235**. Email: **wdlands@eircom.net**   www.alanrogers.com/IR9650

This family run park is located in the heart of Kerry, on the gateway to the Dingle peninsula and just north of the Ring of Kerry and Killarney. Woodlands is an ideal base, only ten minutes walk from Tralee town centre via the town park and famous rose garden. Located on a 16 acre elevated site approached by a short road and bridge that straddles the River Lee, once on site the town seems far removed with a countryside environment taking over. Hedging, trees, grazing fields and the distant Slieve Mish Mountain create the setting. There are 135 pitches including 85 'super' pitches with hardstanding, electricity, water and drainage to the left and centre behind the main building. A grass area for 50 tents is to the right. The park has a landscaped entrance using tropical shrubs and cordyline trees and flower beds have been planted around the park. The owners of Woodlands have designed and equipped their park to a high standard including a clubhouse. The town park is home to the Kerry County Museum and 'Siamsa Tíre', the National Folk Theatre of Ireland with nightly performances. In addition to the river, there is a canal bank walk to Blennerville Windmill.

Facilities

Excellent, heated sanitary facilities include sizeable showers (€ 1 token) and provision for disabled guests. Campers' kitchen. Laundry room with washing machines and dryer. Motorcaravan service point. Club house with café/snack bar. Shop. Games room. TV and adult only room. Internet access. Fenced adventure play area. Off site: The nearby Aqua Dome offers half price admission after 18.00. Golf 6 km. Riding 2 km. Blue Flag beaches on the Dingle Peninsula. Sailing 10 km.

Open: Easter - 30 September.

Directions

Site is 1 km. southwest of Tralee town centre. From N21/N69/N86 junction south of Tralee follow site signs for 2.4 km. to park, 200 m. off the N86 Tralee - Dingle road. Site is 300 m. east of the Aqua Dome GPS: N52:15.673 W09:42.219

Charges guide

Per unit incl. 2 persons	€ 15.50 - € 23.00
extra person	€ 6.00
child (under 16 yrs)	€ 2.00 - € 3.00
electricity (10A)	€ 4.00

Woodlands Park
Touring Caravan & Camping Park

Phone:
0035 3667121235

Email: wdlands@eircom.net
www.kingdomcamping.com

★ ★ ★ ★

Alan Rogers Motorhome Award 2007
Failte Ireland Best Large Park 2007
Best National 4-Star Park 1999, 2000, 2003
Park of the year 2005

IR9600 Glenross Caravan & Camping Park

Glenbeigh (Co. Kerry)

Tel: **066 976 8451**. Email: **glenross@eircom.net**   www.alanrogers.com/IR9600

Its situation on the spectacular Ring of Kerry and the Kerry Way gives Glenross an immediate advantage, and scenic grandeur around every bend of the road is guaranteed as Glenbeigh is approached. Quietly located before entering the village, the park commands a stunning view of Rossbeigh Strand, which is within walking distance. On arrival, a good impression is created with the park well screened from the road and with new stone entrance and gates. With 30 touring pitches, all with hardstanding and electricity, and 6 caravan holiday homes, the park is attractively laid out. There is no catering on site but the Glenbeigh Hotel next door is popular and village shops are near. Not least is Kerry Bog Village where you can go back in time in this reconstructed pre-famine village.

Facilities

Well maintained modern toilet block includes facilities for laundry and dishwashing. Motorcaravan service point. Games room. Bicycle hire. Shelter for campers and new dining area. Off site: Playground at Rossbeigh beach (5 minutes). Watersports and tennis near. Riding and fishing 200 m. Golf 500 m.

Open: 1 May - 23 September.

Directions

Park is on the N70 Killorglin - Glenbeigh road, on the right just before entering the village. GPS: N52:03.524 W09:55.914

Charges 2009

Per person	€ 8.00
child (under 14 yrs)	€ 3.00
pitch	€ 8.00 - € 9.00
electricity (10A)	€ 5.00
No credit cards.	

IR9630 Donoghues White Villa Farm Caravan & Camping Park

Killarney - Cork Road N22, Killarney (Co. Kerry)

Tel: 064 662 0671. Email: killarneycamping@eircom.net www.alanrogers.com/IR9630

This is a very pleasing small touring park in scenic surroundings on the N22 Killarney - Cork road. Set in the countryside surrounded by green fields, yet is only five minutes away from Killarney town. Trees and shrubs surround the park but dominant is a magnificent view of the MacGillicuddy's Reeks. There are 30 pitches for caravans and tents, 20 with hardstanding and a grass area for awnings, electricity (10A), water points and night lighting. One is designated for disabled campers. An unusual novelty is old school desks placed around the site, plus an antique green telephone box. One can also enjoy walking through the oak wood, fishing on the Flesk or visiting the site's own National Farm Museum.

Facilities

The toilet block, a sandstone coloured building, is kept spotlessly clean and houses showers on payment, a good toilet/shower room for disabled visitors, laundry room and dishwashing sinks. Motorcaravan service area. Campers' kitchen with TV. Play area. Bicycle hire. Max. 2 dogs per pitch (not certain breeds). Daily coach tours from park. Off site: Riding, golf and boat launching 3 km. Pub/restaurant 1 km. Killarney town 5 minutes, the National Park is 10 minutes away.

Open: 9 April - 5 October.

Directions

Park is 3 km. east from Killarney town on the N22 Cork road. Park entrance is 500 m. east of N22/N72 junction. From Killarney follow N22 Cork road signs and White Villa Farm finger signs from Park Road roundabout. From Kenmare take R569 via Kilgarvan to the N22, or N71 to Killarney, then the N22 Cork road. GPS: N52:02.837 W09:27.224

Charges guide

Per person	€ 6.00
child	€ 3.00
pitch	€ 6.00 - € 7.00
electricity	€ 4.00

No credit cards.
Seven nights for the price of six.

IR9640 Killarney Flesk Caravan & Camping Park

Muckross Road, Killarney (Co. Kerry)

Tel: 064 317 04. Email: killarneylakes@eircom.net www.alanrogers.com/IR9640

At the gateway to the National Park and Lakes, near Killarney town, this family run, seven acre park has undergone extensive development and offers high quality standards. Pitches are well spaced and have electricity (10A), water, and drainage connections; 21 also have hardstanding with a grass area for awnings. The grounds have been well cultivated with further shrubs, plants and an attractive barbecue and patio area. This is to the left of the sanitary block and is paved and sunk beneath the level road. Surrounded by a garden border, it has tables and chairs, making a pleasant communal meeting place commanding excellent views of Killarney's mountains.

Facilities

Modern, clean toilet blocks are well designed and equipped. Baby room. Laundry room. Campers' kitchen. Comfortable games room. Night time security checks. Winter caravan storage. Off site: Adjacent hotel (same ownership) with bar and restaurant. Fishing 300 m. Boat launching 2 km.

Open: 17 April - 30 September.

Directions

From Killarney town centre follow the N71 and signs for Killarney National Park. Site is 1.5 km. on the left beside the Gleneagle Hotel. GPS: N52:02.594 W09:29.921

Charges guide

Per person	€ 8.00
child (under 14 yrs)	€ 3.00
pitch	€ 8.00 - € 9.00
electricity (10A)	€ 5.00

MAP 9

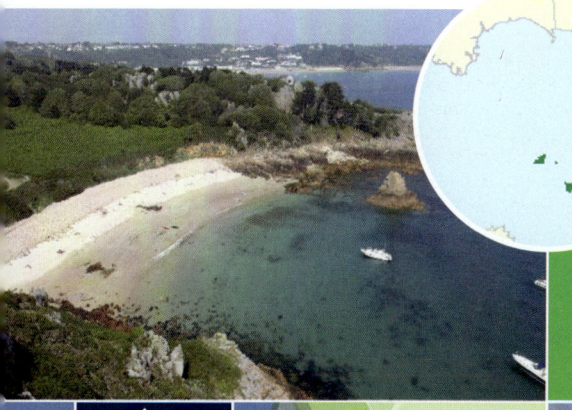

A visit to the Channel Islands offers a holiday in part of the British Isles, yet in an area which has a definite continental flavour. All the islands have beautiful beaches and coves, pretty scenery and fascinating histories.

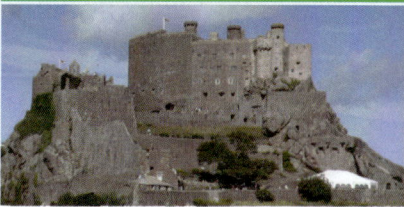

THE CHANNEL ISLANDS ARE MADE UP OF THE ISLANDS OF: JERSEY, GUERNSEY, SARK, HERM AND ALDERNEY

The largest of the Channel Islands is Jersey, which is also the most commercial with more entertainment on offer. It has long stretches of safe beaches for swimming and water-based activities such as windsurfing and banana rides. Caravans and motor caravans are allowed on Jersey, but with a number of limitations (for example, length of stay, width and length of the unit). A permit is required which is obtained as part of the booking procedure with the campsite of your choice. You must book in advance but the campsite owner will advise you on all aspects of your visit.

Guernsey will suit those who prefer a quieter, more peaceful holiday. Caravans and motorcaravans are not allowed here. Guernsey too has wide, sandy beaches plus sheltered coves. The historic, harbour town of St Peter Port has steep and winding cobbled streets, with plenty of shops, cafes and restaurants.

For those who want total relaxation, one of the smaller islands – Sark or Herm, would be ideal. No cars are permitted on either of these islands. Explore on foot, by cycle or horse-drawn carriage.

Shopping on all the islands has the advantage of no VAT – particularly useful when buying cameras, watches or alcohol.

Places of interest

Jersey: St Helier; Jersey Zoo; Jersey War tunnels; Elizabeth Castle; German Underground Hospital in St Lawrence; Samarès Manor in St Clement; Shell Garden at St Aubin; Battle of Flowers Museum in St Ouen.

Guernsey: Castle Cornet at St Peter Port Harbour; Victor Hugo's House; Guernsey Folk Museum; German Occupation Museum; Fort Grey Shipwreck Museum; Saumarez Park.

Sark: La Coupée; La Seigneurie, with old dovecote and gardens; Gouliet and Boutique Caves; Le Pot on Little Sark; Venus Pool; Little Sark Village.

Herm: This tiny island has beautiful, quiet, golden beaches and a little harbour village and hotel. Arrive by ferry from Guernsey for a wonderful day out.

Did you know?

Jersey has been associated with knitting for nearly 400 years.

The Channel Islands were the only part of the British Isles to be occupied by the Germans during the Second World War.

The first road side letterboxes in the British Isles were erected in St Helier on 23rd November 1852.

Herm island is just one and a half miles long and only half a mile wide.

Le Jerriais is the native language of Jersey, a blend of Norse and Norman French.

UK9710 Rozel Camping Park

Rozel, Saint Martin, Jersey JE3 6AX

Tel: 01534 855200. Email: rozelcampingpark@jerseymail.co.uk

www.alanrogers.com/UK9710

This family owned park is within walking distance of the famous Jersey Zoo and the pretty harbour and fishing village of Rozel, where the north coast cliff path commences. The surrounding countryside is quieter than many areas of the island. The park itself is quietly situated at the top of a valley (the French coast can be seen on a clear day) and is surrounded by trees providing shelter. There are two main camping areas providing 130 pitches of which 120 have electricity hook ups (10/16A) and 16 are used for fully equipped tents to hire. Some pitches, mainly for smaller tents are arranged on terraced areas. The remainder are on a higher, flat field where pitches are arranged in bays with hedges growing to separate them into groups.

Facilities

Two first rate, heated sanitary buildings include a bathroom for disabled people with a shower, toilet and washbasin. Family shower room with small heater for cooler weather. Fully equipped laundry. Shop. Takeaway (peak season). Swimming pool (June-Sept) with children's pool and sunbathing areas. Play area. Crazy golf. Games room, reading and TV room. Torches useful. Bicycles for hire can be delivered to the site. Off site: Fishing 1 mile. Beach 2 miles. Riding 3 miles. Golf 4 miles.

Open: 21 May - 9 September.

Directions

Leave harbour by Route du Port Elizabeth, take the A1 east through the tunnel and the A17. At fourth set of lights turn left on A6. Keep in the middle lane. Continue to Five Oaks and on to St Martin's church. Turn right, then immediately left at the 'Royal' pub on B38 to Rozel, continue to end of road, turn right to park. GPS: N49:14.305 W02:03.035

Charges guide

Per person	£ 7.60 - £ 9.00
child (4-11 yrs)	£ 3.80 - £ 4.50
electricity	£ 1.80

UK9720 Beuvelande Camp Site

Beuvelande, Saint Martin, Jersey JE3 6EZ

Tel: 01534 853575. Email: info@campingjersey.com

www.alanrogers.com/UK9720

What a pleasant surprise we had when we called here – the outstanding sanitary building gives campers facilities often associated with top class hotels. A licensed restaurant with covered terrace area is also situated in this building, open morning and evening all season, but perhaps a few less hours at quiet times. There are 150 pitches, 60 with fully equipped tents for hire, but with plenty of space for those with their own. Cars may be parked next to your tent. 100 pitches have electric hook ups (5/10A). Torches would be useful. Car and bicycle hire can be arranged. This family run park prides itself on quality, cleanliness and hospitality.

Facilities

The toilet block is tiled and spotlessly clean, with controllable showers, two fully equipped bathrooms for disabled visitors, and a baby room. Laundry facilities. Games room. TV room. Well stocked shop open 08.00-19.00 during peak times and stocks gas. Licensed restaurant. Outdoor heated swimming pool (41 x 17 ft) with a sun terrace and small waterslide. Play area and large playing field. Evening entertainment. Off site: Beach and sailing 1.5 miles. Fishing, golf or riding within 2 miles.

Open: 1 April - 30 September.

Directions

On leaving the harbour by Route du Port Elizabeth, take A1 east through the tunnel and the A17. At the fourth set of traffic lights turn left on A6. Continue to Five Oaks and on to St Martin's RC church, then right into La Longue Rue, right again Rue de L'Orme then left to site. GPS: N49:12.776 W02:03.369

Charges guide

Per person	£ 6.00 - £ 9.00
child (2-14 yrs)	£ 6.00

Single sex groups not accepted.

UK9770 Vaugrat Camping

Route de Vaugrat, Saint Sampson's, Guernsey GY2 4TA

Tel: **01481 257468**. Email: **enquiries@vaugratcampsite.com**   **www.alanrogers.com/UK9770**

Vaugrat Camping is a neat, well tended site, close to the beach in the northwest of the island. Owned and well run by the Laine family, it is centred around attractive and interesting old granite farm buildings dating back to the 15th century, with a gravel courtyard and attractive flower beds. It provides 150 pitches (6 with electricity) on flat grassy meadows, that are mostly surrounded by trees, banks and hedges to provide shelter. Tents are arranged around the edges of the fields, giving open space in the centre, and while pitches are not marked, there is sufficient room and cars may be parked next to tents. Only couples and families are accepted. It also offers 30 fully equipped tents for hire. Housed in the old farmhouse, now a listed building, are the reception area, and shop where fresh croissants are baked every morning. Upstairs is the Coffee Barn and TV room, with views to the sea, where breakfast is served; one can also sit here in the evenings. There are plans to include caravans and motorhomes subject to permission.

Facilities

Well kept sanitary facilities are in two buildings. The first block is in the courtyard, with hot showers on payment. Unit for disabled visitors with shower, basin and toilet (although there is a 6 inch step into the building). Laundry facilities. Second block near the camping fields provides toilets, washbasins and dishwashing facilities. Shop with ice pack hire and gas (open at certain times by arrangement). Café serving breakfast only. Dogs are not accepted. Torches may be useful. Off site: Bus service within easy reach. Car or bicycle hire can be arranged. Fishing, riding and golf within 1.5 miles. Hotel and bar nearby.

Open: May - September.

Directions

On leaving St Peter Port, turn right onto coast road for 1.5 miles. At filter turn left into Vale Road. Straight over at two sets of lights then first left turn by church. Follow to crossroads (garage opposite) turn right. Carry on past Peninsula Hotel, then second left, signed for site. Site on left after high stone wall (400 yds) with concealed entrance. GPS: N49:29.750 W02:33.259

Charges guide

Per person	£ 7.50
child (under 14 yrs)	£ 5.95
car or boat	£ 1.40

Families and couples only.
Fully equipped tents to hire (details from site).

UK9780 Fauxquets Valley Farm Campsite

Castel, Guernsey GY5 7QA

Tel: **01481 255460**. Email: **info@fauxquets.co.uk**   **www.alanrogers.com/UK9780**

Situated in the rural centre of the island, Fauxquets is in a pretty sheltered valley, hidden down narrow lanes away from busy roads and is run by the Guille family. A car would be useful here to reach the beaches, St Peter Port and other attractions, although there is a bus service each day (20 minutes walk). It was once a dairy farm, but the valley side has now been developed into an attractive campsite, with the old farm buildings as its centre. Plenty of trees, bushes and flowers have been planted to separate pitches and to provide shelter around the various fields which are well terraced. The 86 touring pitches are of a good size, most marked, numbered and with electricity, and there is lots of open space. There are also 15 smaller places for backpackers. The site has 23 fully equipped tents for hire, but there are no tour operators. The Haybarn licensed restaurant and bar provides breakfast, morning coffee and cake and evening meals. There is plenty of room to sit around the heated swimming pool, including a large grassy terrace with sun beds provided.

Facilities

Good toilet facilities have controllable showers, some washbasins in private cabins with a shower, baby bath and changing unit. Dishwashing under cover and a tap for free hot water. Laundry room with free irons, boards and hairdryers. Heated swimming pool (20 x 45 ft) with paddling pool. Restaurant and bar (25/6-7/9). Small shop with ice pack hire and gas. TV room. Table football and table tennis. Small play area and play field. Bicycle hire. Torches useful. Off site: Riding and golf 2 miles. Fishing, sailing and boat launching 3 miles.

Open: May - 15 September.

Directions

From harbour take second exit from roundabout. At top of hill, turn left at 'filter in turn' into Queens Road, then right at next filter. Follow straight through traffic lights and down hill past hospital, through pedestrian lights and straight on at next lights at top of hill. Continue for 0.75 miles, then turn right opposite sign for German Hospital. Fourth left is pedestrian entrance, cars carry on for 400 yds to gravel entrance on left. GPS: N49:28.087 W02:35.305

Charges guide

Per person	£ 5.50 - £ 6.80
child (at school)	£ 2.75 - £ 3.40
electricity (6A)	£ 2.50

Fully equipped tents with fridge for hire.

319

UK9830 Seagull Campsite

The Administration Office, Herm Island GY1 3HR

Tel: **01481 722377**. Email: **camping@herm-island.com**   **www.alanrogers.com/UK9830**

This tiny site, and indeed the island of Herm, will appeal to those who are looking for complete tranquillity and calm. Reached by boat (20 minutes and about £8.50 return fare for adults, £4.25 for children) from Guernsey, the 300 acre island allows no cars only tractors on its narrow roads and paths (no bicycles either). One is free to stroll around the many paths, through farmland, heath and around the coast, where there are beautiful beaches. The campsite is a 20 minute uphill walk from the harbour, but your luggage will be transported for you by tractor. It consists of several terraced areas offering a total of 90 pitches, and 26 fully equipped tents for hire on flat grass areas. There are no electricity hook-ups. One may bring one's own tent and equipment or hire both (but not bedding, crockery and lighting) from the site. Herm is definitely not for those who like entertainment and plenty of facilities, but for total relaxation, with the absence of any bustle and noise it takes some beating! Due to the stony footpaths on Herm, sensible walking shoes are advised.

Facilities

Small, modern, but open, toilet block. Hot showers (£1 payment – there is a shortage of water on Herm). Laundry facility and small kitchen. Freezer for ice-packs. No dogs or pets are allowed. Torches useful. Off site: The harbour village is about ten minutes walk for small shop, gas, a post office, pub, restaurants and café. Fishing on the island.

Open: May - first w/end in September.

Directions

Reached by boat from St Peter Port – report to Administration Office on arrival. Do not take your car as it is unlikely you will be able to park long term in St Peter Port. GPS: N49:28.599 W02:27.398

Charges guide

Per person	£ 5.60
child (under 14 yrs)	£ 2.80
transportation of luggage	£ 7.00

Equipped tents for hire.
Groups of single people not accepted.

UK9870 Pomme de Chien Campsite

Sark GY9 0SB

Tel: **01481 832316**. Email: **ranghill@hotmail.com**   **www.alanrogers.com/UK9870**

The island where 'time stands still' is an apt description of Sark, one of the smallest inhabited Channel Islands, some 45 minutes from Guernsey by boat. Situated five minutes from the shops and ten from the beach, the Pomme de Chien campsite is small with only 50 pitches, of which 8 are occupied by fully equipped tents for rent. The remainder are for campers with their own tents (no caravans, motorcaravans or trailer tents of course). The pitches are large, on fairly level ground, but none have electricity hook-ups. There is a warm welcome from the owners Chris and Jill Rang with the famous charm of Sark. Although you cannot take your car to the island, the Condor service via Guernsey means you can get there in a little over three hours either with your own small tent or of course you could hire one of the site's own (equipment includes everything you're likely to need except bedding and a torch).There is no airport, no cars or motorcycles and (apart from a tractor-drawn land-train up Harbour Hill) the only transport is by bicycle (which must be hired on the island) or horse-drawn carriage. However, all you are likely to need for a tranquil holiday is provided with several small shops, pubs, hotels, restaurants, a Tourist Office and even two banks!

Facilities

Modern sanitary block with free hot showers (large, with bench and hook), toilets and washbasins. Outside washing line. Dogs are not accepted. Torches are necessary. Baggage can be transferred from the harbour to the site by tractor trailer, at a cost of £1 per item. Off site: Bicycle hire 5 minutes. Beach and fishing 10 minutes walk.

Open: May - October.

Directions

Take the tractor drawn 'train' up Harbour Hill (90p; you can walk but it is a ten minute hike). Once at the top take road leading off left, then second right, and follow the lane to the site entrance. Reception is at house with white gates. GPS: N49:26.199 W02:21.798

Charges 2009

Per person	£ 6.50
child	£ 4.50

No credit cards.

Holiday Caravans and Chalets

Over recent years many of the campsites featured in this guide have added large numbers of high quality caravan holiday homes, chalets and lodges. Many park owners believe that some former caravanners and motorcaravanners have been enticed by the extra comfort this type of accommodation can now provide, and that maybe this is the ideal solution to combine the freedom of camping with all the comforts of home.

Quality is consistently high and, although the exact size and inventory will vary from park to park, if you choose any of the parks detailed here, you can be sure that you're staying in some of the best quality and best value caravan holiday homes or chalets available.

Home comforts are provided and typically these include a fridge with freezer compartment, gas hob, proper shower – often a microwave and CD player too, but do check for details. All caravan holiday homes and chalets come fully equipped with a good range of kitchen utensils, pots and pans, crockery, cutlery and outdoor furniture. Many even have an attractive wooden sundeck or paved terrace – a perfect spot for outdoors eating or relaxing with a book and watching the world go by. An efficient heating system is invariably included and some models may also incorporate air conditioning.

Regardless of model, colourful soft furnishings are the norm and a generally breezy décor helps to provide a real holiday feel.

Although some parks may have a large number of different accommodation types, we have restricted our choice to one or two of the most popular accommodation units (either caravan holiday homes or chalets) for each of the parks listed.

The caravan holiday homes here will be of modern design, and recent innovations such as pitched roofs undeniably improve their appearance.

Design will invariably include clever use of space and fittings/furniture to provide for comfortable holidays – usually light and airy, with big windows and patio-style doors, fully equipped kitchen areas, a shower room with shower, washbasin and WC, cleverly designed bedrooms and a comfortable lounge/dining area (often incorporating a sofa bed).

In general, modern campsite chalets incorporate all the best features of caravan holiday homes in a more traditional, wood-clad structure, sometimes with the advantage of an upper mezzanine floor for an additional bedroom.

Our selected parks offer a massive range of different types of caravan holiday home and chalet, and it would be impractical to inspect every single accommodation unit. Our selection criteria, therefore, primarily takes account of the quality standards of the campsite itself.

However, there are a couple of important ground rules:

- FEATURED CARAVAN HOLIDAY HOMES MUST BE NO MORE THAN 5 YEARS OLD

- CHALETS NO MORE THAN 10 YEARS OLD

- ALL LISTED ACCOMMODATION MUST, OF COURSE, FULLY CONFORM WITH ALL APPLICABLE LOCAL, NATIONAL AND EUROPEAN SAFETY LEGISLATION

For each park we given details of the type, or types, of accommodation available to rent, but these details are necessarily quite brief. Sometimes internal layouts can differ quite substantially, particularly with regard to sleeping arrangements, where these include the flexible provision for 'extra persons' on sofa beds located in the living area. These arrangements may vary from accommodation to accommodation, and if you're planning a holiday which includes more people than are catered for by the main bedrooms you should check exactly how the extra sleeping arrangements are to be provided!

Charges

An indication of the tariff for each type of accommodation featured is also included, indicating the variance between the low and high season tariffs. However, given that many parks have a large and often complex range of pricing options, incorporating special deals and various discounts, the charges we mention should be taken to be just an indication. We strongly recommend therefore that you confirm the actual cost when making a booking.

We also strongly recommend that you check with the park, when booking, what (if anything) will be provided by way of bed linen, blankets, pillows etc. Again, in our experience, this can vary widely from park to park.

On every park a fully refundable deposit (usually between £100 and £250) is payable on arrival. There may also be an optional cleaning service for which a further charge is made. Other options may include sheet hire (typically £20 per unit) or baby pack hire (cot and high chair).

UK0380 Wooda Farm Holiday Park

Poughill, Bude EX23 9HJ (Cornwall)
Tel: **01288 352069**. Email: **enquiries@wooda.co.uk**

▶ see report page 41

www.alanrogers.com/UK0380

AR1 – CEDAR – Mobile Home

Sleeping: 3 bedrooms, sleeps 6: 2 double, 2 single beds

Living: living/kitchen area, heating, TV, radio, shower & separate wc

Eating: fitted kitchen with hobs, microwave, oven, grill, fridge/freezer

Outside: table & chairs

Pets: not accepted

AR2 – TREGEA COTTAGE – Bungalow

Sleeping: 2 bedrooms, sleeps 4: 1 double, 2 single beds, pillows & blankets provided

Living: living/kitchen area, heating, TV, radio, shower & separate wc

Eating: fitted kithcen with hobs, microwave, oven, grill, dish washer, fridge/freezer

Outside: table & chairs

Pets: not accepted

Other (for AR1 and AR2): cot and highchair for rent

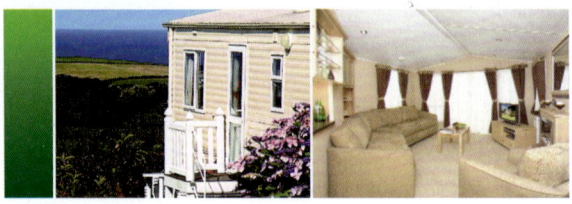

Open: 1 April - 31 October

Weekly Charge	AR1	AR2
Low Season *(from)*	£ 290	£ 295
High Season *(from)*	£ 735	£ 795

UK0790 Harford Bridge Holiday Park

Peter Tavy, Tavistock PL19 9LS (Devon)
Tel: **01822 810349**. Email: **enquiry@harfordbridge.co.uk**

▶ see report page 55

www.alanrogers.com/UK0790

AR1 – 13 CARAVAN HOLIDAY HOMES – Mobile Home

Sleeping: 2/3 bedrooms, sleeps 4/6: 1 double, 2/4 single beds, pillows & blankets provided

Living: living/kitchen area, heating, TV, radio, shower & separate wc

Eating: fitted kitchen with hobs, microwave, oven, grill, coffee machine, fridge/freezer

Outside: table & chairs

Pets: accepted (with supplement)

AR2 – VIXEN TOR LODGE – Bungalow

Sleeping: 2 bedrooms, sleeps 4: 1 double, 2 single beds, pillows & blankets provided

Living: living/kitchen area, heating, TV, radio, shower & separate wc

Eating: fitted kitchen with hobs, microwave, oven, grill, coffee machine, fridge/freezer

Outside: table & chairs

Pets: accepted (with supplement)

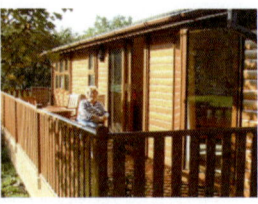

Open: All Year

Weekly Charge	AR1	AR2
Low Season *(from)*	£ 255	£ 325
High Season *(from)*	£ 463	£ 535

UK0970 Cofton Country Holidays

▶ see report page 69

Starcross, Dawlish EX6 8RP (Devon)

Tel: **01626 890111**. Email: **info@coftonholidays.co.uk**

www.alanrogers.com/UK0970

AR1 – EASTDON – Bungalow

Sleeping: 3 bedrooms, sleeps 6: 2 double, 2 single beds, pillows & blankets provided

Living: living/kitchen area, heating, TV, shower & wc

Eating: fitted kitchen with hobs, microwave, oven, grill, dishwasher, coffee machine, fridge

Outside: table & chairs

Pets: not accepted

AR2 – EXE – Mobile Home

Sleeping: 3 bedrooms, sleeps 7: 1 double, 4 single beds, sofa bed, pillows provided

Living: living/kitchen area, heating, TV, shower & wc

Eating: fitted kitchen with hobs, microwave, oven, grill, coffee machine, fridge

Pets: not accepted

Open: All year		
Weekly Charge	AR1	AR2
Low Season (from)	£ 349	£ 275
High Season (from)	£ 695	£ 679

UK1780 Freshwater Beach Holiday Park

▶ see report page 97

Burton Bradstock, Bridport DT6 4PT (Dorset)

Tel: **01308 897317**. Email: **enquiries@freshwaterbeach.co.uk**

www.alanrogers.com/UK1780

AR1 – BUDGET – Mobile Home

Sleeping: 3 bedrooms, sleeps 6: 1 double, 4 single beds, pillows & blankets provided

Living: living/kitchen area, heating, TV, shower & separate wc

Eating: fitted kitchen with hobs, cooker, microwave, oven, grill, fridge/freezer

Outside: table & chairs

Pets: not accepted

AR2 – SUPER DELUXE – Mobile Home

Sleeping: 3 bedrooms, sleeps 6: 1 double, 4 single beds, pillows & blankets provided

Living: living/kitchen area, heating, TV, radio, shower & separate wc

Eating: fitted kitchen with hobs, microwave, oven, grill, fridge/freezer

Outside: table & chairs

Pets: not accepted

Other (for AR1 and AR2): bed linen for rent

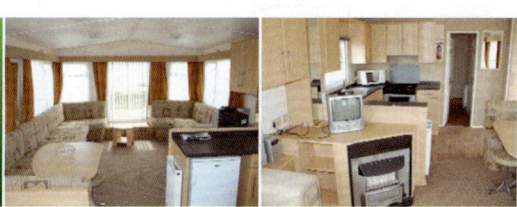

Open: 17 March - 12 November		
Weekly Charge	AR1	AR2
Low Season (from)	£ 210	£ 380
High Season (from)	£ 550	£ 780

UK1810 Newlands Caravan Park

see report page 95

Charmouth DT6 6RB (Dorset)
Tel: **01297 560259**. Email: **enq@newlandsholidays.co.uk**   www.alanrogers.com/UK1810

AR1 – ELITE PINE LODGE – Chalet

Sleeping: 3 bedrooms, sleeps 6: 1 double, 4 single beds, pillows & blankets provided

Living: living/kitchen area, heating, TV, hair dryer, shower & wc

Eating: fitted kitchen with hobs, microwave, oven, grill, dishwasher, coffee machine, fridge

Outside: table & chairs, parasol

Pets: not accepted

AR2 – LYME CARAVAN – Mobile Home

Sleeping: 2 bedrooms, sleeps 5: 1 double, 2 single beds, sofa bed, pillows & blankets provided

Living: living/kitchen area, heating, TV, shower & separate wc

Eating: fitted kitchen with hobs, microwave, oven, grill, fridge

Outside: table & chairs

Pets: accepted

Other (for AR1 and AR2): bed linen, cot and highchair for rent

Open: 5 January - 23 December

Weekly Charge	AR1	AR2
Low Season (from)	£ 350	£ 250
High Season (from)	£ 990	£ 590

UK3850 Rivendale Caravan & Leisure Park

see report page 167

Buxton Road, Alsop-en-le-Dale, Ashbourne DE6 1QU (Derbyshire)
Tel: **01335 310311**. Email: **enquiries@rivendalecaravanpark.co.uk**   www.alanrogers.com/UK3850

AR1 – SENATOR – Mobile Home

Sleeping: 2 bedrooms, sleeps 6: 2 doubles, 1 single bed, pillows & blankets provided

Living: living/kitchen area, heating, TV, radio, shower & wc

Eating: fitted kitchen with hobs, microwave, oven, grill, fridge/freezer

Outside: table & chairs, BBQ

Pets: not accepted

AR2 – ALSOP VIEW – Apartment

Sleeping: 1 bedroom, sleeps 3: 1 double bed, 1 single beds, pillows & blankets provided

Living: living/kitchen area, heating, TV, radio, shower & wc

Eating: fitted kitchen with coffee machine

Outside: table & chairs, parasol, BBQ

Pets: not accepted

Other (for AR1 and AR2): bed linen, cot and highchair for rent

Open: All year excl. 5 - 29 January

Weekly Charge	AR1	AR2
Low Season (from)	£ 250	£ 350
High Season (from)	£ 375	£ 490

Reports by Readers

We always welcome reports from readers concerning sites which they have visited. Generally reports provide us with invaluable feedback on sites already included in the guides or, in the case of those not yet featured, they provide information which we can follow up with a view to adding them in future editions. However, if you have a complaint about a park, this should be addressed to the campsite owner, preferably in person before you leave.

Please make your comments either on this form or on plain paper. It would be appreciated if you would indicate the approximate dates when you visited the site and, in the case of potential new ones, provide the correct name and address and, if possible, include a campsite brochure. Send your reports to:

Alan Rogers Guides, Spelmonden Old Oast, Goudhurst, Kent TN17 1HE

Name and reference number of the campsite (or address for new recommendations):

_____

_____

Dates of visit: _____

Comments:

Reader's Name and Address: _____

_____

_____

_____

Name and reference number of the campsite (or address for new recommendations):

_____

_____

Dates of visit: _____

Comments:

Reader's Name and Address: _____

_____

_____

_____

Open All Year

The following parks are understood to accept caravanners and campers all year round. It is always wise to phone the park to check as the facilities available, for example, may be reduced.

England

UK0018	Bone Valley
UK0030	Ayr
UK0165	Monkey Tree
UK0180	Carnon Downs
UK0255	Sun Valley
UK0270	Mena
UK0300	Colliford Tavern
UK0310	Trekenning
UK0320	Polborder House
UK0430	Padstow
UK0440	Dolbeare
UK0690	Stowford Farm
UK0710	Hidden Valley
UK0745	Riverside (South Molton)
UK0790	Harford Bridge
UK0800	Higher Longford
UK0810	Riverside (Plymouth)
UK0820	Moor View
UK0870	Beverley
UK1250	Woodland Springs
UK1340	Cornish Farm
UK1350	Quantock Orchard
UK1420	Southfork
UK1440	Baltic Wharf
UK1460	Newton Mill
UK1500	Long Hazel
UK1510	Chew Valley
UK1520	Waterrow
UK1560	The Fairways
UK1630	Brokerswood
UK1655	Church Farm
UK1670	Alderbury
UK1700	Devizes
UK1820	Bagwell Farm
UK2030	Wareham Forest
UK2290	Sandy Balls
UK2590	Greenhill Farm
UK2600	Barnstones
UK2800	Alderstead Heath
UK2810	Chertsey
UK2930	Sheepcote
UK2940	Honeybridge
UK2950	Washington
UK2955	Kloofs
UK3030	Tanner Farm
UK3040	Broadhembury
UK3070	Canterbury
UK3090	Black Horse
UK3260	Abbey Wood
UK3270	Crystal Palace
UK3310	Low House
UK3322	Run Cottage
UK3340	Polstead
UK3345	The Dell
UK3382	Rose Farm
UK3385	Applewood
UK3455	Deer's Glade
UK3470	Breckland
UK3520	Searles
UK3575	Stroud Hill
UK3580	Ferry Meadows
UK3690	Bainland
UK3730	Skegness Sands
UK3765	Woodland Waters
UK3815	Lickpenny
UK3845	Clover Fields
UK3910	Teversal
UK3920	Riverside (Worksop)
UK3940	Smeaton's Lakes
UK3945	Milestone
UK4075	Hollyfast
UK4130	Moreton-in-Marsh
UK4170	Tudor
UK4210	Lickhill Manor
UK4300	Poston Mill
UK4400	Stanmore Hall
UK4410	Beaconsfield
UK4430	Oxon Hall
UK5280	Abbey Farm
UK5290	Royal Umpire
UK5505	Stanwix Park
UK5560	Sykeside
UK5570	Wild Rose
UK5705	The Grange
UK5740	White Water
UK5755	South Meadows
UK5800	Ord House

Wales

UK5925	Cardiff
UK5955	Erwlon
UK6045	Gilestone
UK6060	Tredegar House
UK6310	Bacheldre
UK6330	Daisy Bank
UK6590	Beddgelert
UK6600	Bryn Gloch
UK6605	Tafarn Snowdonia
UK6680	James
UK6690	Bron-Y-Wendon

Scotland

UK6870	Glenearly
UK6930	Brandedleys
UK6950	Brighouse Bay
UK7020	Aird Donald
UK7030	Gibson Park
UK7050	Edinburgh
UK7240	Lomond Woods
UK7270	Auchterarder
UK7680	Glenmore
UK7735	Sango Sands
UK7790	Invercoe

Northern Ireland

UK8420	Tollymore

Republic of Ireland

IR8740	Cong
IR8815	Willowbrook
IR9080	Forest Farm
IR9100	Camac Valley
IR9400	Glen of Aherlow
IR9580	Beara The Peacock

Dogs

For the benefit of those who want to take their dogs with them or for people who do not like dogs at the parks they visit, we list here the parks that have indicated to us that they do not accept dogs. If you are, however, planning to take your dog we do advise you to phone the park first to check – there may be limits on numbers, breeds, etc. or times of the year when they are excluded.

Never – these parks do not accept dogs at any time:

UK0065	Wayfarers	UK1490	Greenacres	UK7290	Craigtoun
UK0250	Pentewan Sands	UK2130	Grove Farm		Meadows
UK0302	South Penquite	UK2300	Ashurst	UK8600	Bellemont
UK0860	Whitehill	UK3060	Yew Tree	UK9770	Vaugrat
UK0870	Beverley	UK3120	Gate House Wood	UK9830	Seagull
UK0940	Holmans Wood	UK4100	Hoburne Cotswold	UK9870	Pomme de Chien
UK1075	Golden Coast	UK4160	Christchurch	IR9410	The Apple
UK1130	Hoburne Torbay	UK5550	Limefitt	IR9510	Eagle Point
UK1150	Ruda	UK5890	Glen Trothy		
UK1380	Blue Anchor	UK5980	Moreton Farm		

Sometimes – these parks do not accept dogs at certain times of the year:

UK0010	Chacewater	UK2590	Greenhill Farm	UK5930	Cwmcarn Forest
UK0030	Ayr	UK3095	Little Satmar	UK5995	Caerfai Bay
UK0306	Ruthern Valley	UK3110	Quex	UK6010	Cenarth Falls
UK0490	Mullion	UK3485	Clippesby	UK6280	Aeron Coast
UK0710	Hidden Valley	UK3510	Breydon Water	UK6290	Glan-y-Mor
UK0720	Easewell Farm	UK4180	Ranch	UK6040	Pencelli Castle
UK0850	Galmpton	UK4496	Skipsea Sands	UK6660	Nant Mill
UK0865	Byslades	UK4498	South Cliff	UK6990	Mortonhall
UK1540	Batcombe Vale	UK4520	Flower of May	UK7060	Tantallon
UK1550	Bucklegrove	UK4760	Riverside Meadows	UK7690	Torvean
UK2250	Hoburne Bashley	UK5350	Holgates	UK9710	Rozel
UK2285	Forest Edge	UK5610	Waterfoot	IR8810	Lough Lanagh
UK2470	Southland	UK5710	Doe Park	IR9150	River Valley
UK2500	Heathfield Farm	UK5750	Waren	IR9580	Beara The Peacock

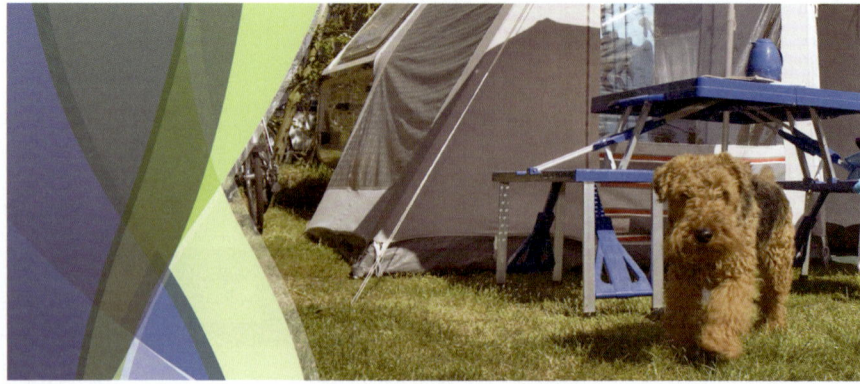

Fishing

We are pleased to include details of parks which provide facilities for fishing on site. Many other parks, particularly in Scotland and Ireland, are in popular fishing areas and have facilities within easy reach. Where we have been given details, we have included this information in the reports. It is always best to contact parks to check that they provide for your individual requirements.

England

UK0165	Monkey Tree
UK0170	Trevella
UK0220	Trevornick
UK0250	Pentewan Sands
UK0270	Mena
UK0302	South Penquite
UK0380	Wooda Farm
UK0415	Trencreek
UK0530	Trethiggey
UK0725	Warcombe Farm
UK0745	Riverside (South Molton)
UK0750	Minnows
UK0810	Riverside (Plymouth)
UK0950	River Dart
UK0970	Cofton
UK1060	Yeatheridge
UK1075	Golden Coast
UK1150	Ruda
UK1390	Old Oaks
UK1460	Newton Mill
UK1480	Home Farm
UK1520	Waterrow
UK1540	Batcombe Vale
UK1545	Cheddar Bridge
UK1570	Northam Farm
UK1575	Unity
UK1580	Warren Farm
UK1590	Exe Valley
UK1630	Brokerswood
UK1640	Greenhill Farm
UK1740	Golden Cap
UK1760	Wood Farm
UK1780	Freshwater Beach
UK2150	Woolsbridge
UK2290	Sandy Balls
UK2360	Hill Cottage
UK2450	The Orchards
UK2515	Nodes Point
UK2610	Bo Peep
UK2700	Hurley
UK2810	Chertsey
UK2820	Horsley
UK2900	Horam Manor
UK2915	Fairfields Farm
UK3030	Tanner Farm
UK3290	Fen Farm
UK3300	Homestead Lake
UK3320	Moon & Sixpence
UK3400	Old Brick Kilns
UK3430	Kelling Heath
UK3455	Deer's Glade
UK3480	Little Lakeland
UK3520	Searles
UK3555	Wyton Lakes
UK3575	Stroud Hill
UK3680	Ashby Park
UK3750	Foreman's Bridge
UK3760	Tallington Lakes
UK3765	Woodland Waters
UK3855	Callow Top
UK3940	Smeaton's Lakes
UK3945	Milestone
UK3970	Glencote
UK4080	Riverside (Stratford)
UK4090	Island Meadow
UK4100	Hoburne Cotswold
UK4140	Winchcombe
UK4150	Croft Farm
UK4170	Tudor
UK4185	Weir Meadow
UK4190	Kingsgreen
UK4210	Lickhill Manor
UK4300	Poston Mill
UK4310	Luck's All
UK4320	Broadmeadow
UK4345	Townsend
UK4380	Fernwood
UK4390	Westbrook
UK4410	Beaconsfield
UK4500	Burton Constable
UK4510	Thorpe Hall
UK4610	Moorside
UK4640	Goose Wood
UK4660	Woodhouse Farm
UK4715	Riverside (Lancaster)
UK4720	Knight Stainforth
UK5280	Abbey Farm
UK5540	Fallbarrow
UK5555	White Cross Bay
UK5600	Pennine View
UK5615	Hill of Oaks
UK5625	Lowther
UK5710	Doe Park

Wales

UK5880	Springwater
UK5945	River View
UK6290	Glan-y-Mor
UK6040	Pencelli Castle
UK6045	Gilestone
UK6245	Morben Isaf
UK6250	Dolswydd
UK6305	Smithy Park
UK6320	Fforest Fields
UK6345	Glanlynn
UK6590	Beddgelert
UK6600	Bryn Gloch
UK6605	Tafarn Snowdonia
UK6670	The Plassey

Scotland

UK6890	Mossyard
UK6910	Hoddom Castle
UK6940	Loch Ken
UK6950	Brighouse Bay
UK7025	Seal Shore
UK7220	The Gart
UK7260	Ardgartan
UK7270	Auchterarder
UK7295	River Tilt
UK7305	Tummel Valley
UK7790	Invercoe
UK7860	Glendaruel
UK7710	Ardmair Point
UK7740	Loch Greshornish
UK7800	Resipole
UK7850	Linnhe Lochside

Northern Ireland

UK8330	Sixmilewater
UK8340	Drumaheglis
UK8405	Cranfield
UK8420	Tollymore
UK8510	Mullynascarthy

Republic of Ireland

IR8815	Willowbrook
IR8825	Lough Key
IR8960	Lough Ree
IR8965	Lough Ennell
IR9100	Camac Valley
IR9230	Nore Valley
IR9470	Blackwater Valley
IR9510	Eagle Point
IR9560	Wave Crest
IR9620	Flemings
IR9630	White Villa

Bicycle Hire

We understand that the following parks have bicycles to hire on site or can arrange for bicycles to be delivered. However, we would recommend that you contact the park to check as the situation can change.

England

UK0025	Roselands
UK0145	Trewhiddle
UK0150	Sea View
UK0255	Sun Valley
UK0306	Ruthern Valley
UK0690	Stowford Farm
UK0750	Minnows
UK0950	River Dart
UK1075	Golden Coast
UK1150	Ruda
UK1250	Woodland Springs
UK1350	Quantock Orchard
UK1390	Old Oaks
UK1490	Greenacres
UK1575	Unity
UK1590	Exe Valley
UK2050	Rowlands Wait
UK2100	Sandford
UK2120	South Lytchett Manor
UK2290	Sandy Balls
UK2315	Riverside (Hamble)
UK2350	Red Shoot
UK2450	The Orchards
UK3325	The Oaks
UK3330	Moat Barn
UK3370	Kessingland
UK3390	Dower House
UK3430	Kelling Heath
UK3485	Clippesby
UK3520	Searles
UK3660	Walesby Woodlands
UK3750	Foreman's Bridge
UK3855	Callow Top
UK3904	Greendale Farm
UK4540	Saint Helens
UK4560	Golden Square
UK4620	Upper Carr
UK5330	Marton Mere
UK5505	Stanwix Park
UK5520	Skelwith Fold
UK5605	Woodclose

Wales

UK5925	Cardiff
UK6040	Pencelli Castle
UK6045	Gilestone
UK6330	Daisy Bank
UK6340	Pen-y-Bont
UK6345	Glanlynn

Scotland

UK6940	Loch Ken
UK6950	Brighouse Bay
UK7000	Strathclyde
UK7230	Trossachs
UK7280	Nether Craig
UK7305	Tummel Valley
UK7740	Loch Greshornish

Channel Islands

UK9780	Fauxquets

Republic of Ireland

IR8740	Cong
IR8790	Carra
IR9130	Roundwood
IR9400	Glen of Aherlow
IR9580	Beara The Peacock
IR9600	Glenross
IR9620	Flemings
IR9630	White Villa
IR9640	Killarney Flesk

Golf

We understand that the following parks have facilities for playing golf on site. Where facilities are within easy reach and we have been given details, we have included this information in the individual reports. However, we recommend that you contact the park to check that they meet your requirements.

UK0220	Trevornick	UK2250	Hoburne Bashley	UK4710	Rudding
UK0380	Wooda Farm	UK2920	Bay View	UK6670	The Plassey
UK0690	Stowford Farm	UK3230	Lee Valley	UK6910	Hoddom Castle
UK0720	Easewell Farm	UK3520	Searles	UK6950	Brighouse Bay
UK1010	Lady's Mile	UK3690	Bainland	UK7060	Tantallon
UK1020	Oakdown	UK4070	Somers Wood	UK7690	Torvean
UK1070	Woolacombe Bay	UK4300	Poston Mill	UK8310	Carnfunnock
UK1575	Unity	UK4520	Flower of May	IR9150	River Valley

Horse Riding

We understand that the following parks have horse riding stables on site. Where facilities are within easy reach and we have been given details, we have included this information in the individual reports. However, we recommend that you contact the park to check that they meet your requirements.

UK0360	Lakefield	UK1370	Burrowhayes	UK2515	Nodes Point
UK0690	Stowford Farm	UK1575	Unity	UK2900	Horam Manor
UK0735	Woolacombe Sands	UK1780	Freshwater Beach	UK6950	Brighouse Bay
UK1060	Yeatheridge	UK2290	Sandy Balls	UK8510	Mullynascarthy

Boat Launching

We understand that the following parks have boat slipways on site. Where facilities are within easy reach and we have been given details, we have included this information in the individual reports. However, we recommend that you contact the park to check that they meet your requirements.

UK0250	Pentewan Sands	UK4500	Burton Constable	UK7740	Loch Greshornish
UK0750	Minnows	UK5330	Marton Mere	UK7800	Resipole
UK1530	Slimeridge	UK5540	Fallbarrow	UK7850	Linnhe Lochside
UK1540	Batcombe Vale	UK5555	White Cross Bay	UK8330	Sixmilewater
UK2520	Thorness Bay	UK5615	Hill of Oaks	UK8340	Drumaheglis
UK2700	Hurley	UK6345	Glanlynn	UK8405	Cranfield
UK3290	Fen Farm	UK6890	Mossyard	IR8825	Lough Key
UK3760	Tallington Lakes	UK6940	Loch Ken	IR8960	Lough Ree
UK4080	Riverside	UK6950	Brighouse Bay	IR8965	Lough Ennell
(Stratford)		UK7025	Seal Shore	IR9510	Eagle Point
UK4150	Croft Farm	UK7260	Ardgartan	IR9560	Wave Crest
UK4210	Lickhill Manor	UK7410	Riverview	IR9610	Mannix Point
UK4310	Luck's All	UK7710	Ardmair Point		

Adults Only

We list here the parks that have indicated to us that they do not accept children at any time during the year, at certain times, or in certain areas of their park.

The following parks have made the decision not to accept children or young adults:

UK0010	Chacewater	*over 30 yrs only*	UK3410	Sandy Gulls	
UK0012	Killiwerris		UK3420	Two Mills	
UK0820	Moor View		UK3450	Little Haven	
UK1250	Woodland Springs		UK3470	Breckland	
UK1355	Lowtrow Cross		UK3575	Stroud Hill	
UK1390	Old Oaks		UK3650	Cherry Tree	
UK1500	Long Hazel		UK3904	Greendale Farm	
UK1510	Chew Valley		UK3980	Longnor Woods	
UK1520	Waterrow		UK4070	Somers Wood	
UK1545	Cheddar Bridge		UK4410	Beaconsfield	*over 21 yrs*
UK1590	Exe Valley		UK4534	Overbrook	
UK1640	Greenhill Farm		UK4580	Foxholme	
UK1680	Plough Lane	*over 21 yrs*	UK4610	Moorside	*over 16 yrs*
UK1770	Bingham Grange		UK5240	Lamb Cottage	
UK2620	Wysdom		UK5510	The Larches	
UK3325	The Oaks		UK5650	The Ashes	
UK3340	Polstead		UK6330	Daisy Bank	

The following parks also do not accept children at certain times or in certain areas of their park:

UK4380	Fernwood		UK4430	Oxon Hall
UK4400	Stanmore Hall			

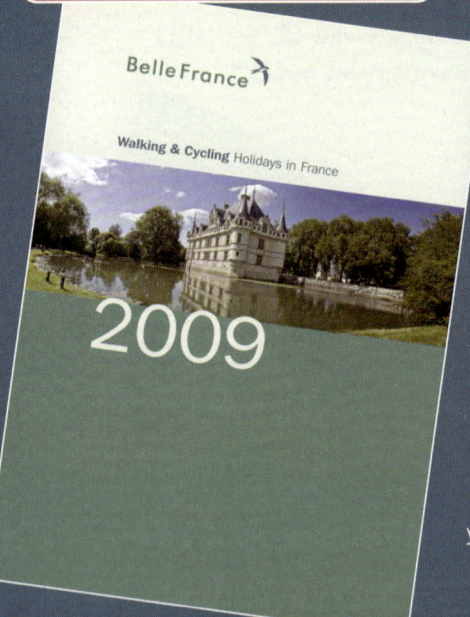

A sign of excellence.

Just one of 200 superb Caravan Club Sites to choose from

Broomfield Farm Caravan Club Site

Caravan Club Sites are renowned for their excellence. With most of those graded achieving 4 or 5 stars from VisitBritain, you can be sure of consistently high standards. From lakes or mountains to city or sea, there are some 200 quality Club Sites throughout Britain & Ireland to choose from.

With over 40 fabulous Club Sites open all year, why stay at home?

Whichever site you choose, you can be assured of excellent facilities and a friendly welcome from our Resident Wardens. Just look for the signs.

Bunree Caravan Club Site

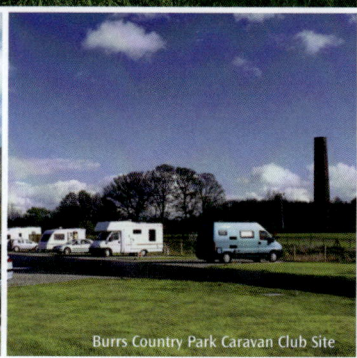
Burrs Country Park Caravan Club Site

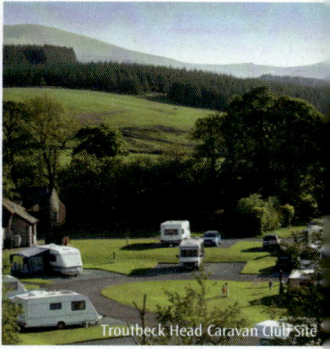
Troutbeck Head Caravan Club Site

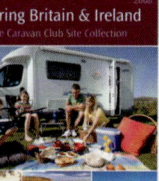

You don't have to be a member to stay on most Caravan Club Sites, but members save up to £7 per night on pitch fees!

Call today for your FREE Touring Britain & Ireland brochure on 0800 521 161 quoting ARG 09 or visit www.caravanclub.co.uk

The Caravan Club, East Grinstead House, East Grinstead, West Sussex RH19 1UA

TRY 3 ISSUES FOR JUST £3

GREAT SAVINGS!
Secure a 20% discount
after your trial ends.

EXCLUSIVE OFFERS!
Get access to unique offers
and discounts.

FREE DELIVERY!
Your copy direct to your
door before it goes on sa
in the shops.

OR

Practical Motorhome

- Touring inspiration and motor caravanning tips
- Common sense advice on maintaining and improving your motorhome
- In-depth motorhome reviews of all the latest models
- The complete motorhome magazine

Practical Caravan

- Holiday inspiration and travel guides for the UK and abroad
- Expert hints and tips to help you holiday better
- Buying advice and in-depth test for towcars and caravans
- Britain's favourite caravan magazine for over 40 years

CALL **08456 777 812** now
or visit **www.themagazineshop.com/caravan09**
or **www.themagazineshop.com/motor09**
Please have your bank details ready and quote AR09

USE CAMPING CHEQUES ON 13 TOP QUALITY UK PARKS
ALL AT £11.95 PER NIGHT

Camping Cheque

flat rate
£11.95
per night
inc. electricity

Cornwall	POLMANTER
	WOODA FARM PARK
	CARLYON BAY
Cumbria	THE QUIET SITE
Devon	RIVER DART COUNTRY PARK
	WHITEHILL COUNTRY PARK
	COFTON COUNTRY HOLIDAYS
Dorset	NEWLANDS
Hampshire	SHAMBA
	RIVERSIDE
Isle of Wight	THE ORCHARDS
Scotland	BRIGHOUSE BAY
Peak District	RIVENDALE

Camping Cheque

559 campsites
24 countries

flat rate
£11.95
per night
inc. electricity

Holiday Savings
Guide 2009

Alan Rogers

www.campingcheque.co.uk

www.campingcheque.co.uk

FREE Holiday Savings Guide

01580 214002

insure4campers.com

Personal travel insurance
European vehicle assistance insurance

Whatever form your camping or touring holiday may take, you'll need proper insurance for complete peace of mind. Our policies provide exactly the right cover for self-drive campsite-based holidays - at fantastic prices!

One call and you're covered

Visit www.**insure4campers.com**

or call us **NOW** for a no-obligation quote
01580 214006

Policies despatched within 24 hours

Alan Rogers

BROUGHT
TO YOU BY
ALAN ROGERS

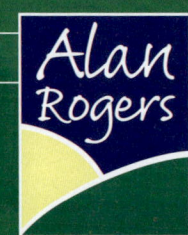

THE CARAVAN & MOTORHOME SHOWS

The UK's favourite caravan and motorhome shows

INTERNATIONAL CARAVAN & MOTORHOME 2009 NEC BIRMINGHAM 13-18 OCTOBER

The UK's biggest selection of caravans, motohomes, trailer tents, holiday homes, awnings, folding campers and of course accessories! The NEC is the first place to see all the latest products, have a great day out and find exactly what you want for your 2010 holiday.

MANCHESTER CENTRAL CARAVAN & MOTORHOME SHOW 2009 MANCHESTER 22-25 JANUARY

Come and see the widest choice of caravans and a great selection of motorhomes from leading UK and overseas manufacturers. If it's a bargain you are looking for, many exhibitors are offering amazing deals that you won't find anywhere else!

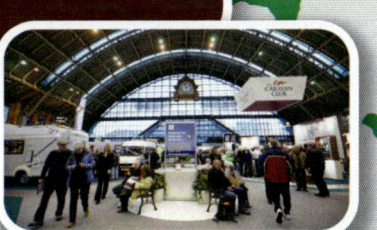

FOR MORE INFORMATION VISIT

www.caravanshows.com

08701 288 288

RED TEXT DENOTES ALL YEAR SITE

Miles 0 5 10 15 20 25
Kms 0 8 16 24 32 40

Parks on this map are featured on pages 12-76 of the guide.
Please refer to the numerical index (page 358) for exact campsite page references.

RED TEXT DENOTES ALL YEAR SITE

WALES
(see map 6)
South Wales

HEART OF ENGLAND
(see map 4)
Gloucestershire

SOUTH WEST ENGLAND

Devon

Somerset

Dorset West

Dorset East

Wiltshire

Isle of Wight

Hampshire

Berkshire

SOUTHERN
(see also map 4)

West Sussex

Surrey

Oxfordshire

Buckinghamshire

Parks on this map are featured on pages 77-123 of the guide.
Please refer to the numerical index (page 358) for exact campsite page references.

SOUTH WEST
(see maps 1 & 2)

Wiltshire

Oxfordshire

SOUTHERN
(see also maps 2 & 4)

Berkshire

Buckinghamshire

Hertfordshire

Hampshire

LONDON

EAST
(see map 4)

Essex

West Sussex

Surrey

SOUTH EAST

East Sussex

Kent

Isle of Wight

4100

2620
2570

2150
2340
2285
2360
2290
1650
1640
1670
SALISBURY *
WINCHESTER *
2130
2250
2310
2350
RINGWOOD *
2300
LYNDHURST *
2380
2320
BOURNEMOUTH *
2280
2500
2450
NEWPORT *
2520
2470
2495
2530
2515
2480
2475
SANDOWN *
RYDE *
PORTSMOUTH *
2315
SOUTHAMPTON *
2690
2700
2750
2810
2800
2820
2895
2885
2960
2940
2930
2900
2915
2920
2955
2960
2930
BRIGHTON *
CHICHESTER *
EASTBOURNE *
HASTINGS *
SWINDON *
OXFORD *
READING *
GUILDFORD *
CRAWLEY *
TUNBRIDGE WELLS *
LONDON *
3270
3250
3230
3280
3120
3030
3040
3090
3095
3100
3060
3130
3110
3290
3285
AYLESBURY *
HARLOW *
CHELMSFORD *
SOUTHEND-ON-SEA *
MAIDSTONE *
ASHFORD *
CANTERBURY *
DOVER *
RAMSGATE *
FOLKESTONE *

A40
M40
A34
A346
A303
A4
M4
A31
M3
A3
A24
M23
M25
A22
A26
A21
A259
M20
M2
A2
A299
A13
M11
M25
A1(M)
A12

RED TEXT DENOTES ALL YEAR SITE

0   5   10   15   20   25
Miles
0   8   16   24   32   40
Kms

Parks on this map are featured on pages 124-140 of the guide.
Please refer to the numerical index (page 358) for exact campsite page references.

Parks on this map are featured on pages 141-184 of the guide.
Please refer to the numerical index (page 358) for exact campsite page references.

RED TEXT DENOTES ALL YEAR SITE

0		20	Miles	40		60
0		32	Kms	64		96

7050
7060
EDINBURGH 6980 7065
6990
7045 7035

6960

BERWICK-UPON-TWEED
5800

5750
5755

SCOTLAND
(see map 7)
7030 SELKIRK
Scottish Lowlands

5770

MOFFAT

Northumberland

DUMFRIES
6910

NORTHUMBRIA

5810

NEWCASTLE
UPON TYNE
Tyne and Wear
SUNDERLAND

6875 5505 CARLISLE
5506

5640

CUMBRIA

5510

Durham

DURHAM 5705
5700

BISHOP AUCKLAND

PENRITH
5670 5625
WORKINGTON 5630 5610
KESWICK 5660 5620 5635
Cumbria 5570 5560
5520 5590 5600
5550
5540 5555
5615 5545 KENDAL 5650
5605

5740 MIDDLESBROUGH
DARLINGTON

5710
5720

4528
4532

4775
4690 4765 4770 4570
North Yorkshire 4580 4534 4590 4550
THIRSK 4560 4620 4540 4520
4760 4760 4740 4780
5350 5271 4715 4660 4638 4640 4545
5270 4720 4670 4630 4640 4610 4510 4498
SETTLE 4750 DRIFFIELD 4496
5272 SKIPTON 4710 BRIDLINGTON
5300 4755 YORK
YORKSHIRE
BLACKPOOL Lancashire
5330 PRESTON **East Riding of Yorkshire**
5295 BRADFORD 4645 4500
HULL
West Yorkshire
5290
NORTH
5360 **WEST** 4700
5280
Merseyside **South Yorkshire**
LIVERPOOL MANCHESTER
PRESTATYN 6660 3660
6655 SHEFFIELD
RUNCORN 3680
Cheshire MACCLESFIELD **Lincolnshire**
WALES NORTHWICH 3840 3920 LINCOLN
(see map 6) 5240 BUXTON 3845 3950 3692 3690
CHESTER CONGLETON 3980 **Derbyshire** 3675
WREXHAM LEEK 3850 3815 3910 **Nottinghamshire** 3940
6680 6670 3970 3945
6700 STOKE 3855 3765
HEART
4415 **(see map 4)**
4380 DERBY 3770
Staffordshire NOTTINGHAM
4410

Parks on this map are featured on pages 185-230 of the guide.
Please refer to the numerical index (page 358) for exact campsite page references.

MORECAMBE ✱
LANCASTER ✱

FLEETWOOD ● 5272
● 5300

BLACKPOOL ● **Lancashire**
5330 PRESTON
5295 ●

NORTH
WEST 5290
(see map 5)

5360 ●
● 5280

Merseyside
LIVERPOOL ●

RUNCORN ✱

Cheshire

✱ CHESTER

HOLYHEAD ✱

● 6640
● 6636

COLWYN BAY PRESTATYN ● 6660
6695 ● 6655
6690 A55
● 6650

North Wales

A494

6635 ●
CAERNARFON ✱ ● 6620
6605
6600

A487 WREXHAM ✱
6590 ● A470 A5
6680 ● ● 6670
6700 ●

6580 ● ✱ PORTHMADOG
BALA ● 6340
6355 ● 6345
6585 ● 4380 4415

6370 ● ✱ DOLGELLAU
4410
4430
SHREWSBURY

RED TEXT DENOTES ALL YEAR SITE 6240 ● **Shropshire** A49

Miles 6245 ● A470 6305 ● ● 4440
0 5 10 15 20 25 6310 ● 6330
0 8 16 3 24 2 40 **HEART**
Kms **(see map 4)**

6290 ●
ABERYSTWYTH ✱ **WALES** A44 4390

A487 LLANGURIG LEOMINSTER
Mid Wales 4345 ●

6280 ● 6250 ●
LLANDRINDOD WELLS ✱ **Herefordshire**
6320 ●

● 6005
CARDIGAN ✱ **West Wales** ● 4300 4310
● 6010 5880 ● 6070 ●
FISHGUARD ✱
LLANDOVERY ● 5955
5995 ● 5960 ● A40 BRECON 4360
A40 6040 ● 5890 ● 416
CARMARTHEN ✱ 6045 ●
HAVERFORDWEST
5992 ● A48
5994 ● A477
5974 ● 5945 ●
5975 ● A470
5980 SWANSEA ✱ **South Wales** 5930 ●
PEMBROKE ✱ 5982 5940 ●
5990 ● 5985 6060 ● NEWPORT
M4 ✱ CARDIFF
5925
● 5927

Parks on this map are featured on pages 231-256 of the guide.
Please refer to the numerical index (page 358) for exact campsite page references.

The following labels appear on the map:

THURSO
WICK
7735
7730
7920
HELMSDALE
7720
ULLAPOOL 7710
7700
A9
FRASERBURGH
7750
DINGWALL
ELGIN
A98
7740
INVERNESS 7690
7540 7550 7530
A835
A96
KYLE OF LOCHALSH 7760
7670
ABERDEEN
Highlands and Islands
Grampian
A87 A82 A9 7680
MALLAIG
NEWTONMORE
BRAEMAR
7850 FORT WILLIAM 7830
7800 7790
7300 7295
SCOTLAND
7305 PITLOCHRY 7280
7810
A9 A90
OBAN
CRIANLARICH
Heart of Scotland
7410 DUNDEE
7310 A85 PERTH
INVERARAY 7270 7290
7260 7220
7230 7320 STIRLING
7860 7240
GREENOCK 7050 EDINBURGH 7060
GLASGOW 6980 7065 A1
7045 6990 7035
7000
A702
BERWICK-UPON-TWEED
IRVINE KILMARNOCK 6960 5800
M74 SELKIRK 5750
7025 7030 5755
CAMPBELTOWN AYR JEDBURGH A1
7010 7015 Scottish Lowlands ALNWICK
A76 MOFFAT A7 A68
A77 NORTHUMBRIA
(see map 5)
NORTHERN IRELAND (see map 8) MORPETH
DUMFRIES Northumberland
NEWTON STEWART 6940 6930 6910 5810
STRANRAER 7020 CASTLE DOUGLAS 6870 5640 A69 HEXHAM
BALLYMENA 8310 LARNE 8320 A75 6945 6880 6875 5505 CARLISLE CONSETT
6890 6900 6950 KIRKCUDBRIGHT 5506 A68
ANTRIM 8330 6885 5510 M6 Durham
BANGOR BELFAST PENRITH 5710
WORKINGTON 5670 5625 5720
5630 5610 5700
5660 5620 5635 5570 A66 5600
5560 5590
8460 A591 5520 5550 5555
A595 5540 KENDAL
8420 5615 5545 5650 4690
5645 5605 North Yorkshire

Parks on this map are featured on pages 257-285 of the guide.
Please refer to the numerical index (page 357) for exact campsite page references.

RED TEXT DENOTES ALL YEAR ROUND SITE

Miles
0   20   40   60
0   32   64   6
Kms

CAMPBELTOWN *

8350 8360
8600
COLERAINE 8590
8340
LONDONDERRY

8310
LARNE
8320

STRABANE
BALLYMENA

A6

A2

A36

8330 ANTRIM

DONEGAL *

OMAGH
COOKSTOWN

BELFAST * BANGOR

A2

NORTHERN IRELAND

A32

8690
8695 SLIGO

N15

N16

8550
ENNISKILLEN

8510

ARMAGH

A7

A24 8460

8750

N17

NEWRY 8420

8730

N5

8825

8405

8810
8770 8790

8815
8780

CAVAN

DUNDALK

N17

N3

N2

N1

8740

N4

ATHLONE 8960

8965

N6

GALWAY *

9100 DUBLIN

PORTLAOISE

IRELAND

NAAS

9140

9460

N18

9420

9080 9160

9130

9230

WICKLOW

9150

N7

LIMERICK *

N8

N9

KILKENNY 9240

N24

9230

N11

TIPPERARY
9370 9400

9410

N21

9550 9650

TRALEE

N20

N8

CLONMEL

9470

WEXFORD *

KILLARNEY

9600 9590 9620
9640 9630

ROSSLARE
9170

9610

9480

N22

9330 9340

9560 9580
9570

9510

CORK

N25

9505 9500

Parks on this map are featured on pages 286-316 of the guide.
Please refer to the numerical index (page 358) for exact campsite page references.

Orkney Islands

* KIRKWALL

7950

* THURSO

Shetland
Islands

LERWICK
7980

Parks on these maps are featured
on pages 284-5 of the guide.

9770
9780

Herm

9830

ST PETER PORT

Guernsey

9870

Sark

CHANNEL ISLANDS

Jersey
9710
9720

ST HELIER *

Parks on this map are featured
on pages 317-320 of the guide.

353

Town and Village Index

Index by Campsite Number

Index - Campsite Number

England

Wales

Scotland

Index - Campsite Number

Index - Campsite Region, County and Name, Advertisers, Images